P9-CJS-958

MVFOL

A HISTORY
OF ENGLAND

COUNTIES OF
ENGLAND AND WALES

MILES

0   20   40   60   80

SCOTLAND

NORTHUMBERLAND

CUMBERLAND   DURHAM

WESTMORLAND

Isle Of
Man

E
N
G   YORKSHIRE

ANGLESEY   FLINT   LANCASHIRE

CAERNARVON   DENBIGH   CHESHIRE   DERBY   NOTTINGHAM   LINCOLN

MERIONETH

MONTGOMERY   STAFFORD   RUTLAND

SHROPSHIRE   LEICESTER   NORFOLK

RADNOR   WARWICK   HUNTINGDON

PEMBROKE   CARDIGAN   NORTHAMPTON   SUFFOLK

BRECKNOCK   HEREFORD   WORCESTER   BEDFORD   CAMBRIDGE

CARMARTHEN   OXFORD   BUCKINGHAM   HERTFORD   ESSEX

GLAMORGAN   MONMOUTH   GLOUCESTER   MIDDLESEX   LONDON

BERKSHIRE   SURREY   KENT

WILTSHIRE

SOMERSET   HAMPSHIRE   SUSSEX

DEVON   DORSET

CORNWALL   Isle Of
Wight

Clayton Roberts
The Ohio State University

David Roberts
Dartmouth College

SECOND EDITION

A HISTORY OF ENGLAND

Volume I
Prehistory to 1714

Prentice-Hall, Inc., Englewood Cliffs, New Jersey 07632

Library of Congress Cataloging in Publication Data

ROBERTS, CLAYTON.
  A history of England.

  Includes bibliographies and indexes.
  Contents: v. 1. Prehistory to 1714 —
v. 2. 1688 to the present.
  1. Great Britain–History. I. Roberts,
David, 1923—. . II. Title.
DA30.R58 1985   941   84-26334
ISBN 0-13-389966-7 (v. 1)
ISBN 0-13-389974-8 (v. 2)

Editorial/production supervision: Sylvia Schmokel
Cover design: Joe Curcio
Manufacturing buyer: Barbara Kelly Kittle

©1985, 1980 by Prentice-Hall, Inc., Englewood Cliffs, New Jersey 07632

All rights reserved. No part of this book may be
reproduced, in any form or by any means,
without permission in writing from the publisher.

Printed in the United States of America

10 9 8 7 6 5 4 3

ISBN 0-13-389966-7   01

Prentice-Hall International, Inc., *London*
Prentice-Hall of Australia Pty. Limited, *Sydney*
Editora Prentice-Hall do Brasil, Ltda., *Rio de Janeiro*
Prentice-Hall Canada Inc., *Toronto*
Prentice-Hall Hispanoamericana, S.A., *Mexico*
Prentice-Hall of India Private Limited, *New Delhi*
Prentice-Hall of Japan, Inc., *Tokyo*
Prentice-Hall of Southeast Asia Pte. Ltd., *Singapore*
Whitehall Books Limited, *Wellington, New Zealand*

Contents

CHAPTER 12   ELIZABETHAN ENGLAND: 1558–1603   279

CHAPTER 13   EARLY STUART ENGLAND: 1603–1640   316

CHAPTER 14   THE ENGLISH REVOLUTION: 1640–1660   341

CHAPTER 15   RESTORATION AND REVOLUTION: 1660–1689   370

CHAPTER 16   WAR AND SOCIETY   397

INDEX   427

Preface

The history of England has exercised a perennial fascination over the minds of mankind. A people who gave us Shakespeare and Newton, created the Common law and Parliament, built the world's largest empire, transformed industry, and defended the liberties of Europe against Napoleon and Hitler cannot be dull or insignificant. But though the fascination remains perennial, the story to be told changes with the mounting literature on the subject. In the past twenty years scholars have written and published a flood of articles and books on the history of England. They have examined or re-examined every event, left nothing untouched, from the building of Stonehenge to the discovery of North Sea oil.

It is our purpose to incorporate this recent scholarship into a history of England that is broad in scope and interpretive in nature.

The time has long since passed when a history of England could be a history of past politics. We have endeavored, therefore, to write a history of society as well as of the state, a task which the works of J. Z. Titow, M. M. Postan, Lawrence Stone, Peter Laslett, E. P. Thompson, Eric Hobsbawm, David Landes, and many others have made possible. Demographers, intellectual historians, social historians, historians of technology, and historians of popular movements have opened up a new world, a world which general histories of England have previously ignored. We have sought to illuminate this broader, richer world, even though it means saying less about the rise and fall of ministries.

We have sought throughout to wed a narrative form to a concern for interpretation, both to trace how and to explain why events came about. Without embracing any single interpretation of English history, we have sought to stress the dominant themes that run through it: the coming of Christianity, the creation of the English monarchy, the growth of English power and empire, the triumph of Protestantism and religious diversity, the winning of political liberty and parliamentary government, the emergence of a capitalistic and industrial economy, the triumph of the scientific method; and, in the twentieth century, the emergence of the welfare state, the decline in English power, the loss of empire, the faltering of the economy, and the decay of religious belief.

The historian's task is by no means limited to tracing such developments; he or she must also study past ages for their own sake. Thus we have sought to explain in terms of the society they served such institutions as the Anglo-Saxon manor, the medieval Exchequer, the Tudor council, the Stuart Parliament, the Hanoverian cabinet, and the nineteenth century economy; as also to portray in their own terms medieval piety. Elizabethan humanism, Augustan manners, Victorian morality, and twentieth century popular culture.

Though we have paid close attention to analysis and explanation, we have not sought to write an abstract and impersonal history. At bottom men and women, with their fervor and heroism, their steadfastness and suffering, their folly and stupidity, their greatness and meanness, make history. We have endeavored to capture those dramatic confrontations, those acts of heroism, those eruptions of passion, and those moments of illumination that give history its vividness, its color, its drama, and that help shape its course.

The help of other scholars has been invaluable to us in the writing of this history. Bryce Lyon of Brown University, Donald Sutherland of the University of Iowa, and Mavis Mate of the University of Oregon read with care and commented upon the chapters on Medieval England. Paul Seaver of Stanford University, Stephen Baxter of the University of North Carolina, Barrett Beer of Kent State University, and Roger Manning of Cleveland State University read with equal care the chapters on Tudor and Stuart England. Sidney Burrell of Boston University kindly loaned us his paper on the origins of the first Bishops' War, a paper whose insights proved most helpful. Henry Snyder of Louisiana State University read chapters 21 through 28, while Peter Stansky of Stanford University, Sheldon Rothblatt of the University of California at Berkeley, and Anthony Wohl and Donald Olsen of Vassar College read the chapters on the eighteenth, nineteenth, and twentieth centuries. To all these scholars we owe a great debt. They qualified our bold assertions, corrected our minor inaccuracies, and questioned our doubtful interpretations. The story as finally told, however, remains ours; we bear sole responsibility for it.

CLAYTON ROBERTS
DAVID ROBERTS

1 The Land and the People

A land shapes its people. Britain is an island and the British are an insular people—closely knit, enjoying continuity of development, conscious of their differences from others, proud of those differences. Britain is also a small island, only 90,000 square miles in size. The Scots inhabit the island north of the Cheviot hills. The Welsh occupy a mountain fastness to the west. The English dwell in the remaining 50,000 square miles (about the size of New England), with a boundary that is 90 percent seacoast.

Because the English occupied a small land, clearly defined by sea and mountains, they achieved political unity long before the French or the Spanish. And because the Channel formed a moat defensive to the realm, the English needed only a navy to repulse invaders. Had England possessed a defenseless land frontier to the east and west, as did Prussia, it too might have developed militaristic traditions. But England was defended by the sea and by its navy, and so Englishmen could oppose standing armies as a threat to liberty. The same sea that surrounds England also penetrates into its harbors, bays, channels, estuaries, and rivers. No Englishman lives more than 70 miles from the sea. The English therefore became a maritime people, not afraid to venture upon the sea in search of profit and power. The most important fact in British history may well be that Britain is an island, and the most important date that moment—about 6000 B.C.—when the North Sea flooded over the lands that joined Britain to the Continent.

Yet the sea can be a highway as well as a barrier. England, because it lies only 21 miles off Europe, escaped the stagnation that insularity often brings. England's location gave it access to the more advanced civilizations of the Mediterranean world. A succession of invaders and missionaries brought agriculture to England, then iron, then Roman government, finally Christianity, the Renaissance, and the Reformation. Then in the sixteenth century the center of commerce and culture moved from the Mediterranean to the Atlantic, and England, once situated on the distant edge of civilization, found itself near the center. It was now well placed to colonize new lands and become the *entrepôt* of the world's trade.

Soil and climate have contributed much to English civilization as well. The lowlands of Britain are uniquely suited for agriculture. The chalk and limestone soil of Salisbury Plain, the Cotswolds, and the North and South Downs offer excellent grazing for sheep and cattle. The heavy clay of the Weald and the Thames Valley yield rich crops of wheat, especially in Oxfordshire. But the most fertile parts of England are the Midlands and East Anglia, where overlapping layers of limestone, clay, and sand have produced a brown, loamy soil of great richness. Sufficient rainfall and sun cause this soil to yield up its riches. The average rainfall in England is about 30 inches a year—rather more to the west, less to the east. Because the rain is distributed uniformly throughout the year, great works of irrigation and the despotic governments needed to build them were not necessary. Though England lies as far north as Labrador, prevailing winds from the southwest bring moderate temperatures. The average temperature in July is 63° Fahrenheit, in January 39°. In the west there is not enough sun to grow wheat, but oats thrive there, as do pasture grasses. Wheat and barley are grown in the Midlands and the east, maize only in Essex where the sun shines oftener. But though the English have too little sun to grow much maize, they are fortunate in escaping the droughts, floods, hurricanes, and blizzards that strike other lands.

This prosperous agriculture, however, prevails only in the south and the east. A line drawn from the mouth of the river Exe in the southwest to the mouth of the river Tees in the northeast divides the lowland zone of England from the highland zone (though the Lancashire plain lying north and west of this line belongs to the lowland zone). South and east of the Exe-Tees line is the England of fertile soil, mild temperatures, valleys and plains, navigable rivers, easy communications. North and west lie Dartmoor, Exmoor, the mountains of Wales, the Pennines, the Yorkshire moors, and the Lake District, a land of mountains, rocks, barren moorland, scanty soil, and short, rushing streams. This division of the land has influenced the history of England through the centuries, creating (except in the nineteenth century) a backward, impoverished, thinly populated northwest, and a heavily populated, prosperous, progressive southeast. Successive waves of invaders have entered to the southeast, driving the native population into the mountain fastnesses of the north and west.

England is also rich in minerals. The tin of Cornwall, which first brought Britain to the attention of the Romans, continued to be a source of wealth until the nineteenth century. After the Romans departed the most important metal became iron, the ore of which is found throughout Britain. Since great amounts of charcoal (wood charred in a kiln from which air is excluded) were

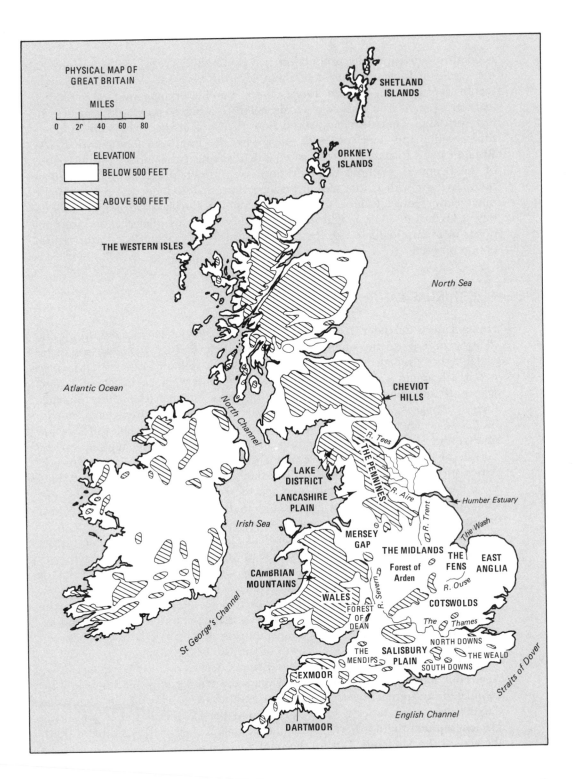

PHYSICAL MAP OF
GREAT BRITAIN

MILES

0   2r   40   60   80

ELEVATION

BELOW 500 FEET

ABOVE 500 FEET

SHETLAND
ISLANDS

ORKNEY
ISLANDS

THE WESTERN ISLES

North Sea

Atlantic Ocean

North Channel

CHEVIOT
HILLS

R. Tees

LAKE
DISTRICT

THE PENNINES

R. Aire

LANCASHIRE
PLAIN

Humber Estuary

Irish Sea

R. Trent

The Wash

MERSEY
GAP

THE MIDLANDS

THE
FENS

EAST
ANGLIA

CAMBRIAN
MOUNTAINS

Forest of
Arden

R. Ouse

R. Severn

WALES

FOREST
OF
DEAN

COTSWOLDS

The   Thames

St George's Channel

THE
MENDIPS

SALISBURY
PLAIN

NORTH DOWNS

THE WEALD

SOUTH DOWNS

Straits of Dover

EXMOOR

English Channel

DARTMOOR

needed to smelt iron, its production was centered in areas rich in forests—in the Weald of Kent, the Forest of Dean, and the Forest of Arden. In the eighteenth century, when these forests were rapidly disappearing, the English learned to smelt iron with coke (coal heated to a high temperature out of contact with air). They also discovered how to use coal to drive steam engines, thus creating the chief source of energy for the Industrial Revolution. It was Britain's good fortune to have vast coal deposits near the surface on both sides of the Pennines. Without this iron and coal, Britain might have remained as poor as Italy; with it, the nation became the greatest industrial power of the nineteenth century. Indeed, the Reverend William Buckland, Professor of Geology at Oxford in 1845, taught that God had brought together coal and iron deposits near Birmingham with the express purpose of making Britain the richest nation on earth.

THE EARLIEST INHABITANTS

Humankind is far older than the island of Britain. Humans emerged during the Pleistocene era, on the open savannahs of Africa, first as *Australopithecus*, a bipedal, erect primate ancestor, and then, over a million years ago, as *Homo erectus*, a hominid with a cranial capacity midway between the gorilla and *Homo sapiens*. If the ability to make tools distinguishes humans from other animals, then *Australopithecus* and *Homo erectus* must be regarded as human. *Australopithecus* made crude chopping and cutting tools from pebbles of lava and quartz, and *Homo erectus* fashioned an all-purpose hand ax by chipping off the outside of the rock until the core had a working edge. The hand-ax culture of Africa spread north—to Morocco by 400,000 B.C., to Abbeville and St. Acheul in France by 300,000 B.C., and perhaps to southeastern Britain at the same time. Coarsely worked hand axes found in Kent suggest the possibility that around 300,000 B.C. humans began to occupy Britain, though the earliest clearly documented occupation occurred around 200,000 B.C.. The human ancestors who first entered Britain were not of the species *Homo erectus*, but of a species intermediate between *Homo erectus* and *Homo sapiens*. Part of the skull of one of them was found at Swanscombe in the Thames Valley. The size of the skull exceeds that of *Homo erectus* and approaches that of modern man. Swanscombe man, who probably lived about 200,000 B.C., manufactured a superior hand ax, a fact which illustrates the close connection during man's early history between technological advances and the growth of the size of the brain.

The development of humans in Britain occurred during the Great Ice Age. Four times during these 600,000 years the temperature fell, the snow accumulated, and great sheets of ice crept southward—as far as the Thames in 325,000 B.C.. Four times it grew warmer and the ice receded. The advancing glaciers molded the northern mountains, reshaped river valleys, and laid down the clay of the Midlands. During the interglacial periods, the seas rose and old land surfaces became sea floors. Humans probably first entered Britain during a warm phase of the second glaciation, in pursuit of the reindeer, the bison, the musk-ox, and the woolly rhinoceros. During the interglacial periods, they hunted red deer, roe deer, wild ox, and wild boar.

Life during the Old Stone Age was, as Thomas Hobbes imagined it to be, "solitary, poor, nasty, brutish, and short." Survival beyond the age of 40 was rare; life expectancy averaged twenty-five years. Of four or five children born, only two or three would survive to maturity. The men spent the day tracking animals while the women and children gathered fruits, roots, and grubs. Because it requires 200 square miles of land to support one person in a hunting society, there were probably no more than 500 people in all of Britain. They huddled in caves, starved when drought drove away game, died of infectious diseases, and fled south when the ice advanced.

Despite these conditions, humans slowly extended their mastery over the forces of nature. The Paleolithic (or Old Stone Age) inhabitants of what is now Clacton, Essex, made their hand axes by striking flakes from a central core. They also discovered that the flakes themselves made useful tools. But the true revolution in toolmaking came when the people of Levallois (near modern Paris) deliberately began to make tools from the flakes. A whole range of specialized flake tools now replaced the all-purpose hand ax. During the third interglacial period this Levalloisian culture spread to Britain.

Closely allied to it was the Mousterian culture, in which flaked tools were struck from small, disclike cores. The makers of these tools were Neanderthals, whose cranial capacity exceeded that of modern humans but whose chinless, heavily-browed faces resembled those of apes. Neanderthal people fashioned skin clothing, used fire, and buried their dead with care. The attention paid to the burial of the dead suggests that humans were now aware of the briefness of their existence on earth and guessed at the presence of unseen powers in the world.

But the future did not lie with the Neanderthals. They and their culture died out by 40,000 B.C., replaced by Cro-magnons who, if suitably clothed, could walk down London's Regent Street today without causing a head to turn. These were true *Homo sapiens*—tall, erect, robust. They transformed the flint industry by producing long, narrow, parallel-sided blades, rather than flakes, thereby discovering the principle of the cutting knife. They also invented a chisel, with which they could work antler and bone into spearheads, harpoons, arrows, and fishing tackle. The chisel was also used to carve and engrave jewelry, for advanced Paleolithic people possessed an esthetic sense not displayed by earlier humans. The most remarkable display of this esthetic sense can be found in the cave paintings of Altamira and Lascaux in southern France, where the artists, with remarkable naturalism, captured the movements of the bison, the reindeer, and the rhinoceros. Paintings such as these are not found in Britain, but the blade culture of France did come to Britain, to the Creswell Crags of Derbyshire, where flint tools for dressing leather and carving bones have been found. Gradually a distinct Creswellian culture emerged, distinct enough to be called the first British culture. And that culture encompassed art, for at Creswell Crags an unknown British artist scratched upon a fragment of bone a naturalistic engraving of a horse's head.

About 8,300 B.C., the Great Ice Age suddenly came to an end. The tundra and steppe, on which Paleolithic people had hunted the bison, the reindeer, and the rhinoceros, gave way to forests—first of birch, then of pine, finally of oak, elm, and lime. This profound change in environment destroyed the foundations of the Paleolithic economy and gave rise to the Mesolithic (or Middle Stone Age) hunter. To survive, humans had to learn to fish, to catch fowl, and to hunt the deer and elk. They now needed dugout canoes, harpoons, fish nets, spears, and bow and arrow. Two cultures, one from the shores of the North Sea (the Maglemosian) and the other from what is now France (the Tardenosian) supplied these Mesolithic skills to Britain. The Maglemosians developed axes and adzes with which to fell trees and make dugouts. They made bows of tapered wood and paddles for their canoes. The Tardenosians were skilled in the manufacture of microliths, or small flints. These microliths were mounted on wooden or bone shafts to make spears, harpoons, and arrows. In Britain these Mesolithic cultures flowed together and gave rise to native cultures, one of which was that of Horsham. The people of Horsham used the microliths of the Tardenosians, adopted the heavy axes of the Maglemosians, and built the first dwelling in Britain—a pit eight feet wide and four feet deep, roofed over with boughs or sod.

THE NEOLITHIC REVOLUTION

Triticum dioccoides is the ancestor of our wheat, *Hordeum spontaneum* of our barley. Both grew wild in the arc of land that extends from Syria through the foothills of Turkey and Iraq to Iran. In these same foothills wild sheep roamed. Here, about 6,000 B.C., sun, soil, water, seed, animal life, and people came together to bring about an economic revolution. Humans learned to cultivate plants and to domesticate animals. No other event before the Industrial Revolution had so profound an influence on human life. The new agricultural economy could support a population ten or more times greater than that which a hunting economy could support. Agriculture allowed a settled way of life, one that gave men and women the opportunity to weave cloth, make pottery, search for metals, and trade their wares.

Various Mediterranean peoples, slightly built, dark, with long, rather narrow heads, carried this new culture up the Danube, through Europe, and across the Channel. Others carried it by sea to Spain, and then along the coasts of Brittany to Cornwall, Ireland, and Scotland. By 3,800 B.C. Neolithic farmers had established themselves on the chalk soil of the Downlands of England. The new culture gradually replaced the Mesolithic hunting cultures, which now disappeared. But though they disappeared, they should not be ignored, for measured by the span of time that elapsed, nine-tenths of the history of humans in Britain concerns the struggle of the Paleolithic and Mesolithic people to improve their crude stone tools, to perfect their hunting skills, and possibly to begin the herding of animals, particularly deer.

The Neolithic colonists did not settle on the heavy clay soils of England, but on limestone uplands, sandy tracts near the coast, and the chalk Downs of southern England, lands which were forest until cleared by the Neolithic settlers. These settlers were a pastoral and nomadic people who tended broadskulled, large-horned cattle. They commonly kept pigs, as also a few goats and sheep. Though the growth of grain was subsidiary to the raising of cattle, they did plant small fields with wheat and barley, first criss-crossing the field with a plow to break up the ground, then cultivating it with hoe and spade. They har-

The interior of a stone hut, over 3,000 years old, at Skara Brae, a Neolithic village in the Orkney Islands (Edwin Smith).

vested the grain with flint sickles and ground it by rubbing a small stone round and round on a larger, concave one. The women produced simple pottery vessels, but there was no weaving; they still fashioned clothing from skins.

At various places on the Downs Neolithic people built camps that served as headquarters. The camps were formed of concentric rings of ditches and embankments, frequently broken by causeways leading into the center. The greatest of these camps was built at Windmill Hill, Avebury. Its outer circle encompassed 23 acres, the inner circle a fourth of that area. The great number of causeways across the circles suggests that the camps were designed to protect cattle from attack. Some camps were places of habitation, but others were merely meeting places for trading, festivals, sacrifices, and the rituals accompanying burials. The houses in which the Neolithic people lived, whether in camps or in isolated settlements, were at first rude pits surrounded by oaken stakes supporting a roof, which was probably made of skins. Later they built houses that were wholly above the ground. To hew the oaken stakes they needed flint axes, and to find the flints large enough for such axes they needed to mine the chalk soil where flint was buried. The Windmill Hill people brought mining to Britain. They sunk shafts 30 to 40 feet into the chalk, and then dug a network of galleries out from the bottom of each shaft. Flink taken from the mines was then manufactured into axes. The flint miners and ax makers of Norfolk, Sussex, and Wessex formed the first specialized industrial community in Britain.

On nearly every ridge in Sussex one could find in Neolithic times a causeway camp, a flint mine, and a cluster of long barrows. The long barrows were designed for the collective burial of the dead; they were between 100 and 400 feet long, between 30 and 50 feet wide, and about 12 feet high. They were built of earth heaped over an unroofed chamber of timber and turf. Within these chambers archaeologists have found skeletons in a crouched position, the scattered bones of other skeletons, and grave goods such as vases and ornaments. They have also occasionally found female figurines and phallic symbols, suggesting that these tombs were in part dedicated to the fertility of man and beast.

To the west, in the Cotswolds, barrows were built by piling smaller stones over elaborate burial chambers built of great stones, or megaliths. These stone vaults, which contained as few as five and as many as fifty persons, could be used for successive burials over many years. The privilege of burial in such vaults was probably limited to the ruling family. The Cotswold gallery graves, however, were not the only megalithic monuments built in the British Isles during Neolithic times. Hundreds were built in Ireland, southwest Scotland, the Western Isles, northern Scotland, the Shetlands, and Orkney. Some had a long passage into a circular chamber; others had chambers built of vertical megalithic slabs, with horizontal slabs breaking the chamber into segments. The stones used in megalithic architecture weighed as much as 4, 8, and 10 tons. The labor of quarrying, transporting, and erecting these great stones suggests the existence of a political unit larger than the family. But more intriguing than the social significance of these monuments is their religious meaning. The grave goods may have been placed there to assist the deceased in his passage into the next world. But the idea of rebirth is also a common one in primitive societies, and the vaults may have been built to protect the spirit of the departed until it could once again enter into a living person. Whatever the belief, it led to the erection of monuments that can still be seen, stark and bold, on the hills of England, Wales, Ireland, and Scotland.

THE EARLY BRONZE AGE

The discovery of radiocarbon dating caused a revolution in the writing of British prehistory. Where it was once thought that the Neolithic people first came to Britain about 2500 B.C., it is now known that they came between 4000 and 3400. Similarly, where it was once believed that the Beaker Folk first came to Britain in 1900 B.C., it is now known that they came as early as 3000. The revolution in dating has led to a revolution in historical explanation. Forty years ago, prehistorians attributed almost all change in Britain to the migration of peoples and the diffusion of ideas, mostly Mediterranean; now they look to developments within the British Isles. In 1940, for example, Professor Gordon Childe argued that the megalithic tombs in Britain were derived from the eastern Mediterranean, but radiocarbon dating shows that such tombs existed in Britain a thousand years before their supposed eastern Mediterranean prototypes. The megaliths of Europe did not have a single origin, but developed independently in Malta, in Portugal, in Denmark, and in Britain.

The same is true of the art of metallurgy. Prehistorians once thought that the Beaker Folk brought a knowledge of metallurgy with them from the Rhine, but archaeological evidence now suggests that they purchased their copper daggers and axes from an Irish metal industry that was already in existence. The art of metallurgy probably traveled originally from Egypt to Spain, from which the megalith builders brought it to Ireland in late Neolithic times. Ireland possessed copper ore, which Irish smiths worked into flat axes and halberds (a combination of an axe and a pike). About 2000 B.C. they began to manufacture these implements in bronze, an alloy of tin and copper, using a ready supply of tin in Cornwall. The Beaker Folk may have brought the idea of a bronze alloy, but they brought neither bronze implements nor the skills to make them. The Irish smiths may have seized on the idea. They created a thriving British-Irish bronze industry that, though constantly influenced by continental ideas, maintained its insular character. Until about 1400 B.C., stone weapons and tools, mostly of flint, continued to be widely used; after that date, the superior bronze daggers and axes drove out the flint ones.

The Beaker Folk who invaded Britain about 3000 B.C., were a nomadic people from the Rhine Valley. Armed with bows and arrows and daggers, they crossed the North Sea and the Channel, occupied most of Britain, and mixed with the Neolithic inhabitants, some of whom adopted the lifestyle of the Beaker Folk. They are called the Beaker Folk after a beaker-shaped pot in common use among them, a pot that may have been used to drink a fermented beverage. The raising of crops played only a small role in their lives, for they were essentially herders. They lived in tents or pits sunk into the ground and covered by wattle, but though their houses were inferior to those of the Neolithic people, their pottery was more skillfully made and they wore linen and woolen clothes, held together by buttons. They buried their dead singly, in graves containing a dagger, a bow and arrow, some ornaments, and a beaker. Over this grave they piled earth in a round mound.

In Wessex, about 1900 B.C., there appeared graves containing riches far beyond those found in ordinary graves. These special graves contained daggers strengthened by flanged sides, slitted cups, gold pendants, bone tweezers, dress pins, and finely designed pottery. Clearly, these were the graves of a warrior aristocracy, who either emerged out of the Beaker society itself or came over from Brittany. The striking similarity between Breton and Wessex graves at this time suggests that they may have been Breton warriors. But whether they were a native or a foreign aristocracy, they reflected the political power and the social distinctions that existed in the densely populated, wealthy Wessex of that time.

STONEHENGE

The wealth, political organization, learning, and religious zeal of Wessex were displayed even more magnificently in the great stone monuments its inhabitants built. The most impressive of these is Stonehenge, which rises boldly and mysteriously out of Salisbury Plain. Like a Gothic cathedral, Stonehenge was built over many centuries. Sometime between 2900 and 2500 B.C., the Neolithic people of Salisbury Plain built Stonehenge I. This was a great ditch with banks built up on both sides, 380 feet in circumference, with an avenue leading out of it. One hundred feet outside the circle, down the avenue, stood a great stone, now called the heel stone. Standing at the center of Stonehenge one can see the midsummer sunrise, or summer solstice, over the heel stone. Within the ditch, there were once four stones that formed a rectangle which stood at right angles to the line of the midsummer sunrise.

About 2000 B.C., the Beaker Folk built Stonehenge II, two concentric rings of large stones placed within the ditch and banks. The Beaker Folk, and the Megalithic people before them, often built such circles of stones on the hills and moorlands of Britain, but never (except at Avebury 15 miles to the north) on so ambitious a scale. At Stonehenge II there were 82 bluestones, each weighing about 5 tons, all of them brought from distant Wales. But the two concentric circles of bluestones were soon taken down by the Wessex

Stonehenge as viewed from the air, showing the trilithons and the sarsen circle (*The Bettmann Archive, Inc.*).

chieftains who built Stonehenge III. They erected one great circle of sarsen stones, each weighing about 25 tons, brought from Marlborough Downs 20 miles to the north. Across the tops of these stones were placed other stones, the lintels, each weighing about 7 tons. This continuous circle was 97 feet in circumference. Within it they erected, in the shape of a horseshoe whose open end faced the heel stone, five great trilithons. A trilithon is made of three stones, two of them upright and the third laid across the tops. The upright stones of the trilithon were 25 feet in height and weighed from 40 to 50 tons each. Sometime later, the builders of Stonehenge III added a horseshoe of free-standing bluestones within the sarsen circle. This impressive structure of bluestone and trilithon horseshoes, surrounded by bluestone and sarsen circles, encompassed by ditch and bank, with avenue and heel stone, formed the great monument whose remains inspire awe to this day.

What did it all mean? That it reflected the compelling power of religion cannot be doubted, for it is hard to find any other impulse that would have led people to build not only Stonehenge, but the great stone circle at Avebury and the mysterious hill at Silbury, which lies near Avebury and is the largest artificial mound in Europe. It is likely that Stonehenge was a temple dedicated to the worship of the sun, for the line of the midsummer sunrise forms the main axis of the whole monument.

But it might be more than a temple. In 1962 an astronomer affiliated with the Smithsonian Astrophysical Observatory, Gerald S. Hawkins, visited Stonehenge, charted 165 recognized Stonehenge I positions (stones, stone holes, mounds), extended lines through 120 pairs of the charted points, and placed this information in a computer. He discovered that Stonehenge I had eleven

STONEHENGE

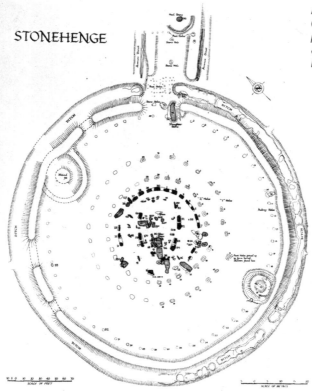

A diagram of Stonehenge (*British Crown Copyright, reproduced with permission of the Historic Buildings & Monuments Commission for England*).

key positions, which pointed to ten of the twelve extremes of the sun and moon (the sun has four extreme positions in a year: midwinter sunrise, midwinter sunset, midsummer sunrise, and midsummer sunset; the moon, because it comes north and returns south twice in a year, has eight, of which Stonehenge I failed to measure only two). He then found that Stonehenge III, with its trilithons and sarsen circle, pointed to eight of these positions. In 1964 he discovered that alignments at Stonehenge pointed to sunrise, sunset, moonrise, and moonset at the equinox (March 21 and September 23). Stonehenge, if Gerald Hawkins is right, was not only a temple but an astronomical observatory.

Such an observatory could have had practical, religious, and scientific uses. It may have furnished a calendar that told people when to plant crops. It may have enabled the priest to summon the people together at the proper time to witness the risings and settings of sun and moon—for all forms of worship require a calendar in order to keep their festivals on the right day. And finally it may have led some people to see a pattern in the puzzling movements of the sun and the moon.

These are matters of speculation. What is more certain is the social and

The sun rising over the heel stone, seen through the sarsen circle (*British Crown Copyright, reproduced with permission of the Historic Buildings & Monuments Commission for England*).

political significance of Stonehenge, for only a society that was wealthy, stable, and politically centralized could have built such a monument. Experiments carried out by the British Broadcasting Corporation indicate that it took 100 men to move one bluestone one mile in a day and 700 men to move one sarsen stone one mile. Based on these calculations, it has been estimated that it required 1.5 million man-days of labor to build Stonehenge. A rude, primitive society could not have organized and administered a labor force of such formidable proportions; nor could a society unskilled in engineering have joined lintels to uprights by such sophisticated techniques as mortice and tenon. Stonehenge is more than a monument to the sun; it is a monument to the skill and organization of the peoples who built it.

THE LATE BRONZE AGE

Between 1700 and 1100 B.C. the Neolithic population of Britain absorbed the Beaker Folk and the Wessex chieftains. The result was the emergence of two new cultures: the Food Vessel culture north of the Thames and the Urn culture south of it. The Food Vessel people got their name from the vases they buried with their dead. They were a pastoral people who made badly fired pottery, used only the simplest of bronze implements, and yet adorned their women with earrings of gold and necklaces of Yorkshire jet. The Urn peoples cremated their dead, whom they buried in urns. They grew flax for linen, wove woolen cloth, to a fineness of 33 threads to an inch, tended their flocks, cultivated wheat and barley and a hoe, and lived in round stone huts, clustered in circles. The Urn peoples eventually spread north, into Yorkshire, Lancashire, and even Scotland, establishing a uniform culture throughout the British Isles. The years that followed, unlike those that saw the arrival of the Beaker Folk and the rise of the Wessex chieftains, were years of calm. Society remained pastoral and the bronze-smiths improved their art.

About 1400 B.C. profound changes occurred both in agriculture and metallurgy. Archaeologists once attributed these changes to the migration of a new peoples from central Europe into southern England, but the evidence for such a migration is slim. Archaeologists now believe that this new culture, called the Deverel-Rimbury culture, was a native development, a development caused by the exhaustion of the soil on the uplands. As a result the inhabitants of England made a concerted attack upon the richer, more demanding lowland soils, soils which could sustain a longer period of use. They now placed more emphasis on the growing of cereal crops, with the result that a well-balanced, mixed farming now replaced the pastoralism of an earlier age. By discovering how to sow wheat and barley in the winter (using the hulled variety of each), farmers provided a steady supply of food throughout the year. These new farmers grew grain in neat, rectangular fields, perhaps a quarter of an acre in size. They enclosed their pastures, the boundaries of which can still be seen in Sussex and Dorset. In these enclosed fields one can, perhaps, see the beginnings of a private property in land. This early agricultural revolution produced more bountiful crops, which in turn supported a population which may have approached a million by the end of the Bronze Age.

The late Bronze Age also witnessed striking advances in the bronze industry. The bronzesmiths of Britain now began to manufacture the slashing sword, the socketed ax, and the pegged spearhead. These were for warriors. For the farmer and householder, they produced sickles, buckets, knives for daily use, and cauldrons for hanging over the fire. And they produced these weapons and tools in greater numbers and more inexpensively than ever. The introduction of iron in 600 B.C. only accelerated a process already begun: the widespread use of metal tools and weapons.

THE CELTS

When did the Celts first enter Britain? The question is difficult to answer, since the word "Celt" refers to a language, not a race or a culture, and a language leaves few traces behind it. It is certain that the inhabitants of Britain spoke Celtic when the Romans came. It is also certain that the Belgae, who invaded the island in the first century B.C., spoke Celtic. And there is solid evidence that the warriors who carried the La Tene culture to Britain in the third century B.C.

were Celts. Most historians would agree that the peoples who brought the Hallstatt culture of Upper Austria to Britain in the seventh century B.C. also spoke Celtic. The Beaker Folk may have spoken Celtic, for they came from the upper Rhine. But there is no way to prove it. What is certain is that the Celtic-speaking peoples who came between the seventh and the first centuries B.C. transformed British life. They brought iron, introduced the use of money, founded kingdoms, instituted the priesthood, and created a new art. Iron, money, kings, priests, and art—hallmarks of modern civilization—emerged with the coming of the Celts.

The Cimmerians, who swept into Europe in the eighth century B.C. from north of the Caucasus, taught the use of iron to the Celts of central Europe. Then, early in the seventh century B.C., some of these Celts invaded England—the warriors with iron daggers and broadswords, the farmers with sickles, axes, and narrow plowshares. Later invaders built two-wheeled chariots with wheels cased in iron and used iron bits for guiding the horses. The Belgae were even more highly skilled in iron work. With their iron axes they could fell timber and with their plow they could even turn over the heavy clay soil of the valleys.

The Celtic inhabitants of Britain also used iron bars as currency. At Glastonbury in the late second century merchants used flat iron bars weighing 309.7 grams as a standard of value and a medium of exchange. The people of Glastonbury, who lived on an island in the marshes of Somerset, raised cereals, bred cattle, made excellent pottery, traded with their neighbors, and gambled away their earnings at dice. The iron bars they used as currency represented a wide economic area, not a political unit. In the next century, the Belgae used minted coins rather than iron bars and introduced into Britain the potter's wheel. By the end of the century, Britain exported grain, iron, tin, leather, and hunting dogs to the Continent.

The people of Glastonbury, who defended their island with palisaded fortifications, were not alone in this concern for defense. Between 1200 and 150 B.C. fortified settlements, particularly on hilltops, dotted the landscape. These hill forts served in part as religious centers, in part as meeting places, and in part as pastoral enclosures, but were principally a defense against an invader, or a stronghold built by a successful invader. The Celts, particularly in the fifth century, came as aristocratic warriors. In thinly populated areas like Yorkshire, they established an oligarchic rule over their own followers. When they confronted a native population, as in the south, they reduced them to the status of tenants. The aristocratic nature of Celtic society is vividly demonstrated by the resplendent graves of the warrior chieftains. They were buried fully clad, with swords and helmets, along with flagons of wine and their two-wheeled chariots. The hill forts of southeast England disappeared when the Belgae created kingdoms strong enough to end the fierce strife of tribe against tribe. The most powerful of these kingdoms was that created in A.D. 25 by Cunobelin, whom Shakespeare transformed into Cymbeline. Cunobelin located the center of his kingdom in Hertfordshire and Essex, but extended his power into Oxfordshire,

An Herefordshire iron age hill fort (Cambridge University Collection, copyright reserved).

the Fens, and Kent. Throughout the southeast people left their hill forts and settled peacefully in homesteads and large unfortified towns.

Julius Caesar, who conquered the Celtic tribes of Gaul, observed of the Celts that there were among them only two classes of people who counted: the warriors and the priests. The priests, who were called Druids, taught that the human soul was immortal and at death passed from one person to another. They also taught that spirits, many of them evil, dwelled in forests, streams, springs, and rocks. They held the mistletoe in particular veneration and chose groves of oak as their special retreat. To protect those who were going into battle or to help those who were ill, they offered human sacrifices. The Druids were more than priests; they were also physicians, teachers, prophets, and judges. They taught young people their magic lore and they were judges in matters of crime and disputed boundaries. Powerful and esteemed, they counselled kings and ruled over people.

The Celtic aristocracy sought pleasure in beauty as well as consolation in religion. Out of Scythian and Greek influences, their artists developed a brilliant abstract art. From the Scythians, who entered central Europe about 500 B.C.,

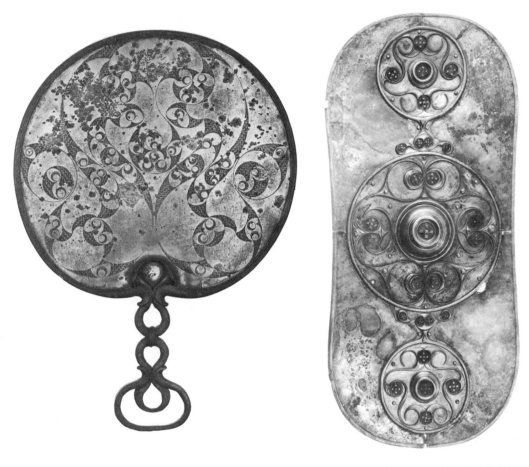

Two examples of Celtic art: the Desborough mirror and a decorated bronze shield (the British Museum).

they learned a decorative vocabulary of curves, countercurves, spirals, and interlaces. From the Greeks they learned new ways of giving expression to living forms. The Celtic artist copied the Greek designs in a free, spontaneous manner, thereby creating a style marked by graceful curves, scroll patterns, and perfect proportions. The artists engraved these ingenious curve patterns on bronze shields, sword scabbards, sacrificial dishes, and mirrors. At Glastonbury the art of the few became the art of the many when potters inscribed these designs on pottery, but the curving patterns of the earlier style now became more purely geometrical. The growing influence of Rome after 20 B.C. caused the symmetry to become even more formal and the designs unimaginative. The Roman invasion itself put an end to this extraordinary art, except in distant Ireland.

Thus, when the Romans arrived in Britain in 55 B.C., it was not an empty land that they found, nor a land inhabited by a rude and ignorant people. Rather, they found a people who enjoyed a settled agriculture, possessed weapons and implements of iron, used money, made excellent pottery, guessed at the meaning of human existence, and strove toward political unity. It was a level of civilization far below that of Rome, but at the same time it was infinitely higher than that enjoyed by the first inhabitants of Britain 200,000 years before.

FURTHER READING

(In this and subsequent lists of Further Reading, an asterisk indicates that the book is available in paperback.)

LLOYD AND JENNIFER LAING. *The Origins of Britain.* London, 1980. A brief, nontechnical introduction of prehistoric Britain; excellent illustrations.

W. GORDON CHILDE. *Prehistoric Communities of the British Isles.* New York, 1972. A wide-ranging, brilliant synthesis, first published in 1940; shows how Continental cultures were adapted to an insular environment.

RICHARD BRADLEY. *The Prehistoric Settlement of Britain.* London, 1978. A study in "settlement archaeology"; summarizes recent work on woodland and grassland clearance, arable and pastoral farming, and field systems.

*PETER FOWLER. *The Farming of Prehistoric Britain.* Cambridge, England, 1983. A survey of the evolution of British farming during the last two millenia B.C.; argues that agrarian history is central to our understanding of the prehistoric world.

DEREK ROE. *The Lower and Middle Paleolithic Periods in Britain.* London, 1981. Technical, yet clearly written; stresses the need for the British Paleolithic to be seen in its European context.

for the British Paleolithic to be seen in its European context.

STUART PIGGOTT. *The Neolithic Cultures in the British Isles.* Cambridge, England, 1954. Though becoming out-of-date, remains the classic account.

BARRY CUNLIFFE. *Iron Age Communities in Britain.* 2nd. ed., London, 1978. A comprehensive survey that covers the whole of Britain and all aspects of Iron Age life.

LLOYD LAING. *Celtic Britain.* London, 1979. A popular introduction, incorporating the most recent scholarship; many illustrations and a useful bibliography.

R.J.C. ATKINSON. *Stonehenge.* London, 1956. Presents the essential facts about the structure and construction of Stonehenge, but also speculates on the inspiration and social conditions that enabled the monument to be built.

GERALD S. HAWKINS., in collaboration with John B. White. *Stonehenge Decoded.* Garden City, N.Y., 1965. An ingenious, though controversial, investigation into the astronomical purposes of Stonehenge.

2 Roman Britain: 55 B.C.-A.D. 450

Late on an August evening in 55 B.C., two Roman legions, some 10,000 men, sailed from Boulogne in eighty ships. Led by Julius Caesar, they reached Dover the next day, where they saw the formidable chalk cliffs lined with Britons. Sailing north a few miles, pursued by the defenders, the Romans finally ran their ships onto the open beach. The Britons waded out into the sea to oppose them. A fierce skirmish followed, until the Britons, outflanked and outfought, fled in panic. The Romans had won a beachhead.

Julius Caesar, a Roman general, an ambitious politician, and the conqueror of Gaul, launched this expedition for a variety of motives. In the first place, he wished to punish the Britons for giving refuge to Celtic rebels fleeing from Gaul. He had also heard of the wealth of Britain, of the gold and silver, the lead and tin, the grain and slaves. Then there was the prestige to be won by adding a new province to the empire, and that province one that lay shrouded in mystery beyond the ocean. Though these motives were personal to Caesar, they reflected the needs and character of the expanding Roman Empire. Economically that empire depended on the tribute exacted from the provinces; politically it was dominated by ambitious generals and senators; psychologically it was sustained by victories and fresh triumphs.

Finding that the Britons were stronger than he had thought, Caesar left within a month, describing the expedition in his *Commentaries* as a reconnaissance. In 54 B.C. he returned with 800 ships and 25,000 men. He now drove inland, forded the Thames, and defeated Cassivelaunus, the most powerful of British kings. But news of an insurrection in Gaul forced his withdrawal within two months, and he never returned. The Roman conquest of Britain was delayed for a century, a century during which the Roman Republic fell, Augustus created the empire, Cicero wrote his famous letters, Christ preached to the world, and St. Paul addressed the Romans.

Augustus, the first Roman emperor, having suffered a disastrous defeat in Germany, resolved that the empire should be contained within its existing boundaries. But Claudius, who became emperor in A.D. 41, and who had led a sheltered life owing to a physical deformity, needed a military victory in order to establish himself in the eyes of the army. He sought that victory in Britain, where the situation demanded action. The great Cunobelin, who had welcomed Roman traders, minted money, established a capital at Colchester, and declared himself *rex Britannorum*, died in A.D. 42. His kingdom descended to two reckless sons, who at once invaded the kingdom of the Atrebates and drove out their king, Verica, an ally of Rome. A failure to support Verica, reasoned the politicians in Rome, would badly damage the prestige of Rome. There were also other motives for an invasion. Since the Rhine garrison had grown dangerously powerful, Claudius decided to weaken it by moving two of its legions to Britain. At the same time the Romans discovered that the suppression of Druidism in Gaul would require its suppression in Britain. For all these reasons, in A.D. 43 Claudius ordered Aulus Plautius to sail against the British with 40,000 men.

Unlike Caesar, who failed on both occasions to discover the port of Richborough in Kent, Plautius sailed directly to this sheltered harbor. His landing was uncontested and his fleet was secure against storm. A sweep through Kent, a contested passage across the Medway, and a march on Colchester was enough to bring down the kingdom of Cunobelin. By A.D. 47 the Romans had conquered the lowlands of Britain and had constructed a cross-country road, later called Fosse Way, that ran from Exeter to Lincoln. By A.D. 61, they had reached the island of Anglesey, a sacred center of Druid mysteries and a center of resistance to Rome. There they slaughtered the Druid priests and the wild, black-clothed women who, like furies, mingled with the priests and urged them on.

The Iceni of East Anglia then rose in revolt against Roman rule. Heavily taxed, conscripted, plundered by corrupt officials, exploited by moneylenders, their lands confiscated, the Iceni soon discovered what it was like to be a colonial people. It took only the flogging of Queen Boudicca, ruler of the Iceni, and the rape of her daughters to spark a rebellion. Other tribes joined the Iceni and fell savagely upon the Romans in Camuldunum (Colchester), Verulamium (St. Albans), and Londinium (London). They massacred thousands —70,000, reported the Roman historian Tacitus. Only the quick march of Governor Suetonius Paulinus from Anglesey saved Roman rule in Britain. With 10,000 legionaries he met and defeated the vast army that followed Queen Boudicca. Boudicca, who led her troops into battle after making a fiery speech to them, escaped captivity by drinking poison (though others reported she died of illness). Nothing now prevented Paulinus from laying waste, with fire and sword, the rebels and their lands.

The Romans accomplished in eighteen years what it took the Anglo-Sax-

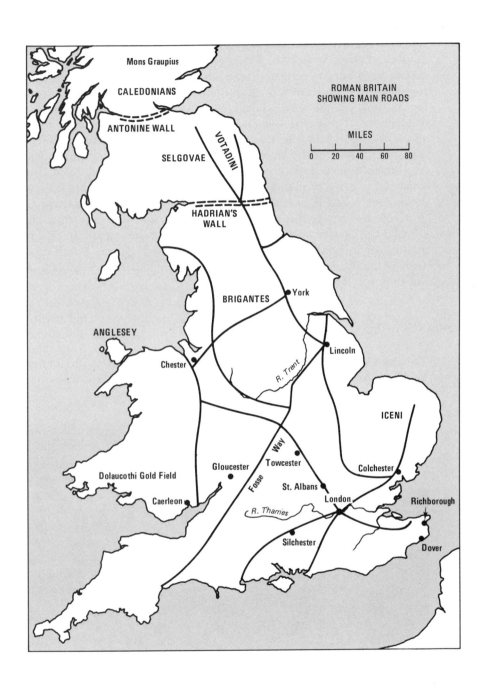

ROMAN BRITAIN
SHOWING MAIN ROADS

MILES

0   20   40   60   80

Mons Graupius

CALEDONIANS

ANTONINE WALL

SELGOVAE

VOTADINI

HADRIAN'S
WALL

BRIGANTES

York

ANGLESEY

Chester

Lincoln

R. Trent

ICENI

Way

Towcester

Colchester

Fosse

Gloucester

St. Albans

Dolaucothi Gold Field

Caerleon

London

Richborough

R. Thames

Silchester

Dover

ons a century and a half to achieve: the conquest of lowland Britain. The explanation for their success lies in their greater political organization and their superior military skills. The Romans were a highly centralized people facing a number of tribal kingdoms. *Divide et impera,* "Divide and rule," was the Roman maxim, and there were many Celtic chiefs who allied with Rome in order to secure themselves against a powerful neighbor. There was military resistance—at the Medway, in the west, during Boudicca's revolt—but the Romans quickly overcame it. The Celtic war chariots made a thundering noise as they dashed across the battlefield, but they were no match for the heavy cavalry of the Romans and useless if the Romans had time to plant stakes and ropes. The Britons attacked with fury and speed but could not disrupt the Romans, who remained in close formation, protected by shields and flexible body armor. The legionaries would then hurl their seven-foot javelins at the enemy, trot forward in wedge formation, thrust with their shields, and stab with their short swords —while the cavalry outflanked and surrounded the enemy. In this manner Roman discipline and superior weapons defeated Queen Boudicca's untrained army at Mancetter in the Midlands. According to report, 80,000 Britons fell, but only 400 Romans.

HADRIAN'S WALL

Though the Romans destroyed the Druids at Anglesey and defeated Queen Boudicca at Mancetter, they still faced two problems: how to govern and how to defend lowland Britain.

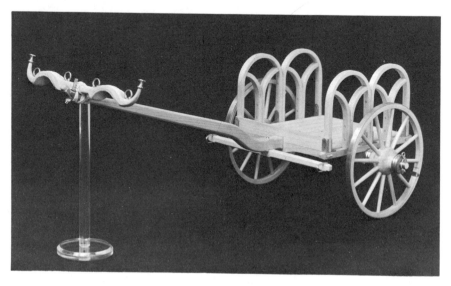

A reconstructed model of a Celtic chariot (National Museum of Wales).

The rebellion of the Iceni led in time to the adoption of milder policies by the Romans and to an attempt to Romanize life in the southeast. But it was not on government by consent that the Romans truly depended; it was on the army. The Roman occupation of Britain was a military occupation. Few Latin-speaking peoples came to Britain other than soldiers and officials, though there were about 60,000 of these. They made up only a small percentage of the population, which was about four million.

Until A.D. 100 the Romans maintained four legions in Britain; after that they kept only three, which meant some 40,000 men. These legions were garrisoned at Caerleon in South Wales, at Chester in the northwest, and at York in the north. Between the garrisons, and between them and London, ran roads that were straight, wide (20 to 25 feet), paved with stone, and kept open the year round. Their purpose was to move troops swiftly from place to place, but merchants soon made use of these roads, which formed a network some 7000 miles in length. Not until the nineteenth century could people and goods travel as swiftly through Britain as during Roman times.

Roman legionaries in battle: a scene from Trajan's column (Evans Brothers Limited).

The Romans were more successful in subjugating the lowlands than in defending the frontier. Britain was a weakly held border province. The Romans did finally conquer Wales by building roads through it and garrisoning forts along the roads. Julius Agricola, who became governor of Britain in A.D. 78, completed the subjugation of Wales. He then turned to the problem of the Brigantes in northern Britain. By the brilliant use of roads and forts (of which there were forty), he forced them to bow to Roman rule.

But further north yet there remained the Votadini, the Selgovae, and the Caledonians. Against them Agricola applied the same methods that had proved so successful in Wales and the north. He marched into what is now Scotland, built forts, and defeated a Caledonian army at the Battle of Mons Graupius, fought somewhere on the edge of the Highlands. Agricola's policy was clear-cut: Rome should protect the south by conquering the whole of the British Isles. But before he could carry out this policy, he was recalled to Rome. Agricola had the good fortune to be the father-in-law of Tacitus, one of the greatest of Roman historians. In his life of his father-in-law, Tacitus praises his wisdom and regrets that he was recalled. There is no doubt that Agricola governed Britain with wisdom and energy, but his forward policy in Scotland might have bankrupted the province. Britain already held 10 percent of the troops of the empire. To hold Scotland also would have demanded four legions, an excessive burden on an economy that could barely support three. Furthermore, that

Hadrian's Wall near Housesteads, extending westwards over the crags (British Crown Copyright, reproduced with permission of the Controller of Her Britannic Majesty's Stationery Office).

fourth legion was needed to shore up the defenses of the empire on the Danube.

The Emperor Hadrian, who visited Britain in A.D. 122, proposed what he believed was a less expensive solution to the problem of defense. It was an engineer's solution: Rome should build a wall from the mouth of the Tyne River to Solway Firth. Between A.D. 122 and 128, Roman engineers constructed such a wall. Built of stone in the east and of turf in the west, it was 73 miles in length, 15 feet high, 10 feet wide at the base, and 7 feet wide at the top. There were numerous turrets, a small fort every mile, and quarters for troops. To the north of the wall was a ditch, 27 feet wide and 15 feet deep. To the south of it was another ditch (a defense against the Brigantes). The Romans designed the wall less to repulse the frontal assault of an invading army than to prevent plundering and raiding, and to separate the Brigantes from their allies in the north. It was not a wall to be defended, like a city wall, but a fortified base from which to launch attacks on the enemy. That it saved on labor is doubtful, for it took about a million man-days to build and required some 9500 men to garrison.

The Romans were not even sure they had built it in the right place, for in A.D. 143 they built another wall, 37 miles long, between the Firth of Forth and the Firth of Clyde. They held this wall, called Antonine's Wall, for about twenty years and then abandoned it. The emperor Severus in A.D. 210 further strengthened Hadrian's Wall, which protected Britain until the legionaries abandoned it in the late fourth century. Hadrian's Wall was the most formidable barrier of its kind in the Roman Empire, but it reflected the limitations of Roman power as much as its greatness.

THE ROMAN TOWN

Defended by Hadrian's Wall and Agricola's forts, the Britons in the south enjoyed 300 years of peace, shared in the famous *Pax Romana*. During those years, the government sought to win the Celtic chieftains over to Roman rule by granting them a measure of local self-government and by holding out before them the charms of Latin civilization. The chosen instrument for both purposes was the town. Mediterranean culture had flowered in the city; Rome had begun as a city-state; it had grown by absorbing other city-states. What more natural than to transmit to Britain its urban way of life through the town.

Veterans from the army established the first four towns, called *coloniae*, at Colchester, Lincoln, Gloucester, and York. The government then conferred on the existing Celtic town at Verulamium the status of a city, under the title of a *municipium*. It may have granted the same status to London, which was located where the Thames River is both narrow enough to be bridged and broad enough to receive ocean-going vessels. The imperial government also grouped the tribes of Britain into cantons, created capital towns for each canton, urged the Celtic aristocracy to live there, and gave to these capitals the status of a town, or *civitas.*

Whether a town was called a *colonia, municipium,* or *civitas,* it had a council composed of wealthy townsmen. The council in turn elected magistrates who dispensed justice and maintained the public buildings, the streets, and the drains. Nor did their jurisdiction stop at the town wall, for the towns of Britain governed the countryside that surrounded them. It was through the town, the council, and the elected magistrates that the Romans disguised the lack of true self-government in Britain.

The town was also an instrument for disseminating the civilization of Rome. Agricola tried to teach the Celtic chieftains Latin and to introduce them to the luxury of the bath and the banquet. To this end he gave liberally to the erection of basilicas and temples. There were in Britain some twenty to thirty large Roman towns, ranging in size from London, with its 15,000 inhabitants, and Silchester, with its 2,500, to the smaller *civitas* with about 1,000. These towns were laid out in the Roman checkerboard fashion, with streets intersecting each other at right angles. In the center was the forum, an open space surrounded by public buildings and shops. There were temples for worship, basilicas for public meetings, baths for public bathing, theaters for plays, and amphitheaters for gladiatorial contests.

In Silchester, the most thoroughly excavated Roman town in Britain, the forum was surrounded by an impressive colonnade. On one side stood a basilica, over 200 feet long and nearly 60 feet wide, adorned with both local and Italian marble. Latin civilization was all-pervasive. The architecture was classical —arches, columns, capitals, entablatures, pediments. There were temples for the worship of the chief deities of Rome. The wealthy built houses of masonry, roofed with tile, and paved with mosaics illustrating Roman mythology. When they grew weary of Silchester or London, they could always travel to Bath, where the Romans had discovered the local hot springs and where they had used the local limestone and the lead of the Mendips to build sumptuous baths and plunging pools, surrounded by arches and colonnades. It was the most splendid spa in Western Europe.

Yet these towns were artificial creations, imposed on people unaccustomed to them. The ordinary British notable preferred life on his country estate to life in town. Aside from London, with its mint, its wharves, its mills, and its radiating roads, no town had a sufficient economic base to support it. The countryside produced only enough food to support itself and the army of occupation. There was no surplus to support a considerable population engaged in trade and manufacturing. The towns were essentially instruments of government, and when the government faltered in the fifth century, the towns decayed.

Because it was a border province, Britain came under the personal command of the emperor, who entrusted its immediate government to a legate, or governor. The governor's duties were largely military, but he also supervised

The Roman baths at Bath, the large rectangular pool (A.F. Kersting, F.R.P.S.).

the *civitates*, directed the building of roads, recruited men for the army, and managed the public post. He also had judicial duties, for he was the court of appeal in lawsuits and exercised original jurisdiction in all cases that involved either Roman citizens, capital punishment, or condemnation to the mines. In later centuries he had a legate to assist him in his legal duties.

There was one field, however, in which the governor was not supreme: finance. A provincial procurator, named by the emperor and responsible to him, collected taxes and paid out revenues. He was assisted by a corps of hated tax collectors. The chief sources of revenue were a tax on land, a poll tax, custom duties, and (after the late third century) a levy of grain to feed the army. The agents of the procurator would assess the amount of the land tax and the poll tax a town and its hinterland should pay. The council and the magistrates would then enforce its collection. It is little wonder that by the third century service as a councillor and magistrate had become more of a burden than an honor.

THE COUNTRYSIDE

The chief instrument for the Romanization of the countryside was the villa. A villa was the center of an agricultural estate, distinguished from the Celtic farmstead by its attempt to imitate the comforts and the way of life of the town.

A fourth-century Roman mosaic at Woodchester (Keith Branigan).

Most of the 620 villas that dotted the southeast were owned by wealthy Britons, not by Romans. When the villa first appeared in the second century, it was unpretentious—a single range of four or five rooms, with a corridor running in front of them, built of stone, timber, and tile. The corridor was important, for it gave the occupants a privacy denied to families huddled together in Celtic round huts. But the great age of villa building occurred in the fourth century. The wealthy Briton then built as many as thirty or forty rooms around one or more courtyards. The hypocaust, a system of central heating with an underground furnace and tile flues, now became the style. Windows were glazed, floors were paved with mosaics, and bath suites were provided. In these villas, of which there were probably seventy-five in Britain, the Romanized Briton enjoyed a standard of comfort that was not achieved again until the eighteenth century.

Around the elaborate house was the economic basis for this luxury—the barns, the cattlesheds, and the quarters for farm workers. Some estates had one or even two thousand acres. Part of the estate might be farmed by slaves; other parts were let out to tenants. Originally these tenants leased land for five years or less, but by the fourth century their legal position grew worse. They became bound to the soil like medieval serfs.

Not all farms were Romanized. Side by side with the Roman villa was the Celtic farm. Historians once thought that the Celts who lived in the countryside lived only on isolated farms, but recent archaeological evidence shows that some lived in villages, which were often associated with a villa. The Celtic field system with its small, rectangular fields survived through the Roman occupation. The Romans, in fact, contributed little to the improvement of farming, though it is possible that they added a coulter (for cutting the turf in front of the plowshare) and a moldboard (for turning over the sod) to the Celtic iron plow. What is certain is the fact that they introduced into Britain the grapevine, the cherry tree, and peas, parsnips, and turnips.

The principal contribution of the Romans was to make Celtic farming more efficient by providing peace, roads, markets, and towns. British farmers raised grain, bred cattle, and grazed sheep. The grain was vital to feed the farmers themselves, the army of occupation, the miners, and those engaged in the making of pottery. But since the government took over half the crop, little money was to be made from selling grain. Cattle raising was more profitable, but not as profitable as raising sheep. It is no coincidence that during the third century British woolens became famous throughout the empire and that during the next century the Roman villa spread across the countryside. Indeed, the villas are concentrated in the Cotswolds, the center of the sheep-grazing industry in Britain. It was the wealth taken from the backs of British sheep that built the Roman villa.

Tacitus believed that gold, silver, and other metals, not grain and wool, would be the reward for conquering Britain. The yield of gold, however, proved disappointing, even though the Romans mined gold for a century in the Dolaucothi mines in Carmarthenshire. Nor was tin to prove the most valuable metal. Before the Romans came Cornwall had exported great quantities of tin, but once the Romans had gained possession of the Spanish tin mines, which they did under Augustus, they undersold the British in the Mediterranean market. The British industry went into decline until about A.D. 250, when the Spanish mines were closed and the Cornish mines once again prospered. It was not tin, however, but lead that proved of greatest value to the Romans. Lead ore was doubly valuable: first for the lead itself, which was used in the construction of baths, water pipes, and coffins, and secondly for the silver which the lead ore of the Mendips, Flintshire, and Derbyshire contained. Within six years of the Claudian invasion the Romans were producing lead and silver from the Mendips. At first the imperial government itself undertook the mining of the ore and the production of lead and silver. But in the second century it leased its rights to private individuals and companies. Pewter is an alloy of lead and tin, and there soon grew up in Britain a flourishing pewter industry that furnished the middle classes with the cups from which they drank their Rhenish wine and local beer. Bronze continued to be widely used, and Britain possessed

An aerial view of Watling Street, the Roman road from London to Chester (Cambridge University Collection, copyright reserved).

both the tin and copper from which to manufacture it. During the first two centuries of Roman rule Britain probably had an unfavorable balance of trade, for it imported large quantities of Roman pottery and Rhenish and Moselle wines. But during the third and fourth centuries the British began to manufacture pottery and drink local beer, at 4 denari a pint, rather than Rhenish and Moselle wines. And Britain exported not only lead and woolens, but leather, hunting dogs, Kentish oysters, and Irish slaves.

THE COLLAPSE OF ROMAN RULE

As it was the power and vigor of the Roman Empire that led to the conquest of Britain in the first century, so it was the feebleness and exhaustion of the empire that led Rome to abandon Britain in the fifth. There were many causes of that exhaustion. The Roman economy in the West depended too heavily on slave labor and tribute from conquered peoples. When imperial expansion stopped in the second century, the supply of slaves and tribute fell. At the same time, a growing army of bureaucrats and soldiers consumed the wealth that was produced; by the fourth century there were some 40,000 bureaucrats and 500,000 soldiers on the payroll and a dwindling number of Romans on the tax rolls. This situation was made more serious by the fact that the population was declining because of war, famine, and plague. The economic crises led the heavily taxed productive classes—the middle classes in the cities and the tenant farmers in the countryside—to desert their employments. To keep the economy going, the emperors enacted laws freezing people in their vocations. During these same centuries, the educated classes turned from Greek humanism and Roman practicality to search for personal salvation through otherworldly religions. The Romans, furthermore, failed to solve the problem of the imperial succession.

In the third century, the army intervened in politics more and more. Commanders even used legions, needed on the frontiers to hold back the barbarians, in private wars to gain possession of the imperial throne. In A.D. 197, the governor of Britain, Clodius Albinus, seeking the imperial throne, crossed into Gaul with part of the Roman army in Britain. The resulting dislocation led to vandalism and looting throughout the north. Septimus Severus, who defeated Albinus and became emperor, immediately strengthened the Wall and gave Britain a long spell of tranquility that was broken only late in the third century, when Saxon pirates in search of booty fell upon the eastern coast of Britain. To defend the land against these pirates, the Romans built forts and signal stations along the coast, from the Solent to the Wash. In the fourth century the Emperor, realizing that military vigilance was the price of empire, created a new official, the Count of the Saxon Shore, and gave him command of the troops that garrisoned these forts and stations. Such defenses proved sufficient against raids, but they were not sufficient to withstand a concerted action by the barbarians. Such an action came in 367, when the Scots from the west, the Picts from the north, and the Saxons from the east assaulted and overran Hadrian's Wall and killed the Count of the Saxon Shore. Only resolute action by the Count Theodosius, a skillful and experienced soldier, allowed the restoration of Roman garrisons at the Wall.

But these garrisons did not remain for long. In 383 Magnus Maximus, a general whom the troops in Britain declared emperor, took part of his army to Gaul in quest of the imperial throne. And in 398 Stilicho, regent of the empire in the west, withdrew troops from Britain in order to wage war against the Visigoth, Alaric. On neither occasion was the Wall abandoned nor Britain entirely depleted of troops. There were clearly enough troops remaining in Britain in 407 to embolden them to elevate one of their officers to the imperial throne as Constantine III and to follow him to Gaul. Constantine III probably left a core of officers and men behind, officers and men whom the Britons expelled in 409. There are two good reasons why the British expelled the remnants of the

Roman army: they wished to rid themselves of the financial burden of the imperial establishment, and they had successfully organized their own defenses. Though no one could have been aware of it at the time, the year 409 marks the end of Roman rule in Britain.

In the fifth and sixth centuries the Britons offered a stout resistance to the Anglo-Saxon invaders, but ultimately were overrun. The failure of the Britons to defend themselves and the obliteration of Latin civilization in Britain raises two fundamental questions: How thoroughly were the Britons Romanized and what did survive of Roman civilization?

The Roman occupation of Britain offers many parallels to the British occupation of India. In the one a Romano-British culture emerged, in the other an Anglo-Indian. In both, the rich and the educated adopted the language, law, and dress of the imperial power, though the peasants remained untouched. Outwardly the Briton was a Roman and the Indian an Englishman, but inwardly the Briton remained Celtic and the Indian Hindu. And when the occupation ended, the inward person won out.

It was in the towns that the Britons were most thoroughly Romanized. Latin was the language of law, government, business, and culture; even artisans knew enough Latin to scrawl words on their pottery. It was the townspeople who wore the toga, drank wine, visited the baths, and gave dinner parties. The depth of Romanization is also reflected in the art of Roman Britain, for classical sculpture and mosaics drove out the abstract art of the Celts (though the Celtic feeling for pattern influenced both the sculpture and the mosaics). Britons worshipped the Roman gods, either in temples dedicated to Jupiter, Juno, and Minerva, or in those dedicated to deified emperors. In the towns, as in the villas, there was a culture truly touched by Rome.

But most Britons—some two-thirds of them—lived neither in towns nor villas. Latin civilization hardly touched them at all; they spoke no Latin and they worshipped Celtic gods in a hundred local shrines. For them, the Roman occupation meant compulsory grain deliveries and taxation. Nor did the towns prove permanent, as in Gaul and Spain. Once the Romans left the towns began to decay—buildings were left unfinished and amphitheaters became local markets. Only where they served an economic purpose did they survive into the fifth century. It was a Celtic Britain that the Anglo-Saxon invaders confronted in A.D. 449.

Their fierce onslaught in the next century and a half swept away nearly everything Roman. All that remained as a permanent legacy were the Roman roads (whose course still determines the direction of many modern highways), town sites (such as London, Canterbury, and York), and British Christianity. Of these legacies, Christianity was the most significant. In the early years of the empire the Romans, tolerant of most religions, persecuted Christianity because of the exclusive claims it made to people's allegiances. Several British martyrs suffered for their faith, most notably Alban, a Roman soldier put to death at Verulamium about 429. But the persecution ended when Constantine embraced Christianity at the opening of the fourth century. In 314, British bishops from London, York, and Lincoln attended the Council of Arles.

Britain also produced a Christian heretic, the learned Pelagius, who taught that man was born free of sin, possessed free will, and had the power to choose between good and evil. This presented a direct challenge to St. Augustine's belief that man, because of his sinful nature, is completely dependent on God's grace for salvation. St. Augustine's teachings became the orthodox teachings of the Church, but Pelagius's ideas became popular in his native land. In order to root them out, the Church in Gaul sent St. Germanus of Auxerre to Britain in 429. His mission was a success; the British Church returned to orthodoxy. It was, therefore, the orthodox faith of Rome that St. Patrick, a Romanized Briton who had studied under St. Germanus at Auxerre, carried into Ireland in 462, and that other Celtic missionaries carried to Wales and Scotland. Here, in the remote mountains and islands of the west, Celtic Christianity survived, to play an important role a century later in the conversion of the Anglo-Saxons.

FURTHER READING

*SHEPPARD FRERE. *Britannia: A History of Roman Britain.* London, 1974. A closely argued, scholarly, superbly written historical narrative, broken at the 3rd century with discursive chapters on the army, administration, towns, countryside, and trade.

PETER SALWAY. *Roman Britain.* Oxford, 1981. Authoritative, up-to-date, judicious, lengthy, and dull; contains an annotative bibliography; best used as a work of reference.

*IAN RICHMOND. *Roman Britain.* 2nd. ed., Harmondsworth, 1963. A first chapter on military history provides a chronological framework for chapters on towns, the countryside, economics, and religion; clear, concise, scholarly.

JOHN WACHER. *Roman Britain.* London, 1978. More heavily dependent on archaeology than Frere, and more concerned with economic and social life.

GRAHAM WEBSTER. *The Roman Invasion of Britain.* London, 1981. An entertaining and scholarly account of Caesar's and Claudius's invasions; contains an ingenious attempt to infer the location of 130 Roman forts from the disposition of troops.

A.L.F. RIVET. *Town and Country in Roman Britain.* 2nd. ed., London, 1964. A delightful account of the British side of Roman Britain; contains an acute analysis of the social background of the villa system.

*DAVID BREEZE, AND BRIAN DOBSON. *Hadrian's Wall.* 2nd. ed., Penguin Books, 1978. The most recent history of the Wall; seeks to show how it came to be, what it was, how it developed, and why it was abandoned.

JOHN MORRIS. *Londonium: London in the Roman Empire.* London, 1982. Not primarily about London, but about Britain as a part of the Roman world; though a brilliant introduction to the world of archaeology, it views the data in terms of people and society.

IVAN MARGARY. *Roman Roads in Britain.* 3rd. ed., London, 1973. A detailed, topographical study of the 7,400 miles of Roman roads; good on the construction of roads; beautiful aerial photographs.

TACITUS. *Agricola and the Germania.* Penguin Books, 1971.

3 Anglo-Saxon England: 450-1066

The history of English civilization—as distinct from the history of mankind in Britain—begins with the Anglo-Saxons, for they, insofar as it can be done, wiped the historical slate clean. Between A.D. 450 and 650 they sailed up the rivers of England, settled on the land, cleared the forests, built villages, and made England theirs. The straight Roman roads and the walls of the Roman towns remained, as did a Celtic population, largely reduced to slavery. But little else remained—except far to the west in Wales, Ireland, and western Scotland, where Celtic kingdoms kept alive the language, the learning, the literature, and the Christianity of the Celts. In time this Celtic civilization exercised an influence on England, but English civilization itself had its roots in the laws, customs, language, and institutions of the Anglo-Saxons. To the years between 450 and 1066 may be traced the boundaries of shires, the diocesan organization of the Church, the location of boroughs, the names of villages, the existence of open fields and manors, the division of England into parishes, the institution of monarchy, and the beginnings of the English language, not to speak of the name "Englaland" itself, the land of the Angles.

THE CONQUEST OF BRITAIN

The Anglo-Saxons came first as pirates, then as mercenaries, finally as colonists. As early as A.D. 287 Saxon pirates plundered the coasts of Britain; by the year 429, they had penetrated far inland. But the permanent conquest of Britain was carried out not by marauding pirates, but by mercenaries brought into the land to protect it. Both Gildas, a Welsh monk, and Bede, a Northumbrian scholar, tell the classical story of this fateful event. Vortigern, the proud ruler of southeastern Britain, called in the Saxons, led by two brothers, Hengest and Horsa, to help defend Britain against the Picts and the Scots. Hengest and Horsa, who may have once served in the Roman army, came in 449 or thereabouts, served Vortigern for six years, quarreled with him over pay, rebelled, established a kingdom in Kent, and (in Gildas's words), "fixed their terrible claws in the eastern part of the island." Historians have long doubted the truth of this story, since Gildas, who wrote shortly before the year 547, was a preacher rather than a historian, and since Bede, who added names and dates to Gildas's account, lived more than two hundred years after the event. But recent archaeological discoveries have confirmed the gist of the story—namely, that the British did invite German mercenaries into the land. The excavation of Germanic cemeteries near York, Lincoln, Norwich, and Ancaster reveal that during the first half of the fifth century Germanic mercenaries lived in these areas. The evidence also suggests that British authorities brought them there. It is quite possible that these mercenaries, like their brethren in Kent, rose in revolt and seized power. The silence of the chroniclers and poets about any great battle for York or Lincoln lends support to this conjecture, since no battle is needed when mercenaries swiftly seize a town.

Had the Anglo-Saxons limited themselves to the seizure of power, their conquest of Britain would have been a mere military occupation, like that of the Romans in A.D. 43 or the Normans in 1066. But the Anglo-Saxons went further; they colonized the land. Aware of how few they were and anxious to strengthen themselves, the mercenaries invited their fellow Germans to join them. They came in boats of shallow draft, narrow beam, and great length; a typical boat was 75 feet long, ten feet wide, and drew two feet of water when unladen. Having neither keel nor mast, they had to be rowed, usually by some 36 oarsmen. In these graceful, swift ships the colonists went up the Thames, up the many rivers that emptied into the Wash, through the Humber estuary to the Trent, and up the Trent to the Midlands. They came in small bands, led by a chief, though on occasion powerful kings formed great confederations. One of the greatest of these was Aelle, founder of the Kingdom of Sussex. Though the chroniclers have recorded the great battles—at Old Sarum, at Dyrham, at Catterick—the true story of the conquest lies in the slow, remorseless advance of small bands of warriors, followed by their wives and children, along the valleys and up the streams of England. They felled the trees, built their rude huts, and plowed the soil. This conquest was slow, extending over two centuries, but because it was slow, widespread, and deeply rooted it meant that the Anglo-Saxons would lay the foundations of modern England.

The Anglo-Saxons who settled in England were a Germanic people who had lived along the shore of the North Sea, from the Danish peninsula to the mouth of the Rhine. The historian Bede divided them into three tribes: the Angles, who came from Angeln on the neck of the Danish peninsula; the Saxons, who came from the lower Elbe; and the Jutes, who came from Jutland, also on

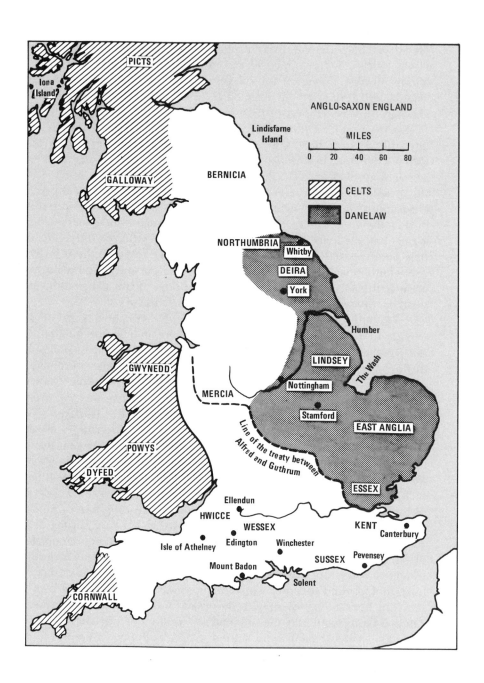

the Danish peninsula. Archaeological evidence supports this distinction among the three peoples. The Angles made a cruciform brooch, the Saxons a saucer-shaped brooch, and the distribution of these brooches shows that the Angles settled in the north of England, the Saxons in the south. Grave finds in Kent, the Isle of Wight, and Hampshire show that Jutes settled in those areas. But three qualifications must be made to the traditional story as told by Bede: first, these tribes had already come into contact with each other near the mouth of the Rhine before they came to England; secondly, there were other tribes who came, particularly the Frisians; and thirdly, the Anglo-Saxons were far more conscious of their common Germanic origins than of these tribal distinctions.

A desire for land drove these people to Britain. The crowded cemeteries and the many habitation sites in fourth-century Angeln and Saxony indicate a growing population. Along the coast of Frisia the sea had eroded the coastline, thus reducing the land available for settlement. And to the west the Franks barred any further advance. The Anglo-Saxons thus took to their boats, crossed the North Sea, and invaded Britain.

They were a pagan and illiterate people, but they were not unskilled in the arts of war and government. Theirs was a warrior society, aristocratic and heroic. Tacitus in the second century described this society, as did, many years later, the author of the epic poem *Beowulf*. The unknown poet who wrote *Beowulf* was probably a Christian who lived in the eighth century, but the society he described and the values he celebrated were those of the fifth century. The strongest bond in that society was that between lord and man. Every chief and every king was surrounded by a company of warriors, called by Tacitus a "comitatus." These warriors, whom the Anglo-Saxons later called "thegns," owed loyal service to their lord; in return, he rewarded them with treasure, arms, golden rings, great estates. When Beowulf returned from killing the monster, his king, Hygelac, rewarded him with land, a hall, and high office. A kingdom's very existence depended on the ability of its king to win battles and thereby to find the treasure and land with which to reward his followers. To betray a lord in such a society earned one perpetual infamy; it was even a reproach to leave a battlefield alive where one's lord lay dead.

The Anglo-Saxon warrior did not know the promises of Christ and could not fall back on the hope of eternal life. For him, life was a swift flight from darkness into darkness. Human destiny lay outside his control—capricious, unknowable, and doom-laden. In such a world the greatest virtues were the heroic ones: courage, endurance, honor, generosity, prowess in battle, boasting at the table, drinking at the feast, and splendor in dress. In great hall, decked with golden tapestries, the tables adorned with golden goblets, Beowulf and his companions feasted, drank, and boasted of their great deeds. As long as fate permitted it, life progressed from battle to feast and from feast to battle. But more important than the transitory joys of life was winning lasting fame for great deeds and for loyalty to one's lord. "Each of us," says Beowulf, "must experience an end to life in this world; let him who may, achieve glory before he dies; that will be the best for the lifeless warrior hereafter."

Inspired by these ideals and driven by the needs of a military aristocracy for land, the Anglo-Saxons finally prevailed over the native British. Yet the British put up a stout resistance, as the slow advance of the Saxons testifies. For some years after 449 the Saxons drove westward, but then, about 500, the British won a great victory at Mount Badon, believed to be near Wimborne in Dorsetshire. Among the British captains at Mount Badon was a brave warrior named Arthur about whom little is known, but around whom, in medieval times, arose the legend of King Arthur, Camelot, Excalibur, and the Knights of the Round Table. The British victory halted the advance of the Saxons for the next fifty years, but after 550 both the Saxons in the south and the Angles in the Midlands and the north resumed their drive westward. By the year 650 eleven English kingdoms had come into existence: Bernicia and Deira in the north; Lindsey, Mercia, and Hwicce in the Midlands; East Anglia, Essex, and Kent along the eastern coast; and Sussex, Surrey, and Wessex in the South.

But what was the fate of the native British? Historians once believed they were largely exterminated, and cited the story of Aelle, who killed all he found inside the fort at Pevensey, "so that not even a single Briton was left alive." Other massacres may well have occurred in Sussex, for there are hardly any Celtic place names there. The fate of the British language also supports the claim that the Britons were exterminated, for only fourteen British words found their way into English. But there is also evidence that casts doubt on the case for extermination. The laws of Kent and Wessex show that the native inhabitants survived as social inferiors, and archaeologists have recognized a British influence on objects found in Saxon cemeteries. River names offer the best clues, for new settlers will, if they displace a native population, change the names of lesser rivers. A careful study of such rivers in England shows that east of a line drawn from the Yorkshire Wolds to Salisbury Plain British river names are rare, but to the west they are more numerous. It was therefore probably in the west that the native population survived in the greatest numbers. Few historians today argue that the Britons were completely massacred or driven out, but most would agree that those who remained were reduced to a condition of servitude. It is no accident that the Anglo-Saxon word for "a Briton" came to denote a slave.

THE CONVERSION TO CHRISTIANITY

Shortly after A.D. 585, a young Roman of aristocratic origins named Gregory saw several boys of fair complexion and fair hair exposed for sale in the Roman slave market. He inquired whether they were Christians or pagans, and was told they were pagans. "Alas," he said, "how sad that such handsome folk are still in the grasp of the Author of darkness, and that faces of such beauty conceal minds ignorant of God's grace!" He then asked what was their race, and was told that they were Angles. "That is appropriate," he said, "for they have angelic faces, and it is right that they should become fellow-heirs with the angels in heaven." Gregory thereupon asked the Pope to send him to Britain to convert the English, but the Pope, pressed by the citizens of Rome, refused to allow this able administrator to leave Rome.

Gregory eventually became Pope himself and promptly initiated his long-cherished project. The time was ripe, for Gregory had recently heard that the English wished to become Christians and knew that Ethelbert, the pagan King of Kent, had married a Christian princess from Gaul. To carry the Christian gospel to the English, Gregory named a close friend, Augustine. Though a man of narrow views and arrogant bearing, Augustine proved able to carry out the greater man's conception. He and nearly forty fellow missionaries reached Canterbury, the capital of the Kentish kingdom, in 597. Within a year Ethelbert received baptism, and so did, shortly afterward, his nephew, the King of Essex. The conversion of Kent and Essex set a pattern for the other kingdoms: first convert the King; the conversion of his loyal thegns would follow, after which missionaries could be sent to preach to the populace. By these tactics, Raedwald of East Anglia and Edwin of Northumbria were converted to Christianity. But the death of a monarch might bring a relapse to heathenism, as it did briefly in Kent, more permanently in Essex and East Anglia, and disastrously in Northumbria. Despite these setbacks, the missionaries sent out from Canterbury persevered in God's work, with the result that by 663 the southeast was permanently won to the Church. The lasting conversion of Northumbria, however, was a task left to the Celtic missionaries from Iona.

In 597, the year Augustine landed in Kent, St. Columba died on the island of Iona. St. Columba was an Irishman of royal birth, impetuous temper, and fervent faith who carried the Christianity of St. Patrick to Iona, a small, wind-swept island off the west coast of Scotland. It was at Iona, among the monks in their beehive huts, that Oswald of Northumbria sought refuge from his enemies, and it was to Iona that he looked for help when he became King of Northumbria in 633. Penda, the fierce, heathen King of Mercia, had driven the missionaries of Rome from Northumbria. Oswald, anxious to restore Christianity to his kingdom, naturally looked for help to the monks who had sheltered him at Iona.

They heeded his call and sent a monk named Aidan. Aidan, instead of founding a bishopric at York, established a monastery on the island of Lindisfarne, off the coast of Northumbria, By doing so he advertised one of the deepest differences between Celtic and Roman Christianity. The government of the Roman Church was centered in the bishop and his diocese; the government of the Celtic church, in the abbot and his monastery. There were other differences. The Roman monk shaved the top of his head in the form of a circle, in imitation of Christ's crown of thorns; the Celtic monk followed the Druid custom of shaving a broad strip from ear to ear. They also dated Easter differently. Both churches agreed that Easter fell on the first Sunday after a full moon after the vernal equinox, but the Celtic church put the vernal equinox on

March 25, the rest of Christendom on March 21. Furthermore, the Celts stubbornly followed an 84-year cycle of such Sundays, a cycle the Roman Church gave up in 457 for a more accurate one of 532 years. Beneath these outward differences lay a deeper, more spiritual difference. The Roman Church emphasized order and discipline, and possessed wealth and power; the Celtic church relied on evangelical fervor, and praised the ascetic life. Aidan offered the perfect example of such a life, trudging the roads of Northumbria on foot, preaching the gospel, admonishing the rich and helping the poor. He and his band of monks, with the constant support of Oswald, rescued Northumbria from heathenism. And his successors, on the death of Penda, also won the kingdom of Mercia to the cause of Christ.

In Northumbria the Roman and Celtic churches now met face to face, for Oswy, who succeeded Oswald as King, had married a Kentish princess who followed Roman usage. It was a practical and urgent problem, for it was most awkward for the King to be celebrating Easter while the Queen was observing Lent. King Oswy therefore summoned a conference at Whitby in 663 to debate the Easter controversy. Colman, a monk from Iona, stated the case for the Celtic Easter; he argued that they dare not change a date which both St. John the Evangelist and the saintly Columba had observed. Wilfrid, a native Northumbrian who had studied in Rome, then presented the case for the Roman dating of Easter; it was a usage observed by the apostles Peter and Paul and by all the world except the obstinate inhabitants of two remote islands. He then asked Colman whether a Celtic saint, meaning Columba, was to be preferred before the blessed Peter, who held the keys to the kingdom of heaven. Oswy at once interrupted. Was it true, he asked Colman, that Christ gave the keys to the kingdom of heaven to St. Peter? Colman answered that it was. Oswy thereupon declared for Rome, "lest, when I come to the gates of the kingdom of heaven, there should be none to open them." Other reasons probably weighed more heavily with Oswy, reasons such as the grandeur of Rome, the strength of Canterbury, and the need for harmony in the realm. This much is certain: The judgment at Whitby ensured that England would not be divided between two different communions and would be united with an undivided Christendom.

The acceptance of Roman usages led to the organization of the English Church as a single body. This task was performed by Theodore of Tarsus, a remarkable man who proved that age need be no obstacle to great achievement. Named Archbishop of Canterbury by the Pope in 669, Theodore, then 67, began the work of organizing the English Church. He had completed it by the time of his death at 88. Theodore was a monk, scholar, and philosopher from Asia Minor, a man seemingly ill-fitted to the task given him; fortunately, he was also a disciplinarian and an autocrat. In twenty years he created a diocesan organization for the English Church. At his death there were fourteen bishoprics extending over the various kingdoms of England. Within the diocese the preponderance of work fell on the bishop. He baptized converts, catechized and confirmed candidates for membership in the Church, made annual visits through the diocese, and supervised the churches that fell within it. And the bishop was to perform these tasks according to Roman ideas of practical efficiency. Theodore told Chad, the saintly bishop of Mercia, that he must abandon the Celtic custom of visiting his diocese on foot, and when Chad objected, Theodore forced him to mount a horse. Theodore also summoned frequent synods, or meetings attended by all the bishops of England, and thereby gave England a synodical organization. The synod that met at Hertford in 672 was the first occasion on which representatives of the English people sat together for debate and decision.

The steadfastness of Augustine, the zeal of Aidan, the prudence of Oswy, and the skill of Theodore all contributed to the conversion of the English, but there were more fundamental reasons why Christianity triumphed so completely. Most important among them was the inadequacy of German heathenism, a religion compounded of animism and magic. The Anglo-Saxons worshipped trees, wells, rivers, and mountains; they felt themselves surrounded by ogres, elves, demons, and goblins. Priests were held to possess magical powers—they could bind the hands of the enemy by chanting spells or free a prisoner from his fetters by incantation. The Anglo-Saxons had their gods, Tiw, Woden, Thunor, and Frig (from whose names came Tuesday, Wednesday, Thursday, and Friday), but they had no ethical system, no answer to the problems of life and death, no cosmology that explained the mystery of human existence.

Christianity, on the other hand, did offer answers to these questions. It provided a cosmology of heaven and hell, offered the promise of eternal life, and preached that it could be won through belief and obedience. It also offered a social discipline useful to a settled, agrarian society: the Church opposed violence, condemned sexual license, defended marriage, defined rights of inheritance, and urged submission to one's lot in this world. The kings of England welcomed a church whose scriptures described and whose government illustrated kingship in action. Monotheism fit better with monarchy than did the many gods and the many local shrines of paganism.

To the inadequacy of heathenism and the relevance of Christianity must be added the prestige of Rome. The rude English looked with awe on the language, art, learning, splendor, and sophistication of Roman Christianity. To choose to become a Christian meant to choose to be part of the civilization of Rome.

THE CREATION OF THE ENGLISH MONARCHY

Next to the adoption of Christianity, the most significant event in Anglo-Saxon history was the creation of the English monarchy. This was achieved in two steps: first by the absorption of the lesser kingdoms into three great ones, Northumbria, Mercia, and Wessex; and then by the triumph of Wessex over the other two. North of the river Humber the kingdoms of Deira and Bernicia

A reconstruction of a Viking ship preserved in the blue clay of the Oslo fjord. In such ships the Vikings descended upon England. It is over 75 feet long, has provision for 16 pairs of oars, with a side-rudder for steering (*copyright University Museum of National Antiquities, Oslo, Norway*).

merged to form Northumbria; south of the Humber, Mercia absorbed the lesser kingdoms that existed there; and in the southwest Wessex expanded at the expense of the Britons. During the seventh century it seemed that Northumbria, under the leadership of three remarkable kings, Edwin, Oswald, and Oswy, would unify all England. These kings were the first rulers to give real meaning to the title of *Bretwalda*, "ruler of Britain," a title other kings had claimed in earlier years and that meant little more than greatest among kings. For a brief moment Oswy extended Northumbrian authority from the Firth of Forth to the borders of Wessex. But in the end Northumbria failed to unify England. Its kings were brave and able, but they faced the insurmountable problem of defending two widely separate frontiers, one in the south against the Mercians and one in the north against the Picts and the Scots.

In the eighth century supremacy passed to Mercia. Of the kings who ruled Mercia, Offa was undoubtedly the greatest. Between 757 and 796 he extended Mercian power through all England south of the Humber, built a great earthen dike to divide Mercia from Wales, established an archbishopric at Lichfield, minted a silver penny, promoted trade with the Continent, and corresponded with Charlemagne. His assumption of the title *Rex Anglorum,* King of the English, was no idle boast. Yet the kings of Mercia were not destined to unite England. Two forces in the ninth century destroyed the work of Offa: the rise of the House of Wessex and the Viking onslaught on England.

Elizabeth II, the present Queen of England, is a lineal descendant of Egbert, King of Wessex, who reigned over that kingdom from 802 to 839. There were earlier kings of Wessex, such as Cerdic and Cynric in the sixth century, but their history is shrouded in legend. It was Egbert who wrested from Mercia supremacy over the lesser kingdoms in the south, who defeated the Mercians at the battle of Ellendun in 825, and who won for himself the title of *Bretwalda.* The basis of the power of Wessex lay in its secure location in the south and its ability to expand into the thinly populated west. It was there that its kings found the lands with which to reward loyal thegns. Yet Wessex might have lost the dominance it won at Ellendun had it not been for the coming of the Vikings.

In the ninth century Viking warriors from Denmark and Norway suddenly attacked the Christian lands of Europe. They sailed up the rivers of Russia, into the Irish Sea, across the Atlantic Ocean, along the coasts of Brittany and France, and into the distant Mediterranean. They were driven by a hunger for land, but even more by a way of life based on plunder. The upper classes of Denmark and Norway had learned to live on the tribute and loot of war and had been taught from youth to love adventure and battle. The Danes first raided England in 793, when they sacked the monastery at Lindisfarne. Other raids followed. They would come on the first east wind of the spring, come in their graceful, high-prowed boats, boats that possessed keel and sail as well as oars, boats with a steering board on the right side (hence starboard). Protected by shirts of mail, helmets, and kite-shaped shields, and wielding great iron battle axes, they plundered the churches and monasteries of the land. In 851 they wintered for the first time in England and in 866 a great army of Danes occupied East Anglia. Within five years this army had overrun Northumbria and Mercia and launched an attack on Wessex.

They came to plunder (which explains why there are now more Anglo-Saxon coins in the museums of Scandinavia than in the museums of England), but when the treasures of England were exhausted they had to find new ways to exploit the country. They therefore turned from loot to land, and began to settle and farm the countryside east of the Pennines. They did not displace the English who were there, but joined them in those thinly populated regions. They substantially added to the racial composition of the present English population, which is principally compounded of Celt, Saxon, and Dane. They also brought with them their own law, their own customs, and their own language. The region where they settled became known as the Danelaw. They significantly influenced the English language, which grew out of a dialect of the East Midlands, where English and Danes had mingled together. As Otto Jespersen, the famous linguist, has observed, an English person cannot *thrive* or be *ill* or *die* without Scandinavian words, which are to language what *bread* and *eggs* are to daily fare.

In 871 Alfred, grandson of Egbert, became sole king of Wessex. He came to the throne at a perilous hour, for the Danes were raiding far and wide through his kingdom. In that first year Alfred fought no less than nine battles against the Danes, though a decisive victory eluded him. He was finally forced to bribe the Danes to leave. They did, but soon returned. In 878, in the dead of the winter, they suddenly marched into Wessex, seized Chippenham, and launched fierce raids into Wiltshire and Somersetshire. The ferocity of these raids forced many to flee from Wessex and others to submit to the invaders. Alfred, however, refused to flee or submit. With a small band of loyal men he retreated to the Isle of Athelney, a remote spot in Somersetshire surrounded by marshes and dense forests of alder.

It was here, legend reports, that Alfred, seeking rest at the hearth of a peasant and brooding over other matters, allowed the cakes the peasant's wife had placed on the hearth to burn. This tale, told in a saint's life two centuries later, is probably pure romance, but it is certainly true that during these seven weeks at Athelney Alfred's thoughts were on public policy, not cakes. During that time he carefully prepared a plan of campaign for the spring. He summoned the *fyrd*, or militia, of Somersetshire, Wiltshire, and Hampshire to meet him in May at Egbert's Stone on the border of Wiltshire and Somersetshire. From there he marched against the Danes at Edington and inflicted upon them a crushing defeat. Three weeks later, Guthrum, king of the Danes, accepted Christian baptism and agreed to lead his army out of Wessex.

The Battle of Edington saved Wessex from destruction, but it did not end the Danish threat. In 885 the Danes in East Anglia broke the peace, which provoked Alfred to seize London the next year. He now made a new treaty with Guthrum, a treaty that divided all England between the Danes and the English. The new boundary ran along the Thames from its mouth to London, skirted north of London to Bedford, then ran diagonally across England to Chester. To the northeast of this line Guthrum ruled; to the southwest, Alfred.

But even this treaty brought no lasting peace, for a new Danish army, crossing from Boulogne, invaded England in 892 and remained there—chiefly in East Anglia—until 896. Thus Alfred, though he had saved Wessex from destruction in 878, had to devote the rest of his reign to the building of a system of defense that would prevent further destruction. He began by building a navy that could intercept the Vikings at sea. Little is known of Alfred's navy except that he himself designed ships that were larger, swifter, and steadier than those of his enemy and that on two occasions his ships won a victory over the Vikings. But his small navy could not intercept all invaders, so Alfred also strengthened his defenses on land. Wessex had nearly met disaster in 878 because of the slowness with which the *fyrd* was mobilized. Alfred therefore divided it into two halves, so that half of his peasant levies could be in the field or garrisoning forts while the other half were at home farming. A similar division among his thegns, the more important military force, made longer campaigns possible. Finally, Alfred began to build a network of fortresses, or *burhs*, throughout his realm. These *burhs* were large enclosures, permanently garrisoned and surrounded by an earthenwork and stockade. They were a place of refuge where the people and their livestock might find safety. No village in Wessex was more than 20 miles from such a fortress.

ALFRED THE GREAT AND HIS SUCCESSORS

It is not without reason that Alfred is the only English king to have been given the title, the Great. He is not called great because of the vastness of his kingdom or the extent of his conquests, both of which were modest, but because of the greatness of his character. He was a man of courage and energy, versatile in his interests, infinitely curious, deeply religious, a lover of books, conscious of the vexations of power but driven by a profound sense of duty. "As long as I have lived," he said, "I have striven to live worthily." His concern for justice led him to issue a lengthy code of laws, in which he collected together the most just laws of his predecessors and added provisions protecting the weaker members of society from oppression. His love for the Church led him to devote half his income to religious uses, to bring the bishops to court to help him govern, and to seek to revive the monastic life which a century of Danish attacks had destroyed.

Of all his endeavors, the most remarkable was his effort to promote learning. On coming to the throne Alfred discovered that hardly a priest south of the Thames could translate a Latin letter into English, even though there were many men who could read English. He therefore resolved that the treasures of ancient literature should be translated into English. He himself struggled to learn to read and write Latin. He also collected scholars from all over Europe to help in his translations. Alfred presided over their work and at times took a hand in it. He began with Pope Gregory's *Pastoral Care*, the basic handbook on the duties of a bishop. He then had Werferth translate Gregory's *Dialogues*, whose tales about St. Benedict he may have hoped would inspire a revival of monasticism. Alfred and his scholars next translated two historical works, Bede's *Ecclesiastical History of the English Nation* and Orosius's *History Against the Pagans*, a history of the world from the creation to A.D. 407. To the translation of Orosius, Alfred added much geographical information about Scandinavia and the Baltic countries, information that reflected his wide interests and keen curiosity. He turned finally to two philosophical works, Boethius's *The Consolation of Philosophy*, which taught that the pursuit of wisdom is the wise man's consolation, and St. Augustine's *Soliloquies*, which taught that contemplation could save a ruler from the sin of pride. For Alfred life had little meaning if divorced from knowledge and reflection.

The head of Alfred the Great from a coin of his reign (*Ashmolean Museum, Oxford*).

Alfred's program for the revival of learning encompassed more than translations; he also encouraged the establishment of schools. His own household became a school for the education of the sons of nobles and commoners. It was his hope that all free-born Englishmen would learn to read English and all those destined for the Church would learn to read Latin. Alfred may also have encouraged the writing of the *Anglo-Saxon Chronicles* in order that his thegns might read the history of their own land. In his code of laws, Alfred borrowed freely from the laws of Kent and Mercia, thereby exhibiting a consciousness that there was an English law. The translation of Bede's *Ecclesiastical History of the English Nation*, which he instigated, further promoted an English consciousness among his subjects. Alfred never lived to see England united under the House of Wessex, but his laws, his translations, and his encouragement of the *Anglo-Saxon Chronicles* helped establish the intellectual foundations of that unity.

The House of Wessex could not have unified all England had not the successors of Alfred proved skillful warriors and redoubtable kings. Because Anglo-Saxon kingship was intensely personal, the success of any reign depended on the abilities of the king himself. At his death in 899 Alfred left his kingdom to his eldest son Edward, a man of energy, purpose, patience, and strategic sense. He adopted his father's *burh* system and consolidated his advance into Danish territories by building fortresses there. In the pursuit of this strategy he was aided by his sister, Ethelflaed, who had married Ethelred, Lord of Mercia. The Anglo-Saxons never held women in contempt as the Normans did, so when Ethelred died in 911, Ethelflaed, as the Lady of the Mercians, continued to govern. She personally led military expeditions and built a series of strategically placed *burhs*. By 918 Edward had captured Stamford and Nottingham and was master of England south of the river Humber. In that same year his sister died, whereupon Mercia and Wessex were united under Edward.

It was Athelstan, son of Edward, who brought the north of England under the Crown of Wessex. If the key to Edward's strategy was the building of *burhs*, the key to Athelstan's was the exploitation of the hostility the Danes felt for the Norsemen who had invaded Yorkshire from Ireland in 919. In 927 Athelstan captured York from its Norse king and established his supremacy in the north. But the gains he won were nearly lost at his death in 939. His successor and half-brother, Edmund, had to surrender much of the north and midlands to Olaf, the Norse king of Dublin. Edmund, however, waited patiently, knowing that the Danish population loathed its Norse masters. In 944 he marched north, expelled the Norse king, and reestablished English rule. He established it so securely that his son Edgar, who ruled England from 959 to 975, could be called Edgar the Peaceable.

ANGLO-SAXON GOVERNMENT

In the creation of the English monarchy, the achievement of geographical unity was only half the story; the evolution of the institutions of kingship was the other half. The earliest kings were hardly more than warrior chiefs, enjoying the loyalty of their personal followers and living off their own estates. Gradually, a tribal, personal kingship became a territorial, institutional kingship. The Christian ceremonies of anointing and coronation set the king apart from other men as God's chosen representative. Public fealty sworn by all men supplemented the personal loyalty of man for lord. A king who could govern his small kingdom in person gave way to a king who acted through royal officials—ealdormen in the shires and port-reeves in the boroughs. The succession, which had gone to the ablest among the royal family, gradually became hereditary in the eldest son. The king's revenue came to include a food rent from all lands, fines from courts of justice, tolls, treasure, and the Danegeld. The most crushing of these impositions was the Danegeld, a land tax the king originally collected in order to buy off the Danes but that later kings collected to support a standing army. The powers of the king went beyond leading his tribe in war; he could now codify old law and declare new, grant land by charters, mint coins, receive and send embassies, and require his subjects to serve in the militia, repair fortifications, and build bridges.

When declaring law or granting land or resolving on war the king nearly always consulted with the Witan, a council of wise men. Its membership was undefined, but on important occasions it would include the ealdormen, the bishops, the leading abbots, the king's chaplains, and household officials. The Witan was an aristocratic body, and the king heeded its advice only because he respected its wisdom and sought its support. On the death of a king the Witan elected his successor, but this election was only a formality—unless the dying king failed to name a successor and the succession was in doubt.

It was the king's household, not the Witan, that made the English monarchy strong. The king had numerous household officials—butlers, seneschals, marshals, chamberlains, and chaplains—but of these only the last two proved important. From the chamberlains, who kept the king's robes, jewels, and money, later grew a financial department that received revenues and made disbursements. From the chaplains who served the king arose in time a secretariat that drew up, in stately Latin, charters for granting land, and issued, in terse English, writs for making known the king's commands.

The emergence of shires and hundreds completed the transformation of a tribal monarchy into a territorial monarchy. In Wessex and East Anglia the various shires either grew out of earlier kingdoms, as in Kent, or out of tribal divisions, as in Norfolk, or out of the area around a town, as in Dorsetshire. During the tenth century the kings of Wessex extended this system of shires into the Midlands. Each shire had a court, or moot, which met twice a year to execute the orders of the king, to declare and enact laws, or dooms, and to give judgment in criminal, civil, and ecclesiastical cases. The ealdorman presided over the shire moot. He was the chief officer of the shire and the leader of its levies in war. He was invariably a powerful nobleman, but named by the king and answerable to him.

When in the eleventh century the ealdorman came to govern several shires, the duty of presiding over the shire court fell to another royal official, the shire-reeve, or sheriff. The sheriff became the vital link between the king and the local courts, for his bailiff presided over the hundred court. The origin of the hundred as a division of the shire is obscure. Eventually, however, the hundred court became the ordinary criminal court of the land, meeting every four weeks, in the open air, to punish cattle thieves or witness the sale of land. King, shire, and hundred formed a remarkable system of local government, a partnership between king and community, with the king commanding the suitors to the two courts to do justice and preserve order. In theory, all freemen could attend the shire and hundred courts; in fact, those who declared the law and ordered the form of proof in these courts were the thegns, bishops, and priests.

The law which thegn, bishop, and priest enforced was the ancient unwritten customs of the people. The Romans regarded law as the legislative act of a sovereign authority, but the Germans held that it was the unchangeable customs of the people. The king and the Witan might codify the law, or even enact new law, but these codes were by no means comprehensive. The great mass of customary law continued to be handed down orally and to be declared by doomsmen in the local courts. That law was also primitive, for it reflected a society where government was weak and the police nonexistent. Since the government could not protect a person, that task fell to his relatives. It was a murdered man's kin, his near relatives, who sought vengeance for his death. A fear of the retribution that the kin would exact provided the principal force for the maintenance of order in early Germanic society.

Gradually, however, the blood feud was transformed into a system of financial compensations. A murderer could escape from the vengeance owed him by paying the kindred of the murdered person a sum of money, a *wergeld* or "life price." This sum varied with the social rank of the murdered person; the *wergeld* of an ordinary man or woman was 200 shillings, of a nobleman or woman, 1200 shillings. Compensation was also paid for injury done to a person. The sums of money varied not only with his or her rank but with the parts of the body injured—for striking off a man's nose one paid 60 shillings; for knocking out a tooth, 8 shillings; for striking off a shooting finger, 15; and for seizing a young woman by the breast, 5. As archaic as this system of justice seems, it was an advance over the exaction of vengeance, and Alfred strove with all his might to replace the blood feud with the *wergeld*.

A kindred could not lawfully seek vengeance or compensation unless the accused person had been found guilty. The procedure by which a hundred or shire court found a person guilty or innocent was formal and elaborate. It began with the plaintiff summoning the defendant to answer the charge brought against him. If the defendant did not appear, he lost the suit by default; if he appeared, the plaintiff recited the charge and swore he did not act out of malice or hatred. Next the defendant swore an oath of denial, and in Anglo-Saxon law a denial was held to be stronger than an accusation. To support his oath the defendant would seek the aid of oath helpers, or compurgators, the number of which depended on the seriousness of the charge. The accused was given thirty days in which to assemble his compurgators, whose oaths carried more weight if they owned more land. These oath helpers did not supply facts concerning the case; they merely swore that the defendant's oath was "pure and not false." If on the appointed day the defendant and his compurgators appeared at court and all swore their oaths, the defendant was cleared. This naive procedure, so open to abuse, worked largely because a defendant known by his fellow villagers to be guilty could hardly find the needed compurgators.

A man who failed to produce the needed oath helpers, who had a record of many accusations, or who was caught in the act of theft had to submit to a different form of proof, the ordeal. Because people regarded the ordeal as a judgment of God, the Church now stepped in. After a fast of three days and a mass in which the defendant was charged to confess his guilt before receiving the sacrament, the accused was subject to one of three ordeals. In the ordeal of cold water the priest adjured God to accept only the innocent in the water, after which the accused was lowered into it. If he floated he was guilty, if he sank (though only briefly) he was innocent. In the ordeal of iron the accused carried a hot iron nine feet, and in the ordeal of hot water he plunged his hand into boiling water to take out a stone. In both he was cleared of the charge if after three days his hand healed without festering. To us trial by ordeal is absurd, but to the Anglo-Saxons, who believed in demons, spirits, spells, and the providence of God, it was justice.

Two developments during these centuries pointed toward a less private conception of the law. The first of these was the extension of the king's peace. To commit a murder or assault in the king's residence was not only a private crime, demanding compensation to the injured party or his kin, but a breach of the king's peace, requiring the payment of a fine to the king. Gradually the king's peace was extended to highways, bridges, churches, and towns; and to special times of the year, such as Christmas and Easter. The king's peace came eventually to include all England for 365 days a year, and the English came to view crime less as a private injury than a public wrong. The second development was the emergence of the presentment jury in the Danelaw, at a time when traditional methods of maintaining law and order were breaking down. In 997 Ethelred enacted a law requiring the twelve leading thegns in each *wapentake* (as the hundred was called in the Danelaw) to swear that they would accuse no innocent man or conceal any guilty one; they were also to arrest all men of bad repute. Upon these jurymen, and not upon the injured party, fell the duty to present to the court the most notorious offenders in the neighborhood.

The most important fact about English law was its popular character. Law was the custom of the people, declared in the courts and handed down from generation to generation. The king, though his initiative brought into existence shire and hundred courts, rarely did justice himself; his duty was to see that the popular courts performed it. Yet, upon closer scrutiny, it becomes apparent that the king's reeves, the bishops, the priests, and the thegns declared the law and superintended justice in these courts. That these courts were more aristocratic than democratic merely reflected the structure of Anglo-Saxon society.

THE STRUCTURE OF SOCIETY

From earliest times, Anglo-Saxon society was aristocratic and lordship was an essential bond holding men together. There were all degrees and ranks of men: the king and those who shared his royal blood, the ealdorman who governed over the shire, the thegn who served in war and owned land and a hall, the *geneat* who paid rent for his land and performed riding service for his lord, the *gebur* who held some 30 acres for which he performed labor services, the cottager with his 5 acres of land, and the slave who was looked upon as property, not a person. The law took notice of the different ranks of men by assigning to each rank a different *wergeld*, a different value to their oaths, and a different *mund*, or fine, for violating the peace of their households. In Wessex the *wergeld* of a thegn was 1200 shillings; of a *ceorl* (which included *gebur* and cottager), 200 shillings; of a Welshman, 120 shillings; of a slave, 60 shillings. In this hierarchy the law also found a place for the clergy: the bishop ranked with the ealdorman, the priest with the thegn. Even traders found a place, for a merchant who crossed the sea three times gained the rank of a thegn.

The thegn played a crucial role in Anglo-Saxon society. He was a powerful warrior, surrounded by retainers, who served the king in battles and at court. In the earlier centuries lordship was a personal relationship and nobility was a matter of birth, but after Alfred's reign lordship became associated with the possession of land and nobility could be won by service to the king. *Bookland*, or land granted by a charter and freed from food rents, became the ultimate reward for service to the king. Law codes, meanwhile, placed ever greater obligations on the thegn in the shire and hundred courts. As a landlord, the thegn became responsible for the maintenance of order in his locality.

During Alfred's reign, every thegn served one month out of three at the royal court, where he found a pattern for his own household. He too had his household officials and his chaplains. He lived (as the excavations at Yeavering in Northumberland show) in a great hall, built of timber, rectangular in shape, and surrounded by a stockade. The hall was furnished with movable trestle tables and had fixed benches along the sides (which were covered with cushions at night for the retainers to sleep on). In the hall men passed the mead horn from hand to hand, feasted, drank, boasted, and quarreled. The playing of the harp and the singing of songs relieved the tedium of a winter's night. During the day the thegn, when not at war or at court, passed his hours hunting the stag, chasing the fox, or hawking, while his wife oversaw the spinning and weaving and the preparation of meals. The epic poetry of the day, such as *The Song of Maldon* and *The Battle of Brunanburgh*, celebrated the heroic virtues of the Anglo-Saxon thegn, but by the eleventh century he had become as much a landlord as a warrior.

The wealth with which the thegn built his hall and purchased his golden goblets and great sword came from the labor of the peasants on his estates. Whether the ancestors of these peasants were free men when they came to England is a question historians continue to debate, for the evidence to answer it conclusively does not exist. There is only some evidence pointing to dependence on a lord, and some pointing to freedom. The many villages named after persons suggest lordship, for the villages were presumably named after the lords who established them. The one-to-one correspondence of manor and village in the south and southwest also suggests lordship, for the manor and its lord must have existed ever since the village was settled. Indeed, the seventh-century laws of Wessex appear to describe a manor, complete with lord and tenant lands.

Yet there is evidence pointing the other way. The existence of peasants—called *sokemen*—who were free to sell their land suggests an earlier time when there were no lords. Similarly, the existence of two or three or more manors in a village in East Anglia and the Danelaw suggests that there were villages before there were manors. The importance of the kindred in law, rather than the lord, and the tenacity with which the custom of the manor was observed also suggest that there had been a time when lordship was less powerful. The theory that best accounts for all these facts is a twofold one: farmers dependent on a lord settled in some parts of England; in other parts, farmers who owed allegiance only to a king. Freedom was especially characteristic of the Danelaw, where the Scandinavian farmer, though subject to personal lordship, enjoyed freedom of tenure on the land.

What is certain is that lordship deepened during these centuries. By gaining the right to collect the king's food rent, a lord could increase people's dependence on him. Law codes increasingly frowned upon the lordless man, preferring to rely on lordship rather than kinship. The violence of the age, particularly during the Viking invasions, persuaded people to commend themselves and their land to the protection of a lord. As a result, by the eleventh century the obligations that fell upon the typical peasant, the *gebur*, were indeed heavy. He could not leave the estate at will. He must labor two days a week on the lord's land, three days at harvest time. He must pay his lord 10 pence at Michaelmas and give him 23 bushels of barley and 2 hens at Martinmas. At Easter he owed him one young sheep or two pennies.

The *gebur* was personally free, possessed rights in the land, and could not be bought and sold. This was not true of the slave, who was at the bottom of the social pyramid. His obligations were unlimited, though custom decreed that his master should give him every year twelve pounds of grain, two sheep, one good cow, and the right to cut wood. For minor offenses he could be flogged, for serious ones mutilated or put to death. The sources of slaves were many: conquered Britons, captives taken in war, men who were driven by the threat of starvation to sell their own children into slavery—though the child's consent was needed if he or she were over the age of seven. The number of slaves in the early centuries was large, but their numbers shrank, both because the Church encouraged men to free their slaves and because the increasing use of money made it easier for a Lord to pay for the labor he needed. The freed slaves thus swelled the number of *geburs* in Anglo-Saxon England.

OPEN FIELDS AND ROYAL BOROUGHS

The Celts used a light plow, no more than a stout beam to which an iron point, or plowshare, was attached, and which two oxen pulled through the soil. This scratch plow was especially effective on light soils, such as the chalk of southern England. Only with difficulty could it turn over the heavy clay of the Thames valley and the Midlands, and yet it was here that the Anglo-Saxons in time settled. Unlike the Celts and the Romans, who emphasized livestock in

Plowman and oxen, a bronze group from Piercebridge, Durham, probably third century A.D. It is an example of the Romano-British scratch plow, or *aratrum (the British Museum)*.

their husbandry, the Anglo-Saxons emphasized grain and for this they needed the rich soil of the valleys. To turn over this soil they needed a heavy plow, with a coulter, or knifeblade, to cut the turf, a plowshare to loosen the soil, and a moldboard to turn it over. As is often the case with technological advances, the heavy wheeled plow developed slowly. The Romans introduced the coulter, which became an integral part of the plow. They may have also introduced the moldboard, since the deep cut a coulter causes makes necessary a moldboard to clear the furrow. With this superior plow the British were able in the last years of Roman rule to cultivate the heavier soils in the valleys. The Anglo-Saxons, who probably adopted this Romano-British plow, made no improvement on it, at least not until the tenth or eleventh centuries when they, or more probably the Danes, added wheels to the plow, thus allowing the plowman to regulate the depth of the furrow. The wheeled plow was especially useful in breaking up virgin clay soil and allowed the penetration of the lowland forests. To pull this plow through heavy clay soil required eight oxen, yoked two by two.

The heavy plow and eight-oxen team transformed agriculture. Because it took valuable time to turn such a plow, the Anglo-Saxons plowed long furrows, often 220 yards long. Since this could not be done in the small, square fields of the Celts, vast open fields had to be adopted. Because no peasant owned eight oxen, plowing became a cooperative effort, with each peasant being awarded strips in the open field. These strips, totaled together, ranged in extent from 16 to 30 acres. They were scattered throughout the field and were probably allotted in proportion to the number of oxen a peasant brought to the plow team. Inequality was therefore written into the open field system. Rather than living on homesteads at the edge of the fields, the peasants lived in villages at the center, where they found protection, shelter, and immediate access to the arable land. At first two fields surrounded the village. One lay fallow in order to recover its fertility; the other was divided into two halves, one of which was sown with winter wheat or rye, the other with spring barley or oats. As the population grew and pressed upon the land, the proportion of land sown with winter and spring crops increased (where the fertility of the soil permitted it) to two-thirds. There were now three fields: one fallow, another sown with a winter crop, and a third with a fast-maturing spring crop.

This blend of corporate enterprise and private ownership extended to the use of the meadow, the commons, and the woods. The meadow, whose hay fed the oxen, was apportioned, strip for strip, according to the peasant's holding on the arable land. On the commons the peasant grazed his cows, which were chiefly used to breed oxen for the plow team; his sheep, which were valuable for meat and wool; and his goats, which furnished milk and cheese. The woods played a major role in the rural economy, for in the woods the peasant found fuel to warm the household, timber to build a cottage, honey to sweeten food and brew mead, and acorns and beechmast to feed the pigs. Swine were more important than sheep in early English husbandry, since they provided the chief source of meat. Though the Anglo-Saxons enlivened their festive occasions with mead and prized their bacon, they could not do without bread and beer. The early English drank beer on a gargantuan scale, which explains why far more barley, which was needed by brewer and baker, was sown than wheat.

Only by relentless toil could the peasant wrest a living from the soil, for yields were low. The most fertile land produced only about 9 bushels of grain

A wheeled plow, as represented in the Bayeux tapestry (*Phaidon Press*).

an acre, compared with some 60 bushels in modern England. In the autumn the peasant plowed the fallow and sowed it with wheat, scattering the seed broadcast, and thereby wasting much of it. During winter he threshed grain, cut timber, repaired stalls for the oxen, and built pig sties. In the spring he plowed again and sowed barley and beans and vegetables. In May, June, and July he harrowed the soil, spread dung, sheared sheep, repaired fences, and made fish weirs. The longest hours of labor came at harvest, when the peasant, with the help of his whole family, reaped the grain with a short sickle and gathered it in. While the men and boys worked in the fields, the women and girls made cloth and clothing, baked bread, brewed ale, butchered the pigs, and tended the garden. It was a life of unremitting toil, broken only by Church holidays, which the peasants—to the anger of the priest—more often used for drinking and making merry than for religious observance.

The material conditions of peasant life were primitive and precarious. Excavations of a few Anglo-Saxon villages show that he and his family lived in a rude timber hut of only one room, about 10 feet by 18, with an open hearth,

An aerial photograph of Padbury, Buckinghamshire. The ridges and furrows, highlighted by the setting sun, are remains of the strips in the medieval open fields at Padbury. Two fields are shown here, divided by a stream: the road and hedges are modern (*Cambridge University Collection, copyright reserved*).

Scenes of Agricultural Life from a Saxon Calendar, c. 1030 A.D. (*the British Library*).

PLOWING THE FIELD

DIGGING AND SOWING

TENDING THE LIVESTOCK

HARVESTING THE GRAIN

MOWING THE HAY

THRESHING THE GRAIN

REPAIRING THE FENCE

the smoke from which found its way out through a hole in the thatched roof. Of privacy and comfort there was nothing. The villagers had few material goods—excavations have turned up only some iron knives, iron combs, bone pins, cattle bells, and loom weights. Not possessing the potter's wheel until the seventh century, the early English made coarse and unshapely pottery. A diet of porridge, bread, and beer kept the villagers alive. When the crops failed, they suffered famine and death.

The manor became the principal institution for organizing economic life in the countryside. Manors varied greatly from place to place, but in essence they were alike: a landed estate, belonging to a lord, with dependent cultivators settled on it. On the classic manor of the Midlands and the South the dependent cultivators enjoyed considerable rights in the land—strips in the arable, the produce of which was theirs, and the use of meadow, commons, and forests. But for these rights they owed the lord heavy obligations. In addition to the usual weekwork on the lord's land (or *demesne*) and rents in money and kind, they had to plow one acre of the lord's land each week during the autumn plowing, three acres more as boon work, two acres more in return for pasture rights, and a further three acres—for which they furnished the seed—as part of their rent. In addition, they did duty at the lord's sheepfold during the winter. Only the custom of the manor prevented the lord from imposing total tyranny on the peasant.

Anglo-Saxon agriculture was not a purely subsistence agriculture, in which the manor produced only enough for its own needs. The invention of the iron ax and the heavy plow allowed the early English to exploit fertile lands no previous peoples had used. It was this wealth that supported not only the monarchy and the Church, but the merchants who from the tenth century onward crowded into the boroughs, or towns, of England. In the sixth century there were no such boroughs, only a few people huddled behind the walls of Canterbury and London; by 1086 there were seventy-one royal boroughs, with their markets, mints, guilds for keeping the peace, borough courts, and borough tenure. It was all very royal, for the King established the mints, granted the right to hold a market, and named the reeve who presided at the borough court. He also granted the land, which could be held for a rent and which could be freely bought and sold. The boroughs were small. London may have had 12,000 inhabitants, York, 8,000, Norwich and Lincoln 5,000 each, and Cambridge 1,300. The origin of these boroughs varied: some grew up around a royal estate, others around a cathedral or great monastery, yet others around the *burhs* Alfred and his successors established. One factor, however, was present in every instance: an increase in trade and in the number of merchants engaged in trade.

The collapse of the *Pax Romana* brought with it the collapse of the currency system, with the result that in Britain in the fifth century the circulation of coins ceased. Without a currency trade became difficult, a difficulty compounded by the unwillingness of traders to face the insecurity of the times. But in the seventh century some order returned, trade revived, and coins reappeared. Penda, from whose name probably comes the word "penny," minted a silver coin, a coin Offa greatly improved in quality. The English began to export wool, cloth, cheese, and slaves to the Continent, in return for glassware, fine pottery, silver vessels, and wine. Though Charlemagne complained to Offa of the poor quality of English cloaks, their fame spread to the eastern Mediterranean. The Viking invasion momentarily interrupted this trade with the Continent, but it opened up a new trade with the Baltic. While London and Southampton based their prosperity on foreign trade, most boroughs drew their wealth from internal trade. There was probably never a moment when peddlers traveling through the land did not sell iron and salt. Gradually a trade in other commodities arose: lead from Derbyshire, cheese from the Vale of the White Horse, eels from the Fenland, ornamented helmets and elaborately fashioned swords from local ironsmiths, and fine cloth from Wessex. It was the merchants engaged in these trades who sought the protection of the King's boroughs and lived on the agricultural surplus created by the open fields of England.

MONASTICISM AND LEARNING

Soon after his arrival at Canterbury, Augustine established the monastery of St. Peter and St. Paul. Within a century monastic houses were established at Malmesbury, Ely, Wearmouth, Ripon, and throughout England. People of all ranks entered these monasteries—kings, royal princesses, Northumbrian nobles, great Churchmen, ordinary peasants. Their zeal for the religious life reflected a profound change in people's view of the world, a change from the pagan ideal of heroic endeavor within the world to the Christian ideal of withdrawal from it. The world was seen as the province of the Devil, whose temptations were to be avoided by withdrawal into a life of contemplation. No one in the seventh century exhibited this life of contemplation to greater perfection than St. Cuthbert, in whom were joined the finest in Celtic and Roman monasticism. As a youth Cuthbert had turned in disgust from the life of a warrior to the Christian ideal. He entered a monastery at Melrose, rose to be its abbot, and then went as abbot to Lindisfarne. Here, in 676, he resolved to attain the perfect life of a recluse. On the small island of Farne, 7 miles away, he built a rude hut, around which he erected a wall of stone and turf that blocked out all but the heavens from his view. There he existed on barley and onions, chanted his psalms and hymns, and won his victory over the flesh.

Peculiar to England were the double monasteries in which a community of monks and a community of nuns lived side by side, under the authority of a woman, the abbess. The greatest of these was the double monastery at Whitby, governed by St. Hilda, whose reputation for wisdom led many to come to Whitby to seek her advice. Under her governance Whitby became a center of

imago   ui   ʊ̅ʊɥ

ɅGIOS
LUCAS

Portrait of St. Luke, from the Lindisfarne Gospels. This black-and-white reproduction fails, of course, to capture the vivid colors of the original (*the British Library*).

learning and a training ground for bishops for the new Church. For widows and for women who did not wish to marry, monasticism brought a range of opportunities hitherto unknown.

Withdrawal into contemplation, however, was not the only ideal cherished by the Church. The Church also saw itself as a pilgrim society carrying God's truth to the people. Cuthbert himself, at the entreaty of the King, the bishops, and the nobility of Northumbria, left the island of Farne to serve once again in the world. In the eighth century the missionary impulse that had led to the conversion of the English now returned across the Channel. English missionaries, led by a West Saxon named Wynfrith, who took the name Boniface, successfully converted the heathen of Thuringia, Hesse, and Bavaria. Though the heathen Frisians massacred Boniface and fifty of his followers in 754, he had accomplished enough by that time to justify the claim that no Englishman before or since has exercised a greater influence on German history.

In the twin tasks of converting the heathen and sustaining the faithful the

The Ruthwell Cross, Dumfriesshire, early eighth century. It stands 18 feet high: the middle relief shows Christ with Mary Magdalene, the lower relief shows Christ healing the blind man. On the narrower side are runic passages from a Saxon poem. "the Dream of the Rood" (*F.S. Cheney, Felixtowe*).

Church was eager to enlist the services of learning and art. Christianity was a religion of the book and could only be expounded by those who could read and interpret the Scriptures. There had been schools in England since the time of Augustine, but learning of more than an elementary kind began with the arrival of Theodore of Tarsus in 669. His school at Canterbury taught Latin and Greek, Roman law, the method of regulating the religious calendar, Church music, and the metrical rules for composing religious poetry. From Canterbury, Aldhelm, a scholar of great ability and a poet of great ingenuity, carried the new learning to Malmesbury, but it never took root there. It was in Northumbria, where the tradition of Celtic learning was strong, that it took root, in the monasteries of Jarrow and Wearmouth founded by Benedict Biscop, a friend of Theodore's and an avid collector of books. The libraries he established made

The Weingarten Crucifixion, from a Gospel book illuminated in England between 1051 and 1065. The jagged outline of the drapery gives a moving impression of the human suffering of Jesus (*The Pierpont Morgan Library*).

possible the work of Bede, the greatest figure in the Northumbrian renaissance.

Bede entered Wearmouth at the age of 7 and spent his entire life there and at Jarrow, in devotion and study. "It has ever been my delight," he wrote, "to learn or teach or write." Before his death in 735, at the age of 63, he had written 36 scientific, historical, and theological works. Medieval Europe remembers him for his theological writings, which were based on the Church Fathers and the allegorical method of interpreting the Scriptures. The greatest of his scientific treatises was *De Temporum Ratione* (On the Nature of Time), in which he popularized the modern practice of reckoning years from the birth of Christ. He is best remembered in modern times for his *Ecclesiastical History of the English Nation,* a work written in a Latin of great simplicity and power. Bede was a born artist, with an incomparable gift for storytelling, a fine eye for the picturesque, and a remarkable ability to weave together information from various sources. He was also an accurate and impartial historian who sought to distinguish between fact and rumor, even though his deep faith led him to relate and to believe in scores of miraculous happenings. A love of learning did not die with Bede, for one of his pupils founded a school at York that educated Alcuin, who in turn traveled to the court of Charlemagne, where he helped that monarch found a palace school.

Art as well as learning graced the Northumbrian renaissance of the seventh and eighth centuries. The Church spared nothing in its effort to make the worship of the Christian God impressive and magnificent: gold chalices, purple alter cloths, silk robes. The same impulse led to the illumination of manuscripts, particularly of the Gospels. In the Lindisfarne Gospel (Gospels), the finest example of the art of illumination, one can see both an Italian influence in the representation of the figures of the Evangelists, and a native influence in the sumptuous decorations on each page. The use of bright, contrasting colors heightened the magnificence of the decoration. Equally remarkable were the sculptures carved on the Christian crosses of Northumbria, particularly those at Bewcastle in Cumberland and Ruthwell in Dumfriesshire. Such crosses marked an open place for Christian worship in an age when there were few churches. The subjects carved on the crosses—Christ as judge, St. John the Baptist, the healing of the blind man—were chosen to instruct the faithful in the truths of Christianity. The fertility of design found in these crosses suggests a remarkable outburst of native talent, though certain of its motifs, such as the vine scroll, suggest a Classical influence. One fact is certain: nowhere in Europe at this time were artists creating sculptures of such dignity and power.

It was the political stability provided by the kings of Northumbria that made this flowering of art and learning possible. When the Vikings destroyed that stability, learning and art perished, and with them the monastic life. Alfred the Great, who once wrote that a king needed to be served by those who fought, those who labored, and those who prayed, sought and failed to revive monastic life. But where he failed, his successors succeeded. During the tenth century, monasteries modeled on the reformed Benedictine houses of France sprang up throughout England. Edgar supported the movement with such enthusiasm that he earned the title Father of the Monks. Between 940 and 1066, some sixty houses for monks and nuns were restored or established in England. Kings and thegns carved out of their lands endowments for religious foundations, with the result that the Church acquired nearly a third of the occupied land of England. The English Church itself became thoroughly monastic, with the regular clergy, or monks, often replacing the secular clergy. A high proportion of bishops were monks.

The revival of monastic life meant the revival of learning. But the glory of this new learning did not lie in the ornate Latin of an Aldhelm or the direct, limpid Latin of a Bede; it lay in the emergence of a literature written in English, a vernacular literature. The origins of this literature can be traced to the seventh century, when Caedman, a herdsman whose talents St. Hilda discovered and encouraged, first applied the rhythms and alliteration of Old English heroic verse to the service of the Christian religion. His successors wrote poems on the workings of Divine Providence, poems of moral exhortation, poems dramatizing the Last Judgment. They also wrote poems celebrating the pagan virtues of loyalty to one's lord and bravery at sea, poems into which were woven Christian themes like the promise of eternal life. During the tenth and eleventh centuries a vernacular literature in prose was added to this poetic tradition. The greatest of these writers was Elfric, abbot of Eynsham, who translated parts of the Old Testament into English and who wrote sermons, pastoral letters, and lives of the saints. He wrote a deliberately rhythmical prose, often alliterative, whose effect was more like that of verse than prose; yet it was also as precise and clear as any Latin composition. Elfric was a gifted teacher, and through teaching and writing he established a new standard of excellence for English prose. Gone were the stilted translations of the age of Alfred.

The Church also turned to music to give splendor and solemnity to religious services. From the time of Theodore the Church had used the Gregorian chant, a style of unmeasured, vocal music, for reciting the psalms. Originally there was only one reciting note, with the voice rising up at the beginning of a phrase and dropping down at the end, but the choirmasters of England developed a system of polyphony, in which the trebles of the boy choristers mingled with the deeper voices of the monks, creating a music of great beauty.

THE SURVIVAL OF THE ENGLISH MONARCHY

The Anglo-Saxon monarchy was a personal monarchy which needed the driving force of an able king to make it work. But it was more than that; it was also a system of administration composed of courts, councils, and officers. Between 978 and 1016 this system of administration was put to a severe test when the reign of an incompetent king coincided with renewed Danish attacks. Ethelred, who came to the throne in 978, inherited many problems from his predecessors—an unstable frontier, the rivalries of powerful ealdormen, a Danish population of unsure allegiance—but many of his difficulties were of his own making. He distrusted his nobles, dealt unfaithfully with men, lacked clear principles of action, vacillated in war, and was a bad judge of character. It is not without reason that he earned the nickname *Unraed,* which was mistranslated in the sixteenth century as "unready," but which means "of no counsel."

The true measure of Ethelred's weakness became apparent when he was confronted by renewed Viking attacks. These began as hit-and-run raids in 980, but became formidable when Olav Tryggvason, a Norwegian of royal descent, led a fleet of ninety-three ships to Folkestone, harried the coasts of Kent and East Anglia, and extorted tribute from its peoples. He returned in 994 with Swein of Denmark and a fleet of ninety-four ships. They unsuccessfully besieged London, and then turned to plundering the countryside of southern England. It was sometime between 991 and 994 that the English resolved to buy off the Danes. In return for 20,000 pounds of silver, Olav Tryggvason sailed away, promising never to return. The policy of paying Danegeld in order to gain a breathing spell in which to organize one's defenses is not a foolish one; Alfred himself pursued it in 878. But the policy is an invitation to disaster if the defenses are not reorganized, and Ethelred failed to reorganize them. Instead he paid more Danegeld, which, according to the chroniclers, rose in amount from 24,000 pounds of silver in 1002, to 30,000 in 1007, to 48,000 in 1012. Nor did these payments protect the country from the ravages of the Vikings, who in 1012 looted the cathedral at Canterbury and murdered the archbishop.

Swein of Denmark now decided upon the conquest of all England. In the summer of 1013 he sailed for England; by autumn the Danelaw had accepted him as king, and before the end of the year all of England had recognized him. But Swein died suddenly in February 1014, and the English magnates asked Ethelred to return as their King, provided "he would govern them better than he did before." He did return, but soon escaped the tribulations of kingship by death. He died in London in April 1016, whereupon the citizens of that city and the great noblemen who were there offered the crown to his son, Edmund Ironside. A deputation of influential ealdormen, bishops, abbots, and thegns immediately set out for Southampton, where they offered the Crown to Swein's son, Cnut. A fierce struggle between Edmund and Cnut ended seven months later with Edmund's death, probably by an assassin. The whole of England, weary of disorder, now rallied behind Cnut. True, he was a Dane, but what the English wanted was a strong king, not necessarily an English king.

The speed with which Cnut established his government offers convincing testimony that the royal administrative system had not collapsed during Ethelred's misrule. And the peace and security that the English enjoyed for the next nineteen years showed what an able monarch could do with that machinery. Cnut was the first ruler of a truly united England, for he had the allegiance of both the Danes and the English. He won Cumberland in the north from the ancient kingdom of Strathclyde, which now disappeared from the map. Cnut made it his deliberate policy to reconcile the Danes and the English. He married Ethelred's widow, Emma of Normandy, issued codes of law based on those of his English predecessors, and named Englishmen to the great earldoms throughout the kingdom. He also promised to govern with the advice of the bishops, who remained unchanged. In 1018 he summoned the leading Danes and Englishmen together at Oxford, where they promised to live peaceably together under the laws of Edgar.

Cnut, who had won his kingdom by the sword, was unwilling to throw away the sword. He established a standing military force, the *housecarls,* and collected an annual tax, the *heregeld,* to pay for them. He likewise maintained a navy, which cost nearly 4000 pounds a year. This expense and the *heregeld* placed a heavy burden of taxation on the English, but in return they had internal peace and security from foreign invasion. That security was the greater because Cnut became King of Denmark in 1019 and King of Norway in 1028. He was the head of a great Scandinavian empire and a monarch of importance in Europe, as was acknowledged when he traveled to Rome in 1027. While in Rome he attended the coronation of the new Emperor, whom he persuaded to reduce the tolls on English pilgrims and merchants traveling through his lands. He also persuaded the Pope to lessen the heavy charge imposed on English Archbishops for receiving the *pallium,* the insignia of office. Cnut died in 1035, at the age of 40, having restored to England those traditions of good government that had arisen during the tenth century.

He left two sons, Harold, who reigned from 1035 to 1040, and Harthacnut, who ruled from 1040 until 1042. Neither carried out his father's wishes or governed with his wisdom. Both used the office to exploit their subjects. Only the sudden death of Harthacnut saved England from an oppressive tyranny. With his death, the Danish line of kings came to an end, for the English summoned Edward, son of Ethelred and Emma, who was half-Norman by birth and who had spent his entire youth in Normandy. His accession marks the first step toward the creation of an Anglo-Norman state and society.

FURTHER READING

*PETER HUNTER BLAIR. *Introduction to Anglo-Saxon England.* 2nd. ed., Cambridge, England, 1977. A scholarly examination of the coming of the Germanic peoples, the creation of the kingdom of England, the development of the English language, and the growth of Christianity.

D.V.J. FISHER. *The Anglo-Saxon Age c. 400–1042.* London, 1973. A fair-minded survey of the period, which convincingly integrates political, economic, social, religious, and cultural developments.

STENTON, F.M. *Anglo-Saxon England.* 3rd. ed., Oxford, 1971. A large-scale, comprehensive history, by a scholar who possesses an unequalled mastery of the sources; as in other volumes in the Oxford History, the bibliography is an outstanding feature.

H.R LOYN. *Anglo-Saxon England and the Norman Conquest.* Oxford, 1962. Well-written, authoritative; especially valuable for its comprehensive account of the economic and social history of the period.

LESLIE ALCOCK. *Arthur's Britain: History and Archaeology A.D. 367–634.* London, 1977. Contains a spirited, extensive, scholarly argument for the historical existence of Arthur.

H.R. LOYN. *The Vikings in Britain.* London, 1977. The best basic introduction to the subject; reflects the author's breadth of knowledge and critical judgment.

*ELEANOR SHIPLEY DUCKETT. *Alfred the Great.* Chicago, 1957. A charming, brief life of Alfred, which distinguishes between legend and history, and successfully places Alfred in his times.

TREVOR ROWLEY, ed. *The Origins of Open-field Agriculture.* London, 1981. Essays by ten historians, archaeologists, and geographers, most of whom argue that open fields evolved in late Saxon times.

DOROTHY WHITELOCK, ed. *English Historical Documents.* 2nd. ed., Oxford, 1979. Contains the major portion of the written sources on which the history of the period is based—chronicles, charters, laws, saints' lives, letters; all the documents are translated.

*BEDE. *A History of the English Church and People.* Penguin Books, 1956. Bede's masterpiece is both a work of art and the fundamental authority for the history of early Anglo-Saxon England.

4 Norman England

William Duke of Normandy was a moderately tall, robust man with reddish-brown hair, massive shoulders, and a harsh gutteral voice. In battle he was fierce and tenacious, at Court majestic and domineering. Before he became known as William the Conqueror, he was known as William the Bastard, for his father, Duke Robert, had never married his mother, Herleve, the daughter of a tanner. Duke Robert had, before he set out on a pilgrimage to Jerusalem, persuaded his magnates to recognize William as his heir. On his father's death in Asia Minor in 1035, William thus became Duke of Normandy. He was then 7 years old. With the help of the King of France he survived his minority, but thereafter his success in withstanding his many enemies was a triumph of character. He possessed an indomitable will, great tenacity of purpose, and the ability to make the right decision at the right time. He was a brutal man, capable of inflicting savage atrocities upon his enemies—at the siege of Alençon he cut off the hands and feet of thirty-two captives. But he was also a calculating man who could combine mercy with ferocity. To great prowess in the field he joined great prudence at the council table, and by means of both he tamed the most turbulent baronage in Europe.

This was the man who in 1066 claimed the Crown of England, raised a powerful army, transported it across the Channel, met King Harold in battle, and defeated him decisively. William's conquest of England gave an abrupt turn to the path of English history. It imposed on England an alien aristocracy, introduced into the kingdom feudal institutions, and linked England—commercially, ecclesiastically, and culturally—with Europe, not Scandinavia.

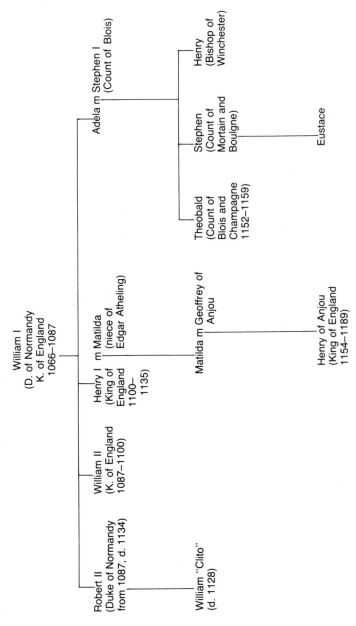

Contenders for the Duchy of Normandy and the Kingdom of England in the Twelfth Century

William I
(D. of Normandy
K. of England
1066–1087)

Robert II
(Duke of Normandy
from 1087, d. 1134)

William "Clito"
(d. 1128)

William II
(K. of England
1087–1100)

Henry I
(King of
England
1100–
1135)
m Matilda
(niece of
Edgar Atheling)

Matilda m Geoffrey of Anjou

Henry of Anjou
(King of England
1154–1189)

Adela m Stephen I
(Count of Blois)

Theobald
(Count of
Blois and
Champagne
1152–1159)

Stephen
(Count of
Mortain and
Boulgne)

Henry
(Bishop of
Winchester)

Eustace

THE CONQUEST OF ENGLAND

Edward the Confessor's death without an heir in January 1066 gave William the opportunity to claim the Crown of England. He was through marriage a first cousin once removed of Edward, but such a connection had never before formed the basis for a claim to the Crown. No English blood, royal or common, flowed in his veins. William also claimed that in 1051 Edward the Confessor had recognized him as his successor and that Harold Godwinson in 1064 had sworn to promote that succession. But Edward, on his deathbed, designated Harold as his successor, and Harold's oath to William had been wrested from him while in captivity. Not a single Englishman raised his voice for William, and the Witan swiftly chose Harold king. Harold accepted the Crown, whereupon William at once branded him a perjuror and usurper. The motives that drove William on were not complicated: he wanted the wealth and power that the Crown of England would bring him. He conquered England for the same reason his Viking ancestors had swept over much of Europe in the ninth century and his fellow Normans had recently conquered Sicily: he sought the spoils of war.

It was a desperate gamble, for the odds were strongly against a small duchy defeating a kingdom of more than a million inhabitants. But luck favored the duke. His two greatest enemies, the king of France and the count of Anjou, died in 1060. As a result the young French king fell into the hands of regents sympathetic to William, and the county of Anjou fell into civil war. The Pope, at odds with the Archbishop of Canterbury and dependent on Norman help in southern Italy, gave his blessing to the venture. The papal banner made an act of robbery appear a noble crusade, and greatly helped recruiting. It was not all luck, however, for William pressed on his preparations with skill and energy. He summoned his magnates, a new and powerful aristocracy in the duchy, and held out to them the prospect of winning lands in England. He recruited knights from all over Europe and gathered a fleet of more than 800 ships in the mouth of the river Dives. By early August, they were ready to sail.

It was not a weak, disintegrating kingdom that William invaded, but a rich, peaceful one, well governed and well defended, with a thriving commerce, an increasing population, and a growing amity between the English and the Danes. Its Church was not famous for scholarship or piety, but neither was it sunk in corruption. Edward the Confessor was not a great lawgiver or an enlightened patron of the Church, but he governed England from 1042 to 1066 with shrewdness and persistence. He was neither an imbecile (as a great historian once called him) nor a saint (though canonized in 1161), but a mediocrity who admired Norman fashions and displayed a remarkable ability to survive in office.

Yet two weaknesses did appear in the structure of the English state during his reign. The first was the rise of the earldoms. Cnut had grouped the shires of England into larger territories, over which he placed an administrative and military officer called an earl. He kept tight control over the earls, but Edward did not, and so the earls came to act with increasing independence. Three of the greatest earldoms, Wessex, Mercia, and Northumbria, became all but hereditary in the families of Godwin, Leofric, and Siward. In 1051 Edward sought to reduce the power of the house of Godwin by rejecting its candidate for the see of Canterbury and naming a Norman clergyman instead. Edward's action provoked a violent quarrel with Earl Godwin, who fled into exile. The next year the Earl returned, appealed to the anti-Norman sentiments of the English, raised an army, overawed the King, and forced him to expel his Norman favorites. Real power now resided in the House of Godwin. Earl Godwin died in 1053, but his sons soon held three of the four greatest earldoms in England. Harold held Wessex; Tostig, Northumbria; and Gyrth, East Anglia. Had the House of Godwin remained united, it might have saved England in the crisis of 1066. But it fell apart in 1065, when the Northumbrians rebelled against Tostig's misrule and Harold agreed to his brother's dismissal and exile. Tostig at once swore vengeance against his brother and sought aid from Harold Hardrada, King of Norway, to regain his earldom.

The second—and fatal—weakness was the lack of a successor to the throne. It was not Edward's incompetence that brought down the old English

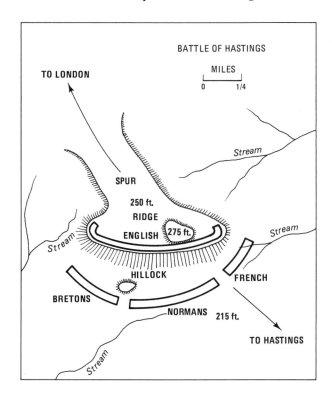

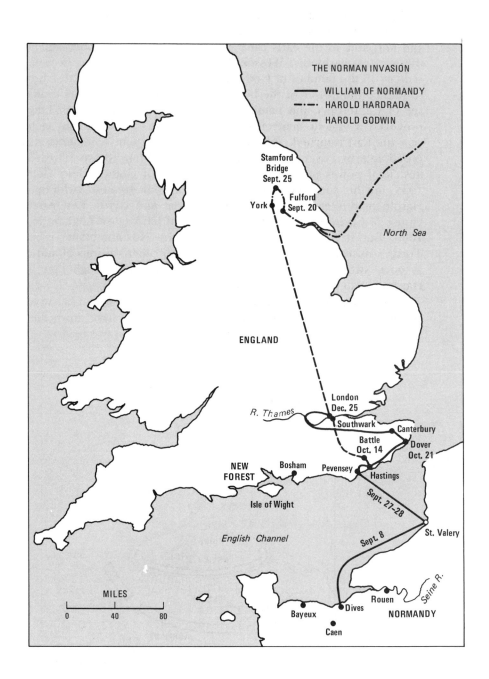

THE NORMAN INVASION

——— WILLIAM OF NORMANDY
—·—·— HAROLD HARDRADA
——— HAROLD GODWIN

Stamford
Bridge
Sept. 25

Fulford
Sept. 20

York

North Sea

ENGLAND

London
Dec. 25

R. Thames

Southwark

Canterbury

Battle
Oct. 14

Dover
Oct. 21

NEW
FOREST

Bosham

Pevensey

Hastings

Isle of Wight

Sept. 27-28

St. Valery

English Channel

Sept. 8

Seine R.

MILES

0   40   80

Rouen

Bayeux

Dives

NORMANDY

Caen

monarchy, but his death without an heir. Legend has attributed his childlessness to a vow of chastity, taken despite his marriage, but there is no contemporary authority for this story. The one certain fact is that he had no heir, and that the only living male descendant of Alfred the Great was Edgar Atheling, a mere boy. The dying King and the Witan therefore chose to entrust the destinies of England to Harold Godwinson, a man of courage, intelligence, affability, great physical strength, and good looks. But his elevation to the throne was an invitation not only for Duke William but for Harold Hardrada to claim the Crown. Harold Hardrada based his claim on a promise made by Harthacnut to Magnus of Norway that Magnus should have the English Crown should he outlive Harthacnut.

Fortune smiled on William of Normandy, for the north wind that pinned his ships to the shores of Normandy in September blew Harold Hardrada's ships south from Orkney to the Humber, where he joined forces with Tostig. The full brunt of the first English blow thus fell on Harold Hardrada, not Duke William. Harold Godwinson marched swifty north, caught the Norwegians by surprise, and defeated them at Stamford Bridge. Harold Hardrada fell in battle, as did Tostig. Of the 300 ships that brought the Norwegians, only 24 were needed to carry back the survivors. The victory at Stamford Bridge on September 25 gave proof of the military might of the English, but it also momentarily

William the Conqueror's army crossing the Channel, a scene from the Bayeux tapestry, commissioned by Bishop Odo of Bayeux. William's half-brother. The tapestry is an elaborate pictorial narrative, from the Norman point of view, of the events leading up to the Conquest and of the Conquest itself. This pictorial narrative is not really a tapestry but rather an embroidery in various colored wool on a background of bleached linen. It is 230 feet long, 20 inches wide, and contains 626 human beings, 190 horses, 41 boats, 37 buildings, and a comet. This superb work of art was probably designed by an artist of the school of Canterbury and almost certainly embroidered in England by English craftswomen (*Phaidon Press*).

weakened that might. Three days after Stamford Bridge, William landed in England. Harold raced back to London, leaving behind many of his archers and much of his infantry. He then hastily raised an army from his own housecarls and the local levies, and marched against William at Hastings. His impetuosity proved his undoing, for delay would have allowed him to bring a larger and better disciplined army against William.

At 9 A.M. on the 14th of October, William launched his first assault on the English, who commanded a ridge that fell off steeply to the east and west but only gently to the south, from which direction the Normans attacked. William had some 5000 troops, Harold perhaps 7000, though many were untrained, ill-equipped recruits. On both sides the soliders wore chainmail and conical helmets, carried shields, and fought with spear and sword. The English also wielded great battle axes, which could cut through chainmail. The Norman knights, unlike the English housecarls, fought on horseback, holding their lances steady at the hip or brandishing them as spears. William first sent his infantry and archers against the English, but the solid shield-wall of the closely packed English troops withstood the assault. He then sent his mounted knights forward, but they fared no better and retreated in confusion. Some of the English thereupon pursued the Norman infantry, only to be trapped and cut down by the Norman cavalry. Unable through the long afternoon to break the shield wall of the English, the Normans twice feigned retreat, each time wheeling on their pursuers and cutting them to pieces. In a final assault on the ridge William sent both archers and knights, the archers sending a shower of arrows high over the shield-wall and the knights charging the now weakened ranks of the English. This time they broke the English ranks, slew Harold and his brothers, and captured the ridge. The Battle of Hastings represented the victory of

The Battle of Hastings: English foot soldiers, armed with heavy axes, oppose the Norman knights amidst a shower of arrows. A scene from the Bayeux tapestry (*Phaidon Press*).

new tactics over old, of a mobile cavalry, supported by archers, over a massed infantry wielding ax and spear.

His victory won, William waited for the submission of the English, but it did not come. He thus began a slow march to Dover, on to Canterbury, westward south of the Thames, devastating the land as he went. Not strong enough to take London, he burned Southwark. He then marched through Hampshire, crossed the Thames, and circled east. Twenty years later his path could still be traced by the devastation he caused. The English, unable to organize a resistance, now submitted. On Christmas Day, in the abbey Edward had built at Westminster, the Archbishop of York crowned William king. William promised to govern as Edward's successor and to maintain his laws. He dismissed only a few Englishmen from office and seized only the lands of those who fell at Hastings. Yet his work was not done. Discontent smoldered, to burst forth in the southwest in 1068 and in the north in 1069. The rebellion in the north posed the more serious threat, for the King of Denmark supported it. With characteristic vigor and brutality, William marched north, captured York, bribed the Danes to leave, and laid waste the land. His troops massacred the rebels, slaughtered livestock, burned stores of food, and destroyed farm implements. Not a single inhabited place remained between York and Durham. He turned 1000 square miles into a wilderness, but the kingdom of England was now his.

FEUDALISM

The mounted knight, which won William a kingdom at Hastings, first appeared in the eighth century in Carolingian France. The invention of the saddle, the bit, and the stirrup made possible the armed warrior on horseback—above all the stirrup, which the West borrowed from the East and which allowed the horseman to withstand the shock of charging against an opponent with a lance. To maintain a mounted knight was expensive. He needed several horses, attendants, a sword, a lance, a kite-shaped shield, high leather boots with spurs, an iron helmet, and armor, which consisted of a one-piece garment of leather stretching from knee to neck and sewn all over with metal rings. His training was costly, for he was a professional soldier, trained from childhood to maturity in the difficult art of fighting on horseback. Maturity was set at 21 (and remained so until very recently), because a man was then strong enough to bear arms.

How to pay for such troops in a rural society where little money circulated and few taxes were collected posed a nearly insoluble problem. Charles Martel and his successors as kings of France solved it by paying their knights in land. From late Roman times, kings had granted lands as a reward for past services, "benefices" they were called. They now made the grant conditional upon future service; the benefice became the fief. It was a contract, but not an impersonal, commercial contract, for the recipient of the land became the vassal of the donor, or lord. The relationship of a vassal to his lord was an honorable and sacred one, entered into when the vassal placed his joined hands between the hands of the lord as an act of homage and then swore an oath of fealty that gave religious sanction to the act of homage. The lord then invested the vassal with his fief. The vassal owed his lord respect, obedience, and service; in return, the lord owed his vassal protection, justice, and maintenance. Out of the union of the fief and vassalage the institution of feudalism was born.

William the Conqueror brought feudalism to England and thereby transformed English society. Institutions tending toward feudalism did exist in Anglo-Saxon England, but the housecarl was not a knight, the hold oath was not an act of homage, and land loaned for miscellaneous services was not a fief. The social revolution wrought by the Norman Conquest was the more complete because the rebellions of 1068 and 1069 led to the displacement of the old English ruling class. Some four or five thousand thegns lost their land and were replaced by Normans. From the beginning, William acted on the feudal principle that there can be no land without a lord and that all the land of England was held of him. He thereupon granted land to some 170 barons, his great tenants-in-chief. He laid down with great exactness the services he demanded in return: a specific number of knights, usually grouped in units of five, for a clearly defined number of days, eventually set at forty. Some tenures were semi-military, owing castle guard or escort duty or the provisioning of troops.

Feudal tenures were originally not hereditary, but simply conditional on the performance of services owed. The land reverted to the lord on the death of the vassal. The vassal's heir could regain the estate only by paying a sum of money called a relief. If the vassal's family became extinct, the land escheated, or returned permanently, to the lord. Because a child could not perform the military services required, the lord took possession of the lands during the child's minority and the child became his ward. If the estate fell to a daughter or widow, the lord had the right to make certain that she married a man who could and would loyally perform the services demanded. Relief, escheat, wardship, and marriage were the feudal incidents. In addition, the vassal owed his lord a sum of money, or aid, when in need. Ultimately the occasions when the lord could automatically demand an aid were reduced to three: the knighting of his eldest son, the marriage of his eldest daughter, and the ransoming of his person.

The king's tenants-in-chief had, in turn, to find the knights the king demanded of them. These numbered between 4,000 and 7,000, for William did not believe he could hold down the English with fewer. A baron might provide the knights demanded of him from his own household knights, but more often he granted lands to knights, who became his vassals. They in turn might carry the process of subinfeudation further by granting lands to others. A great bar-

The stone keep of Rochester Castle, Kent, built by Archbishop Gervase of Canterbury soon after 1126 (*Reece Winstone, Bristol*).

on might possess lands scattered over twenty counties; at the center of his barony was his residence, usually a castle, of which at least eighty-four were built by 1100. The castle was as important a weapon for riveting Norman rule on England as the mounted knight, and as much a part of the feudal scene. William built castles wherever he went and permitted his barons to do likewise. Some of these castles, such as the Tower of London, were formidable structures of stone, but most were simpler structures of wood. A typical castle was composed of a large enclosure, the bailey, which was ditched, banked, and palisaded; within this there was a great mound of earth, the motte, on which stood a timbered tower, or keep. The motte-and-bailey castle served as the home of a great baron, his administrative center, and the stronghold where in time of rebellion he and his household could find safety.

A baron also held his barony together by a court, to which his vassals owed attendance. It was a feudal court in which the lord, by virtue of his lordship, exercised jurisdiction over his vassals in civil pleas, especially those concerning land. To this feudal jurisdiction William's barons soon added a franchisal jurisdiction. Either by usurpation or by a grant from the King they gained control over the hundred courts, which meant particularly jurisdiction over disputes about land, the stealing of cattle, and the hanging of thieves caught redhanded. Much public justice thus fell into private hands.

The Norman Conquest and the introduction of feudalism worsened the lot of women in England, especially those born into the upper classes. In Anglo-Saxon England men and women lived on terms of rough equality with each other. Great ladies took an active part in public affairs. Cyneruth, the tyrannical Queen of Mercia, had her portrait on a silver penny, and Aelfgifu, who bore Cnut two sons, ruled Norway as a regent. At a less royal level, women governed monasteries—not only those exclusively for women, but double monasteries for both men and women. The rights of women were also respected: No woman was forced to marry a man she disliked. Widows enjoyed the custody of their children and were not forced to remarry. If a wife, with her children, left her husband, she could take half their goods. A wife could also sell whatever land she brought to a marriage. Nor was there any rule of primogeniture, by which the whole estate must descend to the eldest son. An examination of thirty-nine wills which have survived from Anglo-Saxon England show that no preference was given to sons over daughters; parents provided equally for both.

Feudal law changed all this. Because an estate must now support knight service, it must descend intact to the eldest son. Feudal society was a society organized for war, a masculine society in which women had little part. Women had no public duties in Norman England; they were neither summoned to the King's council nor allowed to serve as jurors or judges. As a minor, a woman was in the guardianship of her father, who could arrange her marriage, often at the age of 7 or 8. As a wife, she was in the guardianship of her husband. Any land she possessed became his for the duration of the marriage, and she could neither plead in court nor make a will without his consent. Canon law, which specifically allowed wife beating, sanctioned a wife's subjection to her husband. Not until she was a widow did she escape guardianship, but even then she was denied the custody of her eldest son unless she could beg or buy the right of wardship over him. She was given for the rest of her life a third of the estate (the widow's dower), but her lord might force her to remarry—or extort money from her for the right not to remarry. It is true that an unmarried woman or widow could (where there was no male heir) inherit land, do homage for it, defend it in court, sell it, or give it away, but she lost these rights the moment she married or remarried. To defend her great estate, maintain her independence, and escape remarriage, the widowed countess of Aumale paid the King 5000 marks.

DOMESDAY BOOK AND THE MANORS OF ENGLAND

Feudalism was a political institution by which the King paid for military and other services by the grant of land to his vassals. But it was not simply land that he granted; he also granted the tenants on it and the obligations they owed to the lord of the manor. A fief was commonly a bundle of manors, and the manors of England formed the economic base on which feudalism rested. Their wealth equipped the knight and sent him into battle. Payments from the King's own manors and the obligations owed the King by his tenants-in-chief made up the larger part of the King's revenues. Knowing this, in 1086 William sought to ascertain the wealth of his own manors and of those of his tenants-in-chief, with a view to their further exploitation. He sent commissioners into each county to hold sworn inquests at which the sheriff, the barons, and the priest, reeve, and six villeins from each village testified. The commissioners asked them who held the land, what its value was, what stock was on it. "So very thoroughly did he have the inquiry carried out," wrote the Anglo-Saxon chronicler, "that there was not a single 'hide,' not one virgate of land, not even —it is shameful to record but it did not seem shameful for him to do—not even one ox, nor one cow, nor one pig which escaped notice in his survey."

The results of this vast survey were recorded in two volumes, which were placed in the treasury and which gained the name of Domesday Book because its judgments were as final as those handed down on doomsday. Domesday Book provided the King with the annual value of every manor in England and so allowed him to determine what feudal incidents to charge his tenants-in-chief, what rents to collect from his royal manors and boroughs, and what geld to demand from the country. The Book was a testament to the administrative skill of the English government and a record of the introduction of feudalism into England.

A careful reading of Domesday Book shows that the Norman Conquest was a catastrophe for the English. It swept away the thegns of England, only two of whom survived as tenants-in-chief. Nearly half the total income from rents on land, £30,000 out of £73,000, went to the creation of some 170 baronies, which were given to Normans. Nearly a fourth of the income from land went to the royal family and another quarter to some 50 prelates within the Church. Thus less than 250 persons controlled most of the land of England. These princes, prelates, and barons, with their vassals, dependents, and retainers, numbered some 10,000 people. They were a foreign elite imposed on a nation of some two million English. Nor was it only the thegns who suffered; many freemen who had owned their own land and could go with it to whatever lord they wished sank to the level of sokeman or villein. A *sokeman* was a free peasant who owned his own land and therefore could sell it, but who could not take his holding to another lord, for it was tied to the *soke*, or manor. The sokeman (found chiefly in the Danelaw) owed the lord of the manor only rent and suit to court. Domesday Book reveals that in many instances the number of sokemen in the Danelaw fell sharply between 1066 and 1086. The conquest tended to level all men to the condition of the *villein,* a peasant who was tied to the manor on which he was born, who owed weekwork and boonwork, who paid a *tallage* (a tax imposed at the will of his lord), and who must take his grain to be ground at the lord's mill, and his bread to be baked in the lord's oven. The villein was also required to pay his lord a fine on the marriage of his daughter (*merchet*), to give him his best beast on his death (*heriot*), and to answer in the lord's court for any failure to perform the services he owed.

The new landlords sought, wherever possible, to increase labor services and rents. In Hampshire there were at least forty-four manors whose lords demanded more than the values set upon them. The manor of East Meon, for example, judged by the villagers to be worth £60, paid £100. William himself, whose greed for gold was notorious, set the example. Domesday Book shows that he obtained far more revenue from his lands than had his predecessors. The burden on the peasantry was heavier because England still suffered from the devastation caused by the march of William's army and the ruthless suppression of the northern rebellion. Of 1,333 places listed in Domesday Book as "waste," 1,076 came from the devastated counties of the north. There were many manors throughout England that had markedly fewer plow teams than plowlands, indicating a fall in population. Depopulation, the destruction of farm implements, and the slaughter of livestock caused a sharp fall in the value of manors, a decline from which many had not recovered by 1086. The value of the lands of Cambridgeshire was 13 percent less in 1086 than in 1066; in Nottinghamshire, it was 19 percent less; in Derbyshire, 35 percent less; and in Yorkshire, 74 percent less. In about two-thirds of England, values failed to recover their levels of 1066.

These figures are abstract and bloodless. What lies behind them is the rude villein, in his knee-length gown, drawn in at the waist, driving his oxen down the long furrow, toiling from sunrise to sunset, his wife tending the stock and making the cheese, his house a hovel into which livestock freely enter, possessing nothing beyond his farm stock and a few pots and pans, subsisting on wheat or barley loaves in prosperous times, facing starvation in years of famine. On his and his wife's labor the wealth of England largely depended.

One class of persons improved their status—if not their condition—with the coming of the Normans. Slaves made up nearly 10 percent of the population of Anglo-Saxon England; in the next century they virtually disappeared. The Normans found it more profitable to exploit a peasant than a slave. Indeed, by 1200 the Latin word for slave, *servus,* had come to be used interchangeably with *villani,* or villein. The peasants of England had become serfs.

Domesday Book likewise reveals that many of the boroughs of England suffered from the conquest. The population of most towns declined, houses lay waste (478 of them in Oxford), and trade decayed, especially trade with Scandinavia and France, with whose monarchs William had quarreled. William did not trust the English inhabitants of his towns, so in every town he built a great castle to overawe them. At the same time he exploited his boroughs more thoroughly than ever, increasing by 20 to 25 percent the "farm of the borough," that is, the total sum of rents, tolls, and profits of justice due from them.

Yet the Normans were not hostile to towns. In the following century both kings and barons founded new towns, each with its market, castle, and church. From the market they hoped to gain profit; from the castle, increased authority over the countryside. To make life more attractive for the burgess, or town dweller, they granted extensive liberties to both old and new boroughs. Such liberties commonly included the right to pay a fixed rent on, or sell, one's house and land; freedom from *heriot* or relief; freedom of marriage; freedom from excessive tolls; and the right to trial in a borough court. Many new boroughs, because of insufficient trade, fell back to the status of a village, but others became true towns—that is, towns with a permanent market and a mercantile population.

The first thirty years of Norman rule in England with a cruel blow to the inhabitants of both manor and town. But Norman discipline and order, the long peace of Henry I's reign, and a climate that became milder than had been known for centuries allowed the English to emerge from this ordeal stronger and more prosperous than ever.

THE NORMAN CHURCH

The Norman Conquest had nearly as profound an influence on the English Church as on English society. It brought Normans with their reforming ideas into the higher offices of the Church; it created the problem of the place of the Church in a feudal society; and it reinvigorated monasticism.

Having conquered England, William soon secured the dismissal of Archbishop Stigand, a symbol of corruption, and replaced him with Lanfranc, prior of Bec. Lanfranc was a North Italian trained in canon law, a renowned scholar, and a blunt, practical man. By 1087 all the bishops in the English church but one were Normans. Lanfranc, who sympathized with the movement for reform begun by Pope Gregory VII about 1059, saw that two principal reforms were needed in the English Church: ecclesiastical affairs must be freed from the control of all laymen but the king, and bishops must be given stricter control over the clergy. To achieve this first purpose, William, through a Church council, decreed that bishops and archdeacons should no longer preside over "ecclesiastical cases" in hundred or shire courts. This came to mean that all cases concerning clergymen and all cases in which laymen committed moral offenses should come before a court presided over by the bishop or his subordinate. England now had two systems of courts, one secular, one spiritual.

In order to give the bishops stricter control over the clergy, Lanfranc strengthened the cathedral chapter. He brought sees that were once located in the countryside into towns and provided that these newly organized chapters be composed of canons, not monks—that is, of secular clergy, not regular.

Church councils passed legislation that empowered bishops to hold councils, or synods, twice a year and to appoint an archdeacon to help supervise the diocese and preside over the new ecclesiastical courts. Lanfranc also sought to reform abuses within the Church, particularly to end simony and clerical marriages. A Church Council passed legislation forbidding simony, the purchase of ecclesiastical offices, but the practice reappeared in the reign of Henry I. The marriage of priests also proved a difficult problem, for the Anglo-Saxon Church had allowed such marriages. Lanfranc, on this issue, showed himself to be a man of moderation. He agreed that priests who were now married need not put away their wives, but he did insist that no unmarried priest take a wife and no married man be ordained. The deeper problem in the countryside, however, was the lack of parish churches. Much of England was served either by collegiate churches, called minsters, or by rude field churches. The Normans completed the parish system of England, which the Anglo-Saxons had begun. Norman barons and knights, perhaps to expiate the sin of conquest, built churches everywhere, and like the thegns of Saxon times they regarded these churches as their property and claimed the right, known as *advowson*, to name the priests who served in them.

The parish priest performed the mass and met the immemorial needs of a Christian life—baptism, marriage, and burial. The religious feelings of early medieval Englishmen were unsophisticated. God and Christ were close at hand, as were the saints and martyrs. The invisibility of the next world caused little concern, since so much of this world was unseen to the men and women in the parishes. They had never seen London or Rome or Jerusalem; heaven, purgatory, and hell were real to them. Nor did they doubt the inevitability of an afterlife and a day of judgment, which helps explain why the greatest of warriors might suddenly renounce all and depart for Jerusalem. The parish priest was there to help sinful humans win their way to heaven, but a sinner might also seek the intercession of a local saint, to whose shrine he or she would make a pilgrimage. The whole edifice of medieval piety, from parish priest to hermit monk, existed to serve men and women who feared damnation and sought eternal life.

William the Conqueror favored reform within the Church, but he did not intend to surrender control over the Church. Indeed, he fastened his grip more firmly on it by imposing feudal obligations on the lands held by the bishops and the greater abbots. They now held their lands as vassals of the King, and for them they owed knight service, prayers, and counsel. The Bishop of Lincoln, for example, held manors throughout the Midlands and three castles, for which he owed sixty knights. But at the very moment when William sought to feudalize the Church, the Papacy, guided by Gregory VII, sought to assert its independence. Rome claimed the right to hear appeals in all ecclesiastical cases, large and small, and it insisted that the bishop was first a spiritual leader. Gregory even demanded that William, because the Papal Curia had awarded him the Crown in 1066, hold England as a papal fief. William refused. He also forbade appeals to Rome and prohibited the publication of papal decrees in England without his consent. William meant to be master over the Church.

Yet the question remained unanswered: Was the bishop a royal official or a spiritual leader? In an age that deeply revered symbols, this question was seen as a dispute over whether the King or the Archbishop should invest the bishop with the ring and staff, the symbol of his spiritual authority. Whenever William named a new bishop, he first received homage and fealty from him, then invested him with ring and staff. To Gregory VII and to the saintly Anselm, who succeeded Lanfranc in 1093, this was intolerable. Anselm even went so far as to refuse to consecrate bishops the King had invested.

During the reign of the violent and grasping William Rufus (1087–1100), there was no possibility of settling the dispute, for he plundered the wealth of the Church, kept bishoprics vacant so he could enjoy their revenues, and drove Anselm into exile. Henry I (1100–1135) was a different kind of man—more reasonable, more compromising. Anxious to be on good terms with the Church, he soon reached an agreement with Anselm, who had grown tired of exile. At the monastery of Le Bec in Normandy they agreed to a compromise: A bishop should first do homage to the King for his lands; then he should receive the ring and staff from the Archbishop. Henry also agreed that cathedral chapters should elect bishops, but insisted that the election take place under his eye in the royal chapel. Though nominally free, elections were guided by the royal will. In substance Henry I yielded scarcely anything at Le Bec. Bishops remained loyal officials first, giving counsel, going on embassies, administering the Chancery.

It was not in the lives of the bishops, men facing numerous practical problems, that the Church produced its deepest spirituality, but in the lives of countless monks and nuns. In 1086 there were only 48 monastic houses in England and 850 monks and nuns. By 1154 there were 805 houses and 5000 monks and nuns. The twelfth century was the golden age of monasticism in England. The Norman kings did not so much cause this growth as witness it. William founded Battle Abbey on the site of the Battle of Hastings, but he did little else. His chief concern was to secure control over the religious houses. At the conquest there were twelve English abbots out of twenty; by 1089 there were none. The Normans who replaced them brought great energy to the administration of their houses, but they were caught up in feudal obligations and were more interested in breeding scholars and administrators than saints.

The greatest wave of religious enthusiasm came from 1135 to 1154 and was a spontaneous outburst of piety by men and women from every walk of life —though mostly from the aristocracy. The monastic virtues of poverty, chastity, and obedience were attractive chiefly to the well-born. Peasants already lived in poverty, could not afford chastity (for need of the labor of their children), and already owed obedience to a lord. In medieval eyes real poverty was a disgrace; only voluntary or "divine poverty" was a virtue. What the aristocracy sought in monastic life was silence and solitude, a life of ordered calm, liberation from the vexations of life in a troubled world; they also saw in monastic life the highest expression of the Christian life.

Many who could not enter a monastery nevertheless supported them with gifts; in the Danelaw even poor peasants gave an acre of land. Many of these gifts went to Cluniac houses, where the monks in their simple black gowns spent the day in prayer and chanting. But many persons found the continuous chanting and liturgical ceremonies, which the Cluniac ritual demanded, unappealing. They joined the new Cistercian order, which alternated chanting and liturgical ceremony with manual labor and private prayer. The Cistercians deliberately placed their monasteries in remote places, far removed from the temptations of the world. The greatest of their houses, Rievaulx, lay in the wild dales that border the Yorkshire moors. They did not lease their lands to tenants, but farmed them with lay brothers who, though often illiterate, were full members of the house. Monastic life was thus opened to the humble and illiterate, who could never have hoped to become choir monks. The Cistercians, clad in their white or gray gowns, pursuing a life of simplicity and austerity, tending their sheep on the moors, raising buildings of a severe Gothic beauty, soon outnumbered Cluniac monks in England.

The ruins of Fountains Abbey, Yorkshire, founded in the twelfth century by the Cistercians (*Aerofilms*).

But such isolated communities did not meet the needs of the Church in England. To provide better service for the ordinary parish church, the Austin canons were formed. Members of this order lived communally as monks, but served in parish churches. And to meet the demands of women for a conventual life, Gilbert of Sempringham, an English priest, created an order for women who would live communally and simply, like the Cistercians. By 1189 it had fourteen houses, with 960 nuns. Zeal for the monastic life encompassed both town and country and reformed the lives of both men and women.

THE MACHINERY OF GOVERNMENT

Though the Normans introduced feudalism into England, they retained and developed the principal institutions of the Anglo-Saxon monarchy—the chancery, the chamber, the geld, the sheriff, the fyrd, and shire and hundred courts. These institutions gave them the authority they sought and prized.

Under Edward the Confessor clergymen who belonged to the King's Chapel drew up the charters and issued the writs the King needed. The Normans continued and developed these practices. The writs, formerly written in English, they wrote in Latin and used far more freely. At the head of the writing office there appeared in 1078 a "Chancellor," so named because he and his clerks sat in the King's lodgings behind a screen, or *cancella*. In this way the chancery grew out of the chapel and became a distinct branch of government.

The collection and storage of the King's revenues belonged to the Chamber, which under the Anglo-Saxon kings had become more than a domestic treasury in the King's bedchamber. Edward the Confessor had established a permanent treasury at Winchester, whose officials were skilled at striking dies and testing the purity of coinage. The Normans thus inherited the best currency in Western Europe and an elaborate system for assessing, collecting, and storing the King's revenues. These consisted of rents from his lands, feudal incidents and aids, the profits of justice, and the geld. William's own lands produced the greatest revenue. By 1086 he possessed nearly a quarter of the landed wealth of England—an estimated £17,650 out of a total of £73,000 in annual value. But he did not neglect the geld, which had become practically an annual tax on the landed wealth of England. William levied it nearly every year of his reign.

The official responsible for collecting the geld and the rents from royal manors was the sheriff, who now began four centuries of ascendancy in local governments. His chief duty was to collect the King's revenues and account for them at the treasury, but William took from the earls (whose greatness now came to an end) and gave to the sheriffs the duty of summoning and leading the fyrd. The fyrd was national in organization, not feudal, a general levy of all free men to help defend the kingdom. The sheriff also presided over the shire court, read the King's writ to the court, and pronounced the judgment reached by the suitors to the court. No officer was more important to William than the sheriff. Therefore he named Norman barons to the office—strong-willed, ruthless men whose power tended to become extortionate unless curbed by an equally ruthless king.

The Norman kings took great pains to preserve the shire court as the principal point of contact between the king and his subjects. To it the great landowners of the county (a term introduced by the Normans) paid suit. These suitors were the living repositories of the immemorial law of the land. They heard criminal cases, disputes between tenants of different landlords, and actions for wrongs and debts. The Normans continued to use the hundred court to enforce criminal justice, even though many of these courts fell into private hands. By 1272, in fact, over half the 628 hundreds in England were in private hands. Despite this fact, the hundred court remained important as a fiscal unit for assessing the geld and as an instrument for preserving the peace and judging petty crimes. The obligations shire and hundred courts imposed on the people fell on the village, not the manor. It was from the village that the priest, the reeve, and four good men came to the hundred and shire court, there to give the king the information he sought.

The Normans were shrewd enough to adopt many Anglo-Saxon institutions, but they also added institutions of their own. The most important of these new institutions was the Curia Regis, or King's Court. The Curia Regis differed from the Witan since it was a feudal court, to which the King's tenants-in-chief owed attendance and where they might receive trial by their peers. It was an amorphous institution, hardly more than the King, or one authorized to act for him, doing business in an open place. It took many forms. On solemn occasions, such as the great festivals of Easter, Whitsun, and Christmas, William would summon his vassals to attend him. These were great ceremonial occasions, when he would wear his crown amid much pageantry and feasting, and when he and his vassals would do justice and discuss important affairs of state. Such an assembly was called a *Magnum Concilium*, or great council. But the real work of government was done by a small council, those who happened on any occasion to be attending the King. It was most often composed of household officials, administrators of minor baronial rank, and a few bishops and great barons. It guided public policy, managed finances, superintended local government, and tried all but the greatest cases. In its nonfeudal, or national, capacity it tried important criminal and civil cases and heard appeals from hundred and county courts.

Nothing did more to swell the volume of business before the Curia Regis than the growth in the number of pleas of the Crown. "Pleas of the Crown" were crimes of so serious a nature that they were reserved for royal, not local and popular, justice. By Henry I's reign they numbered thirty-seven, and included murder, robbery, rape, arson, and breaches of the King's peace. As the King's peace came to be extended to more places, persons, and times, almost any crime could be seen as a breach of the King's peace, and so a plea of the Crown. At the same time, the feudal concept of felony, which originally meant treachery to one's lord, was extended to all serious crimes. The King had every reason to increase the number of felonies, for the lands of a tenant-in-chief found guilty of a felony escheated to him. Soon, however, the volume of cases that came before the Curia Regis proved unmanageable. William I sought to solve the problem by having sheriffs hear pleas of the Crown in the county courts, and William Rufus by naming resident royal justices in the counties, but the ingenious Roger of Salisbury, chief minister to Henry I, found the permanent solution. He sent royal justices on a tour, or "eyre," of the counties, where they heard pleas of the Crown. These itinerant justices, the ancestors of the modern assize courts, became an essential link between local and central government. The justice they enforced was swift and severe. Roger Basset in 1124 in Leicestershire hanged more thieves than ever before, forty-four in all, and had six more blinded and castrated. Capital punishment and flogging came with the Normans; the Anglo-Saxons preferred fines.

Roger Le Poer, Bishop of Salisbury, who had first sent itinerant justices into the counties, had begun life as an obscure priest in Caen, Normandy. Henry I, struck with the rapidity with which he said mass (so the story runs), brought him to England, where Roger soon exhibited a remarkable talent for business. Shortly after 1107 Henry made him justiciar, in which capacity he governed England during Henry's many absences from the kingdom. Roger of Salisbury was an ambitious man. He amassed great riches, built a splendid castle at Devizes, and promoted his relatives to high office—his son as Chancellor, a nephew as Treasurer, another nephew as Bishop of Lincoln. His greatest work, however, was the creation of the exchequer.

The first two Norman kings adopted and developed the financial machinery of the Anglo-Saxon treasury. But during the reign of Henry I the treasury yielded some of its power to a new institution, the exchequer. The exchequer was a financial board and court, sitting in London, composed of officials called barons of the exchequer, though they were usually not barons in the ordinary sense. Before this board the sheriff twice yearly accounted for his receipts and disbursements. The sheriff would appear before the barons of the exchequer, seated at a table covered by a checkered cloth. The checkered cloth—with its columns of squares representing sums of money—was in effect an abacus, and the accounts of the sheriffs were calculated by moving counters on these columns. In this way the sheriff, who probably could neither read nor write, could be sure he was not being cheated. Having paid the sum he owed, the sheriff received a receipt, a wooden stick or tally with notches cut along the edges to represent sums of money (the wider the notch, the greater the sum). The tally was then split down the middle through the notches. The sheriff kept one half, the exchequer the other. The exchequer was also a court, with procedures of its own, before whom the sheriff must justify his conduct. The exchequer could, and did, impose heavy fines on sheriffs guilty of extortion, but more often it adjudicated disputes about what revenues were or were not owed the King. The sheriff coming to London to answer before the exchequer and the itinerant justice traveling down to the shires to do justice provided two essential links between local and central government. In this close linkage lay the strength of the English government in the twelfth century.

TYRANNY AND ANARCHY

Because his eldest son, Robert, was incapable of ruling both Normandy and England, William I left Normandy to Robert and England to William Rufus, his second son. William Rufus was a jovial ruffian, a splendid knight, and a brutal tyrant, who was called Rufus because of his beefy red face. He was extravagantly generous to his own knights but ruthlessly plundered the Church, whose teachings he scoffed at whenever secure from the danger of death. His one purpose was to wrest Normandy from his brother; in order to pay for the armies to do this, he taxed his subjects unmercifully. His chosen instrument for this task was a household chaplain, the unscrupulous Ranulf Flambard. Flambard transformed the royal administration into a machine for extorting money from the King's subjects. He exploited feudal aids and incidents to the fullest, particularly forfeiture, escheat, and marriage. He also collected arbitrary aids, such as that in 1096 when William Rufus demanded 10,000 marks to pay for a campaign in Normandy. The Church suffered the most. Not only did William Rufus collect arbitrary aids from his Church fiefs, but he left abbeys and bishoprics vacant for long periods of time so that he could enjoy their revenues. William Rufus was an unloved king when he died while hunting in New Forest on August 2, 1100, brought down by an arrow shot by Walter Tirel.

Historians will never know for certain whether Walter Tirel shot the arrow accidentally or deliberately, but the speed with which Henry seized the crown and the favor he later showed to Tirel's family suggest a deliberate act. Henry, who was William the Conqueror's third son, seized the treasury at Winchester the very day William Rufus died. The next day he had a small group of barons "elect" him King and on August 5 he was crowned at Westminster. Though every bit as greedy and autocratic as William Rufus, Henry was less impulsive, more calculating, cleverer, and better educated. He was also far more pious. His piety, however, had little influence on his personal life—he fathered twenty illegitimate children. Prudence was the hallmark of his character, and prudence led him to placate the barons by imprisoning Ranulf Flambard, to appease the English by marrying Edith, a descendant of Alfred the Great, and to issue a Coronation Charter in which he promised to end the unjust exactions imposed by William Rufus.

Contenders for the Crown of England in 1066

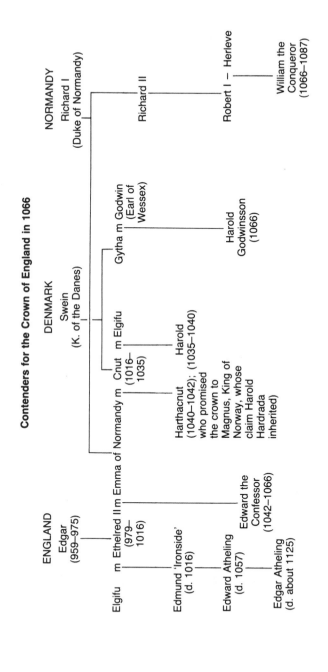

The reign of William Rufus had revealed the potential for tyranny that lay in the vast powers, feudal and monarchical, that William the Conqueror had gathered to himself. There was no institutional check on the King. He might seek the advice of the Curia Regis, but he need not take it. The only check on him, if a check at all, was a moral one: his promise in the coronation oath to rule justly, to protect the Church, to suppress malefactors, and to rule under the law. Henry made such promises more fully than had any previous King. He would end the heavy exactions on the Church, collect only the customary feudal dues, mint only good money, and restore the good laws of Edward the Confessor. He had copies of the charter sent into every shire. But it was only propaganda; he did not keep his promises. He collected more feudal incidents and aids than custom allowed, he resorted to financial oppression, and he created new "forests" from which he collected a multitude of fines.

No grievance weighed more heavily on the English in these years than the forest law. The Anglo-Saxons had no forest law. The Normans, for whom hunting was a passion and venison a means of subsistence, introduced it into England in order to protect the red deer, the roe deer, and the wild boar. By royal proclamation the King could put any stretch of land—usually wooded lands where deer throve—under its law. Most of Essex was a royal forest, and one could walk through royal forests nearly all the way from Windsor to the Channel. By 1200 royal forests covered about a quarter of England. In such forests all game was reserved to the King. The forest law, enforced by foresters, wardens, and verderers, was harsh. There was a 10 shilling fine for hunting deer, and a villein could lose his right hand for resisting a verderer. The law meant a severe economic loss to the English peasant, who sought in the forest the game to supplement a meager diet.

Four typical Exchequer tallies (Public Record Office).

A battle scene typical of the cavalry engagements fought in Stephen's reign. The scene appears on an illuminated manuscript, probably painted at Bury St. Edmunds about 1135. It purports to be a picture of the Saxons defeating the Britons, but reflects more accurately the warfare of the twelfth century (*Pierpont Morgan Library, MS 736, f. 7*).

Two purposes dominated Henry I's reign: the conquest of Normandy and the establishment of a peaceful succession to the Crown. In the first of these he succeeded; but in the second he failed. By 1106 he had wrested Normandy from Robert, who had seized it again on William Rufus's death. But his one legitimate son and heir, William, drowned in 1120 when his ship, its passengers and crew drunk, foundered on the rocks outside Barfleur. This left only his daughter Matilda, for neither custom nor church law permitted the succession of bastards. Henry forced his barons to recognize Matilda as his successor, but they disliked the idea. It was unprecedented for a woman to rule; and Matilda's later marriage to Geoffrey of Anjou made her still less acceptable, for the counts of Anjou were traditional enemies of the Norman Dukes. Thus, when Henry in 1135 died (allegedly from eating too many lampreys) and Stephen of Blois swiftly seized the throne, the barons and the Church accepted him as

King. He was the son of William the Conqueror's daughter, Adela, and one of the largest landowners in England.

Unfortunately for England, Stephen, though good-natured and chivalrous, was naive, weak, temporizing, and incompetent. He lacked both the gift of leadership and the ruthlessness needed by a twelfth-century king. As a result thirty-five years of peace gave way to two decades of turbulence. It was Matilda's bid for the throne in 1138, aided by Geoffrey of Anjou and the King of the Scots, that precipitated civil war. By 1141 her bid had failed, but civil war had spawned feudal anarchy. The great barons played each side off against the other, built unlicensed castles, usurped royal authority, made treaties among themselves, and minted their own coin. The most infamous of these barons was Geoffrey of Mandeville, who converted the fenland abbey of Ramsey into a fortified center from which to pillage the countryside. By exacting bribes and favors from each side in turn, Geoffrey won large estates, an earldom, the hereditary keepership of the Tower, and the heridary office of sheriff in Essex, London, and Hertfordshire. Other lords played the same game. The Earl of York turned Bridlington Priory into a castle and the Earl of Richmond plundered the church at Ripon. The chroniclers no doubt exaggerated the extent of the anarchy, but England clearly suffered from lack of governance. Just as the reign of William Rufus had revealed the potential for tyranny that lay in feudalism if the king were too ruthless, so Stephen's reign revealed the potential for anarchy if the king were too weak.

The accession to the throne in 1154 of Matilda's and Geoffrey's son, Henry of Anjou, ended the anarchy that had disgraced Stephen's reign. The Church played a critical role in Henry's accession. In 1139 Stephen had committed the monumental blunder of attacking Roger of Salisbury and his family. Not only did this paralyze the operation of the exchequer, but it turned the Church away from the King. A few years later Archbishop Theobald, now head of the Church, refused to crown Stephen's son Eustace as his successor; the Archbishop then fled to Anjou. By 1153 Henry of Anjou, now a mature warrior of 19, governed nearly half of France as Count of Anjou, Duke of Aquitaine, and Duke of Normandy. Using Normandy as a springboard, he invaded England in 1153, where a tired Stephen, despondent at his son's death, agreed to a treaty drawn up by the Church. By the Treaty of Winchester, Stephen would reign as King until his death, when Henry would succeed him. Death soon came, on December 19, 1154, and Henry of Anjou became King as Henry II. England waited to see whether he would rule as a tyrant, or as another Stephen, or as a wise and lawful King.

FURTHER READING

R. ALLEN BROWN. *The Normans and the Norman Conquest.* London, 1969. Traditional in approach; defends the catastrophic view of the Norman Conquest; copious footnotes and a bibliography.

AUSTIN LANE POOLE. *From Domesday Book to*

Magna Carta 1087–1216. 2nd. ed., Oxford, 1955. A volume in the Oxford History of England; though becoming out-of-date, it reflects its author's extensive and intensive knowledge of the primary sources.

*M.T. CLANCHY. *England and Its Rulers 1066–1272.* Oxford, 1983. Stresses the interaction between foreign lordship and national identity; vivid anecdotes and apt quotations make it fascinating reading, but a basic knowledge of the period is a prerequisite.

DAVID DOUGLAS. *William the Conqueror.* Berkeley, 1964. A history of the times as well as a biography; learned, authoritative, readable; views the Conquest as a revolutionary event.

H.G., RICHARDSON, AND G.O. SAYLES. *The Governance of Medieval England from the Conquest to Magna Carta.* Edingburgh, 1963. Emphasizes the continuity between Anglo-Saxon and Norman institutions; controversial but a useful balance to Brown and Douglas.

REGINALD LENNARD. *Rural England 1086–1135.* Oxford, 1959. Examines the economic and social structure of Norman England; a work of meticulous scholarship and penetrating insights.

DAVID KNOWLES. *The Monastic Order in England* . 2nd. ed., Cambridge, England, 1963. Traces the development of monasticism from 943 to 1216; its deep learning, power of portraiture, and narrative skill make it a classic.

*EILEEN POWER. *Medieval Women.* Cambridge, England, 1975. A collection of charming and witty essays about medieval women, written by a distinguished medievalist.

V.H. GALBRAITH. *The Making of Domesday Book.* Oxford, 1963. Describes how and why Domesday Book came into existence; rejects geographically arranged returns for feudally arranged returns; contains insights about the period in general.

DAVID DOUGLAS, AND GEORGE GREENAWAY, eds. *English Historical Documents 1042–1189.* Oxford, 1983. Contains chronicles, returns from the Inquest of Sheriffs, entries from the Pipe Rolls, letters from popes and archbishops; reproduces the Bayeaux Tapestry with commentaries on each scene.

5 The Angevins

The twelfth and thirteenth centuries were a creative period in the history of England, an age of growth and new ideas, a fertile age, a true springtime. The population tripled. Technological advances transformed agriculture. The wool trade emerged as the great cornucopia of English wealth. Towns grew in size and won self-government. A renaissance in learning led to the rise of universities. And the kings of England and their judges created a Common Law that was more uniform, rational, just, and equitable. These events have captured the attention of historians, for out of them came modern England. But to those who lived during this time, other events loomed larger: the murder of an archbishop, the ransoming of a king, the loss of an empire. The historian, fortunately, need not neglect the one for the other, for it is the task of history both to show how the present grew out of the past and to examine the past for its own sake.

THE NEW AGRICULTURE

Estimates of the population of medieval England are notoriously unreliable. Historians have varied from 1.1 to 2.5 million in their estimates of the population in 1086, and from 3.7 to 7.2 million in their estimates of the population in 1300, with most accepting the higher figure. But upon one fact all historians agree: whatever the actual numbers, the population tripled between 1086 and 1300. They likewise agree that the cause of this growth was the availability of land, which led to marriages at an earlier age, which in turn led to the birth of more children. But the population could not have tripled in two centuries had there not been enough food. The growth in population depended on a growth in the productivity of agriculture.

Technological advances explain part of the growth in the productivity of agriculture during these years. At the heart of these advances was the replacement of the two-field with the three-field system. Under the two-field system, half the land was planted with grain—wheat, rye, barley, or oats—while the other half was left fallow. The next year the two fields reversed their roles. During the eleventh century, however, there arose in the Frankish lands between the Seine and the Rhine a new system of cultivation, the three-field rotation. It reached England in the late twelfth century. Under this system arable land was divided into three fields. One was sown with a winter crop, such as wheat or rye; the second with a spring crop, such as oats, barley, beans, or lentils; the third was left fallow. The usual rotation was from fallow to winter crop to spring crop. The new system increased the amount of land under cultivation by one-third. On a 600-acre manor, for example, 400 rather than 300 acres would yield a crop. It also decreased the amount of plowing, since keeping down weeds meant plowing the fallow twice a year rather than once, and there was now less fallow. Furthermore, the new rotation spread the plowing, sowing, and harvesting more evenly throughout the year, reduced the chances of the entire crop failing, and added vegetable proteins (beans and peas) to the peasant's diet. Given the pressure of a growing population on the land, there was an urgent need to shift from the two-field system to the three. By the middle of the fourteenth century the three-field system prevailed throughout most of England.

In technological inventions the twelfth century was unusually creative.

Plowing with a team of horses (*the British Museum, MS Egerton 1147*).

The introduction of the overshot vertical waterwheel made the milling of grain by waterpower more efficient. The first windmill ever built in Europe was in operation in 1185 at Weedley, in Yorkshire. Within a century, windmills were commonly used for grinding grain in eastern England. To waterpower and windpower the English then added horsepower. The invention of the horseshoe and the horsecollar made possible the use of the horse in farming and hauling, for the hooves of the horse, unlike those of an ox, are easily broken, and the yoke-harness, well suited to an ox, tends to choke a horse when he pulls hard. The nailed horseshoe, first developed in Siberia, appeared in England during the reign of Edward the Confessor, and the rigid, padded horsecollar, of central Asian origin, appeared a century later. By the early twelfth century horses were drawing the harrow and pulling four-wheeled wagons that now replaced the two-wheeled cart. Not until late in the century, however, were horses used for plowing, and then usually in teams of six oxen and two horses. Gradually horses came to be wholly substituted for oxen. Although an ox can exert the same pull as a horse, it is far slower and has less endurance. Modern studies show that a horse can produce 50 percent more foot-pounds per second than an ox. Thus the plowman grew more efficient as he slowly substituted the horse for the ox.

The immediate gains of productivity made by the new technology were probably modest; far more was gained by reclaiming wastelands. This was rarely done by settling new villages, for most of the villages of England had been established by the time of Domesday Book. It was done instead by the lord expanding his acres at the expense of woodland and waste, and by the tenant adding a few acres to his holdings. This process, called "assarting," went on steadily during these years, and brought increasingly marginal land into cultivation. Land was reclaimed on a grander scale by draining the marshes. In the Fens, some 200 square miles were won from the sea. Such was the land hunger of the age that even the royal forests were colonized. Henry II had drastically increased the royal forests of England, but his successors relaxed the rigors of the forest laws and sought to exact a profit from the colonizers. Reclaimed marsh and forest lands were often rich. This cannot be said of the thin heathland of Norfolk and Suffolk, where grain was grown in the thirteenth century for the first and the last time in English history. Much of the reclaimed land was too barren to invite earlier settlement and too profitless to be farmed later.

The increase in population also led to a concentration on grain at the expense of sheep farming and cattle grazing. In the thirteenth century, England started on the path followed today by many densely populated, underdeveloped nations: it deserted mixed farming for the growing of one or two staple crops. In the Midlands and the south, the traditional regions of mixed farming, some villagers owned no animals. Pasture was converted into arable in order to gain a few more bushels of wheat, rye, or barley.

The pressure of population on the limited resources of England led inevitably to a rise in prices. Wheat, which had sold for 1 shilling, 9 pence per quarter in 1190, rose to 3 shillings, 6 pence in 1203. During the same period, the price of an ox rose from 4 to 7 shillings, and that of a sheep from 5 to 10 pence. During the twenty years after 1210, the price of wheat fluctuated around 3 shillings, then climbed to 6 shillings. Those who benefited most from these rising prices were the great lay and ecclesiastical landlords who produced for a cash market. Thirteenth-century records show that the great earl and the great abbey grew at the expense of the petty knight and the smaller monastery. They grew because they had the land, the capital, the enterprise, and the enlightenment to exploit the buoyant market for wheat and wool. Durng the twelfth century many of these landlords had rented out demesne lands to middlemen at a fixed rent; now they returned to direct management.

It was for men such as these that Walter of Henley wrote his treatise on estate managment, *Husbandry*, in which he admonished the landlord to keep exact accounts and instructed him when to plow and how to harrow. A race of improving landlords arose who turned to more frequent plowing, to better weeding, and to marling, composting, and folding. Marling was the addition of a crumbly, earthy deposit, rich in carbonate of lime, to the soil; composting was the spreading of decayed organic matter on the soil; and folding was the grazing of sheep on the arable after harvest in order to enrich it with their dung. These landlords also experimented with different ratios of seed to soil and with different crops. Gradually wheat replaced rye as a winter crop, and beans and peas (which return nitrogen to the soil) replaced oats as a spring crop.

But this "high farming," as it came to be called, did not lead to extravagant increases in productivity. Yields, by modern standards, remained low. The yield of all grains on the Bishop of Winchester's estates, for example, ranged between 6 and 9 bushels an acre. Today this region yields 40 to 50 bushels an acre. The modest increases that did occur in the thirteenth century arose less from capital investment and technological improvements than from the more intensive exploitation of land and labor. The revival of demesne farming meant the revival, and often the increase, of labor services. The tenants on a manor usually farmed the poorer land with inferior grains. In many areas sheep farming was the landlord's occupation; the poor kept only cows and pigs. The cottagers who worked for hire suffered most as real wages fell. During the thirteenth century the wages of winnowers and threshers on the bishop of Winchester's estate rose by only 10 percent. Given the inflation of these years, this meant a decline of one-third in real wages. For a great landlord a bad harvest meant the difference between profit and loss; for the poor it meant the difference between subsistence and starvation. The manorial accounts of the thirteenth century show that the death rate (measured by the payment of *heriots* to the lord of the manor) rose sharply in years of bad harvest. With the population pressing dangerously close to the margin of subsistence, the poor could stay alive only if there was a good harvest.

WOOL, TRADE, AND TOWNS

Those who grew richest from farming were probably those who raised sheep, for the twelfth and thirteenth centuries saw an unprecedented boom in the export of wool to Flanders and Florence. Flanders in particular was a great buyer of English wool. Its burgeoning population, unable to support itself by agriculture, had turned to industry, and above all to the cloth industry. Because its own wool was too coarse, it imported the finer wool of England. Soon a vast flow of wool crossed the Channel. To ransom Richard I in 1194, the English government exported 50,000 sacks of wool, an amount equal to the fleece of 6 million sheep. In 1273 the English exported 33,000 sacks and in 1304 (the peak year) 46,000 sacks. It was an immensely profitable trade, since wool that could be grown in England at £4 a sack sold in Flanders at £12. No wonder a wool merchant engraved on his window:

I praise God and ever shall
It is the sheep that hath paid for all.

Two breeds of sheep produced the best wool: the smaller sheep of the Welsh border, whose wool was short, fine, and well suited to the manufacture of textiles of a heavy texture, and the larger sheep of the Cotswolds and Lincolnshire, whose wool was long, fine, and well suited to the production of worsteds and serges. Though peasants in pastoral country kept flocks of sheep, the greatest flocks were found on the demesne lands of the great lay and ecclesiastical landlords. There were 29,000 sheep on the estates of the bishop of Winchester and 13,400 on those of the earl of Lincoln. The Cistercians maintained immense flocks in the dales of Yorkshire and the deep valleys of Wales. These great landlords dominated not only the production of wool, but also its distribution. For the sale of their own wool they entered into contracts with Flemish and Italian merchants, often selling their wool two or three years in advance, with the interest for this extension of credit being disguised in the price. The Cistercians regularly entered into such contracts, though forbidden to do so by the Chapter General. These great landlords also sold the wool they collected from the smaller farmers in their districts. They acted as middlemen for the great foreign merchants in London, the greatest of whom were found in the Hanse of London, an association of fifteen Flemish towns. The Hanse of London dominated the wool trade in the twelfth century. In the next century that dominance passed to Italian merchants who, acting as papal tax collectors, came into contact with monasteries short on cash and long on wool. English merchants were also active in the wool trade, both as woolmongers, buying from small farmers, and as exporters, selling abroad. In 1273 English traders carried overseas a third of the wool that England exported.

Wool dominated English trade but was not the only commodity exported. The English also exported grain to feed the cloth workers of Flanders, tin to support the Flemish metal industry, lead to roof the abbey at La Rochelle, and coal to warm the homes and shops of Bruges. In return, they imported cloth from Flanders, iron from Spain, spices from the Mediterranean, and great quantities of wine, for which they had contracted an unquenchable thirst, from France. Before Henry II ascended the throne, England imported her wine from the Seine Valley, but the Angevin connection led to the dominance of the wine of Gascony. Each year, Gascony sent 20,000 tons to England.

Far greater in volume than foreign trade was England's internal trade. Yarmouth sent its herring and Scarborough its cod throughout England. The Forest of Dean sent ironware to the villages of England; Northumbria produced coal to be used in forging, burning lime, evaporating brine, and brewing ale. The Romans had mined coal, but not the Anglo-Saxons; then in the late twelfth century the English rediscovered the value of coal. To feed these miners, fishermen, woolgrowers, and merchants the farmers of England sent grain and dairy products to the towns and to other regions. Though the great majority of men and women engaged in farming and consumed most of what they produced, they did not live in a subsistence economy. In fact, by the close of the thirteenth century the sale of grain commonly accounted for 20 to 30 percent of the profits of a manor. Even the poorest villager needed money to buy salt and ironware.

The trade of England moved along its highways and rivers. Packhorses, carts, and wagons carried goods along arterial roads which, so the law decreed, should be wide enough for two wagons to pass, or for two oxherds to make their goads touch across them, or for sixteen knights to ride abreast. Bulkier commodities, such as grain, coal, timber, and stones, were carried on rivers. Often both road and river were used: the lead for the roof of Waltham Abbey came, all 263 cartloads, from Derbyshire to Boston, from where it was carried by sea to the Thames, then up the Thames and the Lea to Waltham. The products that barges and wagons carried through England were sold in weekly mar-

A wagon and team of horses from a medieval manuscript (*MS Bodley 264*).

kets, at annual fairs, and in the permanent markets of the towns. The ordinary villager bought the ordinary requirements of life at local markets, held one day a week, usually on Sunday. During the twelfth and thirteenth centuries successive kings granted or confirmed 2,500 market charters. The great annual fairs, such as those held at St. Ives in Huntingdonshire or St. Bartholomew in Smithfield, served a much wider area and usually lasted for a week, though sometimes they ran for a month. Merchants came from all over England and from foreign lands to set up stalls and booths, each trade usually being allotted a place. At such fairs one could buy tin from Cornwall, iron from the Forest of Dean, wool from the Cotswolds, and silk, cloth, and spices from abroad. In the fourteenth century these great fairs declined in importance as merchants ceased to attend them and as the towns grew in number and size.

The bulk of medieval trade eventually fell to merchants who traded throughout the year in a particular town. These towns were, in fact, the result of the great expansion in commerce and industry in the twelfth and thirteenth centuries. Between 1066 and 1334, old towns grew in size and new ones were created—160 of them, of which only twenty-three failed to survive. Immigration from the countryside swelled the population in the towns. In Stratford-on-Avon in 1252 a third of the burgesses bore the names of the villages from which they came. Unlike in Anglo-Saxon times, when most burgesses engaged in agricultural pursuits, they now devoted themselves largely to trade and manufacturing. Boroughs had long possessed their own court, or portmoot, over which a royal official, the portreeve, presided; and the sheriff of the county had traditionally collected the rents, fines, and dues that were owed the crown (called the "farm"). But townsmen, who were, in Professor Postan's words, "non-feudal islands in the feudal seas," sought to free themselves from dependence on the shire. They wished to elect their own sheriff and to collect and render to the exchequer their own "farm." Henry I granted both rights to London, but Henry II, who distrusted the independence of towns, withdrew them. Richard I and King John, however, desperately needed money, and so granted to numerous boroughs, in return for money, the right to elect their own sheriff and the right to render their own "farm" to the exchequer.

It was only a step from the right to collect one's own taxes to self-government. During the anarchy of Stephen's reign, the Londoners formed a commune—that is, a sworn association of citizens that would rule the city—but it survived less than a year. Fifty years later, in 1191, the Londoners again formed a short-lived commune. It was again suppressed, but this time one element survived, the office of mayor. From 1193 until today London has had a mayor, and from 1216 onward has elected him annually (except when London fell into the King's hands under Edward I). To assist the mayor in governing London, the citizens also elected a council of twenty-four alderman. By 1215 London was a self-governing municipality, but not a democratic one. Candidates for office came from a clique of merchants, and not all citizens had the right to vote. Medieval town government was intensely oligarchic. Other towns imitated the pattern set by London, though none achieved the same degree of self-government. By 1216 the office of mayor had appeared in a dozen towns.

Outside London the merchant guild fostered the growth of self-government. The merchant guild was an association of all the tradesmen and craftsmen in a town, not merely of the merchants. It included weavers, tailors, masons, carpenters, and goldsmiths, and women as well as men. The purpose of the guild was to enforce a monopoly of trade in favor of its members. Outsiders who wished to buy and sell in the town were subject to tolls and regulations from which guildsmen were free. In Leicester, for example, only guildsmen could buy and sell wool wholesale, and the guild determined that wool wrappers should be paid only a penny a day and food, and flock pullers a penny and a half, without food. The primary aim of the guilds was to further the mercantile interests of its members, but they also served a convivial and ceremonial purpose with drinking and feasting, and a benevolent purpose, with care for the sick and burial of the dead. And in towns such as Bury St. Edmunds and Reading they even became the town's governing body.

By 1216 there were merchant guilds in forty towns. London had none because its various crafts and trades were large enough to form their own guilds. There were guilds of grocers, vintners, fishmongers, mercers, tailors, butchers, pepperers, and—most important of all—weavers. The weavers became so powerful that Londoners tried, though unsuccessfully, to bribe Henry II to dissolve their guild. As other towns grew in size, the all-encompassing merchant guild was replaced by numerous craft guilds. But the purpose served by the guild remained the same: to secure a monopoly of trade for its members.

THE TWELFTH-CENTURY RENAISSANCE

In the age of Bede learning found a home in the monasteries; the renaissance of learning that occurred in the twelfth century found its home in the cathedral cities. The town, the fruit of an expanding commerce, became the scene of a renewed intellectual life, and the cathedral became the center of learning. At the cathedral were libraries, archives, and schools; and in the household of the bishop were men learned in theology and canon law. Every great cathedral—Canterbury, St. Paul's, York, Winchester, Lincoln—had its school, run by masters named by the chapter. The cathedral schools, however, were unable to meet the growing demand for education. Other schools arose, but because education was a monopoly of the Church, the bishop or his deputy had the right to license them. In Stephen's reign, for example, the chapter of St. Paul's threatened to excommunicate all those who presumed to teach in London without a license. Two famous schools, Holy Trinity and St. Martin's, were exempt, but other learned men who set up their own schools needed a license from the master of St. Paul's.

At these schools students studied the *trivium,* the first three of the seven liberal arts: grammar, rhetoric, and logic. Of these subjects, Latin grammar was the most important, for Latin was the medium of speech and writing in the learned world. Men prayed in Latin, preached in Latin, and sang in Latin. By the end of Henry II's reign men also needed to know Latin to negotiate a legal or commerical transaction. In the better schools the study of grammer included the study of classical literature. In the early Middle Ages that literature fell into eclipse, but the twelfth century rediscovered it. Men and women once again read Virgil and Ovid and Cicero, even though this pagan literature, with its frank acceptance of the joys and pleasures of the world, put their souls in peril. The rhetoric taught by Rome had little meaning, for oratory did not play a central role in medieval life. The Middle Ages therefore transformed rhetoric into a study of the rules for letter writing, and manuals appeared on the most perfect epistolary style. The last of the *trivium,* logic (or dialectic, as it was often called), played a smaller role in the twelfth-century renaissance, though gradually, to the great sadness of John of Salisbury, it drove out the study of literature.

John of Salisbury was the most learned man of the age, a perfect model of the literary man. Born in Salisbury sometime between 1115 and 1120, he devoted his life to scholarship. As was the custom of the day, he spent his youth moving from school to school. He studied dialectic under the great Peter Abelard at Paris and literature in the school of Bernard of Chartres. At Chartres he learned to write the purest Latin of the Middle Ages. In 1150 he returned to England, where he entered the household of Archbishop Theobald, served as his secretary, made frequent embassies to the Roman Curia, and became a friend of Thomas Becket. The breadth of his reading in the Latin classics was unequaled in Europe. He deeply admired Cicero, both for his wisdom and for his pure and flexible style. Yet he also admired the Church Fathers, whom he quoted side by side with the classics. In his letters, essays, and history there appeared a Christian humanism that recognized no antagonism between Christian truth and ancient wisdom and that preferred wide reading to narrow logic chopping.

The other four of the seven liberal arts, the *quadrivium,* were those that could be treated mathematically—arithmetic, geometry, astronomy, and music. At the opening of the twelfth century students of the *quadrivium* had little to study—only the scrappy, thin, and often fantastic material in Isidore of Seville's *Encyclopedia,* a book filled with legends about one-legged men in Ethiopia and swans that sang sweetly because they had long, curving necks. The early Middle Ages had lost the knowledge of Greek (even of the alphabet) and with it of Greek science. It was the great contribution of the twelfth century to recover that science, though it did so by a circuitous route. The Arabs in their conquest of the Near East had absorbed the philosophy and science of the Greeks and carried it with them across North Africa to Sicily and Spain. The Christian reconquest of Spain led to the translation into Latin of Greek and Arabic works on science.

In this work two Englishmen, Adelard of Bath and Robert of Chester, played an important role. Adelard was an incorrigible wanderer who studied at Tours, taught at Laon, and traveled to Greece, Asia Minor, Sicily, and Spain. In Spain he translated Ptolemy's *Almagest* and Euclid's *Elements,* thus giving Europe an astronomy that was to last until Copernicus, and a geometry that was not to be improved upon until modern times. Robert of Chester, who became archdeacon of Pamplona in Spain in 1143, translated the *Algebra* of Al-Kwarizmi, thereby introducing both the name and the science into the West. He (or Adelard) may also have translated Al-Kwarizmi's book on arithmetic, which contributed to the adoption of Arabic numerals, with the indispensable zero, by the West. Despite the convenience of this new system of enumeration, the English were slow to adopt it; not until the middle of the sixteenth century do Arabic numerals appear frequently in English records.

In 1125 the English depended for their philosophy and science on Bede's *Chronology,* Isidore's *Encyclopedia,* and two works of Aristotle translated by Boethius. By 1225 they possessed, in Latin, the geometry of Euclid, the astronomy of Ptolemy, the mathematics of the Arabs, the medicine of Galen and Hippocrates, and the complete work of Aristotle. But it was the content of these works, not the method, that they absorbed. Medicine became the study of the writings of Galen and Hippocrates and physics the logical interpretation of Aristotle's treatise. Yet there was in Adelard of Bath a glimmer of the scientific temper of the Greeks and the Arabs. He carefully described an earthquake in Syria and observed that light travels faster than sound. He regarded the worship of authority as an impediment to learning and believed that God was an explanation to be used only when all others failed.

The twelfth century not only rediscovered the Latin classics and Greek science, but also Roman law. In the sixth century the emperor Justinian had codified Roman law, and the code survived in a work known as the *Corpus Juris Civilis.* It nearly disappeared during the early Middle Ages, surviving in only two manuscripts, but in the eleventh century Italian jurists at Bologna revived the study of the *Corpus.* From Bologna a knowledge of Roman law, which firmly buttressed the authority of kings, spread throughout Europe. It even reached England, carried there by a Lombard jurist named Vacarius, whom Archbishop Theobald employed as his legal adviser. Upon Theobald's death, Vacarius went on to Oxford, where he lectured on the civil law, as Roman law came to be called. But no student could make a career in civil law, since the English courts used the Common law. What influence Roman law had on England came largely through canon law, the law of the Church. The twelfth century witnessed the growth, systematization, and study of canon law. Because that law touched on matters of marriage, wills, contracts, heresy, perjury, and sexual offenses, it touched on the lives of all English people.

When Vacarius left Canterbury he went to Oxford, where masters and scholars had begun to assemble, possibly because it was conveniently located where roads going east and west intersected with those going north and south.

In 1167 Henry II, in the middle of his quarrel with Thomas Becket, ordered all English scholars at Paris home. They came to Oxford, where by 1184 there were several faculties, a bookbinder, a note taker, and two parchment makers. To protect themselves from townsmen seeking to fleece them, the masters and scholars formed a guild. The guild, however, provided little protection. In 1209 a town and gown riot forced some 2000 scholars to flee to Reading, Cambridge, and Paris. Those who fled to Cambridge remained there; the others returned after five years, for in 1214 King John compelled the townsmen to recognize that the bishop of Lincoln, or his representative, the chancellor of the university, had jurisdiction over all scholars. The scene was now set for the growth of the universities in the thirteenth century.

THE ENGLISH COMMON LAW

The twelfth century was a legal century, witnessing the revival of Roman law, the development of canon law, and the creation of the English Common law. People now began to reason and to write about the law. Those who served the King at court were intelligent clerics, not illiterate barons, men skilled in Latin

Henry II, from the effigy at Fontevrault, France (*Caisse Nationale des Monuments Historiques et des Sites. Paris; Arch. Phot. Paris/S.P.A.D.E.M.*)

and acquainted with Roman and canon law. But the most important lawyer among them was Henry II himself, the true founder of the English Common law. Henry was the first King since the Norman Conquest to be fully literate. He had received a princely education, spoke Latin as easily as French, delighted in intellectual discussion, and had a passionate interest in history and literature. But he was essentially a man of action, a restless man who displayed an immense capacity for work. He hated idleness and reputedly never sat down except when eating or riding; he stood while at mass and in council (that he might not grow fat, some said). His court was constantly on the move, and many days he sat in the saddle from dawn to dusk, if not attending to business then in hawking and hunting, of which he was inordinately fond. He was stockily built, with reddish hair, a freckled face, and bright blue eyes that became bloodshot when he fell into a rage, as he occasionally did, for he had an ungovernable temper. He also had a fierce determination to govern his lands well and to see that justice was done. Within six months of his coronation he had brought peace to war-torn England, expelled King Stephen's Flemish mercenaries, leveled unlicensed castles, and resumed control of all royal castles. There remained, however, the violence and brutality of the ordinary criminal.

The volume of crime in Angevin England was enormous. In one year the justices at Lincoln dealt with 114 cases of homicide, 89 of robbery, 65 of woundings, and 49 of rape. Yet the machinery for detecting, arresting, trying, and punishing the criminals was wholly inadequate. There was no police force, only a system by which a group of persons was made responsible for producing in court any of its members charged with a crime. This system, known as the frankpledge, required that all unfree men over 12 join together in a group. Should one member be suspected of a crime, the others must produce him in court. If he fled, they must raise the hue and cry, follow, and capture him. Henry II sought to strengthen this system by having the sheriff take "a view of the frankpledge" twice a year in the hundred court—that is, make certain that no unfree villager was living outside the frankpledge.

The method of prosecuting criminals was equally uncertain. The traditional method of accusation was for the injured party, his relative, or his lord to bring the charge before the shire or hundred court and offer to prove it in battle (though the court might grant the accused trial by ordeal). Such appeals, as they were called, often broke down over some technicality, and the accuser, if he failed to prove his accusation, was fined. Furthermore, there might be no specific accuser, but only the suspicion of the countryside. In 1166 Henry II therefore sought a more certain method of accusation. This was the presentment jury, which may have had its origin in Anglo-Saxon times but more likely arose out of Norman practices. At Clarendon Henry II and his council issued an assize (so-called because it was the result of a session or *assisa* of the council), which directed that a jury of twelve men from each hundred and four men from each township should declare upon oath, before the sheriff or itinerant justices, the names of those suspected of robbery, theft, or murder. The presentiment jury was the forerunner of the modern grand jury. But it only indicted the criminal. The determination of guilt still rested on the archaic methods of battle, compurgation, and ordeal.

Trial by battle, a crude and savage procedure, was limited to appeals of felony (where there was an accuser who could prove his oath by the test of battle); compurgation continued chiefly in the Church courts; thus ordeal by water or fire remained the most common form of trial in local and royal courts. Henry II and his justices had no illusions about the irrationality of ordeal. They did not believe that the failure of a trussed man to float when lowered into water blessed by the priest (the normal ordeal for men) proved his innocence, nor that the clean healing of the wounds caused by carrying a red-hot iron (the normal ordeal for women) gave proof of innocence. By the Assize of Clarendon Henry and his council declared that a person of bad reputation, even though he or she survived the ordeal, should be banished from the realm. The true trial jury, or petty jury, first appeared about 1200, when justices gave the accused the option, on the payment of a small fee, of having his or her case decided by a jury. A decree of the Fourth Lateran Council in 1215 dealt the final blow to trial by ordeal, for it forbade priests to participate in such trials. Since the ordeal required the participation of a priest—to bless the instruments of the ordeal—this prohibition made trial by ordeal impossible. During the thirteenth and fourteenth centuries trial by jury became the accepted method of deciding criminal cases.

The use of the jury in civil cases was as great a triumph for rationality and due process of law as was its use in criminal cases. During Stephen's reign and occasionally during Henry's, powerful men seized the lands of their neighbors and would not relinquish them. What was needed was a swift procedure for restoring the land to its original possessor. Henry II and his advisers therefore devised a series of writs, which any free man might purchase from chancery, that commanded the sheriff to empanel a jury that would, before the King's justices, decide the question of possession. One writ provided that the sheriff ask a jury of twelve men whether the plaintiff had recently been wrongfully disposed of his land. If the jury answered yes, the land was restored. A second writ posed this question: Did the plaintiff's father die in lawful possession of the land and was the plaintiff his heir? If the jury answered yes, the heir received the land. A third writ concerned the naming of rectors and vicars to parish churches. The jury was asked who presented the last priest, on the grounds that this person, or his heirs, should represent again. By a fourth writ a jury decided whether land was held by free alms or by a feudal tenure. In every case the jury acted not as doomsmen declaring the law or as compurgators supporting an oath, but as members of the community declaring the facts. They were a jury of recognition, an institution the Normans brought with them and used in compiling Domesday Book. These writs, and the jury action they initiated, were instantly popular and widely used.

The writs, however, only determined who had recently possessed the property, not who rightfully owned it. Questions of ownership were traditionally decided in feudal courts by judicial combat. The plaintiff must do battle, though he himself did not do battle; the contest was between hired champions. It was a crude and inequitable means of settling disputes. In 1179, therefore, Henry II offered a remedy. If Ralph claimed the ownership of land held by Thomas, he could secure a "writ of right" from the chancery ordering the appropriate lord to do justice between Ralph and Thomas. But Thomas, the defendant, now had the right to secure a "writ of peace," which forced Ralph, if he wished to proceed with his claim, to secure another writ ordering the sheriff to appoint four knights who thereupon empaneled a jury of twelve other knights, who then decided which of the two owned the land. The procedure was slow, but it was also rational and equitable, and soon became popular. During Richard's reign, 135 disputes over land were settled by this procedure in one year.

The writs of Henry II's reign were originally designed, not to replace feudal courts with royal courts, but to provide a sanction against abuses in the feudal courts, with the royal courts offering a kind of judicial review. But in fact the system of writs soon brought about the replacement of feudal courts with royal courts. The writ and the jury, by making royal justice available to all free men, swelled the volume of business before the royal courts. In essence there was only one royal court, the Curia Regis, but it took various forms. The gravest cases, such as the trial of Archbishop Becket, took place before the King and his barons in the Great Council, but a small council, or court of *coram rege*, heard most pleas. But this court followed the king around England. To provide a more permanent place of justice and to help meet the mounting demand for royal justice, Henry in 1178 ordered five judges to sit permanently as a court at Westminster. This court was the forerunner of the court of Common Pleas, just as the court of *coram rege*, which followed the King, was the forerunner of the King's Bench. Also sitting in Westminster, in the great hall built by William Rufus, was the exchequer, which dealt with financial litigation. But even these central courts could not begin to meet the insatiable demand for royal justice. Henry therefore sent royal justices to the counties, with the authority to hear a great variety of civil and criminal pleas. Henry I had sent out such itinerant justices sporadically, but the practice died out during Stephen's reign. Henry II now restored the practice and made it normal and regular.

In these courts there gradually emerged one law, common to all England, based on the judgments of successive judges. The law these judges enforced was assumed to be the custom of the people; the judges merely declared what the law was. But their judgments carried weight with the judges who followed them. From at least 1194 onward, clerks in the King's court recorded these judgments on plea rolls. The new Common law even found its first expositor. Some unknown author, traditionally believed to be Henry's able justiciar, Ranulf Glanvill, wrote a treatise entitled *De Legibus et Consuetudines Regni Angliae* (Of the Laws and Customs of the English Kingdom). This treatise contained the first reasoned account of the new legal procedures. The English Common law had come of age.

HENRY II AND THE CHURCH

Henry dealt more successfully with the law than he did with the Church. His relationship with the Church, always turbulent, ended in the tragic murder of Thomas Becket, Archbishop of Canterbury. But it would be a grave mistake to see this dispute solely as a personal quarrel between two proud and passionate men, since behind the personal quarrel lay a fundamental political dispute. Henry desired to recover for the state the powers over the Church it had lost during Stephen's reign. During those years of anarchy appeals to Rome in ecclesiastical cases became common, the election of bishops and abbots was taken from royal control, and ecclesiastical courts extended their jurisdiction over contracts and debts and claimed the exclusive right to try and punish clergy accused of crimes. Furthermore, these practices now enjoyed the blessing of canon law and the support of an aggressive, reforming papal monarchy. Gregory VII and his successors had created a powerful and confident papacy that was determined to protect the independence of the Church.

To assist him in recovering these rights Henry II in 1162 named his Chancellor, Thomas Becket, to be Archbishop of Canterbury. It was the greatest blunder of his reign. Becket, the son of a Rouen merchant who had settled in London, was a townsman, the first of England's great men to be so. He attended one of the city's grammar schools, then entered the household of Archbishop Theobald, with its band of brilliant scholars. But Becket was no scholar; he was a man of action, an energetic administrator, and an agreeable companion. He was also vain, extravagant in his dress, and driven by a thirst for power and success. Recognizing his great abilities, Henry named Becket Chancellor in 1154. To Archbishop Theobald's pained surprise, Becket, as Chancellor, served the interests of the state, not the Church. He became the King's boon companion, organized his Court for him, went hawking with him, and supported him in all his quarrels with the Church. Believing such a man would be useful at the head of the Church, Henry named him Archbishop after Theobald's death.

As Chancellor, Becket had played the role of the King's true servant. As Archbishop, he played the role of protector of the Church. He opposed the King in everything, even in secular matters. But the quarrel that ended in his murder concerned the trial of a clergyman who had committed a crime. The problem of the criminal clergyman was a serious one, for in the twelfth century a large number of men in minor orders were counted as clergymen. Because Church courts could not shed blood and because there were few prisons, a guilty clergyman usually escaped serious punishment. At most he suffered degradation, and usually only had to do some act of penance. Such immunity led disreputable men into the Church. In 1163, William of Newburg estimated that clergymen had committed over a hundred murders since 1154. At a council at Westminster in October 1163, Henry stated that he had the right to punish clergymen found guilty in a Church court. Becket at first refused to consent to this proposition. He refused, that is, until the Pope, not wishing to anger Henry II while quarreling with the Holy Roman Emperor, urged Becket to submit. The Archbishop thereupon agreed to Henry's proposal.

Henry then made the mistake of putting into writing the customs of Henry I's reign, customs Becket and the bishops could only accept if unwritten. At a Council of Clarendon he drew up a series of proposals, called the Constitutions of Clarendon, which forbade appeals to Rome without royal consent, reserved for royal courts pleas of debts, denied the Pope the right to excommunicate the King's vassals and officers without the King's consent, and provided that clergymen found guilty by a Church court be turned over to a royal court for punishment. Becket immediately cried out that this last proposal meant a "double punishment." Nevertheless, he quite unaccountably accepted the Constitutions, that is, until the Pope condemned them. Becket then repented his action, reversed his stand, and opposed the Constitutions.

An enraged and vindictive Henry summoned Becket to a council at Northampton to stand trial, both for delaying justice in a dispute over land held of Canterbury and for failing to account for moneys that passed through his hands as Chancellor. Becket accepted the judgment of the court in the first case, but denied that he needed to account for the moneys since he had been summoned only to answer for the land. Becket then forbade the bishops on the council to sit in judgment on him, whereupon Henry called on the justiciar to pronounce sentence anyway. That night Becket fled to France, where he remained in exile for six years. The real dispute that divided King and Archbishop was not over land or moneys but over the Constitutions of Clarendon. Right, on that vexed matter, lay on both sides. By promulgating the Constitutions Henry upheld royal custom; by opposing them, Becket upheld the laws of the Church.

Thomas Becket remained in exile from 1164 to 1170, during which time a new quarrel embittered relations between him and Henry. To ensure the peaceful succession of his eldest son, Henry had Prince Henry crowned King during his lifetime. The Archbishop of Canterbury being in exile, he had the Archbishop of York and six bishops perform the coronation. This infuriated Becket, for the right to crown a King rested with Canterbury. He immediately secured the Pope's authority to excommunicate those who had participated in the coronation. Henry, probably to prevent the Archbishop and the Pope from placing England under an interdict—that is, suspending all religious services— met with Becket. Nothing was said about the disputes that divided them, but Becket was permitted to return to Canterbury. He did so in December 1170. He then exacerbated the quarrel by excommunicating the bishops who had crowned Prince Henry. Three of these bishops were with the King in Normandy. Their report on Becket's conduct threw the king into a towering rage. "What set of idle cowards I keep in my kingdom," he allegedly said, "who allow me to be mocked so shamefully by a low-born clerk." Four knights of the King's household, without waiting for the King's anger to cool, hurried to England. They found the Archbishop in the north transept of the cathedral, near the choir. There they hacked him to death with their swords.

No event in the twelfth century so profoundly shocked the Christian world. Within two years the Pope canonized Thomas Becket. A cult immediately grew up around St. Thomas: miracles occurred at his tomb, scenes of his martyrdom were depicted in stained glass, and Canterbury became one of the great shrines of Europe. On Henry II the Pope laid many penances: he was to send 200 knights to defend Jerusalem, build three monasteries, and make restitution to those who had suffered for supporting the Archbishop. More important, the widespread horror at the murder weakened Henry in his negotiations with the Pope over the Constitutions of Clarendon. He now retreated on several crucial issues. He agreed not to block appeals to the papal court. He agreed to allow clergymen to leave the realm without his permission. He agreed that papal bulls (commands) could enter the realm without his consent. Above all, he agreed that criminal clergymen should be both tried and sentenced in Church courts, though they must first prove before a royal court that they were clergymen. But Henry did not retreat in everything. He kept the right to consent to a bishop's excommunication of his tenants-in-chief and, most important of all, he kept control over the election of bishops and abbots. Those elections were to be "free" as long as the King's nominees were elected. As the writ to the chapter at Winchester reads:

Henry, king of the English &c. to his faithful monks of the church of Winchester, greeting.

I order you to hold a free election, but, nevertheless, I forbid you to elect anyone except Richard my clerk, the Archdeacon of Poitiers.

THE ANGEVIN EMPIRE

Henry ruled not merely a kingdom but an empire, an empire that extended from the borders of Scotland to the foothills of the Pyrenees. At heart he was a French prince, who was born and buried in France and who spent twenty-one of his thirty-four years as King of England there. From his father he had inherited Anjou, Maine, and Touraine; from his mother, Normandy and England. On marrying Eleanor of Aquitaine he gained Aquitaine, Poitou, and Auvergne as well. In the first ten years of his reign, by marriage, diplomacy, fraud, and force he added the Vexin and Brittany to his empire. As King of England and ruler of half of France, Henry was undoubtedly the greatest monarch in Europe. But these disparate lands were not held together by a central adminis-

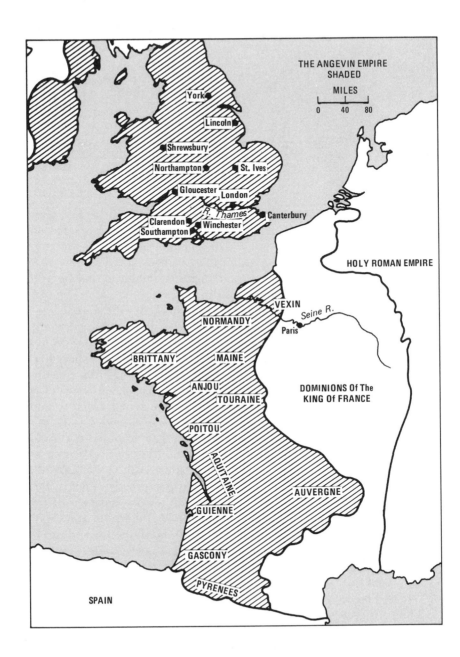

THE ANGEVIN EMPIRE
SHADED

MILES

0   40   80

York

Lincoln

Shrewsbury

Northampton   St. Ives

Gloucester   London

R. Thames   Canterbury

Clarendon   Winchester
Southampton

HOLY ROMAN EMPIRE

VEXIN
Seine R.

NORMANDY

Paris

BRITTANY   MAINE

ANJOU

TOURAINE

DOMINIONS Of The
KING Of FRANCE

POITOU

AQUITAINE

AUVERGNE

GUIENNE

GASCONY

PYRENEES

SPAIN

Hunting with a falcon (*the British Library, Cottonian MSS Tiberius B.V. pt 1, f. 7v*).

tration. Furthermore, Henry held his continental lands as the vassal of the King of France. It was a personal empire, whose existence depended on Henry's energy and skill. Only his own rapidity of movement kept the empire together, for which reason he kept a swift galley in constant readiness at Southampton. Such was his demonic energy and such his ambition, that he even planned to supplant the Holy Roman Emperor in Italy.

But Henry's grand designs were checked by the rebellion of his sons. Henry II gave Henry, Richard, Geoffrey, and John titles and lands, but little income and no authority. Chafing under this tutelage, urged on by their mother (the beautiful, passionate, and willful Eleanor, who was angered at Henry's infidelity to her), and supported by Louis VII, King of France, Henry's sons rose in revolt in the summer of 1173. It was the most serious crisis of Henry's reign. But though the rebellion was widespread, the rebels failed to coordinate their movements. It began in Normandy in July, was extended to Brittany in August, and then to England, where the Earl of Leicester led an invading force of Flemings. Finally, in the spring of 1174 the King of Scotland invaded England. But through a swiftness of movement that astonished the King of France, Henry suppressed each rebellion in turn. He was greatly aided in this by the support of the Church, his royal officials, the towns, and men of property in the counryside. It was the sheriff of Yorkshire who defeated and captured the King of Scotland. Toward his sons Henry showed mercy and to the rebels he granted amnesty, but he surrendered no real power and he demolished the castles of the rebels. From 1175 to 1182 the Angevin Empire was at the summit of its greatness. Yet the work of holding it together was unending. In 1180 Louis VII of France died, to be succeeded by a far more ruthless and skillful king, Philip Augustus. Philip now allied with Richard who, because of the death of the young Henry, had become the eldest son. Richard deeply resented his father's plotting to give the succession to John, his younger brother. On November 18, 1188, Philip in person asked Henry to recognize Richard as his lawful heir. Henry refused. Richard then kneeled to Philip and did homage to him for all the French lands. This act led to open war in which Henry, deserted even by John, suffered defeat. Only his death on July 6, 1189, and the succession of Richard to all his lands saved the Angevin Empire.

WALES, IRELAND, AND SCOTLAND

Had Henry devoted to the subjugation of Wales, the settlement of Ireland, and the conquest of Scotland the energy he spent on holding together his continental possessions, he might have built an empire that would have lasted, instead of one doomed to extinction. The British Isles might then have achieved a unity that has always eluded them.

The very geography of Wales, with its high, rugged mountains, made conquest difficult. In the closing years of William the Conqueror's reign, the Normans briefly conquered North Wales, only to be decisively expelled in 1094. In the south the story was different. Here a few great Norman lords, the marcher lords, who had settled along the borders, or marches, of Wales, slowly occupied the fertile lowlands, building castles and founding towns as they advanced. In the far west, in Pembrokeshire, a group of Flemings displaced the Welsh. By the end of the reign of Henry I, South Wales was practically an Anglo-Norman province. Then, on the accession of Stephen, the Welsh rose in revolt and freed all Wales but Pembrokeshire from English rule. In the following years the Welsh produced two great leaders, Owain Gwynedd in the north and Rhys ap Gruffyd in the south. To Henry II the independence of these two princes was an affront to the dignity of his crown. He therefore led an expedition against Owain Gwynedd in 1157, which led to Owain's rendering homage to Henry for his lands. Rhys ap Gruffyd likewise swore fealty to Henry, but often broke his oath. In 1165, for example, he and Owain revived the struggle for Welsh independence. To suppress this revolt, Henry assembled a great army at Shrewsbury, made up of English knights, contingents from Normandy and Anjou, and Flemish mercenaries. The army marched against Owain, but wet weather, boggy moorlands, and the shortage of supplies forced Henry's army to retire to Shrewsbury. This disaster ended Henry's efforts to subjugate Wales. In the north Owain extended his boundaries to the estuary of the Dee, and in the south Rhys completed the conquest of Cardigan.

The losses in South Wales go far to explain the conquest of Ireland in 1170 and 1171, since it was a handful of frustrated marcher lords who undertook that conquest. Ireland's lack of unity proved their opportunity. In 1014 the last King of Ireland died, and a period of bewildering anarchy followed. It was during this time that Dermot MacMurrough, King of Leinster, a lover of poetry and fine tales, abducted the beautiful wife of the King of Breffni. The King of Breffni replied by supporting a revolt of the Leinster chiefs that drove Dermot into exile. Dermot sought out Henry II in distant Aquitaine and won

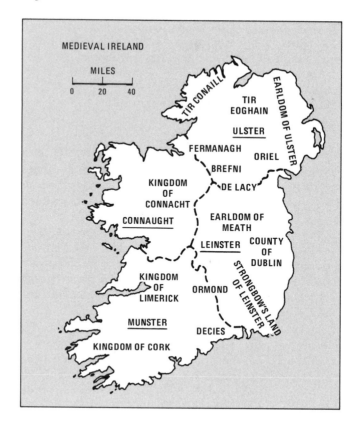

MEDIEVAL IRELAND

MILES

0   20   40

TIR CONAILL

TIR EOGHAIN

EARLDOM OF ULSTER

ULSTER

FERMANAGH

ORIEL

BREFNI

DE LACY

KINGDOM OF CONNACHT

CONNAUGHT

EARLDOM OF MEATH

LEINSTER

COUNTY OF DUBLIN

KINGDOM OF LIMERICK

ORMOND

STRONGBOW'S LAND OF LEINSTER

MUNSTER

DECIES

KINGDOM OF CORK

from him the authority to raise men within his realms. He found such men among the discouraged marcher lords of South Wales, chief of whom was Richard of Clare, Earl of Pembroke, nicknamed Strongbow. Strongbow not only accepted Dermot's offer, but married Dermot's daughter, thus making himself heir to the kingdom of Leinster. In 1170 Strongbow landed in Ireland with 200 knights and 1000 light-armed troops, overran Leinster, captured Dublin, and on Dermot's death succeeded him as King.

His success alarmed Henry II, who did not relish his subjects' carving out independent kingdoms for themselves. He therefore came to Ireland in person, with 500 knights and 4000 archers. Strongbow, preferring to be a secure baron rather than an uncertain king, submitted to Henry and received his lands back as a fief. The plundering of Ireland now began. Henry's deputy, Hugh de Lacy, seized 500,000 acres in Meath; the Fitzgeralds evicted the MacCarthys from Munster; John de Courcy carved out a princely domain in Ulster. Before the twelfth century had ended, the Anglo-Normans governed two-thirds of Ireland. The explanation for their success lies in their superior weapons and discipline.

The Irish soldiers had neither armor nor helmets, and so could not withstand the quick-firing archers and mail-clad horsemen of the Normans. The invaders also had superior fortifications, for they built stone castles as they advanced, castles the Irish found impregnable. The feudal system was then imposed on the conquered lands, and though the native peasants remained to till the fields, they were viewed as an inferior and savage race. The two communities, speaking different languages, remained divided from each other.

The first king of Scotland appeared in 1018, for in that year Malcolm II took the Lothian (the region lying between the Forth and the Tweed) from the Northumbrians. More remote than Wales and more united than Ireland, Scotland preserved its independence against both Norman and Angevin kings. In 1174 it nearly lost that independence because of the rashness of William the Lion, who led an ill-fated invasion of England, only to be defeated and captured. To recover his liberty, William performed homage to Henry II and surrendered to him the strongest castles in Scotland. But the overlordship and the castles Henry won were surrendered by his son, Richard I, in 1189, in return for 10,000 marks he needed to pay for his crusade. Scotland retained its independence, but it did not retain the three English counties of Durham, Northumberland, and Westmorland, which the powerful King David I had seized during Stephen's reign. David I died in 1153, and the next year Henry II demanded of David's sixteen-year-old successor the cession of these counties. Young and inexperienced, Malcolm IV agreed. The boundaries of England and Scotland have remained ever since the Cheviot hills and the river Tweed.

But no border could prevent Saxon and Norman influences from transforming the Celtic kingdom of Scotland into an English-speaking feudal state. In 1066 many English men and women fled to Scotland, among them Margaret, sister of Edgar the Atheling, who eventually married Malcolm Canmore, King of the Scots. Queen Margaret was a remarkable women, devoutly religious, austere in her private life, and deeply conscious that she belonged to the Wessex dynasty. While her husband played at war, she brought English culture to the court and the country. She promoted commmerce with foreign lands, decorated the palace with silk hangings, and introduced a new refinement to the court. Her deepest influence was on the Scottish Church, whose practices closely resembled those of Ireland. She convened councils of the church, discussed the Scriptures with Lanfranc, debated doctrine with the clergy, and brought the Scottish Church into conformity with those of Western Europe. Her career proves that in Scotland, at least, exceptional women were not prevented from engaging in politics and debating theology. But then Scotland was not yet feudal. It was not until David I's reign (1124–1135) that Norman influences entered Scotland, and then they came like a flood. Norman families became prominent; the Celtic system of land tenure gave way to the feudal; the sheriff appeared; an exalted notion of kingship arose; and advances were made toward a centralized administration. Though the Normans never conquered Scotland, Anglo-Norman institutions did.

Queen Eleanor and Richart I, from the effigies at Fontevrault Abbey (*Caisse Nationale des Monuments Historiques et des Sites, Paris*).

RICHARD I AND KING JOHN

Of all the kings of England, Richard I, also called Richard the Lion Hearted, was the least English. Raised in Aquitaine, he spent only six months of a ten-year reign in England, a land he chose to pillage rather than govern. A superb soldier and a spirited chivalrous knight, his one passion was to embark on the Third Crusade and recapture Jerusalem. To secure money and allies for this venture he was prepared to go to any lengths. He sold public offices, released the King of Scotland from vassalage, and ceded Auvergne to Philip Augustus. "If I could find a suitable buyer," he is reported to have said, "I would sell London itself." He set out in the summer of 1190, wintered in Sicily, spent May capturing Cyprus from a Greek tyrant, and arrived before the walls of Acre in June. Acre was a vital seaport whose capture had defied the efforts of the demoralized crusaders already there. Richard, with his siege engines and skillful generalship, captured it within a month. He then marched through the hot, dry countryside toward Jerusalem. He got within 12 miles of its walls, only to find his supplies exhausted and the crusaders torn by dissension. He thus decided to negotiate with the powerful Arab leader, Saladin. In September 1192 Richard concluded a three-year truce with Saladin which gave the Christians access to the holy places of Jerusalem. It was not the brilliant success he had dreamed of, but news that his brother John was plotting with Philip Augustus against him persuaded him to hurry home.

To avoid capture by Philip, he decided to travel through the Adriatic and Central Europe, but this proved his undoing. In Vienna the duke of Austria, with whom Richard had quarreled on the Crusades, captured him. The duke turned him over to his lord, Emperor Henry VI, with whom both Henry II and Richard had quarreled. Henry VI, in need of money, demanded an immense ransom—150,000 marks—for Richard's release. It is a testimony to the wealth and efficient administration of England that the government could raise the money. When Richard had first left for the East he had provided a clumsy system of two justiciars to rule in his absence. It broke down, and he had to send Walter of Coutances to save the situation. It was Walter who, with the help of other loyal servants and Richard's mother, Eleanor, raised the vast sum demanded by Henry VI. They did so by collecting a scutage of 20 shillings on every knight's fee, a carucage of 2 shillings on every hundred acres of land, and a 25 percent tax on the movable wealth of every Englishman. Scutage was a payment of money in lieu of the performance of knight service in person, and became common as subinfeudation created knight fees of one-half, or even one-sixth, of a knight's service. The carucage was a tax on land that replaced the old Danegeld. The fractional tax on personal property was an Angevin invention, first used in 1166 to raise money for the defense of the Holy Land. The fact that the government could govern efficiently in Richard's long absence and now raise the money needed to ransom him is a tribute to Henry II's remarkable administrative reforms.

Richard paid his second visit to England in 1194 to secure the money needed to save his empire from the French king. The single-minded purpose of Philip Augustus was the destruction of the Angevin Empire. But he found his match in Richard, who spent the last five years of his reign resolutely defending it. For this purpose Richard found the feudal institutions of England inadequate, for he needed an army in the field for longer than the forty days a feudal levy customarily served. He therefore raised an army of paid knights (at a shilling a day), of men-at-arms (at 4 pence a day if mounted and 2 pence if not), and of foreign mercenaries who lived for fighting and plunder. It was enormously expensive, but it allowed Richard to defeat Philip Augustus at every turn, until an arrow fired during a skirmish ended Richard's life on April 6, 1199.

By the laws of primogeniture, all Richard's lands should have gone to Arthur of Brittany, son of John's older brother, Geoffrey. The barons of England and Normandy, however, preferred John to a boy of 12, as did John's mother, Eleanor, who won Aquitaine for him. The barons of the Loire preferred Arthur, as did Philip Augustus, who received Arthur's homage for all the Angevin lands in France. John now acted swiftly. He had himself invested as Duke of Normandy in Rouen in April and crowned King of England in London in May. He then threatened to carry on a war that had already exhausted all parties. Philip retreated and granted John, in return for the payment of an enormous relief of 20,000 marks, all Richard's French possessions. John now, as so often, proved his own worst enemy. In August he married Isabel of Angouleme, laid claim in her name to La Marche, quarreled with the barons there, and refused to appear at Philip's court when the barons appealed to him. Philip's court then ruled that John had forfeited all his French lands. This led to war, which John opened with a bold stroke. From Le Mans he marched 80 miles south in two days, surprised those who were besieging Eleanor in the castle of Mirabeau, and captured Arthur and 200 barons. He then forfeited the decided advantage he had won by allowing twenty-two of the prisoners to die of starvation and (according to one story) by murdering with his own hands, when drunk and in a rage, the young Arthur, whose body he threw into the Seine. Arthur's murder cost John all support in the Loire Valley and Brittany and his idleness the next year cost him Normandy. Philip conquered Normandy in 1204, captured the last castle in Anjou in 1205, and secured Britanny in 1206. John, who had fled to England in 1204, now held only a part of Aquitaine.

MAGNA CARTA

In England the early years of John's reign were years of order and peace. The man most responsible for this was Hubert Walter, Chancellor and Archbishop of Canterbury. His death in 1205 was therefore a severe loss to England. It also made necessary the election of a new Archbishop, an election that plunged England into seven years of strife. John wanted the monks of Canterbury to elect the Bishop of Norwich, but instead they elected their subprior. Hearing of this, John commanded them to elect the Bishop, which they did. The monks then took the dispute to Rome, where Innocent III, a Pope dedicated to the supremacy of spiritual authority, set aside the election of both candidates and persuaded the monks to elect Stephen Langton, an English cardinal. John refused to accept such an election and denied Langton entry into England. The Pope replied by placing England under an interdict and by excommunicating John. John retaliated by seizing the property of those who refused to perform the prohibited religious services. For five years the churches were silent, while John plundered their wealth. Then suddenly, in 1213, John surrendered. He accepted Langton as Archbishop, restored the Church its property, and agreed to govern England as a papal fief. He surrendered because the Pope threatened to pronounce his deposition if he did not yield and because Philip planned to invade England. Conscious of his growing weakness at home, he knew that he needed the moral authority of the Church in order to withstand Philip.

From the day he lost Normandy, John had to provide for the defense of England, since the Channel ports now lay in hostile hands. He quickly built a fleet of fifty-one royal galleys and organized the local defenses. The danger soon passed, for Philip turned his attention to the south of France. But this fact did not end the enormously costly military preparations, for John's consuming desire was to recover his French lands. To this end he led an expedition to Gascony in 1206 and allied with the Emperor in 1209. By 1213 the dukes of Brabant and Limburg and the counts of Flanders, Holland, and Boulogne had joined the coalition. The English treasury poured out vast sums for these princes. The plan of attack was carefully thought out: John was to march against the French king from the southwest and the Emperor, with the coalition princes, from the northeast. Unfortunately for John, his Poitivin barons would not fight against the French king and so he had to retreat to La Rochelle. His retreat allowed Philip to throw all his forces against the Emperor at Bouvines, where on July 27, 1214, he routed the armies of the coalition. The Battle of Bouvines ended all John's hopes of recovering his French lands.

The catastrophe of Bouvines made Magna Carta inevitable, for an arbitrary king cannot afford the humiliation of such a defeat. Yet Bouvines only heightened the struggle that led to Magna Carta. That struggle had begun with John's vast and unending financial exactions. He levied a scutage on the slightest pretext, raising the usual rate of 1 mark a knight fee to 2.5 marks in 1204 and 3 marks in 1213. He also placed a fifteenth on all merchandise passing through English ports and twice taxed the movable wealth of Englishmen. He exploited feudal dues by charging exorbitant reliefs and selling wardships to the highest bidder. Henry II and Richard had also exacted great sums from their subjects, yet had not met resistance. The difference in John's case lay in his arbitrary rule, his suspicious nature, and his wanton cruelty. In many ways John was an attractive king. He had an acute intelligence, a sense of humor, great administrative capacity, and a fondness for reading. He liked to do justice in person, though too often he gave the force of law to whatever pleased him. "The law is in my mouth," he once said. He was deeply suspicious of his subjects and so frequently demanded oaths of loyalty from them and hostages to secure those oaths. He took a morbid delight in watching judicial combats and was capable of great cruelty, as when he allowed the wife and son of William of Braose, a favorite who had incurred his displeasure, to starve to death in the dungeon of Windsor Castle.

The events leading to Magna Carta began with a meeting of the barons at St. Paul's Church on August 25, 1213, at which Stephen Langton read aloud Henry I's coronation charter. A year later the barons, mostly from the north, refused to pay the scutage demanded by John, and early in 1215 they gathered under arms at Stamford. From Stamford they marched on London, where in May the citizens opened the gates to them. Originally it was a revolt only of the great barons pursuing their selfish ends, but they were soon joined by the Church, the lesser feudal aristocracy, and the towns. Between the middle of

May and middle of June, Stephen Langton played the crucial role in transforming the purely feudal demands of the barons into the demands of the whole realm. John, who now saw that he was defeated, agreed to meet the barons at the meadow of Runneymede by the Thames, halfway between Staines, where the barons were camped, and Windsor, where John resided. There, on June 15, 1215, John set the seal to the Great Charter, or Magna Carta.

Magna Carta was fundamentally a feudal document, a defense of the interests of a feudal class. It contained clauses limiting reliefs, forbidding the wasting of lands during wardship, removing widows from any compulsion to remarry, and providing that scutage and aids (other than the three customary ones) be levied only with the consent of the great council. But it was more than a feudal document. In the first place, it contained clauses that guaranteed the rights of the Church, the liberties of the towns, and the freedom of movement of merchants. In the second place, it accepted and confirmed the legal reforms of Henry II's reign. The king should not sell, deny, or defer justice to any man; the court of Common Pleas should remain in a fixed place; the possessory writs should be heard more often; no free man should be arrested, imprisoned, or dispossessed "except by the lawful judgment of his equals or by the law of the land." This last clause did not mean trial by jury, as the seventeenth-century lawyers thought, but it did mean trial before a court of law. These clauses in Magna Carta meant little to the villein, for Henry II's reforms applied only to freemen, but as villeinage slowly came to an end, more and more people came to enjoy the protection these clauses offered.

For contemporaries, the significance of Magna Carta lay in the fact that it contained a full and detailed statement of the customs of the time. For future generations its significance lay in the fact that it enunciated the principle that the King is, and shall be, beneath the law. The Angevin kings had created an absolutism that threatened to sweep aside the restraints of feudal custom. Ranulf Glanvill even opened his treatise on the laws of England by quoting the maxim in Roman law that what the prince decrees has the force of law. John's capricious and arbitrary conduct, however, persuaded the English to place their King beneath the law. They even added to Magna Carta a crude mechanism to ensure that he could no longer override it. A committee of twenty-four barons were empowered, with the help of the whole land, "to distrain and distress" the King in every possible way should he violate the charter.

This clause never came into operation, but in September, when the Pope condemned Magna Carta and when John recovered his nerve and began to raise mercenaries, the barons took up arms again, even appealing for help to Louis, son of the French king, to whom they offered the English crown. Civil war raged until John fell ill of dysentery, made worse by a surfeit of peaches and cider, and died on October 18, 1216. The accession of his son Henry, a boy of 9, brought the civil war to an end.

FURTHER READING

FRANK BARLOW. *The Feudal Kingdom of England 1042–1216.* London, 1955. A remarkably well-written narrative, which weaves together political, economic, social, religious, and intellectual developments.

J.L. BOLTON. *The Medieval English Economy 1150–1500.* London, 1980. Comprehensive and clearly written; Bolton gives all points of view on debatable questions, then his own judgments, which are well-balanced and fair.

H.E. HALLAM. *Rural England 1066–1348.* Brighton, Sussex, 1981. Criticizes the orthodox view that by 1300 there was great hunger in England and that famine caused a decrease in population; emphasizes late marriages and technological advances in farming.

CHARLES HOMER HASKINS. *The Renaissance of the Twelfth Century.* Cambridge, Mass., 1927; reprinted by Meridian Books, 1960. A masterful survey of the intellectual achievements of the twelfth century; breadth of scope, deft use of detail, mature judgments, and a sympathy for all human interests make it a classic.

JAMES CLARK HOLT. *Magna Carta.* Cambridge, England, 1965. A major work of historical revision; Holt shows sympathy for King John, criticizes the barons, and underlines the ambiguities of the Charter; contains a good analysis of Angevin government.

———. *Henry II.* London, 1973. A political narrative of the reign, punctuated by extended analyses of the government of England and of Henry's relation with the church; fluently written but insular in outlook.

AMY KELLY. *Eleanor of Aquitaine and the Four Kings.* Cambridge, Mass., 1950. A beautifully written life of Henry II's queen, in which places are vividly portrayed and events dramatically recounted.

DAVID KNOWLES. *Thomas Becket.* Palo Alto, Calif., 1971. A gracefully written biography, concise, wise, learned; at times less than fair to Henry II and less than critical to Becket.

STEPHEN RUNCIMAN. *A History of the Crusades. Vol. 3, The Kingdom of Acre and the Later Crusades.* Cambridge, England, 1954. A distinguished work of scholarship, written with wit, irony, and narrative skill; redresses the Western bias of most accounts.

W.L. WARREN, *King John.* New York, 1961. A reassessment of the reign of King John, in which the flaws in his character are played down; written for the general reader.

6 The Thirteenth Century: 1216-1307

If the twelfth century was the springtime of medieval civilization, the thirteenth century was the high summer. During that century the institutions of medieval life—lord and vassal, manor and guild, castle and cathedral, town and university, tournament and troubadour—reached maturity. A moment of equilibrium was reached when institutions and ideals fashioned in earlier years met the needs of society. The medieval papacy reached its widest power, governing the Church from Sicily to Scotland, from Spain to Norway. The crusading impulse led men to the Holy Land, while the code of chivalry, softened by the courtly ideal, governed the lives of knights. A few scholastic philosophers held that faith could not contradict reason, though the great majority of men and women accepted unquestioningly the truths of their Christian faith. It was a stable society, largely rural, with warfare endemic in the border regions, but peace and order maintained elsewhere by a strong monarchy. England's medieval monarchy, though it faltered during the reign of Henry III, reached the summit of its greatness under Edward I. Within these same years there also emerged one of the most characteristic of medieval institutions, Parliament, an institution that was to survive the age that created it. The story of the thirteenth century, therefore, is one of stability and equilibrium, of splendor and achievement.

BARONS AND KNIGHTS

Medieval society was intensely hierarchical, with the various ranks of men and women arranged in a social pyramid. At the apex stood the King, with a revenue of £35,000 a year, followed by a dozen earls whose incomes ranged from £1,000 to £2,000 a year. Below them were twenty to thirty barons who were wealthy enough to rank among the "magnates of the realm." Most barons had incomes varying from £500 to £1,000 a year. Farther down the social scale came the knights and squires, whose manors brought them anywhere from £20 a year to over £100. Though all knights were formally of the same social class, the great baron towered over the ordinary knight. Most landlords, in fact, never became knights; they remained country gentlemen, content to spend their time managing their estates and hunting. It is difficult to give a modern equivalent for these sums of money, but the immense wealth of the barons can be gauged by comparing their incomes with those of the working classes. A skilled mason might earn £5 in a year, an unskilled laborer £2.5, and a laundress £1. In the thirteenth century wealth was concentrated in the baronial class, and within that class in the hands of a few.

The need for money with which to pay royal taxes, hire retainers, dispense hospitality, and live in splendor drove the nobility to manage their estates carefully. To assist him, a great magnate would have a large household, perhaps of sixty servants, with a council to advise him, auditors to oversee his accounts, a marshal to superintend the stable, a chaplain to say mass, a baker to bake bread, and a brewer to brew beer. The household itself was a small hierarchy, with the lord at the top and a phalanx of grooms at the bottom. The key official was the steward, who decided what crops should be grown, how many halfpenny loaves could be made from a quarter of grain, and whether the

Bodiam Castle near Hauckhurst on the border of Sussex and Kent. The castle is surrounded by a wide moat, fed by the river Rather (*the National Trust*).

reeve was cheating in the delivery of milk and cheese. The steward saw to the collection of rents, accounted for all expenses, and presided at the manorial court. It was a foolish lord who left the steward to his own devices, for they could be unscrupulous. A wise lord took a personal interest in his estates and tenants, learned the extent and fertility of his lands, surveyed the rents and services owed him, and strove to know his servants personally. His lady likewise took an active part in the administration of the household, as the career of the countess of Leicester illustrates. She regularly supervised the immediate household, and when her husband, Simon de Montfort, was in Gascony or fighting in the civil war, she managed the entire estate. Women such as the countess were neither the submissive sheep depicted by the moralists nor the cardboard beauties drawn by the romancers. They were women of spirit and enterprise.

The typical knight or squire, with some twenty-four tenants and 250 acres of demesne land, possessed no such household, and was content to live in an unfortified house, with a hall, a kitchen, and a private room for himself and his lady. The great barons lived in castles that bore little resemblance to the small wooden keeps of the eleventh century. The quest for greater security against siege and for more comfort led to the building of ever larger castles. The castle, once a single building, now became a series of separate buildings surrounded by a protecting, or "curtain," wall. The curtain wall had a walk on top and projecting towers from which archers could fire on anyone who attempted to scale the walls. Within the wall was a stone keep and miscellaneous wooden buildings—a chapel, a kitchen, stables. The stone keep usually consisted of a basement, where stores were kept, a great hall above it, and above the hall the bedchamber of the lord and lady. The hall, with a dais or raised platform at one end and a fireplace in one wall, was the hub of all social activity. It was meagerly furnished, with only two chairs on the dais for the lord and lady, trestle tables and benches, and hangings of painted cloth on the walls. Glass windows began to replace shuttered windows, but even then the hall was usually dark, cold, and cheerless.

The castle afforded the background for a life shaped by chivalry, a system of ethical ideas appropriate to the knight—that is, to a man whose profession was fighting. Among its virtues were prowess in battle, courage, loyalty, fidelity to one's word, and generosity. By the thirteenth century generosity had become the chief virtue. One troubadour declared it to be a disgrace for a man to live within his means; he ought to mortgage his estate in order to entertain and to give presents. These virtues were not only exhibited on the battlefield, they were also celebrated in long narrative poems, the *chansons de geste*. In these songs of great deeds the poet chronicled endless battles and recounted vivid stories of the hero cutting his foes to pieces. But during the twelfth and thirteenth centuries two influences, the Church and the lady, modified this rough masculine code of ethics.

The Church developed the concept of the perfect knight, a devout Christian who served his lawful prince, put down crime, and aided the weak and helpless. It argued that the knights of the realm, like the clergy, formed an order, an order appointed by God to fight in His service. At the same time the courtly ideal appeared in southern France, where lyric poets, called *troubadours*, glorified the great lady, placed her on a pedestal, and made her adoration and service, even from a distance, the greatest good in a knight's life. Carried to Paris and London by Eleanor of Aquitaine and her courtiers, this new ideal became the fashion. Together the courtly and religious ideals transformed the Welsh tales of King Arthur into romances that celebrated prowess in battle, devotion to God, and worship of woman.

In the thirteenth century there were in England between 500 and 1000 knights, among them most of the great magnates of the realm. When life grew tedious, they turned for amusement to the tournament. In the early Middle Ages these tournaments were like pitched battles: The knights would divide into two camps, and then charge each other in a murderous melee. By the middle of the thirteenth century, urged on by Henry III and Prince Edward, a new kind of tournament appeared. The knights now jousted against each other individually, with blunt weapons, before spectators, and according to accepted rules. Tournaments, which had been the training ground for the young knight, now became great social occasions.

Hunting was another favorite amusement. If a baron did not own a private forest, he at least had a park, or area of land enclosed by a paling, where he might hunt deer without royal license. The medieval upper classes also had a passion for hawking, or hunting with the falcon. This sport, like hunting the deer, was reserved for King and nobles alone. The yeoman had to be content with a goshawk and the clergyman with a sparrowhawk. In the long winter evenings the nobility played chess or gambled with dice. Playing cards had not yet appeared in Europe and books were used for devotion, not amusement. The place of the book was taken by the minstrel, who recited, sang, danced, and juggled. Feasting afforded an occasion for hospitality, with silver plates, cups, and spoons, proudly displayed at the high table. There might be elegant dishes, such as larks and woodcocks, but the usual fare was a great plenty of beef, mutton, pork, and poultry, washed down with wine from Bordeaux. So great was the thirst of the upper classes for wine that it amounted to one-third of all English imports.

MANOR AND VILLAGE

The barons and knights of England drew their wealth from land, either from many manors scattered across many counties, or from one carefully managed manor. The manor as an institution reached its greatest extent in the thirteenth century, although the classic manor, with its open fields and meadows, its villeins and cottagers, its weekwork and boonwork, did not prevail everywhere. In much of East Anglia and Kent enclosed fields were normal, and the peasant was often a freeman with little connection to a manor. In Cornwall, the Lake District, the Welsh Marches, and the hilly country of the Pennines, the isolated farm and hamlet predominated. In fact, throughout much of the Midlands and the South, where the classic manor did prevail, there was not necessarily a one-to-one correspondence between manor and village. In Warwickshire in 1279 about half the villages had a single lord of the manor; in the other villages there were two or more manors, each with its lord.

It was the village that dominated the peasant's life, with its small houses clustered around the great stone church, its narrow streets radiating from the village green, its mill, its alehouse, and perhaps a manor house, though often the lord lived elsewhere. Beyond the one-storied, thatched houses, each set in a small garden, stretched the great open fields. The meadows where peasants mowed hay in June lay next to the river. On the commons, a piece of rough pasture land, those peasants fortunate enough to own a cow could put it out to graze. In such villages, containing on the average about 300 persons, the majority of people lived out their lives.

The villagers had a voice in the management of the open fields surrounding them, but where there was but one lord of the manor or a dominant lord, the villagers acted through the manorial court. The manor, not the village, was the working unit of agrarian life. A manor was both a piece of land and a unit of jurisdiction over those who lived on the land. A tenant was also the lord's man; he performed an act of homage in the manorial court on receiving his strips in the open fields. There were many kinds of tenants. The elite among them were the freemen, who owed only a money rent and answered in a royal court for any petty crime they committed. The freemen on a manor might come to 15 percent; all the others were serfs, which meant that they could not leave the manor or marry without the lord's permission and must answer for the tenure of their holdings and for any petty crimes in the manor court.

Even among the serfs there was a hierarchy. At the top were the holders of a full virgate of land (which varied in size from 16 to 30 acres according to the quality of the soil); below them were those who held half a virgate. At the bottom were the cottagers, who held only a small plot of land, about 5 acres; for a livelihood they depended chiefly upon wages paid for their labor by the lord or by a virgater. The greater a serf's holdings, the greater his obligations. The holder of a virgate of land, for example, owed not only a money rent but also weekwork and boonwork. On the manor of Borley in Essex, weekwork meant laboring on the lord's demesne for three days each week between September 29 and August 1; boonwork meant twenty-four days harvesting for the lord between August 1 and September 29. Weekwork and boonwork did not end the burdens resting on the serf. He must also grind his grain in the lord's mill and bake his bread in the lord's oven, for which he paid a fee. On his death his heir must pay a *heriot*, which might be only his best beast, but might also include his cart, pigs, copper vessels, and uncut woolen cloth. He paid a fee at the marriage of his daughter or at his son's leaving to become a priest.

Sowing the seed by hand, a scene from a medieval calendar (*the British Library, Add. MSS 35, 315*).

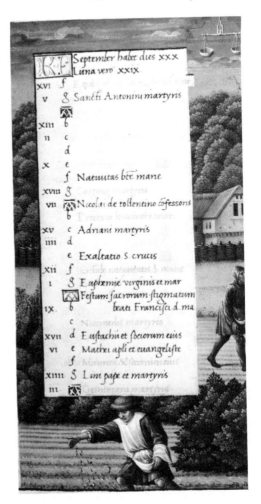

Most grievous of all, his lord might *tallage* him at will, that is, exact whatever sum he wished. Lawyers defended the tallage on the grounds that in theory the serf and all his chattels belonged to the lord.

Yet the serf was not a slave; he possessed rights protected by the custom of the manor. Chief among these was the right to the produce grown on his strips in the open fields. These strips passed on his death to his widow, and on her death to their eldest son (or, in some parts of England, to the youngest). The holding of strips in the open fields brought with it the right to strips in the meadow and "the right of common," which was of great value because it allowed the peasant to graze livestock on the commons proper, on wasteland, and on the arable and meadow after the crops were harvested.

The serf's rights were secured in the manor court, held on a green or under an oak or in the lord's hall, presided over by the lord or his steward, and attended by all the serfs, who declared the custom of the manor and handed down judgments. The manor court had various duties: it controlled the open fields, determined how many cattle each tenant might place on the pasture, witnessed the transfer of land, and punished trespasses and theft. On the manor of Tooting Bec, for example, the court punished one Richard Bradwater, a considerable scoundrel, for letting his pigs trespass on the lord's meadow, for driving another man's cattle from the common pasture, for mowing and taking hay from the lord's meadows, and for assaulting the bailiff. The bailiff was the lord's man, responsible to him for the administration of the manor, but the pivotal officer in the running of a manor was the reeve, who was usually chosen from amongst the wealthier peasants. It was the reeve who saw that workers got up on time, supervised the plowing, kept watch on the threshing, and brought before the manor court those who failed in their duties.

The immemorial rhythm of the seasons dictated the life of the peasant. In January he would spread manure or marl on the fields; in February he would plow in the straw; in April he would plow, in preparation for sowing the spring crops. The seed was scattered by hand from a basket slung around the sower's neck, and the field was then harrowed so that the birds could not eat the seed. The harrow was a wooden frame with teeth projecting from it, which a horse drew over the sown field. In May the peasant worked in his garden; in June he mowed the hay in the meadow, for which purpose he used a long scythe. In July he plowed the fallow a second time. August saw the climax of all his activities, for then the crops were harvested. To mow the barley, oats, and rye the peasant used a scythe, but to cut the wheat he used a sickle. The wheat was cut high up on the stock, leaving the straw standing. Men worked in teams of five,

Harvesting the grain (*the British Library, Royal MSS 2.B. VII, f. 78v*).

Threshing the grain (*the British Library. Add. MSS 88, 126, f. 8v*).

four cutting, and one binding. In the autumn the fallow was plowed for the last time, in preparation for planting winter wheat. During wet weather the grain was threshed, using a flail (two pieces of wood tied together by a leather thong), which the worker swung against the grain, dislodging the kernels. The kernels were separated from the chaff by tossing the grain into the air when there was a strong breeze, the breeze blowing away the chaff and leaving the heavier kernels to fall to the ground. In late autumn the peasant repaired farm implements and gathered wood or peat for winter fuel. During these months the peasant woman toiled as ceaselessly as her husband, growing vegetables, making cheese, brewing ale, spinning yarn, and helping at harvest. Women performed every task known on a manor but that of plowing.

And what standard of life did the peasant gain from this unremitting toil? If he were fortunate enough to own a virgate of land, probably a rude plenty. He might hope to reap 68 bushels of wheat, 95 bushels of barley, and 70 bushels of oats. He would probably sell his wheat to gain the money with which to pay his rent. The barley he would use both to brew ale and make bread, the oats he would either feed to his horse or eat as pottage. But the virgate holders were a minority; there were thousands who had but half a virgate or less. For them life was a continuous struggle to survive. The diet of the average peasant was monotonous. He rarely ate meat, except on special occasions, when chicken or salted beef or smoked bacon would be set on the table. The usual diet was a hunk of bread and a mug of thin ale in the morning, a lump of cheese and bread at midday, and thick soup made of peas and beans in the evening, accompanied by bread, cheese, and ale. He lived in a house made by placing curved uprights, "crucks" they were called, opposite to each other, with a ridgepole running the length of them. Once this framework was up, the walls were built, usually out of wattle-and-daub. A thatched roof kept out the rain and an iron plate on the earthen floor served as a fireplace. There being no

Construction of a cruck house: a pair of crucks with tie-beam (*George Holmes, The Later Middle Ages: 1272–1485, Thomas Nelson & Sons Ltd. 1962*).

chimney and only one or two small windows, the house was smoky, dark, damp, and cold; bags of straw thrown on the floor served as beds.

From this drab existence the peasant found some relief in Holy Days. The Church decreed that these should be many, but the lord of the manor saw that they were few. Aside from Sundays, when light work was often demanded of them, peasants enjoyed the twelve days of Christmas and a few days at Easter and Whitsunday (the seventh Sunday after Easter). At Christmas they feasted at the manor house, drank strong ale, and laughed at the pranks of the mummer's play; at Easter they watched the miracle play performed; on May Day they celebrated with dance, song, games, and more ale. The great occasions of life—birth, marriage, and death—were celebrated with much heavy drinking, along with dances and games. It was not the Merry England imagined by nineteenth-century romantics, but neither was it an England of unrelieved gloom.

TOWN AND GUILD

A serf, by fleeing to a town and living there for a year and a day, could escape bondage. Many became merchants, joined the merchant guild, and prospered. In the thirteenth century, however, a peasant who fled to a town was more likely to become a member of a craft guild. The rise of the craft guilds was the most important change in town life to occur in the thirteenth century. The number and variety of crafts were great: cobblers, saddlers, weavers, tailors, goldsmiths, drapers, tanners, bakers. Each craftsman was limited to the pursuit of his own craft or "mystery." So great was the passion for specialization that in Canterbury the bakers of white bread were forbidden to bake black bread. Medieval shops were small, often not more than 6 feet wide, and were less a store than a workshop. Craftsmen kept no stock, but made goods to order. The primary purpose of a craft guild was to protect the economic interest of its members. No craftsman could work in a town unless he was a member of the guild, which laid down detailed regulations concerning the quality of goods, the method of manufacture, and the price that could be charged. It limited entry into the craft both by requiring a long apprenticeship and by limiting the number of apprentices a master might have. In the thirteenth century appren-

A pause during the harvest (*the British Library, Add. MSS 24, 098, f. 25v*).

tices might hope to become masters, but by the late Middle Ages the great majority could only hope to become journeymen, working for wages the guild set. Custom, not competition, governed economic life in the towns, just as it did on the manor.

The largest guilds were those associated with the manufacture of cloth, an industry centered in towns of the eastern Midlands, especially Leicester. In the manufacture of cloth from raw wool there were four main processes: carding, spinning, weaving, and fulling. The last process, fulling, entailed the beating of the cloth while it lay in a trough filled with water and fuller's earth, the purpose being to thicken and felt the cloth. This was traditionally done by workers treading upon the cloth with their feet, but late in the twelfth century the fulling mill, which used waterpower, appeared. Water was taken from a swift-flowing stream and channeled to a waterwheel, whose axle extended into the mill building. Here projections on the revolving axle alternately raised and let fall heavy wooden hammers, which beat the cloth that lay in a trough of water and fuller's earth. Because of the need for waterpower and because rural labor was cheaper than urban, the clothmaking industry migrated to the valleys of the West Country and the Pennines. The eastern towns kept their importance as market centers, but the migration of their only large-scale industry reduced their prosperity. Despite the exodus of the cloth industry, the towns of England continued to grow. By 1336 there were about 240 towns in England, large and small. London was by far the largest, with perhaps 30,000 inhabitants and with suburbs that extended to the King's palace at Westminster, two miles to the west. York had about 10,000 inhabitants; Bristol, 8,000; Coventry, 6,000; and Norwich, 5,000.

As towns grew in population and wealth they sought to secure themselves behind walls, but building walls was extremely expensive. Therefore, as small a

The Shambles, York. Though nothing in the Shambles is older than the sixteenth century, the narrow street and protruding upper stories give a clear idea of the appearance of a medieval town, crowded within its walls (*Edwin Smith*).

space as possible was enclosed, and it was used to the fullest. The result was narrow streets, with the upper floor of houses built out over them. Because houses were built of wood and roofed with thatch, fires were frequent. In 1189, therefore, the magistrates of London decreed that houses be built partly of stone and roofed with tile. Towns had no drains other than the street itself, which sloped towards the middle. Into the streets people dumped refuse of every kind. But despite the stench, the medieval city, especially London, offered a lively, noisy, colorful, gregarious life. Tradespeople called out their wares and crowds searched for bargains at stalls and open shops. On the river bank, near the wine wharves, public cook shops offered for sale meat, fish, and fowl, roasted, baked, or stewed. Young men enjoyed tilting, wrestling, bowls, cockfighting, and bull-baiting. On May Day Londoners walked out into the meadows and forests, for no medieval town ever lost its rural character. The taverns, as the author of *Piers Ploughman* lamented, were always crowded with tinkers, hackneymen, parish clerks, fiddlers, ropemakers, watchmen, and Tyburn hangmen, laughing and chattering, toasting and singing, until one of them, having drunk a gallon and a gill, rose, staggered, and fell flat on the floor. "The only plagues of London," wrote William Fitz Stephen, "are the immoderate drinking of fools and the frequency of fires."

The townsman lived by different ideals from those of the nobleman. Not being trained as a soldier, he had little taste for war. Communal pride, not reverence for a lord, inspired him. And he could not afford the chivalric ideal of boundless generosity, for his money was his capital. This led the nobleman to condemn the townsman as grasping and stingy. The Church, too, condemned merchants who yielded to avarice. It taught the doctrine of the "just price"—namely, that a tradesman should charge only the price that would allow him to live as his father and grandfather had. It also condemned the practice of buying goods, holding them for some time, and selling them at a higher price. Above all, it condemned usury—that is, the taking of any interest on a loan. This prohibition led the Jews to establish colonies in nearly every major English town and to grow wealthy loaning money to kings, noblemen, and prelates at an average rate of interest of 43 percent. The Jews flourished under Henry II; suffered periodic confiscation of their wealth under Richard, John, and Henry; and were expelled by Edward I in 1290 because they were no longer needed. Their place was taken by Italian bankers, who had devised means to circumvent the ban on taking interest.

BISHOPS, PRIESTS, AND FRIARS

The towns of medieval England contained an astonishing number of parish churches. London had 136, Norwich 50, the small borough of Lewes 8. Their great number reflected the deep piety of the age, just as the great stone church in each village, towering over the cottages, symbolized the central place of religion in the lives of English men and women. It was within these simple, rectangular, high-roofed churches that villagers and townspeople worshipped, usually standing or squatting on the rushes which covered the floor. In these churches the priest droned out the mass, barely intelligible even to those who knew Latin. The peasant understood little, but when the bell rang and the priest held up the blessed bread and wine the peasant probably felt the mystery and dimly apprehended that Christ's body was made anew. Paintings on the church wall portrayed for him the ecstasy of the saved as they were caught up in the arms of angels and the horror of the damned as the devil seized them with flesh-hooks and pitched them into everlasting fire. The fact of death and judgment haunted medieval life, and the Church was present everywhere—at local shrines, at wayside crosses, in bands of pilgrims, in the pealing of bells, in distant church spires.

The Church was also omnipresent in economic life. To the rector of the parish the peasant owed the great tithe in grain, usually the tenth sheaf at harvest, and lesser tithes in cattle, wool, and hay. Because these tithes were often used for purposes other than his support, the parish priest had to depend for his livelihood on the glebe. The glebe was a portion of land, scattered through the open fields, which the priest himself farmed. He kept his beasts on the commons, appeared before the manor court, entered into petty quarrels, and ran the risk of becoming a farmer first and a priest second. But the involvement of the Church in economic life did not end with the priest and his glebe. Bishoprics and monasteries were among the greatest landlords in the realm, owning many hundreds of manors. At Lincoln Cathedral, for example, one canon was rector of Langford in Oxfordshire and enjoyed its greater and lesser tithes, while a second canon was lord of the manor at Langford and collected the rents and services owed him as lord. Despite homilies in praise of poverty, the Church was as insistent upon its rights as any lay lord.

The wealth the Church took through tithes and rents was unevenly distributed. Ecclesiastical society was every bit as hierarchical as lay society. At the apex stood the princely bishops, governing their diocese, ordaining priests, holding synods, and conducting visitations. The wealthiest among them—the two archbishops and the bishops of Winchester, Ely, and Durham—had incomes equal to those of the wealthiest barons. Below the bishop came the rector, who if he enjoyed all the tithes of his parish, was a rich and influential man, equal in status to a knight. But the income of many rectories had fallen into the hands of abbeys, cathedral chapters, collegiate churches, and the king himself. Much of this was inevitable, for in the thirteenth century episcopal officials, royal administrators, and university scholars were not paid wages but were granted rectories, whose incomes they enjoyed though they did not live in the parish. Some clergymen, known as pluralists, amassed two to three rectories. The Church did not try to abolish absenteeism and pluralism, but rather to mitigate the harm by demanding the appointment of a vicar to perform the duties of the parish priest. An ordinary vicar enjoyed an income of about £4 a year, far less than a rector's, but more than the £2½ a plowman might earn.

The vicar ranked economically with the largest holders of land in the open fields. Below him were a mass of chaplains and assistant priests, the lowest paid among the clergy.

The gravest problem in the medieval Church was the ignorance of the clergy. "The ignorance of the priest," wrote Archbishop Pecham in 1281, "casteth the people into the ditch of error." Educated priests were needed to make clear to the ordinary parishioner the meaning of the service and of the symbolism that was everywhere. But most parish priests could barely stumble through the four sermons required of them each year. The dean of Sarum found that five out of seventeen clergymen whom he visited could not interpret the central portion of the service of the mass. Their ignorance is not surprising, for they were largely recruited from the peasant class and received no systematic training. A boy might start as a server to the village priest, rise through the four orders of the clergy, and learn the elements of Latin from a kindly priest. Being of peasant stock, they understood their parishioners, which was their great strength, but the art of making a sermon was beyond them. This they left to the preaching friars.

In 1221 a band of thirteen priests, dedicated to a life of poverty, simplicity, and preaching, crossed the Channel. They were a party of Dominicans, an order founded by Dominic Guzman, a Spaniard, who believed that learning and preaching should be used to combat heresy and to win men to the Gospel. Three years later a smaller band of three Englishmen and six Italians landed at Dover. They brought the faith and teachings of St. Francis of Assisi, a young Italian who preached nothing less than man's duty to live Christ's life anew, here and now. Where St. Dominic labored for the rational conversion of men's minds, St. Francis sought to preach the Gospel by living it. Ultimately it was what the two orders had in common that mattered. Members of both orders were bound by oaths of poverty, obedience, and chastity. They were not, however, monks; they moved freely in the world, especially in the towns, preaching, doing good works, bringing to the thirteenth century a religious ardor no longer found in the monasteries. By refusing to own property, they avoided the trap into which the monasteries fell, the possession of great and corrupting wealth. They lived in crude, unheated buildings owned by their patrons, and depended for their livelihood upon charity. By 1272 there were forty-nine houses of Dominican friars and forty-seven of Franciscan in England. Though forbidden to preach in a parish church without the priest's permission, they could preach in their own chapels and in public. Through such preaching, they revitalized the religious life of England.

THE CATHEDRAL

The cathedral, with its spires and pinnacles reaching for the heavens, with its lofty nave and choir leading irresistibly to the high altar, with its translucent stained glass windows casting a mystical glow over all, expressed most palpably the power and splendor and mystery of medieval Christianity. The Anglo-Sax-

Church of St. Lawrence, Bradford-upon-Avon, one of the finest remains of Anglo-Saxon architecture. The walls are two-and-a-half feet thick and the exterior is enriched with fluted columns and blank arcading (*National Monuments Record, England*).

ons were quite incapable of building such churches. Most of their churches were built of timber; those they built of stone were small, usually without aisles, and crude in construction. Windows were few and tiny, and the masons preferred to bridge the windows with a single stone or with two stones tilted against each other. The true arch was beyond their capability. The coming of the Normans changed all this, for they were not only brave soldiers and energetic administrators, but prodigious builders. Within a century they had built ninety-seven great abbey and cathedral churches, not to mention countless parish churches—an astonishing feat for a country with a population of about 2 million.

The Normans built their churches in the Romanesque style, which developed in Lombardy in the ninth century, when craftsmen rediscovered the art of constructing vaults and arches of masonry. The ground plan of these churches was based on the Roman basilica, or hall of justice. The early Christian basilica was an oblong building, with aisles flanking a wide and lofty nave, ending in a rounded extension or apse, which contained the altar and the bishop's throne (or *cathedra*, hence "cathedral"). Eastern influences led to the addition of cross arms, or a transept, between the nave and the apse. Liturgical demands, largely occasioned by the Cluniac movement, transformed the early Christian basilica into the medieval cathedral. The need to perform services of great solemnity and visual splendor led to larger, more impressive churches with processional aisles. The veneration of saints led to the building of many side altars and chapels. The needs of the monks and canons to perform their religious offices daily led to the extention of the east end beyond the transept, to furnish a choir. Because the laity were not permitted in the choir, a second altar was placed in the nave. The chief elements used in the construction of these churches were giant columns, massive cylindrical piers, semicircular arches, thick masonry walls, small rounded windows, and towers raised over the west front and over the crossing of the nave and transept. The effect created by these elements can be seen in Durham Cathedral, the finest of all northern Romanesque churches. It is an effect of massiveness, strength, vigor, solidity, and plainness of statement.

The greatest problem facing the builders of Romanesque churches was how to cover a wide and lofty nave with a stone roof. Except at Durham, they never solved it. They had to rely instead on timber roofs, which created the danger of fire. The art of stone vaulting, lost with the collapse of the Roman Empire, was recovered only slowly. In southwest France masons solved the

The nave of Durham Cathedral, a magnificant example of Romanesque architecture (*National Monuments Record*).

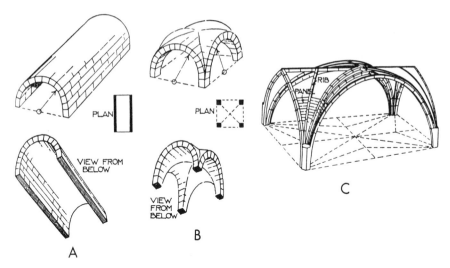

The evolution of Gothic vaulting. A. Roman tunnel vault; B. Romanesque groin vault over a square; C. Gothic ribbed vault over an oblong compartment. (From Sir Banister Fletcher, *A History of Architecture*).

problem of vaulting the nave by placing a series of domes on arches; at Issoire and Poitiers they used a barrel, or tunnel, vault. But tunnel vaulting could not rise very high, since its great outward thrust demanded short, stout walls. The Normans discovered a third solution: the groin vault. If two tunnel vaults intersect each other at right angles, the point of intersection has two transverse arches, two longitudinal, and two diagonal. This is a groin vault and the area it covers is a bay. The builders of Durham Cathedral strengthened the groin vault by placing ribs along the lines of intersection of the masonry, ribs that made the vault less likely to collapse. The ribs also had a dramatic esthetic effect, for they took off directly from the shafts that made up the piers in each bay, thereby giving an unbroken vertical line from floor to ceiling.

If made with a semicircular arch, a rib vault can only cover a square. If used to cover an oblong area, the diagonal arch must be so depressed as to create the danger of collapse—and collapses were frequent in the twelfth century. At Boxgrove Priory, where round arches were used, the builders solved the problem by making the choir twice the width of the aisles and by using every other aisle pier to support the vaulting over the choir. Thus, every bay was a square. But the most effective solution was the use of the pointed arch, which allows more of the desired verticality than a round arch. An oblong area could be covered simply by employing different degrees of pointing. Though more vertical than before, there was still considerable outward thrust. To counter it, the builders of Durham supported the aisles with heavy buttresses and then ran

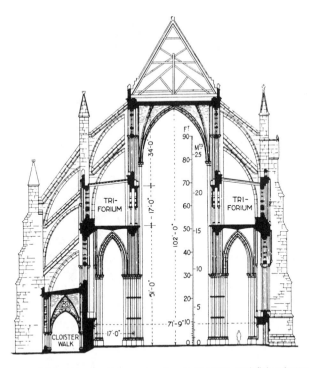

The transverse section of Westminster Abbey, showing buttresses and flying buttresses. (*From Sir Banister Fletcher, A History of Architecture*).

arched, or flying, buttresses from the aisle roof to the walls of the nave above the aisles. By using buttresses builders could reduce the thickness of the walls and increase the number of windows. With the combination of these three elements—the rib vault, the pointed arch, and the flying buttress—the Gothic style was born.

A French architect, William of Sens, first used the pointed arch for construction in England, at Canterbury in 1175, but the most inspired example of early Gothic is Lincoln Cathedral, built between 1190 and 1250. Lincoln contains the high vaulting, the pointed arches, the slender piers, the heavy buttresses, and the narrow lancet windows characteristic of the austere and simple beauty of early Gothic. The Gothic style transformed the inert masonry of the Romanesque (one column at Durham contains enough stone for a dozen thirteenth-century piers) into a system of lines of force, precariously and elegantly balanced against each other. The English never pursued this system with the logicality of the French, who built ever higher vaults over nave and choir, but clung instead to a strong horizontal line in nave and choir, and to the square English east end, where they placed splendid east windows.

The interior of Lincoln Cathedral (*National Monuments Record, England*).

The English did, however, pursue the arts of window tracery and rib vaulting to their logical end. Builders steadily increased the size of windows and by means of stone shafts divided them into arches, circles, and other geometrical shapes. Geometrical tracery dominated the first half of the thirteenth century; during the second half builders turned to curvilinear shapes of great inventiveness. At the same time vaulting became more elaborate, with masons adding to the usual transverse, longitudinal, and diagonal ribs secondary ribs that fanned out from, or ran between, the primary ribs. Their purpose was purely decorative. In fact, historians describe this phase of Gothic architecture as the Decorated to distinguish it from the earlier phase. A third phase, called the Perpendicular, emerged in the early fourteenth century at Gloucester Cathedral. In many ways it was the culmination of earlier developments. Walls that were once mostly stone now became largely glass. Where stonework was retained, it was paneled to resemble window tracery. Over the choir at Gloucester masons created an extremely complicated vaulting and over the cloister they built the first fan vault in England, a vault with ribs that fanned out in a cone shape. The groin vault, which had no ribs, became the fan vault,

The choir and presbytery of Gloucester Cathedral (*National Monuments Record, England*).

which was nearly all ribs. Yet the spirit of the Perpendicular was not flamboyant like the Decorated, but rectangular, plain, sensible, and very English.

The ordinary English cathedral grew like a landscape, having perhaps a Norman nave, an Early English choir, a Decorated east window, and a Perpendicular north transept, but this does not mean that the cathedral was the spontaneous product of devout craftsmen. Every part was designed by an architect, then called the master of the works. He rarely labored with his own hands, leaving that to the master masons, the carpenters, the glaziers, and the sculptors. The sculptors were very much the servant of the architect. In the Norman churches their work was abstract, but with the coming of the Gothic they carved, in a naturalistic manner, foliage, plants, and human figures. The greatest triumph of English sculpture was the west front of Wells Cathedral, where Simon of Wells and others carved 176 full-length statues. These statues do not exhibit the intensity of the sculptures at Chartres, in France, but they do present a veritable "Bible in stone." The cathedrals of England were not the spontaneous creations of humble craftsmen, but they were, and are, monuments to the deep faith and great wealth of Englishmen in the Middle Ages.

THE UNIVERSITY

The university, like the cathedral and Parliament, is a legacy of the medieval world. The medieval university, however, differed in many ways from the modern university. It had few, if any, buildings, no student societies, no athletic programs, and no board of trustees. It was merely a guild of masters of the arts, who established a curriculum of study, provided instruction in it—usually in hired halls, for a fee paid directly to the professor—and offered a degree upon its completion. By 1190 there was such a guild, or *universitas*, at Oxford. It was a poor and struggling one, with the masters subject to the supervision of the Chancellor of the Bishop of Lincoln and the students subject to the harassment of townspeople. By 1300 the scene was transformed. There now existed a privileged, self-confident community of scholars, consisting of some 1500 students and masters. The Chancellor, who awarded all degrees, no longer represented the Bishop of Lincoln but the masters; proctors named by the university and not the town authorities disciplined students. There were four faculties, those of arts, law, medicine, and theology. The growth of Oxford in the thirteenth century resulted from a succession of great teachers, most of whom were Franciscans or Dominicans. Among them were Robert Grosseteste, who became the first rector of the newly arrived Franciscans, and his pupil, Roger Bacon, also a Franciscan, whose inquiring mind turned from grammar and logic to astrology and alchemy, and found there much wisdom and much nonsense. The friars in the thirteenth century gave Oxford a European reputation; Cambridge, however, remained a purely local university.

The students at Oxford ranged in age from 14 to 21 and came to Oxford with a vocational purpose. Four out of five would become priests, a few bishops, others doctors or lawyers or monks. In the beginning they rented lodgings from the townspeople, but in order to escape from the extortions of landlords they banded together and lived in halls of their own. They lodged and dined in these halls, but went out to any teacher in town for instruction, since every teacher was free to set up his own school. Out of these halls gradually emerged the colleges of Oxford, with their endowments, statutes, rules, and buildings. Wealthy benefactors founded three colleges in the thirteenth century and four more in the fourteenth, each with its rooms, dining halls, library, and chapel.

Students were of all types. There was the poor student, who earned a pittance copying for others and who could not afford to buy books for himself; the wealthy student, who in addition to his books possessed a candle, a comfortable bed, and clothes more magnificent than the prescribed gown and hood; the idle student, who drifted from master to master and spent most of his time in the tavern; the perennial student, who put off taking his degree so that he might continue to enjoy the good cheer of Oxford; the dull student, who studied six years and learned nothing; and the serious student, who attended lectures assiduously and read until he fell asleep over his books. Most students had high spirits and empty pocketbooks. The commonest theme in letters home was the need for money, some of which was certainly used for drinking wine in a tavern, after which the students might abuse some woman, mock a townsman, or provoke a riot. In 1354 several students pronounced the wine served them sour and threw the pot at the tavernkeeper, thereby precipitating a riot that lasted one week and led to the death of sixty-three scholars.

To secure a mastership of arts a student had to study, for some six years, the seven liberal arts. The earlier years were spent on the *trivium*, which meant primarily a course in Aristotelian logic. Having completed the study of the *trivium*, a student received the degree of bachelor of arts and went on to the *quadrivium*. The great majority of students never completed the six years required for a mastership of arts, even though that degree was necessary if they wished to go on to study civil and canon law, medicine, philosophy, or theology. To gain a doctorate in theology took another eight years, with the result that few sought the degree. The method of study both in the arts and the advanced curriculums was the same: the close reading of prescribed texts—Aristotle's logical works in the arts course, *The Digest* in civil law, Gratian's *Decretum* in canon law, Abelard's *Sic et Non* in philosophy, and Lombard's *Sentences* in theology. These authorities were read, lectured upon, commented upon, compared, and disputed about. Truth had already been revealed by authority; logic was the special tool for harmonizing any discordances among authorities.

Historians have given the name scholasticism to the philosophy taught in the medieval universities. The name derives from the twelfth-century episcopal schools where this philosophy first emerged. Two great influences shaped scholasticism: the tradition of Greek logic and the doctrines of Christian theology. In essence, scholasticism was an attempt to apply the formal logic of Aristotle, with its syllogisms, definitions, and classifications, to the doctrines of the Church. The force of argument should buttress the authority of faith. This was a bold step away from the dictum of Tertullian, an early Father of the Church, who said: "I believe because it is absurd." Anselm, archbishop of Canterbury under Henry I, was one of the first to employ reason in the service of faith, but with Anselm reason remained subordinate to faith. With Peter Abelard reason appeared to assert an equality. In his famous *Sic et Non* he brought together the conflicting opinions of the Fathers on all the chief points of Christian doctrine. He did so to reconcile them, but the contradictions he exposed seemed to promote doubt. Abelard knew only the logical works of Aristotle. During the thirteenth century Aristotle's *Metaphysics* and works on science were translated. The Church reacted by condemning these works, which contained such heretical doctrines as the eternity of matter. In the 1270s, however, a Dominican scholar, Thomas Aquinas, wrote his *Summa Theologiae*, a work that reconciled reason and faith and synthesized Greek philosophy and Christian theology. Aquinas carried Aristotle's ideas to the furthest point tolerable to the Church—too far, in fact, for the Archbishop of Canterbury, who in 1277 condemned Aquinas's work at Oxford. A year later, however, Aquinas's supporters at Oxford secured his reinstatement. A more formidable critic of Aquinas was John Duns Scotus, a

Franciscan, a professor first at Oxford and then at Paris. He denied that reason could prove the existence of God or that the intellect could comprehend the nature of God. Scholasticism, as perfected by Aquinas in the thirteenth century, asserted the harmony of reason and faith. Duns Scotus, who lived into the next century, reasserted their separation.

HENRY III AND THE PROVISIONS OF OXFORD

While the master masons built their ribbed vaults and the friars preached their sermons and the scholars wrestled with Aristotle, Henry III reigned as King. He came to the throne at 9 years of age in 1216 and reigned until his death in 1272. The dominating theme of his reign was the conflict between his resolve to restore royal authority to what it had been before Magna Carta and the resolve of the barons to force him to take their advice. Because the reissue of Magna Carta in 1217 had dropped the provision for a baronial council, there was no obligation for the King to consult them. Yet during Henry's long minority the barons had grown accustomed to giving him counsel. Therefore when Henry in 1227 declared himself of age, turned for advice to courtiers, employed aliens from Poitou and Savoy, governed through the Household rather than the Exchequer and Treasury, and devised a private seal to circumvent the Lord Chancellor's Great Seal, the barons grew restless. Had Henry governed with conspicuous success the barons might have forgiven him, but he embarked on several wars in France which the barons did not want and which ended in disaster. Henry was a king of extravagant ambitions. Appreciating art, he lavished treasure on the building of palaces and castles; extremely devout, he rebuilt Westminster in the Gothic style. But he never learned to govern, being suspicious, opinionated, obtuse, and fickle. He was deaf to reason and blind to public opinion. His ineptness was particularly awkward at a time when the barons had come to see themselves not merely as tenants-in-chief of a great lord, but as spokesmen for the "community of the realm" to a sovereign king.

Two events precipitated the crisis that led to the Provisions of Oxford in 1258. One was Henry's grandiose scheme, urged upon him by the Pope, to win Sicily for his younger son. Edmund; the other was a run of bad harvests. The year 1255 saw a good crop, but three bad harvests followed. Despite the people's distress, the King pursued his absurd Sicilian venture, raising vast sums from the clergy and a general aid from the kingdom. It was to no avail. No troops were raised and only a fraction of the huge sum promised the Pope was collected. His Sicilian policy bankrupt, bereft of allies, the Church alienated, Henry in 1258 yielded to the demands of a confederation of barons and knights. At a Great Council at Oxford these barons and knights, in the name of the commune of England, forced upon Henry the Provisions of Oxford, a reform program consisting of four chief provisions. There should be, first of all, a permanent council of fifteen, largely baronial, whose advice the King must follow in all affairs of state and who should name the Justiciar, Chancellor, and Treasurer. Secondly, the traditional officers should be restored and all revenues paid into the Exchequer, not into the King's Chamber or its subdepartment, the Wardrobe. Thirdly, a panel of four knights should be chosen in each shire court to hear complaints against sheriffs and other royal officials. Fourthly, the Great Council, whose meeting was now called a "parliament," should meet three times a year. The authors of the Provisions of Oxford were a few powerful magnates, but to gain the support of other classes they offered them benefits, such as an inquiry into sheriffs. But for the country gentlemen an inquiry into the misdeeds of royal officials was not enough; in 1259 they forced the magnates to agree to the reform of abuses on baronial estates as well.

The barons who forced the Provisions of Oxford on the King anticipated some twelve years of reform, but the period hardly lasted two. It came to an end because the King turned against the program and because the barons were too divided to resist him. The leadership of Simon de Montfort, the Earl of Leicester, in the reform movement contributed both to the King's rancor and the barons' divisions. Montfort had come to England twenty years before, a Frenchman ignorant of the English tongue though heir to the Leicester Earldom. Marriage to the King's sister made his fortune, but failure in the administration of Gascony turned the King against him. Montfort was a clear-thinking, methodical, just, even idealistic statesman, but he was also an arrogant and assertive person, who once said that the King should be confined at Windsor as an imbecile. His leadership of the reform movement certainly alienated Henry and prompted him in 1261 to persuade the Pope to release him from his oath to abide by the Provisions of Oxford. Henry then dismissed the Justiciar and Chancellor named by the barons and sent Montfort into exile. The barons did not oppose this, for a powerful group of them had come out against Montfort and the reform program. Henry, however, wasted his advantage by going to France instead of restoring order, ending discontent, and consolidating his authority.

This gave the younger barons an opportunity to invite Montfort to return to England, which he did in April 1263. Civil war was imminent, but neither side was prepared to wage it. They therefore agreed to arbitration by Louis IX of France, who, swayed by Henry's surrender of all claims in France north of the Loire and in Poitou, pronounced unconditionally in favor of Henry. Montfort rejected the judgment, assembled an army, and met the King in battle at Lewes, in Sussex. The King's son, the exuberant Prince Edward, routed the undisciplined throng of Londoners on Montfort's left, but then pursued them so far he could not return before Montfort had won the battle.

Montfort and his allies now created a Council of Nine to govern England, but it was not Montfort's intent to create an oligarchy. He wished rather to govern through the Great Council, meetings of which he summoned in 1264 and 1265. To these parliaments he summoned not only the barons and bishops, but knights of the shire and, in 1265, burgesses from the towns. He sought and found his support in the middle classes and in the clergy, among knights, burgesses, bishops, and scholars. But meanwhile he lost the support of the barons, who believed it disloyal to govern against the King's will and who feared an investigation into abuses on their own estates. The outcome was predictable: At Evesham on August 4, 1265, a royal army overwhelmed Montfort's small band, slew Montfort, and dismembered his body.

The Battle of Evesham swept away the Provisions of Oxford and restored Henry III to full authority. Guided now by his more prudent son, he exercised that authority more wisely during the last seven years of his reign. But Montfort's death and the abolition of the Provisions of Oxford did not mean that the reformers had acted wholly in vain. The idea that affairs of state should be discussed in great councils and that there should be a continuous co-operation between King and barons had taken root in England, not least of all in the mind of Prince Edward himself.

EDWARD I AND STATUTE LAW

Edward I was 35 years old when he came to the throne—tall, lithe, handsome, with a broad forehead and thick black hair. Though he spoke with a stammer, he possessed a ready eloquence. He was a brave and skillful warrior, a conscientious and wise king, and an intense and willful person. Above all, he had a keen interest in the law and a love of order and system. These two qualities led him to systematize the legal traditions of the past, much as Aquinas had systematized the philosophical and theological traditions of the past. The Common law had grown by precedents established by the decisions of judges in innumerable disputes. The King in his Council, of course, was the highest court, a court where remedies could be found for new abuses either by the invention of new writs or by the handing down of new judgments. Edward now chose a different path for establishing such remedies. He chose to modify, alter, and augment the Common law by means of statutes. A statute was a solemn declaration of the law by the King in his Council, and its significance lies in the fact that it could create new law. No doubt Alfred the Great and Henry II did, in fact, create new law, but in theory they were only declaring existing law. It was now recognized by judges, by litigants, and by jurists that the King in Council could create a new law, which would then become part of the existing Common law. Indeed, the growth of the Common law at the hands of the judges became less flexible because enacted law controlled judge-made law.

Edward used the new instrument of statute law for three basic purposes: to check the growth of private franchises, to define feudal relations, and to promote good local government.

There were in medieval England many kinds of courts: royal, ecclesiastical, manorial, borough, and franchisal. In the thirteenth century the Crown grew especially suspicious of the franchisal courts, which were held by private persons and exercised a variety of rights. Such a court might claim the view of frankpledge or the right to hang a thief caught red-handed or the right to summon the community to see if there were any criminals to be presented for trial. Such courts did not fit the theory put forward by Bracton in his *Laws and Customs of England* that all jurisdiction in the realm emanates from the King, that the King is the fountain of justice. The Earl of Warenne challenged Bracton's theory by producing the old, rusty sword with which his ancestors had won their judicial rights, but though history was on the earl's side, Edward acted on Bracton's theory. He launched a searching inquiry into all private jurisdictions, ordering his justices to ask every man by what warrant (*quo warranto*) he held his franchise. In 1278 he gave legislative authority to the principle of *quo warranto* in the Statute of Gloucester, which asserted that no franchise was to be exercised until its holder had justified it before the King's justices. Edward, however, did not intend to destroy franchises, only to limit them. Faced with baronial opposition to the Statute of Gloucester, he accepted a compromise in the Statute of *Quo Warranto* in 1290. By this statute a franchise holder, if he could prove possession since time immemorial, which meant in practice before the accession of Richard I, was entitled to a royal charter confirming his franchise. Franchises continued, but they were brought within an ordered system of royal justice.

Edward I also used statute law to bring order to the law of feudalism. Most land in England was held by feudal tenure, but the cost of armor had become so great and the average knight's fee so subdivided that it became impractical to exact knight service. Even scutage became difficult to collect. Edward acknowledged these changes by replacing the personal obligations of feudalism with territorial obligations. In the Statute of Winchester in 1285, he and his Council declared that all who held land worth £15 a year, whether the tenure was feudal or not, must maintain the horse and equipment of a knight (though a later effort to make all landlords worth more than £20 liable for service on horseback met stout resistance). Edward also cut boldly through the complexities of subinfeudation by declaring in 1290 in the Statute of *Quia Emptores* that henceforth no man could create a new feudal tenure. If B held land of A, he could grant it to C only if he dropped out of the chain and allowed C to hold directly of A. This brought the process of subinfeudation to a halt, and as land escheated to the primary lord all tenures were brought nearer the King.

In enacting these two statutes Edward was not pursuing a consciously antifeudal policy; he was only seeking order. *Quia Emptores* was enacted at the instance of the baronage, as was the Statute of Mortmain in 1279. This statute forbad a layman to sell or grant to the Church, for once land fell onto its hands there was an end to wardship, marriage, and escheat. In theory the proscription was complete; in practice a layman could secure a royal license to sell or grant land to a religious corporation. Knight service may have become an anachronism, but feudal incidents were still prized by King and barons alike.

Resolved to bring good government to his subjects, Edward in 1274 ordered an inquiry into local government. He thereby opened a Pandora's box of complaints against extortionate sheriffs, corrupt bailiffs, negligent coroners, and inept escheators. To remedy these abuses, Edward and his Council enacted the Statutes of Westminster I (1275), Gloucester (1278), and Westminster II (1285), great omnibus statutes that declared illegal a host of abuses. But Edward soon discovered what reformers in every age have discovered, that the evil often lies in corrupt men, not in the system. In 1289, he therefore appointed a special judicial commission to try corrupt justices, exchequer officials, and sheriffs. Before the commission had finished its work, ten justices were found guilty and dismissed. But Edward was not content merely to enact new law and punish corrupt officials; he also appointed new local officials, called keepers of the peace. They were drawn from the local gentry, and it was their duty to keep order, apprehend criminals, and present them to royal justices. Edward went further. In the Statute of Winchester he made the burden of catching criminals and bringing them to justice fall squarely on the whole community. If a hundred failed to bring a murderer or a robber to justice within forty days, it must pay a penalty. Edward meant that his kingdom should be well governed and all his subjects have justice.

WALES, GASCONY, AND SCOTLAND

Edward I made two great contributions toward the creation of the modern English state. One was the development of statute law; the other was the conquest of Wales.

Edward did not launch a premeditated war of aggression against Wales. War came when the proud and ambitious Prince Llywelyn, grandson of Llywelyn the Great, refused to do homage to Edward for his principality and to pay the 3000 marks required annually by the Treaty of Montgomery of 1267. Edward, on his part, was determined to assert his overlordship of Wales. War broke out in July 1277. Edward fought a brilliantly successful campaign; then the war came abruptly to an end in November. The Treaty of Conway followed, in which Edward, not being bent on conquest, allowed Llywelyn to rule a diminished Principality of Gwynedd in north Wales. The treaty proved to be only a truce. Bitter quarrels soon arose between the marcher lords and Llywelyn over the disposition of property and the question of whether Welsh princes should appeal their disputes to Llywelyn or to Edward. It was Llywelyn's brother, David, who precipitated war in 1282 by seizing Hawarden Castle and riding through Wales calling for revolt. All free Wales rose with him.

Edward's campaign in 1283 was as brilliantly successful as that of 1277. There were four good reasons for his success. To begin with, he mixed cavalry and archers in a new and effective way. He used the archers to break the ene-

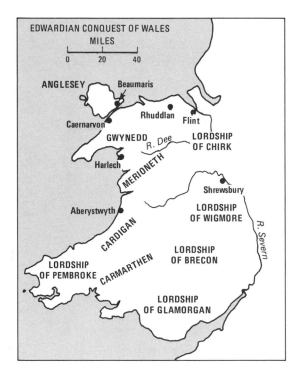

my's cavalry and his own cavalry to pursue the enemy's broken forces. Secondly, he adopted a well-designed strategy of allowing the marcher lords to clear the south while he marched along the north coast of Wales and laid seige to Llywelyn's stronghold in Snowdonia. Thirdly, he had command of the sea, which kept his troops supplied and which allowed him to cut off the island of Anglesey, with its grain, from Snowdonia. Fourthly, he had behind him the resources of an England more united, more populous, and wealthier than ever before. For the core of his army, the cavalry, he relied on the feudal host, but in fact there were in England only a few hundred knights, even though there were thousands of knight fees. Edward therefore increasingly employed a salaried army. The army with which he conquered Wales was composed of levies of free men, who were paid wages and who were divided into battalions of 1000, companies of 100, and lesser groups of 20, each under a designated officer.

The defeat of the Welsh in 1283, the death of Llywelyn that year, and the trial and execution of David in 1284 opened the way for a permanent settlement in Wales. The King through his justices now ruled North Wales, Cardiganshire, and Carmarthenshire directly. Edward introduced English criminal law into the new shires and hundreds that were created in this area, though Welsh tenants continued to hold their land by Welsh law. The rest of Wales remained in the hands of the marcher lords. Each lordship consisted of a large

Caernarvon Castle from the air (*Aerofilms Limited*).

territory occupied by Welsh tenants but centered on an English manor or borough. Nothing, however, did more to guarantee English ascendancy than the line of great stone castles Edward built—at Flint, at Rhuddlan, at Aberystwith, at Harlech, at Caernavon, and at Beaumaris. And with these imposing fortifications, the art of castle building in the West reached perfection. Their designers abandoned the motte-and-bailey principle for that of the concentric curtain wall, a thick, high wall surrounding a large central space. Built into the walls were massive towers, with loopholes from which archers could cover all approaches to the castle. Entry into the castle across the moat surrounding it was defended by a complicated system of drawbridges and gates. By means of these splendid castles Edward fastened his grip upon Wales.

The year 1293 marks a turning point in Edward's reign. Unitl then he pursued goals within his power to achieve; thereafter his unbridled ambitions taxed English resources beyond endurance. Gascony was a case in point. Edward held Gascony as a vassal of the king of France, Philip IV, with whom he maintained good relations until 1293. In that year a dispute arose between English and Gascon ships on the one hand and Norman ships on the other, a dispute Philip sought to settle in his court at Paris. As overlord of Gascony, he summoned Edward to appear in Paris; but Edward, though quick to assert his rights as overlord in Wales, refused to appear. Philip thereupon seized Gascony. Edward replied by planning a great expedition to recover it. He taxed the clergy and laity directly and formed alliances with Flanders, Brabant, and Nas-

Harlech Castle from the south. Originally the sea washed the foot of the rocky hill on which it stands (*A.F. Kersting*).

sau. But the country resisted taxation and the nobility refused to serve in Gascony. In 1297 Edward took an army to Gascony but accomplished little. After five years of negotiations he recovered Gascony, but only on condition that he recognize Philip as his overlord.

The war in Scotland, also the result of Edward's ambitions, explains in large part his failure in Gascony. In 1290 Margaret, the heir to the Scottish crown, died, leaving a disputed succession. This gave Edward an opportunity to assert his overlordship over Scotland by acting as arbitrator in the dispute, an arbitration that the Scottish nobility welcomed. After hearing some dozen claimants, Edward in 1292 awarded the Crown to John Balliol. But the nemesis of power revealed itself; Edward's pride drove him ever onwards. He treated Balliol not as a king but as a puppet, hearing in London appeals from Scottish subjects and ordering Balliol to raise money in Scotland for the Gascon venture. The Scots answered by allying with France in 1295, an act that goaded Edward into laying siege to Berwick-on-Tweed, capturing it, and indiscriminately butchering its inhabitants. He then marched into Scotland, secured Balliol's abdication, and declared himself King.

Edward's triumph proved as empty as it was swift. Led not by a nobleman but by a mere gentleman, William Wallace, the Scottish people defied English power. In 1297 Wallace defeated an English army at Stirling Bridge. Edward avenged this defeat the next year at Falkirk, but did not capture Wallace. Only

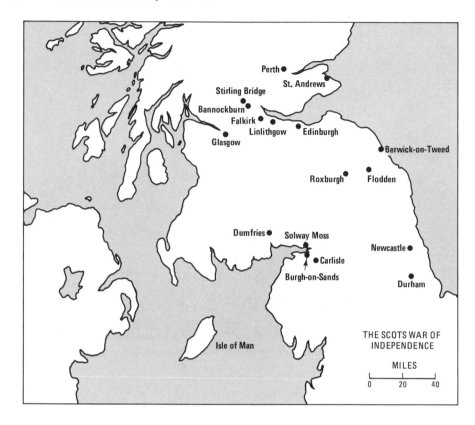

Perth

St. Andrews

Stirling Bridge

Bannockburn

Falkirk

Linlithgow   Edinburgh

Glasgow

Berwick-on-Tweed

Roxburgh   Flodden

Dumfries   Solway Moss

Newcastle

Carlisle

Burgh-on-Sands

Durham

Isle of Man

THE SCOTS WAR OF
INDEPENDENCE

MILES

0   20   40

by sending armies to Scotland in 1300, 1301, 1303, and 1305 was he able to capture Wallace and secure the homage of the bulk of the Scottish nobility. But this work was suddenly undone when in 1306 Robert Bruce, a powerful Scottish nobleman, claimed the Crown of Scotland and put himself at the head of a movement for Scottish independence. Edward set out once again for Scotland, but died, aged 68, at Burgh-on Sands.

Scotland was Edward's greatest blunder. When he came to the throne, he found two kingdoms that had not been involved in a serious quarrel with each other for a century. Before his death he had created antagonisms that were to last for two centuries and a half.

THE ORIGINS OF PARLIAMENT

The war in Scotland and the expedition to Gascony were immensely expensive, thus compelling Edward to summon Parliaments to get the money he needed. The word "parliament" (derived from the French *parler*, to talk) first came into common use in the middle of the thirteenth century, when it described an occasion, not an institution. That occasion was a parleying or meeting between the King and his notables in the Great Council. The composition of the Great Council was much the same as the Curia Regis of the Norman kings: the King himself, the bishops and abbots, and the earls and greater barons, to whom were now added a bureaucratic element, the members of the King's inner council who were neither barons nor tenants-in-chief. It was this body that the barons in the Provisions of Oxford had demanded should meet three times a year. The functions of a parliament were political, judicial, legislative, and fiscal. Parliaments met to give the King counsel—Edward even wrote the Pope that he could do nothing affecting the rights of the realm without such counsel. Parliament was judicially important because it was the highest court in the land, before which all important and difficult cases were heard. Even the ordinary freeman, if he found no appropriate writ to bring his case before the Common law courts, could bring it before Parliament by petition. Under Edward, Parliament became important legislatively, for he sought its assent in the enactment of his great statutes.

Yet it was the fiscal duties of Parliament that transformed it from an aristocratic assembly into a representative institution. And it was the growing scale and costs of war that created those fiscal duties. In the twelfth century the kings of England relied upon their prerogative revenues, among them rents from estates, profits of justice, purveyance (the right to buy provisions at a cheap rate), scutage (money paid to the King in lieu of performing military service in person), and the tallage (an arbitrary tax on the King's demesne and boroughs). The income from these sources, however, was not enough to pay for the mounting costs of wars and foreign ventures. An expedition to France might cost £50,000, nearly double the King's annual revenue. The kings of England in the thirteenth century therefore turned to taxes that were national, not feudal, that fell upon all free men, not just tenants-in-chief. The most important of these was the lay subsidy, a tax assessed upon the income and movable property of all free men. In the year 1207 John collected the first such subsidy, a thirteenth of the income and movable property of all free Englishmen. Henry III levied such subsidies on seven occasions. The King now had at his command revenues many times greater than he had been able to collect from his estates and feudal rights.

To justify such taxation the kings of England pleaded necessity: in a time of emergency the King had a duty to defend the realm and his subjects an obligation to support him in that defense. In the late twelfth century lawyers, both canon and civilian, popularized this doctrine of necessity, which became a common assumption among the political classes. But two questions arose. Who was to judge when an emergency existed? And did necessity override the rights of property? To the first question the canon and civilian lawyers answered that, since the tax touched upon all, the ruler must submit the plea of necessity to the counsel and consent of a representative assembly. And Henry III did seek the counsel and consent of the Great Council to the subsidies he collected. To the second question the lawyers answered that necessity did override the rights of property if the King's subjects assented to the plea of necessity.

During the reign of Henry III lay subsidies were exceptional, and so acceptable, but during Edward I's reign they became regular, and so burdensome. To find the means to recover Gascony, Edward collected lay subsidies in 1294, in 1295, and again in 1296. He also taxed the income of the clergy, a tax which John had first collected, which usually consisted of a tenth of the annual incomes of cathedrals, abbeys, and rectories, and which required the consent of the clergy. In 1294 Edward likewise imposed a customs duty on wool for three years, a tax beyond and above the 6 shillings, 8 pence on every sack of wool exported that Parliament had voted Edward in 1275. These three taxes—the lay subsidy, the tax on the clergy, and the customs—had this in common: They required the consent of those taxed, a consent given only if the King could prove that the realm was in peril.

The clergy were the first to resist Edward's demands, first in 1296 and again in 1297. On both occasions they pleaded the papal bull, *Clericis Laicos*, in which Pope Boniface VIII condemned royal taxation of clerical wealth. Edward replied with a long exposition of the doctrine of necessity, and wrested a subsidy from the clergy by threatening them with outlawry if they did not grant it.

The mounting political crisis came to a head in 1297 when Edward, to gain support for a campaign in Flanders, extended the obligation of personal military service to all men with an annual income from land of £20 or more, ordered all wool in merchants' hands to be seized and sold for his profit, and sought to collect a tax from the laity without their consent. The magnates now joined with the clergy to resist Edward. In a Remonstrance the magnates brought together the kingdom's grievances—the extension of military service, the seizure of wool, lay and clerical taxes—and declared that the war in Flanders was an attack on a foreign realm, not a defense of England, and so did not justify these acts.

In August 1297 Edward sailed to Flanders, leaving behind him Regents to govern the realm. From these Regents the opposition, growing in strength daily, wrested a Confirmation of Magna Carta and the Forest Charter. In this Confirmation of the Charters Edward bound himself never again to take subsidies, increase the customs, or seize property "except by the common assent of the realm." During the last ten years of his reign, Edward, growing ever more grasping as he sank into bankruptcy, repeatedly violated the Confirmation of the Charters. But the principle of consent survived him, to be of incalculable importance in the history of the English-speaking peoples on both sides of the Atlantic.

The Confirmation of the Charters said nothing about how the common assent of the realm was to be secured. During most of the thirteenth century the Great Council voiced that assent. The magnates who sat on that council were the King's natural counsellors, with a right to give the King counsel on all affairs of state, including the necessity of taxation in an emergency. But by

Edward I meets his Parliament in 1295 (*New York Public Library*).

1295 matters had changed; knights of the shire and burgesses from the towns, meeting in Parliament, had been brought into the common counsel, which was needed for the grant of a subsidy or the customs. Four developments brought about this change. In the first place, both Henry III and Edward I imposed military obligations upon all free landholders, not just their tenants-in-chief, thereby instilling in the knights of the realm an awareness of their responsibility for the defense of the realm. Secondly, the new national taxes infringed upon the property rights of all free Englishmen, an infringement that could only be justified by securing the consent to the taxes of their representatives. Thirdly, the consent of the representatives of the shires and towns proved administratively useful in the collection of the taxes. And finally, the baronial opposition, in order to justify its opposition to the Crown, sought the support of the knights and burgesses. The result of these developments was the meeting of the "Model" Parliament of 1295, which included magnates, bishops, councillors, knights of the shire, burgesses from the towns, and proctors elected to represent the lesser clergy. But it must not be thought that the knights and burgesses played a central role in such a parliament. The magnates still resolved whether the King's plea of necessity was valid. Having done so they laid the case of necessity before the knights and burgesses, whose assent was largely formal. Yet the knights and burgesses could insist that the sum granted not impoverish the subject and they might seek the redress of their grievances. From these few and formal duties the later House of Commons was to grow.

FURTHER READING

SIR MAURICE POWICKE. *The Thirteenth Century 1216–1307*. Oxford, 1953. A monumental work, combining an intimate knowledge of those who made history with the grand themes of political life; the vast amount of detail makes it demanding reading.

AUSTIN LANE POOLE, ed. *Medieval England*. Rev. ed., 2 vols., Oxford, 1958. Nineteen essays on various aspects of medieval civilization, such as geography, architecture, towns, armor, costume, coins, heraldry, art, handwriting, and printing.

*DORIS MARY STENTON. *English Society in the Early Middle Ages*. 3rd. ed., Penguin Books, 1962. A charmingly written and scholarly account of English society, with chapters on barons and knights, villagers, towns, the Church, and the arts of peace.

M.M. POSTAN. *The Medieval Economy and Society: An Economic History of Britain in the Middle Ages*. London, 1972. A demographic interpretation of history, arguing that the growth and decline of population shaped prices, wages, and social relations; stimulating and persuasive.

H.Z. TITOW. *English Rural Society*. London, 1969. Half the book contains carefully chosen documents, the other half clearly written introductory essays; favors the Postan thesis.

R. ALLEN BROWN. *English Medieval Castles*. 3rd rev. ed., London, 1976. Long the standard work and still the best; discusses the domestic use as well as the military; excellent illustrations.

DAVID KNOWLES. *The Religious Orders in England*. Cambridge, England, 1948. Continues the history of the Benedictine Order and the Cistercians, to which he adds the history of the rise of the Friars; the prodigious learning is lightly borne.

R.F. TRAHERNE. *The Baronial Plan of Reform, 1258–1263*. Manchester, England, 1932. A detailed and vivid history of the barons' gradually developing plan of reform; highly favorable to the barons, who are depicted as noble and idealistic.

MICHAEL PRESTWICH. *War, Politics, and France Under Edward I*. London, 1972. An important book, partly because it describes the size of armies, the costs of war, and the burden of taxation, and partly because it corrects Powicke's uncritical portrait of Edward.

HARRY ROTHWELL, ed. *English Historical Documents 1189–1327*. London, 1975. Contains chronicles, public records, ecclesiastical records; emphasizes political and legal history at the expense of social, economic, and intellectual history.

7 War
and Crisis:
1307-1399

The fourteenth century brought an end to the expansion which characterized the thirteenth century and witnessed an erosion of the confidence and assured values which then reigned. As early as the second decade of the century, population began to decline and rents to fall. There followed a prolonged and exhausting war with France, in the midst of which the plague descended upon England, reducing its population by nearly a third between 1350 and 1400. Other forces were also at work to undermine the old order. The longbow, first used at Falkirk in 1298, helped to undermine the military basis of feudalism. Economic depression and the unprofitability of demesne farming eroded manorial institutions in the countryside. A distinctive English language promoted a national consciousness that undermined the cosmopolitanism of the early Middle Ages. And finally, a new, wealthy, educated laity, composed of gentlemen, merchants, and lawyers, showed an increasing interest in the material world and expressed a virulent anticlericalism. Out of the crises and dislocations of the fourteenth century arose new values and new institutions—nationalism, capitalism, individualism, anticlericalism—that were to find fruition in the sixteenth century.

Amidst this change there was also continuity. The monarchy remained, for the barons in the reigns of Edward II and Richard II sought not to destroy monarchy, but to capture its machinery. There also remained the medieval ideals of the rule of law and of government by the consent of the communities of the realm, ideals that survived all attacks on them. Out of the decay of the old order emerged a new order, though one which incorporated something of the old.

EDWARD II AND THE BARONS

During the fourteenth century the power of the aristocracy increased as that of the Crown diminished. This process began during the reign of Edward II, who came to the throne in 1307 and was deposed and murdered in 1327. The civil strife and political dissensions of Edward II's reign cannot be attributed solely to his political ineptness, for his father left him problems the ablest of kings might not have solved. The Crown was deeply in debt because of costly wars fought in the past; it was also committed to an aggressive foreign policy in Scotland that could be reversed only with dishonor and continued only with bankruptcy. Furthermore, the barons, whom Edward I had angered with his autocratic rule, were ready to seize any opportunity to recover the authority and privileges they believed to be rightfully theirs. Whether an able king could have solved these problems is doubtful; what is certain is that Edward II was totally unfit to do so. He had no head for business and allowed his feelings to shape

A painting of the coronation of a King, probably Edward II in 1308. The King, whom the Bishop anoints, holds the orb and the scepter (*The Master and Fellows of Corpus Christi College, Cambridge*).

his political conduct. He may have been a homosexual; he certainly fell under the influence of ingratiating young men. He was indifferent to knightly pursuits, preferring such unaristocratic activities as swimming, rowing, play-acting, and thatching barns. He further offended the barons by fraternizing with singers, actors, carters, and oarsmen.

The barons had come to mistrust Edward even before he came to the throne, with the result that they demanded from him an unprecedented coronation oath. They made him swear to observe the laws the community of the realm should determine in the future. But this safeguard could not prevent the new King from displaying his affection for, and placing his trust in, a young Gascon knight of caustic wit and tactless vanity named Piers Gaveston. Though Gaveston flaunted his greatness by walking immediately before Edward, resplendent in purple and pearls, at the coronation, it was not his vanity against which the barons protested but his monopoly of the King's counsel. They regarded themselves as the King's rightful counselors and resented his reliance on court favorites. By March 1310 their resentment had grown so great that they forced upon Edward a committee of twenty-one (seven bishops, eight earls, and six barons), who were to draw up ordinances designed to remove the causes of past misgovernment and prevent their recurrence. In 1311 the committee presented a draft of forty-one ordinances to Parliament and King, who accepted them—the King only reluctantly.

The chief thrust of the ordinances was to prevent "bad and deceitful counsel." The ordinances therefore provided for the removal of evil counselors, the banishment of Gaveston, and the appointment of counselors and royal officials with "the counsel and assent of the baronage and that in Parliament." Far from solving England's problems, the ordinances led only to further strife, for Edward did not intend to abide by them. He tried to name a treasurer without the assent of the barons and he summoned Gaveston back from exile. The more extreme among the barons seized Gaveston, held a mock trial, and executed him in 1312. Two years later Edward, in order to bring relief to the English forces in Stirling Castle, marched north against the Scots. Victory would bring him the popular support he needed to resist the barons; defeat would destroy his prestige. Unhappily for Edward, he failed at the Battle of Bannockburn to protect his archers, who were driven back in confusion on the men-at-arms, who fled from the field in terror. The humiliating defeat at Bannockburn guaranteed the independence of Scotland and compelled Edward to accept new limitations on his power at the hands of the lords ordainers, as the members of the committee of twenty-one were now called.

Between 1314 and 1322 the barons demonstrated that they were hardly more fit to rule England than the King and Gaveston. The Scots countinued their raids into England, taxes and the cost of bread (as a result of crop failures in 1315 and 1316) remained high, and there was no real attempt to implement the ordinances. The explanation for the failure of the barons is threefold. In the first place, they were divided—by personal quarrels, by regional loyalties, and between extremists and moderates. Even their motives were mixed, being an amalgam of concern for good government and the pursuit of selfish interests. In the second place, they sought to govern from outside the Court and Household, where real power lay and where the daily decisions of government were made. Finally, they could not win over Edward, who remained hostile to their endeavors and who soon found a new favorite, Hugh Despenser, to help him throw off their yoke. The favors he showered on Despenser briefly united the barons against the new favorite, and in 1321 a Parliament they dominated ordered his banishment. But the next year he returned to help Edward who, showing an unaccustomed vigor, raised an army and marched against the barons. At Boroughbridge, by combining archers with dismounted men-at-arms and pike-men, he defeated the barons. He promptly called a Parliament at York, which annulled the ordinances and restored the authority of the King.

Edward soon squandered the authority he had regained. The government of the realm fell into the hands of Hugh Despenser and a Household clique. The government did little to remove old grievances. Relations with France and Scotland deteriorated. Meanwhile Hugh Despenser, by trickery and force, built up an empire in South Wales. His territorial ambitions soon united the marcher lords and the northern magnates, whose divisions in 1322 had given Edward his victory. Edward had no idea how narrow the basis of his power was. Otherwise he would not have sent Queen Isabella to France to negotiate a treaty with her brother, the French king. The queen had no love for Edward, who during the last years of his reign had grown to hate her—it was even said he

The alabaster effigy of Edward II in Gloucester Cathedral (*A. F. Kersting*).

carried a knife in his stocking with which to kill her. She now allied, in bed as well as in politics, with Roger Mortimer, a marcher lord who had escaped to Paris from the Tower. With the young Prince Edward (whom Edward had foolishly allowed to join his mother in Paris) at their side, they invaded England in 1326. The magnates of the realm, almost to a man, joined them, as did the King's own brothers. The invaders soon dispersed the royal forces, seized and hanged Despenser, and captured the King.

They then summoned a Parliament in the King's name, which charged Edward with being incompetent, accepting evil counsel, rejecting good counsel, injuring the Church, losing Scotland, and breaking his coronation oath. A delegation from the Parliament demanded that he abdicate in favor of his son, or else his subjects would renounce their homage and fealty to him and his heirs. Edward, astonished at this widespread disloyalty, agreed to abdicate. Nine months later Mortimer's henchmen cruelly murdered him in Berkeley Castle. The deposition of Edward II was an unprecedented and illegal act, for as Bracton had written, God alone could punish a King. Yet it was an act of profound constitutional significance, for by it the community of the realm served notice on future kings that they were to govern by the law, of which Parliament was the guardian.

EDWARD III AND THE HUNDRED YEARS' WAR

Edward III was very unlike his father. Where Edward II delighted in unknightly pursuits, his son loved war, jousting, tournaments, and the chase. Where Edward II surrounded himself with courtiers and artisans, his son sought the comradeship of warriors, magnates, and chivalrous knights. Where Edward II eschewed the advice of his barons, his son sought it and won popularity by conforming to their tastes and ideals. Edward III was not a great king, nor a man of notable foresight or intellectual ability, but he was a brave knight whose ambitions coincided with the temper of the time.

For the first three years of his reign, Edward was under the tutelage of Isabella and Mortimer, who governed England. But in 1330, resentful of Mortimer's hold on the government and disgusted by his mother's behavior, he allied with some of the younger nobility and seized power. He placed his mother in comfortable retirement and had Mortimer tried and hanged. For the first time in twenty-three years, England enjoyed the personal rule of an able monarch. He was a monarch eager to win victories on the field of battle and to prove himself a great warrior. His first efforts were in Scotland, where in 1332 and 1333 he won glorious victories, but he soon discovered that the French were openly supporting the Scots. He thereupon decided (in the words of the historian George Macaulay Trevelyan) that "to pick the famous lily was an enterprise of more profit, ease, and honour than to pluck the recalcitrant thistle."

French support for Scotland was the occasion for the outbreak of war with

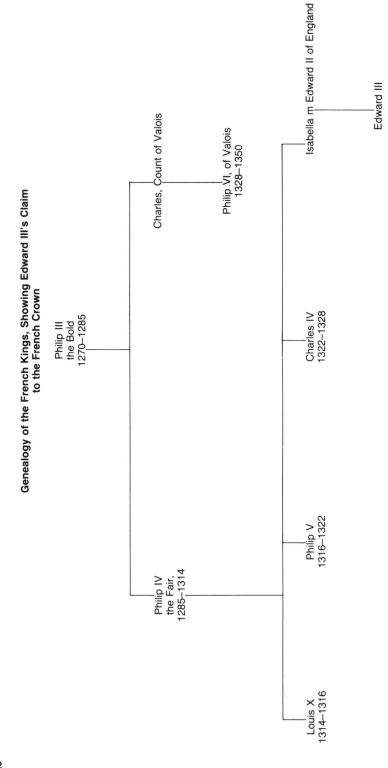

Genealogy of the French Kings, Showing Edward III's Claim to the French Crown

Philip III
the Bold
1270–1285

Charles, Count of Valois

Philip VI, of Valois
1328–1350

Philip IV
the Fair,
1285–1314

Isabella m Edward II of England

Edward III

Charles IV
1322–1328

Philip V
1316–1322

Louis X
1314–1316

France in 1337, but it was not the fundamental cause. Neither was the appeal of the Flemish towns for aid from Edward III against the King of France. Least of all was Edward III's claim to the French succession a cause, for Edward had recognized Philip VI as the rightful successor in 1329 and did not voice his claim until the war was two years old. The fundamental cause of the Hundred Years' War was the determination of Philip VI to subordinate Edward's ducal authority in Aquitaine to his own royal authority and Edward's equally firm resolve to retain his independence there. This was the central issue, but there may well have been deeper motives at work in Edward and his barons: a delight in the excitement of war, a love of the comradeship of the camp, a hope for glory and renown.

Edward opened the war on a grandiose scale. By raining money on them, he built up a great alliance of princes in the Rhineland and the Low Countries; and he won the support of the cloth towns of Flanders by threatening to forbid the export of English wool to Flanders unless they turned against France. But these alliances proved more costly than useful and the revolt of the Flemish towns against their pro-French count proved of little use. Furthermore, the Exchequer soon ran out of money. Edward had nothing to show for the immense sums spent between 1337 and 1341 other than a shattering defeat of the French fleet at Sluys in 1340—and he made little use of this victory.

From 1342 onward Edward pursued a different strategy, one which the resources of England could afford. He conducted raids for plunder and pillage deep into France. It was on such a raid in 1346 that Edward, with a small army

The Battle of Crécy as represented by an illustration in Jean Froissart's *The Chronicles of England, France, and Spain (Bibliothèque Nationale, Paris).*

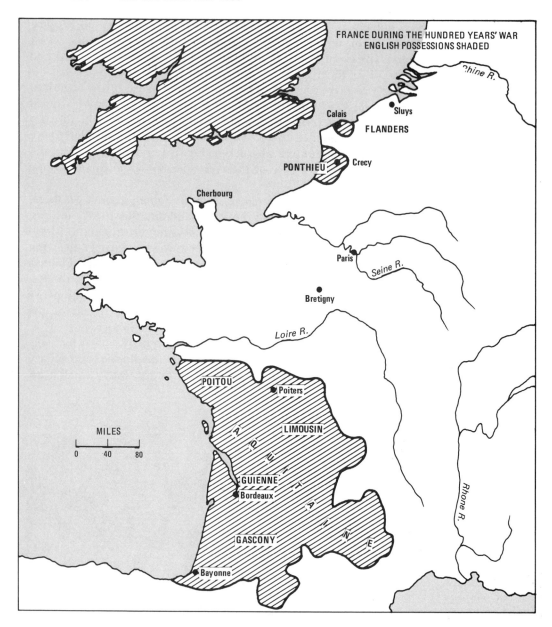

FRANCE DURING THE HUNDRED YEARS' WAR
ENGLISH POSSESSIONS SHADED

of 7000 archers, 1000 lances, and 1700 horse, met the French King, who led a much larger army, at Crécy in northern France. In the battle that followed the skilled English longbowmen broke the charge of the mounted French knights, who were then slaughtered by the dismounted English men-at-war. It was a victory for the tactics Edward I had used at Falkirk and Edward II at Boroughbridge, tactics that rested on the devasting power of the longbow. The longbow was made of yew wood, stood about five feet high, and shot an arrow a yard long. In skilled hands, it could shoot six arrows a minute with a force sufficient, at 200 yards, to pierce an inch of wood or the armor of a knight. The longbow not only won Edward a glorious victory but helped to end 500 years of supremacy for the mounted knight.

Ten years after Crécy, Edward's son, the Black Prince, won an even more resounding victory at Poitiers. Using the same tactics as his father had used at Crécy, he routed the French army and captured the King of France. Political disunity, social unrest, the plague, and marauding bands of English soldiers (called free companies) soon plunged France into a desolation that forced her to sue for peace. By the Treaty of Brétigny in 1360 Edward renounced his claim to the French throne, but in return received full sovereignty over a much enlarged Aquitaine, which now included Gascony, Poitou, and Limousin. In northern France he received Calais, Ponthieu, and Guines. The French further agreed to ransom their King for the vast sum of £500,000, equivalent to the English King's revenues for five years.

The explanation for the remarkable success of the English in these years does not lie solely in the superiority of their tactics. Other factors favored the English, such as the disputed succession in Brittany, the disloyalty of Charles of Navarre to the Valois kings, the simplicity of King John of France, and the remarkable support Englishmen of every class, but particularly the nobility, gave Edward III's continental campaigns. This support was the more effective because Edward no longer sought to raise his armies by feudal levy. He employed instead the indenture system. By this system the King entered into private contracts with different captains, usually noblemen, who undertook to raise a certain number of soldiers for long-term service. The feudal levy was hard to assemble and was undisciplined when it met; the new system encouraged discipline and subordination to the commander. To an increasing extent the war was fought by professional soldiers, for whom fighting was a livelihood.

The remarkable gains confirmed by the Treaty of Brétigny proved to be ephemeral. By Edward III's death in 1377, England had lost all its possessions in France except for the coastal areas around Calais, Cherbourg, Bordeaux, and Bayonne. The truth is England did not have the resources to conquer France, and raids were no substitute for a military occupation. Once France found an able King in Charles V, an able general in Bertrand du Guesclin, and an appropriate strategy in guerrilla warfare, the days of English triumphs were numbered. The English found it increasingly difficult to raise money for campaigns that brought little success and less profit, while France was swept by a great wave of determination to expel the English.

The war in France exercised an important influence on life in England. Though unprofitable overall, because it employed men in unproductive labor, diverted shipping from its normal use, and threw the wool trade into confusion, it did redistribute income. The common soldier drew his wages, the nobility profited by plunder and ransom (the Black Prince gained £20,000 from the ransom of the French noblemen captured at Poitiers), and contractors grew wealthy furnishing the armies with food and clothing. The war also, by provoking a hatred of foreigners, promoted the growth of a national consciousness. But the most profound effect of all was to make a bankrupt Crown dependent on Parliament.

THE EVOLUTION OF PARLIAMENT

At the beginning of his reign, Edward III faced a difficult dilemma. Either he could choose to defend Gascony and go to war against France, in which case he would soon exhaust the resources of the Crown and be forced to rely on taxes voted by Parliament, or he could pursue a policy of peace, in which case he would injure his prestige and provoke the opposition of the barons. He chose war, but the extraordinary demands for money occasioned by war forced him to meet Parliament often, with the result that it grew in power and stature.

By 1307 Parliament existed as a recognizable body of lords and officials, meeting with the King to discuss great affairs of state, to which knights and burgesses were often, but not always, invited. When they came they came as suitors more than participants. From this body during the fourteenth century emerged a Parliament with a hereditary House of Lords and a representative House of Commons, each possessing its powers and privileges. The House of Lords grew out of the feudal obligation of tenants-in-chief to perform suit to court. During the thirteenth century a distinction arose between the greater barons, who received an individual writ summoning them to Parliament, and the lesser barons, who were not summoned, even though Magna Carta prescribed that they should be. Edward I called to Parliament only the greater magnates whom he wished to call, but in Edward III's reign these magnates, now calling themselves peers, demanded that they always be summoned, a demand to which Edward acceded. By the end of the fourteenth century the right to a writ summoning one to the House of Lords became hereditary, descending, as feudal property did, by primogeniture. The King could, and Edward III did, create new peers, either under the older titles of Baron and Earl, or under the newer titles of Duke and Marquess (to which Viscount was added in the fifteenth century). There were in Parliament in the fourteenth century some forty to fifty lay peers, which meant that the spiritual peers, made up of two archbishops, eighteen bishops, and numerous abbots, occasionally outnumbered the lay peers. In 1305 some seventy-five abbots attended, though by the end of the Middle Ages only about twenty came. Judges and other royal officials, who dominated the Parliaments of the thirteenth century, declined in number and power; as many as thirty sat in Edwards I's Parliament, only about ten in Edwards III's, and they sat only as advisers.

The House of Lords exercised various powers: it heard important judicial cases, corrected errors made by lower courts, gave the King advice, consented to taxes, and enacted statutes. The critical moment in the development of these powers came in the reign of Edward II. Under Edward I it was uncertain whether the magnates were present in Parliament as petitioners or decision-makers. Under Edward II the magnates resolved this ambiguity in their own favor; they became the decision-makers and thereby augmented the power of the aristocracy. Since the magnates alone, with the King, were the decision-makers, it followed that the lesser landowners, who did not share such power, could not sit in the House of Lords. Instead, as knights of the shire, they joined the burgesses in the House of Commons.

In 1307 the Commons were not a necessary part of Parliament. Often they were not summoned, and when summoned merely appeared before the King's councilors in Parliament to answer questions. By 1399 they were invariably summoned, met separately in their own House, deliberated, presented common petitions, and voted taxes. Their regular attendance began in the later years of Edward II's reign, when King and magnates vied for the support of the Commons. But it was Edward III's desire for their cooperation in the collection of taxes that ensured they would become a permanent part of Parliament.

At first the burgesses met alone, for the knights of the shire met with the barons and the lower clergy sat as a separate body. It appeared that the English Parliament, like similar bodies on the Continent, would be composed of the three estates (clergy, nobility, and commoners) meeting separately. But it was not to be, since the clergy ceased attending Parliament (preferring to vote taxes in Convocation), and the knights discovered they had more in common with the burgesses than with the barons. By 1339 the knights of the shire, who were elected in the shire court by the leading men of the county, met together with the burgesses, who were elected by the oligarchy of merchants who dominated borough government. It was a development unique in Europe, a development that helps explain why Parliament survived in England when similar institutions disappeared elsewhere.

The first power gained by the Commons was control over taxation. In 1297 the magnates, in the Confirmation of the Charters, had enunciated the principle that the King could not levy any aids, taxes, or prizes without the consent of the realm, though they did not specify how that consent should be expressed. By the reign of Edward III it was established that both Lords and Commons must consent to direct taxes, the chief of which was the "tenth-and-fifteenth," a levy on movable property. The customs, however, was an indirect tax, and Edward III continued, on his own authority, to levy it at a higher rate than Parliament had granted in 1275. The Lords, who were eager for the money with which to wage war in France, went along with Edward, but the Commons, who felt the brunt of the tax, protested. A fierce struggle ensued between Edward and the Commons, a struggle that did not end until 1362, when Edward agreed to a statute which declared that henceforth no charge should be levied on wool without the consent of Parliament. Parliament had established its control over taxation, both direct and indirect.

Had the Commons been content merely to vote or refuse to vote taxes to the King, they would have played a modest role in the public life of England. But they went on to secure legislative power. By the end of the thirteenth century it was recognized that a statute required the consent of the great magnates in Parliament. It was not until Edward III's reign that the Commons, by their regular attendance at Parliaments and by their control over taxation, also secured the right to consent. It came to be held that no statute was valid to which they had not consented. They also gained the right to initiate legislation by transforming their petitions into bills. Any subject of the King had the right to petition the King in Parliament for redress of wrong. The Commons therefore began to frame their own petitions. In 1337 they framed forty-one such petitions, sixteen of which the King answered by incorporating the remedy sought into two statutes. Because the King occasionally agreed during Parliament to the remedy sought in a petition but then later enacted a statute that bore only a faint resemblance to that remedy, the Commons began to insist on the accurate conversion of their petitions into statutes during the meeting of Parliament. The petition thus became the parliamentary bill. The Commons also began to insist on the redress of grievances before they voted the King money. They first acted on this principle in 1340, when they agreed to vote a tax only if the King accepted six petitions they had presented. The King incorporated the petitions into fourteen statutes, and the Commons voted the money. By the fifteenth century it became a regular procedure, one that gave the House of Commons a powerful lever for winning its demands.

Harmony between King and barons characterized Edward's reign—except for two political crises in 1341 and 1376. Both concerned the endeavors of the great magnates to use Parliament to control the King's council, which by the fourteenth century had become an important administrative body, at the center of the government.

Edward's angry attempt in 1341 to make his ministers in London answer for his failures in France provoked the first crisis. He dismissed his Chancellor and Treasurer and summoned John Stratford, the Archbishop of Canterbury, to answer charges brought against him. Edward's deeper purpose was to exercise an unchallenged control over his council and ministers. He met the resistance of the Archbishop, who demanded first that he be tried by his peers in Parliament and second that the magnates should share in the appointment of the King's ministers. The barons supported him in the first demand, and the King yielded to it, thereby taking the first step toward establishing the principle that no lord should be tried except by his peers in Parliament. Edward yielded to the second demand by consenting to a statute that provided for the appointment of his ministers "in Parliament." Six months later, determined not to be deprived of the right to appoint and dismiss his own ministers, Edward issued an ordinance repealing the statute. But he was careful in the future to appoint counselors and ministers who had the confidence of the barons.

Scandal and corruption at court, mismanagement of the war, and military losses in France brought on the crisis in 1376. Responsibility for this state of affairs did not lie with Edward, who had sunk into senility, but with his son, John of Gaunt, Duke of Lancaster, who had seized control of the administration in 1371. John of Gaunt soon surrounded himself with Alice Perrers, the King's unscrupulous mistress, Lord Latimer, an old soldier and royal favorite, and Richard Lyons, a wealthy London merchant, all of whom feathered their nests at the Crown's expense. Led by the Black Prince and the Earl of March, a group of barons, using the House of Commons as their instrument, drove these parasites from office. Peter de la Mare, the Speaker of the House of Commons (and steward of the Earl of March's estates) strode to the House of Lords, where in the name of the House of Commons he accused Lord Latimer and Richard Lyons of a long list of crimes. The Lords found them guilty and sent them to prison, thereby acknowledging that the House of Commons had the right to impeach and the House of Lords to judge ministers of state. Parliament also banished Alice Perrers from the realm and reshuffled the council, adding nine new baronial members to it. But the victory of the reforming barons was short-lived. John of Gaunt won control of the Parliament elected in 1377, and secured the release of Latimer and Lyons, the return of Alice Perrers, and the imprisonment of Peter de la Mare. That same year Edward III died, with Alice Perrers at his bedside, where she stole the very rings off his fingers. Once again an attempt to control the administration from outside the Court and Household had failed, but not before it had left a precedent for the power of impeachment.

THE TRANSFORMATION OF THE MANOR

The same century that saw the rise of Parliament saw the transformation of the manor. Early medieval society was essentially a community of manorial lords, drawing their wealth from a servile peasantry who owed labor services. By the middle of the fifteenth century this system was for all practical purposes dead. Labor services had been commuted into money rents. Land that had been held by servile tenure was now held by *copyhold*—that is, the rent owed was entered upon the manor roll, a copy of which became the title deed. The lord of the manor now leased his demesne rather than cultivating it directly. A class of wealthy peasants, the franklin class, arose, who amassed copyholds and leased demesne lands. The less enterprising peasants became a rural proletariat, working for wages. In the fifteenth century the royal courts began to protect copyhold tenure, thus accelerating the disappearance of the manorial court. A static, servile rural society based on personal obligations gave way to a mobile, free society based on monetary obligations.

The forces that brought about this transformation are difficult to disentangle, for the historical evidence is slight and occasionally contradictory. It was once thought that the emergence of markets and the growth in the supply of money caused these changes, yet in the north of England, farther removed from markets and supplies of money, labor services were commuted early, while in the Midlands and the southeast, nearer to markets and money, labor services were exacted throughout the thirteenth century. A plentiful supply of money was certainly a necessary condition for these changes, but it was not the driving force. That force was the economic depression of the fourteenth century, which led to a decline in manorial profits. The depression was caused in part by Scottish raids into England, the competition of grain from eastern Germany in continental markets, and the waste of resources in war. But the root cause was the decline in population. The turning point came in the years of flood and famine from 1315 to 1317. Until then the population of England had grown; thereafter it began to decline. The onset of a cold spell throughout Europe in about 1300 greatly contributed to this decline. The slow decline of the first half of the century became catastrophic in the second half with the arrival of the Black Death in 1349.

The Black Death was the dreaded bubonic plague, which originated in Central Asia, reached Italy in 1347, and was carried to England in August 1348 by refugees fleeing from Calais to Melcombe Regis in Dorset. In 1349 the plague scoured England. It was spread by the bite of a flea carried by the black rat, and throve in dirty and unsanitary conditions. For that reason it devastated the towns and the poor most of all. It returned in 1361, 1368, and 1375, and was not completely wiped out until the seventeenth century, when the brown rat, which does not carry the plague flea, drove out the black rat, which does. By 1400 the population of England had probably fallen by a third, from 3.5 million to 2.5 million.

The effect of the plague was to accelerate the forces that were already making demesne farming unprofitable. Wages rose, despite the fact that the landlord class in 1351 passed the Statute of Laborers, which established a maximum wage. Its enforcement proved difficult, with the result that wages were twice as high in 1400 as they had been in 1300. After 1375 agricultural prices fell, since there were fewer people seeking to purchase food. The shortage of labor deepened from 1390 onward, making it difficult to find peasants to take up holdings. The first reaction of some landlords was to turn the clock back, to attempt to exact even more labor services. But these attempts met dogged resistance, and soon the great majority of landlords gave up the direct management of the demesne and leased it to farmers. Between 1391 and 1411, for example, demesne farming on the estates of Christ Church, Canterbury, came to an end, the monks preferring to lease their lands.

Once a landlord resolved to lease his demesne, he had no need for the labor services of his tenants, which were then commuted into money rents. The process of commutation began as early as the twelfth century, but was greatly accelerated in the fourteenth. The holding of land by a money rent made the sale of land easier and there soon emerged a prosperous class of farmers, holding by copyhold and leasehold, and a larger class of peasants who held small holdings or none. At Frisby in Lincolnshire in 1381 there were sixteen families, all tenants, the richest of whom was only about twice as wealthy as the poorest. By the end of the fifteenth century there were ten families, of whom three had no land at all and two were wealthier than all the rest. Freedom brought with it inequality.

The unprofitablity of demesne farming was not the only force promoting the slow crumbling of manorial society. The peasants themselves struggled against it. Some lived legally outside the manor by paying an annual fine, or "chevage," to the lord. Many others just fled the village, with the result that their holdings had to be let for smaller rents, often without any labor services. Those who fled soon found employment or a copyhold. In 1377 the Commons complained at length about villeins who conspired together to withdraw their services. Since commutation was not enfranchisement, the peasants had to struggle for their personal freedom. Servile dues and services no longer seemed right to the wealthier peasants, while the lord's control over the village weakened with his leasing the demesne. In the end economic forces asserted themselves; Landlords discovered that the most effective way to retain tenants was to release them from all servile obligations. This process of emancipation was not reversed later, with the result that England entered the modern era some two hundred years ahead of the Continent in the enfranchisement of its peasantry.

THE PEASANTS' REVOLT

Social and economic changes are often slow, piecemeal, unplanned, and unforeseen—such was the decline of villeinage. At other times, often in the midst of the disintegration of old forms of society, men and women seek consciously to refashion society according to firmly held ideals—such was the Peasants' Revolt of 1381. At Mile End, outside London, on a Friday in June, the peasants and artisans of Essex demanded of their King the complete abolition of serfdom and the commutation of servile dues to a rent of 4 pence an acre. The next day at Smithfield the peasants and artisans of Kent demanded that there be no lordship in England but the lordship of the King, that the goods of the Church be divided among the parishioners, and that there be no villein in England, "but all to be free and of one condition." For a brief moment a belief in freedom and equality confronted the traditional view that society ought to be a hierarchy of graded ranks.

The peasants' revolt was not planned; rather, it was a spontaneous, almost accidental uprising, fueled by numerous grievances and sparked by the passage of a poll tax. In 1380 Parliament, growing weary of paying for the war in France with the usual tenth-and-fifteenth, taxes which fell on the propertied classes, passed a poll, or head, tax, which fell on everyone equally, the lowliest villein paying the same as the wealthiest Duke. This patently unjust tax, which Parliament had first employed in 1377, provoked a rebellion only because there existed among the rural workers a mass of resentments and dissatisfactions. They hated the landed classes for attempting to keep down wages through the Statute of Laborers. They hated their landlords for enforcing manorial obligations. They were angry at the wealth and worldliness of the higher clergy. They had visions of better conditions, inspired by wandering hedge-priests, such as John Ball, who asked:

> When Adam delved and Eve span,
> Who was then the gentleman?

One possible factor, the deepening misery of the peasants, did not cause the revolt, for their economic condition was steadily improving. Wages were rising faster than prices; even the landless laborer, because of the shortage of labor, was well paid. Many villeins owned a fair amount of property. The peasants' revolt, like the French Revolution, was inspired by rising expectations and by anger at the slowness with which the old order was reforming itself.

The rebellion began in Essex and Kent in late May. The two bands of rebels soon converged on London, which they entered on June 13. For two days the city was given over to the insurgents, who plundered and burned, opened prisons, destroyed legal records, slew the leading collector of the poll tax, and besieged the King and his ministers in the Tower. Having no standing army, the fourteen-year-old Richard II and his advisers resolved to negotiate. On the 14th the young King met the rebels at Mile End and granted them a charter that abolished villeinage and commuted labor services to a rent of 4 pence an acre. The next day he met the rebels once again at Smithfield, when the intrepid Mayor of London, William Walworth, pulled Wat Tyler, the leader of the peasants, from his horse and slew him. The courageous young King then ordered the rebels to disperse, which they promptly did, since respect for the monarchy ran deep. The crisis at London was over. But the King and his noble advisers had no intention of fulfilling the concessions they had granted. When a deputation of villeins came to Richard to ask him to confirm the charter he had granted, he replied: "Villeins ye are still and villeins ye shall remain."

The revolt was by no means confined to London. In Hertfordshire the tenants of the Abbey of St. Albans besieged the abbot, insisting on their rights to hunt in the woods, fish in the river, grind their corn at home, and sell land among themselves. At Bury St. Edmunds in Suffolk the tenants broke into the Abbey and for a time extorted their liberties from the abbot. In Norfolk a rebel army plundered Norwich, marched to Yarmouth, and systematically destroyed manorial records. At Winchester in Hampshire and at Beverley and Scarborough in Yorkshire, the unprivileged rose against the privileged. As late as September there was a rising in Wiltshire, though throughout most of England these rebellions had been suppressed by the end of June and the concessions granted to buy off the rebels withdrawn. The peasants gained nothing by their revolt. In fact, the fear created by the crisis probably hindered the process of emancipation. The peasants failed because they had no political power, no allies among the gentry or nobility or wealthy merchants. They had only their revolutionary ideals of freedom and equality.

JOHN WYCLIF AND LOLLARDY

The last quarter of the fourteenth century witnessed a religious crisis as deep as the social crisis, a crisis associated with the ideas of John Wyclif. It is almost impossible to demonstrate a causal connection between the two. Wyclif's ideas had no apparent influence on the peasants in 1381, though the social stresses of the time may have led some to embrace Wyclif's ideas. What is certain is that both the social and the religious revolt were directed against the traditional ideas of order, degree, authority, and lordship.

John Wyclif came from a modest landed family in Yorkshire and pursued a distinguished career as a scholar at Oxford. He became a third master at Balliol College, took his bachelorship of divinity in 1368, and proceeded to his doctorate in 1372. He held in succession various country livings, where he was rarely resident, to which he added a canonry at the collegiate church of Westbury-on-Trym, whose duties he failed to perform. Oxford was his home and study his passion. Like William of Ockham, he believed that religious belief had to be taken on faith and that God's will is inscrutable and His power infinite. From Archbishop Bradwardwine he learned to emphasize God's grace and help rather than man's free will. From Richard Fitzralph he borrowed the theory of dominion—namely, that the lawful exercise of lordship, or dominion over men, depends on grace; that is, on the righteousness of the person who exercises it. And like Marsilius of Padua he appealed to Scriptures and secular authority rather than to canon law and papal authority.

From 1378 onward, frustrated in his hope for greater preferment and appalled at the scandal of the two Popes (for the Great Schism began in 1378), he followed the logic of his ideas ever deeper into heresy. Both the Pope and the English bishops condemned his views, but his theory of dominion won him the support of the anticlerical party, led by John of Gaunt, who protected him. John of Gaunt later deserted him when he began to publish works that described the Church as a community of true believers and questioned the doctrine of transubstantiation (which asserts that the priest in the sacrament of the mass transforms bread and wine into the flesh and blood of Christ). Wyclif found safety in retirement to his rectory at Lutterworth, where he died and was buried in 1384, though in 1428 the bishop of Lincoln had his bones cast into the river Swift.

Wyclif's ideas were not systematic, nor did he recognize the revolutionary implications of many of them. Yet he did enunciate a number of dangerously heretical notions. First, he urged the theory of dominion; righteousness, not legal forms, gives the clergy their dominion and property, and it was for the secular authorities to decide if a clergyman had fallen from righteousness. Like Martin Luther, Wyclif never attacked secular lordship and had no sympathy with the peasants who did. Secondly, he urged that the Church was a community of believers, not an ecclesiastical hierarchy, a position that led him to deny the authority of the Pope and the rest of the hierarchy. Thirdly, in place of tradition, reason, and authority, he substituted a reliance on Scripture and individual conscience. Fourthly, he concluded that God had predestined some, "the elect," to salvation and others, "the foreknown," to the pains of hell. Fifthly, he questioned the very heart of the medieval Church by denying transubstantiation. He regarded the doctrine as crude and untrue, though (again like Luther) he clung to a belief in the real presence of Christ in the sacrament of the mass. Christ was present in the same sense that the King was present in England. Lastly, his belief in predestination led him to reject the Church's mediatory and sacramental role. How could a priest forgive sins if God alone could do so? In his learned, scholastic way, John Wyclif touched on all the later Protestant doctrines but the central one—justification by faith alone.

Wyclif's ideas were made momentarily dangerous by their confluence with a rising tide of anticlericalism. Anticlericalism is not irreligion, but rather hostility to the power and wealth of the clergy. The roots of fourteenth-century English anticlericalism were various. To begin with, there was repugnance at corruption in the Church, at pluralities, nonresidence, greed, pride, and the flaunting of great wealth. It is unlikely that these abuses were substantially greater than in earlier centuries, but there was now an absence of any redeeming religious fervor, such as the Cistercians brought to the twelfth century and the Franciscans to the thirteenth. The clergy grew more worldly, monks took more meals, regularly violated the rule against eating meat, kept domestic servants, and received cash allowances; nunneries became boarding houses for the noble and wealthy. Then there was the rise of an educated, prosperous, confident, articulate laity—landowners, merchants, lawyers—who resented the financial exactions and moral demands made upon them by the Church. Their jealousy of the wealth of the Church was probably greater because their income from land was declining. Finally, there was an English hatred of a foreign Pope. During much of the fourteenth century the popes resided at Avignon and were seen as tools of the French. Furthermore, the Papacy in the fourteenth century interfered more often than ever in the English Church, through provisions, annates, and appeals. The Pope now insisted on his right to name, or "provide" candidates for English bishoprics, canonries, and rectories; and the number of such benefices reserved for the Pope increased greatly. At the same time it became customary for bishops to pay the first year's revenue of the see, or "annates," to the Pope. Appeals of ecclesiastical cases to the papal court were not new, but they were more obnoxious when made to Avignon.

Anticlericalism found expression in many ways, in the poetry of Chaucer and Langland, in the Crown's seizure of the wealth of the Bishop of Winchester, in Parliament's attempt to impose a tax of £50,000 on the Church, and in

Parliament's declaration that King John had had no right to make England a tributary of the Pope. But the most permanent expression of the spirit is found in the Statute of Provisors of 1351 and the Statute of Praemunire of 1353. The Statute of Provisors allowed the King to expel from a benefice any person whom the Pope had wrongly named to it and to place his own candidate in it. The Statute of Praemunire declared that no Englishman should in a matter over which the King's court had jurisdiction sue another Englishman in any court outside England. The main intent was to prevent suits in papal courts over the right to name to benefices. It was not the King who sought these statutes but the landowners in Parliament, who believed that papal provisions threatened their own rights. These same lesser patrons secured new statutes of provisors in 1365 and 1390 and more stringent statutes of praemunire in 1365 and 1393, but the total effect was less to weaken the Pope than to strengthen the King. Both Edward III and Richard II used the statutes as bargaining counters in their negotiations with the Papacy. The Pope continued to provide men to benefices, often those the King nominated, and the volume of appeals to Rome remained the same, though none to the injury of the Crown. But it all occurred with the King's permission. As Pope Martin remarked, "It is not the Pope but the King of England who governs the Church in his dominions."

Anticlericalism led some men and women, a few even at Court, to adopt Wyclif's views. These men and women came to be called Lollards, but Lollardy reflected a religious tradition wider than anticlericalism and older than Wyclif. It drew on an ancient tradition of puritanical criticism of the pomp and pride of great Churchmen and on a desire, largely felt by the artisan and merchant, for a religion that was less legalistic and mechanical. Wyclif contributed to this tradition in two ways, by gathering a group of scholars around him at Oxford who kept his ideas alive for a generation, and by sponsoring the translation of the Bible into English. During Richard II's reign there was a political Lollardy at Court and an academic Lollardy at the university, but both proved frail plants. The moment John of Gaunt abandoned his anticlerical policies, the bishops were free to launch their counterattack. They began by purging Oxford of Lollardy, but Lollardy still found some sympathy among the lower clergy, the gentry, traders, and artisans. In 1395 some knights of the shire presented a bill of Lollard demands in Parliament. Richard II suppressed the petition, but kept in his Household men known to favor Lollardy. It was only with the accession of the House of Lancaster that the full force of the government was turned against the Lollards and that men of substance abandoned them. In 1401 Parliament passed a Statute for the Burning of Heretics, a statute that empowered the Church to condemn and the state to burn heretics. Despite this statute, Lollardy survived among the humble and the poor, among bakers, millers, weavers, laborers, in the west of England, in the Chilterns, in the Stour valley, and in Yorkshire. It survived underground throughout the fifteenth century, to help prepare the soil for the reception of Lutheran ideas in the sixteenth.

THE EMERGENCE OF AN ENGLISH NATIONALITY

The decision of the Lollards to translate the Bible from Latin into English reflected a profound change in English life. Before the fourteenth century English society was cosmopolitan and English culture Latin or French. Churchmen moved freely through Christendom; the knights of many countries fought in the East; Latin was the language of learning and French of the Court and the law. The aristocracy spoke French and all others English, so dividing the country. Then in the fourteenth century those forces already at work creating an English nationality quickened. Before the end of the century an English language, an English literature, an English art, and an English habit of thought had stamped itself on these island peoples.

In 1350 French was still the language preferred by the upper classes but during the next fifty years English ousted its rival. The hatred for things French engendered by the Hundred Years' War no doubt hastened this process. In 1362 Parliament sought to make English the language of the law; in 1363 the Chancellor for the first time opened Parliament in English; and the earliest known will in English dates from 1387. In the previous 250 years there had been many English dialects. It was, ironically, one of the most poverty-stricken of these, the East Midland dialect, that finally prevailed. Its victory arose largely from the fact that it was spoken in the region where London and the universities lay, but some credit for its victory must be given to the genius of Geoffrey Chaucer, who used it in his works.

Chaucer, who was the son of a London wine merchant, pursued various careers as a page in a noble household, a soldier in the French wars, a member of embassies to Italy and France, a commissioner of the customs, and a clerk of the works. His career made him a man of the world, with a remarkable insight into human character. He was also a scholar who had steeped himself in the literature of France and Italy and used that knowledge to raise English poetry to the first rank. His first masterpiece was *Troilus and Cresyde*, a narrative poem in which he gave flesh and blood to the thin characters of Boccaccio's tale and in which he portrayed with humor and pity the glory and tragedy of youth. His greatest masterpiece was *The Canterbury Tales*, left uncompleted at his death, in which he portrayed a cross-section of English society. He painted the rich merchant, the hunting monk, the lecherous summoner, the worldly friar, the prosperous franklin, the poor scholar, and the Wife of Bath, one of the great comic characters in English literature. In his understanding of character, his breadth of sympathy, his tolerance and humor, his sense of drama, and his vivid imagery Chaucer began a tradition that later found expression in Shakespeare and Dickens.

William Langland, a poor London clergyman in minor orders, began a different but equally powerful tradition in English thought and letters. In his poem, *The Vision of Piers Ploughman*, he expressed a religious earnestness, a moral fervor, an outrage at wrongdoing, and a suspicion of wealth and learning that formed what was later to be called the Puritan conscience. He also expressed a hatred for idleness and a belief in the virtue of hard work that was later to be called the Protestant work ethic. *The Vision of Piers Ploughman* is an account of the disillusionment experienced in this world by Piers, the ploughman, an honest seeker after truth. The poem paints the corruptions of wealth, attacks the money-grubbing friar, exposes the uselessness of pilgrimages, and satirizes learning in the guise of a fastidious scholar who cannot stand the plain fare of ordinary doctrine. Truth, the good life, God, and salvation were not to be found, the honest Piers discovers, in great wealth or subtle doctrine, but in honest labor and the service of Christ.

The late fourteenth century proved to be a seminal age not only for poetry but for the drama. During the late Roman Empire, the Church had condemned the theater, yet the liturgy of the Church contained within it a dramatic element. In the tenth century that element was extended into the rudiments of a play; on Easter one group of priests would represent the women approaching the tomb and another group the angels guarding it, and a dialogue would follow. By the thirteenth century these liturgical plays had grown so large that an entire church was devoted to their performance. The Church now became alarmed that the dramatic element was growing stronger than the religious. In the fourteenth century it therefore removed the drama from the Church and placed it in the nearby precincts. Drama now became secularized; actors spoke English, not Latin. They were no longer priests but members of guilds formed to produce such plays. Instead of brief liturgical speeches, playwrights wrote a longer dramatic script. They also introduced into the biblical stories which lay at the center of their plays characters and comic incidents not found in the Bible. On feast days, especially that of Corpus Christi, the guilds would perform a series of biblical plays at various places around town. Each play was mounted on a platform, fitted with wheels, and so drawn from place to place. With these religious plays began a dramatic tradition that not even the Puritans' attack on the theater in the seventeenth century could stifle.

It was also during the late fourteenth century that the Englishness of English art (to borrow a phrase from the eminent historian of art, Nikolaus Pevsner) found expression in the Perpendicular style. In architecture the peculiarly English qualities were those of angularity, compromise, and illogicality. The English saw space as angular, not plastic; they added wall to wall and rectangle to rectangle rather than molding space as the French did. The square-ended chancel, the square towers of parish churches, the hammerbeam roof, and the porches added to cathedrals all proclaim this quality. The quality of compromise lies at the heart of the Perpendicular style, for though it is called perpendicular its essence is a compromise between the vertical and the horizontal line. Window tracery and paneling made up of tier upon tier of arches and blank arches, forming a grid of horizontal and vertical lines, distinguish the Perpendicular, as do low-pitched roofs and flat-topped towers. Not for the English the tremendous vertical thrust of Chartres or the lofty spires of German churches;

they preferred balance and matter of factness. But they were often illogical, as the interlaced arches, lopsided vaults, and extended west facades give evidence. No French architect would have made a west facade wider than the width of the church, but many English architects did.

In sculpture and manuscript illumination also the Perpendicular style won out. In their alabaster altars and panels, late medieval artists carved long, lean, thin-faced figures not unlike those found in the illuminations of the Psalter of St. Albans, with its gaunt, stiff, motionless figures. The English had not always exhibited such restraint, for the tracery and sculpture of the Decorated style showed a flowing, even flamboyant line. But whether the line was flamboyant or elongated, it was always a line. Both styles were linear, anticorporeal, unfleshly, a denial of the body. This does not mean that English artists were not keen observers, for the margins of the illuminated manuscripts of late medieval England are covered with birds and beasts and with little scenes of every day life—a man beating down acorns for his pigs, hounds chasing a hare, a windmill, a wrestler. English art leaned to the informative rather than the imaginative, to fact rather than fancy, to the reasonable rather than the dogmatic.

It was not only in art but also in science that the English worshipped fact and looked to experience. The twelfth-century renaissance had led to the recovery of Greek science, but that science was based on the premise that, as in geometry, truths can be logically deduced from self-evident principles. The Greeks relegated the careful observation of the natural world to a secondary role. It was the remarkable achievement of a group of Oxford philosophers in the thirteenth and fourteenth centuries to transform the Greek geometrical method into the modern experimental method. They did so by joining the process of induction to that of deduction.

Robert Grosseteste, Chancellor of Oxford and later Bishop of Lincoln, was the first scholar to advance such a theory of scientific investigation and explanation. He held that the study of nature was a double procedure: To reach a generalization one must begin with sensory experience; one must gather particular facts and generalize from them. From such generalizations the scientist must, by a process Grosseteste recognized to be intuitive, establish a theory that has explanatory power. But this is not enough. The theory must then be proved by deducing from it a number of consequences, whose actual occurrence is then tested by an appropriate experiment. Not only did Grosseteste see the importance of experiment, but he grasped the importance of mathematics. Mathematics could be used to describe what happened and to correlate the variations in the effects observed. It was a tool for describing events in the world of experience.

The most important of Grosseteste's students was Roger Bacon, who became a member of Grosseteste's circle in 1249. Bacon's chief contribution was to apply the double method of induction and deduction to the study of light, especially the rainbow. He first collected all like instances of such a phenomenon, sought the common nature of them, and then deduced that the colors were created by the refraction of sunlight through individual drops of water. He too found mathematics indispensable. "All categories," he wrote, "depend on a knowledge of quantity, concerning which mathematics treats, and therefore the whole power of logic depends on mathematics."

In the early fourteenth century the ideas of Grosseteste and Bacon were taken up by a group of scholars at Merton College, Oxford, one of whom, William of Heytesbury, formulated for the first time a correct law of uniform acceleration. He declared that a body accelerating uniformly will cover in a given time exactly the distance it would have covered in the same time had it been moving constantly at the speed it reached at the middle moment in time. While William of Heytesbury studied motion another Oxford scholar, William of Ockham, turned his attention to the methodology of science. He launched a radical attack on the excesses of scholastic philosophy. He rejected the final causes, essences, and substances of Aristotle, and asserted the principle of economy—namely, that in seeking to explain nature, one should not unnecessarily multiply concepts. He likewise declared that such concepts as "redness" or "squareness" or "goodness" were purely mental constructs, which the mind forms from its experience of particular red objects, square objects, or good conduct. Only through experience of individual things can one gain a certain knowledge of the real. By the fourteenth century it had become clear that the English habit of thought was not deductive, as in France, nor metaphysical, as in Germany, but empirical. The English desired to dwell among things.

RICHARD II AND THE DEFEAT OF ABSOLUTISM

The fourteenth century ended, as it had begun, with a profound political crisis. In 1399, as in 1327, the English deposed and murdered their king. In 1327 it was Edward II; in 1399, Richard II. Richard came to the throne in 1377, a handsome boy of 10, the only son of the Black Prince. During the first five years of his reign, the government of the realm rested with a baronial council that sent costly and fruitless military expeditions to France and lost command of the sea to a Franco-Castilian fleet. During the years from 1382 to 1386 Richard matured, slowly built up a royal party, and began to entrust real power to his personal friends. He made Michael de la Pole, the son of a wealthy merchant, Chancellor in 1383 and named Robert de Vere, a vainglorious and tactless courtier, hereditary Chamberlain. On both he showered estates and titles. Richard soon showed himself to be an intelligent and sensitive man. He was a connoisseur of art, music, and literature, and had a flair for fashion in dress. He is said to have introduced the use of the handkerchief into England. But though a man of culture, he was no king. He was tactless, impulsive, alternately lethargic and energetic, and totally lacking in political realism. He was no judge of men or circumstances. As a consequence, he failed to defend England against France, wasted resources on John of Gaunt's Spanish ambitions, and

The left panel of the Wilton Diptych, showing Richard II kneeling in prayer. The Wilton Diptych, painted in the late fourteenth century, is one of the earliest masterpieces of English painting (*the National Gallery, London*).

angered the barons by allowing the government to fall into the hands of favorites.

The barons were not, however, prepared to relinquish the power they had won under Edward III and increased during Richard's minority. In the Parliament of 1386 the Lords and Commons demanded that Richard dismiss his Chancellor and Treasurer. Richard replied that he would not remove the least boy in his kitchen on account of them, but was forced to back down when Parliament refused to vote the money he needed unless he would dismiss the two officials. Parliament went on to impeach Michael de la Pole for corruptly using his office for profit and for neglecting the defenses against France. They likewise established a commission of reform that would hold power for one year and told Richard that Parliament might depose a king who governed against the law and without the advice of the peers. Richard was too proud to submit for long to this indignity. In 1387 he restored Pole, marched into the Midlands, raised forces, and pressured his judges into declaring that the commission of reform was illegal and Parliament had no right to impeach his servants without his consent. The judges also declared that those responsible for the commission and the impeachment deserved execution. The barons, led by the Duke of Gloucester, the Earl of Warwick, and the Earl of Arundel, promptly raised an army, overawed the King, personally accused or "appealed" the King's leading advisers, and demanded that a Parliament meet to pass judgment on them. In the ensuing Parliament, called the Merciless Parliament, the barons completed the work they began in 1386. In response to the "appeals" brought by the "appellant lords," Parliament dismissed, exiled, imprisoned, or executed the King's servants and judges. Richard's circle of friends was shattered, and the Lords Appellants emerged supreme.

The Duke of Gloucester and his allies remained in power for a year, slowly losing favor through their incompetence, when suddenly, in May 1389, Richard declared himself of full age and free to govern personally. He did so for the next nine years, in a conciliatory and restrained manner. He did not recall those exiled by the Merciless Parliament. He allowed the Appellant Lords to remain on the council. He restored English power in Ireland. He pursued a popular anti-Papal policy. But the appearance of tranquillity was misleading, for he fashioned a core of loyal Household officers and built up a party among the moderate barons. Even more alarming was the development of his political ideas. The long tutelage he had suffered during his youth had awakened in him a desire to be independent and to govern by means of the royal prerogative.

The humiliations suffered in 1386 and 1388 heightened that resolve. Slowly he came to see that the absolute power of the King was the best answer to the problems of government in the fourteenth century. He declared that the laws were in the King's breast and that he alone could make law. In 1391 he obtained a declaration from the Lords and Commons that the King's prerogative was unaffected by previous legislation. In 1392 he revoked the liberties of London because the city refused him a loan. He also, through the system of retainers used by the barons, raised a private royal army that wore his emblem of a white hart.

By 1397 Richard felt strong enough to strike. In July he arrested Gloucester, Warwick, and Arundel and summoned a Parliament, which met under the gaze of soldiers wearing the white hart. Parliament, upon appeals brought by lords of the King's party, executed Arundel, banished Warwick, and condemned Gloucester, who died in his prison at Calais, probably murdered. The next year Parliament met at Shrewsbury, where Richard persuaded it to vote that the royal person was inviolable and that it was treason to act against the royal prerogative. Parliament also voted him a subsidy on wool for life, rather than for the usual one or two years, and delegated its authority to a

The Descendants of Edward III

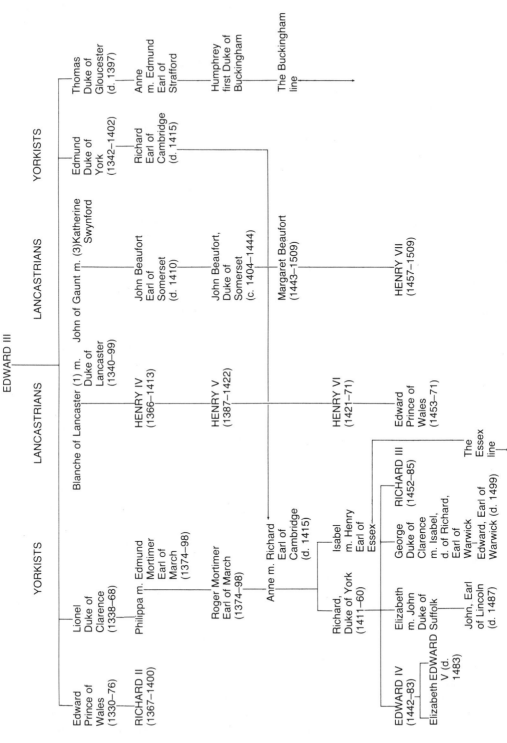

(Edward III had 12 children. Two sons died in infancy; three daughters died unmarried; a daughter Isabella married into the Coucy family; another daughter, Mary, married into the Montfort family.)

commission of eighteen, thereby rendering itself temporarily powerless. Richard now possessed the absolute power of which he had dreamed.

During the last two years of his reign, the King's conduct approached political madness. He pursued a fantastic design to gain the Imperial throne by bribing the Electors of Cologne and the Palatinate. He extorted large loans from the rich. He sought to exercise strict control over local government by appointing subservient "yes-men" as sheriffs. He made use of courts of law that did not administer the Common law. He extorted from suspected persons sealed, blank charters which, if the givers offended him, he could later fill in as he wished. All this made him unpopular with the politically powerful classes. But his greatest blunder was to confiscate the lands of John of Gaunt, Duke of Lancaster, on his death in 1399, thereby denying Henry Bolingbroke, Gaunt's eldest son, his rightful inheritance. By this act Richard not only angered the greatest magnate in England, but alienated all the barons; for whose lands were safe if the King might seize them at will? Richard compounded his blunder by journeying to Ireland at this moment, leaving the kingdom in the hands of his incompetent uncle, the Duke of York. Henry Bolingbroke, Duke of Lancaster, whom Richard had exiled the year before, now seized the occasion to lead an expedition to England to recover his inheritance. He landed in the north, where the two most powerful families, the Percys and the Nevilles, joined his cause. As he marched south, even the duke of York came over to his side. Richard rushed back from Ireland, but when he landed at Conway he found only a small band of supporters. He might have fled to Ireland or Gascony, but was duped into surrendering by Bolingbroke's promise that he would remain King if Bolingbroke received his rightful inheritance.

At some moment during his invasion of England, Henry of Lancaster resolved to seize not only his lands but the throne. He now put his plan into operation by taking Richard to London, imprisoning him in the Tower, summoning a Parliament in his name, and wresting an abdication from him. The day after Richard abdicated, Parliament, meeting in the presence of Bolingbroke's armed retainers, heard Richard's deed of abdication read, along with thirty-three charges against him. Henry, Duke of Lancaster, then stood up to claim the Crown by right of descent, conquest, and Richard's misrule. His claim by descent was weak; the right of conquest was a two-edged sword; and the argument of unfitness could be turned against any future king. Yet Henry prevailed because he had the realm behind him. No doubt it was the military forces at his command that allowed him to depose Richard, but he chose to remove the King by means of Parliament. Previous Parliaments had removed evil counselors and so established a precedent that Henry now chose to follow. As Henry IV he ruled England by a title Parliament had confirmed. Hereditary monarchy now bore a blemish on its escutcheon.

A few months after Henry came to the throne, Richard's supporters rose in revolt. Henry quickly crushed the revolt and resolved that it was too dangerous to allow Richard to live. Lancastrian propaganda declared that Richard starved himself to death at Pontefract Castle, but it is more likely that heavy chains, systematic torture, insufficient food, scanty clothing, and cold killed him. Richard suffered the same fate as Edward II and for a like reason. Both sought to place their personal government above the laws of the realm and the counsels of the great magnates.

FURTHER READING

*GEORGE HOLMES. *The Later Middle Ages 1272 –1485.* New York, 1966. A useful introduction for those reading about the period for the first time; especially good on the institutions of government.

*A.R. MYERS. *England in the Late Middle Ages.* Revised ed., Penguin Books, 1966. A volume in the Pelican History of England; a short survey but skillfully compressed and fuller on political events and the arts than Holmes.

MAY MCKISACK. *The Fourteenth Century 1307– 1399.* Oxford, 1959. A comprehensive, scholarly, gracefully written history; encompasses social, economic, and intellectual developments as well as political; contains a comprehensive bibliography.

G.L. HARRIS. *King, Parliament, and Public Finance in Medieval England to 1369.* Oxford, 1975. An important recent monograph that traces the failure of feudal revenues to meet the costs of war, the rise of public taxation, and the capture of the control of taxation by Parliament.

EDUOARD PERROY. *The Hundred Years' War.* London, 1951. A masterly work of synthesis and interpretation; treats the Hundred Years' War as a whole, not as a chapter in English history.

ANTHONY TUCK. *Richard II and the English Nobility.* London, 1973. A political history of the reign based on the most recent scholarship; depicts Richard as neither insane nor an exalted monarchist, but as insensitive to the consequences of his actions.

PHILIP ZEIGLER. *The Black Death.* New York, 1969. A very readable, scholarly account of the beginnings, course, and effects of the Plague; follows the Plague across Europe but concentrates on England.

RODNEY HILTON. *Bond Men Made Free: Medieval Peasant Movements and the English Rising of 1381.* London, 1973. Though Hilton devotes half the book to other medieval social movements, he argues that the 1381 Revolt differed from them and could only have occurred in marketoriented southeastern England.

T.H. LLOYD. *The English Wool Trade in the Middle Ages.* Cambridge, England, 1977. A detailed, thoughtful, important study of the wool trade from the twelfth century through the fourteenth.

A.C. CROMBIE. *Robert Grosseteste and the Origins of Experimental Science.* Oxford, 1953. A pioneering work that stresses the medieval roots of the Scientific Revolution.

8 Lancaster and York: 1399-1485

The fifteenth century opened with the seizure of the Crown by the House of Lancaster, continued with its capture by the House of York, and ended with its seizure by the House of Tudor. During the first half of the century the English renewed the Hundred Years' War with France, won a glorious victory at Agincourt, and then lost the fruits of that victory in a long, costly, inglorious series of small defeats. By 1453 England had surrendered all its possessions in France but Calais, and its mercenary soldiers came home to contribute to the outbreak of the Wars of the Roses in 1455. Civil war now replaced foreign war, as rival factions of powerful noblemen struggled to gain control of the government. Never were the great magnates of the realm more powerful, never was the King more feeble, never was the government in so great a disarray. Yet Edward IV, of the House of York, in twelve short years after 1471 went far toward reversing this trend. He made the monarchy stronger than it had been since the reign of Edward I and began to restore order in the countryside. The fifteenth century presents the anomaly of a Crown, checked first by Parliament, then by an aristocratic council, then by civil war, suddenly reasserting itself and recovering its independence. The century also presents the anomaly of profound economic changes amid economic depression, and growing literacy amid cultural decadence. It was the century in which England, from being a nation that exported a primary product, raw wool, became a nation that exported a manufactured product, woolen cloth. The wealth that the great clothiers made from this industry went into the building of parish churches, the founding of chantries, the establishment of grammar schools, and the purchase of books.

HENRY IV AND THE FOUNDATIONS OF LANCASTRIAN RULE

Well might Shakespeare have Henry IV declare, "Uneasy lies the head that wears a Crown," for his short reign was a troubled one. The difficulties that marked his reign did not arise from any defect in Henry's character, for he was an able King, a tenacious soldier, a statesman capable both of patience and decision. The fault lay in the circumstances surrounding his coming to the throne. His uncertain title encouraged plots against him. Inadequate revenues made him dependent on Parliament. The magnates who placed him on the throne expected him to govern according to their wishes. His criticisms of Richard for governing by a clique, extorting money, not waging war, and spending extravagantly bound him to an opposite course of action. Henry faced the usual problems of a late medieval King, but a King weakend by an uncertain title.

Henry's troubles began in the autumn of 1400 when Owen Glendower, a Welsh gentleman descended from the ancient Welsh nobility, led a revolt against English rule. The rebellion spread rapidly through Wales because Welsh tenants resented their exploitation by English landlords. Henry's troubles grew more serious when Sir Edmund Mortimer, uncle of Richard II's legitimate heir, the Earl of March, joined the rebellion. The crisis grew ever graver when the Percys, the mightiest family in the north of England, also joined. The Percys had helped Henry gain the throne, but they were now angry that he had not paid them the money he owed them as wardens of the Scots Marches and that he had not allowed them to ransom Scottish prisoners taken in battle. In 1403 Glendower, Mortimer, and the Percys joined together in a bizarre scheme to overthrow Henry and partition England among themselves. Henry met this threat with unusual swiftness. He marched north to Shrewsbury, intercepted the Percys before they could join with Glendower, and defeated them. He had surmounted the deepest crisis of his reign, though he had to suppress a second uprising in the north in 1405 and only slowly regained the many castles lost in Wales. By 1408, however, he was firmly seated on the throne.

In these early years Henry was buffeted by blows from other quarters. Parliament, and the House of Commons in particular, criticized him for his failure to defend the coasts against French raids, for his extravagant Household expenditures, and for his gifts of land to courtiers. Against such criticism, often unjustified, Henry was virtually powerless, for though in theory he enjoyed all the prerogatives of a King of England, in practice his authority was much diminished. During his reign the House of Commons reached the zenith of its power in medieval times. The causes of this development were various. By the end of the fourteenth century Parliament had evolved into its modern form, one in which the Commons were as essential a part as King and Lords. Henry suffered all the weaknesses of a usurper. His income of £90,000 a year was smaller than Richard II's, which was £116,000. And though he enjoyed the revenues of the Duchy of Lancaster, he had to meet the heavy expenses of garrisoning Calais and suppressing rebellion. His financial needs placed him at the mercy of the House of Commons, who refused in 1404 to vote him additional taxes unless it could appoint the treasurers to administer it. It also demanded that Henry remove four members of his Household and name in Parliament a continual council with whose advice he would govern. Henry reluctantly agreed.

In 1406 the demands of the House of Commons were equally crippling to the prerogative. In return for a shilling increase in the customs, Henry agreed to nominate his councilors in Parliament, to govern with their advice, and to allow the Commons to name auditors to audit the money voted for the war. Henry was unable to control his own administration without the consent of a council whose nomination had been imposed upon him. In 1407 the Commons wrested from Henry an acknowledgment of its sole right to initiate money bills. But these gains did not mean that the English monarch suddenly became subordinated to Parliament. Henry struggled against these limitations on his power and threw them off when the opportunity arose. The Commons retained the right to initiate money bills, but it did not again seek to impose a council on the King. What it really sought was to control taxation, not the government; it wanted less taxes, not more power.

After 1408 different factors shaped English politics. The military danger posed by France, Glendower, and the Percys diminished. The King grew ill and dispirited. His son, the ambitious Prince Henry, grew more restless in his desire to take his father's place. He allied himself with the powerful Beaufort family, half-brothers of the King. Through the Beauforts he sought to win control of the Council, which fell once more under aristocratic domination. The authority of Parliament now receded as politics became a struggle of rival aristocratic factions for control of the Council. The ambitions of Prince Henry were the chief ground for these quarrels, but there were also genuine differences of opinion over the wisest policy toward France. In 1411 the Prince favored seizing the opportunity offered by divisions in France to resume the war; but his father steadfastly pursued a policy of peace. It was even rumored that the Prince might engineer the King's abdication, but in 1412 Henry roused himself and with the help of Archbishop Arundel ousted the Prince and Thomas Beaufort, who was Chancellor, from the Council. Twice that year the Prince came to London with a retinue of men, presumably to use force, but nothing came of the threat. Henry died peacefully in March 1413, still King, but having done little to solve the deeper problems that beset the monarchy. His supreme achievement was to have survived and to have handed on the Crown to his brilliant son.

HENRY V AND THE WAR IN FRANCE

Henry V came to the throne at the age of 25, young, energetic, courageous, a soldier-king who in the next ten years governed England with firmness, justice, and honor. He was a devout monarch, who heard mass often and vowed to go

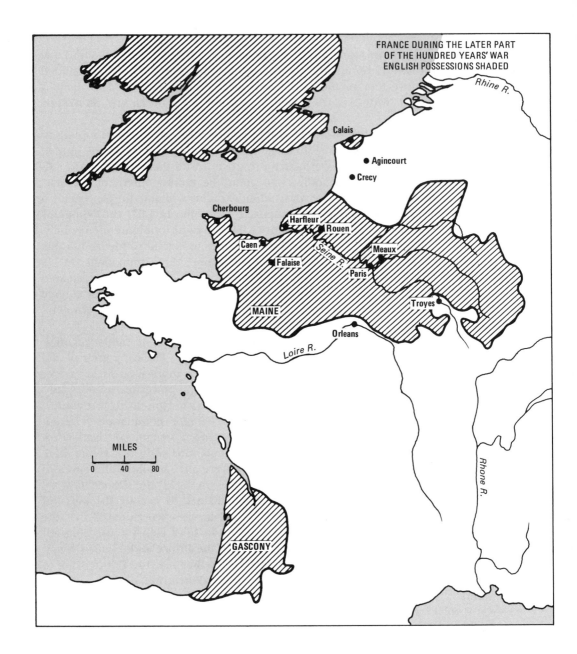

FRANCE DURING THE LATER PART
OF THE HUNDRED YEARS' WAR
ENGLISH POSSESSIONS SHADED

Rhine R.

Calais

● Agincourt

● Crecy

Cherbourg

Harfleur

Rouen

Caen

Seine R.

Meaux

Falaise

Paris

MAINE

Troyes

Orleans

Loire R.

MILES

0   40   80

Rhone R.

GASCONY

on a crusade. He was, as Shakespeare wrote, "the mirror of all Christian Kings." This was how most of his contemporaries and the Elizabethans saw him, but modern historians have discovered another side to his character. He was, in their judgment, cruel, domineering, selfishly ambitious, and sanctimonious. Whichever portrait comes closer to the truth, one fact is certain: Henry V dedicated his entire reign to one great cause, the conquest of France.

Political disorder in France presented an open invitation to resume the war. The King, Charles VI, was old and mad, with the result that political power had fallen into the hands of great princes of the realm, like the Duke of Burgundy and the Duke of Orléans. Since 1407, when the Duke of Burgundy had connived at the murder of the Duke of Orléans, the feud between these families had divided all France into Burgundians and Armagnacs (as the Orléanists were called). In September 1413 the Duke of Burgundy fled Paris to his domains in the Low Countries, leaving Paris in the hands of the Armagnacs. Henry thus had a splendid opportunity to recover England's lost lands in France, and perhaps win the crown itself. He needed little prompting, for ever since 1411, when he sent a small force to France on his own initiative, he had wanted to do this. On becoming King he promptly entered into secret negotiations with the Duke of Burgundy to secure his neutrality and opened negotiations with the Armagnacs to cloak England's preparations for war. In August 1414 an English delegation to Paris proposed that Henry should marry Charles VI's daughter, Catherine, and receive in full sovereignty Normandy, Touraine, Maine, Anjou, Britanny, Flanders, and all Aquitaine. The French refused this outrageous demand. Henry made a similar demand in June 1415, with the added threat that if the French refused he would recover those territories with the sword, and also seize the French Crown. The French again refused, whereupon Henry joined his troops at Southampton. The motives that drove Henry to war were many: to win glory and fame, to increase the power of the English Crown, to still discontent at home with great victories abroad, and to enforce a claim in whose righteousness he believed. To the historian today the English claim to the French Crown and lands appears flimsy and fabricated, but Henry never doubted the rightness of his cause.

With 2,000 men-at-arms and 6,000 archers, Henry sailed from Southampton in August 1415. It was a carefully planned expedition, reflecting Henry's mastery of detail and organization. He first besieged Harfleur, which fell after five weeks, the first town ever captured by the English by means of cannons. Though the long siege had depleted his forces, most of them falling to dysentery, he determined to march north to Calais, thereby revealing the weakness of the French. The French, convinced that Henry had overreached himself, blocked his advance at Agincourt, which lay less than 30 miles from Crécy, the scene of Edward III's great triumph. There, on St. Crispin's Day, the 25th of October, a tired, wet, hungry English army confronted a French army five times its size.

The French made some disastrous mistakes. They chose to fight in a narrow defile between the forests of Agincourt and Tramecourt, thus making their superior numbers useless. Stung by a rain of arrows from the English archers, they foolishly launched their cavalry against English archers who were well protected by stakes driven into the ground. They then sent heavily armored soldiers on foot through deep mud against the English foot soldiers, who repulsed them, whereupon lightly armored English archers infiltrated the broken ranks and destroyed the French with hatchets and axes. Furthermore, the

French kept their crossbowmen at the rear, where they were useless. The English, on the other hand, extended their longbowmen forward on both flanks. The rout of the French army was complete. Indeed, toward the end of the day, fearing a counterattack, Henry ordered the slaughter of thousands of French prisoners. Before the day was over the French had lost 5000 killed, including three dukes, five counts, and ninety barons, with another 1000 taken prisoners. The English lost less than 300 men. Henry had won a victory more dazzling than Crécy or Poitiers, and all the bells of England rang in celebration.

Henry had won the battle but not the war, a fact he was too good a soldier not to recognize. When he returned to France in 1417, he pursued a strategy of besieging, one by one, the chief fortified towns of Normandy. In eighteen months of long, careful sieges he captured Caen, Falaise, Cherbourg, and Rouen, but his success was only made possible by the Duke of Burgundy's advance on Paris, which the Duke captured in 1418. It was at this point in the war that the two French factions, alarmed at Henry's successes, sought a reconciliation. It was short-lived, for an adherent of the Dauphin (the French King's son), murdered the Duke of Burgundy in 1419, plunging France once more into strife. The new Duke of Burgundy, thirsting for revenge, allied with Henry and forced on the mad King of France in 1420 the Treaty of Troyes. By the Treaty of Troyes Henry was to marry the King's daughter, Catherine, and to succeed to the throne of France on the King's death. Henry spent the remainder of his short life in the wearisome task of besieging French towns. It was the dysentery he contracted during the long siege of Meaux that brought his life to an end in August of 1422.

Henry V's death proved fortunate for his reputation, for he had embarked upon a hopeless enterprise. The Crown's debts were piling up, since current revenues were not enough to pay for a single one of his campaigns. Now to the cost of the campaigns was added the cost of administering occupied territories. Parliament also grew restive at the heavy financial demands made upon it. Henry's objectives had always been more dynastic than national; he was more concerned with his own rights than with the nation's true interests. His early death helped to conceal this fact and to cause succeeding generations to remember him simply as the triumphant warrior-king.

HENRY VI AND THE DECLINE OF THE MONARCHY

During the long reign of Henry VI (1422–1461) the power and dignity of the English monarchy declined to its lowest ebb. A long minority contributed to this fact, for Henry, the son of Henry V and Catherine, was only nine months old when he came to the throne. Nor did his coming to maturity in 1437 check the decline, for Henry grew up to be a pious, gentle, well-meaning recluse, with no capacity for politics. During these forty years of royal impotence, the government fell into the hands of a Council dominated by the great magnates of the realm. The Lords in Parliament named the first Council, but the Council perpetuated itself thereafter by electing new members without consulting Parliament. Never before in English history had the aristocracy enjoyed such an ascendancy in government. And on the whole they exercised that power well, particularly during the first twenty years of Henry's reign.

The King's wise and respected uncle, the Duke of Bedford, carried on the war in France; Parliaments regularly voted the needed subsidies; the courts of law administered justice; the more turbulent barons went to France in search of plunder and ransoms. The most disruptive influence in these years was the fierce rivalry between the Duke of Gloucester, an adventurous soldier, a patron of literature, the King's uncle, and an ambitious and maladroit politician, and Cardinal Beaufort, Bishop of Winchester, a man of enormous wealth and much cunning, the King's great-uncle, and an enigmatic figure in politics. Gloucester and Beaufort continually intrigued against each other, but their quarrels never flamed into open conflict. When they threatened to, the Duke of Bedford hurried over from France to extinguish the flames.

The aristocratic Council found that it had as much need of Parliament as had the kings in the fourteenth century. Parliament tenaciously defended its right to vote extraordinary taxes, and in 1450 it revived the power of impeachment. In two particular ways the Commons during these years extended its powers. It established the practice of introducing petitions worded in the exact form of the proposed statute, and it won the right to consent to *all* legislation. Judges now ruled that no bill could become a statute without the consent of the House of Commons as well as of the King and Lords. The continued importance of the Commons and the growing power of the landed gentry led in 1430 to a statute that limited the right to vote in county elections to those who held a freehold worth 40 shillings a year. This statute, designed to maintain the House as a preserve for wealthy landlords and merchants, effectively disenfranchised the copyholder and leaseholder, men of "small substance and no worth." The importance of the Commons also led nonresidents to seek election from the boroughs. Where the boroughs once returned only their most prominent citizens, they now returned lawyers, gentlemen, Household officials, and civil servants. By 1472 at least half the borough representatives were not citizens of the borough they represented.

The influence of the Crown, however, did not destroy the independence of the Commons; frequent opposition to the Crown demonstrated this. More powerful than royal influence was the influence exercised by great lords, both over elections and over the conduct of members when elected. In Yorkshire the Percys and Nevilles dominated elections; in Norfolk, the powerful Duke of Norfolk. But the influence of the great magnates was not an overriding one. In 1450 the Duke of Norfolk was unable to secure the election of Sir Roger Chamberlain from Norfolk. Most members were rich, independent-minded squires, and if they often supported the lords of the Council, they did so more from an identity of interest than from political subservience.

It was in fact the refusal of Parliament to pour money into the bottomless pit of the French war that finally brought an end to that imperial venture. In theory the army in France should have been paid out of the revenues raised there. On his deathbed Henry V urged Bedford to win the support of the French by good government, but Bedford's wise laws for the occupied territories proved unavailing. His administration, which extended over all France north of the Loire, met with passive resistance everywhere. The annual deficit of £30,000 a year became unendurable. In 1428, when England besieged Orléans, the government could send only 2700 men as reinforcements. All that France needed for victory was to shake off the apathy which the devastation caused by English arms had created. It was a saintly peasant girl from Domremy, Joan of Arc, who accomplished this task. Guided by mystic voices that bid her free France, she used her remarkable powers of persuasion to convince Charles VII that he could recover his kingdom and that she was the instrument to accomplish it. With an army that Charles placed in her hands, she relieved Orléans. From that moment the French drove the English ever northward, though Joan herself, captured by the Burgundians and sold to the English, was burned as a heretic and witch.

The French now took care not to expose their armies to the successful English combination of archers and men-at-arms, and they made better use of their artillery. The point of no return came in 1435, when the English at the peace conference of Arras refused to give up Paris or Henry's claim to the French throne. Their obstinacy drove the Duke of Burgundy to desert them and to join the King of France. With the Duke as an ally, the English could barely hold their own; without the Duke, their defeat was certain. In 1436 the French drove the English from Paris, in 1450 from Normandy, in 1453 from Gascony. Nothing was left of the English dominions in France but Calais.

Defeat abroad, as it does in all ages, embittered politics at home. The Duke of Bedford died in 1435, thus removing a restraining hand. Cardinal Beaufort, a realist at heart, finally saw that the cause was hopeless and listened to the peace party in the Council. The militant Duke of Gloucester favored continuing the struggle—a popular view since it was easy to persuade men that the losses arose from bungling and treachery, not superior French resources. Soon the Beaufort faction found an ally in William de la Pole, Earl (later Duke) of Suffolk, a court favorite on whom Henry VI poured offices, lands, titles, and commercial privileges. Politics now moved out of an aristocratic Council that coopted its own members into a Court where the King's favorites ruled. In 1444 Suffolk won a two-year truce in the French war by agreeing to the marriage of Henry VI to the King of France's niece, Margaret of Anjou. Margaret, a spirited, willful, passionate young girl, quickly persuaded her gentle husband to surrender Maine to the French. With the Crown debts at £400,000 and the Crown revenues a mere £30,000 a year, it was inevitable that England should reduce its garrisons in Normandy and that Normandy should easily fall to France, as it did in 1449 and 1450.

Parliament and the populace did not see the fall of Normandy as inevitable; they saw it as a disaster whose authors should be punished. The soldiers at Portsmouth lynched the Bishop of Chichester. The House of Commons impeached the Duke of Suffolk, who sought safety in flight, only to be captured by the mutinous crew of a royal ship and beheaded. Six months after Suffolk's murder, the men of Kent rose in rebellion under the leadership of Jack Cade. Cade's rebellion was a general movement of disaffection, provoked by financial corruption, administrative incompetence, the decline of trade, and the loss of the war. The rebels came largely from the trading centers in Kent, where the export of cloth had declined between 1448 and 1450 from 2,078 pieces of cloth to 237. Among the rebels were workers in cloth, shipmen, tradesmen, three members of Parliament, seventy-four gentlemen, and some peasants. Though the rebels demanded the repeal of the Statute of Laborers and the protection of the royal courts for the land of the poor peasants, their chief demands were more political than social. They wanted the removal of evil councilors, an end to corruption, an improvement in the method of collecting taxes, and the return of royal lands granted to favorites. The rebels terrorized London for three days but could not gain the Tower. The King met with the rebels, raised an army, attacked them, and routed them. Because no one above the rank of knight joined the revolt and because the rest of England remained quiet, the revolt did not become a civil war. But civil war was soon to come, and the greatest magnates of the realm enlisted themselves in it.

THE WARS OF THE ROSES

From 1455 to 1485 a factious nobility and a weak King plunged England into a civil war that historians have called the Wars of the Roses. Few events in history have been more wrongly named. The error began with Shakespeare, who in a memorable scene in *Henry VI* had the Duke of York pluck a white rose, the emblem of his House, and the Earl of Somerset a red rose, the emblem of the House of Lancaster, to signify their opposition to each other. Drawing upon this scene, Sir Walter Scott named these wars the Wars of the Roses, but the scene was pure invention. In fact the red rose was not the emblem of the House of Lancaster, but of the House of Tudor. The misconception goes deeper, for the cause of the wars did not lie in a disputed succession to the Crown but in the feebleness of Henry VI and the factiousness of the nobility. Richard, Duke of York, did not at first seek the Crown but only power at Court. Nor is it correct to date the wars from 1455 to 1485, for in effect the wars came to a close in 1471.

The Wars of the Roses were first of all a struggle for power among contending factions of noblemen, a struggle in which the lower and middle classes took no part. But they were more than this. They were also a period in which private warfare, intimidation, injustice, and violence prevailed in the counties.

ENGLAND IN THE FIFTEENTH CENTURY

MILES

0   20   40   60   80

Newcastle ●

York ●
Leeds ● ✕ Towton
Halifax ● ● Moor   Hull ●
         ● Wakefield
WEST RIDING   ✕

R. Trent

● Lincoln
Nottingham ●   Boston ●

Shrewsbury ●   Lynn ●   Norwich ●
                         R. Ouse   Yarmouth ●
Birmingnam ●   ✕ Leicester
         ● Bosworth Field
Coventry ●   ✕ Northampton ● Cambridge
R. Severn
● Tewkesbury   Bedford ●
Gloucester ●   Oxford ● ✕ St. Albans
                         ✕ Barnet
R. Thames
● Bristol   London ●

Salisbury ●

Southampton ●

Exeter ●

Plymouth

The roots of this mounting disorder can be traced far back into the fifteenth century, even into the fourteenth.

It was the decay of feudalism in the thirteenth and fourteenth centuries that made room for a new system of relationships between lord and man. Feudal relations were based on the vassal holding land of the lord; the new system, which historians have called "bastard feudalism," was based on the lord's man, or retainer, receiving a wage or pension. Because a retainer often wore the livery, or household uniform, of the lord he served, he came to be known as a liveried retainer. Such retainers often signed an indenture promising to serve a lord for life or for a number of years. The system of liveried retainers appeared as early as Edward I's reign, but it was in the fifteenth century that it became a scourge on the countryside. The growing concentration of property in the hands of a few great families, the return of undisciplined troops from France, and the feebleness of the King promoted its growth. Private wars between armies of liveried retainers became the ultimate weapon for settling disputes. In 1445 a quarrel between Sir William Bonville and the Earl of Devon flared into the Battle of Exeter; the Nevilles and the Percys fought a pitched battle at Stamford Bridge in 1453; the Duke of Norfolk in 1469 besieged Caistor Castle with an army of 3000 men; and Lord Molyns in 1450 attacked John Paston's manor house (as Paston recounts it) with

> a thousand persons . . . arrayed in manner of war, with cuirasses, coats of mail, steel helmets, glaives, bows, arrows, large shields, guns . . . ladders, and picks with which they mined down the walls, and long trees with which they broke up gates and doors, and so came into the said mansion, the wife of your beseecher at that time being therein, and twelve persons with her; the which persons they drove out of the said mansion and mined down the walls of the chamber wherein the wife of your beseecher was, and bare her out at the gates and cut asunder the posts of the house, and let them fall, and broke up all the chambers and coffers in the said mansion.

Over-mighty subjects used force not only to seize castles and manor houses, but also to intimidate courts of law. A great lord might appear at court with forty or fifty retainers in order to "maintain" his cause or that of a dependent. Any man bold enough to bring a lawsuit against a great lord or one of his allies might find that no counsel would serve him, that no witness would appear for him, and that the great lord had named the justices of the peace who were to try him. A powerful lord might bribe the jurors or intimidate the justices or, as Lord Fanhope did as a last resort at Bedford Town Hall, simply break up the meeting of the court with armed men.

Two qualifications must be made to this picture of anarchy and injustice. Livery and maintenance largely afflicted the countryside, not the towns; and the extent of the disorder may appear greater than in earlier centuries simply because it was better reported. There are no Paston letters for the thirteenth and fourteenth centuries. Yet these are only qualifications. The fact of social disorder is writ large over the history of the middle decades of the fifteenth century, as a petition before Parliament in 1459 makes clear. The petition complains of robberies, ravishments, extortions, oppressions, riots, and wrongful imprisonments that were universal throughout the land.

While the Lord Moleyns and the Lord Fanhopes of the age were besieging manor houses and invading courtrooms, the greatest lords, led by the House of York and the House of Lancaster, were fighting for political power. This struggle had its roots in two circumstances: the feebleness of the King, who could not prevent defeat abroad or disorder at home, and the irresponsibility of the aristocracy, who sought to exploit his weakness for their own gain.

Richard, Duke of York, the greatest landowner in the kingdom and a descendant of Edward III, placed himself at the head of the opponents of the Court. Edmund Beaufort, Duke of Somerset, a descendant of Edward III through John of Gaunt, led the Lancastrian forces at Court. Between 1450 and 1455, as the King fell into madness and then recovered, Yorkists and Lancastrians alternately controlled the Court.

In 1455 this struggle for power erupted onto the battlefield. At St. Albans in May a Yorkist army defeated the Lancastrians in a battle that traditionally marks the beginning of the Wars of the Roses. Somerset fell in the battle, and York siezed the opportunity to win for himself the protectorship of England. He did not hold it for long, for the Queen, now the leader of the Lancastrian forces, soon recovered power at Court. The years 1456 to 1459 were relatively quiet, but only because both sides were preparing for a new resort to arms. The crisis came in 1460, when the Duke of York's ally, Richard Neville, Earl of Warwick and Captain of Calais, launched an attack across the Channel. The fortunes of war now fluctuated wildly. At Northampton in July the Yorkists triumphed over the Lancastrians. At Wakefield in December the Lancastrians

The parish church of Lavenham, Suffolk, one of the great fifteenth-century wool churches of East Anglia (*National Monuments Record, England*).

defeated the Yorkists in a battle in which Richard, Duke of York, met his death. In February 1461 the Lancastrians won another victory at the Second Battle of St. Albans, but their triumph was short-lived. On March 29 the new Duke of York, Edward, decisively defeated the Lancastrians in a savage, seven-hour battle in a blinding snowstorm at Towton Moor. The Lancastrian cause never recovered from this defeat.

Beneath this kaleidoscope of changing military fortunes one can glimpse a deeper reason for the Yorkist victory. They profited from the reaction against Lancastrian misrule. The failure to maintain a royal fleet had alienated the merchants, whom Warwick enlisted in the Yorkist cause. The lack of good government, the burdensome collection of purveyance, repeated demands for money, and mounting corruption increased the government's unpopularity. The vindictiveness of the Lancastrians in the Parliament of 1459, when they voted numerous Acts of Attainder against Yorkist lords and knights, frightened the upper classes. As a result, when Warwick landed the men of Kent welcomed him, and when Edward marched into London the crowds cheered him. Indeed, the executions carried out by the Lancastrians after the battles of Wakefield and St. Albans and the plundering of the countryside by the Queen's army finally overcame the reluctance of the Yorkist party to remove Henry VI from the throne. In the autumn of 1460 the Yorkists could only persuade Parliament to name Richard, Duke of York, protector of the realm and heir to the King. In March 1461 a Yorkist Council and an assembly of London citizens at Clerkenwell acclaimed Edward King of England by hereditary right. The Yorkist claim to the throne was a strong one, but they would not have enforced that claim had Henry VI proved to be an able king.*

To a large extent, Edward IV owed his throne to his cousin, the Earl of Warwick, and he very nearly lost it by alienating this powerful and able politician, who stood for no principle more exalted than his own power. In a moment of infatuation Edward married the beautiful Elizabeth Woodville, a young lady from an obscure family. He then poured favors on her father, and on her five brothers and seven sisters. The rapid rise of the Woodvilles, along with Edward's determination to ally with the Duke of Burgundy, infuriated Warwick, who favored an alliance with France and the preservation of his own power. His fury finally drove him to raise the Neville forces in the north, to seek the assistance of Louis XI of France, and even to ally with his detested enemy, Margaret of Anjou. In the autumn of 1470 Warwick landed in England with an army and compelled Edward, who had insufficient forces, to flee to the Netherlands. Warwick the kingmaker now restored Henry VI to the throne, even though he had become a permanent imbecile. Warwick was unable, however, to hold the power he had seized. Edward raised a large force in the Netherlands, sailed up the Humber in 1471, and at Barnet on Easter Sunday in a thick mist defeated and slew Warwick. A few weeks later it was announced that Henry VI

---

* For the strength of the Yorkist claim see the genealogical chart on page 182.

had died in the Tower "of pure displeasure and melancholy," though he was probably murdered. Edward was now the undoubted King of England, beholden to no kingmaker.

EDWARD IV AND THE RESTORATION OF ROYAL POWER

Edward IV was a most unlikely person to restore the Crown to its former ascendancy. He was tall, handsome, affable, and indolent, a dissolute young soldier who loved wine, women, and magnificent clothing. Yet he began the revival of royal power that the Tudors carried to completion in the sixteenth century. Tradition has established the year 1485 as the beginning of modern English history, but 1471 makes more sense, for the Tudors built on the foundations Edward IV laid down.

Edward succeeded where others had failed for at least three reasons. In the first place, he had none of Henry VI's feebleness, nor did he suffer—as Henry IV had—from an uncertain title. The House of York, the descendants of Edward III's second son, always had a stronger claim to the throne than the House of Lancaster, the descendants of Edward III's third son. Furthermore, no serious pretenders to the Crown were alive—the Yorkists had seen to that by murdering Henry VI in the Tower and by slaying his young son, Edward, at the Battle of Tewkesbury (fought two weeks after the Battle of Barnet). But what mattered more was Edward's vigor and intelligence. He was an active King, who for several years went himself on judicial progresses through the countryside, suppressing disorders and seeing that justice was done.

Edward also succeeded because he made the Crown financially independent. The Lancastrians, by granting royal lands to favorites and waging wars that interrupted the trade on which the customs depended, drove the royal revenues down to a point where the Crown was dependent on Parliament. Edward reversed this trend. He added to the lands of the Crown the lands of the Duchy of Lancaster, which Henry VI had allowed to fall into the hands of Cardinal Beaufort. Then he made certain that all the lands which fell into his hands by escheat or forfeiture remained there. He also persuaded Parliament to vote him the customs for life, which freed him from the necessity of summoning Parliament every year or two in order to renew it. As great as these revenues were, they were not enough to allow the Crown to wage war. The pursuit of peace became the key to financial independence. Edward dared not relinquish English claims to the French throne and French territories too swiftly, for they were still popular. He therefore summoned Parliament in 1474 and allowed it to vote him a large subsidy for an invasion of France. In 1475 he launched the invasion, but then quickly allowed Louis XI to buy him off. By the Treaty of Picquigny, Louis promised to pay Edward an immediate sum of 75,000 gold crowns and an annual pension for the rest of his life of 50,000 gold crowns. Louis also permitted English merchants to renew their trade with Gascony and other parts of France. Peace brought trade, and trade an increase in the customs. From 1475 onward Edward was free from any dependence on parliamentary grants.

The third reason for Edward's success lay in the clamor of the middle classes for order and in their aversion to taxation. The Wars of the Roses had caused enough violence and injustice, and enough damage to trade, to make the middle classes, both in the countryside and in the towns, yearn for a strong king. Nor were they alarmed that Edward IV met only six Parliaments in twenty-two years. The public had lost confidence in parliaments that were only tools of factions. And their hatred of taxation made them welcome a king who would "live of his own." Peace abroad and low taxes at home caused the merchants of London to prosper. So great was the satisfaction of the mercantile community that they even acquiesced in the forced loans, or benevolences, which Edward levied on those who had grown rich in trade and industry but escaped the traditional taxes.

The institutions through which Edward exerted his royal power were the Council, the Chamber, the office of Secretary, and the Court. In his Council Edward made greater use of knights, justices, sergeants, and attorneys, and less use of magnates. The Council became a body of trusted men, dependent on the King, advising him, and carrying out his will. It recovered some of the judicial powers it had lost at midcentury. Ever since the fourteenth century it had sat in the Star Chamber as a court; the difference now was that a strong King backed its efforts to suppress, by fines and imprisonment, the violence of the times. Conciliar government was even extended to the Marches of Wales, where the Prince of Wales's Council enjoyed wide powers, and to the north, where Richard, Duke of Gloucester, on becoming King, created the King's Council in the north. More important than the Council in the daily administration of the realm, however, was the Household, particularly the Chamber. Edward used the Chamber to administer his royal lands, thereby escaping the cumbersome procedures of the medieval Exchequer. He also made extensive use of the Secretary, who was always a member of the Council, and who dealt with correspondence on every matter and issued warrants under the signet seal. Yet Edward clearly understood that government was more than Star Chamber decrees and warrants under the signet. He sought by the magnificence of his person and Court to exalt the monarch above his subjects.

How far Edward sought to exalt the monarch is hard to say, but an acute observer of the political scene, Sir John Fortescue, voiced his opinion on the rightful powers of the monarch. Fortescue was a chief justice of the King's Bench and a Lancastrian who was captured at Tewkesbury. Edward pardoned him and named him to the Council. Fortescue then wrote the first political treatise in the English language, *The Governance of England.* In it he argued that no kingdom could prosper where the King was poor and his subjects nearly as wealthy. He therefore urged that the King build up the royal demesne by resuming alienated lands and that his subjects be prevented from accumulating large estates by marriage alliances or other means. He also urged that the King rely on a Council that was not dominated by the greatest lords in the land. These arguments, however, did not mean that Fortescue believed that the King of England should be absolute. He drew a favorable contrast between England, a limited monarchy, and France, an absolute monarchy. He declared that the King of England rules by laws which he cannot change at his pleasure and which are made with the "assent of the whole Kingdom." Fortescue's purpose was to rescue the King from his subservience to the great lords, not to make him an absolute monarch, ruling above the law.

DEPRESSION AND ECONOMIC CHANGE

The political turbulence of the mid-fifteenth century caused a decline in trade that added to the woes of a people already suffering from an agricultural depression. During the fifteenth century the price of wheat and barley continued to drop, trade with the Netherlands was disrupted, and trade with Gascony was temporarily halted by the French. Yet depression did not prevent a fundamental change in English commerce. From being chiefly an exporter of a raw material, wool, England became chiefly an exporter of a manufactured commodity, woolen cloth. In 1350 it exported 30,000 sacks of wool a year; in 1485 it exported only 10,000 sacks. Meanwhile the export of woolen cloth rose from 4,774 cloths (a cloth was 24 yards long and 2 yards wide) in 1354 to 30,000 cloths in 1400 and 50,000 in 1485. The fifteenth century demonstrated that fundamental economic change is consonant with prolonged economic depression.

The forces working for this transformation were various. The most important may well have been the high export duties levied on wool. From 1363 a group of merchants called the Company of the Staple had maintained a permanent garrison, or "staple," at Calais. Edward granted them a monopoly of the export of wool so he might more easily tax wool. This tax was £2 a sack, or a fourth of the price of the wool. English cloth, on the other hand, paid only a trivial duty. This gave the English clothier an immense advantage over his Flemish competitor, who had to pay at least a fourth more for his wool. There was also the fact that England produced at home, close to the Cotswolds and dales of Yorkshire, where the best wool in Europe was produced. The declining profitability of agriculture also promoted the manufacture of cloth, for many peasants, finding no work in the fields, turned to the spinning wheel and loom. Finally, the guild system did not restrict the English industry as severely as it did the Flemish. Originally the English cloth industry existed in the towns, in Coventry, York, Norwich, and Salisbury, but the difficulty of bringing together the weaver who wove cloth, the fuller who fulled it, the dyer who dyed it, and the shearman who finished it, each with his own guild, proved very great.

As the market for cloth expanded, as the need for waterpower for fulling emerged, and as the restrictions of the guilds grew more irksome, the manufacture of cloth moved to the countryside.

This led to the rise of the great clothier, the entrepreneur who purchased wool from the farmer, took it to the cottages for the women and children to card and spin, carried the yarn to the weaver to weave into cloth, then took the cloth to the fuller to be fulled, the dyer to be dyed, and the shearman to be finished. His last act was to place the cloth on packhorses to be carried off to market. Such an enterprise required great sums of capital, a clothier willing to take risks, freedom from guild regulations, and laborers who would work for wages. The system came to be called the "putting-out system" and its emergence marks the advent of capitalism in English industry.

England, as George Holmes has observed, was the Japan of the later Middle Ages, exporting cheap, serviceable cloth all over the Western world, just as the Japanese export their Toyotas and Sonys. England sold cloth to the Hansards, who carried it to Novgorod; to the Italians, who carried it to Byzantium; and to the merchants of the Netherlands, who carried it to central Europe. The English came to resent the fact that foreigners dominated the trade in cloth, a commercial nationalism that found expression in 1437 in *The Libel* [meaning little book] *of English Policy.* The author argued that foreigners could not do without English wool and cloth and therefore must submit to the English or starve. He urged that England exploit its command of the Channel to stifle the trade of the Italians and the Hansards. But the governments of the 1440s and 1450s did not have the naval power to challenge the Italians and Hansards. An attempt by Robert Sturmy to send ships loaded with wool, tin, and cloth to Pisa met with fierce reprisals by the Genoese. An attack on a Hansard fleet in 1449 led to the seizure of all English goods in the territories of the Hanseatic League and the closing of the Danish Sound to English shipping. The 1450s were the bleakest decade in English trade. The government quarreled with the Duke of Burgundy, who controlled England's most important market, the Netherlands. Gascony, to whom the English had sent wheat and cloth in return for wine, was lost. Even the export of cloth declined in this decade. It is no wonder that the merchants supported Edward in his bid for the Crown.

And they were well repaid. As King he restored to the Hansards their former privileges and gained Louis XI's permission for a resumption of trade with Gascony. The export of English cloth began its sensational rise, which continued under the Tudors. And though Edward restored the privileges of the Hansards, the total trade in the hands of foreigners was less than two-thirds of that in the hands of the Merchant Adventurers, the English company to whom Henry IV granted a charter in 1407 and who dominated the export of cloth.

The depression and the economic changes of the fifteenth century affected the different classes in different ways. The laborers and peasants who worked for hire held their own, since wages remained high and prices stationary. Peasants with small holdings in the West Riding, the West Country, and

East Anglia could supplement their incomes by spinning and weaving. The more enterprising peasant could rise by leasing the lord's demesne. In these years the copyholder who worked his own land and kept sheep, hens, pigs, cattle, and bees prospered more than the large landowner who grew a cereal crop. These years witnessed the rise of the yeoman class. The name "yeoman" was once reserved for the freeholder peasant, but now it came to be applied to all prosperous peasants, whether they held by freehold, copyhold, or leasehold.

It was the large landowners who suffered the severest economic decline during these years. A few of the greatest families survived by accumulating, through marriages, more land, but many baronial families went down. A few avoided bankruptcy by marrying the daughters of rich merchants or by participating in trade, for it was in commerce that wealth was made. Not all merchants, however, grew wealthy. Many towns in England declined in population and wealth during the fifteenth century. Others prospered, like Bristol, with its trade to Ireland and Spain, and with the cloth industry of the West Country behind it; and Southampton, where the Italian galleys came with their silks, satins, furred gowns, spices, sugar, and gems, and returned with wool, cloth, hides, and metal. But the most prosperous town of all was London, whose merchants controlled the rural cloth industry and dominated the Merchant Adventurers. In 1334 London had 2 percent of the taxable lay wealth of England; by 1515 it had 9 percent. But not all Londoners prospered. The master weaver became a hired hand and the craft guilds lost much of their power to the oligarchic merchant companies such as the mercers (those who dealt in textiles), grocers, and drapers. It was the successful merchant who prospered and who used his burgeoning wealth to erect parish churches and build oak-beamed houses.

LATE MEDIEVAL CULTURE

Civil war and economic depression prevented the aristocracy from building on a grand scale, while most of the great cathedrals and abbeys of England had been built in earlier centuries. The wealth of England, therefore, now found employment and the piety of Englishmen found expression in the building of parish churches, especially in East Anglia, the West Riding, and the Cotswolds. Here the clothier and woolman devoted their wealth to the building of resplendent parish churches. Responding to the increasing nationalism of the time, patrons and architects built these churches in the uniquely English Perpendicular style, with large porches, timber roofs, richly carved choir stalls and rood screens (screens separating the nave from the chancel), and square towers crowned with pinnacles at the four corners. The piety of the age also found expression in the endowment of chantries. A chantry was a chapel where a priest said masses for the repose of the souls of the dead. A wealthy man might endow a chantry college, where a staff of priests said masses in perpetuity for his soul and those of his family. A less wealthy man would found a chantry chapel in a cathedral or parish church, a chapel built with all the profuse decoration of the Perpendicular style. Originally a brass effigy of the donor covered the floor above his tomb, but the growing ostentation of the time led to more elaborate chantry tombs. The tomb now became a chest, rising above the floor, surmounted by a recumbent effigy, usually in alabaster, of the deceased. The finest of these effigies, such as that of Richard Beauchamp in Warwick Chapel, were works of art that exhibited the powerful realism of fifteenth-century sculpture.

The chantry chapel reflected many of the qualities of late medieval religion—its individualism, its preoccupation with death, its reliance on the intercession of the Church. Many of the merchants who endowed a chantry seemed less concerned with the glory of God than with the future of their souls, and the elaborate tombs they built witnessed less to Christian truth than to their own material worth. Chantries also reflected the unusual fascination of the fifteenth century with death. Wall paintings in churches depicted death as a skeleton, reaping his grim harvest, and the Scottish poet William of Dunbar lamented in a famous poem

> Unto the Death goes all Estates,
> Princes, Prelates, and Potentates,
> Both rich and poor of all degree:
> Timor Mortis conturbat me.*

This preoccupation with death may have arisen from the growing attractiveness of this world, joined to the constant presence of death in an age of war and plague. Whatever the reason, men and women increasingly sought the intercession of the Church, and did so in an age when the Church stressed free will and the efficacy of good works, of which few were more efficacious than the offering of masses for the swifter progress of souls through Purgatory. The fear of death also promoted the cult of Mary, who might intercede with Christ for sinful man. Paintings on walls and rood screens portrayed Mary in a most worldly and lively manner.

In comparison to earlier centuries, the fifteenth century was intellectually sterile. There were fewer students at the universities and no great issues. Reginald Pecock, the outstanding scholar of the century, illustrated this sterility. He was a Welshman and fellow of Oriel College, Oxford, who rose to be Bishop of Chichester and who wrote over forty works. He was a scholastic philosopher who had immeasurable confidence in the power of formal logic and the validity of the syllogism. His chief concern was to refute and convert the Lollards. He attacked the Lollards for their dependence on Scripture alone and sought to restore the harmony of reason and faith that St. Thomas Aquinas had asserted and Duns Scotus and Ockham repudiated. But the day was rapidly

* The fear of Death doth trouble me.

passing when exercises in formal logic could either persuade people or reveal new truths.

The intellectual sterility of the age was paralleled by a decline in the quality of courtly verse. This came about partly because the patrons of letters were too busy waging war, partly because allegories and chivalry were as threadbare as scholasticism, and partly because the final "e" in the English language, pronounced in Chaucer's time, had become mute. This last development made Chaucer's lines seem variable and so led his disciples to produce careless, clumsy verses. But though courtly letters declined, popular literature flourished —in the ballad, the carol, the morality play, and letter writing. The fifteenth century was the great age of the narrative ballad, which was usually meant to be sung. Those about Robin Hood reflected many features of the time—the popular hatred of sheriffs, respect for the yeoman class, and faith that the King will do justice. The carol began as a song for a dance, in which the dancers sang the refrain, but the connection with dancing had disappeared by the fifteenth century. Carols kept the refrain and a lyrical quality but they now expressed a religious sentiment. They were written for Christian festivals, especially Christmas, and were usually joyous in mood, though occasionally melancholic. To the miracle play, which reached its height about 1425, was now added the morality play, in which the dispute lay between abstract virtues and vices. The masterpiece among morality plays was *Everyman*, in which Death summons Everyman to God. One by one Everyman's worldly companions forsake him, until only Good Deeds is left to accompany him to his last ordeal. The ballad, the carol, and the play were part of an oral tradition, but the gradual growth of literacy led for the first time to the practice of letter writing. The letters of the Paston family of Norfolk contain some of the finest English prose of the age—plain, direct, vivid.

Margaret Paston, one of the Norfolk Pastons, assumed that any man fit to be put in charge of the household's bread and beer could write, and Sir Thomas More a generation later estimated that half the population could read (he must have been thinking of London). One of the principal causes of this widespread literacy was the foundation of grammar schools during the fourteenth and fifteenth centuries. In 1382 William of Wykeham founded a grammar school at Winchester, a certain proportion of whose students should be "the sons of noble and powerful persons," a provision that was the germ of the great English public (in American terms private) schools. In 1440 Henry VI established an equally splendid grammar school at Eton. Noblemen, men and women of lesser ranks, town corporations, and guilds all established schools. By the end of the century there were from 300 to 400 schools scattered throughout England.

During these same years there arose on the north bank of the Thames, between the city of London and Westminster, four great Inns of Court, where the Common law judges and lawyers received their legal education. These institutions came into being when associations of lawyers purchased the inns, or townhouses, of great noblemen and religious societies. In these inns the students slept, dined, disputed, and studied the mysteries of the Common law. The lawyers and apprentices who composed the Inns of Court had an exclusive right to plead in the royal courts. The Inns of Court made the fifteenth century a golden age of pleading.

The grammar schools and the Inns of Court produced an ever-increasing number of educated laymen, a process that was greatly accelerated by the introduction of the printing press into England. William Caxton, a successful merchant with literary tastes, learned the art of printing in Flanders. He set up the first press in 1476 in the precincts of Westminster Abbey. The first books he published reflected the medieval taste in literature—lives of saints, books of devotion, romances, the works of Chaucer. Indeed, by publishing Malory's *Morte d'Arthur* he helped perpetuate the taste for medieval romance. Malory fused together in a coherent and simple manner the various Arthurian ro-

The Smith Company enacts the trial of Christ in the streets of Coventry
(*Victoria and Albert Museum*).

mances. He was indifferent to the supernatural elements, such as the quest for the Holy Grail, but he idealized the chivalric elements. He made Arthur not only a chivalrous knight but a national hero. His romance was the first great work of poetic prose in England.

The tastes of the English in the fifteenth century were conservative, their intellectual disputes sterile, and their courtly verse clumsy. Yet beneath this outward decadence social and educational forces were creating an educated lay public, both in the upper and middle classes, that in the next century would welcome the new learning and art of the Italian Renaissance.

RICHARD III AND THE FALL OF THE HOUSE OF YORK

But for the chance death of Edward IV and the rapacity of Richard III, the House of York would have been on the throne when English scholars brought the new learning from Italy. But Edward died suddenly at the age of 40, worn out, not by work, but by a feverish pursuit of pleasure. He was succeeded by his son Edward, a mere boy of 12. The young prince was controlled by the Queen Mother, behind whom stood the grasping, ambitious, numerous, and unpopular Woodville family. To forestall their triumph, Richard, Duke of Gloucester, the King's brother, marched swiftly south, seized the Prince, won control of London, and had the Council declare him protector of the realm.

Gloucester succeeded because he had the support of many councilors and noblemen and because most Englishmen feared the civil disorders that would arise under a minority. In the next months, however, Richard overreached himself. He had Lord Hastings, the last of Edward IV's trusted councilors, executed. He had Dr. Shaw declare at Paul's Cross and the Duke of Buckingham announce at the Guildhall that Edward IV's marriage was invalid, his children illegitimate, and Richard therefore the rightful heir. The next day Parliament meekly agreed that Edward's marriage was invalid and Richard rightfully King. On July 6 Richard was crowned as Richard III. A month later the two young princes, Edward V and his brother Richard, Duke of York, were probably smothered to death in the Tower, most likely on Richard's orders. Richard's seizure of the throne was the most ruthless of many violent acts committed during the fifteenth century, but it was the work of an ambitious, nervous politician, not a moral ogre. Shakespeare's picture of Richard as physically and mentally deformed, a "crouchback" with his right shoulder higher than his left, is false, a piece of Tudor propaganda to justify the accession of the House of Tudor. Richard III was a courageous soldier, an able administrator, and a man of culture. Yet the many attempts to whitewash Richard of the guilt of murdering the two princes carry little conviction. No one will ever know for certain who ordered their murder, but the evidence points more clearly at Richard than at anyone else.

The murder of the two princes—rumor of which soon spread abroad—

broke the Yorkist party. The Duke of Buckingham, once Richard's ally, now raised a rebellion against him in the west of England, a rebellion Richard swiftly suppressed. Buckingham paid the ultimate penalty for failure in medieval England; he lost his head. The object of Buckingham's rebellion was to bring Henry Tudor, Earl of Richmond, to the throne. This man now became Richard's most formidable foe. Through his mother, Margaret Beaufort, Henry had inherited the Beaufort claim to the throne—an uncertain claim, for it came through John of Gaunt's illegitimate children. Henry had fought at Tewkesbury in 1471 for the Lancastrians, from which battle he had fled to Britanny to await his chance. The growing unpopularity of Richard's rule now made his chances seem less hopeless. The executions of Earl Rivers, Hastings, Buckingham, and others had greatly narrowed Richard's basis of power. His resort to forced loans further increased the hostility to him. When Henry Tudor sailed from France with 2,000 men in August 1485, he met little resistance. Richard's men at Milford Haven, where Henry landed, far from opposing Henry, put themselves under his command. Henry then marched through Wales and the Midlands to Leicester, where on August 22 he met Richard in the battle of Bosworth Field. Henry was outnumbered, but the Earl of Northumberland, who commanded Richard's right wing, refused to fight, and Thomas Lord Stanley, who was formally allied with Richard, deserted with all his men to Henry. The defection of Stanley spelled certain defeat for Richard, who died fighting for his crown. The crown itself rolled underneath a hawthorne bush. Lord Stanley picked it up and placed it on the victor's head.

FURTHER READINGS

*JOHN A. THOMSON. *The Transformation of England.* London, 1983. A clear, accurate, comprehensive survey, which emphasizes those developments that transformed rather than perpetuated medieval society.

E.F. JACOB. *The Fifteenth Century 1399–1485.* Oxford, 1961. A large compendium of facts rather than a coherent interpretation; does bring together in one place the fruits of recent research; the bibliography runs to 110 pages.

R.L. STOREY. *The End of the House of Lancaster.* London, 1966. A lively, readable book that argues that the Wars of the Roses were the outcome of the antisocial urges of bastard feudalism.

A.R. BRIDBURY. *Economic Growth: England in the Later Middle Ages.* London, 1962. Challenges the orthodox view that sees economic decline in these years; argues that the Black Death stimulated enterprise.

F.R.H. DU BOULAY. *An Age of Ambition: English Society in the Late Middle Ages.* London, 1970. A social history that both scholar and general reader may read with pleasure and profit; contains fascinating chapters on "Class," "Marriage and Sex," and "Attitudes Toward Authority."

RICHARD BARBER, ed. *The Pastons: The Letters of a Family in the Wars of the Roses.* Penguin Books, 1984. The letters of a family who rose to eminence in Suffolk; they offer a rich and intimate glimpse of these turbulent years.

J.L. KIRBY. *Henry IV of England.* London, 1970. Not a personal biography but a careful, judicious, detailed history of the reign; particularly valuable on the King's finances.

CHARLES ROSS. *Edward IV*. London, 1974. A vivid, profound, yet critical study of Edward IV, which has become the standard history of the reign.

PAUL MURRAY KENDALL. *Richard the Third*. New York, 1956. A sympathetic life of the much-maligned monarch; an appendix argues that Buckingham, not Richard, ordered the murder of the princes in the Tower.

A.R. MYERS, ed. *English Historical Documents 1327–1485*. London, 1969. Contemporary sources on politics, the government, the Church, and economic and social developments, all linked together by introductions that form an important work in their own right.

9 The Reign of Henry VII: 1485-1509

The kingdom which Henry VII won at Bosworth Field was a thinly populated though rich and fertile land. The Venetian ambassador found it a pleasant land of rolling hills and beautiful valleys, of wide meadows and agreeable woods, with a great plenty of water everywhere. He found the climate healthy, for the cold in winter was less severe than in Italy and the heat in summer less oppressive. The heat was less in summer because of the rain which, he observed, "falls almost every day during the months of June, July, and August." He thought the riches of England—its fertile soil, its wool, its tin and lead, its fish and wild fowl—greater than that of any country in Europe. He thought more land should be put under the plow, but observed that this negligence was made up for by the enormous number of animals—deer, pigs, cattle, and above all sheep. What most struck him as he traveled from Dover to Oxford was the emptiness of the English countryside. "The population of this island," he wrote, "does not appear to bear any proportion to the fertility and riches."

When Henry VII ascended the throne, some 2.2 million people occupied a land that had supported between 4.5 and 6 million at the end of the thirteenth century. The Black Death and related diseases had decreased the population of England to a mere 2.1 million during the years from 1400 to 1430. It remained at that level until about 1470, when first slowly, then more swiftly, it began to rise. By 1600 it had reached 4 million, nearly what it had been three centuries before. Thus the dramatic events of Tudor England were played out against a backdrop of a growing population whose numbers slowly destroyed the fifteenth-century world of cheap food and high wages.

These 2.2 million people were not divided into a few self-conscious classes, but into many ranks and degrees of men and women. The most profound distinction lay between those who owned land and those who did not. Among the landowners of England in 1500 there were some 50 noblemen, 500 knights, 800 esquires, and 5000 gentlemen (not to speak of the King, who owned about 5 percent of the land, and the Church, which owned over 20 percent). The nobility were set off from the other landowners of England by their titles, their seats in the House of Lords, their great households, and their wealth. The wealthiest peer in the realm, the Duke of Buckingham, enjoyed an income of £6000 a year; the average income of a peer was probably £1000 a year. They led their lives in public, amid a mass of underemployed servants, in huge drafty halls, dispensing hospitality on a magnificent scale. Husbands and wives occasionally lived apart, keeping separate households in different parts of the country. They sent their children to wetnurses at birth, then to servants to be reared, and finally to another lord's household to learn "courtesy." The want of affection in family life helps to explain the ease with which children became pawns in marriage alliances. In the late fifteenth century, this style of life began to give way to a domestic style. Increasingly the lord's family retired to private chambers to dine, and in the 1490s peers began to build houses for comfort rather than defense. These houses were one of the earliest signs of the country-house civilization that was to dominate England for the next 400 years.

After the nobility came the gentry, who consisted of all the landowners of England below the peerage and above the yeomanry. Contemporaries often, but not invariably, distinguished three ranks within the gentry: the knight, the esquire, and the gentleman. The knights were the fewest and the wealthiest. There were some 500 knights in England in 1500, with an average income of about £200 a year. Below them were the "esquires," a name originally applied to the younger sons of knights, but now applied to any considerable landowner who did not aspire to knighthood. In 1500 there were some 800 squires in England, men whose incomes averaged £80 a year. The title "gentleman" originally described the younger sons and brothers of esquires, but came to be applied to a large group of minor landowners, some 3,000 to 5,000 in number. They were distinguished from the esquires chiefly by the fact that an esquire owned one or more manors, while a gentleman merely owned land within a manor. Most gentlemen had an income of £10 to £20 a year.

The gentry class as a whole represented an amalgamation of the knightly class of the thirteenth and fourteenth centuries with two new groups, merchants and lawyers who had purchased land, and yeoman farmers who had accumulated enough land to seek gentility. Formally, one became a gentleman when the College of Heralds recognized one's right to bear a coat of arms, a right recognized with increasing frequency in the fifteenth century. But in reality gentility was defined by a way of life based on the ownership of land and unsullied by manual labor. It was also distinguished by cultivated manners, a proper education, and a comfortable house. A wealthy merchant or yeoman would purchase the land; his properly educated son would acquire the status. "Gentility," said Lord Burghley, Queen Elizabeth's great minister, was "nothing but ancient riches."

Beneath the gentry were the yeomen, the peculiar glory of England, the descendants of the franklins of Chaucer's time. It is as difficult to define yeoman as it is to define gentry. Different records often called the same man "yeoman" and "husbandman." Generally speaking, a yeoman owned or leased a farm of 100 or 200 acres and rented additional pasture, whereas the husbandman farmed about 10 to 30 acres. A yeoman's livestock might be ten times as numerous as the husbandman's and his income greater than many a gentleman's. He filled his house, not with gentility, but with bacon, eggs, butter, and cheese. The husbandman rarely owned any land; his economic well-being depended on the fixity of his tenure and his landlord's willingness not to raise the rent. In an average year a husbandman with 30 acres might produce a crop worth £3 13s 4d, pay 12s 6d rent and 10s tithes, and be left with £2 12s 10d.

At the bottom of the pyramid were the cottager and the laborer, those who worked for wages, probably two out of every three Englishmen. They were not an industrial proletariat, for the cottage and acre or two of land they rented were an important part of their livelihood. A laborer with only an acre of land might, by thrift and hard work, rise in the world. Yet life for most of them was harsh and precarious. They lived in cottages with but a single room, often only 10 feet by 8. When the harvest was good and bread cheap they survived; when it was not, weakened by hunger, disease might sweep them away (the expectation of life at birth was about 35 years, compared with 70 today). Despite the harshness of life, suicide (which the church condemned) was rare; expectations were low and there were compensations such as a sense of belonging to a place, a leisurely pace of work, a close-knit family, a cycle of holy days, and the oblivion offered by a cheap and plentiful supply of ale.

Nine out of ten people lived in the countryside, but much of the wealth of England was to be found in the towns. During the fourteenth and fifteenth centuries there was a remarkable advance in urban wealth. In 1334 urban wealth was 7 percent of the wealth of the country; by 1524 it was 15 percent. Equally remarkable was the growing ascendancy of London. In the early fourteenth century it was three times wealthier than the richest provincial city, Bristol; by 1520 it was ten times wealthier than the richest provincial city, which was now Norwich. It had 60,000 inhabitants, whereas York, Bristol, and Norwich had but 10,000 each and a dozen other towns but 5,000. The Venetians were filled with admiration at the riches of London. They wrote home about the fifty-two goldsmith shops in Cheapside, filled with treasures that the shops of Rome, Milan, Florence, and Venice together could not rival. The Venetians said nothing about the squalid streets where the poor lived, but there were many such streets. London exhibited the same wide gulf between rich and poor that the countryside did. The bottom three-quarters of the population owned only 4 percent of the total wealth of the city, while the top 5 percent owned 80 percent. In Coventry eleven persons owned 44 percent of the wealth, while half the population owned nothing other than the rags they wore and a few pieces of board as furniture. And during the late fifteenth century town governments grew ever more oligarchical. The new charter for Bristol, for example, put an end to what little popular control had existed. Inequality of wealth and increased social distinctions were the hallmarks of the society Henry VII governed from 1485 to 1509.

ENGROSSMENT AND ENCLOSURE

It is a curious but indisputable fact that the growth of individual liberty was a chief cause for the growth of inequality. In the twelfth century serfdom had stamped a rough equality on the villeins of England, most of whom had rights in some 30 acres of land. The gradual disappearance of serfdom, the commutation of labor services into money rents, the appearance of a market in land, and the renting of the manorial demesne made possible the erosion of this equality. The enterprising peasant steadily accumulated land. Others went to the wall and became landless laborers. The engrossing of farms—the adding of farm to farm—proceeded from generation to generation, either by the natural process of inheritance and marriage or by the purchase of land. By 1500 villeinage was practically extinct. The important distinction now became one of wealth, not legal status; the line ran between the well-to-do peasant who owned or leased land and the landless laborer who worked for wages. The village of Wigston Magna in Leicestershire offers an example of such a rural society. Two great absentee families owned 60 percent of the land, the Church owned 3 percent and the peasants 37 percent, but out of some eighty peasants only twenty owned any land. Under the Tudors the pace of engrossing increased. A few individuals bought more and more land, making it more difficult for a growing population to find land. Indeed, engrossing was probably a greater social problem than enclosing, for it went on throughout England, while enclosure was limited largely to the East Midlands.

Enclosing was the process by which the lord of a manor or a tenant bought up all the strips adjoining his, put a hedge around them, and farmed this compact, closed field separately from the open fields. Throughout the fifteenth century individual tenants had, by exchanging strips and by purchasing them, consolidated their holdings in this manner. It made for a more efficient agriculture, as was demonstrated by the fact that enclosed land sold for 50 percent more than unenclosed land. Against such enclosure neither the moralist nor the statesman inveighed, but it was very different when the lord of the manor consolidated large stretches of the open field, evicted his tenants, and converted the land to pasture, on which he put great flocks of sheep. Even worse was the landlord who enclosed all or part of the village common, thus depriving his tenants of the right to pasture their animals on it. Moralists and statesmen condemned such enclosures. In 1489 Parliament passed an act forbidding the conversion of arable into pasture and the pulling down of houses. The government feared that enclosures would swell the number of vagrants,

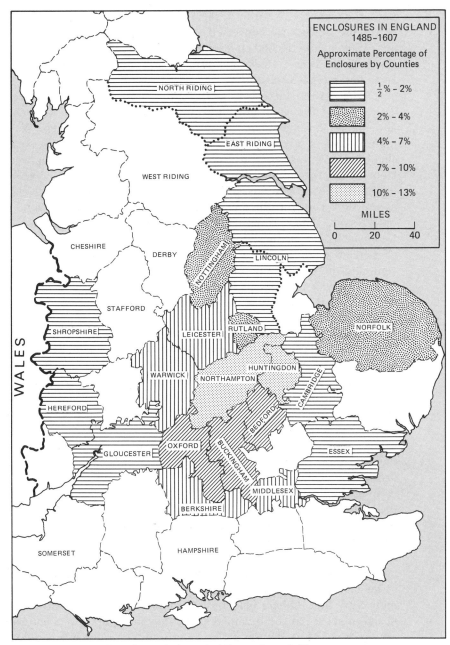

ENCLOSURES IN ENGLAND
1485–1607

Approximate Percentage of
Enclosures by Counties

	½% – 2%
	2% – 4%
	4% – 7%
	7% – 10%
	10% – 13%

MILES

0   20   40

NORTH RIDING

EAST RIDING

WEST RIDING

CHESHIRE

DERBY

NOTTINGHAM

LINCOLN

STAFFORD

SHROPSHIRE

LEICESTER

RUTLAND

NORFOLK

WARWICK

NORTHAMPTON

HUNTINGDON

CAMBRIDGE

HEREFORD

BEDFORD

W A L E S

OXFORD

BUCKINGHAM

GLOUCESTER

ESSEX

MIDDLESEX

BERKSHIRE

SOMERSET

HAMPSHIRE

Adapted from E. F. Gay, *Quarterly Journal of Economics*, vol. 17.

reduce the amount of grain needed to feed England, and deplete the supply of
men for the fighting forces. The enforcement of the act was left to the initiative
of landlords, with the obvious result that it was not enforced. Within a few

years the owner of Stretton Baskerville turned out eighty people, let their houses tumble down, and converted the arable fields into pasture. Between 1485 and 1500 nearly 16,000 acres were enclosed in Northamptonshire, Warwickshire, Oxfordshire, Buckinghamshire, and Berkshire, of which over 13,000 acres became pastureland.

The driving force behind the conversion to pasture was economic gain. The demand for wool and mutton, and hence the price of each, rose higher and higher, making it increasingly profitable to raise sheep. Wages remained high, making it advantageous to turn from arable farming to pasture. A single shepherd, with his boy and dog, could tend a whole flock, replacing a hundred laborers on the arable. The profits from sheep farming were immense; the temptation to turn to sheep farming irresistible. Those who yielded were not, as was once thought, the merchant who had recently bought land and sought a quick profit. Those responsible for turning arable into pasture were the old, well-established families. In Leicestershire the ancient squirearchy carried out 67 percent of the enclosures, the monasteries 17 percent, the nobility 12 percent, and the Crown 2 percent. But though the "new men" did not enclose the land and evict the tenants, a new spirit did. Landlords came to regard their lands more as a source of wealth and less as a means to support a numerous tenantry useful as a military force.

A landlord who wished to turn to sheep farming would begin by evicting the leaseholders from his demesne and enclosing it for pasture for sheep. This presented few problems, for most leases were short. But sheep farming demanded more land than the demesne, so the lord set out to acquire land from his tenants. These were of three kinds: the freeholder, who paid a token rent and enjoyed complete security of tenure; the customary tenant, who held by a great variety of tenures; and the tenant-at-will, who held his land on his lord's terms at his lord's pleasure. The customary tenants were the most numerous, about three out of five. Some held their land by the "custom of the manor," which was recorded on the manorial court roll. Others possessed a copy of the entry on the manorial court roll and were called copyholders. But the distinction between a customary tenant without a copy of the manor roll and one with a copy was far less important than the conditions enrolled there. Some customary tenants held their land for only one lifetime. An enclosing landlord need only await the tenant's death to seize his land. Others held by inheritance, but with an uncertain entry fine (the sum paid by an heir to succeed to his lands). A landlord could evict such a tenant by demanding an impossibly high entry fine. Others held by inheritance and a fixed entry fine. They were nearly as secure as the freeholder, but they made up only a minority of customary tenants. Thus, by calling in leases, evicting tenants-at-will, awaiting the death of a copyholder, and imposing high entry fines, a determined lord could create a great sheep run, to his profit and his tenants' misery.

In 1516 Sir Thomas More in his *Utopia* cried out that the sheep, once so meek, now devour the very people themselves. His lamentation was exaggerated, for much of England was untouched by enclosures. In the highland zone of the west and north the arable, always small, had long been enclosed. In the wood-pasture regions within the lowland zone, arable fields had also been long enclosed. Kent had never known open fields, and pasture for cattle and pigs in Essex and Suffolk was already enclosed. Along the east coast of England was a marshland that harbored an agricultural world of its own. The only counties seriously affected by enclosure were in the Midlands, extending from Leicestershire and Warwickshire south through Northamptonshire and Oxfordshire to Berkshire. Leicestershire affords a typical example of the extent of enclosures. It lay in the heart of open field England, with possibly 95 percent of its land under cultivation. Of the enclosures that occurred in Leicestershire 48 percent took place before 1485, 43 percent between 1485 and 1530, and 9 percent thereafter. The climax was reached about 1510. During the entire period only about one-tenth of the open field arable was converted to pasture, a fact that appears to make Sir Thomas More's lament seem excessive. Yet it was not, since enclosures, partial and complete, touched one village out of three. Of 370 villages in Leicestershire, 140 suffered from a complete or partial conversion to grass. Forty of these villages were completely enclosed and became deserted, part of the lost villages of England. The fact that economic distress of this magnitude did not lead to revolt can probably be explained by successive waves of the plague, which reduced some of the villages to small, decaying communities. There were few to be evicted, and they could find vacant tenures or employment elsewhere. Where there were many to be evicted the distress was great, though the wealth of the nation increased.

INDUSTRY: URBAN AND RURAL

There was a second reason why enclosing and engrossing did not lead to social revolt during the reign of Henry VII: the English economy was a dual economy in which the peasant worked in both agriculture and industry. In the uplands of Wiltshire and Suffolk they wove cloth, in Cornwall and Devon they mined tin, in the north they mined coal, in the West Midlands they manufactured nails. Of these rural industries, the woolen cloth industry was by far the most important. It was centered in the West Country (Gloucestershire, Wiltshire, and Somersetshire), in East Anglia (particularly Suffolk), and in the West Riding of Yorkshire. These were areas of pastoral farming, where agriculture placed fewer demands on the villager than did the cultivation of the arable. The cloth industry in Hertfordshire, for instance, disappeared in the sixteenth century when that county turned to the growing of grain. Though the great bulk of cloth produced went into the home market, exports also rose spectacularly, making the cloth industry of Wiltshire and Suffolk dependent on foreign markets. A new phenomenon appeared in the English economy: periods of unemployment caused by fluctuations in a distant market.

During the 1490s there were several changes in the location of the industry. The areas around Halifax and Leeds replaced York as the center of the industry in Yorkshire, while in the West Country it came to be centered on Exeter. But there were no changes in basic organization. The great capitalist clothier continued to dominate, putting out the wool to be spun and the yarn to be woven in lonely cottages from Cornwall to Cumberland. Nor were the clothiers averse to agreeing to a price for the weaving of cloth—a price that drove the weaver to work long hours to earn his livelihood.

There were many other industries in England besides cloth making. It is even possible that the building industry (if one includes the quarrying of stone within it) employed as many as the cloth industry. Between 1480 and 1540 there was a great resurgence in church building. In the 1500s the nobility and gentry also began to build country houses, while thousands of small gentry and prosperous yeomen rebuilt their homes. Next to the building trades came the exploitation of the mineral wealth of England. By 1500 miners had already opened most of the coalfields, but the working life of a medieval pit was short because of the inability of miners to control flooding. Then in 1486, at Finchdale in Durham, water-powered pumps were first used to pump out the mines. Between 1490 and 1510 tin production in Cornwall and Devon, which had been stagnant, doubled. This increase came about largely because shaft mining replaced open cast mining, a change that meant the triumph of the capitalist entrepreneur. Where a peasant once needed only a pick and shovel to mine tin, costly equipment now became necessary, equipment that only a rich merchant or enterprising landlord could furnish. The lead industry in the Mendips also prospered in the 1490s, for the demand for lead as roofing material for churches and houses proved insatiable.

The metal trades likewise flourished. Birmingham, reported John Leland in Henry VIII's reign, resounded to the noise of smiths making knives, bits for horses, cutting tools, and nails. But the richest men in Birmingham were the butchers and tanners. The leather industry in England was probably more important than the metal crafts, for leather was used for shoes, clothes, belts, buckets, and bellows. The industry was centered in the Midlands and London, where cattle were raised and butchered for the food market. Many early Tudor enclosures, in fact, were undertaken for cattle grazing, not sheep runs. Finally, there was the shipbuilding industry, which Henry VII fostered with carefully placed subsidies. The first subsidy went to Bristol, the home of William Canynges's bustling, expanding shipyard. Canynges, who owned 3000 tons of shipping, kept a hundred carpenters and workmen busy. But though Bristol was preeminent, every harbor and inlet in England echoed to the hammers of the shipwright.

Industry was not wholly rural. One-third of the population of Coventry and Norwich was engaged in the cloth trade and every town had its butchers, tanners, tailors, cobblers, chandlers, brewers, and hatters. A large town would contain up to a hundred different trades, a medium-sized town about sixty. The small craftsmen, however, never became as wealthy and powerful as the merchants. Of the twelve great amalgamated companies in London, only the clothworkers were not traders. The craft guilds in London and elsewhere grew less and less influential—and more and more monopolistic.

Hours of work in industry (and in agriculture too) were long. A statute in 1495 provided that between March and September the worker should be at work before five in the morning and should leave between seven and eight in the evening, with half an hour for breakfast and an hour and a half for dinner and a nap, a total of fourteen to fifteen hours, with two hours of break. From September to March every craftsman and laborer should work from daybreak until nightfall. There were variations. The master cappers at Coventry had a twelve-hour day all year around, and the building trades in London worked from 5 A.M. to 7 P.M. between March and September, and from 6 A.M. to 6 P.M. between September and March, though they had only an hour and a half off for meals.

These hours seem intolerable, but there were mitigating circumstances. The pace of work was slow, not being geared to the machine. There were some thirty-five holy days beside Sundays. And there was widespread underemployment. It is likely that the average workweek was only three days a week, which made the twelve- to thirteen-hour day bearable. But it also made the problem of poverty more acute. A master craftsman earned about 6 pence a day, his assistant 5 pence, and a laborer 4 pence. In Coventry, a journeyman capper received 2 pence a day, but was probably furnished meat and drink. Assuming that a laborer worked only three days a week, his income for a year could not have exceeded 50 shillings. Of this he might pay 5 shillings a year to rent two rooms, a small open-roofed hall and an inner chamber. A pair of shoes would cost a shilling—three days' wages. In all, a workingman might spend 4 shillings on clothing for himself and his family. Fuel and light cost little, for fuel could be picked up in wooded country and rushlights could be made at home for nothing. It is clear that the workingman spent about 90 percent of his income on food and drink. Bread was the staple, eaten with cheese. Meat rarely appeared on his table, though fish, especially the herring, often did. Because consumer goods were almost nonexistent, the laborer had little to spend his money on but beer and ale, which explains why he spent so many hours in the alehouse. When the harvest was good, prices low, and the workweek long, the laborer prospered as he never did again until the eighteenth century. But when the harvest was bad, prices high, and employment slack, he suffered far more than the rural poor, having no acre of land to fall back on.

COMMERCE: FOREIGN AND DOMESTIC

Though England's overseas trade was less than a tenth of its coastal and internal trade, it exercised a disproportionate influence over the economy. Between 1470 and 1510 the export of cloth overseas tripled, from 30,000 cloths a year to 90,000, thus enriching the clothier and merchant, giving employment to the weaver, and driving up the price of wool. The soaring price of wool in turn led landlords to convert their arable into pasture. The greatest fortunes in this trade were made by the merchants who exported the unfinished, undyed wool cloth to Antwerp. They were found chiefly in London and were organized in the Company of the Merchant Adventurers. By the early sixteenth century, cloth and raw wool accounted for 90 percent of all English exports, the remainder being made up of coal, tin, lead, grain, and fish. In return, England imported wine from Gascony and oil, soap, alum, and dyestuffs from Spain (the necessary raw materials for the cloth industry).

English ships carried only half the cloth exported; the Hansards and the Italians carried the other half. English merchants had no success in breaking the Hansard monopoly of trade in the Baltic, but they did penetrate the Mediterranean, establishing a profitable trade with Pisa. Henry VII himself invested £8000 in wool to be exported to Pisa. The shipping lobby in Parliament was by no means content to leave so much foreign trade in alien hands; it secured the passage through Parliament of two navigation acts. The first, in 1485, forbade the import of Gascon wine in foreign ships, the second, in 1489, forbade the import of Toulouse woad—a plant producing a blue dye—in foreign ships. The second act also required English exporters to use English ships whenever possible. Economic nationalism thus made its first inroad into the cosmopolitanism of medieval commerce.

Though great fortunes were made in overseas trade, coastal and internal trade were probably worth ten times as much. English sailors were busy carrying coal from Newcastle southward, grain from Yarmouth northward, stone and slate along the coast of Devon, wood from Essex to London, all in small ships of 10 tons or more. Through the rivers of England this trade extended far inland. There were four great river systems: The Thames, the Great Ouse, the Severn, and the Trent, each with its tributaries. Ships from Lynn would carry wine, fish, salt, and coal up the Great Ouse, then along the Cam to Cambridge. Down the Severn came barges with coal from Shropshire. Along the Trent went ships carrying grain to the lead-mining districts of Nottinghamshire and Derbyshire. Much inland trade, however, went by road. Surviving records from Southampton in the middle of the fifteenth century show that 6,689 carts left that town during four years, and 223 pack horses. Pack horses carried the cloth of the Cotswolds to London and the wool of Cumberland and Westmorland over the Pennine moors to Newcastle. A carrier could average 20 miles a day, with each horse carrying four pieces of cloth. One of the busiest roads in England was that which carried grain from Cambridgeshire and Bedfordshire to London. Major towns such as Coventry, Leicester, and Bedford could only be reached by road.

Roads were also used to carry goods to the great fairs of England. In the early sixteenth century there were 352 principal fairs, of which the greatest was the Stourbridge Fair in eastern England. It lasted for five weeks, from August 24 to September 29, and at it one could purchase linen yarn, flax, silk, bread, ale, wine, fish, salt, hay, grain, pitch, tar, coal, and numerous other commodities. The weekly market, however, played a more significant role in the life of the average person. There were 760 market towns in England, each with the right to hold a market once a week. On average, a person would have to walk some 7 miles each way to market, carrying eggs, butter, and chickens. He or she would then have time to sell these provisions, buy some woolen cloth, ask for the news, gossip with friends, and return home. A market was the lifeblood of a town, the loss of which meant ruin.

The many licenses granted for annual fairs and weekly markets during Henry VII's reign give proof of a marked increase in internal trade. But neither this increase nor the spectacular expansion in foreign trade can be attributed to Henry, for he had no clear commercial policy and even on occasion sacrificed trade to political considerations. Powerful economic forces, not Henry VII, created this prosperity. Yet Henry had the good sense to allow those economic forces free play. Above all he avoided war, which during the middle of the century had gravely interrupted trade and which under his son would interrupt it again. He not only avoided war but made treaties that promoted trade—treaties with Denmark in 1490, with the Netherlands in 1496, with France in 1497, and with Spain in 1499. These treaties were not the product of a modern king pursuing enlightened economic policies; they were the product of a medieval king anxious to increase his customs, to maintain the loyalty of London, and to defend his realm by fostering shipping and thereby the navy.

Henry VII proved farsighted in one respect. He licensed John Cabot, a Genoese by birth and Venetian by citizenship, to search for unknown lands beyond "the eastern, western, and northern seas." Since the reign of Henry V the seamen of Bristol had carried provisions to Iceland and brought back dried cod. Between 1480 and 1490 they sailed even farther out into the Atlantic, in search of the legendary Isle of Brasil, with its valuable dyewood. They may have even reached Newfoundland in 1490. These voyages, and Cabot's later, were made possible by fundamental improvements in the design of ships. Ever since the twelfth century, Europeans had sailed in single-masted ships, low and broad, with a single, square-rigged sail. During the fifteenth century they developed the two- or three-masted ship, with a high, pointed bow to resist heavy waves and a three-cornered lateen sail on the mizzen mast. The new ships, twice the tonnage of the old, could sail closer to the wind and withstand heavier seas. By the close of the century ship captains also had the mariner's compass, with its pivoted needle and compass card.

With such ships and with such a compass, John Cabot set sail into the North Atlantic in search of a northwest passage to the wealth of the Far East. The men of Bristol dreamed of their city becoming the great *entrepôt* for the distribution of the spices of the East to the markets of Europe. On his first trip, in 1496, storms drove Cabot back. The next year he reached Newfoundland and probably a portion of the North American seaboard. On his third trip, in 1498, he took five ships, one of which Henry VII himself equipped, but he never returned. His son Sebastian then took up the quest for the northwest passage, sailing in 1508 as far as Hudson's Bay. On his return in 1509 he found the old King dead, which ended this age of English exploration, for the new King preferred wars in Europe to voyages of discovery in the Atlantic.

THE CONSOLIDATION OF POWER

Henry VII served England well in two important ways: he brought peace, which allowed commerce to thrive, and he repaired the fabric of the English monarchy, which under Henry VI had fallen apart. Yet it was by no means certain in 1485 that he would survive to do either, for his situation was precarious. His claim to the Crown was weaker than the Earl of Warwick's or the Earl of Lincoln's, both Yorkists and both alive.* The Yorkists were strong in the North and in Ireland. Margaret of Burgundy, Edward IV's sister, longed for Henry's overthrow. If Henry could seize the throne by force, so could others. But though Henry's situation was precarious, his tenacity and sagacity were great. Henry was a hardheaded and unemotional King whom exile had taught patience and craft. Though suspicious of men, he was slow to anger and willing to forgive. His portrait by Sitium is a picture of craft: thin lips, a high-bridged, pointed nose, hooded eyelids, high cheekbones. This picture of prudence and calculation led earlier historians to describe Henry as the first modern King, but nothing could be further from the truth. His tastes, values, beliefs, and recreations were medieval. He heard two or three masses a day, founded two convents, delighted in ceremony and pomp, loved to hawk and hunt, lived in the company of earls and barons, and bequeathed enough money to the Church for 10,000 masses to be said within a month for the salvation of his soul.

Henry's first task was to consolidate his power. He continued many Yorkists in office, married Edward IV's eldest daughter, Elizabeth, had Parliament recognize the succession to be in him and his heirs, and made a progress through the North, suppressing a minor revolt along the way. But all this he did as King, not in order to become King. Immediately after the Battle of Bosworth, he proclaimed himself "Henry by the grace of God, King of England." He delayed his marriage to Elizabeth in order to prove that he governed by his own right, not hers. And he asked Parliament, which he summoned as King, to confirm the succession, not his title. Henry's most effective claim to the throne came from his possessing it. The Battle of Bosworth settled the question of who was rightful King of England, and contemporaries saw the hand of God in Henry's victory.

* For Henry VII's, the Earl of Warwick's, and the Earl of Lincoln's claims see the genealogical chart on page 182.

The bust of Henry VII by Pietro Torrigiano (*Victoria and Albert Museum, Crown Copyright*).

One year after Bosworth, Henry was in full command of his kingdom. Not only was his authority accepted throughout the country, but the birth of a son, Arthur, joined in one person the rival houses of Lancaster and York. Henry, however, knew his throne was not secure. The Yorkists, supported by the indefatigable Margaret of Burgundy, kept plotting his overthrow. Because Henry kept Edward, Earl of Warwick, the only direct male representative of the House of York, in the Tower, the Yorkists had to put forward pretenders. The first of these was Lambert Simnel, a gentle ten-year-old boy, son of an obscure tradesman, whom the Yorkists passed off as the Earl of Warwick. They found support for him in Dublin, where he was proclaimed Edward VI. Margaret of Burgundy sent 2000 highly trained German troops to help. Led by the Earl of Lincoln, the Yorkist army landed in Lancashire and marched on London. But the English, tired of civil war, refused to join the invaders, whom Henry VII trounced at East Stoke on June 16, 1487. Many leading Yorkists, including the Earl of Lincoln, met death in battle. The young Lambert Simnel fell captive to Henry, who made him a scullion in his kitchen.

The Battle of Stoke did not end the plotting of the Yorkists. They found a new pretender in Perkin Warbeck, the son of a Tournai merchant, who claimed to be Richard, the younger of the two princes thought to have been murdered in the Tower. No one believed in this imposture except those who wished to make use of Warbeck, but these included the Holy Roman Emperor, the King of France, Margaret of Burgundy, and the King of Scotland. Perkin Warbeck attempted to invade England on three occasions—a landing in Kent in 1495, a raid from Scotland in 1496, and a landing in Cornwall in 1497. On the last occasion he was captured, taken to London, imprisoned, and finally, at the rumor of yet another plot, executed. The same rumor led Henry to execute the Earl of Warwick, whose only crime was to be the son of Edward IV's brother. Even with the deaths of Warbeck and Warwick the Crown was not entirely secure, since the Earl of Lincoln's brother still wandered about the Continent. Henry nevertheless faced no more armed challenges after 1497.

It was Henry's good fortune that when he came to the throne there was no ruler in France, the Low Countries, or Scotland strong enough to wage war against him. Louis XI of France had died in 1481, leaving the Crown to Charles VIII, a boy of 13. The ruler of the Low Countries was also a minor. A faction of nobles murdered James III of Scotland in 1488, leaving a royal minority. Before long, however, Henry had to face the central issue of England's relations with France. The medieval tradition of hostility to France remained strong and deep, a tradition Henry kept alive by joining the title of King of France to that of King of England. But the last half of the fifteenth century had seen the European scene transformed. France, united by Louis XI, had become three times stronger in men and revenues than England. Claims that may have made sense in the reign of Henry V had become unrealistic.

France now threatened to annex Brittany, a territory that would give it mastery over the whole southern shore of the Channel. Faced with this situation, Henry entered into a network of anti-French alliances which Spain, recently formed from the union of Aragon and Castile, had fashioned. When these alliances turned out to be ropes of sand, Henry acted alone, sending 6,000 troops to help the Breton nobles preserve their independence. Then in 1491 Charles VIII married Anne of Brittany, who had inherited the duchy at her father's death in 1488. Henry replied by preparing for a full-scale war against France. Parliament readily voted him £100,000. Men, ships, guns, and tents were assembled. In October 1492 Henry led an army out of Calais to besiege Boulogne. But within a month he made peace with France. By the Treaty of Etaples the two kings agreed to remain at peace with each other, not to support the other's enemies, and to allow their subjects to trade on equal terms. In addition, Charles VIII agreed to pay Henry £5000 a year for the next fifteen years. Like Edward IV before him, Henry had preferred a profitable peace to a ruinous war.

The crisis in Brittany and the Treaty of Etaples made it possible for Henry to marry his daughter and sons into the royal houses of Scotland and Spain. The crisis in Brittany led Spain to look to England for support in resisting the growing power of France. In March 1489 Spain signed the Treaty of Medina del Campo with England, whereby both kingdoms agreed to go to war against France. Spain failed to keep its side of the bargain, but Henry gained from the treaty what he wanted, the marriage of his son Arthur to Catherine, the daughter of Ferdinand and Isabella. It was not until 1501 that Arthur and Catherine were finally wed, amidst jousting, dancing, and play acting. Five months later Arthur died. Unwilling to lose the Spanish alliance, Henry immediately proposed that his second son, Prince Henry, marry Catherine. After many vicissitudes and the arrival of a papal dispensation, the marriage took place in 1509. Some years before Henry had wed his daughter Margaret to James IV of Scotland, a marriage made possible by the Treaty of Etaples. As long as England was at war with France, there was little prospect of peace with Scotland, France's ancient ally. The marriages of Henry's children into the royal houses of Europe brought him what every new dynasty craves, recognition and acceptance. The Crown now sat more easily on his head.

THE REVIVAL OF ROYAL POWER

Henry VII did not create a new monarchy, nor did he make any permanent innovations in the existing one. Indeed, there was no need for him to do so, for the feebleness of the monarchy in the fifteenth century did not arise from a lack of institutions or powers. It arose from the lack of a strong King at the center and from the financial dependence of the King on Parliament. During his reign Henry corrected both faults.

To begin with, he made certain that he governed his Council and that his Council did not govern him. This does not mean that he refused to appoint great magnates of the realm to his Council. In fact, his Council did not differ from those of his predecessors: about one-fourth were peers, one-fourth bishops and abbots, and one-half knights, lawyers, clergymen, and Household officials. There were probably more laymen and fewer clergymen than before— reflecting a more secular society—and there were fewer nobles on the inner council that attended the King daily. What really mattered was the fact that Henry, like Henry II and Edward I, summoned whom he wished to Council and they became his servants.

The functions of the Council also remained the same: to advise the King in matters of policy, to help him in the administration of the realm, and to give judgment in cases brought before it. But under Henry the judicial work of the Council did assume a different character from before. The development of the Court of Chancery from the fourteenth century onward had relieved the Council from hearing petitions in civil cases. An Englishman who failed to get justice in the Common Law courts could now appeal to Chancery for equity. But the judicial work of the Council hardly diminished, for it extended its work through a number of committees. One committee, the Council Learned, fined men for breaches of the law. Another committee, established by a statute in 1487, helped enforce the laws against livery and maintenance. A third committee, established in 1495, proceeded against corrupt jurors. And a tribunal established in the Household, the future Court of Requests, provided swift justice for poor men (though few who used it were poor). Henry did not create these committees and courts in order to deprive the Common law courts of their jurisdiction; he created them in order to make the machinery of the Common law work more effectively.

Henry VII knew as well as did Edward IV that no King could be powerful who was financially dependent upon Parliament. He therefore took measures to increase the revenues of the Crown, measures that met with astonishing success. By inheritance he gained the lands of Lancaster, York, and Tudor; by forfeiture on acts of attainder he amassed yet more land. Through an efficient administration of these lands he increased his revenues from £10,000 to £40,000 a year. Because of the growing volume of overseas trade, a result of the pursuit of peace, his revenues from the customs rose from £32,000 to £42,000. His revenues from the sale of wardships rose from £343 in 1491 to £6,163 in 1507. By imposing heavy fines on those who violated the law and by selling pardons, he greatly increased the profits of justice. Receipts from the sale of pardons averaged £3,000 a year between 1505 and 1508. During the last years of Henry's reign, the zeal of the Council Learned in collecting debts and levying fines aroused much fury against its chief members, Edmund Dudley and Sir Richard Empson, but receipts from money owed under bonds rose from £3,000 a year in 1493 to £35,000 in 1505. In all, Henry's revenues increased from £52,000 a year to £142,000. These revenues did not pass through the archaic, slow, rule-ridden Exchequer, but through the efficient Chamber, whose accounts Henry patiently checked, page by page.

Henry's increased revenues were important to him not only because they gave him independence, but because they allowed him to give his subjects relief from taxes. During the first half of his reign Henry raised about £22,000 a year from direct taxation. These taxes were heavy enough in 1497 to provoke a large number of Cornishmen to rebel, kill a tax collector in Taunton, march on London, and camp on Blackheath. Henry, who would never negotiate with rebels under arms, attacked and slew 2,000 of them. But he learned from this event that his subjects wished him "to live of his own." During the second half of his reign he taxed his subjects only once, in 1504.

The most difficult task Henry faced was to tame his mighty subjects. Historians once believed that he did this through the Court of Star Chamber—that is, through the whole Council acting judicially, enforcing swift justice on great men guilty of riot, retaining private armies, and maintaining, through intimidation, cases before the royal courts. Now it is true that the Council met—and had met since Edward III's reign—in the Star Chamber of Westminster Palace and there enforced a swift justice, with no jury, no counsel for the defendant, and no right against self-incrimination. But during Henry's reign the government rarely initiated a prosecution. Of 194 cases that came before the

Council, most resulted from a petition by one subject against another and concerned such matters as the possession of land and the rights of municipal bodies. The few cases the government initiated concerned rioting and the corruption of juries, and they were usually sent on to the Common law courts for trial. The Council never once fined a peer for maintenance or retaining.

The chief instrument on which Henry relied to restore order was the justice of the peace. There was nothing revolutionary in this, for the justices of the peace had been charged since the fourteenth century with keeping order. What was new was the vigor and care with which Henry, his Council, and his justices on circuit supervised their work. The justices of the peace were unpaid local gentlemen, and to that extent independent, but they could also be dismissed, and no gentleman wished to suffer that blow to his prestige. Justices of the peace were most unlikely to carry out measures of which they deeply disapproved, such as anti-enclosure laws, but the gentry of England in the late fifteenth century did desire to see the restoration of law and order. Parliament passed acts in 1495 that empowered justices of the peace to remove suspected men from juries and to try without a jury men accused of taking part in riots or unlawfully giving liveries. In 1504 came Henry's celebrated statute against liveries, which repeated the condemnation of retaining found in Edward's statute of 1468, but improved the procedure for enforcing the law. Justices of the peace were now to report all violations to the King's Bench or Council for prosecution there. In the ensuing years of Henry's reign the justices of the peace sent numerous indictments for retaining to the King's Bench, who prosecuted the offenders.

But not once during the first twenty years of Henry's reign was a peer charged with retaining. This was no accident. Henry knew that the system of retaining liveried servants was deeply embedded in English society. He sought, in fact, to make use of the system to promote his own power. A lord who was loyal to him and who had many retainers was a force for order in his country. Furthermore, it was to the King's advantage that armed retainers should be available for military purposes. In 1492 he raised an army for the war against France by granting commissions to lords who in turn enlisted men. But toward the end of his reign Henry took more energetic action. For retaining 471 men, Lord Abergavenny was indicted before justices of the peace in Kent and tried before the King's Bench, which in 1507 found him guilty and fined him. Henry's favorite device for taming great subjects was the exacting of bonds from those guilty of some offense, bonds which were then pledges of their future good behavior. These bonds ranged from £2,000 to £5,000, sums a lord would forfeit if Henry decided he had not remained loyal. Henry rarely enforced such bonds, but the threat of doing so ensured fidelity. The prosecution of Abergavenny and the exacting of bonds, however, did not bring an end to retaining and disorder in England. The deep-seated willingness of Englishmen to resort to violence could not be eradicated overnight. Not until the end of the sixteenth century did more peaceful habits prevail. As late as 1578 the retainers of Lord Rich, some twenty-five strong, attacked Edward Windham in London in broad daylight. Though Henry VII did not bring order to England, he did begin the long struggle by which the Tudors made England one of the most orderly kingdoms in Europe.

THE NEW LEARNING

While the Tudor kings strove to bring order to England, the scholars were busy propagating the new learning of the Italian Renaissance. Scholasticism was essentially the application of reason, understood as formal logic, to received authorities, such as the Bible, St. Augustine, Aristotle, and Galen, with the purpose of reconciling them and glorifying God. The new learning, or humanism, as it came to be called, was quite different. It was the application of reason, understood as a knowledge of language, to human experience with the purpose of promoting virtuous conduct. The humanists turned from logic to language, from theology to rhetoric, from Aristotle to Plato, from medieval compendiums to the original Latin and Greek. The first Englishman to show a serious interest in humanism was Thomas Chaundler, warden of New College, Oxford. In 1475 he invited an Italian scholar to lecture on Greek at Oxford. Attending the lectures was William Grocyn, who went to Italy between 1485 and 1491 to improve his knowledge of Greek. With him was another Oxford student, Thomas Linacre. Grocyn returned to Oxford to lecture on Greek; Linacre, who had also studied medicine while in Italy, returned to translate Galen and found the Royal Society of Physicians. The example of Linacre and Grocyn led the young John Colet, son of a wealthy London merchant, to study in Italy. He returned to Oxford in 1496, where he delivered a series of lectures on the Epistles of St. Paul. He had read the letters in the original Greek and he gave a direct, human explanation of them, rather than the allegorical and anagogical interpretations beloved by the scholastics. The conservatives cried out against such novel methods, fearing they might promote heresy and worldliness. Their fears appeared justified when Erasmus of Rotterdam, eventually to become the greatest scholar of his age, came to Oxford in 1497 to study Greek and went on to translate the New Testament from Greek into Latin. His translation corrected the Vulgate (the authorized version) in a manner that tended to undermine the scriptural authority of the Papacy and the priesthood.

Though the opposition of the conservatives to the new learning was dogged, both at Oxford and Cambridge, it ultimately prevailed. Among the forces causing that triumph two were paramount: the growing secularism of education and the printing press. During the fourteenth and fifteenth centuries the foundation of Winchester and Eton and the establishment of grammar schools by civic corporations and guilds broke the Church's monopoly over education. The prosperous years of the late fifteenth century witnessed a striking increase in the number of schools established by towns and wealthy merchants. But there were no changes in the methods of teaching until Magdalen College School, founded in 1480, became a center for teaching grammar by more enlightened methods. Magdalen was soon eclipsed by St. Paul's School, London, which John Colet founded in 1508. To prevent ecclesiastical interference, he persuaded the dean and chapter of St. Paul's to surrender supervision of the school to the Mercer's Company of London. With Erasmus's help, Colet planned a new kind of school, open to all who had talent and free of charge. New grammars in English and Latin were written; new subjects, such as Greek, geography, and natural history, were introduced; the classics were studied in the original; and the barbarous Latin of the scholastics was banished. Though Colet opposed clerical interference, he designed an education whose chief purpose was to promote a Christian way of life. It was not long before Eton and Winchester began to emulate St. Paul's.

William Caxton had established his press at Westminster in 1476. Soon there were other presses, at Oxford, at St. Albans, at London. By 1500 at least 360 titles had been printed in England, and 30,000 throughout Europe. Few of the books published in England furthered the study of the classics, but many of those from abroad did. In the long run printing promoted the growth of a wide reading public and made possible the large private library. By 1520 it was possible to buy books by Erasmus for 6 pence, a day's wage for a craftsman. The revolutionary ideas of the humanists would never have circulated so rapidly had it not been for the printing presses.

What John Colet accomplished for the grammar school, Bishop Fox achieved for the universities. In 1517 he founded Corpus Christi College, Oxford, the first college dedicated to humanistic studies. Corpus Christi emphasized the value of a correct understanding of the original text, in sharp contrast to the scholastic method of formal disputations upon the *Sentences* of Peter Lombard or the works of Duns Scotus. The ideals of Bishop Fox received official sanction in 1535, when the government issued royal injunctions that suppressed the study of canon law, encouraged the study of Greek, classical Latin, Hebrew, mathematics, and medicine, abolished the use of medieval compendiums, and urged that the "frivolous questions and obscure glosses" of the scholastics be put aside. Scholasticism persisted in the universities for many decades to come, but the officials responsible for enforcing the royal injunctions could report on their second visit to New College that they found the quadrangle filled with the pages of Duns Scotus, the wind blowing them into every corner.

Medieval education was essentially vocational. The universities trained priests, the Inns of Court lawyers, the town schools scriveners (professional copyists or writers). There now emerged, however, a new educational ideal, the production of the accomplished gentleman trained to serve the state. The rough values of the chivalric code slowly yielded to the values of restraint and good taste. A concern for the development of self-reliance and self-expression gradually replaced the corporate and ascetic ideals of medieval Christianity. At the same time, the nobility and gentry became less willing to leave government to clergymen born of humble stock. At a banquet early in Henry VIII's reign an old gentleman swore he would rather his son be hanged than study letters. "Gentlemen's sons," he declared, "ought to be able to blow their horn skillfully, to hunt well, and to carry and train a hawk elegantly; but the study of letters is to be left to the sons of peasants." Richard Pace, Henry VIII's secretary of state, promptly replied: "If your son were called upon to answer a foreign ambassador, he would but blow his horn, if he were educated according to your wishes, and the learned sons of peasants would be called upon to reply. And they would be placed far ahead of your hunting and hawking son."

Closely allied to the ideal of the accomplished gentleman was that of the scholar who devoted his talents to the service of his prince. Of these the finest example in England was Sir Thomas More, author of *Utopia* and Lord Chancellor of England. Sir Thomas was born in Milk Street, Cheapside, London, the son of a prosperous lawyer. He attended St. Anthony's , one of the best grammar schools in the city, and then went on to Oxford, where he studied Greek under Linacre. On returning to London he studied law at the Inns of Court, became a friend of Erasmus, gained renown as a man of wit and learning, married, and established a household in Chelsea, where he gave his three daughters an education in Latin, Greek, arithmetic, and music that was unrivaled in that age. He also wrote *Utopia*, an account of an imaginary commonwealth located somewhere between Brazil and Ceylon. In Book One of *Utopia* More attacks the rich and powerful in all their guises, whether as usurer, engrosser, encloser, or depopulator, whether as idle courtier, venal monk, ostentatious lord, or warlike prince. The root of all these evils he finds in greed, sloth, and the insatiable pride of men. To overcome greed and sloth and to discipline pride men must, as the Utopians did, abolish private property, eat in common dining halls, wear a common uniform, receive a common education, and accept a common obligation of daily toil. More was not a modern socialist, for he found the root of evil in human nature, not economic institutions, but he did believe that only where property was held in common could pride and greed be held in check.

MEDIEVAL AND MODERN

Fifty years ago historians divided medieval from modern English history with the accession of Henry VII in 1485. Today no historian would do so, for it has become clear that Henry VII did not create a new monarchy. He merely restored the old English monarchy, and in doing this he only followed in the steps of Edward IV. Edward first strengthened the Council, relied upon the Star Chamber, amassed land, restored financial solvency, and made use of the justices of the peace. Furthermore, it is pure legend that Henry VII spurned the nobility and allied with the middle classes, that he suppressed livery and maintenance by means of a newly created Star Chamber, that he pursued a new

A map of Utopia, from the 1518 Basle edition of Sir Thomas More's masterpiece (*New York Public Library*).

diplomacy based on deceit and cunning, or that he had completely restored order by his death in 1509.

Yet a powerful argument can be made for the fact that between 1470 and 1510 deep economic, social, and intellectual changes augured a new age. In 1470 the population began to recover, thus ending the shortage of people and abundance of land that had characterized the previous century and a half. Prices began to rise, and with them rents. The landed gentry slowly recovered the incomes they had once enjoyed, while the workers, especially after 1520, began to suffer an erosion in their incomes. The process of the engrossment and enclosure of land, begun about 1470, reached its height about 1510. It was also in 1470 that the great expansion in foreign trade began, giving a powerful push to the wool industry. The wealthy merchants used their riches to purchase land, thus swelling the ranks of the gentry and obscuring the line between mercantile and landed wealth. About 1490 gentlemen began to build gracious homes with wainscotting and glass windows, thus creating the setting for a country-house culture that was to dominate England for the next four hundred years. The printing press which Caxton brought to England in 1476 made it possible for the country gentlemen to collect a private library, and the new learning that Grocyn and Linacre and Colet brought from Italy ensured that Cicero and Seneca, not Duns Scotus and Peter Lombard, would dominate that library. Henry VII did not create a new monarchy, but forces over which he had no control were creating a new England.

FURTHER READING

S.T. BINDOFF. *Tudor England.* Penguin Books, 1950. A beautifully written, thought-provoking essay on the problems facing the Tudor monarchs and the solutions they found.

G.R. ELTON. *England Under the Tudors.* Rev. ed., London, 1974. A magisterial survey, incorporating the most recent research, by England's leading authority on the Tudors; contains a useful bibliography.

C.S.L. DAVIES. *Peace, Print and Protestantism, 1450–1558.* London, 1976. A thorough, precise, dependable survey, written in a vigorous, lively style; the approach is more traditional than the title suggests.

J.D. MACKIE. *The Early Tudors, 1485–1558.* Oxford, 1952. One of the few volumes in the Oxford History of England that is a pleasure to read; better on politics than economics and on men than institutions; contains a full bibliography.

STANLEY BERTRAM CHRIMES. *Henry VII.* Berkeley, 1972. Not an intimate biography, but a perceptive study of the impact of Henry VII upon the government of England; deals the final blow to the belief that Henry was a "New Monarch."

R. B. WERNHAM. *Before the Armada: The Emergence of the English Nation.* New York, 1966. A study of English foreign policy from 1483 to 1588; an interpretative history distinguished by compelling, close-knit arguments.

MAURICE BERESFORD. *The Lost Villages of England.* London, 1954. Argues that enclosures, not the Black Death, led to the abandonment of villages and that most villages were abandoned in the mid-fifteenth century, not from 1488 to 1517.

ALISTAIR FOX. *Thomas More: History and Providence.* New Haven, Conn., 1983. Demolishes the myth of an ever gentle, witty, saintly More; yet does not deny the nobler side of More in bringing out the darker side.

SIR THOMAS MORE. *Utopia.* Translated and edited by Robert M. Adams. New York, 1975. A penetrating analysis of European society and an imaginative description of a community freed from temptation by the abolition of private property.

C.H. WILLIAMS, ed. *English Historical Documents 1485–1558.* New York, 1967. Contains original sources on government, religion, the structure of society, and daily life in town and country.

10 War and Reformation: 1509-1547

Pervasive economic, social, and intellectual forces do not alone shape history. Often chance or the whims of an individual monarch or the counsels of a powerful minister intervene to alter the course of history. The history of England in the early sixteenth century offers a splendid illustration of this truth. Without doubt a rising population, a prosperous wool trade, an emerging gentry, the printing press, and the new learning combined to produce a new society—more secular, more peaceful, more individualistic. But that society was also shaped by the whims of Henry VIII and the counsels of Thomas Cromwell. Had Henry not sought a divorce from Catherine, even at the cost of breaking from Rome, England might not have become a Protestant nation; and had Cromwell not counseled him to use Parliament as an instrument for breaking from Rome, that institution might have counted for less in the sixteenth century. Even more, Henry's vainglorious pursuit of war, by impoverishing the Crown, made its future dependence on Parliament more certain. Rarely have the whims, passions, prejudices, and pride of a monarch so dominated the history of a reign and had consequences more significant for the future.

Henry was no ordinary monarch. Nature had endowed him with remarkable physical and mental gifts. He had a swift, nimble mind, learned mathematics easily, knew Latin and French, understood Italian, discoursed with Sir Thomas More about astronomy, and corresponded with Erasmus about divinity. He was the first English king to receive a Renaissance education, studying Homer and Virgil, reading much in Cicero, and drawing wisdom from the histories of Thucydides and Tacitus. As befitted a Renaissance prince, he was astonishingly versatile in his accomplishments. He was an excellent horseman. He could draw the bow with greater strength than any man in England and was rarely unhorsed in his favorite sport, tilting. He delighted in hawking, wres-

231

Henry VIII, magnificently attired and imperious in countenance, painted by an unknown artist (*National Portrait Gallery, London*).

tling, and dancing. His greatest passion may well have been for music. He performed with skill on the lute, organ, and harpsichord, and had a strong, sure voice. He composed music, writing two five-part masses, many instrumental pieces and part songs, and an anthem, "O Lord, the Maker of All Things," which is still sung in English cathedrals. He brought Italian musicians to Court, who introduced sacred music in the Renaissance style.

Accompanying these varied talents was a character marked by exuberance, flamboyance, prodigality, a love of life, and captivating charm. But the charm could rapidly turn to anger, for Henry was a high-strung, unstable person. He was utterly sure of himself, totally devoted to his own interests, selfish and egotistical, with a streak of cruelty markedly different from his father's clemency. He began his reign by executing two of his father's ministers and continued it by executing his own. He executed two wives, several earls, a duke, and a countess, and he ordered the execution of three cardinals. As Sir Walter Raleigh wrote two generations later: "For King Henry the Eighth, if all the Patterns and Pictures of a merciless Prince were lost in the world, they might all again be painted to the life, out of the story of this King."

No one in 1509, when Henry came to the throne, saw or foresaw this cruelty. All they saw was a young King, 17 years of age, extraordinarily handsome, tall, square-shouldered, with auburn hair, a fair complexion, and a round face.

To almost all his people he brought deliverance from the oppressive financial exactions of Henry VII. On the second day of his reign, Henry threw Edmund Dudley and Sir Richard Empson, the chief tax collectors of his father's reign, into the Tower; sixteen months later he had them executed on a purely fictitious charge of treason. Henry then devoted himself to pleasure, leaving the routine business of government to his almoner, Thomas Wolsey. His days were filled with hawking and hunting, tilting and jousting, wrestling and tennis; his nights with revels and pageants, singing and dancing, gambling and feasting. "The King," it was said in 1515, "is a youngling, who cares for nothing but girls and hunting and wastes his father's patrimony."

WAR AND DIPLOMACY

Henry had not been on the throne more than two years before he faced a critical decision. Should he continue his father's policy of peace and no Continental entanglements or should he pursue a policy of war and conquests in France? His advisers counseled peace, as did More and Erasmus. Henry, however, chose war—not that he needed any prompting, for he was young, athletic, vain, eager to help the Pope and to prove himself in battle. In 1511 he joined the Holy League, composed of the Pope, Spain, Venice, and the Swiss, a league formed to drive France from Italy. The next year, at the King of Spain's urging, Henry sent 18,000 men to northwest Spain, with the intention of marching into Aquitaine. But Ferdinand, the King of Spain, never sent the men and supplies he had promised; instead he took the opportunity to capture the kingdom of Navarre to the east. The English army suffered through the hot, wet Spanish summer at Fuentarrabia, where the soldiers drank wine as though it were beer until they came down with dysentery. Against Henry's orders, the army finally boarded their ships and came home. Ferdinand meanwhile compounded his treachery by making a separate truce with France.

The next year Henry decided to act without Ferdinand. The Emperor Maximilian sent him 2,000 men and the Pope secretly bestowed on him the title of King of France. Parliament voted the necessary money; Wolsey organized the supplies and prepared the ships. In June Henry landed at Calais with 25,000 men. From there he marched slowly south, captured the small town of Therouanne, and won a skirmish against a French cavalry force. Henry next besieged Tournai, which fell in September. He returned home with his French standards, his glory, and two French towns in his possession. For this trivial accomplishment he had spent £922,000, a vast sum for a king whose ordinary revenue was only £150,000 a year.

The organizer of victory was Thomas Wolsey, who now began his meteoric rise to power. Wolsey, the son of an Ipswich butcher, had gone to Oxford, become a fellow of Magdalen College, and entered the service of the Archbishop of Canterbury as a chaplain. In 1507 he left the Archbishop to enter royal

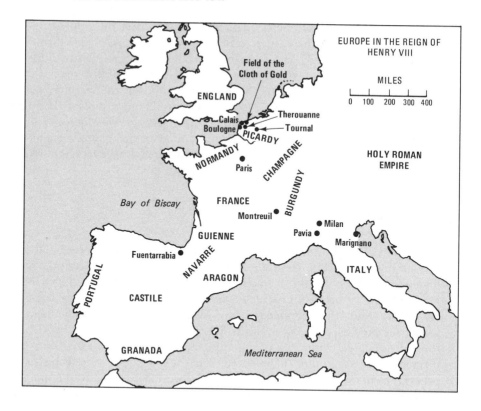

service, where by dint of an enormous appetite for work, a swift judgment, a sharp eye for detail, and daily attendance on the King, he became Henry's chief minister. In 1514 the organizer of victory became the architect of a successful peace. Henry still wanted war, but the forces working for peace proved too strong for him. The new Pope made peace with the King of France and urged his allies to do likewise. Lack of money with which to fight new battles and a desire to be revenged on Ferdinand prompted Henry to make a separate peace before his father-in-law could. In August 1514 England and France signed a treaty that left Tournai and Therouanne in English hands and provided for the payment of the arrears due on the pension granted to the kings of England by the Treaty of Etaples. The marriage of Henry's sister Mary to the aged Louis XII of France cemented the peace. Wolsey's skillful negotiations had rescued something from a military venture designed to bring Henry glory, not to protect the nation's interests.

From 1514 to 1529, while Henry hunted and played the lute, Thomas Wolsey attended to the business of government, especially to the conduct of foreign policy. His motives were complex. In part he was the late medieval churchman, seeking to serve the Papacy and hoping for a Cardinal's hat, even for election to the Holy See itself. In part he was the King's true servant, seeking to give expression to Henry's love of glory and action. In part he was the humanist, who knew the cost of war and sought to bring peace to Europe. At all times he was the proud, meddling diplomat who could not endure not being at the center of affairs.

His first masterpiece was the treaty with France in 1514, but that peace collapsed in 1515 with the death of Louis XII and the accession of Francis I. The adulation Europe gave to the handsome young French king stung Henry to jealousy, which Francis's reconquest of Milan and his glorious victory at Marignano only heightened. Francis then sent John Stuart, Duke of Albany, to Scotland, where he took power from Henry's sister, the regent Margaret. Henry once again clamored for war against France, but Parliament in 1515 voted too little money. Wolsey therefore proposed to wage the war by hiring Swiss mercenaries and granting subsidies to the Emperor. The Swiss and the Emperor took the money but failed to act. Wolsey next sought to organize a league of the Pope, the Emperor, and the King of Spain against France, only to see it collapse when Charles, the new King of Spain, signed the Treaty of Noyon with Francis in 1516.

Wolsey then turned to a policy of *rapprochement*, which met with success. In 1518 England and France signed a treaty in London whereby England returned Tournai to France in return for 600,000 crowns. Wolsey then transformed this treaty into a collective security pact that required all signatories to come to the aid of the victim of aggression. This early idea of a concert of Europe probably meant little to the other powers, but England during the next two years sincerely sought to make it work. Herein lies the meaning of the resplendent meeting of Henry VIII and Francis I in the summer of 1520 on the Field of the Cloth of Gold in northern France. For two weeks Henry and Francis and their noblemen jousted and wrestled and banqueted, the only anxious moment coming when Francis threw Henry at wrestling. For Wolsey it was more than a piece of Renaissance display; he hoped that the friendships formed there would lessen the hatred of the English for the French and the French for the English.

The imposing diplomatic edifice built by Wolsey between 1518 and 1520 collapsed in 1521. It could not survive the fierce rivalry between Francis I, King of France, and Charles V, ruler of Spain, the Netherlands, Austria, and Naples, and recently elected Holy Roman Emperor. The impending struggle between these two superpowers governed all diplomacy from 1520 onward. England had no immediate interest in the outcome, for the quarrel concerned distant Italy. Yet Henry's martial ardor and Wolsey's desire to be at the center of affairs drew England into the conflict. In the autumn of 1521 Henry signed a treaty with Charles V which provided that each should invade France with an army of 40,000 men. This Anglo-Imperial treaty demonstrated clearly that though Wolsey might execute foreign policy, Henry decided what it should be, and Henry was determined on war, not peace. A number of motives led him to ally with the Emperor rather than France: Charles V represented the traditional

Anglo-Burgundian, anti-French alliance; he had promised to help Wolsey win election as Pope; and he controlled the Netherlands, the major market for English cloth. Beneath these practical motives lay Henry's dream of winning the crown of France, of marrying his daughter Mary to Charles V (as the treaty provided), and of seeing his descendants inherit "the whole monarchy of Christendom."

From 1522 to 1525 England waged desultory war against France, expended huge sums of money, brought misery to thousands of innocent French peasants, and accomplished nothing. In 1522 an army pillaged and burned villages in northern France. In 1523 a larger army drove within 50 miles of Paris, only to have to retreat for want of money and support from its allies. The lack of money led Henry and Wolsey in 1524 to open secret negotiations with France, but then came news of Charles's crushing defeat of Francis I at the Battle of Pavia in February 1525. Henry now descended like a jackal on his prey. He urged that he and Charles march straight on Paris, where he should be crowned King of France and his daughter wed to Charles. But Charles, penniless and anxious for peace, refused. Nor was Henry able to field an army. His attempt to collect a benevolence, euphemistically called an amicable grant, failed miserably. The English refused to pay and even threatened insurrection. Henry could not find the money to pay the dowry to support Mary's marriage to Charles, with the result that Charles declared himself free from the engagement and married Isabella of Portugal. An enraged Henry now made peace with France, allied with the League of Cognac (formed to oppose Charles), and in 1528 declared war on Charles, though he had not the means to wage it and had (in order to protect English trade) to agree to a local truce for the Netherlands.

In all these twistings and turnings Henry and Wolsey paid little attention to the principle of the balance of power, since they more often supported the stronger power. Nor was much attention paid to England's true interests, for both Henry and Wolsey had forgotten the cardinal principle of Henry VII's foreign policy—that England should not concern itself with affairs on the Continent unless its interests were immediately threatened. Personal pique, grandiose dreams, and a love of meddling guided English foreign policy for twenty years. It was a policy that failed at every turn because England had not the men or wealth to stand against the two colossi of Europe.

THE DIVORCE

It was not merely anger at Charles V that led Henry to ally with the League of Cognac and declare war. He also wanted to rescue Pope Clement VII from the Emperor's grasp so that the Pope would be free to grant him a divorce from his wife, Catherine. Since the Emperor was Catherine's nephew, he insisted that the Pope not annul his aunt's marriage.

Henry first made public his desire for a divorce in 1527, but he had begun to think about it several years earlier, driven by his concern for the succession and his love for Anne Boleyn. Catherine had given Henry only a daughter, Mary, and there was no hope after 1525 that she would again bear a child. This put the succession in jeopardy and threatened civil war, for only once had a Queen sought to rule England—Matilda in the twelfth century—and her reign had led to anarchy and war. So desperate was the situation that Henry thought of putting his bastard son, Henry fitz Roy, duke of Richmond, on the throne. But this also posed dangers, so Henry thought it better to seek a legitimate son by a new marriage. Henry's anxieties over the succession became inextricably mixed with his passion for Anne Boleyn. Some time between 1525 and 1527, Henry fell violently in love with this 19-year-old daughter of Sir Thomas Bo-

Portrait of Anne Boleyn (*Bettmann Archive*).

leyn, one of his ministers. Anne, who had been brought up at the French court, was not particularly beautiful, but something about her—her beautiful eyes perhaps, or her long black hair which she wore loose—captivated Henry. Tradition says that Anne resisted becoming Henry's mistress, but in fact Henry did not seek a mistress. He sought a wife who would bear him a son.

To considerations of prudence and passion were soon allied those of conscience. Henry became convinced that his marriage had never been lawful and that he and Catherine had lived in sin for twenty years. Catherine had previously been married to Henry's brother, Arthur, and the Book of Leviticus declares: "If a man shall take his brother's wife, it is an impurity: he hath uncovered his brother's nakedness; they shall be childless." True, they had a daughter, Mary, and Deuteronomy, also a part of Scripture, enjoins a man to marry his brother's widow. But in Henry's mind Catherine's numerous still-births and miscarriages were a sign of the curse of Leviticus. When Henry proclaimed to the world that his conscience was troubled, he was not being hypocritical. He had read, thought, and talked himself into a belief in the justness of his cause. A sense of righteousness is one of the most powerful weapons in the arsenal of the egotist, and Henry's egotism was unbounded.

Henry first sought to secure a divorce in a court secretly convened by Wolsey in May 1527. Wolsey's intention was to pronounce the marriage invalid, a sentence the Pope would then confirm. But in late May the Emperor's troops sacked Rome and took the Pope—the timid, vacillating Clement VII—prisoner. There was no hope that Clement would confirm the sentence, for Charles V was adamantly opposed to the divorce. Henry and Wolsey turned to several improbable schemes, such as a dispensation for Henry to take a second wife and a proposal that Wolsey, as vicar for the captive Pope, grant the divorce. But none of these solutions gave Henry the guarantee he sought for the legitimacy of his children by a second marriage. He and Wolsey therefore sought a papal commission for a court in England that could pronounce a final judgment in the case. Clement VII readily granted to Wolsey and Cardinal Campeggio, a famous Italian canon lawyer, a commission to hear the case and pronounce judgment, but he would not agree that their judgment should be final. Intense pressure from England and the triumph of French arms in 1528 led Clement to give Campeggio a second commission that forbade any appeals in the case. But Campeggio was to show this commission only to Henry and Wolsey and then destroy it, which he did.

After many delays, the trial opened in May 1529 at Blackfriars in London. Catherine appeared in person, denied that her marriage to Arthur had been consummated, protested against the court, and appealed to Rome. The trial came to an abrupt end in July when Campeggio adjourned its meetings. Before it could meet again, Clement, reacting to the defeat of French arms in Italy in June, called a halt to the court's proceedings and recalled the case to Rome. It was a humiliating turn of events for Henry, who promptly made Wolsey the scapegoat. He accused him of *praemunire*, then later of treason. Only by dying on his way to his trial and certain condemnation did Wolsey escape the executioner's ax.

In 1530 Henry's quest for a divorce entered a second stage. He now sought to browbeat the Pope into granting it. Henry was convinced of the rightness of his cause, for Leviticus was divine law and a Pope, though he might dispense with canon law, could not dispense with divine law. To prove this he sent English agents abroad to solicit the opinions of the universities, to ransack libraries, and to gain the support of bishops, canonists, friars, scholars, and rabbis. Unfortunately for Henry, the tide of scholarly opinion flowed against him. Church Fathers, earlier popes, eminent canonists, and humanists all interpreted Leviticus to forbid marrying a brother's widow, except in the case Deuteronomy described (a brother dying without children), which was Henry's case (for Arthur died childless). The prohibition against such a marriage was only canonical, and the Pope might dispense with canon law. Henry's efforts to browbeat the Pope probably received a more fatal blow from the Emperor's power than from any defect in Henry's case. Henry's agents in Rome repeatedly warned the Pope that a denial of the divorce would mean the destruction of Papal authority in England. In 1532 Henry even threatened to cut off the flow of annates (payments made to the Pope by bishops on their appointment to office) to Rome. But the Emperor was near at hand and Henry far away. The pope preferred to placate the man who was in a position to take over the Papal States and who might embrace Lutheranism to win popularity with his German subjects.

Clement VII hoped delay would anger neither Henry nor the Emperor, but this tactic finally led Henry to launch a campaign to recover his case from Rome and submit it to an English court. His wish to gain a favorable decision was not the only impulse leading to this action: There slowly matured in Henry's mind the belief that no Englishman should be summoned before a foreign court, that ecclesiastical cases should not pass out of the province of their origin, that the Pope had usurped a jurisdiction that was not his, that the undivided allegiance of a subject was owed his King, and that God had entrusted the King with the government of the Church. When Henry first voiced these ideas in the summer and autumn of 1530, they met with opposition from his counselors, his clergy, his notables, and his ambassadors. He therefore strove to delay any judgment in Rome, fearing an adverse judgment before he could revoke his case to England. He spent the next two years cajoling, persuading, threatening, and compelling Council, Parliament, and Convocation to acknowledge his authority over the Church. In 1531 he demanded that Convocation recognize him as "protector and only Supreme Head of the English Church," which they did after adding the saving clause, "as far as the law of Christ allowed." In 1532 he bullied Convocation into surrendering its legislative independence by granting the King a royal veto on the making of canons. That same year he persuaded Parliament to suspend the payment of annates to Rome. By 1532 it is probable that Henry would have asserted his supremacy over the Church even if Clement had ruled in his favor. He was now possessed by the imperial idea of a sovereign king ruling over church and state.

The most immediate obstacle to the achievement of that ideal and to the winning of a divorce in an English court was Archbishop Warham, a strong defender of the Church. In August 1532 the Archbishop died, and Henry named in his place the pliant, obscure Thomas Cranmer. In December Anne Boleyn became pregnant, which made swift action mandatory, for the expected son must be legitimate. In January 1533 Cranmer secretly married Henry and Anne. In March Parliament passed the Act of Appeals, which cut off all appeals to Rome and trumpeted the imperial idea in its preamble. In May Cranmer heard the divorce case and pronounced Henry's marriage to Catherine null and void. In June Anne Boleyn was crowned Queen of England. Henry had all he wanted—a new Queen, supremacy in the Church, sovereignty in the state—all, that is, but a son, for Anne Boleyn in September gave birth to a girl, the future Queen Elizabeth.

PARLIAMENT AND THE BREAK WITH ROME

No man, even though he be a king, even though he be Henry VIII, could carry through by himself so great a revolution as removing an entire kingdom from obedience to Rome. To accomplish it, Henry needed either the support or the acquiescence of his subjects, particularly of the more powerful ones who sat in Parliament and Convocation. He won that support and gained that acquiescence by exploiting the anticlericalism of the Commons and by taking advantage of the weakness of the Church.

The roots of this anticlericalism lay in the ordinary person's disgust at the power, wealth, pomp, privileges, and corruption of the clergy. By pleading "benefit of clergy," a criminal clergyman, even one in minor orders, could escape hanging and win his liberty after a few months in an episcopal prison. The privilege of sanctuary allowed criminals to find safety for forty days in any church or churchyard, and if they reached a great sanctuary, such as Westminster Abbey, they could stay forever. Worse yet was the power that the clergy exercised in ecclesiastical courts over matters of matrimony, morals, and the probate of wills. It was not Christian charity that guided the judges in these courts, but a narrow legalism and a jealous regard for their fees. In 1514, for example, a London merchant, Richard Hunne, refused to pay a mortuary fee to his rector, who thereupon sued him in a church court. Hunne retaliated by suing the rector in a secular court. The bishop of London answered by charging Hunne with heresy and throwing him into the Lollards' Tower at St. Paul's, where he was later found hanged. A coroner's jury accused three ecclesiastical officials of the murder, but the Church prevented their being brought to trial. The case created an uproar in London, led to an attack on benefit of clergy in the 1515 Parliament, and revealed the depth of Londoners' hostility toward the clergy.

The wealth and pomp of the higher clergy did nothing to endear them to Englishmen. The Church owned nearly one-third of all the land of England and enjoyed an additional income from compulsory tithes. This wealth was most inequitably distributed: The wealthiest bishops received as much as £3,800 a year and the most prosperous rectors about £75, while the average vicar received £9 and lowly curates less than £5. Great monasteries, cathedral chapters, and laymen had appropriated many of the tithes meant to support the parish clergy, leaving the parish duties to poorly paid, often ignorant curates. A clergyman would often collect three or four benefices, adding the evil of pluralism to that of absenteeism. The epitome of all these evils, of ostentation, greed, pluralism, and absenteeism, was Thomas Wolsey. He became Dean of Lincoln in 1509. Archbishop of York in 1514, Abbot of St. Albans and Bishop of Bath and Wells in 1518. In 1524 he substituted the bishopric of Durham for Bath and Wells and in 1529 Winchester for Durham. He now held the richest abbey and the wealthiest bishopric in England. His income was £35,000 a year, about six times that of the wealthiest peer. Some of this came from taking bribes when naming men to offices, the sin of simony. In disregard of his vow of celibacy he had several daughters and a son, heaping on his son offices worth £2,700 a year, thus adding nepotism to his other sins.

Thomas Wolsey also accumulated great powers which he exercised in a manner certain to exacerbate the antipapalism of the English. In 1515 the Pope named Wolsey a cardinal, in 1518 he granted him the powers of a Papal Legate. Using these powers, Wolsey governed the Church more autocratically than ever before. He superseded the powers of abbots, bishops, archbishops, and Convocation. He moved cases from episcopal courts to his legatine court. He appointed foreigners—five of them by 1529—to bishoprics. He left bishoprics vacant and drew the revenues himself. Because his legatine powers were papal, his abuse of those powers excited hatred against the Pope. His arrogance revived the laity's dislike of the Pope's meddling in English affairs, while his autocratic government of the Church led many clergymen to wonder if subjection to Rome was worth it.

Wolsey not only provoked anticlericalism and antipapalism, but he left a gravely weakened Church behind him. Bishops reduced in numbers and authority and kept from all corporate action for twelve years could offer little opposition to the King. Furthermore, the bishops were the King's men, as were most of the deans and archdeacons. In Edward I's reign the Pope nominated two of three Archbishops of Canterbury; in 1344 twenty-five of the sixty-eight members of the cathedral chapter of Lincoln had been named by the Pope. Thereafter papal influence declined. In the late fifteenth and early sixteenth centuries, the way to a bishopric was service to the King, who nominated all of them. By 1444 not one member of the Lincoln chapter had been nominated by the Pope. These bishops, deans, and archdeacons, moreover, were more often trained in canon law than theology and more often engaged in administration than pastoral care. Despite some evidence of a revival of episcopal leadership in the 1520s, the bishops remained the King's men, unable long to resist the combined pressure of Crown and laity.

In 1529 Henry VIII chose to ally himself with the anticlerical forces in England. He disgraced Wolsey, the cleric, and replaced him as Chancellor with Sir Thomas More, a layman. He summoned Parliament and allowed it to attack clerical abuses. The House of Commons, which was as freely elected as any Tudor Parliament, represented the middle orders in society, the gentry, the merchants, and the lawyers, on whom the Tudors came to depend. The Commons at once passed statutes regulating mortuary dues, prohibiting excessive fees for probate of wills, and limiting pluralism. The House of Lords, where the bishops and abbots had a majority, reluctantly agreed. Henry then went on to harass the Church in other ways. In December 1530 he charged the entire clergy of England with the crime of *praemunire*, that is, with exercising a foreign jurisdiction in England through their ecclesiastical courts. In return for a fine of £118,000 Henry pardoned them, and early in 1531 he asked Parliament to register the pardon as an act.

Henry's harassment of the Church had been an impulsive, hit-and-miss affair. This changed in December 1531, when Henry brought Thomas Cromwell into the inner circle of his councilors. Cromwell came from an urban world. He was born at Putney, west of London, the son of a blacksmith and fuller. He received no formal education but traveled in Italy and the Netherlands, where he served as a soldier, a merchant, and a solicitor, gaining some knowledge of the law and much knowledge of the world. In 1516 he entered Cardinal Wolsey's Household, where he managed the suppression of twenty-nine religious houses, whose lands were used to endow a school at Ipswich and a college at Oxford, both founded by the Cardinal. He won election to the 1529 Parliament, where he led the attack on clerical abuses and won the notice of the King. Guided by Cromwell and using Parliament as his instrument, Henry now ended the legislative independence of the Church and cut off its financial and judicial ties to Rome.

The attack began with a complaint against those clerical abuses that the House of Commons, guided by Cromwell, had drawn up in March 1532. The Commons presented the complaint to Henry, who sent it to Convocation for a reply. Their reply angered Henry, who swiftly presented them with an ultimatum: they must agree that all future clerical legislation should receive the King's assent and that all obnoxious legislation in the past should be annulled by a royal commission. Convocation refused, provoking Henry to cry out, now we see that the clergy are "but half our subjects, nay, and scarce our subjects." Henry threatened an act of Parliament ending their legislative independence unless they agreed. A browbeaten, half-empty Convocation finally submitted to the King's demands in a document known as The Submission of the Clergy.

That same year Parliament attacked the financial ties with Rome. The government brought into the Commons a bill that would temporarily halt the payment of annates. The bill passed the Commons only after the first recorded division of that House in history, and it passed the Lords only after Henry went down to Parliament three times. The bill also declared that should the Pope refuse to consecrate a nominee, the nominee might be consecrated by English authority alone.

The ultimate logic of Cromwell's legislation found expression in the Act in Restraint of Appeals of 1533, the most important single piece of legislation passed in the sixteenth century. There had been a plan merely to pass an act empowering an English court to rule on the divorce, but Cromwell made it a general statute that brought all ecclesiastical jurisdiction under the King's control. The preamble to the act, which Cromwell wrote, declared emphatically that England was a sovereign state, free of all foreign jurisdiction, within which the King was supreme. The Act of Supremacy of 1534, which declared the King to be the supreme head of the Church in England, and the Act in Restraint of Annates of 1534, which annexed annates to the Crown permanently, only confirmed the revolution which the Act in Restraint of Appeals proclaimed.

RESISTANCE AND REBELLION

Henry spent 1535 enforcing the new religious settlement. The instrument he used was an oath contained in the Act of Succession of 1534, an oath which was to be administered throughout the realm and which required Englishmen to acknowledge the validity of Henry's marriage to Anne and the invalidity of his marriage to Catherine. Most people, though not enthusiastic, acquiesced in the new settlement, either out of delight at seeing the clergy humbled, or from a deep loyalty to the King, or from a real concern that there be an heir to the throne, or from fear of the King's wrath or, what must have been the case with most ordinary people, from an inability to see that any revolution had occurred. The old religion remained unchanged, the mass was performed, the sacraments were available.

Yet some did resist. The first was Elizabeth Barton, the Nun of Kent. She was a poor servant girl, probably an epileptic, who became a visionary and prophetess, with a large popular following in Kent. She told Henry to his face that the divorce was wrong, and not long afterward she prophesied that he would be deposed within a month if he married Anne Boleyn. The government at once arrested her and several monks of Canterbury who had managed her visions and prophecies. Because the judges ruled that her offense did not amount to treason, Henry had Parliament in 1534 pass an Act of Attainder against her and her associates, who were promptly executed. As always, Henry was careful of the law and careless of justice.

Elizabeth Barton, the first martyr for the old religion, was soon joined by two far more famous ones, John Fisher, Bishop of Rochester, and Sir Thomas More, author of *Utopia*. Bishop Fisher, who had defended Catherine at her trial with spirit, learning, logic, and audacity, was the only bishop to refuse to take the oath of succession. For this Henry sent him to the Tower, where he joined Sir Thomas More, who had resigned the chancellorship in 1532 and refused to swear the oath in 1535. More and Fisher were willing to swear to the succession but not to the condemnation of the first marriage, for that implied a denial of papal supremacy. To refuse an oath was not treason in English law. Henry therefore kept the two men in prison until Parliament had passed an act making it treason maliciously to deny the King's title (which now included supremacy in the Church). At his trial More defended himself brilliantly, but his judges, by ignoring the word "maliciously" and by accepting perjured evidence, found him guilty. They also found Bishop Fisher guilty, and the executioner's ax fell on Fisher in June and More in July. It also fell that spring on six Carthusian monks, a Brigettine, and a secular priest. These executions revealed the implacable resolve of Henry, but the most impressive fact about them is their fewness. The vast majority of the English submitted to the new order in the Church.

They did, that is, until the autumn of 1536, when a combination of political, economic, local, and religious grievances caused a major rebellion in Lincolnshire, Yorkshire, and Cumberland, a rebellion soon called the Pilgrimage of Grace. It began in Lincolnshire, where some peasants, craftsmen, parish priests, and gentlemen rose in revolt on October 1. Within two weeks the revolt spread to Yorkshire, where Robert Aske, a gentleman in the employment of the powerful Percy family, asserted his leadership. It was a popular rather than a noble movement, but behind the commoners stood many of the nobility. The grievances of the rebels varied widely. The nobility resented Thomas Cromwell's ascendancy at Court and his attack on their "liberties" and franchises. The gentry resented the Statute of Uses, which forbade them to settle their estates in a trust, for the "use" of their heirs. The peasants, suffering from bad harvests, resented enclosures and high rents. Everyone hated the subsidy of 1534, which royal commissioners were then collecting. But the chief grievances were religious. One set of royal commissioners was at work dissolving the smaller monasteries and another set enforcing the Protestant-leaning religious instructions recently issued by Cromwell. These changes, along with the denial of Papal supremacy, deeply offended the conservative populace of the North. Rumor compounded their discontent. It was said Henry would rob the parish churches of their plate, reduce the number of parish churches, seize all the gold in the country, and tax those who aped their betters by eating white bread.

Because the King possessed no standing army, the rebels at first met with success. They seized Lincoln on October 5 and occupied York on October 13. By October 24 Robert Aske had 30,000 armed men at Doncaster. On December 2 he gathered a great council at Pontefract to draw up demands that reflected the Pilgrims' grievances. They demanded the dismissal of Cromwell, the repeal of the Statute of Uses, a halt to enclosures, fair rents, an end to heretical innovations, the restoration of suppressed monasteries, the recognition of Princess Mary's place in the succession, and an acknowledgement of the Pope's primacy in the Church.

But the rebellion ended in failure. No great peer joined the movement, nor did it ignite any Yorkist sentiment. In Yorkshire an undercurrent of class hatred between gentlemen and peasants emerged to divide the Pilgrims. Henry's policy of deceit and delay effectively disarmed the Pilgrims while he raised an army from the loyal counties south of the Trent. The Duke of Norfolk, whom Henry placed in command of his forces, promised Robert Aske and his allies a pardon and a hearing of their demands. Robert Aske at once tore from his breast the five wounds of Christ, the insignia of the Pilgrimage of Grace, and ordered the Pilgrims to disperse. Indeed, the chief explanation for the failure of the rebellion lies in the loyalty of the Pilgrims themselves, who saw themselves as petitioners to the King, not as rebels. They failed to perceive that beneath Henry's fair words lay a determination never to treat with "false traitors and rebels," who should be punished for the "detestable and unnatural" sin of rebellion.

A second wave of rebellions in January and February gave Henry the opportunity he sought to wreak vengeance. In the spring of 1537 Norfolk seized and executed rebels throughout the North, with an intent to instill in the people a terror of the King's power. In Cumberland seventy peasants were hung from trees in their gardens. The monks of Sawley were hung on a long timber extending from the steeple of their church. Despite the promise of a pardon and after a mockery of a trial, Robert Aske was executed. In all the government executed 178 Pilgrims, not a great number for an age that regarded rebellion as an unspeakable sin, but enough to deter others in the North from further rebellion for a generation. Though the Pilgrims did not attain their ends, their ill-fated rebellion may have checked a trend toward Protestantism in 1535 and 1536. It probably also led to a drastic change in the power structure of the North. Henry and Cromwell now chose to rely on the gentry and the Council of the North, not on the nobility and great magnates like the Earl of Northumberland.

THE DISSOLUTION OF THE MONASTERIES

The dissolution of the smaller monasteries, those worth less than £200 a year, had helped precipitate the Pilgrimage of Grace; the failure of the Pilgrimage in turn hastened the downfall of the larger monasteries. Those monastic houses which had joined the revolt were promptly declared forfeit, and in 1539 Parliament passed an act assigning the wealth of all monasteries to the Crown. The dissolution of the smaller monasteries in 1536 and the larger ones in 1539 did not arise from the corruption and decay of monastic life, though the visitors sent to the monasteries by Cromwell in 1535 found enough of both. There was scandal—drunkenness and lewdness—though not more than in earlier times. More serious was a loss of a sense of vocation. The monks gave little charity, maintained few schools, promoted little learning. They were sunk in routine and riddled by worldliness. But all this had little to do with their dissolution. Cromwell's visitors wrote their reports to justify a decision already reached.

Henry persuaded Parliament to dissolve the monasteries because he coveted their wealth. The English Church owned about 30 percent of the wealth of England, and the monasteries possessed fully half of that. It was a rich plum, ripe for the picking. And Henry desperately needed money. The massive taxation in the 1520s had been wasted in war. During the 1530s Henry was reluctant to ask Parliament to vote subsidies, for he sought other favors of it. Inflation now began to bite into the royal income, and the cost of defending the realm against the Catholic powers mounted. The result was the decision to seize the wealth of the monasteries.

The monks suffered little, being given a pension of £5 a year, a greater sum than many curates earned. The nuns suffered more, for the male-dominated society of that age would give them only £2 a year. The friars, whose houses were also dissolved, received nothing. There was a considerable loss to the nation in the realm of art and learning. Images, jewelry, metalwork, and reliquaries were melted down; libraries dispersed; and splendid buildings destroyed. The dissolution also led to an attack on popular religious observances, with the dismantling of shrines and the destruction of miraculous images. And since monasteries existed so that monks might pray for the souls of their founders, it became harder for people to defend the Catholic doctrine of intercessory prayer.

The chief recipient of this wealth was the King, whose revenue increased by over £100,000 a year, a sum equal to the total royal income at the beginning of Cromwell's ministry. Cromwell's aim was to use this wealth to endow the Crown in perpetuity. Had he accomplished this aim he would have gone far towards making the Crown absolute. Henry had more generous aims. On the day Parliament passed the act for assigning the revenues of the larger monasteries to the Crown, Henry rushed through both Houses a bill, whose preamble he wrote. In it he promised to spend the money for the support of the Church, the maintenance of almshouses, the promotion of learning, and the maintenance of highways. He fulfilled few of these purposes. He did establish six new bishoprics, endow five Regius professorships, establish a college at Cambridge, and create half a dozen smaller endowments; but this was all he had to show for the immense fortune that passed through his hands. In the end Henry neither permanently endowed the Crown, as Cromwell hoped, nor promoted learning and religion, as the humanists hoped. Instead he wasted this enormous fortune on an enterprise Erasmus and More thought the most foolish of all—war.

In 1542 Henry plunged into war against Scotland and France, a war that was to cost nearly £3 million. To help pay for it, he sold two-thirds of all monastic lands between 1543 and 1547. Some of the land, 2.5 percent of it, he gave to great courtiers like the Duke of Norfolk or to great ministers like Cromwell. The officials of the Court of Augmentations, the financial body set up to administer the revenues of the monasteries, gained the most. Sir Richard Rich, the Chancellor of the Court and the man whose perjured testimony destroyed Sir Thomas More, received fifty-nine manors, thirty-one rectories, and twenty-eight vicarages. The Treasurer of the Court, Sir Thomas Pope, gained thirty manors, and the Auditor, William Cavendish, gained enough land to lay the basis for the fortune of his family, the future Dukes of Devonshire. The entire operation vividly illustrated Sir Thomas More's observation that government is nothing but a "conspiracy of rich men procuring their own commodities under the name and title of the commonwealth."

Most (97.5 percent) of the land was sold (1,527 grants out of 1,593), and at a good price, twenty times the annual value of the land. The nobility purchased some, as did merchants, lawyers, and civil servants. The gentry, however, purchased the bulk of it, probably two-thirds, and most of them purchased the land to round out their existing estates. The picture of "New Men" coming into the country, buying the land, and rack-renting their tenants is largely a myth, not only because the "New Men" were not that numerous, but because the monks and the old gentry were as adept at raising rents as the new men. In an age of inflation only a fool or a saint would not raise rents. As time passed some of the monastic lands fell into the hands of wealthy yeomen, who rose into the ranks of the gentry. These families, along with those merchants, lawyers, and civil servants who bought land, swelled the numbers of the gentry. In Essex in the hundred years after the dissolution the number of gentry families rose from 144 to 336. The Church was the loser and the gentry the winner in the great plunder of the monastic estates.

The dissolution of the monasteries also contributed to the emergence of new attitudes and policies toward the poor. In theory the monasteries played a central role in the relief of the poor—they distributed alms at the monastery gate and supported hostels, leper houses, asylums, and hospitals. But in practice the monasteries in Henry VIII's reign gave less than 5 percent of their money income to charity. Their dissolution, therefore, did not create the problem of poverty that confronted the Tudors. The problem was serious, for there were 20,000 to 30,000 unemployed in a population of less than 3 million, men and women who became beggars, vagrants, and criminals. In the 1530s there appeared a group of preachers and pamphleteers, many of them close friends of Thomas Cromwell, who urged that it was the duty of the state to provide for the poor. They came to be called "Commonwealth men" and they envisaged the creation of a paternalistic state, one that would check enclosures, establish schools, and care for the poor. They urged Cromwell and the King to use the monastic lands for these purposes, but Henry's delight in war wrecked their proposal. The only positive result of the commonwealth movement in the 1530s was the passage of the Poor Law of 1536. This law rested on a distinction between those capable of work but unable or unwilling to work—the sturdy beggar—and those too old or sick to do so—the impotent poor. The 1536 law made the parish responsible for employing the sturdy beggar and caring for the impotent poor. One principle the law insisted upon: Begging was wrong and should be punished. The medieval church had extolled begging, as much for the merit gained by the donor as for the relief given the recipient, but the Protestant ideas that were now flowing into England rejected "good works" and regarded begging as an abomination to be punished by whipping and branding.

THE TUDOR REVOLUTION IN GOVERNMENT

The decade of the 1530s, which saw the break from Rome and the dissolution of the monasteries, also witnessed changes in government so profound that Professor G. R. Elton of Cambridge has called them revolutionary. In 1953 he published a book entitled *The Tudor Revolution in Government,* in which he asserted that a twofold revolution had occurred in the 1530s. On the one hand, England became a sovereign state, owing obedience to no outside authority, with supreme power placed in the King in Parliament. On the other hand, England replaced a medieval, personal, Household administration with a modern, national, bureaucratic administration. The architect of both revolutions was Thomas Cromwell.

It was Cromwell who wrote the preamble to the Act in Restraint of Appeals, where under the term "empire" he asserted the national sovereignty of England:

> This realm of England is an Empire, and so hath been accepted in the world, governed by one Supreme Head and King having the dignity and royal estate of the imperial Crown.

The body of the act gave practical effect to this claim by ending all papal jurisdiction in England. But the Tudor revolution went beyond the mere abolition of papal power in England; it also asserted the supremacy of statute law over natural and divine law. Sir Thomas More declared that he could not obey an act of Parliament if it contradicted the laws of Christendom, but this medieval view no longer prevailed. The placing of sovereignty in the King acting through Parliament was of profound significance, for it meant that England would remain a limited monarchy, that the King would govern through laws made with the consent of his subjects and not through proclamations issued on his own authority. "We at no time," said Henry, "stand so highly in our estate royal as in the time of Parliament."

Accompanying the revolution in government was a revolution in administration. Cromwell took the administration of finances away from the Chamber, which was dependent on the personal activity of the King, and placed it in a series of courts, each with its own officials, seals, office, and responsibilities. He elevated the position of Secretary (which he obtained in 1534) over all other offices, gave it control of finances, foreign affairs, defense, and religion, and relegated the Chancellor and Lord Privy Seal to a secondary place. He transformed the inner ring of the Council into a formal Privy Council, with only twenty members, a clerk, an agenda, and regular meetings. In these ways, Cromwell transformed a personal Household administration into a modern bureaucratic one less dependent on the King.

That a transformation in government occurred during these years is certain, but earlier developments had prepared the way for that transformation and not all of the changes were permanent. King and Parliament, through Statutes of Provisors and Praemunire, had already limited papal power in England; judges ever since 1450 had recognized that Parliament could make new law, unmake old, and control judges in their interpretation of existing law; and only the determined resistance of Parliament prevented Henry and Cromwell from dangerously strengthening the power of proclamation. And during Elizabeth's reign it was the old Exchequer, not the new financial courts created by Cromwell, that became the center of financial administration—though the Exchequer adopted some of the procedures of the new courts. These facts only modify, they do not negate, the picture of a transformation of the English state. Cromwell's reforms were the decisive step in an evolution that extended from the middle of Edward III's reign to the middle of Elizabeth's, and created a sovereign state with a modern administration.

By creating a royal navy, Henry VIII strengthened the state in a more material way. Even here he built on a revival of English seapower that Edward IV and Henry VII had begun. Henry VII left his son five warships, a number Henry VIII increased to forty-five. Furthermore, heavy guns, capable of sinking ships, were now mounted on the warships, which led the design of warships to diverge from that of merchant vessels. These new warships were built in royal dockyards at Deptford and Woolwich which Henry established and supervised. He had a passion for ships and knew the speed, tonnage, and armament of every vessel in the navy. But he did not rely solely on the navy for defense. He also constructed a chain of forts along the coasts and strengthened the garrisons at Hull and Berwick. The navy and the forts were an outward sign of an inward resolve to be independent and sovereign.

Rome was not the only obstacle to Henry's sovereignty. There were also those great "liberties" and franchises, most of them in the North, where the King's writ did not run, and a bishop or lord ruled. Cromwell attacked them with his customary vigor and ruthlessness. In 1536 he obtained an Act of Parliament that for all practical purposes abolished the franchises and "liberties." Then in 1537 he devised a new Council of the North, a permanent council dominated by royal officials, heeding the dictates of London and governing the five northern counties. For the first time in history, all English people became subject to the King's immediate government.

Henry also extended his power into Wales. Ever since Glendower's rebel-

The Great Harry, the flagship of Henry VIII's fleet (*Bettmann Archive*).

lion, Wales had been a tangled web of marcher lordships and a separately organized principality. The marcher lordships, which were virtually petty kingdoms, afforded a refuge for criminals and were a source of endless trouble. Wolsey sought to solve the problem in 1525 by reviving the Council of Wales, but it proved ineffective. In 1536 Cromwell cut the Gordian knot by securing legislation that abolished the marcher lordships and the separate principality. Parliament annexed some of the marcher lordships to English counties; the rest became part of Wales, which Parliament now divided into twelve counties. Within these counties Welsh law was abolished, English law extended, justices of the peace introduced, the use of English required in judicial proceedings, and twenty-four members of Parliament allotted. The Welsh did not oppose this consolidation with England, for they regarded these acts of union as an emancipation from those disabilities they had suffered since the reign of Edward I.

Henry VIII was far less successful in Ireland, where English power, at flood tide in the twelfth century, had slowly ebbed away since. By 1485 that power extended only through the Pale, a coastal area extending 50 miles north of Dublin. Real power rested with Gerald Fitzgerald, Earl of Kildare, whom

Henry VII continued as Lord Deputy until 1494, when he replaced him with an Englishman, Sir Edward Poynings. Henry instructed Poynings to conquer Ulster and to give Ireland a new constitution. Poynings failed utterly in the first task, but he did persuade an Irish Parliament to agree that henceforth it should meet only with the King's consent and should discuss no measure not first agreed to by the King in Council. Poynings Law, as it came to be called, ended the legislative independence of Ireland for 300 years.

Henry VIII soon found, however, that he did not have the money to hold Ireland by force, so he brought Kildare back to rule Ireland. Rule Ireland he did, and his son after him, until 1534, when complaints from the enemies of the Fitzgeralds, chiefly the Butlers, led Henry to imprison the Earl of Kildare in the Tower, where he died of natural causes. His death provoked his son to rise in rebellion, a rebellion easily suppressed by a small English army, supported by the Butlers. Cromwell then urged Henry to enforce an antipapal policy in Ireland. Lord Grey, the new deputy, persuaded the Irish Parliament to pass an Act of Supremacy for the Irish Church, to dissolve the monasteries, and even to recognize Henry as King rather than lord of Ireland. This last measure was necessary because many of the Irish had regarded the Pope as King of Ireland and the King of England as his viceroy, a distinction that the break from Rome made unacceptable. English rule in Ireland remained nominal, yet the fall of the Kildares in 1534 marked a turning point in Irish history. From that moment onwards the initiative lay with the English Crown, not with the Irish; and the Irish were now divided from the English by religion as well as language and culture.

SCOTLAND AND FRANCE

As few as were Henry's achievements in Ireland, they shone brightly in comparison to his failures in Scotland, where a combination of arrogance and inaction defeated several splendid opportunities to unite the two kingdoms. The first came early in the reign, in 1514, when James IV, faithful to his treaty with France, led a large army across the border. At Flodden, just inside Northumbria, the Earl of Surrey outmaneuvered James and dealt him a shattering defeat. James himself and most of the Scottish aristocracy met death in battle. But Henry, besieging distant Tournai, lost the opportunity to seize Scotland. He could rest assured, however, that Scotland was no longer a danger to England, for his sister Margaret was mother and regent to the 17-month-old James V.

English influence in Scotland did not survive for long. James V, who proved to be vehemently anti-English, married a French princess, Mary of Lorraine, in 1538. James also refused Henry's counsels to despoil the Church; instead he listened to the militant Cardinal Beaton. Thus, when Henry in 1541 dreamed once again of invading France, he sought first to fasten the back door. He sought to do this through negotiations, but all efforts failed, largely because

James refused to come either to York or London. Henry exploded in anger and ordered Norfolk to raid Scotland, which he did in October 1542, leaving a trail of devastation behind him. James, however, was provoked rather than intimidated and sent an army of 10,000 Scots across the border. At Solway Moss an English army of only 3,000 drove the Scots, riven by internal dissension, into a

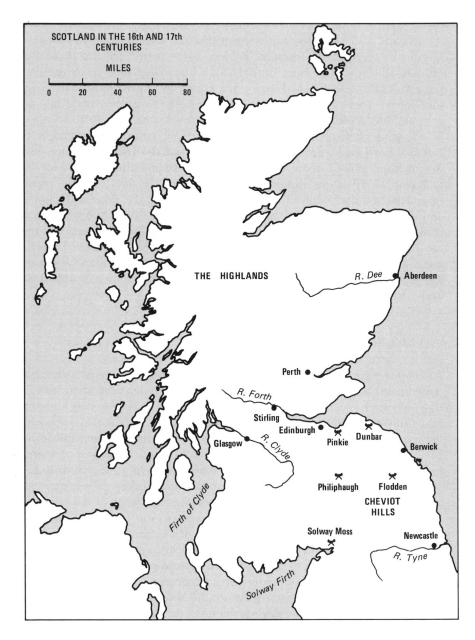

SCOTLAND IN THE 16th AND 17th CENTURIES

swamp. It was a rout more than a defeat, for the English, while losing only seven men, captured seven Scottish lords and five hundred gentlemen. News of the defeat, so men reported, caused the death of James V, who left behind a 7-day-old daughter, Mary Stuart.

The victory at Solway Moss gave Henry an incomparable opportunity to unite England and Scotland. The new regent of Scotland, the Earl of Arran, was prepared to cooperate. There was an Anglophile party in Scotland; Cardinal Beaton was in prison. Thus negotiations were begun for the marriage of Prince Edward to the infant Mary. But Henry promptly overplayed his hand. He sought custody of Mary, he placed English garrisons in Scotland, and he asserted an English sovereignty over Scotland. The result was a reaction in Scotland in favor of France. Between July and December 1543, Cardinal Beaton and his allies regained control and renewed all treaties with France. At this point Henry ought to have launched a major invasion of Scotland; instead, he sent the Earl of Hertford north on a punitive expedition, with instructions to burn and pillage, and to put to the sword every man, woman, or child who resisted. But Hertford's raid, which the earl himself opposed, only stiffened resistance to Henry's ambitions.

The primary reason why Henry did not launch a massive attack on Scotland was his infatuation with war on the Continent. He appears not to have lost his desire for military glory or his dreams of the reconquest of English lands in France. It is true that in part he attacked France because it persisted in aiding the Scots, but his main motive was to win a great victory there. The fact that Francis I and Charles V, after a decade of friendship, went to war again in July 1542 gave Henry the opportunity he sought to meddle once more in Europe. Early in 1543 he entered into an alliance with the Emperor which envisaged the winning of Burgundy for the Emperor and Normandy and Guienne for Henry. That summer Henry declared war on France and that autumn he and the Emperor planned a campaign for the next year, in which each would put 40,000 men into the field. The Emperor was to march on Paris through Champagne, and Henry along the Somme.

In July 1544 an English army of 48,000 men, accompanied by a huge supply train and the aging, corpulent Henry carried on a litter, marched out of Calais. It was the largest army ever sent to the Continent, equal to two-thirds of the population of London, and far too cumbersome to sweep through Picardy toward Paris. Henry therefore used it to besiege Montreuil and Boulogne, a decision that provoked Charles V, or gave him a pretext, to sign a separate and profitable peace with France. Boulogne fell in September, a costly toy for the soldier-king, since it not only cost over a million pounds to win and secure but proved a stumbling block to the conclusion of peace. The war dragged on for another year, during which French troops landed on the Isle of Wight, only to be cut to pieces by the local militia. These dismal campaigns came to an end in 1546, when England and France agreed to a treaty of peace. By this treaty England was to keep Boulogne for eight years, at which time France was to buy it back for 80,000 crowns. For this hollow triumph Henry had spent over £2 million.

To raise this huge sum, and another million spent on the Scottish war, Henry resorted to various expedients. He raised £1,200,000 by direct taxation, £300,000 by loans and benevolences, and £800,000 by the sale of monastic lands (thereby permanently impoverishing the crown). The final expedient was debasement of the coinage. The government invited individuals to bring their coin into the mint, where it was melted down and recoined with more alloy. The mint returned to the person coin of a greater face value, which would mean an immediate profit for him, though eventually prices were bound to rise. The government's profit came from charging forty to eighty times the usual fee for the process. In this way the Crown earned £450,000, while ruining the coinage, promoting inflation, destroying confidence in the government, and injuring the economy.

Henry died in January 1547, still owing £750,000 to bankers in Antwerp, from whom he had borrowed £1 million to help pay for futile and pointless wars. He also died with Scotland unconquered and openly at war with England —in 1545 the French even slipped 3,500 troops into Scotland. The last seven years of Henry's reign were a monument to wrong choices, lost opportunities, arrogance, vainglory, and prodigality.

THE GROWTH OF PROTESTANTISM

When Henry died he left behind a Regency Council whose members were largely Protestant and whose ascendancy practically guaranteed a Protestant England. Was this deliberate? Or accident? Or some combination of the two?

Of Henry's orthodoxy as a young King there is no question. With the help of More and Fisher he wrote and published a famous reply to Luther, a book that went through many editions and earned him the papal title of Defender of the Faith. But the break with Rome caused him to lean on servants whose Catholic faith was less orthodox than his, particularly Archbishop Cranmer and Thomas Cromwell. Cromwell made himself indispensable to Henry by his skill in management; Cranmer won the King's lasting affections by his modesty, subservience, good manners, and sound scholarship. Both men were moderate reformers and persuaded Henry in the mid-1530s to move toward Lutheranism. They were aided in this by the international situation, for in 1533 France, on whose alliance Henry had depended since 1527, began to turn toward Spain. Henry thereupon opened negotiations with the Lutheran princes of Germany. These negotiations failed, but not before they had influenced the first statement of faith of the new Church of England, the Ten Articles of 1536.

These articles were a compromise between the old faith and the new. While they defined in an orthodox manner three of the seven traditional sacraments (baptism, penance, and the mass), they omitted all mention of the other four (confirmation, marriage, holy orders, and extreme unction). Some passages were drawn nearly verbatim from Lutheran sources, but the Ten Articles stopped short of the Lutheran doctrine of justification by faith alone. Salvation was to be gained, as the Catholics taught, by faith and good works. More important than the Ten Articles were the Injunctions which Cromwell as vice-regent of the Church issued in 1536 and 1538. These ordered that a Bible be placed in every parish church, that images be removed, that the clergy teach the Paternoster and the Ten Commandments, and that there be quarterly sermons based on the Scriptures. Cromwell, like Cranmer, sought a simple, pure faith based on Scripture, declared by the King, and accepted by all without disputes over abstruse doctrines.

Henry soon drew back. In 1537, freed from any dependence on the Lutheran princes by the outbreak of war between Charles V and Francis I, he issued *The Institutions of a Christian Man*, usually called the Bishop's Book. The four lost sacraments reappeared, though the emphasis on scriptural authority remained. The strongest check to Protestantism, however, came in 1539, a year of acute crisis. The signing of a treaty of peace by Charles V and Francis I in 1538 precipitated the crisis, as did the Pope's decision finally to excommunicate and depose Henry VIII. Fearing an assault by Catholic Europe, Henry mustered the county militia, strengthened defense works, readied the beacons, and visited his ships at Portsmouth. Fearing rebellion at home, he executed every Yorkist he could lay his hands on. Henry Pole, Henry Courtenay, and Sir Edward Neville lost their heads for no greater crime than being descendants of Edward III. Henry also had Parliament pass the Act of the Six Articles to placate Catholic opinion. These articles upheld transubstantiation (the belief that the priest in the Mass changes the "substance" of the bread and wine into the body and blood of Christ), the need for confession, the sanctity of vows of chastity, the justness of private masses, the sufficiency of communion in one kind, and the illegality of clerical marriages. The act declared that any person who denied transubstantiation should suffer death.

The crisis of 1539 led Thomas Cromwell to renew his efforts to find Henry a new wife. Henry had tired of Anne Boleyn, who after giving birth to a girl, Elizabeth, miscarried a boy. Henry's eyes soon fell on another lady of the Court, Jane Seymour. Determined to be rid of Anne, he accused her of adultery, construed adultery to be treason, and had her executed. Anne was certainly flirtatious, but she was probably not adulterous. Jane Seymour gave Henry the son he had overturned the Church to gain, but she died giving birth to Edward. In late 1537, Henry was once again a widower. A search for a French princess having failed, Cromwell urged Henry to marry Anne of Cleves, whose father, though no Lutheran, was allied with the Lutherans. In January 1540 Anne of Cleves arrived in England, where Henry, appalled at her plain face and dull wits, went through the ceremony only for the good of the realm. But he declared he had never consummated the marriage and soon found a pretext for divorcing "the Flanders' mare." These events occurred when the conservative action at court, led by Bishop Stephen Gardiner and the duke of Norfolk, was growing strong. In July they struck at their greatest enemy, Thomas Cromwell, whom the nobles hated as an upstart, the clergy as a despot, and the conservatives as a radical. Henry allowed himself to be persuaded that his faithful minister had sought to lead the kingdom into heresy and agreed to an Act of Attainder which condemned him to death. Henry chose an attainder rather than a trial because a trial would have allowed Cromwell to defend himself. Cromwell was beheaded in July 1540, and Henry lost the best servant he ever had.

Though Henry in the Six Articles and the King's Book (issued in 1543) clung to orthodox Catholic doctrine, his subjects began to embrace Lutheranism. Lutheran books first entered England in 1520. They met with a favorable reception, for the soil had been prepared by three earlier movements: Lollardy, the New Devotion, and humanism. In 1520 there were still Lollard communities in Buckinghamshire, Essex, London, Birmingham, and Coventry. Most of the heretics dragged before Church courts in the 1530s were Lollards, not Lutherans. But the Lollards were neither politically nor intellectually important and could not by themselves have brought about significant changes in the Church. More important was that lay piety called the New Devotion, which arose in the late fifteenth and early sixteenth centuries.

With the growth of towns there emerged a population that objected to the calculating, mechanical aspects of late medieval Catholicism. They cultivated an inner spiritual life and sought a religion that would reconcile God the righteous judge with the individual's longing for salvation. This new lay piety became explosive when allied to the new critical scholarship of the humanists. Not a single one of the first generation of humanists became a heretic, but by attacking abuses in the Church, by reducing Christianity to its basic simplicities, by translating the New Testament anew, and by emphasizing the importance of the Scriptures they paved the way for Protestantism. Protestantism was a religion of the Book, and Erasmus dreamed of the day when all women might read the Gospels, when "the countrymen might sing them at his plow, the weaver chant them at his loom, the traveller beguile with them the weariness of the journey."

Lutheran ideas found their first home with scholars and merchants. The first Lutheran cell in England was at Cambridge, where scholars, among them Thomas Cranmer and Hugh Latimer, met at the White Horse Tavern to discuss the new ideas coming from Germany. Lutheran ideas likewise throve in London, especially among merchants who traded with the Continent. Two forces caused these ideas to spread beyond these groups: the Bible and the printing press. It was a dedicated, solitary Cambridge scholar, William Tyndale, who produced the first successful New Testament in English, but he could not have done so without a patron in London and the security of service as a chaplain to the Merchant Adventurers abroad. Though the City Council of Brussels condemned, strangled, and burned Tyndale in 1536, his New Testament prompted Miles Coverdale in 1535 to translate the Old and New Testaments

William Tyndale's bibles being smuggled into England (*Bettmann Archive*).

into English. Thomas Cromwell persuaded Henry in 1536 to place Coverdale's Bible in every parish church. Within a year, the Bishop of Hereford admitted that many lay people knew the Scriptures better than the clergy. The Bible could not only be read in the parish church, but could, because of the printing press, be purchased, even by the artisan. When William Malden's father sought to prevent him from joining with others to read the Bible, he rebelled:

> Then, thought I, I will learn to read English, and then I will have the New Testament and read thereon myself, and then had I learned of an English prymer as far as Partis sapientia, and then on Sundays I plied my English prymer. The May-tide following, I and my father's prentice, Thomas Jeffrye, laid out money together and bought the New Testament in English, and hid it in our bed straw and so exercised it at convenient times.

In that Bible hid in the straw, and in many others like it, one can find a truer explanation of the growth of Protestantism than in acts of Parliament or articles of faith. Nor was it only Bibles that were printed. Between 1525 and 1547, English printers published 800 editions of religious works, many of them strongly Protestant.

By 1547 there were numerous Protestants in the Council, at Court, in the Church, and throughout the kingdom—even in distant Yorkshire, where a third of all wills omitted the traditional invocation of the Virgin and the saints. Whether Protestantism would have made such gains had Henry not broken from Rome is a question no historian can ever answer for certain, but it is sure that the denial of papal supremacy, the dissolution of the monasteries, the destruction of Becket's shrine, the placing of an English Bible in every parish church, and the naming of reformers like Hugh Latimer to bishoprics could not help but promote Protestantism. Nor did the fall of Cromwell greatly alter the situation. Within eight months Henry regretted that he had sacrificed his ablest minister, and he did not rigorously enforce the Six Articles. The disgrace of Katherine Howard soon weakened the Catholic party at Court. The Duke of Norfolk's triumph over Cromwell had been cemented by Henry's marriage in 1540 to Norfolk's niece, Katherine Howard. Katherine was young, pretty, lively, a delight to the aging Henry. But her delight in Henry was not so great and she generously granted her favors to others—the evidence was unmistakable—and paid for her folly with her head. Henry then took his sixth wife, an older woman, a widow, Katherine Parr, who not only nursed him during his last days but openly expressed Erasmian, if not Protestant, opinions.

There remains the question of Henry's own religious beliefs during these years. These can be reconstructed from the corrections he made both to the Bishops' Book and the King's Book. Throughout both he rejected any uncompromising statement of justification by faith alone, defended the efficacy of good works, clung to the doctrine of transubstantiation, and persisted in a belief in purgatory. But joined to this instinctive conservatism was a mind remarkably open to radical ideas. He rejected confession and belittled the role of the priest. A belligerent anticlericalism runs through all his comments. By the year 1546 this radicalism led him to propose to the French ambassador that he and the French King abolish the mass in their realms. The remark may have been a jest, but a truly devout Catholic would not have made it. Furthermore, in the same year Henry empowered Cranmer to draw up a new service book that would omit such ceremonies as crawling to the Cross on Good Friday, and Henry attacked the whole idea of intercessory prayer by asking Parliament to pass an act confiscating the wealth of the chantries. Given these facts, it is not difficult to explain why he named two reformers, John Cheke and Richard Coxe, to be tutors to the young Prince Edward and why he left a Regency Council that was predominantly Protestant.

But Henry's open-mindedness only explains why he was *willing* to do these acts. His immediate motives were more practical. He named Cheke and Coxe because they were able scholars; he sought the chantry lands for their wealth, and he destroyed the Catholic party at Court because their leaders had played with treason. Norfolk's son, the poet-soldier Earl of Surrey, had by his arrogant behavior, his open contempt for the King's ministers, and his foolhardiness in quartering his own arms with those of Edward the Confessor infuriated Henry. Surrey dragged his father and the Catholic party down with him. In December 1546 Henry struck Norfolk's and Bishop Gardiner's names from the Regency Council. In January he secured the condemnation and execution of Surrey. Norfolk escaped this fate only because Henry himself died on the day appointed for the duke's execution. Henry died on January 27, 1547, from varicose ulcers that had plagued him for years. It was, therefore, from motives of statecraft—from a desire to prevent faction in the new reign—that Henry left behind him a Regency Council dominated by Edward Seymour, uncle of the new King and a Protestant. But he would not have appointed a Council dominated by Seymour had he not been willing to entertain new ideas in religion.

Further Reading

*G.W. HOSKINS. *The Age of Plunder: King Henry's England 1500–1547*. London, 1976. An unusual book that combines the erudition of an economic historian with the passions of a populist and radical; excels in the discussion of agriculture and rural life.

*G.R. ELTON. *The Tudor Revolution in Government*. Cambridge, England, 1953. An important, scholarly work that may exaggerate the extent of Thomas Cromwell's influence over the King and the revolutionary character of the administrative changes of the 1530s.

JASPER RIDLEY. *Statesman and Saint: Cardinal Wolsey, Sir Thomas More, and the Politics of Henry VIII*. New York, 1983. A fascinating work that challenges legend by depicting Wolsey as a sincere, efficient administrator and More as a persecutor of heretics.

J.J. SCARISBRICK. *Henry VII*. London, 1968. A detached, level-headed, scholarly, detailed, and critical reassessment of Henry; attributes to the King policies Elton attributes to Cromwell.

A.G. DICKENS. *The English Reformation*. London, 1964. Now the standard work on the English Reformation; combines precise scholarship with an admirable impartiality and a readable style.

PHILIP HUGHES. *The Reformation in England*. Vol. 1, *The King's Proceedings*. New York, 1951. A solid, factual, impartial history by a Roman Catholic; the narrative is distinguished by clarity and dramatic interest.

JOYCE YOUINGS. *The Dissolution of the Monasteries*. London, 1971. A brief account of the Dissolution, joined to forty relevant documents; a useful synthesis of recent research.

STANFORD LEHMBERG. *The Reformation Parliament 1529–1536*. Cambridge, England, 1970. An account of the seven sessions of Parliament that created the Church of England and passed equally important social legislation.

GEORGE MACAULAY TREVELYAN. *Illustrated English Social History*. Vol. 1, *Chaucer's England and the Early Tudors*. London, 1949. A delightful book, written by a master of English prose; captures the quality of life in an earlier, rural England.

MURIEL ST. CLARE BYRNE, ed. *The Lisle Letters*. Abridged by Bridget Boland. London, 1983. Contemporary letters that cast a flood of light on fashions, falconry, etiquette, patterns of speech, and the relations of husband and wife, parents and children, and masters and servants.

11 Protestant and Catholic: 1547-1558

Edward died too soon and Mary came to the throne too late to accomplish their purposes. Edward was 9 years old when he ascended the throne in 1547 and 15 when he died of pulmonary tuberculosis in 1553. Mary was already 37 when she ascended the throne, probably too old to bear the child she desperately needed for her design to make England Catholic again. But though neither monarch lived long enough to accomplish his or her purposes, their reigns were pivotal in the history of England. It was during these years that the balance fell decisively on the side of Protestantism and capitalism. The flood of Protestant literature, the abolition of chantries, the Second Book of Common Prayer, the steadfastness of the Marian martyrs, and the identification of Catholicism with Spain all drove England irreparably into Protestantism. At the same time the suppression of Ket's rebellion, the fall of Somerset, and the collapse of the Commonwealth party meant the triumph of competition over custom, of the market price over the just price, and of the pursuit of private gain over the enforcement of social justice. These pivotal years in the growth of Protestantism and capitalism were also a seed time for two other movements: overseas expansion and hostility to Spain. The collapse of the market for woolen cloth at Antwerp led the English to sail south into the Atlantic and north into the White Sea in search of markets and raw materials, thereby beginning the long era of overseas expansion. The English also, during these years, turned away from two centuries of enmity and hostility toward France. Catholic Spain became the hated enemy and remained so for a century.

SOMERSET AND REFORM

In his will Henry VIII left the government of England to the entire Regency Council. This arrangement survived scarcely three days; Edward Seymour, the King's uncle, promptly seized power as Lord Protector and had the young King name him Duke of Somerset. The Council, taught by the Tudors to prize the rule of one man, readily agreed. The Duke of Somerset was somewhat of an enigma. He was liberal in his ideas but greedy and ambitious; an able general but an incompetent politician; tolerant of other men's opinions but arrogant in his own conduct; an idealist in politics but without the tact, patience, and judgment to put those ideals into effect.

The most immediate problem facing him was Scotland, and his handling of it revealed both his idealism and his shortsightedness. He offered the Scots a union of both kingdoms, cemented by the marriage of Edward and Mary Stuart, with home rule and free trade for both nations. But the Scots saw in this project only a design for conquest. They refused it and turned for help to France. Somerset would have been wise at this moment to have allowed the Scots to be Scots; instead, he invaded with 18,000 men, defeated the Scots at the Battle of Pinkie in September 1547, and then grappled with the now familiar problem of how to turn a victory into a conquest. Like Henry VIII before him, he failed to solve the problem; the English government had neither the troops nor the money to occupy Scotland. In 1548 a French fleet brought 6000 troops to Scotland and carried Mary back to France, where she married the dauphin. By the autumn of 1549 there were no English garrisons left in Scotland.

The Duke of Somerset was not a fervent Protestant, but—unwittingly perhaps—he promoted the growth of Protestantism. He did so in three ways: by allowing the free circulation of Protestant ideas, by confiscating the chantries, and by allowing the introduction of the first Book of Common Prayer.

Somerset, who disliked religious persecution, persuaded his first Parliament to repeal the treason and heresy laws of earlier reigns. Swept away were the Treason Act of 1534, which made spoken words treason, the Six Articles of 1539, the Act for Burning Heretics of 1414, and all restrictions on printing the Scriptures. The result was a torrent of Protestant writings—pamphlets, sermons, psalms, devotional works, plays, ballads. Somerset had hoped that liberty would bring calm, but it brought instead a flood of disputation that extended from the bishop's palace to the tavern. The tumult spilled over into image breaking, with the result that the Council ordered the removal of all images and relics from the churches. On a loftier plane, foreign scholars brought the ideas of the Swiss reformer Ulrich Zwingli to England. Martin Bucer of Strassburg became a professor of theology at Cambridge; Peter Martyr, an Italian, occupied a similar chair at Oxford. A Polish Protestant, John à Lasco, became pastor of a refugee church in London.

It was a need for money, not Protestant zeal, that led the government to dissolve the chantries, though the preamble to the Chantry Act of 1547 did attack the idea of purgatory and the saying of masses for the dead. The Chantry Act of 1547 was wide in scope. It not only dissolved 2,374 chantries, but also 90 colleges, many of which ran schools, 110 hospitals and almshouses, which cared for the poor, and all the religious guilds, including those that supported the famous mystery plays. The confiscation of these lands brought the government £610,000, about a fifth as much as the monasteries had brought. But this second dissolution had a far greater effect on the ordinary person's life, for it lessened the role of the Church in society. Private citizens refounded the grammar schools; the municipalities took over the hospitals and almshouses; and the guilds, which had often promoted the veneration of saints, disappeared altogether. The Chantry Act both hindered a revival of Catholic devotion and hastened the secularization of English society.

Thomas Cranmer, as painted by G. Fliccius (*National Portrait Gallery, London*).

In 1548 the government resolved to reimpose uniformity of worship on the land. In September Archbishop Cranmer presented a new Book of Common Prayer to Parliament. It was a masterpiece of compromise and a miracle of English prose. Nearly everything in it was a direct translation of some older piece of liturgy. Cranmer kept old rites, such as confession and extreme unction for the dying. Priests still wore their traditional vestments, and there was still a railed-off altar in the east end of the church. But in two ways the Prayer Book moved toward Protestantism. Common prayer became a fact, for the congregation participated in worship as it had never done before. This dialogue between priest and people gave expression to the Protestant doctrine of the priesthood of all believers. Secondly, the Prayer Book took a Protestant view of the sacrament of the mass, or eucharist. To a Catholic, Christ is corporally present in the host and each mass reenacts Christ's sacrifice on the Cross; according to the 1549 Prayer Book Christ's death at Calvary was a full and sufficient sacrifice, which the communion service commemorates rather than reenacts. Though Cranmer worded this matter so darkly that even Catholic bishops could accept the Prayer Book, the conservative villagers of Cornwall and Devonshire found it altogether too new and strange.

In 1549 Parliament passed an Act of Uniformity that required all clergymen to use the new Book of Common Prayer. When in June the book was introduced into Sampford Courtenay in Devonshire, the incensed villagers forced the priest to celebrate the mass in the old style. Neighboring parishes joined the rebellion, as did the Cornish, who, speaking Celtic, found the English language as incomprehensible as the Latin and less familiar. The rebels drew up a manifesto demanding the Latin mass, the restoration of old ceremonies, the suppression of the English Bible, and the return of the Six Articles. The Protector handled the rebellion with the same humanity that marked all his actions, but the rebels refused to disperse at his promise of a generous pardon. Finally in August the Council sent orders, whose harshness was concealed from Somerset, for the suppression of the rebels. With the help of reinforcements from London, the local landowners, many of them holders of monastic lands, annihilated the rebels. Those who were not slaughtered on the battlefield were hung from gallows as a warning to others.

KET'S REBELLION

While the villagers of Sampford Courtenay were forcing their priest to say mass in the old style, the copyholders of Norfolk were tearing down the fences on the land of John Flowerdew, a hated lawyer turned country gentleman. John Flowerdew sought to divert the rioters by paying them 40 pence to demolish the fences of his enemy, Robert Ket, a prosperous tanner who owned land worth about £50 a year. When Ket heard of the complaints against his enclosures, he agreed to tear them down. Even more, he vowed to join with the rebels and help them to revenge the harm done by the enclosure of common pasture. He became not only their companion but their captain. Under Ket's leadership the rebels, swollen in numbers to 16,000, marched on Norfolk, captured the city, and established a camp on Mousehold Heath overlooking it. Robert Ket was far removed from the stereotype of a modern revolutionary. He was not young, alienated, unsuccessful, and intellectual; rather, he was 57 years of age, a grandfather, unschooled, a member of an ancient family, a successful tanner, and the owner of two manors. His motives must remain a mystery; one can only guess that he was a decent man, with a keen sense of justice, who was carried forward by the enthusiasm of his compatriots.   See   Beer

Apart from Ket, the rebels in Norfolk were composed of the "poor commons," that is, of customary tenants and copyholders, for whom the enemy was the landowning gentry and noble classes. In July 1549 the rebels drew up a list of twenty-nine demands, which they sent as a petition to the King. Their chief demand was that their landlords not be allowed to overstock the commons with their sheep and cattle or to enclose the commons for their own use. The enclosure of arable land was not a grievance, for East Anglia was mainly enclosed country. But the enclosure of the commons for pasture for the lord's sheep was a grievance, second only to the lord's overstocking the commons, thus lessening the tenant's right to graze his sheep and cattle there. The rebels also demanded a reduction of rents and entry fines to the levels of 1485. There were numerous complaints against the clergy, and demands that clerical incomes be cut, that tithes be paid in cash, not kind, and that in each parish there be a resident clergyman, able to preach. Most radical of all were a series of demands that the people participate in local government, an activity hitherto reserved for the gentry.

Ket's rebellion was the most serious challenge made during the century to the Tudor establishment, and its deeper causes lie in both the economic and the intellectual climate of the age. It was, in the first place, a result of a growing population, one that generated both inflation and unemployment. It was the unemployed in Norwich who helped the rebels capture that city. But the chief problem was inflation. The price of foodstuffs rose over 10 percent a year between 1540 and 1550, allowing the tenant to sell on a rising market while paying a fixed rent. The landlord could maintain his real income only by breaking the customary rents and entry fines or by putting more sheep on the commons. During the third and fourth decades of the sixteenth century entry fines rose by 100 percent. No doubt there were instances of rack-renting—of rents raised two- and threefold—but most landlords barely kept pace with inflation. This fact, however, was of little consolation to the tenant who saw his rents rise in violation of the custom of the manor. As one of them said to his landlord: "My bargain was but to pay for my taking £6 13s 4d yearly. . . . You can require no more."

In truth many peasants during these years, especially those with large holdings, prospered, rebuilt their houses, inserted windows, replaced a few sparse wooden forms with comfortable furniture, and began to sleep between linen sheets rather than on straw. Yet a rebellion did break out, in part because of the intellectual climate. The Duke of Somerset openly expressed sympathy for the poor. And a Commonwealth party arose, which denounced enclosures, condemned rack-renting, opposed excessive entry fines, and preached against human greed. Hugh Latimer, who lashed out at covetous landlords before the King at Westminster and before large crowds at St. Paul's Cross, was the most eloquent of these men, but John Hales, who headed a commission in 1548 to investigate breaches of the laws against enclosures, was the most active. Latimer's sermons and Hales's commission were politically unwise, for the oppressed will revolt sooner from hope than from despair. As one councilor put it, "Are victuals and other things so dear? . . . they have lived quietly above sixty years, pastures being enclosed. . . . What is the matter then? By my faith, Sir, liberty, liberty."

A. F. Pollard

A political vacuum in Norfolk allowed the rebels a momentary triumph. There was no local nobleman who could organize the forces of the gentry. The rebels eventually met defeat because they saw themselves as petitioners to the King and Lord Protector, not as revolutionaries. They neither sought to establish a commune in Norwich nor to widen the revolt. It was only a matter of time, therefore, before John Dudley, the Earl of Warwick, leading the King's forces, slaughtered the rebels at Dussindale. Ket's severed head was placed on the battlements of Norwich as a reminder to its citizens of the fate of a rebel in Tudor England.

Ket's rebellion had two immediate consequences: it led to the fall of Somerset and it spelled the eventual doom of the Commonwealth party. By his sympathy for the poor and his inability to maintain order, Somerset had forfeited the support of the only class on which he could hope to depend—the landowners. The Earl of Warwick, having won the King's confidence and now leading an army, seized the opportunity to engineer a *coup d' état.* Through the Council, he seized power, sent Somerset to the Tower, and persuaded the King to create him Duke of Northumberland. Somerset's fall led to the collapse of the Commonwealth party. Hales's enclosure commission came to an end. The Court ceased to extend its patronage to preachers of the social gospel. Parliament even passed a statute asserting the right of lords of manors, subject to certain safeguards, to appropriate wastes and commons. The gentle Somerset had failed in his endeavor to halt the steady growth of capitalism in agriculture.

THE ECONOMIC CRISIS OF 1551

Wool and woolens accounted for four-fifths of all English exports. During the first half of the sixteenth century the number of cloths exported rose three times over, from 50,000 in 1500 to 147,000 in 1550. The great bulk of this cloth was sent to Antwerp, where it was finished and dyed, and reshipped to the German market. This trade to Antwerp increased markedly with the debasement of the English coinage in 1543. A Flemish merchant who had to pay

27 Flemish shillings for an English pound in the 1530s could purchase one for 21 shillings in 1547, and for 15 shillings in 1551. Since prices did not keep pace with falling exchange rates, English cloth became a bargain. Then in 1551 the bubble burst; English exports abroad fell to 85,000 cloths. The Earl of Warwick's decision to reduce the value of English coinage precipitated the collapse. English coins with a face value of a shilling were now to circulate at 6 pence. Just as the debasement of the coinage had stimulated exports, so its revaluation harmed them.

But the causes for the decline in cloth exports were wider and deeper than the revaluation of the coinage. Overproduction had led to a glut on the Antwerp market. Economic depression in Europe, religious persecution in the Netherlands, and the outbreak of plague, which killed many English merchants at Antwerp, all contributed to the decline. A decline in consumption at home made the economic crisis even deeper, because about one-third of all English cloth was sold in England. A series of bad harvests at this time depressed sales, for whenever the harvest was bad the price of bread rose, causing householders to spend more on bread and less on cloth. The crisis that now overwhelmed English clothiers and merchants was severe—and it cried out for a solution.

Sir Thomas Gresham, the royal agent at Antwerp and a member of the Merchant Adventurers, offered one solution: the export of all cloth should be channeled through London and the Merchant Adventurers should be allowed to regulate the flow of cloth at Antwerp. The proposal was characteristic of the Merchant Adventurers, a company which had dominated the trade in cloth since the late fifteenth century and which belied its name by never acting adventurously. It opened no new markets, made no voyages of discovery, and was slow to adopt double-entry bookkeeping and marine insurance. The gist of Gresham's proposal was incorporated in a bill in 1553, but Parliament, for fear of an outcry from the other ports of England, did not pass it. Yet the Merchant Adventurers squeezed out the merchants from other ports and assigned quotas to the remaining London merchants. They also persuaded the government to restrict the privileges of the Hanseatic merchants in London, a measure popular with the people.

Since 1471 the Hansards, as the Hanseatic merchants were called, had paid only 1 shilling on each cloth exported, whereas the English had to pay 1 shilling 2 pence; furthermore, the Hansards did not need to pay the shilling in the pound on general commodities, which English merchants had to pay. Supported by these privileges, the Hansards monopolized the Baltic trade; they handled about a quarter of all English exports. Northumberland now revoked their privileges. But neither of these measures solved the problem facing the English cloth industry. The Merchant Adventurers merely shared out a smaller market, and the English were not strong enough to drive the Hansards (whose privileges Mary restored) from the Baltic. True, the export of cloth did recover from its lowest point, but it remained throughout Elizabeth's reign at a level about 20 percent below that reached in the 1540s.

A bolder solution was to escape dependence on a single market by finding new markets overseas. Because Spain was hostile, because the Turks dominated the Mediterranean, and because the Hansards monopolized the Baltic trade, there were few places to turn other than southward, down the coast of Africa. In 1551 a group of London merchants sent Thomas Wyndham, in *The Lion*, 150 tons, to the Atlantic coast of Morocco, from which he brought back sugar, dates, almonds, and molasses. In 1553 Wyndham sailed farther south, to Guinea, where he found gold and pepper. In 1554 a larger squadron, under the command of John Lok, sailed to the Ivory Coast and Gold Coast and brought back gold, tusks, grain, and slaves. Lok's employers realized a 1000 percent profit on their capital, and Lok became the first Englishman to engage in the nefarious trade in black slaves.

But the English wanted more than gold and ivory and slaves; they wanted to capture the trade with the Orient that had made Portugal wealthy. Since English ships were too small to round the Cape of Good Hope and since all attempts to find a northwest passage had failed, the English resolved to search out a northeast passage. In 1553 three ships under the command of Sir Hugh Willoughby and Richard Chancellor sailed north around the coast of Norway. Willoughby, who became separated from Chancellor, sailed eastward along the Russian coast, ran into the island of Novaia Zemlia, failed to skirt north of it, wintered in the river Arzina, and froze to death there with his entire crew. Chancellor was luckier. He turned south into the White Sea, anchored at Archangel, and traveled overland to Moscow, where he won the respect and friendship of the Tsar, Ivan the Terrible. The Muscovy Company, which sponsored Willoughby and Chancellor, never found the northeast passage to China, but they did open a trade with the Russians, who sent such valuable commodities as wax, tallow, furs, cordage, and timber to England in return for English cloth. And the search for a market for English cloth had been one of the chief motives of the voyage. As Richard Hakluyt, the great Elizabethan publicist of voyages of discovery, wrote: "Our chief desire is to find out ample vent for our woollen cloth."

However important these oceanic trades might be in the future, their immediate impact was slight. The prosperity of England continued to rest on the excellence of the broadcloth manufactured in Somersetshire and Gloucestershire, on the cheapness of the kerseys produced in Yorkshire, on the coal shipped south from Newcastle, on the iron manufactured in the Weald, on the shipbuilding in the Thames, on the leather industry in the Midlands, and on a revival of markets at home and abroad, a revival only peace and good harvests could bring.

THE ASCENDANCY OF NORTHUMBERLAND

John Dudley, Earl of Warwick and after 1551 Duke of Northumberland, was the son of the Edmund Dudley whom Henry VIII had executed to appease the people. John Dudley pursued a distinguished military career in the last years of

Henry VIII's reign, when he proved himself a man of energy, ruthlessness, and stout courage. He also had great political ability, which he coupled to a fierce ambition for power and a naked greed for wealth. In his ambition and greed he did not so much differ from the "new men" of his age as surpass them in vehemence and success. He was a master of intrigue, who originally brought all factions on the council together in opposition to Somerset. He won over the Catholic members by leading them to believe he meant to prevent further religious changes. But once Somerset was in the Tower, he turned away from the path of compromise and moderation. In February 1550 he secured the dismissal of the Catholic members of the Council and turned toward extreme Protestantism. Far from drawing the English together, this decision divided them and cost Northumberland the support of a large part of the propertied classes. He now had to look elsewhere for backing, and he found it in three sources: in the young King, in his fellow councilors and their retainers, and in the Protestant clergy.

The starting point in Northumberland's advance to power was the King himself. Edward VI was one of the most gifted and one of the most obnoxious of the Tudors. He was a lively, good-looking boy, with fair hair and gray eyes. He was intellectually precocious, knew Greek well, wrote essays in French, and understood diplomatic affairs. But he was also haughty, arrogant, and pious. He was a faithful attender of sermons, where he took copious notes. If he spent too long at play, he would reprove himself. On one occasion only is he report-

The Young Prince Edward (*Bettmann Archive*).

ed to have laughed. It was over the mind of this precocious, pious young King that Northumberland in 1551 gained complete ascendancy. He brought Edward into Council meetings and urged him to dispense with the countersignatures of ministers on documents. He freed the King from the restrictions of a minority only to bind Edward closer to himself. But Northumberland never felt secure as long as Somerset, the King's uncle, lived. He therefore had Somerset tried by his peers on trumped-up charges that he had attempted to overthrow the government. Somerset was found guilty, and executed on January 22, 1552. Although the people dipped their handkerchiefs in his blood, supposing it to have the virtue of a martyr's, the Council readily agreed to Northumberland's rule.

Northumberland relied heavily for support on his fellow councilors. In Somerset's time only the Protector had been allowed to recruit his own retainers; now councilors and other courtiers were given licenses to do so. The government even paid for 800 professional cavalrymen, who were retained by some of Northumberland's henchmen. At the same time, lord lieutenants entrusted with the command of the local militia, previously only named in an emergency, were named throughout the whole country. Through this office the Earl of Bedford dominated the West Country, the Earl of Pembroke Wales, and the Earl of Northampton the Midlands. It was in Edward's reign, as much as in Henry's, that the foundations were laid for the "new" aristocratic houses—the Russels gained the Bedford earldom, the Herberts that of Pembroke. Northumberland also needed to reward his adherents on the Council, and this task proved costly. To his credit, he reduced the cost of government by ending the war in Scotland, surrendering Boulogne to France for 400,000 crowns, amalgamating Cromwell's courts of Augmentation and First Fruits with the Exchequer, and seeking to reduce governmental expenditures. But inflation and the cost of the navy defeated all attempts to reduce expenditures to the old peacetime level. To keep the government solvent, Northumberland sold Crown lands, and to ensure the loyalty of his followers he gave them away. Between 1547 and 1553 the government sold or gave away £833,000 worth of Crown lands, an amount that would have brought in £40,000 a year, or a fifth of what the Crown gained from land in 1548. Of this amount, more than half was given away. It was the price of loyalty.

Northumberland, who turned toward Protestantism more from calculation than conviction, was prepared to use anything to buttress his power. In the end, however, he did more to strengthen Protestantism than Protestantism did to strengthen him. Between 1550 and 1553 Protestantism put down roots that Queen Mary found impossible to uproot.

The government began by ordering the suppression of all service books other than the Book of Common Prayer and the destruction of all remaining religious statues and paintings, an order that led to the destruction of priceless books and manuscripts and of other treasures of medieval faith and art. The government next drew up new rules for the ordination of the clergy that transformed the priest endowed with divine grace into the minister appointed to preach, teach, and conduct worship. These steps foreshadowed the conversion of the mass into the communion, which was given full expression in the second Book of Common Prayer of 1552. Archbishop Cranmer sent the first Prayer Book to Martin Bucer, the German theologian, whose extensive criticisms influenced Cranmer and the other authors of the Second Book of Common Prayer. They were now governed by the principle that everything without scriptural basis should be omitted. They abolished the very name of mass and placed the communion table east and west in the church, not altar-wise. The Prayer Book now included the Zwinglian wording, "Take and eat this in remembrance that Christ died for thee"; and it declared that kneeling at communion did not imply any adoration of the sacrament. A Second Act of Uniformity in 1522 not only enforced the use of the book on the clergy, but required the attendance of everyone in the parish at church on Sunday. If they were absent they were fined.

The new Church had a liturgy, but it lacked a creed. In late 1552 Cranmer and his colleagues repaired this deficiency by drawing up the Forty-two Articles. The articles were Lutheran in their emphasis on justification by faith alone and Calvinist in their assertion of the doctrine of predestination—that is, the doctrine that God has decreed whom of humankind He shall bring to everlasting salvation and whom He shall deliver to damnation. In 1553 the young King gave his assent to this uncompromisingly Protestant formulation of faith.

The new liturgy offered the government, desperately in need of money, another excuse to plunder the Church of its vestments and plate. Many of the clergy joined in, even stealing the lead off the roofs of their churches. Northumberland himself continued the despoiling of episcopal lands Henry VIII had begun. He used the immense lands of the bishopric of Durham for his own support. The sordid behavior of Northumberland and his friends undoubtedly offended many people, just as the newness of the liturgy caused resentment. But meanwhile the vested interest in the new order grew, and the new liturgy reinforced the Protestant beliefs that Cromwell's English Bible had fostered. At Edward's death the majority of people were not yet ardently Protestant, but neither were they any longer ardently Catholic.

THE ACCESSION OF QUEEN MARY

In February 1553 the consumptive Edward fell seriously ill; by May his feet were swollen and he was coughing up a black, fetid sputum. On July 6 he died, praying with his final breath, "Lord God, deliver me out of this miserable wretched life." The King's illness confronted Northumberland with a crisis, for by an Act of Parliament and Henry VIII's will the Crown should descend on Edward's death without heirs to Mary Tudor. The accession of Mary would destroy Northumberland's power, if not his life. He therefore persuaded Edward to draw up a will leaving the Crown to the male heirs of Lady Jane Grey, who was a granddaughter of Henry VIII's sister Mary. Northumberland then married his son Guildford to Lady Jane. Edward's will was based upon the assumption that a woman could transmit a claim to the Crown, but could not herself succeed to it. When it became apparent that Edward would die before Guildford and Lady Jane could have a son, the will was changed to read "Lady Jane and her male heirs." Northumberland and Edward then browbeat the judges into drawing up the will and the councilors into signing it. Four days after the King's death, the Council proclaimed Lady Jane Queen of England.

But Northumberland's plot failed because he was unable to imprison the Princess Mary. He summoned her to Edward's deathbed on July 4, but fearing arrest, she fled to Framlingham in Suffolk, where she had herself proclaimed Queen, and set about raising troops. Northumberland at first remained in Lon-

Mary Tudor, as painted by Antonio Moro (*Museo del Prado, Madrid*).

don, probably because he did not trust the other councilors. Finally, on July 14, he set out with a small army. But no battle ensued, for the duke's small army melted away at the news of the thousands who rallied around Mary. Initially there was some hesitation to declare for her, and had she been in prison few would have dared to do so. But once the bandwagon started rolling, there was an outpouring of support. The sailors at Yarmouth forced their captains to declare for Mary. Sir Nicholas Throckmorton at Northampton, who sought to prevent Mary's proclamation as Queen, had to flee for his life. On July 19 the Council in London proclaimed Mary Queen, after the Earl of Arundel had lectured it on the importance of hereditary succession, always a persuasive argument with landowners whose lands were inherited. In the end even Northumberland at Cambridge threw his cap in the air for Queen Mary. Never was there such rejoicing for a Tudor as greeted Mary when she entered London. Yet the populace cheered her because she was a Tudor, not because she was a Catholic. The English rallied to her because they prized order, peace, and a lawful succession, not because they wished to return to Rome. Mary's tragedy was that she did not perceive this fact.

Despite the terrible epithet, Bloody Mary, which posterity has fixed to her name, Queen Mary was a strangely attractive figure. She possessed strength and dignity, as revealed in her resistance to Northumberland's efforts to make her give up the mass. She had courage and judgment, which she displayed at Framlingham. She was gentle and merciful, as she proved by executing only three persons for Northumberland's conspiracy (the duke and two fellow conspirators). She spoke Spanish, French, and Latin, could read Greek and Italian, sang well, and played several instruments. Though she rose early and though her diet was spare, she was not priggish like her brother. She delighted in fine clothes and jewels, enjoyed dancing, loved music, gambled at bowls and cards. But these amiable qualities were overshadowed by her stubborn devotion to high principles. She was, as Christopher Morris has observed, the only adult Tudor with a genuine conscience and the only Tudor who did her country indisputable harm.

Her single-minded purpose was to bring her subjects back to Rome. Since her Protestant half-sister, Elizabeth, seventeen years her junior, was waiting in the wings, Mary saw that she must marry and give birth to an heir. This led to the gravest blunder of her reign, for she refused to marry the two English candidates. Instead she chose Philip of Spain, son and heir of Charles V, the most powerful monarch in Europe, and a member of the same family as Catherine, Queen Mary's mother. The choice proved a disaster, since the English—despite the safeguards written into the marriage treaty—feared they would become subject to Spain, as the Scots were to France. Bishop Gardiner, a Catholic and now Lord Chancellor, opposed the marriage. So did many councilors. The House of Commons petitioned against it, though Mary cut short the Speaker, declaring, "Parliaments were not accustomed to use such language to the kings of England." She then dissolved Parliament.

The dissolution of Parliament made it impossible for the people to oppose the marriage except by rebellion. Mary signed the marriage treaty in January 1554, and rebellion promptly broke out. The conspirators in the west, in Wales, and in the Midlands failed to rise, but Sir Thomas Wyatt, a Kentish landowner, a former sheriff, and son of the famous poet of the same name, made nearly enough headway in Kent to make up for the rest. He led 3,000 armed gentlemen toward London. Wyatt and his allies emphasized the patriotic issue and concealed their Protestant sympathies. Hatred of Spain was their rallying cry and a Courtenay marriage their goal. On January 29 some 600 Londoners joined the rebels, shouting "We are all Englishmen." Had Wyatt marched straight on London, it might have opened its gates. But he did not reach Southwark until February 3, by which time London Bridge was closed. Meanwhile Mary rushed to the Guildhall where, in a speech nearly as eloquent as any of Elizabeth's, she appealed to the loyalty of her subjects.

Mary's appeal and Wyatt's delay tipped the scales against the rebels. A royal army hastily raised from the royal guards and, ironically, from the retinues of Northumberland's henchmen crushed Wyatt's dwindling army in Fleet Street. Mary now ordered some 100 persons executed, including the lovely Lady Jane Grey, who was quite innocent of any involvement. She imprisoned Princess Elizabeth, but her councilors warned her not to execute Elizabeth without clear evidence of her complicity, and that evidence was lacking. In April 1554 a new Parliament confirmed the marriage treaty and in July Philip arrived in London. By her courage Mary had surmounted the second major crisis of her reign, but the rebellion was not without effect. It helped to identify Protestantism with an anti-Spanish, English patriotism in the minds of the English people.

THE RETURN TO ROME

Mary took the first steps toward a reunion with Rome even before Wyatt's rebellion. In October 1553 a freely elected Parliament repealed all the religous legislation of Edward's reign, but it would not revive papal power, restore the Church lands, or reenact the heresy laws Somerset had repealed. It was a substantial achievement to have destroyed the Edwardian reformation at one blow, but it was not enough for Mary. Nor was it enough for Reginald Pole, to whom Mary now turned for assistance. Pole, in whose veins royal blood ran, was an unswerving Catholic, whom Parliament in Henry VIII's reign had attainted for treason. He spent twenty years in exile, during which time he gained a reputation for wisdom and learning, narrowly missed election as Pope, and fell hopelessly out of touch with conditions in England. In 1554 the Pope sent him to England as papal legate with power to end the schism. Parliament, however, would not admit him until he produced a papal dispensation to holders of Church lands solemnly promising them that they would not be disturbed in the possession of those lands. Pole brought with him such a dispensation, which Parliament inserted into the act repealing all the antipapal legislation of Henry VIII's reign. Parliament not only consented to this reunion with Rome, but also revived the heresy laws of earlier years.

The various statutes passed by Parliament did not mean a Catholic revival. Foreign residents reported that people only appeared to be Catholic out of fear. In London priests were mocked in the streets and church services ridiculed. The government had to eject 2000 clergymen (about a quarter of the total) from their livings—mostly for taking wives, which an act of Parliament in Somerset's time made legal. An underground Protestant congregation existed in London, with several subsidiary congregations. Passing statutes was not enough; the government must also actively eradicate Protestantism and create a new and vital Catholic faith. The first task it sought to accomplish by terror. On February 4, 1555, the government burned at the stake John Rogers, the translator of the Bible. He was the first of 286 martyrs to the Protestant faith to be burned at the stake. The great majority of these were laborers, artisans, and shopkeepers, for many of the wealthier Protestants, over 800 of them, had fled to the Continent. Fifty of these 286 martyrs were women, mostly poor widows. A large proportion were in their twenties or teens; most were from the southeast of England. Only twenty-one clergymen met death by fire, but among them were Archbishop Cranmer, Bishop Ridley, and Hugh Latimer, who were burned not at Smithfield in London, where most of the martyrs met death, but at Cornmarket in Oxford.

Responsibility for these burnings does not lie with Philip, who advised against them—though more from policy than conscience. He wanted to avoid the unpopularity such burnings would bring him in England; he had no scruples at burning 1300 heretics in Holland during the same period. Stephen Gardiner, the Lord Chancellor, soon tired of the burnings, though Edmund Bonner, Bishop of London, displayed an open relish for the task. Reginald Pole, a humanist scholar deficient in humanity, did nothing to mitigate the burnings. The chief responsibility for the fires rests with the Queen herself, who acted not out of cruelty, but out of a passion for true religion. It was her high-mindedness that sent so many of her subjects to the flames.

The policy of persecution failed totally. Far from turning men and women away from heresy, it created sympathy for the heretics. At the burning of John Rogers, reported the imperial ambassador:

> Some of the onlookers wept, others prayed to God to give them strength, perseverance and patience to bear the pain and not to recant, others gathered the ashes and bones and wrapped them in paper to perserve them, yet others threatened the bishops.

Demonstrations of sympathy became so frequent that a proclamation forbade them under penalty of death. The London authorities sought to keep apprentices and servants at home on execution days. Until the fires of Smithfield began to burn, Protestantism had been associated with selfseeking politicians; now it was associated with courage and human fortitude, a courage and fortitude John Foxe depicted vividly in his *Book of Martyrs.* It became the most widely read English classic of the next hundred years. The Marian martyrs taught the English a contempt for fashion, an independence of outlook, a willingness to challenge the establishment, and a trust in God that were to create a deep tradition of individualism and protest in English life.

Their success depended in part on the shortness of Mary's reign and on her failure to create a missionary movement. Persecution when allied to missionary zeal can succeed, as the Counter-Reformation on the Continent was to prove. But Mary, reigning before the full tide of the Counter-Reformation had swept across Europe, created no active program of evangelism. All she did was to restore monastic life at two monasteries and found two houses for nuns and two for friars. This backward-looking policy offered no hope of success and ensured that Hugh Latimer's words to Nicholas Ridley, as they were about to be burned, should prove true: "Be of good comfort, Master Ridley, and play the

The burning of Hugh Latimer and Nicholas Ridley at Oxford, from an illustration in Foxe's *Book of Martyrs* (*the British Library*).

man. We shall this day light such a candle by God's grace in England, as, I trust, shall never be put out.''

THE SPANISH CONNECTION

The Queen's marriage was the most sterile event of a sterile reign. Mary sought in Philip a man who could reciprocate her love, a husband who could give her a child, a consort on whose strength she could lean, and a Catholic who would help her lead England back to Rome. But Philip, though outwardly an attentive husband, was a cold and scheming man who had married Mary solely to bring England into the Habsburg conglomerate. He came to England in July 1554 and Mary enjoyed a brief hour of happiness. It did not last. The arrogance of Philip and of the Spaniards who accompanied him soon angered the English. Philip refused to allow the English to trade directly with the Spanish colonies. There were brawls in the streets of London between Spaniards and Englishmen. Philip confided to a friend that he found Mary unattractive, lacking "all sensibility of the flesh." Her one hope was to have a child, and she soon persuaded herself that she was pregnant. The expected birth kept Philip, who was eager to depart for Spain, which he had just inherited from his father, tied down in London. By August 1555, however, even Mary had to admit that some dropsy or tumor near the womb had misled her. Philip was now free to depart. He left in September, not to return again until the spring of 1557, and then for only a short time. Philip brought Mary no affection, gave her no child, left her to govern the kingdom alone, and was shortly to quarrel with, and be excommunicated by, the Pope. It was a sterile marriage, leading to an alliance that brought England defeat and disgrace.

In January 1557 war broke out between Spain and France, and in March Philip crossed over to England to draw that kingdom into the war. Mary, who was overjoyed at his arrival, believed it her duty to bring England into the war. She summoned her councilors individually and threatened them, "some with death, some with the loss of their goods and estates, if they did not consent to the will of her husband." But they, seeing no purpose in the war and knowing that England was not prepared, resisted her threats. They resisted, that is, until the King of France supported the madcap attempt of Thomas Stafford to become protector of England. Stafford sailed to Scarborough in two ships, captured the castle, and proclaimed himself protector. This incident gave the English a reason for war, which the government declared in June.

The war began with a spectacular victory for Philip, but soon turned into defeat for the English. On New Year's Day a formidable French army appeared before the gates of Calais, while a French fleet blockaded the port. Short of food and ammunition, the garrison surrendered within a week. In the remaining ten months of Mary's reign Philip did nothing to recover it for England. The loss of Calais was no tragedy for England, for it was expensive to garrison and useless. But the loss of a town held for 200 years was a humiliation that

the people could not excuse and that led Mary to lament that at her d
word "Calais" would be found engraved on her heart. The war was un
In the spring of 1558 Parliament voted Mary only a single subsidy and a fifteenth, forcing her to rely on a forced loan. The loan met with strong opposition: Forty Worcestershire gentlemen appeared before the Council on a single
day for refusing to pay it. Elsewhere troops and sailors deserted or mutinied.
War and defeat had confirmed the worst fears of the opponents of the Spanish
marriage.

Mary fell ill in the summer of 1558, worsened in October, and was compelled by her council in early November to acknowledge Elizabeth as her successor. Prematurely aged, frustrated in all her hopes and ambitions, maddened
by the thought that Elizabeth would succeed her, she died on November 17.
Mary's tragedy lay in the fact that her heart was Spanish and Catholic, whereas
the hearts of her subjects were English and Protestant. She lacked the redeeming virtue of the other Tudors who, for all their faults, instinctively understood
and shared the aspirations, hopes, fears, predilections, and prejudices of their
subjects. Of all the Tudors probably none understood those aspirations better
or shared more closely those hopes, fears, predilections, and prejudices than
Elizabeth, now Queen of England.

FURTHER READING

WHITNEY R.D. JONES. *The Mid-Tudor Crisis
1539–1563.* London, 1973. Successive
chapters deal with the dynastic, political
and constitutional, social and economic,
and diplomatic aspects of the crisis; contains a useful bibliography.

W.K. JORDAN. *Edward VI.* 2 vols., London,
1968, 1970. A detailed history of the
reign, not a biography; the narrative is
splendid but the praise of Somerset,
denigration of Northumberland, and at-
tribution of responsibility to Edward is
unconvincing.

H.M.P. PRESCOTT. *Mary Tudor.* 2nd ed., New
York, 1952. The standard biography,
characterized by sensitivity and understanding, and written with a novelist's
skill.

*JASPER RIDLEY. *Thomas Cranmer.* New York,
1962. A sensible, readable, scholarly life
that seeks to explain Cranmer's
inconsistencies by his belief that one
owed the King obedience.

BARRETT BEER. *Rebellion and Riot: Popular Disorder in England During the Reign of Edward*

VI. Kent, Ohio, 1982. A study of the
Western and of Ket's rebellions; analyzes
the nature of rebellion as well as describing these two.

PETER RAMSEY. *Tudor Economic Problems.* London, 1963. An admirable introduction to
Tudor economic history; especially good
on prices, overseas trade, and textiles,
weaker on agriculture.

JOAN THIRSK, ed. *The Agrarian History of England and Wales.* Vol. 4, *1500–1640.* Cambridge, England, 1967. An impressive,
authoritative, collaborative work; contains useful chapters on farming techniques, enclosures, farm laborers, prices,
profits, rents, and rural housing.

D.M. LOADES. *The Oxford Martyrs.* London,
1970. A thought-provoking book that
concentrates on Cranmer, Ridley, and
Latimer, but also discusses the policy of
persecution and its role in creating a
Protestant England.

JOAN SIMON. *Education and Society in Tudor England.* Cambridge, England, 1966. Challenges the view that the Reformation was

a disastrous setback to education; argues that Edward's reign saw the evolution of locally governed schools inspired by humanistic ideals.

PEARL HOGREFE.   *Tudor Women: Commoners and Queens.* Ames, Iowa, 1975. A lively discussion of the role of women in English life, with fascinating portraits of individual Tudor women.

12 Elizabethan England: 1558-1603

Elizabeth came to the throne at a perilous hour. The kingdom was at war, Calais lost, the Treasury empty, the coinage debased, trade depressed, and the nation deeply divided by religion. Forty-four years later, at her death in 1603, the nation was Protestant, the Church established, the Crown respected, the coinage sound, the navy victorious, domestic peace secured, trade expanded, new lands discovered, and the poets and playwrights flourishing. It was a remarkable achievement. Queen Elizabeth alone was not the author of the glories of the Elizabethan age; also at work was the genius of the English people, which by some mysterious alchemy blossomed then as never before or since. Yet that genius could not have blossomed had not Elizabeth, who was one of the wisest monarchs who ever ruled the land, preserved peace at home and warded off invasion from abroad. She held the ring, so that other men and women could sail to Virginia, circumnavigate the globe, compose madrigals, paint miniatures, write *The Faerie Queene*, build Hardwick Hall, and perform the plays of Shakespeare.

ELIZABETH AND THE CHURCH

Elizabeth was 25 years of age when she rode to her coronation, a tall, athletic figure, with golden hair and flashing eyes, and much vanity. She was a born queen. Within a month, reported the Spanish ambassador, she was more feared than her sister and as absolutely obeyed as her father. Her imperious will she no doubt received from her father and from an upbringing that was, though precarious, very royal. The dangers that beset her during Edward's and Mary's

Queen Elizabeth in 1575, by an unknown artist (*National Portrait Gallery, London*).

rule taught her to bury her emotions and to conceal her thoughts. The finest of Renaissance educations gave her a fluency in Latin, French, Spanish, and Italian; while an ancestry that blended the royal blood of York and Lancaster with the aristocratic blood of the Howards, the gentry blood of the Tudors, and the merchant blood of the Boleyns made her what she boasted she was, "mere English."

Her first act of state showed her to be a good judge of men. Three days after gaining the Crown she named William Cecil to be her Secretary of State. Cecil, trained as a lawyer, came to the fore under Somerset. He went on missions abroad, became Secretary, sat in every Parliament since 1547, and by his pliancy survived Somerset's fall and Mary's accession. He was a moderate Protestant, secular in outlook, cautious in conduct, and eminently judicious. Elizabeth also had the good sense to name no religious zealot to the Council. She kept eleven of Mary's councilors and added seven new ones. There was only one churchman, who soon resigned. As befitted the Queen's secularism, it was a council of laymen.

The first task facing the Queen and her Council was to settle the religious question. Elizabeth herself was not committed to any creed; indeed, she kept her religious convictions so private that historians have wondered if she had any. What is certain is that she was guided in the settlement of religion by a desire to restore unity among her subjects. She knew that she could not choose

Roman Catholicism, because too many of her subjects hated Rome. She might have preferred Henrician Catholicism, but this was impossible since there were no longer any clergymen who would support the mass without Rome. The only alternative was to turn to Protestantism.

To this end the government introduced into Parliament in 1559 an Act of Supremacy and an Act of Uniformity, the first making Elizabeth, not the Pope, the supreme governor of the Church and the second requiring the use in every parish of a Book of Common Prayer based upon the Prayer Book of 1552, though modified to satisfy the Queen's more conservative views. The two great obstacles to this new settlement were the Catholic bishops and some conservative lay peers in the House of Lords. The lay peers, though not the bishops, acquiesced in the renunciation of the Pope's supremacy, but the lay peers balked at any major alteration in Catholic worship. The government, therefore, took measures to secure the passage of the Act of Uniformity through the Lords. It arranged during the Easter recess a theological disputation, heavily weighted towards the Protestant side. It imprisoned some of the more outspoken Catholic bishops and discouraged others from attending the House. It then introduced into the Lords its Act of Uniformity, which passed by the slim margin of three votes. The Queen, with the help of the House of Commons, had obtained a Protestant religious settlement.

The Elizabethan Prayer Book of 1559 was a compromise between the Queen and the reforming party in the House of Commons, and a compromise in which Elizabeth surrendered most. But though she accepted the second Prayer Book, she insisted on certain amendments to it. To the wording of the second Book, "Take and eat this remembrance . . . ," she added these words from the first Book, "The body of our Lord Jesus Christ, which was given for thee . . . ," thereby restoring an assertion of the real presence in the liturgy. She also added a rubric that required the wearing of vestments by clergymen. Four years later Convocation passed the Thirty-nine Articles, a declaration of faith based on the Forty-two Articles of Edward's reign. Though ambiguously worded, the Thirty-nine Articles were a statement of Calvinist doctrine. Thus it is not too great a simplification to say that the English Church emerged out of the Reformation Catholic in ritual, Calvinist in doctrine, and royalist in government.

ELIZABETH AND SCOTLAND

At her death Mary Tudor left Elizabeth a nation divided by religion and a realm at war with France. Elizabeth solved the religious problem by compromising with the reformers. She ended the war by renouncing, in the Treaty of Câteau-Cambrésis of April 1559, all but the slightest hope of regaining Calais. But the same treaty that freed England from war left the French free to take measures against the Calvinist rebels in Scotland. For a decade Mary Guise, mother of Mary Queen of Scots, had ruled Scotland, aided by French troops and French officials. In 1559 she became alarmed that discontent against Catholicism might merge with discontent against French rule. She therefore forbade all unauthorized preaching. But this action sparked the very rebellion she hoped to prevent, for in May John Knox arrived in Scotland and set it aflame with his preaching. The Protestant nobility, jealous of the French, eager to seize Church lands, and organized as the Lords of the Congregation, now rose in open rebellion.

They appealed to Elizabeth for assistance, which placed her in a dilemma. To send assistance would be to violate the Treaty of Câteau-Cambrésis and to risk war with France at a time when England had no allies. It would also mean supporting rebels against their rightful ruler, an action Elizabeth found repugnant. Yet not to send assistance would mean the probable defeat of the Lords of the Congregation and the creation of a continual Franco-Scottish-papal threat from the north. Elizabeth chose to intervene, though in her characteristically hesitant, dilatory manner. In August 1559 she sent money; in the autumn, powder and cannon. When the French threatened to send more troops to Scotland, Elizabeth sent a fleet north to intercept them, a fleet which in January 1560 destroyed the French fleet off the coast of Scotland.

Elizabeth still held out against sending an army, but the weakness of the Lords of the Congregation compelled her to send 8000 men across the border in March—all the time protesting to the French ambassador that she had sent neither fleet nor army. This last show of force, combined with the death of Mary Guise in June, finally persuaded the French to leave. The Treaty of Edinburgh, signed by the English, French, and Scots in July 1560, provided for the withdrawal of all English and French troops from Scotland and the placing of the government of Scotland in a Council of Nobles. The Treaty of Edinburgh was a far greater triumph for England than the victories of Flodden or Pinkie, for it secured England's back door, ushered in a century of peace, and paved the way to an eventual union of the two kingdoms.

Mary Queen of Scots, who returned to Scotland in 1561 at the death of her husband, Francis II of France, refused to sign the Treaty of Edinburgh because Elizabeth would not amend it to recognize Mary, who was the great-granddaughter of Henry VII, as Elizabeth's successor. Thus began a long duel between the two queens. Mary, who in the eyes of good Catholics was already rightfully Queen of England (because Elizabeth was illegitimate), refused to recognize Elizabeth as Queen until Elizabeth recognized her as successor. Elizabeth, for her part, refused to invite her own assassination by recognizing a Catholic as her successor. The two queens were a study in contrast. Mary was clever, impulsive, high-spirited, and well educated in music, dancing, and horsemanship; Elizabeth was wise, prudent, cautious, and learned in languages, theology, and politics. In Mary emotions proved stronger than intellect; in Elizabeth intellect ruled. The fate of Mary illustrates the hazards of allowing the emotions to rule.

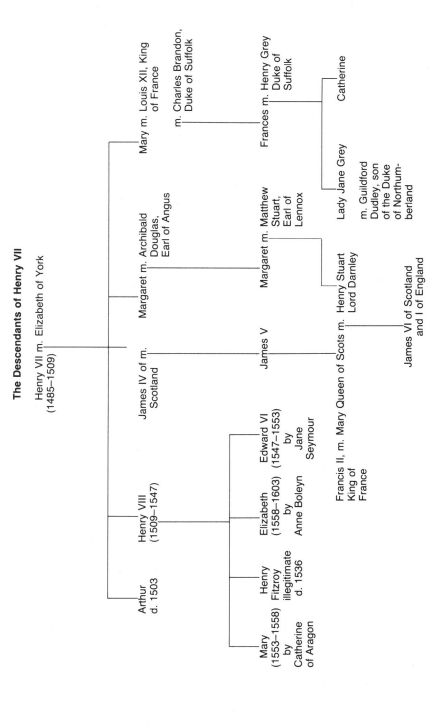

The Descendants of Henry VII

Henry VII m. Elizabeth of York
(1485–1509)

To strengthen her claim to the English Crown she married Lord Darnley, a descendant of Henry VII, but turned from him when she found him to be vain, greedy, crude, and vicious. Darnley's jealous temperament drove him to murder Mary's secretary, David Riccio, whom he believed to be her lover. Less than a year later, in 1567, the wild and dissolute Earl of Bothwell, with the alleged complicity of Mary, avenged Riccio's murder by strangling Darnley and blowing up his body in a nearby cottage. Historians will never be able to prove Mary's complicity in this crime, for the originals of the famous Casket Letters that incriminate her have disappeared. Guilty or not, Mary's subsequent conduct was damning enough. Under the pretense of an abduction, she fled with Bothwell to his castle, where she later married him. This was more than the dour Calvinistic Scots could endure. They deposed her, and when she took arms against her deposition, they drove her from the realm. In 1568 she fled to England.

Because Elizabeth deeply revered the divinity that hedgeth a Queen, she sought to secure Mary's return to Scotland as Queen. She opened negotiations with the rulers of Scotland; she demanded proof of Mary's complicity in Darnley's murder; she urged Mary's return. But all her efforts failed, for the Protestant regents of the infant James VI, son of Mary and Darnley, would not take back a papist and murderous Queen. Since it was dangerous to allow Mary to go abroad, where she might serve as the spearhead for an invasion of England by the Catholic powers, Elizabeth had no alternative but to keep her under house arrest for the next nineteen years.

THE CATHOLIC THREAT

The presence of Mary in England heightened the Catholic threat to the new Anglican Church and to Elizabeth's continuance on the throne. A number of forces combined after 1569 to produce three years filled with plots and rebellions. There was Mary's plotting and intriguing; the sullen discontent of the nobility of the north, feudal-minded, provincial, Catholic; and the fury of the more conservative councilors in London at the ascendancy of Cecil. In addition, there was the growing impatience of Pope Pius V at the continuance of a heretic on the English throne, and the growing hostility of Spain, freed by the decline of French power from any need for England's friendship.

In 1569 these forces led to the Revolt of the Earls in the north. The revolt proved a fiasco since the various parties in it utterly misunderstood one another. There probably would have been no rebellion at all had there not been a Court conspiracy in the south. In London a set of disgruntled noblemen devised a plan to marry Mary to the Duke of Norfolk, overthrow Cecil, subjugate Elizabeth, proclaim Mary heir to the throne, and restore Catholicism. The Duke of Norfolk, though a Protestant, agreed to the plan. The conspirators opened negotiations with the Spanish ambassador and correspondence with the

Earls of Northumberland and Westmorland. In September Norfolk fled to his estates, with the intention, it was thought, of raising the north. But his courage left him. Summoned back to London by Elizabeth, he submitted, entered the Tower, and wrote his brother-in-law, the Earl of Westmorland, to call off the uprising. The Earls of Northumberland and Westmorland had taken Norfolk's initial flight from London as a signal to turn from vague plotting to deliberate planning. They set October 6 for the rising, but abandoned it when they heard of his surrender. What finally drove them to open rebellion was the Queen's summons to appear at Court. Fearing for their lives, they rose in rebellion. Behind this decision lay the grievances of the great magnates of the north, who regarded themselves as the Queen's natural councilors, resented the extension of central authority into Percy and Neville country, and remained Catholics at heart. Collecting their loyal tenants, the two Earls marched to Durham Cathedral, tore down all signs of Protestantism, celebrated the mass, and then marched southward with 3,800 foot and 1,600 horse. They demanded that Catholicism be restored, Cecil be tried, Norfolk freed, and Mary recognized as heir to the throne. But as they marched south they discovered that the Catholic nobility of Yorkshire and Lancashire were deaf to their appeals. Their resolution cracked. They turned northward, disbanded their troops, and fled to Scotland long before the royal army, marching north, could meet them in battle. The rebellion failed because its aims were uncertain and its geographical base narrow. In the next months 450 rebels were hanged, proof that Tudor centralization was stronger than northern feudalism.

One reason for the weakness of the rebels was the Pope's delay in excommunicating and deposing Elizabeth, an action that would have justified their taking up arms against her. It was not until February 1570 that Pope Pius V finally excommunicated Elizabeth, deposed her, and absolved her subjects from allegiance to her. It came too late for the northern rebels, but it gave moral sanction to the plotting of Roberto Ridolfi, a Florentine merchant-banker in London. Ridolfi in 1571 concocted a scheme for replacing Elizabeth with Mary on the throne and for restoring the Catholic Church. Mary gave her approval, the Pope hailed it with enthusiasm, Norfolk let himself be talked into it, and Philip II agreed to it—though he insisted the rebels should rise before he sent troops. Before Ridolfi could make any progress, the government uncovered the plot and arrested the plotters. Norfolk, whom the Queen had pardoned for the Northern Rebellion, was now beheaded. For its part, Parliament passed a statute making it high treason to declare that Elizabeth was not entitled to the throne or to describe her as heretic or schismatic.

The most serious Catholic threat to the Church of England and Elizabeth came not from the fumblings of northern earls or the hare-brained schemes of Florentine bankers, but from the dedication of English missionaries trained in Catholic seminaries at Douai and Rome. In 1574 the first three of these heroic missionaries arrived; by 1578 there were fifty of them; by 1580 over a hundred, many of them Jesuits. With their coming the Counter-Reformation finally reached England. Among the missionaries were men like Edmund Campion, a gentle, eloquent scholar, who came only to preach the gospel and who disclaimed all political purposes. But there were others, like Robert Parsons, a man of action and intrigue, who could not resist dabbling in politics. Since both the pure idealist and the subtle politican posed a threat to the English Church, the government took drastic action. In 1581 Parliament passed a bill which punished "recusancy"—that is, absence from the parish church on a Sunday—with a fine of £20 a month, rather than the 12 pence a week provided in the Act of Uniformity of 1559. In 1585 Parliament passed a bill making it treason for a Catholic priest to be in England. During Elizabeth's reign some 250 persons died for their Catholic faith. The Queen, who professed she did not wish to make windows into men's souls, held she was punishing crimes against the state, not heresy. In most cases, however, this was true only because Parliament had defined adherence to the Catholic faith as a crime against the state. Queen Elizabeth was no apostle of religious toleration; she believed in conformity to the Church as by law established. By 1603 the strict measures she and Parliament adopted to enforce conformity had helped to reduce the number of Catholics in England to 250 priests and 35,000 laity.

THE PURITAN THREAT

Elizabeth's task was doubly difficult because she had to wrestle with the Puritan threat from within the Church while resisting the Catholic threat from without. The word "Puritan" first came into use in the 1570s, but the movement itself, a movement to purge the Church of the impure Roman practices that disgraced it, emerged in the 1560s. To the Puritan the litmus test for the godliness of any practice was its presence in Scriptures. If it were not found there, it should be abolished. In 1563 the Puritans just failed to carry in Convocation articles that would have replaced the bright vestments worn by the English clergy with the black gown of Geneva. But this Vestiarian Controversy was only the prelude to a deeper conflict. In 1570 Thomas Cartwright, professor of divinity at Cambridge, delivered a series of lectures critical of the English Church. The lectures led to Cartwright's dismissal and to fierce pamphlet warfare. Cartwright and other Puritans attacked the authority of the bishops and demanded the introduction of a presbyterian church government, one in which authority lay with ministers and elders meeting in presbyters. Elizabeth, who hated the Puritans and who saw that an attack on the bishops' authority was an attack on hers, acted quickly to suppress them. She defeated their measures in Parliament and sent their leaders into exile.

Militancy having failed, the Puritans embarked on a new strategy. They sought to convert the membership of the Church through periodic meetings of ministers, to which the laity were invited. These "prophesyings," as they were called, spread throughout the southeast. In these meetings the ministers urged the exclusive authority of the Scriptures, the sanctity of conscience in their interpretation, and the doctrine of predestination. The exaltation that came from believing they were among the elect gave the Presbyterians the strength to persevere in their endeavors to purify the Church. Out of the prophesying movement of the 1570s grew the classical movement of the 1580s, an attempt to introduce a presbyterian organization into the Church. Clergymen met together in local conferences, or "classes," where the Book of Common Prayer was amended and candidates for the ministry, elected by the congregation, were put forward for consecration. The Puritans also held district conferences, and even national ones. Elizabeth recognized the dangers inherent in these movements. She ordered Archbishop Grindal in 1577 to suppress prophesying, and when he refused, suspended him. On the death of Grindal in 1583, she named the anti-Puritan John Whitgift as Archbishop. He resolutely enforced conformity on the clergy and rooted out the classical movement. The Puritans then turned to Parliament for help, organizing in 1586 and 1587 a parliamentary campaign that foreshadowed the parliamentary action by which the Puritans in the seventeenth century wrested power from the monarchy. But Elizabeth stood firm and defeated their every effort.

Those Puritans who could not wait for the Church to be reformed founded a separate church, a congregation of true believers gathered together to worship God, owing allegiance to no authority but God. One of the first of these was Robert Browne, a preacher of great ability who in 1581 founded a separate congregation at Norwich. But the government soon drove the Brownists to Holland. By the end of Elizabeth's reign the separatists were few in number and unimportant, while the Presbyterians were in disarray. But Elizabeth did not solve the Puritan problem, she merely buried it. Puritanism continued to spread among the gentry and among the citizens of London, to smolder there until it burst into flame again under James I.

ECONOMIC RECOVERY

Next to settling religion and securing Scotland, the gravest problem facing Elizabeth and her ministers was the recovery of the economy. It was doubly grave because the Tudors believed that economic distress not only caused personal suffering but imperiled public order, since distress drove husbandmen and cloth-workers to riot and rebellion. The first measure the government undertook was the reform of the coinage, a reform begun during Mary's reign. The government called in debased and mutilated coins and issued new ones whose face value corresponded to the value of the silver in them. The operation was brilliantly successful; it ended the monetary chaos and created a stable currency. In 1563 the government had Parliament legislate on a whole array of problems. It passed statutes regulating the making of cloth, encouraging farming, discouraging enclosure, prohibiting the importation of luxuries, aiding shipping, and creating a "political Lent"—Wednesdays and Fridays when people would eat fish, thereby promoting the fishing industry. But the greatest piece of legislation passed that year was the Statute of Apprentices, which made the guild regulations of earlier years national. It erected property qualifications that barred the sons of the poor from entry into most trades, enforced a seven-year apprenticeship in all trades, even husbandry, and established compulsory apprenticeship on the land for unattached youths. It also empowered the justice of the peace to regulate wages, though only the maximum rate, not the minimum. It became a crime to pay more, not less, than the justices laid down. The Statute of Apprentices was a backward-looking law, an attempt to perpetuate medieval regulations by making them national. It was not strictly enforced; the justices neglected the apprenticeship provisions and seldom set wages.

It is doubtful that these measures, except for recoinage, contributed much to the steady economic growth during Elizabeth's reign. The causes of this growth were different and various. The chief of them was a growth in population that fueled a rapid inflation. Prices rose 60 percent during Elizabeth's reign, thus driving landed gentlemen to seek new means by which to exploit their lands. It also caused prices to rise faster than wages, thereby swelling profits, encouraging enterprise, and allowing the accumulation of capital. The increase in population—it rose from about 3 to 4 million—helped the clothing industry. The growing ostentation of the upper classes supported the luxury trades. England's freedom from civil war and from tolls and regulations permitted trade and industry to thrive. War abroad after 1585 stimulated the metal industry, which produced pikes and corselets, cannon and muskets.

Nine people in ten earned all or part of their livelihood from agriculture, and it was improvements in farming that allowed England to feed a growing population. Nothing illustrates better the widespread desire to improve yields than the sale of Thomas Tusser's *Five Hundred Points of Good Husbandry.* Between 1557 and 1580 it went through five editions. Increasingly farmers applied marl (sand, silt, or clay containing calcium carbonate) to their land, intensified the manuring of land, and alternated pasture and arable. Because grain prices rose more rapidly than wool prices, there was less pressure to enclose land for pasture, but toward the end of the reign there arose a movement to enclose land in order to improve tillage. John Norden, a writer on agriculture, estimated that enclosed land was 1.5 times more productive than unenclosed land. Hops, one of the new crops introduced during the century, could only be grown on compact fields.

Productivity during these years steadily increased. In the thirteenth century a farmer could produce only 6 to 12 bushels of wheat on an acre; the Elizabethan farmer could produce from 16 to 20. In 1500 sheep averaged 28 pounds and cattle 320 pounds; by 1610 the sheep and cattle raised on royal estates in Wales averaged 46 and 600 pounds. Without such improvements England could never have surmounted the Malthusian crisis that a growing population inevitably creates.

The manufacture of cloth continued to dominate the industrial world. Its organization remained unchanged; the capitalist clothier continued to be the dominant figure. Several new inventions did increase productivity: a stocking frame on which stockings could be knitted more rapidly, and the Dutch loom, which made possible swifter production of narrow goods like ribbons. But what really saved the cloth industry was the New Draperies, a type of cloth introduced by Flemish immigrants fleeing from Spanish persecution. The New Draperies were a lighter woolen cloth, made from longer fibers, and attractive to customers in the Mediterranean. At the same time the weavers of Lancashire began to weave a cloth out of linen and cotton, called "fustian," which also found a wide sale.

The most spectacular development occurred not in cloth but in coal. The gradual disappearance of forests led Londoners to turn to coal to heat their homes. This led to a boom in the mines around Newcastle, from which coal was carried to London. The growing use of coal in panning salt, refining sugar, manufacturing glass, and boiling soap helped the boom. These industries themselves required great capital investments. The salt works at Wear, for example, required an investment of £4000. Most of this capital came from rich merchants, but some of it came from the aristocracy. Twenty-two percent of the aristocratic families of Elizabethan England owned iron works. While no one discovered how to use coal to make iron—a discovery of the eighteenth century—many turned to the blast furnace, which produced cast iron by pouring the molten metal into forms. It was a great improvement over the older process in which a lump of malleable iron was hammered into shape. Elizabeth's reign also saw the introduction of rolling mills for the production of sheet metal and of drawing mills for the production of wire. By the end of the reign the English metal industry, heavily supported by the government, was producing cannon much sought after on the continent.

Though industry expanded, commerce stagnated. Cloth still dominated English exports, and though the Antwerp market momentarily recovered in the 1560s, war, religion, and politics soon destroyed it. The sack of Antwerp by Spanish troops in 1576 sealed its fate. The Merchant Adventurers now looked elsewhere for an entrepôt—first to Hamburg, then to Emden, finally to Middleburgh in Zeeland. Though willing to move their entrepôt, they were not ready to admit other English merchants to the trade. In 1564 the Merchant Adventurers secured from the government a monopoly of the export of cloth to Europe. Toward the end of Elizabeth's reign competitors appeared to challenge the monopoly, but Cecil, though he sympathized with the cause of free trade, dared not weaken a company upon which the government depended financially. Yet Cecil, now Lord Burghley, did see the ultimate solution to England's commercial crisis when he suggested that her exports should not be sent to one place, but to "sundry places."

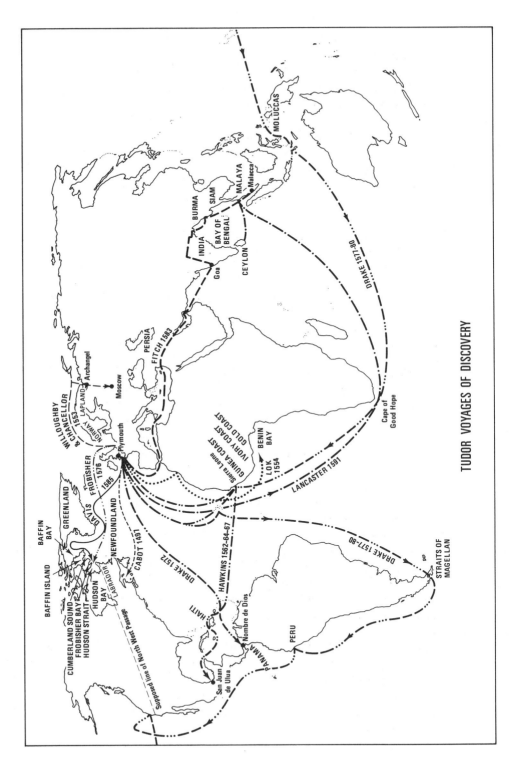

TUDOR VOYAGES OF DISCOVERY

BAFFIN ISLAND
BAFFIN BAY
GREENLAND
CUMBERLAND SOUND
FROBISHER BAY
HUDSON STRAIT
HUDSON BAY
LABRADOR
NEWFOUNDLAND
Supposed line of North West Passage

CABOT 1491
DAVIS
FROBISHER 1576
1585
WILLOUGHBY & CHANCELLOR 1553
NORWAY
LAPLAND
Archangel
Moscow
Plymouth
DRAKE 1572
HAWKINS 1562-64-67
DRAKE 1577-80
HAITI
San Juan de Ulua
Nombre de Dios
PANAMA
PERU
STRAITS OF MAGELLAN

PERSIA
FITCH 1583
INDIA
BURMA
SIAM
BAY OF BENGAL
Goa
CEYLON
MALAYA
Malacca
MOLUCCAS

DRAKE 1577-80
LANCASTER 1591
Cape of Good Hope
Sierra Leone
GUINEA COAST
IVORY COAST
GOLD COAST
BENIN BAY
LOK 1554

THE VOYAGES OF DISCOVERY

The first move to find "sundry places" was exploitation of the new German, Baltic, and Russian trades, made possible by the decline of the Hansards. By 1560 the Hansards had lost control of the export of English cloth to northeast Germany, a trade taken over by English merchants who in 1579 formed the Eastland Company. The company's trade to the North Sea and Baltic was only an eighth of the Merchant Adventurers', but it was a useful market for English cloth and a valuable supply of timber. The high hopes that the Muscovy Company cherished of monopolizing trade with Russia and of capturing that of the East proved illusory. The Dutch found a shorter way to the markets of Russia through the Baltic and the Tsar refused the company's request to exclude the Dutch. In 1562 the Muscovy Company sent Anthony Jenkinson on a daring overland trip from Moscow to Persia, only to discover that anarchy in Central Asia made an overland route from Moscow to China impossible. The Muscovy Company finally gave up all thought of trade to Asia and watched its trade with Russia, where English cloth was too expensive, dwindle to ten ships a year.

The bolder solution was to strike out into the Atlantic in search of the northwest passage to China. In 1576 Martin Frobisher, a rough, cantankerous man, but an experienced navigator, set out in two ships of 25 tons each in search of that elusive goal. He returned with news that he had found a passage and with ore that the goldsmiths thought contained gold. This led to the first great speculating mania in English history. The Queen herself speculated in Frobisher's next two voyages. But the ore proved to be barren and the passage only led into Hudson's Bay. A man of far greater scientific interests than Frobisher's, John Davys, then took up the quest. On his third voyage in 1587 he cleared up the confusion that existed among Greenland, Friesland, Labrador, and Baffin Island, and found four different passages westward. But, he reported, they were too choked with ice to be navigable.

The Elizabethans then turned to the East. In 1580 the Muscovy Company sent Arthur Pett and Charles Jackman to seek once again a northeast passage, but ice stopped them as it had stopped Willoughby in 1554. Other merchants turned to the eastern Mediterranean. In 1581 they formed the Turkey Company, later called the Levant Company. In 1583 they sent Ralph Fitch overland to India, Burma, Siam, and distant Malaya. He returned with wondrous stories, a shadowy agreement with Akbar of India, and a report that the obstacles to a land route were insuperable. The indefatigable Elizabethans now turned to the passage around the Cape of Good Hope, defying the Portuguese monopoly of the southern Atlantic. Between 1591 and 1601 they sent out three expeditions that suffered incredible losses. From the crews of the three ships sent out in 1592, only one sailor, happily picked up by a Dutch ship, survived. But they persevered, and in 1600 a group of London merchants formed the East India Company, which was to become the greatest trading company in English history.

The East India Company was a joint-stock company, not a regulated company. In a regulated company each merchant traded on his own private stock; in a joint-stock company they pooled their stock and then divided up the profits in proportion to their investments. The great cost of trade to distant lands made the joint-stock company a necessity; its invention, in turn, made it possible for gentlemen and peers to invest in trade. The Muscovy Company was the first joint-stock company in English history, but it fell on bad days and reverted to a regulated company. The East India Company was the first successful joint-stock company, the distant parent of the modern corporation.

One particular trade proved unsuccessful, and its failure led the English to turn from trading to raiding. In 1562 John Hawkins, son of a Plymouth merchant, sailed to Guinea, purchased 400 slaves, and carried them to Haiti, where he sold them and some English manufactures. He returned home with sugar, hides, gold, and pearls. Backed now by the Queen, Hawkins made two more voyages, but on the second of them, in 1568, a Spanish fleet fell on him at the Mexican port of San Juan de Ulua. Hawkins in the *Minion* and his friend Francis Drake in the *Judith* escaped and made their way back to England, though only fifteen of the crew of the *Minion* survived. The battle of San Juan de Ulua turned the seamen of England into the enemies of Spain. A war of reprisals began. Drake in 1573 captured the silver of Peru as it crossed the isthmus of Panama, silver worth £20,000. He then sailed through the Straits of Magellan, raided the defenseless Pacific Coast for silver, crossed the Pacific, purchasing spices in the Moluccas, and sailed into Plymouth Sound in 1580 with the richest cargo ever brought into an English port. Other privateers sought to emulate his success, but few did. For all its romance, privateering proved unprofitable to most and diminished the supply of capital in England.

The Elizabethans also lost substantial sums in efforts to plant colonies abroad, but from these endeavors the English learned lessons that were later to pay rich dividends. Three motives drove the English to plant colonies: a desire to tap the fabulous wealth of foreign lands—the gold, silver, ivory, pearls, and spices; a desire to rid England of its beggars, rogues, vagabonds, and cutpurses; and a desire to establish new markets for manufactures, especially cloth. Not merchants, but a small group of Devon gentlemen—Sir Humphrey Gilbert, his half-brother Sir Walter Raleigh, and their cousin Sir Richard Grenville—undertook the first ventures. In 1578 Gilbert secured from the Queen a patent to settle in North America. In 1583 he sailed with three ships and two frigates to Newfoundland, which he claimed for England, and then to the mainland with three ships carrying the prospective colonists. One was wrecked on the rocks; a second sank on the way home; a third reached England. Gilbert, who believed that "we are as near to heaven by sea as by land," went down with the second ship.

Sir Walter Raleigh, a brilliant soldier, a consummate courtier, an accomplished poet, and a master of English prose, now took up the task. He sent out two small ships in 1584, which landed on Roanoke Island. Raleigh at once christened the land Virginia in honor of the virgin Queen. In 1585 he sent out seven ships under the command of Sir Richard Grenville, but the colonists were soldiers, not settlers, and spent their time looking for gold and pearls, not farming. In 1586 they returned home with Drake's fleet. The next year 150 colonists, 17 of them women, went out to Virginia in a fleet commanded by John White. The plan was sounder, for land was to be distributed to the settlers, but the outcome was more tragic. The concentrated effort needed to repulse the Spanish Armada in 1588 prevented John White from returning to the colony until 1590. When he did, he found only an abandoned stockade. The Elizabethans had not learned that with colonies, as with the planting of woods, it takes twenty years before a profit can be realized.

THE WAR AGAINST SPAIN

It was not Drake's raid on Panama or Raleigh's colony in Virginia that led to war with Spain, but events in the Netherlands. In 1567 Philip II resolved to assert his authority in the Netherlands, even at the cost of their historic liberties, and sent out the Duke of Alva with 50,000 troops. A great Spanish army in the Netherlands was as alarming to the English as a great French army in Scotland. Elizabeth responded by seizing five Spanish ships carrying money from Genoese bankers to Alva, which a storm by chance blew into English ports. She decided to borrow the money herself. Alva then seized all English ships and goods in the Netherlands and declared an embargo on English trade. Elizabeth retaliated in kind. Spain had now clearly replaced France as the national enemy of England.

Elizabeth did not wish war, and so patched up her quarrel with Spain. Between 1574 and 1585 she sought by diplomacy to diminish the threat that Alva and his army posed. She supported the liberties of the Netherlands and she secured, through a prolonged courtship of the Duke of Alençon, the French King's brother, the friendship of France. But the collapse of the United Netherlands in 1579, the Spanish conquest of Portugal in 1580, and the submission of Henry III of France to the Guises and Spain left England the sole remaining obstacle to Spanish supremacy in Europe. The crucial question facing Elizabeth was this: Would Philip II use the Netherlands, once the Dutch were conquered, as a platform for launching an invasion of England? She decided he would and so in 1585 sent 5000 foot and 1000 horse to aid the Dutch rebels. This warlike act, in turn, persuaded Philip that he must defeat England if he were ever to subdue the Dutch.

Philip's decision to invade England was made easier by the execution of Mary Queen of Scots in 1587, for he had no desire to dethrone Elizabeth, only to place a French princess on the throne. Elizabeth pretended to be, or truly was, angry at her ministers for carrying out the execution of Mary, but there was no alternative. In the four years before her execution there had been four serious plots, and Mary herself was deeply implicated in the last of these, the Babington plot. Elizabeth's feigned anger at her ministers, if it was feigned, served the purpose of preventing France from going to war to avenge Mary's death.

Hitherto Elizabeth, by her patient diplomacy and interminable marriage negotiations with Archduke Charles of Austria and the Duke of Alençon, had kept the House of Valois and the Habsburgs apart. But the passions of the Counter-Reformation now brought them together. England, with the assistance of the Dutch rebels, stood alone. Only its insularity, its navy, and its trained bands defended her. Fortunately for England, its navy possessed the best ships in Europe. The Queen had employed John Hawkins to design new ships, which were longer and narrower than the usual galleon, and so capable of mounting more guns and sailing closer to the wind. They were also smaller, faster, handier, and without the towering castles at bow and stern. Sir William Wynter armed the ships in an equally revolutionary fashion. He replaced the iron man-killing demicannon, which threw a 30-pound shot a short distance, with the brass ship-killing culverin and demi-culverin, which threw an 18- and 9-pound shot up to 1000 yards. By 1588 Elizabeth had twenty-five such galleons, well-manned by sailors whose wages she raised from 6s. 8d. a month to 10s. Behind the fleet stood the trained bands, spirited gentlemen and staunch yeomen who were better armed and better trained than the medieval villager. Since 1573 the government had armed and trained only the ablest villagers. During the winter of 1587 and 1588 the English, in preparation for the Spanish assault, repaired town walls, placed cannon around seacoast towns, built a system of beacons, and readied themselves for battle.

Philip's strategy was to send an invincible fleet into the Channel to transport the Duke of Parma's 30,000 troops from the Netherlands to England. Philip began to collect such a fleet in Cadiz harbor in 1587, but Sir Francis Drake, ever audacious, sailed into the harbor and "singed the King of Spain's beard" by destroying some thirty large ships. Ever persistent, Philip assembled another armada at Lisbon. In the summer of 1588 it sailed for the Channel— 20 great galleons, 4 galleys of Portugal, 4 galleasses of Naples, 4 great West India-men, 40 large merchantmen, 34 pinnaces, and 23 freighters, 130 ships in all, with 8,000 sailors and 14,000 soldiers. They sailed slowly up the Channel, in a crescent formation, the stronger ships on the outside. Against this great Armada the English brought a fleet containing about the same number of men-of-war, but also many hastily armed ships from the creeks and harbors of the south coast, perhaps 200 ships in all. The English made contact with the Armada on July 12, avoided a general melée, and bombarded the Spanish ships from a 300-yard distance. But Spanish discipline was excellent; the crescent did not break, and the English culverins and demi-culverins did little damage. The Armada sailed steadily up the Channel, only to reveal the fatal miscalculation of the entire campaign. The Duke of Parma's troops, which had shrunk to 17,000, had no way to reach the Armada, for the only deepwater port on the Channel, Flushing, was in English hands. Had Parma sought to transport his troops to

The Ark Royal, one of the new, longer, more maneuverable galleons in the English fleet (*British Library*).

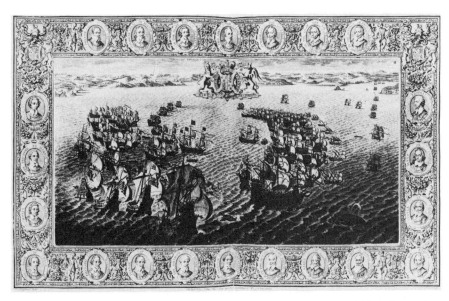

The Armada in its crescent formation, from a near-contemporary tapestry (*British Museum*).

the Armada in the few barges he had, the Dutch and English flyboats would have decimated them in the shallow waters of the coast.

On July 28 the Armada sought refuge in Calais harbor. This was the beginning of the end. The English sent in fireships, which disrupted the closely packed vessels of the Armada. The Spanish ships fled north, ran out of shot, and were defenseless against the English culverins and demi-culverins firing at short range. Many of the ships that escaped the English broadsides met disaster on the northwest coast of Scotland when a gale swept down on them. Only half the ships that sailed from Lisbon ever crept back into a Spanish port. The Spanish lost half their fleet but they did not, wrote a contemporary Englishman, "so much as sink or take one ship, bark, pinnace, or cockboat of ours, or even burn so much as one sheepcote in this land." The defeat of the Armada showed that England could, with its fleet, singlehandedly defend itself against the mightiest of monarchs. The boost to national confidence was immense.

ELIZABETH AND THE GOVERNMENT OF ENGLAND

In the reign of Charles I the people looked back on Elizabeth's reign as a golden age of good government. For once the human propensity to nostalgia was right, for under Elizabeth the English monarchy did function harmoniously and effectively. There were two keys to this success: the wisdom with which Elizabeth used Crown, Court, and Council to administer the realm, and the skill with which she used Parliament and the justices of the peace to bring her subjects into a partnership with herself.

Reverence for the Crown reached its zenith under Elizabeth, who exulted in the divinity attributed to her and exploited it shamelessly. A cult of the Queen arose in popular literature, portraying Elizabeth as a Goddess-Queen. But she was an accessible Goddess-Queen, for rarely did a summer pass that Elizabeth did not travel on a progress through her realm, displaying warmth and delight at the compliments showered on her. She used wisely the immense powers that the Crown brought her—powers to name ministers and judges, to summon and dismiss Parliament, to conduct diplomacy, to govern the Church, and to enforce order. Her deepest instinct was to use these powers to promote unity in the realm, not to pursue partisan or personal policies. Only once did she appear to yield to personal impulse. In the first years of her reign she fell deeply in love with Robert Dudley, whom she had first met at Edward VI's Court as a girl of 16. In 1562 the mysterious death of Dudley's wife, Amy Robsart, who either leaped into, fell into, or was pushed into a staircase well, presented an opportunity to consummate that love in marriage. But Elizabeth drew back. She saw the folly of marrying a man hated by most of her courtiers and suspected of murdering his wife. She turned from Dudley, saying, "I will have here but one mistress and no master."

There were factions in Elizabeth's Court—a peace party led by Cecil, whom the Queen created Lord Burghley, and a war party led by Dudley, whom she made Earl of Leicester—but the Queen kept these factions under firm control, using the one to check the other. She never surrendered her judgment to a great Court favorite, as did James I, but rather supported or opposed a favorite as the balance of factions dictated. She also used the Court and her vast patronage to secure the loyalty of the great families of England. There were in Elizabethan England some 2500 peers, gentlemen, and the younger sons of peers and gentlemen who aspired to a place at Court or in the Household or in the government. To assuage their appetite for place and profit, the Crown had at its disposal about 1200 places, along with pensions, leases, monopolies, and lesser offices. Elizabeth distributed this patronage prudently, with the result that by the end of her reign peers and gentlemen were turning from conspiracy and rebellion in the countryside to faction and intrigue at Court as the final arbiter in politics.

The Privy Council played a central role in the government of the kingdom. Elizabeth reduced it from the unwieldy size favored by Queen Mary to a maximum of twenty members. Most of them were great ministers of state—the Treasurer, the Secretary, the Lord Keeper, the Chamberlain, the Admiral. It was their duty to preserve law and order, to maintain the armed forces, to conduct foreign relations, to regulate agriculture, industry, and trade, and to advise the Queen. Elizabeth named men of probity and energy to it, none more so than William Cecil, who served ten years as Secretary and twenty-five years as Treasurer. Cecil was a patient man, occasionally unscrupulous, with an unquenchable thirst for work and little taste for fame. His partnership with the Queen lasted until his death in 1598, a partnership whose equal cannot be found.

The Queen and Council could make their will felt throughout the land only by means of the justices of the peace, those unpaid amateurs, some forty in every county, on whom the government had laid a bewildering variety of duties, from enforcing law and order to regulating the economy. Every three months the justices of a county met together for two or three days to deal with civil and criminal affairs. These quarter sessions served as a kind of local parliament where the grievances of the community could be voiced. The justices invariably showed great courtesy to the Queen, but beneath this courtesy lay a fierce localism. If the justices disapproved of an order from the Council, they thwarted it by delay and subterfuge. The only sanction the Queen had was dismissal, though often those dismissed had to be named again. In Norfolk, of seventy-five J.P.s dismissed forty were later reappointed. During the sixteenth century, with the decline of the military power of the aristocracy, local government fell into the hands of the gentry. And though the gentry displayed a growing devotion to the Queen, the immediate focus of their loyalties was the county, where they married, intrigued, quarreled, and governed. This partnership between the Queen and the gentry succeeded because they had a common goal in preserving order, protecting property, and defending the realm.

Parliaments were no part of the regular government of the realm. In forty-four years Elizabeth met Parliament only thirteen times, usually for only two months. Her frugality kept them infrequent, for she managed to live on her ordinary revenue, which came to about £200,000 a year. When later in the reign it fell short of her needs, she sold crown lands, in all about £800,000 worth. Occasionally extraordinary expenses and the need for new laws did impel her to summon Parliament, which during the whole reign voted subsidies that averaged about £50,000 a year. Elizabeth had definite ideas about what Parliament should do: it should vote the taxes needed, pass the laws submitted to it, and when asked, give advice. Above all it should not discuss "matters of state," which included religion, the succession, and her marriage. But members of the House of Commons, alarmed at the lack of a successor to the throne and eager to reform religion, persisted in debating these matters. No member was more forward in doing so than the passionate Peter Wentworth, who in 1576, again in 1587, and a third time in 1593 brought forward religion and the succession. "Sweet indeed is the name of liberty," he declared, "and the thing itself a value beyond all inestimable treasure." But he ended his life in the Tower while Elizabeth, through gracious speeches, furious lectures, and masterful management preserved her conception of Parliament's duty.

Profound changes below the surface, however, were making that success hollow. The gentry were invading the House of Commons. In the fifteenth century the House contained one gentleman to every four townsmen; in Elizabeth's later Parliaments there were four gentlemen to every townsman. To meet the clamor for seats in the House, Elizabeth created 62 new ones, raising the size of the Commons to 462. The center of gravity in Parliament gradually moved from the House of Lords to the House of Commons, but the aristocracy recouped its losses by acting as patrons to the parliamentary boroughs.

A gentleman or lawyer eager to win the prestige and advantages that a seat in Parliament offered had first to find a patron who could secure his return from a borough. The new membership of the House was far better educated than its predecessors—252 members of the House in 1593 had been either to a university or an Inn of Court. They were prosperous, confident, experienced, educated; and they slowly built up a corporate spirit and rules of procedure. Many matters were now debated in committees. Bills were read and voted on three times before being sent to the Lords. Most ominous of all, the House often held back the subsidy bill until the Queen had assented to other bills. The constitutional conflicts of Stuart England did not spring suddenly into existence; their roots lay deep in the England of Elizabeth.

THE RISE OF THE GENTRY

The gentry's invasion of the House of Commons was a reflection of a fundamental social change: the rise of the gentry in numbers, wealth, education, and aspiration. Society was still intensely hierarchical, but individual social mobility increased dramatically. When Shakespeare wrote,

Take but degree away, untune the string,
And hark what discord follows.

he not only praised degree, priority, and rank, but confessed that they were often disregarded. In his day many of the gentry could trace their ancestors to enterprising yeomen who, by purchasing parcels of land and making favorable leases, had raised their incomes from about £100 a year to £200 or £300. Their sons in turn dressed in velvet breeches and silken doublets, attended an Inn of Court, offered hospitality, purchased coats of arms, and called themselves gentlemen. But even more of the new gentry came from trade, industry, law, and government. Having made their fortunes in these professions, they bought manors and joined the gentry. Not only did the numbers of the gentry swell, so did the wealth of the class as a whole. Old and new families alike bought up manors from the Church and the Crown. In Norfolk the gentry's share of the 1,572 manors in the county rose during the sixteenth century from 977 to 1,181. The nobility in the later years held 159 manors, the Crown 67, the Church 91, and colleges, hospitals, and other institutions 30. Across all England the gentry probably increased their share of the land from a quarter in the fifteenth century to nearly a half by 1640, almost wholly at the expense of the Church and the Crown.

Though the gentry advanced, the aristocracy did not decline. Conditions in Elizabethan England favored the entire landed class, though admittedly the nobility were slower to take advantage of them. There were various ways to obtain a higher income from land: one could raise rents and entry fees; negotiate shorter, often annual, leases; enclose open fields; throw farms together; or farm the demesne oneself. Rising prices made it particularly worthwhile to enclose uncultivated land such as forests, marshes, and moors. Timber became highly profitable with the growing demand for wood for building. The enterprising industrial squire dug coal, mined lead, and manufactured iron. Recent studies show that landed revenues rose substantially between 1560 and 1590, in some cases more than doubled, and that between 1590 and 1620 they rose much more than prices. The overall increase between 1530 and 1620 was usually threefold, and often more.

The nobility and gentry lavished their new wealth on the building of country houses that were more spacious, more comfortable, more impressive, and more elegant than those in which their fathers had lived. The English built more country houses between 1575 and 1625 than in any comparable period. These houses, with their great windows, their high pitched gables, their wreathed chimneys, their private apartments, their plastered ceilings, and their oak paneling, were usually built on an E- or H-shaped plan. A central porch gave access to the house, with the hall itself on one side, balanced by apartments on the other, giving a pleasing symmetry to the main front. The greater houses would have a long gallery, flooded with light, where an increasingly wealthy and self-conscious gentry would hang their family portraits. The lesser gentry would more often purchase miniature paintings, a delicate and refined

Hardwicke Hall, "more glass than wall" said contemporaries (*A. F. Kersting*).

art that Nicholas Hilliard, son of a citizen of Exeter, carried to a point of perfection. The Elizabethan country house, with its great square windows and its dramatic skylines was a direct adaptation of late Perpendicular church architecture to domestic purposes. But as the age advanced and the influence of Italy increased, the English added classical detail (usually learned from Flemish copybooks) to the Gothic structure. The result was not wholly pleasing, since the ornament ceased to flow naturally from the design and became something applied only for fashion's sake. These houses, of which Burghley House offers a fine example, proclaim the ostentation, the extravagance, the self-consciousness, and even the vulgarity of a newly enriched landed class.

A willingness to offer hospitality was a prime mark of gentility. Sir William Holles, for example, during the Christmas season allowed any man to stay three days in his house without asking whence he came or where he was going. A fat ox was slaughtered each day. Hospitality could be lavish. At a banquet given for the Archbishop of York and other guests, Sir William Fairfax served sixteen dishes at the first course and fourteen at the second. To entertain the Queen on one of her progresses could be ruinous: The earl of Leicester spent £6000 entertaining the royal household at Kenilworth. The households of the wealthier gentry and nobility were immense. The Earl of Derby had 118 servants who, with guests, consumed 56 oxen and 535 sheep a year; the household expenses came to £2,895 annually. The Elizabethans were extravagant in many other ways. They bought costly furnishings, imported velvets and silks, and wore splendid clothing. When gentlemen wore doublets sewn with pearls

Burghley House, Northamptonshire, one of the two country houses built by William Cecil, Lord Burghley (*Country Life*).

they wore, so the saying went, "whole estates on their backs." Death did not end their conspicuous consumption, for they were buried in splendid marble tombs in the parish churches of the land.

A love of learning, or at least of the advantages that learning brought, characterized the Elizabethan gentleman as much as a love of ostentation. By Elizabeth's reign it became clear that men grew in power because they were educated at a university or an Inn of Court. There was Sir Thomas Smith, for example, son of a farmer, who became a professor of civil law at Cambridge, served Edward and Elizabeth as Secretary of State, and retired into the country with many manors. To check the flood of lesser men into government, Lord Burghley even thought of proposing a law requiring the nobility to send their sons to a university, but the nobility needed no such law. Under Elizabeth the sons of noblemen and gentlemen poured into the universities. Enrollment at Oxford rose from 191 a year between 1571 and 1580 to 340 a year between 1581 and 1590 and then fell, finally leveling off at about 300 a year.

The presence of the sons of gentlemen had two effects on the universities: it accelerated the triumph of a humanistic curriculum over the scholastic one, and it abetted the triumph of the college over the university. The study of rhetoric increasingly replaced the study of logic, while the reading of printed books—Cicero, Virgil, Erasmus, Bodin—replaced attendance at lectures. The rise of the college, with its own tutors, helped destroy the university lecture. In the fifteenth century Oxford students lived in some fifty halls; by 1558 only eight of them remained. They were replaced by colleges, which offered the student not only a residence, but a library, tutors, lectures, and a chapel. They even offered instruction in modern history and modern languages. Here students read Aristotle's *Politics* and Thomas Marshe's *Mirror for Magistrates.* The frivolous may have jangled their spurs in the quadrangles and diced, wenched, hunted, and tippled, but many others learned wisdom and virtue. The universities helped to transform a military aristocracy into an aristocracy with political ability. But it was only for the men. There was no place at the universities for women, and the splendid humanistic education that More's daughters and Lady Jane Grey and Elizabeth herself had received died out during the Queen's reign.

YEOMEN AND HUSBANDMEN

Below the gentry came the yeomanry, "An estate of people," wrote Thomas Fuller, "almost peculiar to England, living in the temperate zone betwixt greatness and want." The lawyers persisted in defining them as 40-shilling freeholders who farmed their own land, but in fact many yeomen leased land from others. The status of a yeoman was economic and social, not legal. He was simply a prosperous farmer who did not aspire to gentility. He usually farmed over 100 acres, and through improved husbandry, conversion to grazing, attendance at markets, and the employment of laborers earned a substantial income, perhaps £100 to £200 a year. During the sixteenth and the early seventeenth centuries yeomen prospered as never before. By 1640 they may have held from one-quarter to one-third of the land of England, much more than the one-fifth they held in the fifteenth century and the one-tenth they held in the nineteenth. They ate wheaten bread, bought feather beds, added internal staircases to their houses, sent their sons to grammar school, served in the trained bands, and won acclaim for their honesty, independence, pride, and sturdiness.

Far more numerous were the husbandmen, who held some 30 acres as copyholders or one or two acres as cottagers. Though they lived close to the margin of subsistence, they survived the price rise of the sixteenth century because they lived on the land. From the flax they grew they made their smocks, from the hides of their cattle they made jackets and jugs, from the horns of cattle their mugs, from the coarse hemp they grew they made their shoes and candlewicks. For medicine they used the herbs that grew in the fields or in their gardens. In good times they ate bread made from barley and rye, in bad times bread made from beans, peas, and oats, with some acorns mixed in. Their houses were still the old-fashioned gabled, thatched cottages, with clay, loam, rubble, and wattle filling up the spaces between the timbers. "These English," wrote a Spaniard, "have their houses made of sticks and dirt, but they fare commonly so well as the King." One reason they fared well was the "white meat" they added to their diet, that is chicken, geese, hares, and rabbits.

As the century progressed, the copyholders became fewer and the lease-holders more numerous, and by the end of the century the leasehold had replaced the copyhold as the characteristic tenure. Not all rural people worked in agriculture. In Gloucestershire, for example, only two-thirds were employed in farming; others were at their forges or looms. Many of these rural laborers worked for wages, either in the fields or as servants in great households, but few facts distinguish Elizabethan England more from modern England than the fact that independent producers outnumbered wage earners by two to one.

There existed in Elizabethan England a greater harmony among classes and a freer intercourse among them than in any other age. The Elizabethans no doubt believed in rank and degree, but they mixed together without undue self-consciousness or suspicion. The sons of gentlemen sat in the same grammar school with the sons of yeomen and artisans. The son of a yeoman might even, as did John Smyth of Nibley, enter Magdalen College as the companion of a young lord, Lord Berkeley. Even the lowly husbandman, whom William Harrison declared to "have neither voice nor authority in the Commonwealth," had a role in the village. He served as churchwarden, ale-conner, and constable. And he was active in the Court Leet, where agricultural policy was determined and petty justice done. He frequented the public inn or alehouse, where he drank the common ale while the squire caroused on French wines. John Hawkins introduced tobacco into England, which was smoked in a pipe. At 3 shillings an ounce smoking was expensive, but it became customary for an inn or alehouse to provide a common pipe. It was passed from customer to customer, thus placing tobacco within the reach of all.

BEGGARS AND VAGABONDS

The Elizabethan gentleman may have mixed easily with the yeoman and husbandman, but he had a contempt for, and a fear of, the beggar and the vagabond. Vagrancy, the problem of beggars wandering through the countryside, was not peculiar to the sixteenth century, but during this time the ranks of the vagrants were swollen by demobilized soldiers from Henry VIII's wars and by surplus retainers from noble households. There were probably from 20,000 to 40,000 vagrants or vagabonds in England, divided into those searching for work and those determined to avoid work at all costs–the rogue element. The rogues numbered some 300 to 400 in a county and moved in groups of two or three or in bands of forty or fifty. They ranged from the professional beggar, who could make as much as 14 shillings a day (at a time when the average daily wage of a laborer was 6 pence), to the thief and the murderer. They terrorized the county, stole sheep and cattle, frightened the magistrate, and taxed the slender resources of the constable, whose duty it was to arrest them. Too often when the constable raised the hue and cry for their arrest, his fellow villagers ignored him, saying "I have other business at this time." Of all vagrants it was the gypsies who aroused the most distrust. They first entered England at the beginning of the sixteenth century. Their dark skins, their dealings in the occult, and their claim to see into the future created the deepest suspicion. Parliament even passed a statute condemning those who remained in England to death. They nevertheless remained and managed to survive.

Poverty presented a far more serious problem to the Elizabethans than vagrancy. There were two causes for the widespread poverty of these years. The first was a population that grew faster than opportunities for employment, driving landless younger sons and unemployed clothworkers into the towns looking for work or alms. During Elizabeth's reign probably a quarter to a third of the population of most towns were the begging poor, enjoying only occasional employment. Another third were wage earners, regularly employed, but liable to swell the ranks of the destitute when a slump hit. The second cause of poverty was inflation. Between 1500 and 1640 the real wages of workers dropped by 50 percent. With wages falling it is not surprising that parents sent their children out to work, often when only 5 or 6, and usually in the textile trades. The cruelest time for the poor came when a succession of bad harvests drove up the price of bread, as happened in the 1590s. In 1596 in Newcastle 32 poor folk died of starvation in the streets; elsewhere they were less acquiescent and rioted.

Fearing the vagrants and the poor, the early Tudor Parliaments struck out ferociously. In 1495 Parliament declared that beggars should be placed in stocks for three days, whipped, and then returned to their place of origin. In 1531 Parliament first distinguished between the impotent poor and the able-bodied poor. The old, the lame, the feeble, and the blind were permitted to beg, but the able-bodied poor, even if seeking employment, were forbidden to beg. Tudor ferocity reached a peak in 1547 when Parliament decreed that any man or woman who remained unemployed for three days or more should be deemed a vagrant, branded with a V, and enslaved for two years. The cruelty of the statute made it a dead letter from the beginning, and in 1550 Parliament repealed it. But just twenty-two years later Parliament ordained whipping and boring through the ear as punishment for the first offense of vagrancy, condemnation as a felon for the second offense, and death for the third. This time the act was enforced. In Middlesex between 1572 and 1575 forty-four vagabonds were branded, eight set to service, and five hanged. Yet the act marked a watershed in the poor law history of England, for it recognized that there were unemployed able-bodied men who were not vagrants, and it recognized the need for compulsory contributions from parishioners to provide for the relief of the deserving poor. An act in 1576 even empowered parishes to provide hemp, flax, and iron on which the able-bodied unemployed could work.

The 1572 and 1576 acts served Elizabethans adequately until the great famine of the 1590s. Then fear of riots, allied to an uneasy conscience at the neglect of the poor, prompted Parliament to pass the Poor Law of 1598, which it reenacted in 1601 with slight alterations, and which governed the relief of the poor for 250 years. The act established overseers of the poor in each parish and empowered them to provide suitable dwelling places for the destitute, to set to work persons with no obvious means of maintenance, and to bind in apprenticeship poor children. They could also tax the parish for the necessary funds to carry out these tasks. On the assumption that these tasks would be performed, the government decreed that "no person shall go wandering abroad and beg in any place whatsoever, by license or without, upon pain of punishment as a rogue."

The parishes of England, however, enforced the Poor Law only in times of emergency. Of the great sums spent on poor relief before 1660, taxation provided only 7 percent. The rest came from private philanthropy. The Reformation did much to turn charity toward the relief of the poor. Before the Reformation, 45 percent of London charity was devoted to religious purposes; afterward only 7 percent. Of the money given to relieve the poor, the nobility and gentry gave a quarter, the tradesmen 10 percent, the yeomanry 6 percent, and the lower clergy but 1 percent. By far the greatest amount, 56 percent, was given by the merchants. Even more important than this temporary relief were the charitable trusts established for the rehabilitation of the poor. Here the merchants gave 86 percent. Without the generosity of the merchants, the government would never have solved the problem of poverty.

THE ASCENDANCY OF LONDON

The merchants, whose largess kept the poor from submerging, lived in towns spread across the country, some in manufacturing towns such as Coventry with its capmakers and Sheffield with its cutlers, others in market towns such as Stratford and Bedford. Three towns, Norwich, Bristol, and York, each contained between 10,000 and 20,000 inhabitants; Exeter had between 5,000 and 10,000; a host of other towns numbered about 5,000. Towering over all these towns in size, numbers, wealth, power, and importance was London. Approaching 300,000 inhabitants by the end of the reign, it was at least ten times more populous than any other English town. It was the largest city in northern Europe. The annual value of its customs was twenty times greater than Bristol's, the second port of the realm.

London began east of the Tower and ran westward along the Thames to Westminster, the builtup area never extending more than a mile or a mile and a half north of the river. The city east of the Tower consisted of filthy, narrow passageways and alleys, inhabited by sailors, victuallers, tavernkeepers, and rogues. The Tower, with its walls, turrets, wharf, and cranes, was a world of its own. Between the Tower and London Bridge were wharves, warehouses, gabled houses, churches, and a river crowded with ships. London Bridge, with its

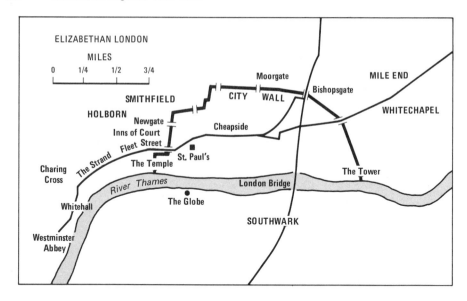

twenty arches and its fine shops and houses lining the roadway, was the only bridge that crossed the Thames at London. To cross the river elsewhere, or to travel up and down it, one had to hire a wherryman.

West of London Bridge rose medieval St. Paul's, with its three-portaled west front and its spire rising high above London. Around St. Paul's were crowded the bishop's palace, the dean's house, a brewhouse, a bakehouse, and Peter's College, which the Elizabethans turned into Stationers' Hall, the center of the publishing trade. Walls and gates still encircled the old city, and within Bishopsgate and Moorgate were the large gardens and sumptuous houses of the richer merchants. Northward were open spaces, where the citizens went "a-maying," the militia exercised, and John Stow, the chronicler of Elizabethan London, trudged for milk as a boy. To the west of the city, along the Strand, ran the great houses of the peers—Essex House, Arundel House, Somerset House—each with its private stairs leading to the Thames. Finally, beyond the hamlet of Charing came the City of Westminster, where two royal palaces, Whitehall and Westminster, attracted all those concerned with government.

Though the government sought to prevent the growth of London, it probably doubled in size during Elizabeth's reign. Throughout the city great houses were pulled down and the sites devoted to small tenements paying large rents. Lord Rich turned St. Bartholomew's Priory into profitable tenements. Outside the city walls, suburbs sprang up. At the beginning of the reign, when much Church property was thrown on the market, rents were low. By its end, with many thousands flooding into the city, among them William Shakespeare and Christopher Marlowe, rents were high. London was a magnet for all who would make their fortunes. Sir John Spencer, for example, came from Suffolk to London, engaged in the Levant trade, became Lord Mayor, and left a fortune to his daughter.

The influence of London was even greater than its size would suggest, for from it the judges on circuit went out every year and to it members of Parliament came every few years. It contained the Inns of Court, which now became finishing schools for gentlemen as well as professional schools for lawyers. To Westminster country gentlemen carried their endless legal quarrels and to Southwark, south of the Thames, they and others went to see the latest plays. From Stationers' Hall books and pamphlets went out to the four corners of the realm. But London's economic influence was most resented. The London merchant controlled the trade of provincial towns, compelling the Norwich draper, for example, to bring his cloth to Blackwell Hall if he wished to sell it abroad. Even more hateful was the London moneylender, into whose clutches fell many a country squire and provincial merchant. Because credit did not keep pace with the growth of trade, moneylenders commonly charged 10 percent interest.

The formal structure of the London government remained unchanged: there were twenty-six wards in which the freemen (and one had to be a member of a guild to be a freeman) voted for the aldermen and common councilors. From two aldermen nominated by the city companies, the freemen elected a mayor. Real power resided in an oligarchy of wealthy merchants, who exerted their control through the twelve great city companies, or liveried companies. Each company was an association of various trades, and the companies continued to enforce apprenticeship regulations, regulate markets, maintain standards of quality, act as benefit societies, and give sumptuous banquets. London, like other chartered towns, enjoyed self-government, but the Crown looked to the city magistrates, as it did to magistrates in the countryside, for help in regulating employment, controlling prices, maintaining order, relieving the poor, collecting taxes, and mustering men for defense.

As the Elizabethan age progressed, the London magistrates grew more Puritan in outlook. They came to regard the performance of plays as "a great hindrance to the service of God" and as "a great corruption of youth with unchaste and wicked matters." They asked the Lord Chancellor to prohibit the performance of plays, but he refused, commenting that Her Majesty sometimes took delight in plays. Ten years later, the Court of Aldermen declared that the youth of the city were greatly corrupted by the wanton things they saw on the stage, but the theater throve in the 1590s as never before.

THE ELIZABETHAN WORLD PICTURE

In 1576 James Burbage, head of the Earl of Leicester's company of actors, built the first theater in London, near Shoreditch, outside the city wall. Others followed—the Curtain, also in Shoreditch in 1577; the Rose, south of the Thames in 1588; the Swan in Southwark about 1595; and the Globe, also in Southwark, in 1598. The shape of these theaters derived from the innyards which had served as their predecessors. They were round or octagonal, with the pit open to the sky, and tiers of covered galleries running around the pit, except the part occupied by the stage. The stage was a large platform jutting out into the yard, divided into an outer and inner stage, with the inner stage often curtained off. Costumes were elaborate, boys took women's parts, properties were few, and scenery nonexistent. These were public theaters, where the populace crowded into the pit and gentlemen sat in the galleries. There were also private theaters in the houses of nobles and at Court. In 1583 Queen Elizabeth's Master of the Revels formed a company of players to perform plays for the Queen and her Court.

In the sixteenth century a number of forces flowed together to produce the Elizabethan poetic drama, the greatest glory of the age. The medieval morality play developed into the Tudor interlude, a play concerned with education rather than salvation and containing both realistic and comic elements. The influence of the Classics also led playwrights to create English comedies, drawing themes and characters from the Roman dramatist, Plautus. The Classics likewise led them to write the first tragedies, for there were no tragedies among the miracle and morality plays. Seneca was the model here, with his somber treatment of murder, violence, and lust. At the same time, there arose at Court,

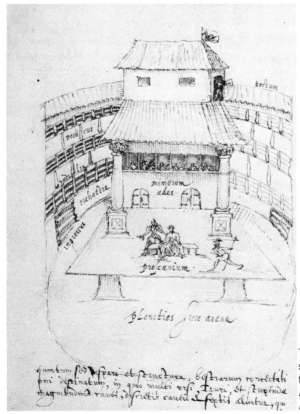

The Swan Theatre, Southwark, showing the pit, the galleries, and the outer and inner stage (*University Library, Utrecht, Ms. 842, fol. 132 recto*).

in the houses of noblemen, and in the universities, an audience that could appreciate more sophisticated plays than could the public that crowded into town innyards and on to village greens. What brought all these forces together was the appearance of the University Wits, university graduates who, not wishing to enter the Church, turned to playwriting for a living. The greatest of them was Christopher Marlowe, whose first two plays, *Tamburlaine* and *The Tragical History of Dr. Faustus,* fell like a thunderclap on the Elizabethan stage. Until Marlowe, English tragedy lacked both a blank verse eloquent enough for its purposes and themes that spoke to the concerns of the Elizabethans. Marlowe introduced a highly charged blank verse, rich in images of power and violence and colored by exotic names from the geographical discoveries of the age. His themes were new. The human intoxication with power is the argument of *Tamburlaine,* the thirst for ultimate knowledge of *Dr. Faustus.* Both reflected the Renaissance concept of *virtu,* the human being as master of his destiny, challenging even the gods who control fortune's wheel.

Christopher Marlowe's death by violence in 1593 prevented him from writing a great corpus of plays or perfecting his blank verse. These tasks William Shakespeare accomplished. Shakespeare was born at Stratford-on-Avon in 1564, of yeoman stock, attended the local grammar school, led a rather reckless life, and then wandered to London, where he became an actor, playwright, and member of the Lord Chamberlain's men, who played at the Globe. It is one of the strangest accidents of history that this superb craftsman, this professional man of the theater, should also have been a universal genius, with an uncanny knowledge of the human heart and a poetic gift unrivaled in the history of English literature. During the 1590s he brought to perfection the romantic comedy, with its counterpoint of poetry and wit, its lively heroines, its delicate treatment of love, its satire on male vanity, and its gallery of comic characters —Bottom the Weaver, Sir Andrew Aguecheek the fool, and the strutting Malvolio. During the 1590s he also matured his cycle of history plays, with their exploration of the problem of order and authority, their study of the relation between moral character and human conduct, and their glorification of England and the House of Tudor. In the greatest of these plays, *Henry IV,* Parts I and II, Shakespeare successfully combined the political with the comic. The center theme was the education of Prince Hal, the future Henry V, but Sir John Falstaff, the richest comic creation in English literature, captures the play. This colossus of the Boar's Head tavern was a vain, pompous, lying braggart, but no man ever showed a greater gusto for life.

In the 1590s Shakespeare also began to experiment with tragedy. His first was *Romeo and Juliet,* brilliantly dramatic but less profound because it was a tragedy of circumstances rather than of character. Then, between 1599 and 1606, he wrote his great tragedies, *Julius Caesar, Hamlet, Othello, King Lear,* and *Macbeth,* tragedies filled with moral ambiguities, with guilt and retribution, with the tragic paradoxes of human nature. They were tragedies in which virtuous men were destroyed by flaws in their characters: Brutus by his political innocence, Hamlet by his irresolution, Othello by his credulity, King Lear by his vanity, Macbeth by his ambition. In these plays, as in all his works, Shakespeare reveals his infinite curiosity about human nature, his remarkable ability to create character, his skilled craftsmanship, his mastery of the English language, and, perhaps most important of all, his sympathy with human beings in all their shapes, kinds, degrees, heights, and depths.

What Shakespeare achieved for drama Edmund Spenser accomplished for poetry. Out of diverse elements—Classical examples, Renaissance Latin verse, the Italian and French vernacular, the traditions of Chaucer—he created a new poetry, one without ragged rhymes, and one that observed a propriety of tone, diction, and verse form. At the Merchant Taylor's school in London he discovered the ideal of the perfect gentleman; at Cambridge he became both a Puritan and a humanist; in Ireland, where he served for twenty years as a civil servant, he learned to distrust as well as admire the courtier. It was in Ireland that he wrote his greatest work, *The Faerie Queene,* an English Protestant humanist epic, in which medieval romance, the Classical epic, Platonic and neo-Platonic ideas, Protestant idealism, and English folklore and patriotism were drawn together to present a poetic comment on the human condition.

In Elizabethan England poetry and music lived in close association. The English thus gave the madrigal, a popular musical form imported from Italy, a warm reception. The madrigal was an unaccompanied polyphonic vocal piece about love or bereavement or the beauty of nature. Some forty collections of madrigals were published during the generation after 1590. Nearly as popular as the madrigal were solo songs accompanied by the lute. Never did music thrive in England as under Elizabeth. The tailor sang in his shop, the shipboy chanted at his oar, and the guest was expected to join the singing after supper. Nor was it all vocal and secular music. William Byrd, whom Elizabeth made organist of the Chapel Royal despite his Catholic faith, wrote music for the virginal, the organ, and the viol consort. He helped introduce from Italy the motet, a choral composition on a sacred text, usually without accompaniment. For depth of feeling and for perfect blending of musical form with the meaning of the verse William Byrd had no equal.

The Elizabethan age was also glorious for its prose—indeed, the English language today is what the Elizabethans made it. New words poured into the language, "furlough" and "drill" from the Low Countries, "embargo" and "breeze" from Spain, and countless Latin and Greek words to express abstract ideas. The richness of English prose can be seen in Richard Hakluyt's *The Principal Navigations, Voyages, Traffiques and Discoveries of the English Nation,* but the masterpiece of expository prose was Richard Hooker's *Of the Laws of Ecclesiastical Polity.* Hooker not only disputed the Puritans' insistence on scriptural justification for every practice by pleading the cause of tradition and utility, he also presented a comprehensive view of the Church, the State, and the divine order of things. In a prose that was reasonable, majestically ordered, calm, and dignified, he argued that natural law, which our reason apprehends and which comes from God, provides a light as useful as scriptural law in governing our lives.

In the plays of Shakespeare, the poetry of Spenser, and the prose of Hooker one can discern an Elizabethan picture of the world, a picture far different from the modern scientific one. To begin with, there was a dualism between the spiritual and material worlds, though it was not the dualism of Descartes, who separated mind and body. Rather it was a Platonic dualism, in which the spiritual continually interpenetrated the material and in which there were a thousand correspondences between the two realms. As Spenser wrote:

> For of the soul the body form doth take:
> For soul is form and doth the body make.

Within each realm the Elizabethans saw an hierarchy: in the spiritual realm, God in the trinity, the nine orders of angels, the minor spirits, and the soul of humans; in the material world, the high heavens, the ninefold division of the heavens, the earth, and the human body.

To the Elizabethans matter was made up of substance and qualities, either of which could, by priest or magician, be altered. It is a belief that justifies the alchemist's dream of transmuting lead into gold, makes reasonable the doctrine of transubstantiation, forms the basis of the astrologer's belief that all things draw their qualities from the stars, and helps explain why the witchcraft mania reached a height during the Renaissance. In such a world there were two great roads to knowledge, the magical and the poetic. There was ordinary magic, as practiced by the astrologer and alchemist, and black magic, as practiced by the witch or by a Doctor Faustus who had sold his soul to the devil. More honored than the magician was the poet, who was prophet, seer, sage, and teacher all in one. His metaphors were not adornments of language, designed to entertain; they were a revelation of the truth about a mysterious world. Human beings played a central part in that world, for they had both body and soul, and so could bridge the gap between the material and spiritual worlds. Nor had modern psychology yet reduced people to machines. They possessed free will, that free will which lies at the center of Shakespeare's tragedies. Richard Hooker presented a perfect picture of man as the Elizabethans saw him. He possessed gross appetites, for he had the taint of Adam on him, but he also possessed free will, which could curb those appetites. He likewise possessed reason, or mind, which could perceive the good and which could direct the will, thereby allowing man to embark on the path of virtue. Of necessity man was a member of society, or the body politic, which the Elizabethans saw as hierarchical. In the eighteenth century Rousseau declared that the very laws of nature make men equal; with equal confidence Hooker in the sixteenth century declared that the very laws of nature make them unequal. It is unnatural to rebel against the sovereign, to show irreverence to the bishop, to show disrespect to rank and degree.

Take but degree away, untune the string,
And hark what discord follows.

POSTLUDE

The last decade of Elizabeth's reign was a sad postlude to a glorious age. The costly war against Spain dragged on; Parliament stormed against monopolies; the Irish revolted; and politics became a sordid scrimmage for place, with the greatest loser, the Earl of Essex, rising in rebellion.

The defeat of the Armada marked the beginning, not the end, of the war. It was fought on many fronts and outlasted the Queen herself. The chief theater was the Netherlands, where 6000 English troops helped Prince Maurice secure Dutch independence. The war spread into France, where Elizabeth sent five expeditions to help Henry of Navarre assert his claim to the French throne against the House of Guise. It spread to Ireland in 1595, when the Irish rebelled and Philip II sent an armada of 100 ships and 10,000 men to assist them. But the wind remained obdurately Protestant, for a gale dispersed the fleet as soon as it set out. The English also sought to make the sea a theater of offensive warfare by attempting to invade Portugal, blockade Spain, conquer Panama, and destroy Cadiz. All but the last expedition failed, for the English had not yet learned how to use seapower effectively over long distances. The war was expensive, costing over £4 million. Parliament voted £2 million in subsidies, taxes which weighed heavily upon a country beset by bad harvests and the plague (which descended on England in 1592, 1602, and 1603). The other £2 million the government raised from ordinary revenue, from the sale of crown lands, from higher customs duties, and from the concealed taxation of monopolies.

In order to encourage inventions and the introduction of manufacturing processes from abroad, the government often granted a monopoly of their use to the inventor or innovator. But the need to reward officers and courtiers and a faith in the virtues of regulation led the government to grant monopolies to individuals engaged in long-established trades—or, if not an actual monopoly, then the right to regulate those engaged in a trade. There was hardly an article in common use—coal, soap, starch, iron, books, and wine—not affected by monopolies. Prices rose, the search warrants came out, the courtiers grew fat, and the public suffered. In 1601 Parliament exploded: member after member rose to denounce the monopolists. Since it was the Queen's right to grant monopolies, it seemed that the constitutional confrontation between Prerogative and Parliament, which the Queen had so long avoided, must come. But Elizabeth knew when to yield and how to be gracious. She told the Speaker that no monopoly which a court of law did not vindicate should continue and she made a golden speech to 140 members of the Commons who crowded into the council chamber at Whitehall. "Though God hath raised me high," she told

London in 1600 as depicted by C. J. Visscher (*British Museum*).

them, "yet this I count the glory of my crown, that I have reigned with your loves."

There is little reason to believe that Elizabeth reigned with the loves of her Irish subjects. Though she was personally indifferent, the persecution of Catholics raged on during her reign, giving a religious character to Irish resistance to English rule. In 1580 the English confronted Earl Gerald of Munster, who declared himself a rebel and invited a Spanish force to Ireland. By devastating the country, burning the harvest, and massacring herds of cattle, the English defeated Gerald, who was captured and killed. Of his vast lands Raleigh received 16,000 hectares and the poet Spenser an extensive demesne.

The most formidable challenge to English rule came from Hugh O'Neil, Earl of Tyrone, who had spent some years in London and understood the courts of both England and Europe. He saw that the Irish could win their independence only if they united and ceased fighting each other. From his stronghold in Ulster he rose in rebellion in 1595. He armed his men with muskets, defeated the English at Contibert and the Yellow Ford, moved freely through Ireland, and wore out the Earl of Essex, who bore down on him with 16,000 men. The truce Essex made—virtually abdicating English rule in Ireland—

came abruptly to an end in 1600 when Lord Mountjoy, a far abler soldier than Essex, landed with an army of 20,000 well-equipped English troops. In Ulster he adopted the policy that had proved successful in Munster: the killing of cattle and the burning of harvests. Tyrone replied by seeking the help of Spain, which sent 4,000 men to the southern port of Kinsale. Mountjoy promptly besieged the town, which compelled Tyrone to march south, often at 40 miles a day, to lay siege to the besiegers. At the request of the Spanish commander, at the entreaty of his ally, Hugh O'Donnel, and against his better judgment, Tyrone attacked Mountjoy's army and suffered defeat. That day's disaster ended all hopes for a free, united Ireland. He submitted to the English and ended his days in Rome.

The Earl of Essex, who had made so disastrous a truce in 1599, returned home to face the wrath of the Queen. Robert Devereux, Earl of Essex, had won the aging Queen's favor in the 1590s with his youth, his charm, his handsome face and figure, and his brilliance of style. He also became the hero of men of action by his forwardness in arms, particularly at Cadiz in 1596. But Essex, a man of moods and impulses, sought more than favor at Court and esteem as a soldier. He sought to fill the political vacuum created by the deaths of Leicester, Walsingham, and Burghley. He desired greatness, a desire that brought him up against the ambitions and abilities of Robert Cecil, the small, hunchedback son of Lord Burghley. During the 1590s there arose a fierce rivalry between Essex and Cecil. For every vacancy Essex had a candidate whom he promoted, for his greatness depended on his ability to promote his clients. His military reputation brought him important new offices—Master of the Ordnance and Earl Marshal—but a military reputation can only be supported by military success. He therefore went to Ireland in 1599, with greater resources and wider powers than any Lord Deputy before him. But in six short months he squandered them and negotiated a truce with Tyrone that was tantamount to surrender. In September he suddenly returned to England, against the Queen's express orders, and burst in upon her at Nonsuch Palace. The Queen handled the matter with her usual skill. She did not imprison the Earl, but committed him to the custody of a friend. Nine months later a special court tried and sentenced him to the loss of his offices and detention during the Queen's pleasure.

The Queen also suspended Essex's lease of the customs on sweet wines, an action that threatened his financial ruin. She hoped this might goad him into reform, but it only goaded him into treason. Early in 1601 he and his friends perfected a plan to seize the Court, the Tower, and the city as a means of imposing their will on the Queen. On Sunday morning, February 8th, Essex with about 200 followers galloped into the city, crying, "For the Queen! The Crown of England is sold to the Spaniard! A plot is laid for my life!" But the city did not rise, the Court was forewarned, the conspirators failed, and Essex was captured. Within ten days a court of his peers had condemned him for treason; within another week the executioner's ax robbed him of life. His was the most egotistical and wasted of Elizabethan careers.

Essex's death left power in the hands of Robert Cecil, who now opened negotiations with the Scottish Court for the succession of James VI of Scotland, though the Queen could never bring herself to name him as her successor. Elizabeth died on March 24, 1603, resisting death as she had resisted all major decisions. Unable to eat or sleep, she refused either to go to bed or take any medication for two weeks. She lay there, on her cushions, silent, miserable. Then life escaped her and Tudor England came to an end.

FURTHER READING

*D.M. PALLISER. *The Age of Elizabeth: England Under the Later Tudors 1547–1603.* London, 1983. Contains chapters on population, social structure, agriculture, trade, government, religion, and culture; most helpful on social structure; defends the responsible capitalism of the age.

WALLACE MACCAFFREY. *The Shaping of the Elizabethan Regime* and *Queen Elizabeth and the Making of Policy.* Princeton, 1968 and 1982. The first volume describes the restoration of political stability, the second elucidates English foreign policy; narrowly political in scope but written with insight, clarity, and elegance.

PENRY WILLIAMS. *The Tudor Regime.* Oxford, 1979. Explores the world MacCaffrey ignores, the world of administration, finance, the militia, monopolies, enclosures, poor laws, penal laws, and crime.

*SIR JOHN NEALE. *Queen Elizabeth.* London, 1934; reprinted New York, 1957. As readable as a novel, yet filled with illuminating and accurate information.

*A.L. ROWSE. *The England of Elizabeth: The Structure of Society.* London, 1950; reprinted Madison, Wis., 1978. A brilliant portrayal of Elizabethan society from the Queen to the merchant and yeoman, written with insight, imagination, passion, and prejudice.

*GARRETT MATTINGLY. *The Armada.* Boston, 1959; reprinted Cranburynswick, New York, 1979. The narrative of the naval action is clear, swift, informed, and exciting; the book also places the naval action in its European context.

*E.M.W. TILLYARD. *The Elizabethan World Picture.* New York, 1944; reprinted New York, 1959. A brief, admirable summary of the conception of the world held by the educated Elizabethan.

*BORIS FORD, ed. *The New Pelican Guide to English Literature.* Vol. 2, *The Age of Shakespeare.* Penguin Books, 1982. A general survey of the English literary renaissance, with particular studies of individual poets and dramatists; the major emphasis is on Shakespeare.

*RICHARD HAKLUYT. *Voyages and Discoveries.* Edited and abridged by Jack Beeching. Penguin Books, 1982. Selections from Hakluyt's contemporary and now classic account of the Elizabethan voyages of discovery.

13 Early Stuart England: 1603-1640

The accident that James I was "the wisest fool in Christendom" and Charles I a proud, aloof absolutist should not be allowed to obscure the fact that powerful, latently dangerous forces were undermining the Tudor monarchy. Even had a monarch with Queen Elizabeth's prudence and sympathies come to the throne, there is no reason to believe that he or she could have maintained the Tudor ideal of government—a financially independent Crown ruling in partnership with the nobility and gentry. There were too many developments sapping the foundations of the Tudor monarchy. To begin with there was inflation, which steadily cut into the revenues of the Crown, until the King could no longer "live of his own." Secondly, there was the rise of the gentry in numbers, wealth, education, experience, and power. Thirdly, there was the growth of a Parliament that possessed rules, procedures, committees, a corporate spirit, and self-confidence. Fourthly, there were the Puritans, dissatisfied with the Church, certain of their righteousness, guided by God, strong of will, slowly growing in numbers. Finally, there were the lawyers, active in provincial towns as well as London, growing wealthy, crowding into Parliament, jealously guarding the Common law, eloquent, willful, and willing to challenge any King who violated the law.

Yet history cannot be written in the subjunctive mood; the historian must write about what did happen, not about what might have happened. What did happen between 1603 and 1640 was a clash between two unwise and incompetent kings and their aggressive subjects.

THE ACCESSION OF JAMES I

For a King who believed he reigned by divine right, James had a preposterous appearance. He was short, with spindly legs and an ungainly head, a figure made more ridiculous by the heavy quilted doublet he wore to ward off the assassin's dagger. His tongue was too large for his mouth, which caused him to stutter and to drink awkwardly. But though he cut a poor figure, he was intelligent. He had a retentive memory, a quick though coarse wit, a love of scholarship, and a shrewd realism about people and affairs. In Scotland, where he had tamed the nobility and disciplined the Presbyterians, he had proved himself a wily, pragmatic, successful ruler. As he rode south in 1603, he had every reason to be pleased with himself. But his self-satisfaction deceived him, for his reign in England was to be as disastrous as his reign in Scotland was successful. He did not understand England as he had Scotland. Furthermore, certain defects in his character came to the fore as he grew old. He exhausted the Treasury with generous gifts to favorites. He had a passion for the chase, which led

Portrait of James I, attributed to Gheeraerts the Younger (*Governors of Dulwich College*).

him to neglect the government while pursuing deer in Theobalds Park. He made long speeches to Parliament in which he put forward theoretical claims to absolute power. Above all, he surrendered his judgment to Court favorites who possessed neither sense nor ability.

James clashed at once with the House of Commons. In 1604 he ordered the Court of Chancery to declare the election of Sir Francis Goodwin from Buckinghamshire null and void, alleging that he was ineligible as an outlaw. James's action was not unprecedented, for Chancery had decided disputed election returns in Elizabeth's reign. It was the Commons who acted in a radical manner by declaring Goodwin lawfully elected and by demanding the right to decide their own election returns. James exacerbated the quarrel by telling the Commons that they derived their privileges from him. This provoked them to draw up *The Form of Apology and Satisfaction,* in which they declared that they held their privileges by right, not by the grace of the King, and that they, not Chancery, were to decide election returns. The Commons never actually presented the *Apology* to James, but they did, after much bargaining, persuade him to agree that the House of Commons was a proper judge of its own returns, thereby acknowledging a principle important to the independence of any legislative body.

The Commons went on to assert its independence from the Crown in many other ways, and James's inexperience aided them. James, unlike Elizabeth, did not have able privy councilors in the House of Commons to manage it. There were only three privy councilors in his first Parliament, four in his second. He also named Speakers who lacked experience and respect. Nor did he help his ministers any by his frequent absences from London during sessions of Parliament. James's dereliction of duty allowed the House of Commons to seize the initiative. Its members limited the Speaker's room for maneuver by passing rules governing when a bill might be read. They made increasing use of committees, and in 1607 stumbled on the device of the committee of the whole. When the House met as a committee of the whole, the Speaker left the chair, all members could attend, and debate was much freer. By 1610 it was customary to refer many important matters to the committee of the whole; by 1620 nearly all significant business came before it. Meanwhile the leaders of the opposition began to meet privately to plan their tactics in Parliament. By the 1620s the privy councilors could hardly make themselves heard in the House of Commons.

In the *Apology* the Commons told James he could not alter religion except by consent of Parliament, but this did not prevent him from seeking a compromise between the bishops and the Puritans. On his arrival in London the Puritans presented him with the Millenary Petition (so-called because a thousand clergy allegedly signed it), in which they asked that the sign of the cross not be used in baptism nor the ring in marriage, that the Sabbath should be kept holy, and that there should be more preaching, fewer pluralists, and less use of the oath *ex officio* (by which suspects must give evidence against themselves). James I, who was an ardent Calvinist except in matters of church government, promptly summoned a conference at Hampton Court between the Puritans and the bishops. Except for a fierce outburst against Presbyterian church government, which led him to declare prophetically, "No Bishop, no King," James played a neutral role. The conference was by no means a total victory for the bishops, but the final outcome was, since James, once the conference ended, lost interest. He allowed the bishops, who dominated the commissions named to enforce the conference's decisions, to make sure that some of them were not carried out. The bishops revised the Book of Common Prayer in their own interest and secured passage through Convocation of new canons, one of which required the clergy to subscribe to the royal supremacy, the Thirty-nine Articles, and the revised Prayer Book. Ninety clergymen refused to subscribe and lost their benefices, but most Puritans conformed, being resolved to reform the Church from within. They had allies in the House of Commons who in 1610 presented a petition to James on behalf of the ejected ministers. During James's reign the Puritans were unhappy, but they were not yet rebels.

James also sought to play the peacemaker with his Catholic subjects. A tolerant man himself, he had when in Scotland promised English Catholics a greater toleration. He did not fulfill these promises; instead, he issued a proclamation ordering all priests to leave the country and he continued to collect recusancy fines. At that very moment Spain deserted the Catholics of England, signing a peace with England that gave no protection to English Catholics. Exceedingly frustrated by these events, a half-dozen Catholic gentlemen plotted to blow up the King, the House of Lords, and the House of Commons on November 5, 1605. The explosion would be a signal for rebellion throughout the land. They hired a Catholic soldier of fortune, Guy Fawkes, to place thirty-six barrels of gunpowder in a room underneath the House of Lords. The powder might well have gone off at the opening of Parliament had not one of the conspirators revealed the plot to the government. On the night of the 4th, palace guards, sent to search Westminster Palace, found Guy Fawkes and his barrels of gunpowder. The other conspirators fled, raised a rebellion, and were captured. Along with Guy Fawkes, they were tried and executed for treason.

The Gunpowder Plot created the annual celebration of Guy Fawkes Day, promoted antipopery for a century and more, and provoked the passage of further penal laws against Catholics. But its significance does not end there. It was, in fact, the last fling of a politically engaged Catholicism. With its failure, Catholics turned away from treason and thereby made possible the existence of a respectable Catholic community in England. This development was abetted by a new oath of supremacy, which included an express denial of the Pope's authority to depose kings. Those Catholics who took the oath, and they were many, became practically, if not legally, exempt from recusancy fines. And once James embarked on a pro-Spanish foreign policy, he was less inclined than ever to enforce the penal laws against Catholics. The 35,000 Catholics of 1603 became the 50,000 Catholics of 1625.

JAMES AND THE LAW

By 1606 James was secure on the throne. He had governed for three years lawfully and successfully. The Gunpowder Plot had created a strong reaction in his favor, and Parliament had cheerfully voted him three subsidies. The truly bitter constitutional conflicts that marked the later years of his reign had not yet appeared. But their root cause, insolvency, had. The near-bankruptcy of the Crown was James's doing, not Elizabeth's. Elizabeth had left a net debt of only £100,000, less than Mary had left her. By 1606 James had increased the debt to £600,000. James spent lavishly and gave prodigally. His wife, Anne of Denmark, loved extravagant clothes and new jewels. James and Anne had two sons and a daughter, each of whom must have a household. The Court delighted in sumptuous banquets and spectacular masques. James gave gifts and pensions to his favorites, most of them Scotsmen. At the reception of the Spanish embassy he gave away more plate than Elizabeth had in her whole reign. It could not continue; James must either retrench or increase his revenues.

Robert Cecil, the King's chief minister, did not push retrenchment with any vigor since he profited from the King's prodigality. As the treasury fell deeper into debt, the glories of Hatfield House rose in Hertfordshire. Since Cecil, whom James made Earl of Salisbury, dared not pursue retrenchment, he had to increase the King's revenues. This he did by various expedients, one of which was to increase custom duties. In 1608 he issued a new book of rates, by which duties on 1400 articles were increased from 30 to 40 percent, yielding an additional £70,000 a year. He could do this because judges in the Bates case in 1605 had ruled that the Crown might, in the exercise of its prerogative to regulate trade, increase custom duties. Salisbury, however, made no pretense that the Crown was regulating trade; the Book of Rates was palpably designed to raise revenue. These "impositions," as the additional duties were called, provoked a storm in Parliament in 1610 and 1614. If the King's claims were allowed, one M.P. cried out, "we are but tenants at his will of that which we have."

The fury of the House of Commons led James to dissolve Parliament, both in 1610 and 1614. That fury also helped cause the failure of the Great Contract in 1610, the one constructive effort made to modernize the King's finances. Salisbury proposed that the King surrender the right of wardship (the right to profit from the custody of tenants who were minors) and the right of purveyance (the right to purchase food at less than market prices) in return for a permanent annual grant of £200,000. The negotiations were nearing success when the quarrel over impositions and James's sudden demand for an immediate supply of £500,000 doomed them to failure. The King was now committed to raising his revenue by impositions, grants of monopolies, forced loans, and other projects of doubtful legality and certain unpopularity.

The illegality of these financial expedients raised two fundamental questions: Was the King bound by law? And who was to declare what those boundaries were? Though James defended the divine right of kings in his *The True Law of a Free Monarchy*, he never asserted that his powers were absolute. In 1610 he acknowledged that, he could not make law or collect subsidies without the consent of Parliament. The constitutional struggles of early Stuart England were not over sovereignty—that is, the location of supreme power, for most people regarded their government as a mixed government of King, Lords, and Commons in which there was no supreme power. The struggle was rather over the extent of the prerogative, a term more familiar to English ears than sovereignty. Prerogative was the sum of all the King's lawful powers, and the question that now arose was who should declare its extent.

The most obvious answer was the judges, who in 1610, for example, informed James that he could not use proclamations to make new law or introduce new penalties for violating old laws. James acquiesced in their judgment, but the burden placed on the judges only raised a further question: Should the judges, as Sir Francis Bacon urged, act as the King's good servants, or should they, as Sir Edward Coke urged, act independently of the King? Sir Francis Bacon, son of a Lord Keeper, was a man of great wit and learning, an essayist of genius, a propagandist of the new scientific method, and a scheming courtier who rose to be Lord Chancellor by his services to James. Sir Edward Coke, son of a Norfolk lawyer, was an irascible, prejudiced, and marvelously learned lawyer, who as Attorney General had furiously prosecuted Essex and Raleigh, and whom James named as Chief Justice of the Common Pleas in 1606. A year later, in 1607, Archbishop Bancroft complained to James that the Common law courts, by issuing "writs of prohibitions," took cases away from the ecclesiastical courts. He suggested that the King, as the fountain of justice, could withdraw cases from both jurisdictions and try them himself. James liked the suggestion and referred it to his judges. Coke replied that the King was not learned in the laws of England, that cases concerning life and property were not to be tried by his natural reason but by the artifical reason of his judges, who were learned in the law. The other judges unanimously followed Coke, and James never again sought to act as a judge himself.

But he did seek to influence the judges. In 1615 an obscure preacher by the name of Edmund Peacham was accused of treason for hinting (in notes for a sermon he never delivered) that James would be smitten with sudden death. James, who was so frightened that he thereafter slept every night barricaded behind feather beds, sought to consult separately with his judges about the case. Coke at first refused to answer, because the King might in this manner pressure the judges. Coke finally answered, but the next year, in a case concerning the King's right to grant licenses to hold pluralities, he resisted the King once more. James sought to delay the case in order to consult with the judges. Coke, on his knees before the King, refused to admit that the King might delay a case. James thereupon dismissed him from office, a severe blow to the independence of the judiciary.

Coke replied by securing election to the House of Commons in 1621, where he took up a cause that carried within it the seeds of a far deeper conflict. If the judges could not be trusted to declare the law rightly, then Parliament must do so. In 1610 and 1614 the House of Commons had condemned impositions as illegal. In 1621 it declared numerous patents of monopoly illegal. In 1624 Parliament even passed an Act of Monopolies, which forbade the King to grant a monopoly to a private individual. This act was the first instance in English history of Parliament legislating away a prerogative of the king.

GOVERNMENT BY COURT FAVORITES

To prodigality, a rather amiable vice, James added the vice of partiality to Court favorites. While Salisbury lived, which was until 1612, he held in check James's passion for Court favorites, but thereafter there was no restraint. James turned to Robert Carr, an athletic and handsome young Scotsman, whom he made Viscount Rochester and then Earl of Somerset and on whom he lavished lands and office. But Somerset soon fell from power, for it was discovered that his wife, the nymphomaniac Lady Essex, had poisoned Sir Thomas Overbury to prevent him from revealing information that would obstruct her divorce from the Earl of Essex and her marriage to Somerset.

Power and influence now fell to the Howard family, the Earls of Northampton and Suffolk, who carried corruption, which had increased during the last years of Elizabeth's reign, to new heights. They pilfered the treasury and sold offices and honors. But they were soon eclipsed by George Villiers, son of an obscure Leicestershire knight. Villiers had a tall and beautifully proportioned body, dark chestnut hair, an exquisitely curved mouth, and dark blue eyes. In France he had perfected his skill in dancing, music, dueling, and horesemanship. James first saw George Villiers in 1614 and immediately fell in love with him. Within a year he bestowed a knighthood upon him. In 1617 he created him Earl, in 1619 Marquis, and in 1623 Duke of Buckingham. He doted on him, flirted with him, kissed him, and embraced him in a manner that made James's homosexual proclivities obvious to his contemporaries. The King's kissing his favorites, wrote Sir Anthony Weldon, "in so lascivious a mode in public . . . promoted many to imagine some things done in the retiring house that exceed my expressions."

James's subjects were quite willing to overlook his sexual preferences, but they could not stomach the lavish distribution of wealth and honors to Villiers, his family, and his clients. Queen Elizabeth had used the power of patronage to weld Court and country together. She had won loyalty by rewarding service. James used the power of patronage to reward flatterers and favorites. A widening gulf arose between Court and country, with the nobility offended at their exclusion from office and the increasingly Puritan gentry and merchants outraged at scandals at Court.

More dangerous yet was James's reliance on the advice of Buckingham rather than the advise of his Privy Council. James allowed the Council to grow from nineteen members in 1610 to thirty-five in 1620, a quite unwieldly number. He also spurned its advice, declaring in 1618, when some councilors opposed him, that he would do as he saw fit "without following the advice of fools." That resolve led to a bitter confrontation with Parliament in 1621. Parliament met under the most inauspicious circumstances: The country suffered from economic depression, there was anger at the extravagance of the Court, and there was fury at the bloodsucking monopolists. The Court had granted some 700 monopolies to favorites. An English man or woman could not wash with soap or starch clothes or purchase a beaver hat or salt food or drink wine or buy playing cards or read the Bible without supporting a monopolist. Led by Sir Edward Coke, the House of Commons searched out the worst offenders and impeached them before the House of Lords. They likewise turned the medieval weapon of impeachment, which had lain dormant during Tudor years, against Sir Francis Bacon, ostensibly because he took bribes at the Court of Chancery, in fact because he had licensed so many monopolies. Bacon found little support in the House of Lords, since a group of "opposition lords" had emerged, a phenomenon unknown during Elizabeth's reign. The Lords found Bacon guilty of taking bribes, fined him, imprisoned him during the King's pleasure, and declared him incapable of holding office.

The King's troubles did not stop with the attack on the monopolists. The House of Commons also launched an attack on his foreign policy. In 1620 the Thirty Years War burst upon Europe, with Spain invading the lands of Frederick, Elector of the Palatinate, who in 1618 had been elected King of Bohemia. He quickly lost the Bohemian Crown and not long after the Palatinate. The English public rallied to his cause not only because he was a Protestant, but because he was the husband of James's daughter Elizabeth, beloved as "the Queen of Hearts." James, ever the pacifist, hoped to avoid going to war in his son-in-law's cause. By offering his son Prince Charles to the Spanish Infanta in marriage, he hoped to persuade Spain to restore Frederick's lands. It was a quixotic plan, which the House of Commons promptly spurned. The Commons wanted war against Spain, and when it met in the autumn of 1621, petitioned for such a war. James, who had appeared to want such a petition, suddenly reversed his position and told the Commons, as Elizabeth had before him, that it had no right to discuss high matters of state. This provoked the Commons to draw up the Protestation of 1621, in which it declared that religion and foreign policy were proper subjects for debate in Parliament. James replied by dissolving Parliament and by ripping the offending protestation from the journals of the House of Commons with his own hand.

James was able to dissolve Parliament because he had found in Lionel

Cranfield, a London merchant, a financier of genius. By retrenching expenses and by managing the revenues more efficiently, Cranfield restored solvency to the Crown. Yet within three years the courtiers, led by Buckingham, impeached Cranfield (now Earl of Middlesex) and drove him from office. Middlesex's fault in Buckingham's eyes was his opposition to a war with Spain, a war which the Duke now desired. It was an astonishing reversal in the Duke's foreign policy, for only the year before he and Prince Charles had embarked on a romantic expedition to Madrid to woo the Infanta. Buckingham believed he could recover the Palatinate by negotiating a Spanish marriage, even though Philip IV of Spain would never have compelled his cousin, the Emperor, to restore the Palatinate to Frederick, whom both Philip and the Emperor regarded as an heretic. In fact the Emperor soon granted Frederick's lands to Maximilian of Bavaria, a Catholic. Buckingham and Charles returned from Spain in October 1623, seething with rage and resolved on a war against Spain. Buckingham quickly formed an alliance with the leaders of the opposition in Parliament and bullied James into asking the House of Commons whether he should break off relations with Spain. James thus conceded to Parliament the very right to discuss foreign policy he had denied it in 1621.

Because Middlesex opposed a war that would destroy all his efforts at economy, Buckingham and Charles engineered his impeachment, which led James, now old and ill but still shrewd, to tell them that they would live to have a "bellyfull" of impeachments themselves. Parliament enthusiastically embraced the war against Spain, but voted only enough money to wage it at sea, an odd way to recover lands in central Europe. Furthermore, they voted that the money be used only for the war, and they named the treasurers who were to spend it. In 1624 the Duke and the Prince taught Parliament to discuss foreign policy, to control expenditures, and to impeach ministers, a curious end to ten years of government by Court favorites.

CHARLES I AND THE ARTS

At the death of James I in March 1625, Prince Charles, a young man of 25, came to the throne. Charles had a Scots accent, a falsetto voice, and a stammer that caused him to keep acquaintances at a distance. He was a nervous, shy man, with perfect manners, a gentle disposition, great dignity, and an exact sense of duty. He proved to be a dutiful husband, a good father, and a disastrous king. He lacked the common touch that would have allowed him to communicate with his subjects, and he had none of his father's shrewd intelligence. Though he displayed a great devotion to principles, those principles were narrow, just as his sense of honor was self-regarding. He had all the obstinacy of a weak man and a pronounced distaste for compromise. His high concept of the nature of kingship separated him from even his closest advisers. It was his tragedy to seek to enforce those high prerogative notions his father had merely

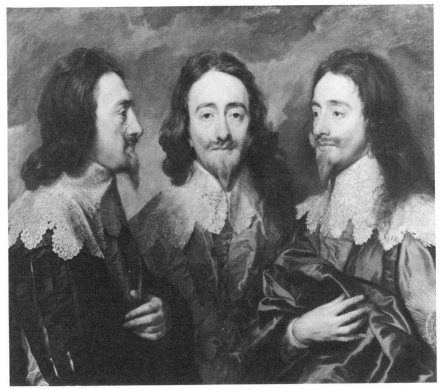

Charles I in Three Positions, by Sir Anthony Van Dyke (*Her Majesty the Queen, Copyright Reserved*).

talked about. He did so conscientiously rather than forcefully, sadly rather than with exuberance. He was, wrote William Laud, "a mild and gracious prince who knew not how to be, or be made, great." The sadness was written on his face. When the sculptor Bernini saw Van Dyck's portrait of Charles, painted in 1637, he remarked, "Never have I beheld a countenance more unfortunate."

Though Charles was unfit to be a king, he would have made a splendid director of an art gallery. He showed superb taste and intelligence in purchasing the paintings of the great Italian masters, of Titian, Tintoretto, Mantegna, and Raphael. He showed equal judgment in commissioning works from the Flemish artists Anthony Van Dyke and Peter Paul Rubens. Van Dyck propagated the cause of absolutism with his flattering, idealistic portraits of Charles, the Queen, and their Court, while Rubens' sketches for the ceiling of the Banqueting Hall represented the apotheosis of monarchy. The new florid style differed markedly from the delicate realism of the miniaturists, who continued to paint the portraits of the nobility and gentry of England. In architecture there occurred an even more marked divorce between Court and country. As their architect, James and Charles employed Inigo Jones, a Londoner who

The Queen's House, Greenwich, built by Inigo Jones for Henrietta Maria (*Country Life*).

enjoyed the patronage of the Earl of Arundel and who learned the pure classical style of Palladio while studying in Italy. Jones built the Queen's House at Greenwich and the Banqueting Hall at Whitehall in an uncompromising classical style—bold, perfectly proportioned, refined, and elegant. He made no concession to the hybrid style called "King Jamie's Gothic," which can be seen at its best in the Earl of Salisbury's Hatfield House. It was this hybrid style, however, this mixture of Gothic and Renaissance elements, and not Inigo Jones's work, that dominated English architecture for the next generation.

Inigo Jones might have built more buildings had Charles not employed him in devising masques for the delight of the Court. A masque was a short, allegorical, dramatic entertainment, with elaborate scenery and costumes. Both Charles and Henrietta Maria occasionally took part in them. In the 1630s many composers concentrated on writing music for the masques at Court, while the madrigalists continued to write for a gentry who preferred simple singing to the ornate, ceremonial masque. The masque had a harmful effect on the theater. To please the tastes of a Carr or a Villiers, Ben Jonson, the greatest of Jacobean dramatists, devoted his efforts to the preparation of elaborate masques, and drama degenerated into spectacle. Even before the emergence of the masque, the theater, which in the time of Shakespeare had portrayed noble men in tragic circumstances, had turned to the bawdy and the horrific, to satire and melodrama. In *The Alchemist*, for example, Ben Jonson satirizes Sir Epicure Mammon, a newly enriched gentleman, and Tribulation Wholesome, a hypocritical Puritan. Playwrights ceased to grapple with moral questions and devoted themselves to amusing sophisticated courtiers with lewd comedies, which sneered at moral virtues. They thereby delighted the courtiers but angered the Puritans, who when they gained power in 1642 closed down the theaters.

The noble themes and moral issues the theater ignored found a home in poetry. The Jacobean age was one of tension, tension between contending faiths, between the new and the traditional, between Gothic and Renaissance

Hatfield House, built for Robert Cecil, Earl of Salisbury, when he was James I's chief minister (*Country Life*).

art. It was also an age passionately interested in exploring distant worlds and new ideas. All of this found expression in a metaphysical poetry marked by paradoxes, sharp antitheses, bizarre words, and strange metaphors. The greatest of the metaphysical poets was John Donne, Dean of St. Paul's, who had begun life as a Catholic and a lawyer. No metaphor was too extravagant for his passionate imagination. Thus he opens one of his finest poems:

> Go and catch a falling star,
> Get with child a mandrake root,
> Tell me where all past years are,
> Or who cleft the Devil's foot,
> Teach me to hear Mermaids singing,
> Or to keep off envy's stinging.

In the writing of prose the same tensions and richness of imagination can be found in works such as Robert Burton's *Anatomy of Melancholy*. Yet the most remarkable writer of the age, Sir Francis Bacon, took a different path. He published in 1597, 1612, and 1625, collections of essays modeled on those of Montaigne in France and characterized by a perfectly balanced, lucid, economical prose. Yet Bacon's work probably had less influence on his age than Sir Walter Raleigh's *History of the World*, published in 1614. Raleigh taught a generation of English men and women, especially the Puritans, not to look backward to a golden age, not to regard kings as particularly favored by God, but to look forward and to use the power of the state to promote God's cause and England's. Three years before the publication of Raleigh's *History* the King James Version of the Bible appeared, the most influential book ever published in England. It drew on the English language at a time when it had reached a zenith of vigor and richness, and it taught that language to three centuries of readers. At the same moment Shakespeare retired from playwriting. The two events marked the end of the Elizabethan age in literature and of the national unity which that literature reflected.

CHARLES I AND PARLIAMENT

The key to the first three years of Charles's reign was the complete ascendancy of the Duke of Buckingham. As powerful as the Duke was under James, he was even more powerful under Charles. And he again misused that power. He sent an army under Count Mansfeld to recover the Palatinate, but it landed in the dead of winter on the Island of Walcheren, with no money and few rations, and was soon wiped out by disease and starvation. He negotiated Charles's marriage to a French princess, Henrietta Maria, but—in violation of Charles's earlier promise—made the suspension of the penal laws against Catholics part of the treaty. He compounded this fault by sending ships to help France suppress the Protestants at La Rochelle. As a result he was quite unable to manage the King's first Parliament, which met in 1625. Angered at the failure of Mansfeld's expedition and alarmed at the marriage treaty, the Commons voted only two subsidies (worth about £140,000) for the war. Even more, when Charles became King they voted the customs duties for only one year—not, as was customary, for life. They wanted to settle the matter of impositions first. The Lords rejected the bill as injurious to the Crown, with the result that no bill passed. There was no time for compromise, because Charles dissolved Parliament the moment he heard that Coke and others intended to attack Buckingham himself.

During the next year a favorite who enjoyed supreme power found that he could not evade supreme responsibility. Only a brilliant success in diplomacy and war could vindicate Buckingham in Parliament's eyes. Instead he stumbled from one folly to the next. An expedition sent to Cadiz to intercept the Spanish treasure fleet was a disaster—the ships were decayed, the provisions inedible, the sailors cowardly, and the soldiers drunk. Buckingham then allowed a series of petty quarrels with France to lead to a declaration of war against that powerful kingdom, even though England was still at war with Spain. Little wonder that the House of Commons refused further taxes and voted an impeachment against Buckingham. It accused him of monopolizing offices, of accepting exorbitant gifts, of neglect of duty, of mismanagement. Since few if any of these faults were crimes, Charles would have been wise to allow the impeachment to come to a trial before the Lords. But fearing the revelations a trial might elicit, he chose a different strategy. He claimed full responsibility for all the Duke's actions, thus challenging the legal principle that the King can do no wrong, a principle that placed responsibility for all decisions on the King's ministers, not on the King. To save the Duke from a trial before the Lords, Charles dissolved Parliament, even though it meant losing four subsidies. Buckingham's impeachment was the first step on a path that led to the establishment of the responsibility of ministers to Parliament.

Denied the four subsidies he sought, Charles resolved to collect a forced loan. He did so with unprecedented ruthlessness, dismissing Chief Justice Crew for refusing to declare the loan legal and imprisoning seventy-six persons who refused to pay it. Five of these, all of them knights, sued out a writ of habeas corpus, demanding to know for what cause they were imprisoned. The Court of King's Bench replied that the King had a right to imprison men without stating a reason, and returned the five knights to prison. The war against France led to other grievous measures. Throughout southern England the troops intended for France were billeted on ordinary families and martial law introduced to discipline the recently impressed, ill-paid, starving troops. Thus, in the minds of the people martial law became associated with the forced loan, and both with arbitrary government.

The £236,000 raised by the forced loan was quite inadequate to wage war against France, a war Buckingham once again bungled. In 1628 financial exhaustion forced Charles to meet a new Parliament, twenty-seven of whose members had been among the seventy-six imprisoned for refusing the loan. The House of Commons did not waste its time impeaching Buckingham but went straight to the matter of defining the law. It drew up a Petition of Right which declared that no man hereafter shall be compelled to pay any tax, gift, loan, or benevolence not voted by Parliament; that no free man shall be kept in prison without cause being shown; that soldiers and sailors shall not be billeted on men without their consent; and that civilians shall not be subjected to martial law. The House of Lords sought to add a clause saving that "sovereign power wherewith your Majesty is entrusted for the protection, safety, and happiness of your people." Coke, speaking in the Commons, objected: "I know that prerogative is part of the law, but 'sovereign power' is no parliamentary word." The Lords gave way and accepted the petition without a saving clause. Charles then tried to shuffle off the petition by not giving his consent in a legal form, but the Commons insisted upon and finally secured his full legal consent.

The Petition of Right was a major triumph for the cause of liberty. In medieval England a "liberty" had a geographical connotation; it was an area governed by a great abbot or an earl palatine, into which the sheriff might not enter. It was the signal achievement of the English to turn the medieval idea of a private liberty, of a particular franchise, into the modern ideal of a public liberty enjoyed by all. A liberty became a general right that the government must not invade. The law which defined this right circumscribed the government. By

1603 the English began to speak of a "fundamental law" that was a check on arbitrary government, though they were unclear what this fundamental law was. It was not the Common law, though Coke on occasion referred to the Common law as "fundamental" and identified it with the laws of nature. Yet Coke acknowledged that Parliament by statute could change the Common law. It would be closer to the truth to say that by fundamental law the English meant that part of the Common law that was identical with the laws of God and the laws of nature.

In the seventeenth century morality and law were still fused together; the law recognized actions that were evil because prohibited and actions that were evil in themselves. Antiquity as well as morality gave sanction to the law. Indeed, the Common lawyers pleaded precedent more often than morality, and appealed to the ancient laws of England more often than to the laws of God and nature. The historical sense of the Common lawyers was naive by nineteenth-century standards: they did not recognize change through time. They believed in an ancient constitution that went back before the Norman Conquest, to time immemorial, when people were wiser and better. Coke, for example, traced Parliament back to the time of King Arthur. In truth, there was no clear idea of the fundamental law; it was a confusion of the Common law, moral law, and the immemorial laws of England. There were only two certain truths: Parliament, as the highest court in the land, had the authority to declare what the law was, and the King was beneath the law.

Having condemned arbitrary government, the Commons went on to attack incompetent government. It drew up an inflammatory Remonstrance calling for Buckingham's dismissal. Charles at once dismissed Parliament to save his favorite, but he could not prevent John Felton, a Suffolk gentleman brooding over the state of the realm and over the Duke's refusal to grant him a captaincy, from driving a dagger into the Duke's heart. Charles, momentarily grief-stricken, resolved to carry on Buckingham's policies, which meant meeting Parliament once again in 1629. The session came quickly to grief over two divisive issues: the continued collection of tunnage and poundage, and the promotion of Arminian clergymen who preached high prerogative notions.

Charles did not believe that the Petition of Right prohibited him from collecting tunnage and poundage (the custom's duties on a tun* of wine and a pound of merchandise). He therefore continued to collect them, and threw into prison merchants who refused to pay. He also refused to allow any condemnation of a clergyman by the House of Commons to hinder his advancement. In 1628 he named Richard Montagu Bishop of Chichester, even though the Commons in 1625 had condemned Montagu for publishing Arminian views. Dr. Arminius was a Dutch theologian who held that man by his own free will could

---

* A tun, or barrel, equalled 252 gallons.

help determine the destination of his soul, a view deeply offensive to the Calvinists. Those who held this view were branded as Arminians. Charles also gave a handsome benefice to Roger Manwaring, who had incurred an impeachment in 1628 for preaching that it was an offense against the law of God to refuse to pay the forced loan. When the Commons in 1629 came to the aid of the merchants who had refused to pay tunnage and poundage, Charles decided to dissolve Parliament. To delay the dissolution, members of the House forcefully held the Speaker in the chair while the House voted three bold resolutions: anyone paying tunnage and poundage, anyone advising its collection, and anyone introducing innovations in religion was "a capital enemy to this kingdom and commonwealth." This revolutionary scene enacted, they released the Speaker and went home.

THE ELEVEN YEARS OF PREROGATIVE GOVERNMENT

The turbulence of the House of Commons in 1629 persuaded Charles to govern without Parliament. To do this he must take one of two paths: either make himself an absolute king and rule through a standing army and a professional bureaucracy—as Richelieu was showing the King of France how to do—or rule within the letter of the law, exploiting every ancient and ambiguous power of the Crown. Possessing no standing army or professional bureaucracy, Charles chose the latter path. The success of his endeavor, therefore, depended entirely upon his success in reducing the costs of government and increasing the revenues of the Crown.

The economies Lord Treasurer Weston ordered did much to reduce expenses, but not nearly so much as the abandonment of Buckingham's war policies. In 1629 England made peace with France, and in 1630 with Spain. During the next decade, as Gustavus Adolphus of Sweden marched into Germany to save Protestantism and as the Dutch resumed their struggle for independence, Charles stood by, a neutral. His policy was not popular with his subjects. England "never throve so well," said Coke, "as when at war with Spain." Royal policy was even less popular when it became known that Charles, under the mask of neutrality, was aiding the Spanish. Every year from 1630 onward Spain, which found it difficult to run the Franco-Dutch blockade in the Channel, sent its gold and silver to Plymouth. Charles then reshipped it through Dover to the Spanish Netherlands, where the money was used to pay a Catholic army to destroy Dutch Protestantism.

On the other side of the ledger was an increase in the revenues of the Crown. Lord Treasurer Weston and Attorney General Noy proved infinitely fertile in expedients. They raised £150,000 in two years by fining landowners worth £40 a year or more who had failed to apply for the honor of knighthood. They revived obsolete medieval forest laws and fined those who had cut timber and cleared wastes on what had once been royal forests. A Commission on De-population fined those who enclosed fields. A new Book of Rates increased the customs duties, which were collected even though never voted by Parliament. The government fined the City of London £70,000 for a technical infraction of its charter—colonizing Londonderry in Ireland. And Lord Treasurer Weston found an excuse for reviving the sale of monopolies. In order to satisfy the Merchant Adventurers, Parliament had exempted companies from the 1624 act forbidding the grant of monopolies. The Crown therefore now granted monop-olies to companies established for the production of alum, soap, coal, salt, and bricks. By the end of the 1630s the government collected nearly £100,000 a year from monopolies, and court favorites a like amount. The poor paid for this through higher prices, which gives the lie to any talk of Stuart paternalism. Charles and his ministers never helped the lower classes; even their attempts to restrain enclosure seem designed more to raise fines from the gentry than to help the tenants. The Earl of Worcester had no difficulty obtaining permission to enclose Wentwood Chase in return for a loan to the King.

All the financial expedients before 1635—with the possible exception of impositions—were legal. In that year, the government extended to the whole kingdom the traditional right to demand ships, or the money to purchase ships, from the seaports. Both Elizabeth and James had collected ship money from the ports, and there might even have existed a medieval precedent for collect-ing it from inland towns, but there existed no precedent whatever for collecting it year after year from inland towns, as Charles did. The tax was equitably assessed, efficiently collected, and properly spent on the navy, but the funda-mental issue was political, not technical. If the King could on his own authority establish an annual non-Parliamentary tax, then the central constitutional issue of the age would be decided in favor of the Crown. A wealthy Buckinghamshire gentleman, John Hampden, therefore refused to pay the 20 shillings assessed on his lands at Stoke Mandeville.

His case came before the twelve Common law judges in the Exchequer Chamber in 1637. The attorney general declared that in an emergency the pre-rogative could not be bound by law and that it was for the King to decide when an emergency existed. John Hampden's attorney, the brilliant Oliver St. John, replied that the prerogative is at all times bound by the law, otherwise an En-glishman's life and property were not secure. The judges ruled in favor of the King by the narrowest margin, seven to five, with Chief Justice Finch calling the English monarch "absolute" and declaring that all acts of Parliament were void which restrained the King's power "to command his subjects, their per-sons and goods." When the Venetian ambassador heard the verdict, he de-clared that this meant royal absolutism and the end of Parliament in England.

The widening gulf between the Court and the country could also be seen in religion. Charles was the first monarch raised from birth in the English Church, and its devotions had a singular appeal to him. His artistic tastes led him to admire the beauty of its ceremonies, and his love of order led him to despise the rantings of the Puritans. From the moment he ascended the throne Charles identified himself with the Arminians—those clergymen who favored ritual and ceremony, who entertained ideas of free will, and who defended the prerogative. But it was not until 1633 that he could name the ablest of these clergymen, William Laud, as Archbishop of Canterbury. Laud, the son of a master tailor in Reading, rose rapidly in the Church through his scholarship and administrative skill. He was a small, blunt, honest, ruthless man, who as Chancellor of Oxford University had driven out the Puritans and established the "beauty of holiness." He now sought to do the same throughout the realm. Using all the authority at his command, he enforced the wearing of vestments and the performance of rituals. The altar should stand in the east end of the Church, protected by an altar rail, not in the middle of the church, where parishioners could leave their hats on it. Priests should wear vestments, have candles on the altar, and bow at the name of Jesus. All this was anathema to the Puritans, though not as horrid as the idolatrous practice of placing statues of the Virgin Mary in some churches.

Laud not only enforced ceremonies on the Church, he suppressed preaching. A group of Puritans—merchants and gentlemen—had bought up the tithes and patronage rights of many parishes in England. They then appointed fervent Puritan ministers to these livings. Using the power of Star Chamber, Laud dissolved their organization and suppressed their activities. He also declared war on Puritans who maintained "lecturers" in the churches of England. In many places a town corporation or a private individual would appoint and pay lecturers to preach on a Sunday afternoon as a supplement to the preaching—if any—of the parish priest. Since the lecturers were usually Puritans, Laud sought to suppress them. Laud's vigorous use of the Court of High Commission and the Court of Star Chamber brought both into disrepute. It also aroused the anticlericalism of the English, for these courts were used to chastise noblemen for immorality, degrade knights for libeling bishops, and rebuke chief justices for being lenient on Puritans. It did not make the laity any happier to see four bishops sitting on the Privy Council.

Closely allied to anticlericalism was antipopery, and the Queen's party at Court exacerbated that sentiment. The Queen did not shape policy, but she did set the fashion at Court—and that fashion centered on Rome. Papal envoys moved freely at Court, priests celebrated mass daily, and several fashionable ladies converted to Catholicism. The gulf between Court and country grew wider and wider, a gulf tangibly symbolized by Charles's proclamation in 1632 ordering all gentlemen without a London house to remain in the country. One gentleman who came up to London anyway was fined £1000.

Though politically unpopular, Charles's policies were financially a success. The Crown was able to collect over £400,000 a year, an income adequate to meet normal expenditures. By 1636 Charles had obtained nearly £200,000 from ship money. By 1638 he was nearly out of debt, and the Crown jewels were taken out of pawn.

ECONOMIC DEPRESSION

The King's subjects did not share in this prosperity, for the 1620s and 1630s were a period of chronic economic depression. Early in James's reign it appeared that prosperity would prevail, for the Anglo-Spanish treaty of 1604 and the Truce of 1609 in the Netherlands brought a boom in trade. By 1614 the export of cloth was a fourth greater than in 1600, and cloth sent to northern Europe made up 90 percent of English exports. Then James I suddenly embraced the plan of Sir William Cockayne to export only dyed and finished cloth. In July 1614 James forbade the Merchant Adventurers to export unfinished cloth, and granted to the King's Merchant Adventurers, a new company formed by Cockayne and other merchants, the sole right to export finished cloth. The project seemed reasonable, for the dyeing of cloth made up 47 percent of its cost and fulling 5 percent. Why should the Dutch rather than the English profit from these processes? Unfortunately for the English cloth industry, Cockayne and his friends did not have the capital or the technical skill to dye and dress cloth. Their true purpose was merely to wrest the monopoly of exporting cloth away from the Merchant Adventurers, and James had listened to them only because they promised him £300,000 a year from their profits. The Dutch immediately retaliated by refusing to receive dressed and dyed cloths. Unable to sell abroad, the new company ceased to buy at home. There were 500 bankruptcies reported among clothiers and soon the unemployed weavers in Wiltshire and Gloucestershire rioted. By 1617 the King's Adventurers admitted their failure and were dissolved. James restored to the Merchant Adventurers their monopoly of the export of cloth. But the damage had been done; in three years exports had fallen by a third.

After a brief recovery in 1618, a still deeper crisis overwhelmed the cloth industry in the 1620s. The immediate cause was an outburst of currency manipulation by local princes in Germany and eastern Europe. By debasing their currencies, they made imports more expensive and so priced English cloth out of the market. In the Baltic the export of English cloth fell by two-thirds between 1618 and 1622. By 1624 the monetary confusion came to an end, but then the disruptive effect of the Thirty Years' War began to be felt. Even more harmful was the competition of the Dutch. Expensive English cloth could not compete with the lighter, cheaper Dutch cloth. Between 1606 and 1640 the number of pieces of woolen cloth exported from London fell from 120,000 to 45,000. Adding to the distress was a series of bad harvests in the 1620s and 1630s that drove people to spend their meager incomes on high-priced grain, not on cloth or other manufactures.

The depression did not hit everyone with equal force. The coal industry continued its spectacular advance. By 1640 England produced three times as much coal as all Europe. The growth of the coal trade meant an increase in coastal shipping, since sea transport, which was twenty times cheaper than wheeled transport, carried most of the coal. During the first twenty years of

James's reign the merchant marine grew as rapidly as during the last twenty years of Elizabeth's. Hardest hit, of course, was England's largest industry, the woolen cloth industry. "Where the clothiers do dwell or have dwelt," reported a contemporary, "there are found the greatest number of the poor." Wages in the cloth industry were low, but unemployment was a greater scourge. The western counties, where the Old Draperies had their roots, were particularly hard hit. The Old Draperies were heavy cloths, made of short-fibres, that looked much like a modern blanket. They now gave way to the New Draperies, a worsted product, much lighter, in which the weave could be seen in the finished fabric. The New Draperies throve in East Anglia, where the wealth of Norwich led James Harrington to call it "another Utopia."

An increasing polarization of society also occurred, with the rich growing richer and the poor poorer. Between 1600 and 1640 the population increased by 25 percent, creating an inflation from which men of land and trade profited. But those dependent on wages grew poorer. The real earnings of a laborer born in 1580 were only half the real earnings of his great-grandfather. The average industrial wage was hardly enough to maintain life, with the result that children had to be sent to work. In the second decade of James's reign the purchasing power of building craftsmen and agricultural workers reached the lowest point in the whole of recorded history (which extends from 1300 to the present). The opulent country homes and the exquisite college quadrangles that the Jacobeans built rested on the sweat of impoverished, exploited workers.

Pressed by the petitions of private traders and by the alarm expressed in Parliament, the government in 1622 named a commission of three commercial and financial experts to inquire into the causes of the depression. One of them, Edward Misselden, argued that the chief cause was the "want of money" and that this want of money arose from the fact that English coin was undervalued in relation to foreign currencies. Being undervalued, foreign merchants purchased it, thereby creating a substantial drain of English coin to the Continent. A second member of the commission, Gerard Malynes, agreed that the flow of English coin out of the country was the cause of its troubles, but believed that the drain was a result of speculation by foreign bankers. It remained for the third member of the commission, Thomas Mun, to see that it was not the undervaluation of English coin or speculation by foreign bankers that caused the drain on English coinage: it was an adverse balance of trade. He wrote:

> For it is a certain rule that in those countries beyond the seas which send us more of their wares in value than we carry unto them of commodities, there our monies are undervalued in exchange, and in other countries where the contrary is performed, there our money is overvalued.

Lionel Cranfield, in his practical manner, had long come to the same conclusion. "Trade is as great as ever," he told the Commons in 1621, "but not so good. It increases inwards and decreases outwards." The facts supported his contention. In 1621 imports into England were higher than during the years of prosperity before 1614, but the export of cloth had fallen well below average. Thomas Mun's brilliant memorandum was a landmark in English economic thought, for it laid the basis of mercantilist economic theory. But the government wanted practical proposals, not theories. Thomas Mun's advice to secure a favorable balance of trade was hardly more useful than Malynes's and Misselden's advice to regulate the rate of exchange. The government clearly did not have the mechanism to regulate the rate of exchange, but did it have the power to secure a favorable balance of trade?

THE EXPANSION OF ENGLAND

Among their recommendations Malynes, Misselden, and Mun urged that the government protect and encourage the colonial trade, the fishing industry, and the merchant marine. They urged, in short, diversification. In the course of the next eighty years this diversification turned an adverse balance of trade into a favorable one, but progress was slow and, under the early Stuarts, owed little to government. Yet a beginning was made, largely by private enterprise, in three directions—in the development of the Mediterranean and East Indian trades, in the exploitation of the Newfoundland fisheries, and in the planting of colonies.

The Jacobeans firmly established that trade with the Mediterranean which the Elizabethans had begun. Many factors explained their success: the decline of Venice; the vulnerability of the Dutch flyboat in distant, pirate-infested waters; the attractiveness of the New Draperies which drove out the expensive Italian textiles; and the market for herring, which became England's chief export to Italy. The Mediterranean was the first region in Europe where English ships captured a significant share of the local trade. Ships of the Levant Company were often away for a year or more, selling from port to port. The large amounts of capital such voyages required were the reason for the company's high entrance fees, exclusiveness, and monopolistic practices.

The entrance fee for admission to the East India Company, £50, was also high, but the returns from the first voyages justified it. The first four ships, sent out in 1601, brought back a million pounds of pepper and spices, and returned the investors 95 percent. But the infant company was harassed by difficulties. It had too little capital and unsuitable ships. The demand for European goods in India was slight and the market for pepper in Europe was unstable. The Dutch, who sent out sixty-five ships in 1601, provided stiff competition. But the English company persevered. The high returns on the early voyages made it easier to attract capital, and the company itself built the ships it needed. It broadened its trade to include indigo and calicoes as well as pepper, paying for these goods with bullion it got by reexporting spices, indigo, and calicoes to Europe. It also engaged in a port-to-port trade in Asia and established trading posts, or "factories," at Surat in 1612 and Ormuz in 1622. In 1623 the Dutch massacred all the English traders at Amboyna in the Spice Islands, but the practical English nevertheless reached a modus vivendi with the Dutch: The Dutch could have the Spice Islands, the English would concentrate on India. In all these endeavors the Crown gave the company little help. Indeed, in 1604, in 1617, and again in 1635, James and Charles, in violation of the charter of the East India Company, licensed rival traders to India.

For the training of seamen, Newfoundland, "the India to the west of England," was far more important than India. In 1615 the Newfoundland fisheries employed 5,000 men and 250 ships; by 1640 they employed 10,000 men and 450 ships. A multilateral trade centering on Plymouth arose, in which merchants imported salt from Spain, sent fishing fleets out to Newfoundland, sold the salted fish in Spain and the Mediterranean, and bought wine, sugar, and salt in return. Newfoundland conformed more closely to the principles of mercantilism than did any other trade. Yet all attempts to colonize Newfoundland were a failure. The weather was too wretched, the fishermen too hostile, and the Crown too unreliable. In 1637 six small settlements forfeited their charters when Charles I granted the whole island to the Duke of Hamilton and Sir David Kirke, neither of whom had made any effort to colonize it.

More successful was the colonizing of Ulster with Scottish and English settlers. In 1607 the earls of Tyrone and Tyrconnel, fearing for their safety, fled abroad. Their lands were seized by the government, which then found excuses for confiscating the lands of other chiefs and their tenants. By 1609 the Crown had seized all six counties of modern Ulster. The land was then divided into parcels of 1000, 1500, and 2000 acres and leased to English and Scottish "undertakers," persons who would undertake to plant their lands with English and Scottish settlers. This proved so difficult that the undertakers often ignored the stipulation that they bring in only English and Scottish tenants, with the result that many Irish remained as tenants on land they once owned. Yet many Scottish Presbyterians did come, seeking freedom for their religion. The city of London also planted English settlers in the northern half of the County of Derry, henceforth known as Londonderry. By 1629 there were 13,000 English and Scottish families in Ulster, cultivating the best land and living side by side with the Irish who had been despoiled of their land. Thus was created the problem of Ulster, which has found no solution to this day.

The resolution to plant settlers in Ulster was taken at Whitehall; the resolution to plant colonists in Virginia was taken in a low-ceilinged, paneled room in Sir Thomas Smith's house in Philpott Lane. Sir Thomas Smith was Treasurer of a syndicate of London merchants who formed a joint-stock company to colonize Virginia. They obtained a charter from the King, raised capital from tradesmen, merchants, bishops, and great lords, and sent out three vessels and 144 men in 1607. Their hope was for a quick profit, comparable to that gained by the East India Company. Like the Elizabethans, they hoped to find gold and silver and new trade routes, but they were far more conscious of the need to grow commodities in the New World, such as timber and hemp and silk, that would prevent the loss of bullion now spent to purchase them from others.

The first colonists, mostly adventurers, wasted their time treasure hunting, with the result that half of them died during the first winter. When their distress became known in England, an unexpected wave of enthusiasm for the colony swept the country. For the first time the idea of colonization, as opposed to treasure hunting and the discovery of trade routes, seized the English people. Offers of capital and personal service flowed in, allowing the company to send out 500 settlers in 1609. But disaster struck again, for they were sent out with insufficient food and found the earlier colonists starving. The winter of 1609–10 was the "starving time," with the famished colonists eating the bodies of the dead, even killing the living for food. It was "a miserie, a ruin, a death, a hell," said one of the sixty survivors.

There were three principal reasons for the disaster: The company failed to send a year's supply of food with each colonist; it clung to the common ownership of land; and it found no commodity worth exporting to England. After 1610 it remedied these faults. It sent out sufficient supplies, gave 50 acres to every person who went to Virginia, and discovered tobacco. In 1612 John Rolfe (who married Pocahontas) experimented with the growing of tobacco and sent his new product to London. It sold immediately, and within a decade tobacco became a valued money crop. Its cultivation became the labor of black slaves, who were brought into the colony from 1619 onward. By 1635 Virginia had 5,000 inhabitants and a secure economic base, but the company that founded it, having invested £300,000 in the venture, became insolvent in 1623. In 1624 James confiscated its charter and Virginia became a Crown colony.

In 1608 a congregation of Puritan separatists, desiring to escape Archbishop Bancroft's persecution, left Scrooby Manor, Nottinghamshire, for Leiden in Holland. By 1620, however, they feared that they were losing their English identity and sought some place in the New World for the liberty they desired. From the Virginia Company they secured a patent to settle on the northern side of the Delaware Bay and from a syndicate of London financiers they got the capital to sail to America. It was an alliance of profit and piety, as the complement of the *Mayflower* reflected—the ship carried 35 pilgrims and 66 adventurers to Cape Cod, where it inadvertently made landfall in November 1620. Within five months, 50 of the 101 were dead. Yet none of the colonists chose to return to England, even though the system of communal ownership was not given up until 1623. Plymouth Colony thereafter survived on farming and fur-trading. In 1637 there were fewer than 600 colonists.

The great migration of Puritans to New England occurred after 1629 and centered on Massachusetts Bay. In March 1629 the Privy Council granted a charter to the Massachusetts Bay Company to settle the lands between the Charles and Merrimac rivers. The company was ostensibly secular in its aims, but a majority were Puritans like John Winthrop, who led the first emigrants. Winthrop was a Suffolk squire, a man of legal training and cool temperament, who had lost his office as attorney for the court of wards because of his Puritan convictions. "Evil times are coming," he wrote in 1629, "when the church must fly to the wilderness." In the summer of 1629 he arrived in Salem, with eleven ships and 900 settlers. Though 200 died the first winter and as many returned home, many others came during the next decade—driven by hunger for land, bad harvests, economic distress, and Archbishop Laud's persecution. All the stockholders of the company emigrated to Massachusetts Bay, where they surrendered the government of the colony to an oligarchy of the members of the separatist churches. That oligarchy immediately established a religious tyranny as harsh as, and more efficient than, Laud's in England. It was to establish a purer church, not religious liberty, that the Puritans came to New England.

To escape Puritan intolerance Roger Williams, a Salem clergyman, founded a colony in Rhode Island. At the same time, the Puritan peer Lord Brooke established a colony at Connecticut. One colony was not Puritan. In 1632 Lord Baltimore, a Roman Catholic who had once served James as Secretary of State, gained from Charles I a charter to settle the northern part of Virginia. There he established a colony based on religious toleration and an English manorial social structure. Between 1629 and 1642 some 60,000 Englishmen came to the New World, about half of them to the Puritan colonies. They were too few to have any impact on the English economy, but they were enough to begin one of the most remarkable transformations in modern history. In 1603 the English-speaking peoples of the world numbered about 4 million; today they number nearly 300 million.

FURTHER READING

*J.P. KENYON. *Stuart England.* Penguin Books, 1978. A narrative of political events written with verve and boldness of judgment; marred by its unqualified revisionist view of early Stuart parliaments and its neglect of social and economic history.

*BRIAN COWARD. *The Stuart Age.* London, 1981. Focuses on politics and religion, but also discusses economic, social, and cultural developments; less a narrative of events than a guide to the changing views of historians on these events.

*CONRAD RUSSELL. *Parliaments and English Politics 1621–1629.* Oxford, 1979. An important revisionist study that argues that consensus, not conflict, characterized the 1620s; for the traditional story see Perez Zagorin, *Court and Country* (New York, 1970).

PAULINE GREGG. *Charles I.* London, 1981. The best life yet written; does not conceal Charles's weaknesses but neither does it dismiss him as a knave or a fool.

J.G.A. POCOCK. *The Ancient Constitution and the Feudal Law.* Cambridge, England, 1957. A study of the common-lawyer's belief in an immemorial constitution and of the scholar's discovery of feudalism.

WILLIAM HALLER. *The Rise of Puritanism.* New York, 1938. A history of puritanism from 1570 to 1643 as seen through its popular literature; argues that the Puritans by their preaching gained a hold on the middle and lower orders of society.

*G.E. MINGAY. *The Gentry: The Rise and Fall of a Ruling Class.* New York, 1976. Traces the gentry from their beginnings in the late Middle Ages to their decline in the nineteenth century; better on their role as landlords than on their role as a political elite.

CHARLES WILSON. *England's Apprenticeship 1603–1763*. New York, 1965. An authoritative, pleasantly written economic history that surveys agrarian, industrial, commercial, and financial developments.

J.A. WILLIAMSON. *A Short History of British Expansion*. Vol. 1. 4th ed., New York, 1956.

Part III focuses on the outburst of colonizing energy from 1606 to 1634; a robust patriotism informs the narrative.

GRAHAM PARRY. *The Golden Age Restor'd: The Culture of the Stuart Court 1603–1642*. Manchester, England, 1982. A study of the relationship between politics and the arts and of the spread of Classical aesthetic values in courtly circles.

14 The English Revolution: 1640-1660

From the English revolution sprang two ideals that profoundly shaped English —and Western—society during the next three centuries: the ideal of individual liberty and the ideal of representative government. In the minds of the English liberty meant limited government. The powers of the executive should be limited by Common and statute law, and the powers of the legislature by natural law and the fundamental laws of England. Government should be thus circumscribed in order to protect the liberties—civil, religious, economic, and intellectual—of individuals. By the end of the century John Locke gave a classic expression to this ideal in his *Second Treatise on Government*, wherein he argued that the very laws of nature guarantee to men and women rights which no government might invade.

Closely allied to the ideal of limited government was that of representative government—namely that the representatives of the nation should have a decisive voice in the exercise of those powers which the government might lawfully exercise. By no means did this mean democratic government, for a nation might be represented in various ways. In medieval times Parliament represented the communities of the realm—the Church, the peers, the shires, and the boroughs. In the seventeenth century, people came to view Parliament as representing those with "an interest in the nation"—that is, those who owned property. Not until the nineteenth century did Parliament represent all men and not until the twentieth century all women. But whatever the form of representation, the demand arose that Parliament have a decisive voice in the shaping of public policy. The English revolution did not permanently secure the supremacy of Parliament or end all dangers of arbitrary government, but in succeeding centuries the English, building on the past, won both limited government and representative government, the two indispensable pillars of a free society.

THE CAUSES OF THE ENGLISH REVOLUTION

A revolution is a rapid, profound, violent change in society. If the change is slow, historians call it an evolution, if superficial a coup d'état, if nonviolent merely rapid change. Historians and sociologists have been unable to agree on the exact set of circumstances that cause a revolution, but they do agree that four elements are usually present: the emergence of a new class or classes, the existence of numerous grievances, an ideology that justifies resistance, and a collapse of power at the top.

It was an alliance of the landed and the professional classes that precipitated the English revolution. It is unlikely that in 1540 either group would have been bold enough or strong enough to have made a revolution, but since that time they had grown in numbers, wealth, experience, and power. Between 1540 and 1640 the number of peers rose from 60 to 160, of baronets and knights from 500 to 1,400, of esquires from about 800 to 3,000, and of gentlemen from about 5,000 to 15,000. Thus the landed classes tripled in numbers during a century in which the population merely doubled. They also grew wealthier. Between 1536 and 1636 the Crown and the Church lost lands worth £6.5 million, most of it purchased by the gentry. Between 1530 and 1630 the standard of living of the average gentleman in Warwickshire increased by nearly 400 percent. Four-fifths of the members of the House of Commons in 1640 had incomes over £1000 a year. Not only were they wealthier, but they were better educated, had profited from a century's experience in Parliament, and had established their power in the counties through the quarter sessions. They were closely allied with the lawyers, whose numbers rose 40 percent between 1590 and 1630, and with the merchants, whose numbers and wealth in London alone were formidable.

The landed classes and their allies would not have revolted had not political, fiscal, economic, and religious grievances driven them to do so. At the dissolution of Parliament in 1629, Charles announced his intention of ruling henceforth without Parliament and showed he meant it by throwing the firebrands of the last Parliament, men such as Sir John Eliot, into the Tower. He kept Eliot there until his death in 1632. The cessation of Parliament and the more exact supervision of the justices of the peace in the counties would have passed unnoticed a century before, but the rising expectations of the landed classes now made them unendurable. Charles's rule was all the more unendurable because of the fiscal exactions that accompanied it. Ship money threatened every person's property; fines for failing to be knighted irritated the gentry; the enforcement of the forest laws angered the nobility; the tripling of the revenues from wardship injured those who held land by feudal tenure. These exactions were irritating, not oppressive, for the English landed classes were probably the most lightly taxed in Europe. What they feared was that future exactions would rob them of their property and make the King financially independent. Obnoxious to all classes were the numerous monopolies Charles had granted, a hidden tax on everyone and a denial of freedom to those who wished to enter a particular trade or manufacture.

Charles's prerogative rule brought a religious as well as a political reaction. Charles and Laud sought to restore the power of the bishops. They brought four of them into the Council and gave others a more active role as justices of the peace. The Laudian bishops in turn sought to revive ritual and ornament by bringing the communion table back into the east end of churches, by encouraging the use of stained-glass windows, by requiring the clergy to wear the surplice, and by ordering the laity to kneel at the altar when receiving communion. These measures were accompanied by a counterrevolution in theology, in which an Arminian emphasis was placed on free will, good works, and the clergyman's role as intercessor between humans and God. All this was anathema to the Puritans, but it also deeply offended the anticlericalism of most Englishmen, whether Puritan or not. Above all, it created a fear that the King and Laud intended to bring England back to Rome, a fear the Queen's power at court and the King's pursuit of a pro-Spanish foreign policy doubly compounded. Charles's persecution of the Puritan clergy had the fault that it was not ruthless enough to suppress them, yet was ruthless enough to enrage them. Archbishop Laud dragged William Prynne, John Bastwick, and John Burton, a lawyer, a doctor, and a clergyman, before the Star Chamber for having libeled the bishops in their pamphlets, and the court ordered them imprisoned and their ears cropped. At the cropping of their ears the crowds in Palace Yard cheered them on and some dipped their handkerchiefs in their blood. Despite the persecution there were still, on the eve of the revolution, forty-six Puritan lecturers in London delivering sixty sermons a week.

No matter how burdensome their grievances, a people will not revolt unless emboldened, united, and justified by a common ideology. In England two ideologies, that of the Common law, and that of Puritanism, served these purposes. The idea that the Common law, from Magna Carta to the Petition of Right, defended the liberties of individuals and the inviolability of property was deeply felt and pervasive. At the Inns of Court gentlemen absorbed the principles of the Common law and as justices of the peace they applied the rule of law. But appeals to the laws of England proved useless when Parliament in 1641 began to encroach on the King's legal powers. Some publicists appealed to the ancient constitution which had existed before the Normans introduced the tyranny of kings and nobles into England in 1066. But more important than the myth of the Norman yoke was the argument from natural law, particularly that the safety of the people was the supreme law of the land, *salus populi, suprema lex*, and that the people, through Parliament, must determine when their safety was threatened. In seven popular pamphlets written in 1642 Henry Parker propounded this doctrine in order to justify Parliament's resistance to the King.

Even more than legalism, Puritanism gave the Parliamentarians the absolute confidence in the righteousness of their cause necessary to carry through the revolution. At the heart of Puritanism lies a belief in the superiority of biblical truth and individual conscience over the dictates of authority. After a century of wrestling with the problem of the obedience owed to princes, the Puritans concluded that resistance to a wicked prince was both legitimate and necessary. In numerous sermons they preached that whenever the prince violated God's law, obedience to him must give way to obedience to God and conscience. Little wonder that Charles complained, "If the pulpits teach not obedience . . . the Crown will have little comfort of the militia."

James Harrington, a contemporary, wisely observed that "the dissolution of this Government caused the War, not the War the dissolution of this Government." Had power not collapsed at the top, the Parliamentarians would never have found themselves in a position to resist Charles. There were two causes for the collapse of royal power, one long-term and structural, the other immediate and disastrous.

Because Henry VIII had squandered his wealth on foreign wars, because Somerset and Northumberland had sought the support of Parliament, and because Elizabeth had preferred to govern by "love-tricks," the Tudors failed to create the institutions of an absolute monarchy. Charles inherited a Crown that was militarily, financially, and administratively weak. In the 1530s there was some thought of creating a standing army, but once Northumberland had, as an economy measure, paid off his Italian and German mercenaries, there was no further attempt to create one. Nor could Charles look to the military power of the aristocracy for help, since its military power had deteriorated with the decline of clientage and retaining. The financial weakness of the Crown stemmed from the failure to develop alternate sources of revenue once the monastic lands had been sold. Charles sought to remedy this fault by various fiscal devices, but they produced only enough revenue to allow him to stagger on in time of peace. They did not produce enough to pay for a royal bureaucracy, with the result that Charles was administratively dependent on the gentry in the counties and the merchants in the towns. His administrative impotence was visible in his inability to assert his authority over the forests, to extract the full amount of ship money, to suppress lecturers, or to censor the press. In the 1630s, when efforts at censorship were at their height, only one-third of the books published were censored.

But prerogative government might have continued for many years had Charles not committed the blunder of stumbling into war. In 1637, without consulting the Scottish Privy Council or the Scottish Parliament, he extended "the beauty of holiness" to Scotland in the form of a new liturgy resembling the English one. It led to riots in St. Giles Cathedral that spilled over into the streets of Edinburgh and spread to other towns. This violent explosion of popular opinion was all the more dangerous because Charles's economic and financial policies had angered the nobility and the merchants. The Act of Revocation of 1625, an attempt to recover all Church lands lost since the Reformation, persuaded the nobility that their lands and inheritances were no longer secure. Unprecedentedly high taxes, among them a 5 percent tax on all interest paid on loans, infuriated the merchants. The nobles and merchants now allied themselves with the Presbyterian ministers. They, and tens of thousands of other Scotsmen, swore a national covenant to assert the right of Parliament and the General Assembly of the Church to determine ecclesiastical policy.

In 1638 the General Assembly took the further step of abolishing bishops in the Scottish Church. Charles was willing to revoke the new liturgy, but not to tolerate the abolition of bishops. In 1639 he raised an army and marched north, only to see his troops, who had no heart for the campaign, melt away. The First Bishop's War ended in the humiliating Treaty of Berwick. Charles now summoned his ablest minister, Thomas Wentworth, the Earl of Strafford, from Ireland. Strafford urged him to meet Parliament, which he did in April 1640. But the Commons refused to vote money until grievances were redressed, so Charles sent it home. Charles and Strafford now confronted both a war in Scotland and a taxpayers' revolt in England. The collection of ship money fell off, the city refused to lend the King money, the Treasury rapidly emptied. The indomitable Strafford persevered with the Second Bishop's War, but with no success. The unwilling English troops met defeat in August at Newburn, and the Scots occupied Durham and Northumberland. In England, as later in France and Russia, military defeat and financial bankruptcy proved the prelude to revolution. Bereft of money, his kingdom occupied, Charles agreed to summon a Parliament.

THE FAILURE OF REFORM

The Parliament that met in November 1640 was not the narrow clique the royalists later said it was. Inflation had increased the number of 40-shilling freeholders in the counties to over 180,000. Elizabeth's creation of new boroughs and Parliament's willingness to broaden the franchise in older boroughs meant that there were 50,000 urban voters. In short, the House of Commons in 1640 directly represented one out of every four adult males. Furthermore, for almost the first time in English history an election centered on great issues. At Great Marlow all the contestants were gentlemen, but the two opposition candidates stood for "liberty," and with the help of shopkeepers and artisans defeated the Court candidates. The old royal and aristocratic patronage system broke down. The Earl of Salisbury could not secure the return of his nominee at St. Albans, and the number of courtiers, and officials in the Long Parliament, as it came to be called, was only forty-nine.

With high hopes and a firm resolve to make changes, the newly elected members arrived at Westminster in November. One of them, Edward Hyde, later a royalist, declared it to be "a dawning of a fair and lasting day of happiness to this Kingdom." The members came resolved to secure their property, to establish the supremacy of the Common law, to rid the Church of popish innovations, to reduce the influence of the bishops, to put foreign policy on a Protestant track, and to guarantee regular sessions of Parliament. By the summer of 1641 Parliament, united in nearly all votes, had accomplished these purposes. It had condemned as illegal ship money, impositions, distraint of knighthood, and the revival of ancient forest laws. It had removed from the Crown the power of taxation without consent and of arrest without trial. It had abolished all the prerogative courts—Star Chamber, the Court of Requests, High Commission, the Council of the North, and the Council of Wales. It had stopped the persecution of Puritans and reversed the policies of the Laudian clergy. It had passed a Triennial Bill that guaranteed the meeting of Parliament at least once every three years. To prove that it meant business it had impeached Strafford, Laud, and the ship money judges for high treason.

It was the impeachment of Strafford that revealed the first break in the unanimity of Parliament and provided the first sign that Charles's consent to these measures was insincere. The House of Commons impeached Strafford and the House of Lords imprisoned him out of anger at his brutality and fear of his ability. Strafford was a fierce man who had urged that John Hampden be whipped and had threatened to hang four Aldermen for refusing to lend the King money. In May 1640 he told Charles that, "being reduced to extreme necessity," he was "loosed and absolved from all rules of government," and could do "all that power might admit." The House of Commons, the city, the Scots, and the populace were determined to have Strafford's head, but the managers of the impeachment could not prove him guilty of treason. They lacked both the laws and the witnesses to do so. The House of Commons therefore turned to an Act of Attainder and condemned him to death legislatively. Fifty-nine members voted against the attainder, the first crack in the unaminity of the House. Charles signed it, an act he ever afterward regretted, but it was information that Charles had plotted to bring the army down from the north to crush Parliament and release Strafford that led the House of Lords to pass the attainder. On May 10 Strafford lost his head on the scaffold, as arbitrary an act as any that Charles had committed.

During the next year four circumstances conspired to ruin all efforts at reform and to plunge England into civil war: Charles's refusal to be a limited monarch, the Irish rebellion, the demands of the Root and Branch party, and the emergence of a royalist party.

Charles displayed his reluctance to be a limited monarch not only by plotting with the army, but by spurning the advice of the leaders of Parliament. The leadership of the House of Commons had fallen into the hands of John Pym and Oliver St. John, of the House of Lords into the hands of the Earl of Bedford and Viscount Say and Sele. These men were not strangers, for they had worked together in the 1630s in the Providence Island Company. They now undertook, in return for office, to manage Charles's affairs for him in Parliament. In February 1641 rumor made Bedford Lord Treasurer and Pym Chancellor of the Exchequer. If any stratagem could have saved the cause of reform it was this undertaking, but Charles preferred to listen to the advice of the Queen and of the gentlemen of the bedchamber. He refused the offer and set out for Scotland in search of an army. He spent the autumn of 1641 in Edinburgh, conceding to the Scots control of their church and their executive, but finding no army. It was then that the Irish rebellion broke out.

In the summer of 1641 his successors in Ireland disbanded the army of 9000 Irish papists Strafford had hoped to use to subdue the Scottish rebellion. Having been paid less than half what was owed them, the troops went home, taking their weapons with them. With the weakening of the forces of order, Catholic priests flocked into the country, stirring up discontent. In October the O'Neils of Ulster rose in revolt and a band of Catholics unsuccessfully sought to seize Dublin Castle. The rebellion grew out of thirty years of English land-grabbing, treachery, exploitation, and religious persecution. It led to the massacre of some 10,000 English Protestant settlers, a number magnified by rumor in London to 200,000. Though their differences were profound, King and Parliament agreed that the rebellion must be suppressed. But who was to command the army to crush it? If the command lay with the King, he might use the army to crush Parliament; if the command lay with Parliament, it might use it to rob the King of his power. The Irish rebellion turned a struggle to enforce the law on the King into a struggle to wrest power from him.

This became evident in November 1641 when the House of Commons appealed to the nation in the Grand Remonstrance. The Grand Remonstrance, 204 clauses long, was a catalog of all the grievances of the past decade, to which were attached two demands: that the King name ministers in whom Parliament might confide and that a synod of the most grave and pious divines be called to reform the Church. The second demand expressed the determination of the Puritans to abolish bishops and reform the liturgy. As early as December 1640, 15,000 citizens of London had presented a petition to Parliament for the abolition of episcopacy "with all its roots and branches." Parliament debated the merits of the petition in February, but then laid it aside. Not until summer did a small body of enthusiasts introduce a Root and Branch Bill into the House, a bill the moderate majority, led by Pym, amended to provide for the government of the Church by nine laymen named by Parliament. The alliance of the Root and Branch enthusiasts with the partisans of Pym led to an attack on the Book of Common Prayer. Few people wished to defend the bishops, but many wished to preserve the liturgy. Among these a party for the King first appeared. In the long night of debate on the Grand Remonstrance they spoke against this radical document, and when the vote was finally taken, late at night on November 22, 148 members opposed it. It carried by only 11 votes. The two sides that were to wage civil war had emerged.

In December 1641 the House of Commons passed a Militia Bill that transferred control of the militia from the Crown to a Lord General appointed by Parliament, thus widening the gap between royalists and parliamentarians. In the same month the radical Puritans in London gained control of the Common Council and promptly established a Committee of Public Safety to control the city militia. Charles meanwhile plotted a military coup. He named the brutal Colonel Lunsford to be lieutenant of the Tower and attempted on January 4, 1642, to arrest the five leading members of the House of Commons. Charles came to the House in person to make the arrest, accompanied by courtiers, their swords jangling at their sides. But the five members had fled. The leaders of the House were now forced to demand control of the militia and nomination of the King's ministers, both to ensure their own safety and to protect the gains of the past year. Charles refused both and fled to York. In March Parliament turned its Militia Bill into and ordinance and began raising forces. In June Charles issued commissions of array for the raising of forces in every county. By August civil war had broken out.

Of the members of the Commons, 302 remained in London, supporting Parliament; 236 fled and supported the King. All attempts to explain this division on the basis of class structure have failed. On both sides there were merchants and lawyers, on both sides old landed families and new, on both sides the rich gentry and the mere gentry, on both sides rising and declining families. In truth, the propertied classes were divided within themselves. The more timid and conservative grew frightened at the political radicalism of Pym, at the religious radicalism of the preachers, at the enclosure riots in the countryside, and at the mobs that surged around the Houses of Parliament in moments of crisis. The only decisive correlation that can be established—aside from the fact that the royalists were eleven years younger—concerns religion. In Yorkshire, for example, over a third of the royalist gentry were Catholic and over half of the Parliamentarians were Puritans. All the peers who sided with the Commons, one quarter of them, favored religious reform. Whatever else it was, the English revolution was a Puritan revolution.

ROUNDHEADS AND CAVALIERS

At Nottingham, in a howling gale and amid torrential rain, Charles on August 22, 1642, raised his standard and called on all Englishmen to rally behind him. Four years later, in April 1646, he rode out of Oxford to surrender himself to the Scots, a defeated king. The chief reason why Charles suffered defeat in the first civil war, which lasted from 1642 through 1645, was his lack of resources. His support came largely from the economically backward north and west, from the larger landlords and their tenants, from Roman Catholics and monopolists, from devoted adherents of the Anglican Church, and from impoverished gentlemen in search of military pay and the chance of plunder. Many supported him only out of personal loyalty, as Sir Edmund Verney, a monopolist, who re-

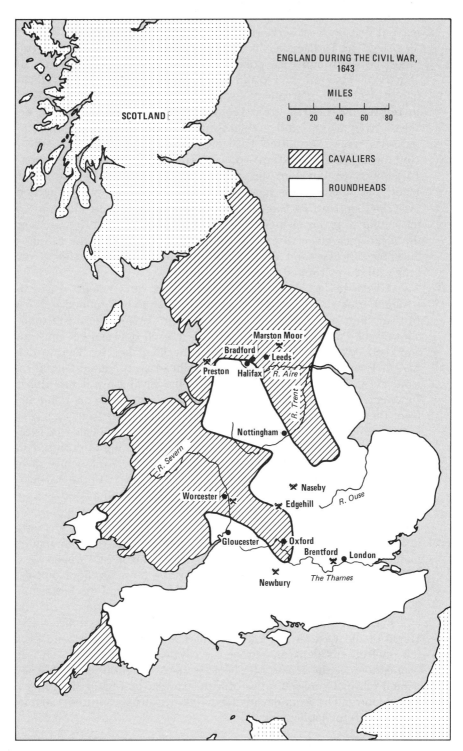

ENGLAND DURING THE CIVIL WAR, 1643

MILES

0   20   40   60   80

CAVALIERS

ROUNDHEADS

SCOTLAND

Marston Moor
Bradford
Leeds
Preston
Halifax
R. Aire
R. Trent
Nottingham
R. Severn
Naseby
Worcester
Edgehill
R. Ouse
Gloucester
Oxford
Brentford
London
Newbury
The Thames

marked that he must serve the King since he "had eaten the King's bread" for 30 years. The Parliament, on the other hand, was strong in the prosperous and industrial south and east, possessed the navy, most of the ports, and the machinery of taxation, and could rely on the vast wealth and efficient trained bands of London. Parliament's support came largely from Puritans determined to reform the Church, from yeomen and tradesmen anxious to better themselves, from artisans and clothiers angry at economic regulations. In Sussex the industrial areas supported Parliament, the agricultural areas the King. The clothing towns of Yorkshire—Leeds, Halifax, and Bradford—were wholly for Parliament. In Wiltshire the gentry supported the King, the clothiers Parliament. The sailors in the navy rose up against their royalist officers and turned over their ships to Parliament. When the revolution spread from Parliament to the countryside, an element of social division appeared. It was summed up in the nicknames given to each side: the royalists became the Cavaliers—swashbuckling officers—and the Parliamentarians the Roundheads—common citizens with close-cropped hair.

Given the fact that Parliament had the greater resources and would grow stronger each month, Charles should have marched immediately on London. Instead, after a victory over the Roundheads at Edgehill in October 1642, he allowed the Parliamentarian army to place itself between his army and London, and then delayed three weeks before attacking the city. During that time the Earl of Essex, commander of the Roundhead army, raised 24,000 men, mostly from the London bands, who withstood the royal army at Brentford. The next summer the Cavaliers planned a three-pronged attack on London, one army from the north, a second from the west, and a third from Oxford. It was the most intelligent strategy of the whole war, but Charles failed to execute it with daring and audacity. Instead he insisted on attempting to capture Gloucester in his rear before attacking London, but he lacked the artillery and spent the summer besieging Gloucester in vain. By September of 1643 the war had reached a stalemate which John Pym sought to end by inviting in a Scottish army.

That autumn he convinced Parliament to pay the high price the Scots asked for their aid—£30,000 a month and the establishment of Presbyterianism in England. The price was worth paying, for the Scottish army that entered England in January 1644 tipped the balance in favor of Parliament. On July 2, 1644, in the evening, amid thunderstorms, on Marston Moor outside York, the combined forces of the Scots, the Yorkshire levies, and the Eastern Association, 27,000 in all, defeated 18,000 royalists under Prince Rupert, the King's nephew. Early in the battle Prince Rupert's cavalry successfully drove back the Horse of the Eastern Association, when suddenly a small band of cavalrymen fell on Rupert's flank and drove his cavalry from the field. This allowed the commander of the Horse of The Eastern Association, an East Anglian squire named Oliver Cromwell, to reform this cavalry and break the ranks of the royalist infantry. The Roundheads slew 4000 royalists, captured 1500, and won all of the north for Parliament.

Marston Moor might have led to a final victory that year had not the Earl of Essex allowed his army to be trapped and cut off in Cornwall and had not the Earl of Manchester allowed a royalist army half the size of his to escape at Newbury. In truth, neither Essex nor Manchester had much heart for the fight. Essex always took his coffin with him on a campaign and Manchester remarked that even if they defeated Charles ninety-nine times, he was King still, but "if the King beat us once we shall be hanged." By passing a self-denying ordinance that would deprive all peers and members of the House of Commons of their commissions, Parliament got rid of Essex and Manchester. They then, in April 1645, named Sir Thomas Fairfax as general of a New Model army—a professional army, recruited nationally, not tied to any locality, and officered by men who because they feared God feared no man.

The New Model army proved itself at the Battle of Naseby in June 1645. At Naseby, which lies halfway between Leicester and Northampton, Fairfax and 14,000 men confronted Prince Rupert with 9,000. Prince Rupert wished to avoid an engagement until reinforcements arrived, but Charles overruled him. Rupert's cavalry quickly broke through the Parliamentarian cavalry on the left flank, but then dashed away to plunder the baggage train. Meanwhile Cromwell's cavalry, on the other flank, broke the opposing Horse, regrouped, and swept down on the flank of the royalist infantry, cutting them down as they ran. At the end, Puritan discipline proved more powerful than Cavalier brilliance, and the King no longer had an army to put into the field. Half of Charles's army at Naseby was paraded through the streets of London in triumph.

THE RISE OF INDEPENDENCY

Parliament found it easier to defeat the King in battle than to secure the goals for which it fought: the establishment of a constitutional monarchy and the creation of a Presbyterian Church. It failed in the first because Charles, though defeated and captured, preferred intrigue, delay, deceit, and unfaithfulness to submission. It failed in the second because of the rise of Independency.

The original purpose of the Puritans was to reform the Church of England. For this reason Parliament in June 1643 nominated an assembly of divines to meet at Westminster to discuss the Thirty-nine Articles. In September 1643, persuant to the Solemn League and Covenant, a group of Scottish divines joined the assembly. The Westminster Assembly now set out to reform the English Church "according to the Word of God, and the example of the best Reformed Churches." They drew up a Directory of Worship, Puritan in character, which Parliament accepted and which replaced the Book of Common Prayer. A majority of the assembly also favored a presbyterian organization of the English Church, one in which the presbytery, composed of ministers and elders, would ordain ministers and maintain discipline. In March 1646 Parliament decreed the establishment of Presbyterianism throughout the land.

But this nascent Presbyterian Church was stillborn. There was little enthusiasm for it in the country; there was a large party opposed to it in Parliament; and the army stood firmly against it. The real genius of English Puritanism lay in voluntary efforts by each congregation, within a church governed by a Parliament distrustful of all clerical power. To voluntarism and anticlericalism was now added a third force: belief in liberty of conscience. In order to reform the Church, the Puritan preachers had demanded the liberty to preach God's word —but what they sought was reformation, not liberty. Yet they preached with too much vehemence that all human beings were equal in sin, that all might hope for redemption, that all should look within themselves for the immanent Christ. It is not surprising, therefore, that some listeners drew the logical deduction that all people possessing reason might study God's word and discover the truth. This Christian humanism found its noblest expression in the work of John Milton, who declared in 1644:

> And though all the winds of doctrine were let loose to play upon the earth, so Truth be in the field, we do injuriously, by licensing and prohibiting, to misdoubt her strength. Let her and Falsehood grapple: who ever knew Truth put to the worse, in a free and open encounter.

But many others—sons of squires, wealthy merchants, tradesmen—likewise urged that every person must find the truth for him or herself. Even the Anglican clergyman Jeremy Taylor, in his *Discourse of the Liberty of Prophesying*, declared that because "we see through a glass darkly, we should not despise or condemn persons not so knowing as ourselves." The rapid growth of literacy, the great increase in printing, the end of censorship, and the end of Star Chamber all promoted a multiplication of religious opinions and religious sects.

The greatest danger to Presbyterianism came when these new ideas infiltrated the army. At the beginning of the war command of the county militias went to men of social rank, but gradually plain russet-coated gentlemen, rich merchants, even tinkers and draymen replaced them. In the county committees, as well as in Parliament, there appeared two parties: one cautious, defensive-minded, intolerant of dissent; the other aggressive, determined to win the war, and tolerant of dissent. In time they came to be called the Presbyterian party and the Independent Party. Among the greatest of the Independents was Oliver Cromwell, who urged that the "state in choosing men to serve it take no notice of their opinions." He took none and created an army that could defeat a king. The radical sects—Baptists, Seekers, Ranters, and Quakers—saw the Church as the gathering of the faithful in individual congregations or meetings, separate from the state. The Independents, on the other hand, favored a national church that would propagate the Gospel. But unlike the Presbyterians, they would grant the radical sects freedom to worship outside it.

The moment of truth came in the spring of 1647 when Parliament persisted in its design to impose Presbyterianism on the country and ordered the army to be disbanded with its wages unpaid. Both material and spiritual interests drove the army to resist, to elect agitators from each regiment, and to form a Council of the Army, composed of two officers and two agitators from each regiment. In June they seized Charles (whom Parliament had bought from the Scots) and presented their demands to Parliament: liberty for tender consciences and the sale of royalists' lands to pay the wages owed them. In August the army occupied London and in September they opened negotiations with the King. Cromwell's son-in-law, General Ireton, drafted a moderate settlement, called "The Heads of the Proposal," which provided for the election of a Parliament every two years, gave Parliament control of the army and nomination of the King's ministers for ten years, and guaranteed toleration of all Protestant churches, even the Episcopal.

Charles would have been well advised to have accepted it, but he refused, saying, "You cannot do without me." He then fled to Carisbrooke Castle on the Isle of Wight, where, though under house arrest, he opened negotiations with a group of Scottish noblemen. In December he signed an Engagement with them, according to which Charles, in return for a Scottish army, promised to establish Presbyterianism for three years and to suppress the Independents. Charles, however, refused to swear the Covenant, which caused the Scottish Church and army to refuse their support. The Scottish noblemen nevertheless began to raise an army to invade England.

Unfortunately for the King, royalist rebellions broke out in Kent, Essex, and South Wales before the Scots were ready to march. Fairfax promptly suppressed the rebellions in Kent and Essex, and Cromwell marched swiftly into South Wales to destroy the rebels there. In these regions the gentry supported the rebellions, but not the common people. In July the Scottish army, 21,000 strong, mostly the servants of noblemen, crossed into England. Cromwell, now given sole command, marched north with barely 8,000 men, crossed the Pennines at the Aire Gap, and fell upon the Scottish army as it straggled southward, foraging for supplies. His men cut them to pieces and the second civil war came to an end.

The leaders of the army reluctantly came to the conclusion that there could be no treaty with Charles Stuart, that man of blood. Cromwell, who often procrastinated, finally decided in late November that it was necessary to give impartial justice to all offenders. At this point, Parliament reopened negotiations with Charles, who conceded to them a Presbyterian Church and parliamentary control of the army for the next twenty years. It was too late. In December the army council sent Colonel Pride with a company of musketeers to purge Parliament. He arrested or frightened away 140 members, leaving a "rump" of barely 50. For the next four years, the Rump cloaked government by the army.

Though the King was the fountain of all justice, the Rump created a Court of High Justice to try him. Though treason could only be committed against the King, the Rump declared it treason to levy war against Parliament.

Few men were willing to serve on the Court of High Justice, but Cromwell and others bullied them into doing so. On January 20, 1649, Charles was brought before the court, where he refused to answer the charges against him and denied that the court had any jurisdiction over him. After a short mockery of a trial, the president of the court pronounced Charles guilty of treason for having violated the fundamental law of England and having waged war against Parliament. On January 30 he was led to a scaffold erected before Whitehall Palace, where the executioner cut off his head, not to the cheers but to the silence of the populace. He acted with great calm and dignity, but his nobility on that memorable scene could not erase the fact that the army had openly and publicly, not by poison or a dagger, brought an English king to account for his misdeeds.

THE COMMONWEALTH

Having defeated the Scots, purged Parliament, and executed the King, the Independents now abolished the House of Lords and established a commonwealth. Formal power rested in the Rump, real power in the army. But just as the victorious Puritans had broken up into Presbyterians and Independents, so the victorious Independents in the army now broke up into Grandees and Levellers. The Levellers were a group of radicals who believed in republicanism, religious toleration, equality before the law, the abolition of tithes, the election of sheriffs, and the sovereignty of the people. The most courageous among them was John Lilburne, a Durham gentleman who grew up as a London apprentice. For defying the Star Chamber he was flogged through the streets of London and put in the pillory, from which he harangued the crowd against bishops. He went on to serve as a captain at Edgehill, to become a colonel, to suffer imprisonment in 1645 for defying the Presbyterians, and to write numerous Leveller manifestoes.

The Levellers, who enjoyed great influence with the agitators, had engineered the seizure of the King, the march on London, and the holding of a remarkable series of debates at Putney in October 1647. The debates centered on "The Agreement of the People," a proposed constitution drawn up by the Levellers which they put forward as a social contract for a new government. It proposed the abolition of monarchy and of the House of Lords, the establishment of religious liberty by a fundamental law that not even the legislature could alter, and the placing of all power in a House of Commons which all freeborn Englishmen should elect every two years. The debate focused on the proposal to grant the vote to all freeborn Englishmen, by which the Levellers meant all adult males who were not criminals or apprentices or servants. Colonel Rainsborough put the case for the Levellers when he declared that: "The poorest he that lives hath as true a right to give a vote as well as the richest and greatest." General Ireton, speaking for the Grandees, dissented. He declared that the vote was rightly restricted to those who have "a permanent fixed interest in this Kingdom"—namely, "the persons in whom all land lies, and those in corporations in whom all trading lies." The fear of the Grandees was that the poor would use the vote to level all estates. As Colonel Rich observed, "You . . . have five to one in this Kingdom that have no permanent interest. . . . There may be a law enacted, that there shall be an equality of goods and estates."

Colonel Rich wrongly characterized the Levellers, for they believed in private property and its protection. It was only privileges such as monopolies and primogeniture that they opposed. The Levellers sharply distinguished themselves from the Diggers, who advocated communal cultivation of land and who in 1649 seized a plot of land at St. George's Hill near London and sowed it with parsnips, carrots, and beans. Their leader was Gerrard Winstanley, a religious zealot who believed that "True freedom lies where a man received his nourishment and preservation, and that is in the use of the earth." The Council of State immediately sent soldiers to expel Winstanley and his twenty or so followers.

As long as he needed their help, Cromwell was reluctant to suppress the Levellers. As late as November 1648 he warned a friend against supporting the King and Presbyterians out of an empty fear of the Levellers. But four months later, after the execution of the King, he and his fellow officers struck at the Levellers. "You have," he said as Lilburne was hurried away to prison, "no other way to deal with these men but to break them in pieces. . . . If you do not break them they will break you." He promptly suppressed a Leveller mutiny at Burford and sought to silence Lilburne, who proved quite irrepressible. Two London juries acquitted him of libel, so the government had to keep him in prison by fiat. The Cromwells, Fairfaxes, and Iretons, gentry all, were determined that the tenants must not be equal to their landlord.

In the ferment of new ideas the civil war brought, one thinker came to conclusions markedly different from the Levellers'. He was Thomas Hobbes, son of an Anglican clergyman, an Oxford graduate, tutor to the second Earl of Devonshire, and an admirer of Euclid's geometrical thought. When the civil war broke out, he thought it discreet to retire to Paris. Hobbes agreed with the Levellers in one matter, that government was formed by a social contract among all men, not by divine institution. But where the Levellers appealed to natural law, he appealed to utility. Men create government to avoid miseries of the state of nature, for in the state of nature there was no industry, no arts, no letters; the life of man was "solitary, poor, nasty, brutish, and short." Only by agreeing to form government and to grant absolute and irrevocable power to a sovereign—be it a person or a council—could man escape the miseries of the state of nature. Hobbes proclaimed these ideas in 1651 in a book entitled *Levi-*

athan, which shocked the orthodox with its materialism and the liberals with its absolutism, but proved to be one of the great classics of Western political thought.

Hobbes's was a lonely voice. The real challenge to the Levellers came from those who believed that God's grace gave men power to rule. The English revolution produced two traditions of thought that have characterized revolutionary politics ever since. One asserts that political power resides in the people, the other that it resides in the pure and the righteous. John Lilburne believed that all men were equal before Christ, and so should enjoy an equal vote. But the army chaplains held that the power of God made men fit to rule, that grace gave men power. They held that grace was not universal, but was granted by God only to those whom He elected to salvation. They believed that good and religious men ought to rule over the wicked and irreligious. In the hands of the chaplains, this doctrine contained a large element of antiprofessionalism: they attacked lawyers, clergymen, and professors for their pretensions, high fees, tithes, and pride, which meant nothing if they had not received the grace of God.

In the hands of John Milton, belief in government by the elect took on a more intellectual guise. In *De Doctrina Christina* and *The Tenure of Kings and Magistrates,* Milton argued that Adam by his disobedience brought servitude upon man, but Christ had set him free again to distinguish true from false, good from evil. By reason and discourse the laws of God could be discovered, being discovered they could be taught, being taught they could be heeded, and being heeded they could lead to redemption (for Milton was an Arminian). Liberty of study and discourse was therefore vital to redemption, yet "liberty," wrote Milton, "hath a sharp and double edge fit only to be handled by just and virtuous men." Thus, though he argued that kings and magistrates were below the law, he urged that not everyone is capable of making law, but only "those Worthies which are the soul of the enterprise." Milton did not say how those who were the soul of the enterprise should be discovered, but both Ireton and Cromwell suggested that those worthy of rule were those to whom God gave success in battle.

The army suppressed the Levellers, but granted the religious liberty in which all Independents believed. Church courts ceased to function and compulsory attendance at the parish church was abolished. The result was a riot of religious sects. There were the Baptists, who believed that not until a person was an adult should he or she choose a church; the Ranters, who believed that God's grace made humans incapable of sin; the Antinomians, who believed that neither faith nor belief need precede God's gift of grace; the Seekers, who went from church to church seeking the truth; and the Quakers, who taught the doctrine of the inner light, that within each man and woman is something divine. Women during these years gained in stature because of the greater equality sectarian congregations granted them. Though the army rejected democracy, it embraced religious liberty.

THE TRIUMPH OF PROPERTY

Not only in the religious sphere but also in the economic, individualism triumphed. No moment is more critical in a people's history than when a traditional society, governed by custom, status, the just price, and a sense of community, gives way to a market society, in which the individual is free to sell land, goods, labor, and talents at the highest price the market will pay. The cake of custom is broken and the forces of supply and demand prevail. In England this transformation came slowly, between 1300 and 1700, but the decisive steps were taken in the 1640s and 1650s. During those years the forces of capitalism were freed from the interference of the Crown. In 1646 Parliament abolished tenure by knight service and the Court of Wards, thus freeing land from its feudal obligations. It had already abolished the Court of Star Chamber, thus making it impossible for the government to enforce the laws against enclosure. It swept away all monopolies, thus ending the interference of courtiers in manufacturing and commerce. The government ceased to regulate wages or enforce guild regulations. It adopted a modern system of finances based on excise and land taxes. Whoever else gained in the English revolution, the landlord, the manufacturer, and the trader certainly did.

In economic thought as well as in economic policy a fundamental change occurred. Medieval ideas of a just price, of the wickedness of usury, of community responsibility gave way to economic individualism. "A man's Labour also," declared Thomas Hobbes, "is a commodity exchangeable for benefit, as well as any other thing." He even suggested that a man might sell his person into slavery if he wished; and he wondered that anyone would consider it "an injustice to sell dearer than we buy." The Reverend Joseph Lee maintained that where government regulation had failed, the free play of the market would succeed. The Levellers likewise extolled freedom from all restriction on trade and favored (as did later the Jacobins in France and the Jacksonians in America) the widest possible distribution of property, so that every individual could support his freedom. It was James Harrington, the author of *Oceana*, a Utopian work published in 1656, who first perceived the fundamental political importance of property, especially of property in land. He put forward a theory of a balance of property—that is, that the government of a state must correspond to the distribution of landed property. If less than 300 persons held the land, a monarchy was appropriate; if less than 5000, an aristocracy; if over 5000, a republic. But Harrington was no Marxist, for he believed political action could shape the economic basis of society. To support the existing Commonwealth he favored an agrarian law that would, by limiting primogeniture, ensure the widest possible distribution of property.

The Rump Parliament never passed an agrarian law, but it did pass the Navigation Act of 1651 to protect the property of English merchants engaged in foreign trade. The act prohibited the import into England of goods from Asia, Africa, and America unless brought in English ships, required that imports from Europe be brought in English ships or those of the country in which the goods originated, and forbade foreigners to participate in the coastal trade or bring in fish or salt. The act was aimed at the Dutch, who with their efficient flyboat, their modern banking, and their powerful navy dominated trade from the Baltic to the Bay of Biscay. In 1648, for example, the Dutch had secured the right of free passage in the Baltic for their ships, while the English had to pay dues. In the seventeenth century power and profit were closely allied, and the English now resolved to break the Dutch monopoly. The Dutch resisted, refusing to allow the English to search their ships in the North Sea and to cease trading with the English colonies in North America. The result was the outbreak of war in 1652.

The English added forty-one new ships to the navy, nearly doubling its size. An English government for the first time in history consciously and deliberately used its seapower to promote commerce—but at great cost. At the height of the Dutch war the navy cost £1.5 million a year, money gained by selling crown, episcopal, and royalist lands. Between 1649 and 1653 the sale of confiscated lands and fines on royalists produced over £7 million. Led by Robert Blake, a general turned admiral, but an admiral of genius, the English defeated the Dutch in a series of naval battles and crowded Dutch ports with merchantmen that dared not run the English blockade. In 1654 the Dutch signed the Treaty of Westminster, in which they acquiesced in the English Navigation Act. That same year the English signed a treaty with Portugal which transferred the monopoly of trade with the Portuguese from the Dutch to the English. Treaties in 1654 and 1656 gave English merchants entry to Swedish ports on terms of equality with the Dutch. Of equal importance was the capture of 1700 Dutch vessels during the war, thereby making it possible for the English merchant marine to carry the goods that the Navigation Act required it to carry. Power did mean profit in the seventeenth century.

OVERSEAS EXPANSION

Revolutions tend to release in a people a fund of energy and a sense of righteousness that finds expression in expansion. The new gospel must be carried to all countries. As Admiral Blake told the king of Spain in 1651, "All kingdoms will annihilate tyranny and become republics." For Cromwell, the spread of true religion was the goal that led him to urge peace with the Protestant Dutch. But he used his power to carry Protestantism and respect for the Commonwealth to Ireland, to Scotland, to the colonies, and to Jamaica and Dunkirk.

To suppress the Irish rebellion, Parliament in 1642 passed the Adventurers' Act, which promised the lands of the Irish rebels to those who would pay for their conquest. This naturally infuriated the Irish, who put three separate armies into the field—an Irish Catholic army led by Owen Roe O'Neil; an army of the "Old English" settlers, mostly Catholics, led by Thomas Preston; and an

army of English Protestant settlers, led by the Earl of Ormond. As so often in Irish history, division enfeebled the Irish and allowed the English to conquer them. In 1646 O'Neil won a stunning victory, but jealousies between him and Preston prevented the Irish from crushing Parliament's troops. The next year 8000 men of the New Model army wiped out Preston's army; in 1649 they defeated Ormond's. It was then that Oliver Cromwell came to Ireland. The rebels still had 40,000 men in arms against the English Parliament, mostly in garrisons throughout the land.

Cromwell attacked the problem with his usual vehemence and skill. He besieged, assaulted, and captured Drogheda, then put to the sword every man in the garrison. He did the same at Wexford a month later. As always, he gave the credit to God. "I am persuaded," he wrote, "that this is a righteous judgment of God upon these barbarous wretches who have imbued their hands in so much innocent blood." He also hoped that the slaughter of the garrisons at Drogheda and Wexford would encourage others to surrender. Most of them did, and by 1650 Cromwell had captured all the ports and most of the towns of Ireland. His son-in-law Ireton directed the savage campaigns that completed the conquest of Ireland. To pay the soldiers who fought and the adventurers who financed these campaigns, the English confiscated Irish lands, even of Anglicans like Ormond and Presbyterians like Inchiquin. In all they confiscated 11 million acres and gave them to the adventurers and soldiers. Before this confiscation two-thirds of the land was in the hands of Catholics; after it not more than a third. Protestants also took a chief place in industry, commerce, and the liberal professions. The Cromwellian settlement created a deep and lasting cleavage in Irish society between Protestant and Catholic. Nor did the Independents bring the saving grace of religious liberty. "If by liberty of conscience you mean a liberty to exercise the Mass," said Cromwell to the Governor of Ross, "where the Parliament of England have power, that will not be allowed of."

Cromwell likewise conquered Scotland, but he showed far more mercy to his fellow Protestants. Charles I lost his few friends in Scotland when his negotiations with the Irish Catholic clan of Macdonalds drove the Earl of Argyll (a Campbell) and the Scottish Estates to negotiate the Solemn League and Covenant with England in 1643. Charles had one loyal friend in Scotland, however, the Earl of Montrose, a military genius whose marches and countermarches, winter campaigns, and Highland troops nearly won all of Scotland for the King. But the Scottish army marching home from Naseby trapped Montrose at Philiphaugh and routed him. The Duke of Hamilton now sought to rescue the King by the Engagement of 1647, but he had the power of the Church against him and met defeat at the Battle of Preston.

The Earl of Argyll and the Presbyterian clergy now reigned supreme. They banned from public life and from office all who had supported Montrose or taken the engagement. But they could not swallow the execution of Charles, even though they had practically led him to the scaffold. The Scottish Parliament at once hailed Charles's eldest son as Charles II and persuaded him, when he arrived in Scotland, to swear the covenant. Cromwell pleaded with the Scottish to give up their royal puppet: "I beseech you in the bowels of Christ, think it possible you may be mistaken." But they did not, so Cromwell marched north with an army, became trapped at Dunbar between the sea and the hills, but won a resounding victory because the Scots left their unassailable position and because they failed in the heavy rain to light the tapers needed to fire their matchlock muskets. After the victory Cromwell marched to Edinburgh and then to Perth, deliberately leaving the way open into England. The Scots fell into the trap. They marched south, only to discover that the English, fearing Cromwell and disliking the Scots, did not rise. At Worcester, on September 3, the anniversary of Dunbar, Cromwell defeated the Scots. God had conferred His "crowning mercy" by ending all civil strife in Britain.

For nine years the English governed Scotland justly, efficiently, and honestly. The Presbyterians continued to worship in their accustomed manner. The merchants enjoyed all the trading privileges of Englishmen. And Scotsmen sent thirty members to the Protectorate Parliament in London. Yet it was expensive government, for the cost of the army of occupation was enormous—£6000 a

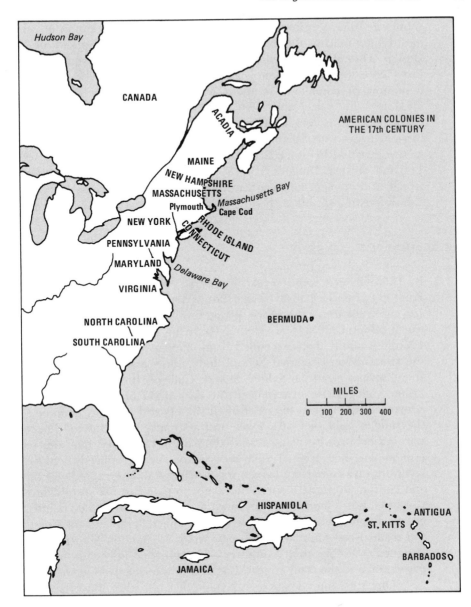

month. The Presbyterian clergy never truly welcomed the union with heretics in the south and heartily welcomed the Restoration when it came.

The Commonwealth also used its power to regain the allegiance of those colonies that had recognized Charles II—Virginia, Maryland, Barbados, Bermuda, and Antigua. The government sent out a strong fleet under the command of Sir George Ayscue, who forced Barbados, Antigua, and Bermuda to submit in 1651, Virginia and Maryland in 1652. The retention of existing colonies did not exhaust the ambitions of Cromwell, who embarked on the Western Design. Though its immediate purpose was to punish Spain for its attacks on Providence and Association Islands, its deeper purpose was to break Spain's monopoly of commerce in the Caribbean. In 1655 Cromwell sent General Venables with a fleet and 2000 men (who were to become colonists) to seize Hispaniola from Spain. They failed and so took Jamaica instead, which provoked war with Spain. It was an imprudent war, since it necessitated immense expenditures to guard and convoy English vessels in the Channel. Yet England did win Dunkirk from Spain, a bridle to the Dutch and a base from which to dominate northern Europe. Cromwell's greatness at home, observed Edward Hyde, was but a shadow of his glory abroad.

THE SEARCH FOR CONSENT

By 1653 Oliver Cromwell had arrived at the center of the English revolution. For forty years he had lived in Huntingdonshire, a modest Puritan gentleman, serving as justice of the peace, promoting lectureships, and managing an estate worth about £300 a year. He was born in 1599 into a junior branch of the Cromwell family that descended from Thomas Cromwell's sister. He attended the Huntingdon Grammar School under the fearsomely devout Dr. Beard and spent several years at Sidney Sussex College, the most puritanical of Cambridge colleges. He experienced the dark night of the soul, when he became convinced that he was the chief of all sinners and certainly damned. Then came the sudden light of God's grace and assurance of salvation. The outbreak of war and his prowess as a cavalry commander catapulted him into fame. He recruited able men, trained them incessantly, and introduced them to the newest tactics in cavalry warfare (which was to charge uninterruptedly at the opponent and cut him down with naked steel, not to pause to fire pistols into his ranks). Cromwell was a modest, rough-hewn man, who wanted to be painted warts and all, a cautious, even conservative man, whom religion and the pursuit of God's will made a revolutionary. Each new victory—Marston Moor, Naseby, Preston, Drogheda, Dunbar, and Worcester—strengthened his belief that God had prepared him and the army to lead England to the New Jerusalem.

Oliver Cromwell was a reluctant dictator who always sought a civilian scabbard in which to conceal the sword. From 1649 to 1653 the Rump Parliament cloaked the rule of the army, but Cromwell and the army eventually quarreled with the Rump. Cromwell, ever a practical man, saw that the Commonwealth could survive only if it were made popular and the royalists reconciled to it. He saw the need to win popularity by reducing taxes, granting amnesty to the royalists, allowing—within limits—religious toleration, and instituting political and legal reforms. But the Rump raised taxes to pay for the Dutch war, passed an amnesty ordinance that was riddled with exceptions, re-

Oliver Cromwell, portrait by Samuel Cooper (*Sidney Sussex College, Cambridge*).

fused to accept the Independents' demand for religious liberty, strictly licensed books, and instituted draconian legal reforms, such as the provision that adultery be punished with death. It also obstructed the political reforms sought by Cromwell and the army, who believed that new elections were necessary. The Rump therefore reluctantly bowed to military pressure and brought in a bill for the dissolution of Parliament and the holding of new elections. Then suddenly the army changed its mind, fearing that new elections would produce an even more conservative House of Commons. In order to prevent the passage of the bill for a dissolution and new elections Cromwell hastened to the House with a file of musketeers. He denounced the members, declared them unfit to be a Parliament for God's people, called in the musketeers, and cried out: "Depart I say, and let us have done with you. In the name of God, go."

The expulsion of the Rump inaugurated a new search for some form of consent to the rule of the army. General Lambert favored a council of state, a written constitution, and then later a Parliament. General Harrison proposed a nominated council of seventy saints, in imitation of the Jewish Sanhedrin. Cromwell chose a variation of Harrison's proposal: a Parliament of 140 members, chosen by the army from names put forward by Independent congregations throughout the land. The Parliament of Saints was the apotheosis of the idea that the godly should rule. Though they came to be called the Barebones Parliament after Praise-God Barebones, a leather seller and prominent member of the assembly, the social composition of this Parliament was not unlike earlier ones. It met in July and set furiously about the work of reform. Though there was not a lawyer in the House, the members decided to abolish the Court of Chancery. Extremists even spoke of replacing the Common law with the law of Moses. They also voted to establish civil marriage and to abolish lay patronage; and they began an attack on tithes, to the dismay of the gentry who had stolen many of them. The irresponsibility of the radical wing of the Parliament of Saints persuaded Cromwell and the moderates that the godly could not govern. Where he once had to do with knaves, Cromwell declared, meaning the Rump, he now had to do with fools. In December Cromwell and the moderates engineered the dissolution of Parliament.

Cromwell now turned to General Lambert's proposals: a written constitution with something monarchical in it. On December 12, 1653, Cromwell accepted The Instrument of Government, the only written constitution in English history. It provided for a Lord Protector, who should be Cromwell, a Council of State, to which it named the generals and their friends, and a Parliament, to be elected every three years by those in the counties with estates worth £200 a year and by the boroughs, which now included Manchester and Leeds. Ireland and Scotland should each send thirty members to the Parliament. It declared that there would be an army of 30,000 and a revenue of not less than £1.3 million, and it guaranteed toleration for all religions but popery, prelacy, and those sects which "under the profession of Christ, hold forth and practice licentiousness." Cromwell accepted The Instrument of Government because he saw a need for "healing and settling," for reconciliation and the restoration of order. He would act as a constable to keep the peace of the parish. In the next six years the Protectorate accomplished much: Administration was efficient and honest; the Court of Chancery was restored and its fees lowered; judges obtained legal security of tenure. A Commission of Triers ensured that godly and learned men were named to parish ministries and local Commissions of Ejectors removed clergy guilty of drunkenness or blasphemy. In 1655 Cromwell even allowed Jews, whom Edward I had expelled in 1290, to settle in England and worship freely. There was probably never a time when the Gospel was preached in England with more energy, eloquence, vigor, variety, and freedom than during these years.

But this fact made little difference when the first Protectorate Parliament met in 1654. Its social composition resembled earlier Parliaments, as did its habits of independence. It immediately attacked The Instrument of Government as illegal, and ninety republican members refused to swear a recognition of loyalty to the Protectorate. Cromwell expelled them, but the remaining members stood firm. They had three fundamental objections to the new regime: it made the executive financially independent of the legislature; it maintained a vast army; and it granted toleration to heretical sects. The members of the first Protectorate Parliament were not about to abandon financial control of the executive, acquiesce in a standing army, or accept religious toleration. It was busy drawing up a new constitution when Cromwell dissolved it in January 1655.

The dissolution inflamed public opinion throughout the country and led to several uprisings. Almost no one liked The Instrument of Government. The republicans viewed it as the establishment of monarchy. The royalists preferred the House of Stuart. The Levellers found it too aristocratic. The Fifth Monarchists believed it to be ungodly. The Fifth Monarchists were those who believed that there had been four universal monarchies in history and that Christ's return, which was imminent, would inaugurate the fifth and last. Nearly all the Puritan preachers believed in the millennium, that is that Christ would ultimately return to earth and rule for a thousand years. But they drew no political conclusion from this fact. The Fifth Monarchists did. They believed that the reign of Christ upon earth was shortly to begin and that it was the duty of the elect to remove hindrances to Christ's rule. The existing rulers were wicked and must be rejected. During the 1650s many Levellers, disheartened at their impotence, and many sectarians, disillusioned by the disbanding of the Parliament of Saints, drifted into the Fifth Monarchist camp. The modern historian finds the Levellers a source of perennial interest because they were the harbingers of democracy, but the Fifth Monarchists were more characteristic of the revolutionary fervor of this deeply religious age.

Cromwell's answer to the near anarchism of the Fifth Monarchists and the incipient rebellion of the royalists was to institute military government. In June 1655, on the advice of Generals Lambert and Desborough, he divided the country into eleven parts and placed a major-general with 500 picked cavalry over each. The purpose of the major-generals was to prevent rebellion and ensure that the local magistrates did their duty. They commanded the militia, purged town corporations, enforced religious toleration, exhorted and bullied justices of the peace, and prohibited race meetings and cockfights, places where royalists met to plot rebellion. The more zealous among them went beyond this original purpose and sought to enforce virtue on the people, strictly enforcing the Sabbath and punishing swearing and drunkenness. To pay for this military tyranny the government imposed a 10 percent tax on the property of all royalists, an arbitrary tax that proved quite inadequate and frightened all property owners.

The major-generals exerted all their influence to elect dependable members to the Parliament that met in 1656, and failed. Even after the Council of State had prevented 100 of the members from taking their seats, the Parliament turned on the government. It refused to approve the militia bill necessary to continue the regime of the major-generals. It passed a law bristling with penalties against Catholics. It fell upon James Naylor, a Quaker who rode into Bristol on a white donkey, saying he was a new incarnation of Christ. The Parliament sentenced him to be flogged, branded, and bored through the tongue. The savage and illegal persecution of Naylor led to a desire for a second chamber to check the House of Commons and the discovery of a plot to assassinate Cromwell led to speculation about who would succeed him should he be killed. A group of moderates therefore persuaded Parliament to present to the Protector The Humble Petition and Advice. The Humble Petition provided for a hereditary kingship in the family of Cromwell, an upper house whose members Cromwell should name and the House of Commons approve, a permanent revenue that should not exceed £1.3 million, and a prohibition against Cromwell's excluding men from Parliament. The fierce opposition of the army to the idea of kingship led Cromwell to reject the crown, but the other provisions of The Humble Petition and Advice came into effect, including the right of the Lord Protector to name his successor.

When Parliament assembled in January 1658 Cromwell permitted the 100 excluded members to return and named many of his friends in the Commons to the upper house. The effect was to destroy any hope of winning a majority in the Commons and to allow the opponents of the new constitution to capture control. Cromwell thereupon dissolved Parliament within three weeks. "Let God be Judge between you and me," he cried out. He died on September 3, 1658, before Parliament could meet again. For ten years he and the army had searched for consent, but searched in vain. The English were too wedded to their parliamentary liberties and too fearful of religious liberty. There was no disguising the fact that the Protectorate was in fact a military dictatorship.

THE RESTORATION

Two forces eroded the foundations of the Protectorate even before Cromwell's death removed the one man who could hold the army together: nostalgia for the old monarchy and financial bankruptcy.

The revolutionary pendulum swung to its farthest leftward point with the Barebones Parliament, and then began to swing back to the right, first to the restoration of government by a single person in The Instrument and then to an upper house in The Humble Petition and Advice. But public opinion swung even faster, driven by a hatred of high taxes and meddling major-generals. The Cony case in 1654 showed how little protection property enjoyed. Cony was a merchant who refused to pay a customs duty arbitrarily levied on silk. The council sent him to prison and prevailed in the case by dismissing one judge and jailing Cony's counsel. It was the Hampden case played over again. There was also deep resentment at the major-generals who replaced the gentry, the "natural rulers" of the counties. Slowly the logic of events led men of property to unite and caused the revolutionaries to divide. Religion ceased to be the greatest cause, and the recovery of their old liberties became the greatest good. As Edmund Chillenden, once a Leveller and a Fifth Monarchist, put it, "Pish, let religion alone; give me my small liberty."

In the summer of 1658, at a time when its military reputation abroad was higher than ever, England was racing toward bankruptcy. The debt stood at £1.5 million and the sailors were owed more than £500,000 in back pay, the soldiers more than £300,000. The Humble Petition and Advice limited the government to £1.3 million a year, when in fact it needed £2.5 million. Since there were no more crown, episcopal, and royalist lands to be sold, the money must be raised by the customs, excise, or assessment. The customs rose from £140,000 in 1643 to £502,000 in 1659, but the New Book of Rates was so high it throttled trade and reduced revenue. The excise, a tax on beer, meat, salt, soap, and starch, introduced by John Pym in 1643, fell largely on the poor. There was little hope of increasing revenues from it, so the government sought to increase the monthly assessment, a tax on rents, annuities, and offices, also introduced in 1643. It was modeled on the ship money tax and marked the first time in English history that the gentry were made to pay a substantial proportion of taxation. But all efforts to raise a million a year on the assessment failed. The Humble Petition and Advice even declared that no part of the revenue should be raised by a land tax. Having been taxed over £80 million during the interregnum, an average of £4 million a year, the English were ripe for a tax strike.

The Protectorate swiftly disintegrated after Oliver Cromwell's death. His eldest son, Richard, succeeded him and summoned a Parliament elected on the old franchise. In April 1659 that Parliament voted that the army council might not meet without its approval, whereupon the army forced Richard to dissolve Parliament. The army then abolished the Protectorate, sent Richard into retirement, and called back the Rump to screen its rule. But times had changed. The Rump itself insisted on controlling the army, and so the army dissolved it in October. Angered by this act, George Monck, commander of the army in Scotland, resolved to march into England. On January 2, 1660, he crossed the Tweed with 10,000 men, thereby destroying the unity on which the rule of the army depended. General Lambert marched north to repulse him, but his troops, unpaid for weeks and conscious of the odium they bore in the nation, deserted. Lambert's army melted away. Monck, whose troops had been paid through February, marched on to London. For motives that are undiscoverable, Monck decided to enter into an alliance with the City of London and to summon back not just the Rump, but all the members of the Long Parliament. He admitted the excluded members, however, only after they had pledged to dissolve the Long Parliament and order elections for a new one—a pledge they kept. Everywhere the electors of England returned royalists; even the Presbyterians, under the pressure of eleven years of military rule, had become royalists. The new Parliament met in April, restored the House of Lords, and invited back the House of Stuart.

Charles II made his return easier by promising, in the Declaration of Breda, an amnesty, liberty of conscience, the payment of wages owed soldiers and sailors, and the recognition of sales of land made since 1642, all subject to confirmation by Parliament. On May 29 Charles entered London, escorted by 20,000 troops. The church bells pealed, flowers covered the streets, wine ran freely, and Londoners crowded windows and balconies to see their king come home.

Though the House of Stuart returned, it returned to a kingdom much altered from that over which it had ruled in 1640. The English revolution left a lasting legacy to future generations, a legacy that was religious, political, and intellectual. In the religious realm it created English nonconformity. Because Cromwell seized power and held it for eleven years, Puritanism was able to put down roots so deep that no amount of persecution after 1660 could dislodge it. England became irremediably divided between Anglican and Dissent, Church and Chapel. Those who persisted in attending the Chapel brought to English public life an independence, a nonconformist conscience, that did much to make England the home of liberty and individuality. Politically, the revolution ensured the defeat of absolutism and the permanence of Parliament.

The most significant fact about the Restoration was that the English restored their Parliament before they restored their king. And it was a Parliament that had learned to rule—to create new financial departments, to establish committees of trade, to administer the Church, and to conduct foreign policy. The Committee of Both Kingdoms during the civil war anticipated the modern cabinet. Habits of government gained over two decades were not easily cast off. Finally, there was the ferment of ideas that raged during these twenty years, ideas that were not lost because they were not immediately realized. The Independents' cry for liberty of conscience, the Levellers' demand for democracy, Milton's plea for freedom of the press, Lilburne's insistence that all governments be under the law, the merchants' demand for freedom of enterprise, and the army's experiment in republicanism, all survived in the realm of ideas, not to speak of the religious ferment which saw the emergence of ideas of free grace, free will, and the inner light. During the twenty years of the English revolution, 22,000 sermons and pamphlets were published in England. The kingdom could never be the same again.

FURTHER READING

*ROBERT ASHTON. *The English Civil War: Conservatism and Revolution 1603–1649.* London, 1978. An original interpretation as well as a textbook; his sensible judgments are a useful antidote to many an overstated thesis.

C.V. WEDGWOOD. *The King's Peace, 1637–1641* and *The King's War, 1641–1647.* New York, 1955, 1959. A vivid and splendid narrative, punctuated by shrewd and sensitive portraits; Wedgwood examines the motives of men rather than the underlying causes of the revolution.

*LAWRENCE STONE. *The Causes of the English Revolution 1529–1642.* London, 1972. Stone does analyze the underlying causes

with an essay on "Theories of Revolution," a summary of the controversy over the rise of the gentry, and an interpretive essay on the causes of the revolution.

ANTHONY FLETCHER. *The Outbreak of the English Civil War.* London, 1982. A scholarly, detailed narrative of events from 1640 to 1643, which emphasizes the leadership of John Pym and his exploitation of papist and royalist plots.

J.S. MORRILL. *The Revolt of the Provinces: Conservatives and Radicals in the English Civil War, 1630–1650.* New York, 1976. An interpretation of the revolution from a provincial perspective, arguing that local concerns led to neutralism and a desire for peace and reconciliation.

AUSTIN WOOLRYCH. *Battles of the English Civil War*. London, 1961. Contains attractively written accounts of Marston Moor, Naseby, and Preston, together with a study of military and political developments from 1642 to 1649.

BLAIR WORDEN. *The Rump Parliament*. Cambridge, England, 1974. Provides a coherent account of the politics of the Rump, a penetrating analysis of its membership, and a sharp revision of the reasons for its dissolution in 1653.

G.E. AYLMER, ed. *The Interregnum: The Quest for Settlement, 1646-1660*. Hamden, Conn., 1972. Consists of a graceful introduction and eight essays by distinguished historians that sum up the most recent research.

*CHRISTOPHER HILL. *God's Englishman: Oliver Cromwell and the English Revolution*. London, 1970. The most recent life of Cromwell, by an historian who knows the age of Cromwell more intimately than any living historian.

*CHRISTOPHER HILL. *The World Turned Upside Down: Radical Ideas During the English Revolution*. Penguin Books, 1975. An immensely learned and sympathetic guide to the Familists, Seekers, Diggers, Muggletonians, Quakers, Baptists, and Ranters who called into question every traditional belief and ancient institution.

15 Restoration and Revolution: 1660-1689

A powerful argument can be made for the proposition that 1660—not 1066 or 1485 or 1688—is the most significant date in English history. The argument would not rest on the fact of Charles II's restoration, but on the fact that a number of other developments reached fruition in 1660 and created the modern world. The English ceased to speak of "the King *in* Parliament," suggesting there was some mystical harmony to be achieved, and spoke of "the King *and* Parliament," thereby acknowledging that they might differ. The last relic of feudalism ended in 1660, when Parliament confirmed the abolition of knight service and wardship, and voted the King an excise on beer in their place. The modern, untrammeled freehold tenure came into existence. Commercial and manufacturing enterprises likewise became untrammeled as guild regulations and monopolies disappeared. An act of 1663 repealed medieval prohibitions on regrating and engrossing, thus allowing speculators to corner a market. The modern standing army came into existence when Charles decided to keep the Coldstream Guard on foot. The modern pattern of meals—breakfast, lunch, and dinner—emerged, and tea and coffee began to replace beer and ale at the table. Men's dress became modern as doublet and cloak gave way to coat and waistcoat. The modern theater, with its proscenium arch and women playing women's parts, sprang into being. In 1666 the Great Fire burned the old Gothic London to the ground, allowing Sir Christopher Wren to rebuild its churches in a classical style. Modern London is still in part Wren's London.

The profoundest change of all came in the realm of thought. The scientific revolution, tangibly embodied in The Royal Society of London for Improving Natural Knowledge, founded in 1662, swept away the hierarchies and correspondences, the essences and accidents, the crystalline spheres and occult qualities of the medieval world picture and replaced it with a modern cosmology. If a modern Englishman were to sup with Ben Jonson in a tavern, their conversation would be plagued by misunderstandings. But if he were to converse with John Dryden in a coffeehouse, he would find that they shared the same language and presuppositions. For modern man the age of Newton, not the age of Bede or Chaucer or Shakespeare, marks the backward edge of time.

THE SCIENTIFIC REVOLUTION

The picture of the natural world which the scientific revolution shattered was a strange and complicated one. Its astronomy derived from Claudius Ptolemy, who lived in Alexandria in the second century A.D. Ptolemy taught that the earth was motionless at the center of the universe, that around it were ten concentric crystalline spheres carrying the planets and the stars, and that beyond the tenth sphere lay the high heavens. Angels kept the spheres in motion, and all bodies moved in perfect circles at uniform speeds. To make this picture fit the observed motion of the stars and planets, Ptolemy invented a complicated system of epicycles, eccentrics, and equants. Medieval people took their physics from Aristotle, who taught that heavy objects fall to the earth more swiftly than light ones, that a uniform force applied to an object will move it at a constant speed, and that an object will immediately stop if the force acting on it ceases. In Aristotelian physics an arrow should drop to the ground the minute it leaves the bowstring. The chemistry of the age was based on the writings of the Greek philosopher Empedocles, who taught that matter consisted of four elements—fire, air, water, and earth. Later writers argued that the planets and stars were made up of a fifth element (or "quintessence"), an ethereal substance that grew more pure as one traveled away from the earth.

The towering figure in physiology was Galen, a physician born in Asia Minor in the second century A.D. He did not believe that blood circulated in the body; it merely ebbed and flowed like the tides. The dark red blood of the veins carried nutriment to the muscles; the bright red blood in the arteries carried spirits to all parts of the body. There were three spirits: the natural spirit which flowed from the liver, the vital spirit which flowed from the heart, and the animal spirit which flowed from the brain. Galen was quite ignorant of the glandular system, so he put forward a system of four humors, or bodily fluids: blood, phlegm, yellow bile, and black bile. Their imbalance caused disease. The physician's duty was to restore the balance, which he did by purging and bleeding. The commonest form of diagnosis was "water-casting," or examination of the urine, since the imbalance of the humors could be discovered from the color of the urine.

These curious, complicated, mistaken, and nonsensical ideas dominated human life for nearly two thousand years, until the development and application of the experimental method swept them away. The ancient Greeks were proficient in mathematics and the medieval scholastics were adept at formal logic, but neither had ever stumbled on the experimental method, which lies at the heart of science. The experimental method consists of the careful observation and precise measurement of the natural world, the induction of general ideas from these observations, the deduction of further propositions from these general ideas, and the testing of these ideas and propositions by going once again to nature.

Robert Grosseteste in the thirteenth century had recognized the importance of induction—that is, of deriving general ideas from the particulars observed—and of verification—that is, of testing those ideas by further investigation. But his thought had more influence in fourteenth-century Paris and fifteenth-century Padua than in England. It remained for Sir Francis Bacon, courtier and politician, philosopher and essayist, to advocate once again the empirical, inductive road to truth. In his *Novum Organum*, published in 1628, he declared that reason "left to itself, ought always to be suspected," and that logic "by no means reaches the subtilty of nature." "Our method," he wrote, "is continually to dwell among things." He urged that axioms be derived from particulars and tested by further experiment. Bacon failed, however, to appreciate the importance of deductive reasoning and mathematics to the scientist, an oversight which René Descartes, a contemporary French philosopher, corrected. Descartes, whose thought was wholly deductive, discovered a one-to-one correspondence between the realm of number (algebra and arithmetic) and the realm of space (geometry). A copy of his work on geometry excited the mind of the young Isaac Newton at Cambridge University.

Even before Bacon and Descartes had published their works, an Italian scholar, Galileo, a professor at the University of Padua from 1592 to 1610, had combined their approaches in the study of mechanics. He was the first true experimentalist, the first modern scientist. In England that distinction must go to William Harvey, son of a prosperous Kentish yeoman, who studied at Cambridge and Padua, and in 1628 published a book which demonstrated that blood circulated through the body. He showed that the heart, which acts as a pump, is the starting point of the blood, and not the liver, as Galen thought. He showed that the valves in the veins permitted the blood to flow only toward the heart and those in the arteries away from the heart, so that the flow was continuous and in one direction. His decisive argument was a quantitative one. He calculated that the volume of blood pumped from the heart in an hour was in excess of the weight of a man, and concluded that it must therefore circulate. His book, *On the Motion of the Heart and Blood*, was initially rejected in England and abroad, but ultimately it made all of Galen's physiology obsolete. Even more important than his conclusions were his methods. For twenty years he conducted painstaking experiments, dissecting fish, eels, frogs, pigs, and dogs. He was the first experimental physiologist.

What William Harvey did for physiology, Robert Boyle sought to do for chemistry. Boyle was the son of the immensely wealthy Earl of Cork, and his father's wealth allowed him to build a splendid laboratory in his London home and to devote his life to science. He experimented with the air pump and established the relationship between the volume and pressure of a gas at a constant temperature—a relationship known today as Boyle's law. In 1661 he published *The Sceptical Chemist*, a work that swept away the ancient Greek belief in four elements and the scholastic belief in essences and qualities. Boyle believed that the differences between substances could be explained in terms of the different arrangements of the ultimate particles of which all matter was composed. Because he rejected the idea of chemical elements, Boyle failed to establish the foundations of modern chemistry, but his revival of the atomic hypothesis made it easier for Antoine Lavoisier to do so a century later.

Isaac Newton, the solitary child of a small landowner in Lincolnshire and a mathematical genius who quickly became professor of mathematics at Cambridge, made the supreme contribution to European science. He brought together in one great synthesis the new astronomical ideas of Copernicus and Kepler and the new physical ideas of Galileo. As early as 1543 Copernicus, a Polish mathematician, had argued that the planets orbit around the sun, not the earth, and that the apparent movement of the stars and sun is the result of the daily rotation of the earth. Kepler demonstrated in 1619 that the planets move in ellipses, not circles, and showed that the squares of the times taken by any two planets in their revolutions around the sun were in the same ratio as the cubes of their average distances from the sun. Meanwhile, Galileo had discovered the concept of inertia—that is, he had shown that a body in motion will remain in motion unless an outside force works against it. Galileo's discovery demonstrated a need for some force to keep the planets from moving off in a straight line through space.

Isaac Newton is said to have grasped the clue while idly watching an apple fall in the orchard of his Lincolnshire home, where he had fled in 1665 to escape the plague. If an apple on the highest hill or in the deepest mine is attracted to the earth, why not the moon also? He then formulated his two laws of gravitation: The force between any two bodies is directly proportional to the product of their masses and inversely proportional to the square of the distance between them. He proved his laws mathematically using an early form of calculus that he invented. The moon falls toward the earth and away from a straight line by about .0044 feet per second. Since the moon is 60 times farther from the center of the earth than is the earth's surface, $60^2 \times .0044$ should give the speed of a falling body at the earth's surface—which it does, 16 feet in the first second. Newton had demonstrated an identity between the mathematically deduced and the empirically observed, the ultimate achievement in science.

Newton did not publish his calculations immediately, because he was not certain that the mass of the earth could be taken as concentrated at its center. But some years later several members of the Royal Society fell to discussing why planets should move in an ellipse. One of them, Edmund Halley, went down to Cambridge to seek an answer from Newton. Newton replied that he

Sir Isaac Newton, portrait by Sir Godfrey Kneller (*National Portrait Gallery*).

had already solved the problem, but then had to confess he had mislaid his notes. He thereupon wrote out another solution. Prodded by Halley, he published it in 1687 in *Principia Mathematica*. In this work he showed that a planet travels in an elliptical orbit because the force of gravity exactly counter-acts the force of inertia, and that the force of gravity is proportional to the product of the mass of any two particles and inversely proportional to the square of the distance between them. A few simple, universal laws of motion now replaced the crystalline spheres, angles, epicycles, eccentrics, equants, and prime movers of Ptolemaic astronomy.

CAUSES AND CONSEQUENCES

Historians have found it easier to chronicle than to account for the rise of modern science. Why did the development of this powerful method for apprehending the truth reach fruition in Europe in the seventeenth century? Why not in ancient Greece or imperial China?

Marxist historians have offered one explanation: it was the result of economic changes in the sixteenth and seventeenth centuries. Not until the bourgeoisie had broken the feudal order could science serve the cause of capitalist production. The weakness of the economic interpretation lies in the fact that the great scientists of the time—Copernicus, Galileo, Harvey, Newton—were motivated primarily by curiosity, not be economic forces. Yet economic forces, though not basic, were favorable. The voyages of discovery produced technical problems of navigation that led to improved quadrants, maps, and chronometers. William Harvey, a practicing physician, was concerned with the health of his patients. Wealthy merchants and financiers promoted scientific education. Sir Thomas Gresham, for example, established Gresham College in 1597, three of whose seven chairs were devoted to scientific subjects. It was a principal center of scientific activity in the early seventeenth century. Thomas Sprat, the first historian of the Royal Society, praised the practical objects of the society, which were "to increase the powers of all mankind and to free them from the bondage of errors." Bacon put the matter more succinctly: "Knowledge is power."

Those historians influenced by the German sociologist Max Weber have sought to connect the rise of science with Protestantism. The explanation suffers from the undeniable fact that many of the greatest European scientists were Catholic and that Harvey, Boyle, and Newton were moderate in their religious views, not Puritan. Yet English Puritanism was not hostile to science; the Puritan revolution stirred up people's minds and made them inquisitive. At Oxford a group of Baconians moved into the university behind the Parliamentary armies. Cromwell's brother-in-law became warden of Wadham College; his physician became warden of Merton. Other scholars, such as Christopher Wren, Robert Boyle, Robert Hooke, and John Locke, attracted to Oxford, formed a group that became the nucleus of the Royal Society in 1662. Restoration England was not puritanical, but neither did it suffer from the Counter-Reformation Catholicism that crushed science in Catholic Europe after 1660.

The real explanation for the scientific revolution lies in the history of ideas. By the sixteenth century Europeans, having appropriated the knowledge of antiquity, were led to study nature itself. Furthermore, medieval science had reached an advanced stage of complexity. Scientists devised ever more epicycles to make the theories of the ancients square with nature, until those theories collapsed under their own weight. At the same time, people began to ask different questions of nature: not *why* an object fell to earth, but *how* it fell. In an increasingly secular society, concern shifted from metaphysics to physics. But perhaps the most fundamental explanation lies in the conjunction of two intellectual traditions, that of Greek deductive thought, going back to Euclid, and that of English inductive thought, going back to Grosseteste. The merging of these two traditions at fourteenth-century Paris, sixteenth-century Padua, and seventeenth-century Cambridge created the experimental method.

The consequences of the scientific revolution were profound, but slow in working themselves out. The new experimental method did not immediately increase either human wealth or health, as Bacon had hoped. Harvey's momentous discovery had no immediate practical result. Not until the nineteenth century was there a close alliance between science and technology. Improved agricultural methods in the late seventeenth century owed little to science. There was one striking exception: Boyle's law describing the relationship of the pressure, volume, and temperature of gases allowed Henry Newcomen in Queen Anne's reign to invent the atmospheric engine, the forerunner of the steam engine. In this case knowledge was power, undreamed-of power.

The new science likewise slowly eroded belief in magic. There was no place in its cosmology for witches who could cause illness in others, astrologers who sold talismans to guard against witches, village wizards who could cure diseases, or wise women whose charms and spells warded off misfortune. Tudor and Stuart England was a land filled with magic. There were magical herbs for weariness, charms to keep weeds out of grain, wassails to bless apple trees, amulets to protect soldiers, divinatory systems to ascertain the price of corn, and magical formulas to keep away pests. Religion was the great rival of magic, and the Reformation, by taking a good deal of magic out of religion, left a vacuum the astrologers and village wizards filled. But magic could not survive a science that demanded that all truths be demonstrated and a mechanistic philosophy that saw the world as composed of small, indestructable particles formed into larger bodies whose inertia and attraction could be measured exactly. The world of nature was a vast mechanical system governed by a few simple laws.

It was not natural science alone that caused the decline in magic; the social sciences helped. French mathematicians formulated laws of probability and English scholars drew up mortality tables. In 1662 John Graunt attempted to construct tables that estimated life expectancy. In the second half of the seventeenth century the word "coincidence," in the sense of the simultaneous occurrence of causally unrelated events, first appeared. To this nascent statistical sense was joined a new spirit of self-help, a new confidence in human initiative, even a belief in progress. Agricultural writers campaigned against "the pattern of ancient ignorance" and politicians rejected the appeal to precedent. "There be daily many things found out and daily more may be," wrote Sir Robert Filmer in 1653, "which our forefathers never knew to be possible."

The new science also transformed the nature of religious belief, though that was not the intention of men like Robert Boyle and Isaac Newton. They were religious men who repudiated the skeptical doctrines of Thomas Hobbes. Newton spent much of his later life studying the prophecies of Daniel and the Apocalypse of St. John. Yet the picture he drew of a universe subject to immutable natural laws had no room in it for miracles. It also weakened belief in intercessory prayer and diminished faith in divine inspiration. A wise Providence, operating by physical causes, now replaced the revelations, inspirations, miraculous cures, and divine interventions of past years. But only with an educated elite; belief in a miraculous religion continued among the people at large, just as belief in magic continued in the villages of England well into the nineteenth century. One of the chief consequences of the scientific revolution was the creation, between 1680 and 1720, of a gulf between the enlightened few and the superstitious many.

The new science also weakened the appeal of poetry. In literature the age of poetry gave way to the age of prose, the age of Milton to the age of Dryden. John Dryden was a poet and dramatist who thought judgment more important than imagination, and rhyme more important than metaphor. To the Elizabethans the poet was a seer and prophet, and metaphor a revelation of the truth. To Dryden and his contemporaries, metaphors were an adornment to language and poetry an entertainment. "King Oberon and his invisible army of fairies," wrote Thomas Sprat, are "false chimeras." Even the style of preaching altered, as clarity and simplicity drove out richness and imagery.

To this development there was one notable exception. John Milton, blind and disillusioned, his hopes of a regenerate England crushed, retired to his house in Jewin Street to write *Paradise Lost*, the greatest poetic epic of the English language. To its composition he brought a mind stored with all the biblical, classical, medieval, and modern learning of his time and a verse that was dignified, flexible, charged with emotion, and capable both of simple directness and sublime heights. Milton set out to "justify the ways of God to men," and did so by arguing that virtue can only be achieved by struggle, and that the fall of Adam and Eve was therefore inevitable, since passive virtue, without the challenge of an imperfect world, cannot release the greatness in man. For Milton a cloistered virtue was no virtue at all, and for Milton the pursuit of virtue was the most heroic enterprise of all.

RESTORATION SOCIETY

Restoration society set little store on the pursuit of virtue and much on wit and pleasure. The Court once again became the center of society and the King the center of the Court. Charles II was an easygoing, pleasure-loving, tolerant, careless, and sensual King, without any spark of religious enthusiasm. He had his first mistress when he was 18 and a succession of them thereafter, who bore him fourteen bastard children. He was a man of fashion who told his Council in 1666 that he intended to alter his dress and soon appeared in a coat and waistcoat, from which the modern coat and vest derive. He also popularized horse racing at Newmarket (where he introduced the Barbary stallions) and yachting for pleasure (which was hitherto a Dutch pastime). He and a group of Restoration wits also set the moral tone at Court, a tone that was coarse, libertine, debauched, and witty. Charles acquired a bawdiness of conversation that became habitual with him, and his wit and easy manners became a model for others.

The wit and bawdiness of the Court spilled over into the theater. Some of the Court wits wrote plays, others were patrons of playwrights. The result was a theater that appealed to the Court and the fashionable around town, and plays that satirized all bourgeois virtues, especially marriage. Playwrights ridiculed the country squire, the London merchant, and the faithful husband. William Wycherly did so brutally in *The Country Wife* and George Etherege more cheerfully in *She Would If She Could.* John Dryden captivated the Restoration rakes with his *Marriage à la Mode,* but won even more popularity with a bombastic tragedy after the French fashion called *The Conquest of Granada.*

Technically the Restoration theater saw notable advances. Theaters were now completely roofed over, with footlights, drop curtains, and painted scenery. The proscenium arch came into use, which gave the stage the "picture frame" appearance it retained well into the twentieth century. Women's parts were now taken by women, not young boys, and men of fashion often came to see the actress rather than the play, even though her talents were often little greater than her virtue.

To the Puritans the Great Plague in 1665 and the Great Fire in 1666 must have seemed to be God's chastisement of the English for their wickedness. The plague struck in May 1665 and lasted until the end of the year, during which time over 68,000 Londoners died. The wealthy fled London, leaving the poor to die in their squalid, rat-infested slums. Little wonder it came to be called the "poor's plague." The plague had waned and the wealthy had returned when a second disaster befell London. In September 1666 a strong east wind drove an accidental fire in Pudding Lane through the city. The fire raged for five days and destroyed the whole city between the Tower and the Temple: 13,000 houses and 89 churches went up in flames, though few deaths resulted.

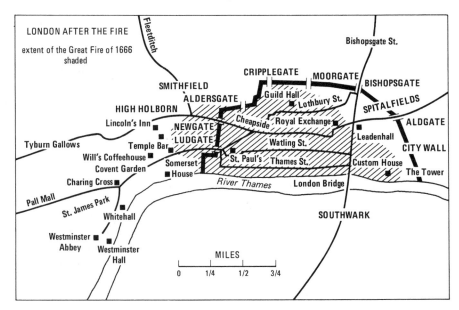

LONDON AFTER THE FIRE

extent of the Great Fire of 1666 shaded

The fire and the rebuilding of London did little to cause the disappearance of the plague in England, for it disappeared in towns where there was no fire. The chief cause of the disappearance of the plague was probably the fact that the modern brown rat extirpated the medieval black rat, and the brown rat does not carry the plague-flea to nearly the same extent as the black rat.

Though the fire did not end the plague, it gave Sir Christopher Wren an opportunity to rebuild the churches of London. Wren had not been trained as an architect. His father, Dean of Windsor Chapel, had sent him to Oxford, where he studied mathematics and astronomy and where he put before the authorities 53 inventions, theories, and mechanical improvements. He went on to become a professor of astronomy and a founder of the Royal Society. But he also dabbled in architecture, designing the Sheldonian Theater in Oxford. Thus when the fire created the necessity to rebuild St. Paul's Cathedral and countless parish churches, a royal commission named Wren chief architect. He resolved to break completely from the past, to turn away from the Gothic to the classical. It was, however, the classical style he had studied in Paris, a blend

St. Paul's Cathedral, London, designed by Sir Christopher Wren (*British Tourist Authority*).

of the classical and baroque. The dome of St. Paul's, one of the most perfect in the world, is classical in its reposeful outline, as is the colonnade around the drum that supports it. But the façade, with its coupled columns and two fantastic turrets, is baroque, as is the interior, with its colossal niches set in the piers and outer walls, giving an undulating effect to choir and aisles. St. Paul's was built in the grand manner, of white Portland stone, its dome rising high above the city, but it is never overpowering in scale or ostentatious in detail. It retains something of the good sense and good manners of the English. The same is true of the fifty-three city churches Wren designed. The exteriors have a dignified simplicity—a plain rectangle, with an elaborate steeple rising in front of it. The interiors show more ingenuity of design, more interlocking effects, creating a spatial polyphony appropriate to the age of Purcell. Yet Wren always kept in mind the need to plan his space as an auditorium. This meant that some of the mystery of the Gothic was lost, but that the practical needs of worshippers were met.

As Paris was the model for monumental architecture and white Portland stone its material, so Amsterdam was the model for domestic architecture and red brick its building material. In London a ground plan evolved that became standardized by the end of the seventeenth century. Houses were built in terraces or rows (unlike the detached *hôtels* in which Parisian merchants lived). Each house would have an entrance on one side leading straight to the staircase. On each floor (of which there were three of four), there would be one large front room and one large back room. In the basement were the rooms for the servants—thus creating the upstairs-downstairs gulf in English society. This ground plan proved so useful that it remained practically unaltered until the end of the Victorian age. There was little splendor but much comfort in these houses. The furnishings added to the comfort. Pottery and glass replaced pewter and wood at the table; and many families came to use knives, forks, mirrors, and pocket handkerchiefs. The high-backed chair came into vogue, as well as the small settee just wide enough for two persons to sit intimately together. Rich fabrics upholstered the chairs and settees, and elegant walnut replaced sturdy oak. Silver coffeepots and teapots served the new beverages and grandfather clocks kept the time. The pocket watch appeared, but it was more decorative than accurate. Yet it might tell a gentleman when to leave his coffeehouse, where he met his friends to discuss commerce or politics.

It was commerce that paid for all. A tax on coal entering the port of London, for instance, paid for the rebuilding of St. Paul's between 1675 and 1710. The years from 1660 to 1700 were among the most expansive in English history. Exports rose from £4.1 million a year to £6.4 million, and imports from £4.4 million to £5.8 million, thus turning a trade deficit of £.3 million into a surplus of £.6 million. Reexports, particularly tobacco and sugar, accounted for a fourth of exports. Cloth, which in 1660 accounted for 75 percent of the value of exports, accounted for less than 50 percent in 1700. America, the West Indies, India, and the East provided a third of all imports. Between 1600 and

1700 calico imports from the East grew from 240,000 to 861,000 pieces. By 1700 the Royal African Company was sending 100,000 slaves a year to America and the West Indies. The growth of commerce led inevitably to the growth of shipping, which rose from 175,000 tons in 1660 to 340,000 tons in 1688.

The Navigation Act of 1660, which repeated and strengthened the provisions of the 1651 Act, and the Staple Act of 1663, which required colonists to purchase their European goods from England, did much to promote this growth, but only because they worked with, rather than against, other economic forces. Political stability, social mobility, the absence of internal regulation, freedom of enterprise, developing industries, a productive agriculture, and a powerful navy helped. Twice during these years, in 1665–67 and 1672–74, England demonstrated that armed aggression could promote commerce by going to war against the Dutch. "What we want," said George Monck, now Duke of Albemarle, "is more of the trade the Dutch now have." By 1700 England had overtaken the Dutch as the greatest commercial power in Europe, and people of all ranks were prospering. The price of sugar fell by half, farmers were exporting their surplus grain to Europe, and the East India Company investor was earning 20 percent on his capital.

RURAL SOCIETY

The historian would be ill advised to push the argument for the modernity of Restoration England too far, since life in the village went along as it had for centuries—and would continue to do so until shattered by the Industrial Revolution. Most people lived in villages, 74 percent by Gregory King's estimate. Another 16 percent lived in towns whose average size was about 1000 inhabitants. Only the remaining 10 percent, who lived in London, lived in a truly urban environment. Villages ranged in size from 200 to 500 inhabitants, with a middle-sized village containing about 400. England was thus a land of villages set among green meadows and ploughed fields, held together by a network of small market towns, the whole network centered on the vast metropolis of London.

The social structure of the village rested on the family, or household. In the village of Goodnestone in Kent, for instance, there were sixty-two households containing 277 persons. A household was composed of the father, mother, children, and servants, but not of grandparents or uncles or aunts. Where there were many servants, the household might be quite large. In Goodnestone there were 23 persons in the household of Edward Hales, Esquire. The household of the average husbandman, however, was small—the two parents, one or two children, and a single servant. Even the humblest families had a servant who helped work the land. To every farm there was a family, and therefore marriage was the entry into full membership in village society. The men and boys did the ploughing, carting, hedging, and the heavy work of the harvest;

the women and girls prepared meals, made the butter and cheese, baked the bread, brewed the beer, looked after the cattle, and took the fruit to market. At harvest everyone went out into the field, for in a northern climate, where there was only one crop a year, swift harvesting was critical. Even a gentleman might break the first rule of gentility, not to work with his hands, and join in.

Traditional agriculture required a pool of labor to help with ploughing and harvesting. This was furnished by the laborer, who had no holdings in the land other than the garden around the cottage in which he and his family lived. In Goodnestone there were a dozen such families. They could never have survived on the wages paid for agricultural labor, but they supplemented that income with industrial labor, mostly spinning yarn, though in some parts of England they worked as miners and nailers. Industry made it possible to put enough people on the land to meet the seasonal needs of agriculture.

In the village of Goodnestone there were 3 households of gentry, 12 of substantial yeomen and husbandmen, 14 of husbandmen, 9 of craftsmen (two carpenters, two brickmakers, a weaver, a shoemaker, a tailor, and a grocer), 12 of laborers, and 12 of paupers. The families of the craftsmen and laborers were smaller than those of the yeomen, and the families of the yeomen were smaller than those of the gentry. (The gentry had an average of 3.5 children, the yeomen and husbandmen 2.9, the tradesmen 2.3, the laborers 2.1, and the paupers 1.8). The poor simply could not expect to live long enough to have as many children as the rich. Most of the land in Goodnestone was farmed by a dozen substantial families of yeomen and husbandmen. Of the villagers born in humbler households, 52 went on to serve in larger households (16 in gentry households, 34 in yeomen and husbandmen households, and 2 in tradesman households). When they entered these households they entered a circle of affection, and though it could turn into a scene of hatred it was always human and intimate. In traditional society the scale of life was small, and the place of one's work was usually the place of one's residence. The patriarchal authority of the male head of the household was unquestioned, be he a gentleman or a laborer.

The average villager need not fear starvation, but neither could he or she look forward to a long life. In the late seventeenth century the life expectancy of a person at birth was only 32 years (in Britain in 1951 it was 65.8). If a man could reach 21, however, he might look forward to thirty more years of life. Early death was a common occurrence in Stuart England; between a third and half of all burials registered in the seventeenth century were of "sons and daughters." Most of these were carried away by disease, not starvation. The evidence of parish registers suggests that in England, unlike in France, the specter of starvation had been removed. John Graunt showed that of 229,250 burials in London in 1661, only 51 starved—and London had a mass of paupers. The English villager had enough to eat, and there was considerable reason for his despising the French peasant for eating black bread and wearing wooden shoes.

The English did not starve because population was kept within bounds.

Late marriages and high infant mortality ensured that families were small. When a son married, he left his parents' household and started one of his own. If he were not in a position to do this, if there were no plot of land, no cottage, no apprenticeship available, then he did not marry. The average age of brides was 24, of bridegrooms 28. Given the short life expectancy of the time, it was unlikely that they would have over five children. The average was four children, and so the population could barely replace itself, since half the babies born did not survive until the age of 20. It is an error to think that the Industrial Revolution brought an increase in infant mortality. A baby born into a Glasgow slum in 1879 had a better chance of surviving than a baby born into the rural, prosperous village of Clayworth in Nottinghamshire in 1679.

The population was also kept down by the personal discipline of the villagers. The rate of bastardy in Stuart England was about 3.6 percent, compared with 4 percent today. Fornication and adultery did occur and there were whores, but most men and women were chaste until marriage. Nor did the Restoration, despite the lewdness of the Court, bring any change in morality. The Church universally condemned sexual intercourse outside marriage. On the surface, the fact that in one parish 42 percent of the babies were born in the eighth month, and in another 28 percent, might seem to contradict this strict sexual morality, but this surprising fact can be explained by the custom of couples cohabiting after the contract to marry, which usually preceded the ceremony by three weeks.

This strict sexual morality was taught from the pulpit. Village society was an oral society, for most people were illiterate. In the county of Surrey in 1642, no less than two-thirds of the males over 18 had to make a mark rather than sign their name to a protestation of loyalty to Parliament. But though they could not read, they attended church. The villagers of Stuart England were literal Christian believers, who looked on the Christian religion as the explanation of life. In Goodnestone all but sixteen villagers took communion at Easter, and the sixteen promised to make amends at Whitsuntide. It was at church that they learned what was going on in England and distant Europe. The preaching parson was indispensable to the social life of the village. It was also the parson who preached those doctrines of subordination to superiors that prevented social unrest in a society dominated by status. In 10,000 parish churches, after Matins on Sunday the priest taught the youth of the parish a catechism which enjoined upon them the Fifth Commandment, to honor thy father and mother, and extended the commandment to submission to all governors. Even the Shorter Catechism of 1644, a Puritan one, preached obedience to superiors. Lilburne might urge that all men were equal, but the clergy taught that they were not, and that obedience was owed to one's superiors.

THE RESTORATION SETTLEMENT

Obedience was very much a part of the settlement between church and state hammered out by Charles and Parliament between 1660 and 1665. The settlement in the state was based on a balance of government, a balance in which the privileges of Parliament offset the prerogatives of the Crown. Executive power was given to Charles, though not in the full measure that his father had enjoyed it. The prerogative courts (Star Chamber, Requests, High Commission, and the Councils of the North and Wales) were not restored, and Parliament stood readier than ever to impeach ministers of state. In 1662 Parliament voted that the command of the militia should reside in the King, but since he was to exercise it through the lord lieutenants, it became in fact the armed forces of the propertied classes. A rebellion of Fifth Monarchists in 1661, however, gave Charles II an excuse to retain a regiment of horse and a regiment of foot, which became the nucleus of a standing army. The army grew from 5000 men in 1660 to 8500 in 1685. But Charles's executive and military powers were of little use if he were financially dependent on Parliament. The crux of the Restoration settlement lay with finances.

It was Parliament's intention to make the King financially independent. It therefore looked at the expenses of the Crown, found them to have been about £1.1 million a year from 1637 to 1641, added £100,000 to cover increased expenses, and voted Charles II an annual revenue of £1.2 milion. Unfortunately for Charles, these revenues came to only £900,000. In 1662 Parliament sought to correct its miscalculation by voting Charles a hearth tax, which brought his permanent revenue to £1,082,000. For any expenditure above this sum Charles was dependent on Parliament, since benevolences, forced loans, and ship money remained illegal. By voting a duty on wine and an excise on beer, Parliament raised Charles's revenue to £1.3 million in 1671, but the duty expired after eight years and the excise after six. During Charles's reign a precarious financial equilibrium supported an unsteady balance of government.

Parliament made no attempt to establish an equilibrium or balance in the Church. Charles had promised in the Declaration of Breda to grant "liberty to tender consciences," but he and his chief minister, Edward Hyde, now Earl of Clarendon, made the mistake of postponing the settlement of the Church from the Convention Parliament (which came to an end in late 1660) to the Cavalier Parliament (which was elected in the spring of 1661). The royalists won an overwhelming victory in those elections; only about sixty Presbyterians won seats. Thus Clarendon's scheme to include the Presbyterians within the Church, and Charles's to tolerate them outside the Church, came to nothing. The country squires, smarting from years of subservience to Puritan preachers, brought back bishops, Prayer Book, surplices, altars, and lay patronage. In 1661 they passed the Corporation Act, which required all municipal officeholders to take the sacrament of the Lord's Supper according to the rites of the Church of England. In 1662 they passed an Act of Uniformity that restored the Book of Common Prayer, required all clergymen to assent to everything contained in it, fined those who administered the sacrament without episcopal ordination, and required all schoolmasters to be licensed by the local bishop. The Conventicle Act of 1664 imposed heavy penalties on any person who attended a "conventicle," that is, a religious service other than that provided by the Church of England. The Five Mile Act of 1665 forbade Nonconformist clergymen to come within five miles of any corporate town. The Nonconformists branded these acts the Clarendon Code, even though Clarendon did not approve of the later acts. With the passage of the Act of Uniformity, 2000 clergymen, one in five in the land, resigned their benefices. Thus was born the Dissenting community in England.

The most remarkable feature of the Restoration settlement was the economic, political, and social power it gave the gentry of England. Though some royalists had sold their land to pay huge fines, the bulk of royalist landlords retained their land. There was no social revolution in the countryside comparable to that in France in 1789. The Militia Act, which required the lord-lieutenants to recruit infantrymen from those worth £50 a year and cavalrymen from those worth £500, placed the sword in the hands of the landowners, at least in relation to the lower classes. The dominance of the gentry in finances was equally clear. They refused to continue John Pym's monthly assessment, which meant that the Crown's income was based on the excise and the hearth tax which fell unfairly upon the lower classes. The parish church likewise fell under the influence of the local squire, and Anglicanism became the religion of the landed classes. Dissent was relegated to merchants and shopkeepers, or to poor artisans like John Bunyan, whose *Pilgrim's Progress,* written in a Bedford jail, reflects the tribulations of a Puritan seeking truth in the reign of Charles II. The landed classes were triumphant and the financial independence of the Crown precarious. The lesson for Charles was clear: If he were to have a successful reign, he must govern in alliance with the gentlemen of England.

THE FAILURE OF THE RESTORATION SETTLEMENT

As long as Charles depended on Clarendon's advice, the government of the realm was lawful, dignified, and Anglican. Admittedly, the royalists hated Clarendon, whom they blamed for their neglect at Court, and admittedly the mercantilist lobby hustled him into a war against the Dutch, which he mismanaged. In 1667 the Dutch even sailed into the Medway, burst through the chain protecting the naval yard at Chatham, sank six English ships, and towed two others back to Holland. The disgrace at Medway led the House of Commons to impeach Clarendon in the autumn of 1667. Charles, who found Clarendon's hectoring sermons insufferable, urged the impeachment, which proved to be a mistake, since the impeachment of Clarendon was the next step after the impeachment of Buckingham on the path to vesting in the House of Commons the power to dismiss unpopular ministers.

Clarendon's fall in 1667 opened the way for Charles's personal government. Gradually he gathered around him a group of ministers who would serve his purposes. At their head was Sir Thomas Clifford, a vigorous advocate of the recent Dutch war and a suspected Catholic. As secretary, Charles employed the Earl of Arlington, who had been Clarendon's chief enemy at Court and who was also suspected of being a Catholic. Then there was the Duke of Buckingham, a buffoon who played at being a statesman and who had friends among the Independents. The ablest minister was Ashley Cooper, who had Presbyterian sympathies and was to become the Earl of Shaftesbury. Finally, there was the Earl of Lauderdale, who likewise had Presbyterian sympathies but who devoted himself solely to Scottish affairs. Because the initials of these five men spelled CABAL, pamphleteers then and historians later have treated them as a cabinet council, but they were not. They were a motley group of servants who were willing to carry out Charles's personal policies. It was the tragedy of the House of Stuart that its monarchs, unlike those of the House of Tudor, harbored personal predilections that ran counter to the prejudices of the English. In the case of Charles II, three predilections set him at odds with his subjects. He admired the Catholic Church and believed that Catholicism was the only decent religion for a prince—though he had the good sense to put off embracing Catholicism until he was on his deathbed. Secondly, his years in exile had taught him to admire things French and he had no fear of the growing power of France. Finally, he had no objection to exercising arbitrary power to achieve these goals. Fear of popery, fear of France, and fear of arbitrary government were to make his reign a tumultuous one.

The Treaty of Dover in 1670 and the Declaration of Indulgence in 1672 proved that these fears were not chimeras. In late May of 1670 Charles, accompanied by Clifford and Arlington, traveled to Dover, where he met his sister, wife of Louis XIV's brother. The French ambassador to England was also present. During the next two weeks they negotiated the secret Treaty of Dover, in which England promised to join France in an attack on the Dutch and to send sixty warships to carry out a landing on the coast of Holland. In return, France would pay Charles £250,000 a year, pay for the 6000 English troops fighting with the French army, and once the Dutch were vanquished, cede to England the Dutch island of Walcheren and port of Cadzand. A second clause to the treaty provided that Charles should declare himself a Catholic, in return for which Louis would pay him £167,000 and loan him 6000 troops to suppress any rebellion that might occur.

To enter on so costly a war with so little help from France was a foolish gamble, but Charles must have been carried away by the enthusiasm of the Catholic faction at Court and by his own desire to crush the Dutch. He secured money from Parliament by drawing up a public treaty with France that made no mention of his religious conversion. Even with this grant, the government was too deeply in debt to wage war, so Charles in January 1672 ordered the stop of the Exchequer—that is, he ordered the Exchequer to suspend payment of government debts for one year. Two months later England found a flimsy pretext for declaring war on the Dutch, though Charles found numerous excuses for not declaring himself a Catholic. As close to helping Catholicism as he dared sail was the issuance of a Declaration of Indulgence that suspended all penal laws against Nonconformists and Catholic recusants. An alliance with France and the toleration of Catholics were to go hand in hand.

Charles's great gamble failed. The Dutch fleet mauled the English fleet so badly at Southwold Bay that it could not carry out a landing on the Dutch coast. The Dutch breached their dikes to keep the French armies from overwhelming them. The war dragged on, to the dismay of Charles and his courtiers. In February 1673 Charles was forced to ask Parliament for yet more money. Parliament refused to vote it unless Charles revoked the Declaration of Indulgence, which was seen as a challenge to the rule of law and to the legislative supremacy of Parliament. Charles yielded and revoked the Declaration. But this was not enough for Parliament, which went on to pass the Test Act, which required every officer of state—civil or military—to receive the sacraments of the Church of England and to denounce the doctrine of transubstantiation. To gain £1,240,000 to continue the war, Charles swallowed even this. But the war, always unpopular, went badly the next year. When Parliament met again in au-

Charles II, portrait by J. M. Wright (*National Portrait Gallery*).

tumn 1673 and winter 1674, it blew the cabal apart by the threat of impeachments; it also forced Charles to make a separate peace with the Dutch in
February 1674, a peace which returned both countries to the status quo before
the war. The war had cost England over £6 million and gained it nothing.
Charles's gamble failed and government by royal favorites came to an inglorious end.

Charles now turned to Sir Thomas Osborne, a Yorkshire gentleman of
considerable financial ability and great political acumen. Charles created him
Earl of Danby and appointed him Lord Treasurer. Danby's strategy was to create a Court party in Parliament and to govern through it. He formed an alliance with the bishops and adopted a staunchly Anglican domestic policy. He
also made good use of the power of patronage. By 1678 over a hundred members of the House of Commons held office at Court and another forty had pensions from the excise. But several forces conspired to defeat his strategy of a
union between Crown and Church, buttressed by royal influence. In the first
place, Anthony Ashley Cooper, now the Earl of Shaftesbury, a man small in
stature but great in spirit, formed a Country party that set itself against the
Court and sought relief for Protestant Dissenters. Secondly, Charles—quite
against Danby's advice—steadfastly pursued a foreign policy that acquiesced in
the growth of French power. In 1676 the French captured Condé and
Bouchain, in 1677 they seized Cambray and St. Omer, in 1678 they defeated
the Dutch at Cassel. Parliament began to clamor for war against France, only to
be told by Charles that war and peace were none of their business. In 1678
Charles yielded to the clamor for war by signing a treaty with the Dutch. In an-
ticipation, Parliament voted the money to raise an army, but no declaration of
war followed. Instead, 7,000 soldiers camped on Hounslow Heath outside London, creating the specter of government by a standing army. At the same time
fear of papists at Court mounted, for Charles welcomed Catholics there and his
brother James, Duke of York, openly proclaimed himself a Catholic.

Fear of popery, fear of France, and fear of arbitrary government mingled
together in the autumn of 1678 to produce the outburst of hysteria that
greeted Titus Oates's tale of a popish plot to kill the King and place his Catholic brother on the throne. Titus Oates was a consummate liar and unconsciona-
ble rogue who had learned enough gossip at the Jesuit College of St. Omer to
be able to tell a convincing story. His tale of a plot to murder the King, burn
London, and establish popery was a fantastic one, but fear of a popish successor, supported by France, led men and women to believe it. Danby might well
have survived the hysteria unleashed by Titus Oates had not Ralph Montagu,
the former English ambassador to France, produced a letter in which Danby, in
Charles's name, asked Louis XIV for a subsidy of 6 million livres annually for
three years, since Charles, having promoted peace with France, could not hope
for supplies from Parliament. The Commons thereupon impeached Danby and
the Lords sent him to the Tower, where he remained for the next five years.
Charles's acquiescence in the growth of French power had destroyed Danby's
scheme of governing through a Court party in Parliament.

For the remainder of his reign, Charles acted as his own chief minister and conducted a remarkably skillful campaign to defeat all efforts to exclude his brother from the throne. In the spring of 1679, again in the autumn of 1680, and once again in the spring of 1681 the followers of Shaftesbury introduced bills into Parliament to exclude James from the Crown. These parliaments, and the elections to them, were marked by turbulent political warfare, out of which emerged two distinct political parties. The followers of Danby became the Tories, so branded by their opponents because their opponents regarded them as no better than Irish horse thieves, or Tories. The followers of Shaftesbury became the Whigs, so named by the Tories, who regarded them as no better than Scottish, covenanting rebels, or Whiggamores. Though these political battles were fierce, the final outcome of the exclusion crisis did not depend on them. Charles was able to defeat exclusion because he was able to prorogue, dissolve, and never meet Parliament again. And he was able to do this because increasing revenues from customs, excise, and hearth tax gave him a precarious financial independence. Between 1681 and 1685 Charles triumphed over his opponents, but the balance of government established at the Restoration lay in shambles.

THE REIGN OF JAMES II

The recklessness of the Whigs in the 1680s, their open challenge to hereditary monarchy, and their willingness to join in a plot to murder Charles at Rye House as he rode back from the spring races at Newmarket in 1683 (a plot Charles discovered and prevented) provoked a royalist reaction that carried James to the throne and financial independence. On his accession James promised the Council that he would protect the Church of England, maintain the government of the realm as established by law, and not interfere with property. A loyal Parliament then voted him the same permanent revenue they had voted Charles II (though increasing yields from the customs, the excise, and the hearth tax made it worth $1.5 million a year), and an additional £400,000 a year for five years. The only opposition to his succession came from the Duke of Monmouth, Charles II's favorite bastard son. With a few other hot-headed Whigs he landed in June 1685 in Devonshire, marched into Somersetshire, raised a ragged army of farm laborers and clothworkers, and proclaimed himself King. It was a hopeless rebellion that James swiftly and bloodily suppressed with his regular army. That autumn Chief Justice Jeffreys came into the southwest at the head of an assize court. The officers of the court seized hundreds of people and gave them hurried trials. Jeffreys bullied witnesses, cowed prisoners into silence, and misdirected juries. Before the Bloody Assize had finished its work, it had executed 300 suspected rebels and sentenced hundreds more to transportation to the colonies.

In the autumn of 1685 James found himself in a powerful position: the treasury solvent, the army victorious, the Church loyal, Parliament obsequious, the Tories rejoicing, and the Whigs broken. Within three years he had thrown it all away and fled into exile. His fundamental error was to break the alliance with the Church of England that was (as Danby had urged) the surest and only support of the Crown. In some ways, James was better fitted than Charles to be a King. He was less debauched, less careless, more loyal to his friends, and a better administrator. But he did not possess a grain of political sense. He was narrow-minded, rigid in temperament, and lacking in imagination. At Oxford in the 1640s he had learned ultraroyalist ideas that he never forgot. He was an obstinate, opinionated man who believed that his father had lost all from too great a display of leniency. Above all he was a zealous Catholic, whose chief purpose was the propagation of the Catholic religion. He himself admitted on one occasion that had he treated religion as a private matter he could have been one of the most powerful kings ever to reign in England, but since God had called him to the throne he must sacrifice everything to His service.

James initially sought to act through Parliament. In November 1685 he demanded that it repeal the Test Act, but quickly had to dissolve Parliament to prevent it from passing a resolution against the employment of Catholics. James now turned to the use of his prerogative, to the policy of dispensing with the Test Act in particular cases. He encouraged Sir Edward Hales, a colonel in the army and a Catholic, to arrange a collusive action. Hales's coachman, Godden, sued him for violating the Test Act. James hastily dismissed the more uncooperative judges, with the result that eleven of the twelve who heard the case acquitted Hales and declared that it was "an inseparable prerogative in the Kings of England to dispense with penal laws in particular cases." James now replaced Protestant with Catholic officers in the army, named the Catholic Strickland to command the fleet, and sent the Catholic Earl of Tyrconnel to rule Ireland. With Tyrconnel he sent sixteen new Catholic judges and councilors. He secured the installation of Catholics or Catholic sympathizers as bishops of Chester and Oxford. He also revived the Court of High Commission under the name of the Ecclesiastical Commission. The commission immediately suspended the Bishop of London, an outspoken Protestant, and launched an attack on the universities, those twin citadels of Anglicanism. It dismissed the vice-chancellor of Cambridge for refusing to grant a degree to a Benedictine monk and it expelled twenty-five recalcitrant fellows of Magdalen College, Oxford, for refusing to elect a Catholic as president. James then named a Catholic as president and turned the college into a popish seminary.

The granting of particular dispensations was a clumsy procedure. James therefore issued a Declaration of Indulgence in April 1687 which suspended both the Clarendon Code and the Test Act, and granted liberty of worship to both Catholic and Protestant dissenters. The declaration was a direct challenge to the reign of law in England, for there was a wide difference between the dispensing power, in effect a pardon granted in advance, and the suspending power, in effect the repeal of a law passed by Parliament. Even James regarded the exercise of the suspending power as only a temporary solution. For a permanent solution he desired Parliament to repeal the penal laws. But when he closeted himself with members of Parliament, he found they would not agree to repeal the Test Act. He therefore dissolved Parliament in July and set about securing the election of one that would. He sought to purge the commissions of the peace in the counties and the corporations in the towns, and to replace staunch Anglicans with Dissenters. All deputy-lieutenants and justices of the peace were asked if they would consent to the repeal of the penal laws and vote for those who would repeal them. If they would not, they were dismissed. In his eagerness to win a sympathetic Parliament James canceled borough charters, sacked town corporations, deprived noblemen of their lord-lieutenancies, and dismissed justices of the peace. His reckless pursuit of a Catholic England took him far along the road to arbitrary government.

The strategy of wooing Dissenters failed. They distrusted a gift brought to them by a man who had branded them as rebels and heretics for twenty years. James soon discovered that he could not trust his own nominees to send men to Parliament who would vote to repeal the Test Act. He thus turned back to his prerogative. In May 1688 he reissued the Declaration of Indulgence, only this time he ordered all clergymen to read it from their pulpits on two successive Sundays. This order finally drove the Church of England to desert its belief in nonresistance and passive obedience to all kings, however wicked. The Archbishop of Canterbury and six other bishops presented James with a petition asking him not to force the clergy to read the declaration, since it was based on a power to suspend law that seemed to them illegal. On reading the petition, James declared: "This is a standard of rebellion," and threw the seven bishops into the Tower. The cause of the Seven Bishops now became the cause of the whole nation. James charged them with seditious libel and brought them before the King's Bench on June 30. After a nine-hour trial, the jury—which included the King's brewer—acquitted the bishops. The shouting of the crowd, the ringing of bells, the discharging of guns, and the lighting of bonfires greeted their acquittal.

THE GLORIOUS REVOLUTION

That same night Arthur Herbert, disguised as a common seaman, set off from London with an important letter for William, Prince of Orange. It was an invitation to him, signed by seven eminent Englishmen, to bring an army to England. The seven signatories were representative of the political nation. Henry Compton, the suspended Bishop of London, spoke for the Church. The Earl of Danby led the Tory party and the Earl of Devonshire the Whig. Edward Russell and Henry Sidney represented the more radical Whigs, while the Earl of Shrewsbury and Lord Lumley were recent converts from Rome. Two forces drove these men to this treasonous act. One was mounting grievances—the laws of the land suspended, independent judges dismissed, Parliament dissolved, a standing army encamped on Hounslow Heath, the universities purged, Catholic officers brought into the army, Jesuits brought i˙ ᴄo the Council, charters overthrown, and the gentry thrown out of local government. The second force was the birth of a son to James and Mary of Modena on June 10, 1688. Grievances that can be borne when temporary become intolerable when made permanent. The birth of a son meant that James's elder daughter Mary, wife of the Prince of Orange and a Protestant, would not become Queen of England on James's death. Instead, James Edward, who would surely be raised a Catholic, would succeed.

William, Prince of Orange, the grandson of Charles I, the husband of Mary, and the taciturn leader of the military forces of the Dutch Republic, readily accepted the invitation to bring an army to England. Several motives prompted him to do so. To begin with, he desired to protect his wife's interests in the throne, which the birth of James Edward threatened—wrongfully threatened if the rumor were true that Mary of Modena had never been pregnant and that a foundling had been smuggled into her bed in a warming-pan. William may also have sought the Crown of England for himself, but if he did it was less for the tinsel repute a Crown brought than for the ability it brought to bring England into the European coalition against Louis XIV. Ever since the Dutch had called him to the office of Stadtholder in 1672, William had devoted his life to combatting the growing power of France. In 1688 there was the danger that James might abandon his neutrality and ally himself with Louis. In January James demanded the return of the English and Scottish regiments serving in Holland. William might have acquiesced in an England that was Catholic; he could never acquiesce to an England that fell into the French orbit.

Bringing an army to England was a gamble, a gamble that succeeded because several events worked toward success. Among them were William's careful preparation, Louis XIV's folly, the Protestant wind, James's vacillation, and the English people's unanimity.

William had no intention of relying on a spontaneous uprising of the English people; he regarded the expedition solely as a military operation. He engaged the English and Scottish regiments in the service of the Netherlands and recruited soldiers from Sweden, Brandenburg, Württemburg, and Switzerland. To protect his rear he secured the support of the Netherlands and several German states, along with the neutrality of Spain, the Empire, and the Pope. It was not so much William's skillful diplomacy that won this support as Louis XIV's folly. Louis's attempt to foist his candidate on the archbishopric of Cologne caused the Empire, Spain, and the Pope to remain neutral, and his prohibition of Dutch exports to France drove the Dutch to support William. Yet the Dutch, fearing invasion, wavered until the middle of September, when Louis's decision to send his army to the upper Rhine freed the Netherlands from fear of a French army. They immediately contributed troops and ships and agreed to pay for the Swedish and German troops William had recruited.

On the first of November 1688 William's army sailed for England, 11,000 foot and 4,000 horse, in 200 transports escorted by 49 warships. The plan was to slip by the English fleet and so avoid a battle that might arouse the patriotism of the English. The elements favored the plan. A strong east wind blew William's fleet down the Channel while preventing the English from clearing a badly chosen anchorage off Essex; when the English finally came clear, the wind dropped and it lay becalmed for two days, after which a southwesterly gale blew the invaders into Torquay and the English back into Portsmouth. William landed safely at Torquay on November 5, Guy Fawkes Day.

Had James marched resolutely on William he might have defeated him in battle, for he had an army of nearly 30,000 men. Instead, he marched to Salisbury, paused, heard rumors of disaffection in the army, held a council of war, and then resolved to return to London. That night John Churchill, Earl of Marlborough, and 400 other officers rode out of camp and joined William in Exeter. The leaderless English army fell apart, while English nobles raised the counties for William. The nobility took the lead in the revolution, but nineteen out of twenty people were behind them. Almost no one rallied behind James, despite frantic concessions made that autumn. The crux of the matter was a free Parliament. When William landed at Torquay he issued a proclamation in which he announced that he had come at the invitation of certain prominent Englishmen in order to secure the meeting of a free Parliament. In August James had issued writs for the election of a Parliament, but in September he had canceled them. By late November James had resolved on neither concessions nor resistance, but on flight. Sending his wife and son ahead of him, he attempted on December 11 to escape abroad. He even bungled his flight, being captured by fishermen and brought back to London. He was pleasantly surprised when William granted his request to retire to Rochester and posted no guards at the back of his house. On December 23 he fled to France, a broken-down, feeble, empty shell of a King. A day later 60 peers, meeting in London, asked William to take over the administration of the realm and to issue letters for the election of a Parliament. On December 26, 300 former members of the House of Commons concurred in this request.

THE REVOLUTIONARY SETTLEMENT

The Convention Parliament met on January 22, 1689, and during the next year drew up a settlement in Church and State that Edmund Burke a century later regarded as one of the most perfect works of man. The first issue that faced the convention was the succession to the Crown. The Tories clung to the principle of hereditary monarchy like limpets to a rock, but they were divided among those who were for restoring James on conditions, those who were for a regency, and those who were for granting the Crown to Mary alone. The Whigs subjected the various Tory solutions to a barrage of criticism, and William let it be known that he would return to the Netherlands if not given a share of the Crown. The Lords held out the longest, but finally agreed with the

Commons that King James II had "endeavored to subvert the constitution of his kingdom by breaking the original contract between king and people," had "violated the fundamental laws," had "abdicated the government" by his flight, and that "the throne is thereby vacant." The two Houses thereupon voted to grant the Crown to William and Mary jointly, with the administration in William's hands.

But they made the grant conditional. When on February 13, in the exquisitely proportioned splendor of the Banqueting Hall, they offered the Crown to the two monarchs, they first secured their assent to a Declaration of Rights. The Declaration asserted that it was illegal to suspend or dispense with the laws, to collect taxes by prerogative, to maintain a standing army without the consent of Parliament, to interfere in parliamentary elections, to tamper with juries, or to impose excessive fines or bail. In December Parliament turned the Declaration of Rights into the Bill of Rights, adding two new provisions. The first declared that no Catholic could succeed to the Crown; the second placed the succession in the children of William and Mary, then in those of Anne (Mary's younger sister), and finally in those of William should he marry again.

The Declaration and the Bill of Rights contained almost no new law. In this sense the Glorious Revolution was really a Glorious Restoration, the restoration of a constitution James had invaded. England had new monarchs, but not a new monarchy. This was true if one ignores the financial settlement that accompanied the political settlement, but one should not. Parliament in 1690 repudiated once and for all the ancient principle that the King should "live of his own." It voted William and Mary the customs revenues for only four years, not for life, and it voted a permanent revenue (including the customs) which fell at least £200,000 short of peacetime expenditures. All this it did knowingly, not from ignorance or confusion. It deliberately voted an inadequate revenue in order to secure frequent Parliaments. The Bill of Rights protected the liberty of the subject; the financial settlement guaranteed the power of Parliament.

The settlement of the Church, like the financial settlement, marked a break from the past. Reluctantly, almost surreptitiously, the Church of England squires granted religious toleration to Protestant Dissenters. Parliament passed the Toleration Act of 1689, which ordered that the penal statutes should not be enforced on Nonconformists. Parliament could hardly do less to reward the Nonconformists for refusing to follow James. Toleration came in the back door, a matter of political convenience not philosophical principle. It did not extend to Catholics, nor did it remove the political disabilities of the Dissenters. The Test Act remained in force.

The Declaration and Bill of Rights amounted to a contract between King and subjects. It was a historical embodiment of the Whig doctrine of a "social contract," a doctrine John Locke publicized in 1690 in his *Two Treatises on Civil Government.* Locke, who was the son of a Puritan attorney, attended Westminster School and Oxford University, joined the Royal Society, and became physician to the fiery Earl of Shaftesbury. It was during the turmoil of the Exclusion Crisis that he composed the *Two Treatises*, but not until 1690 did he dare publish them. Like Hobbes, Locke believed that man once lived in a state of nature, but he painted a much less gloomy picture of the state of nature. As God's creature man possessed reason, and reason made him capable of cooperating with other men and of discerning the laws of nature, the chief of which guaranteed a man life, liberty, and property. But though the state of nature was not as barbarous as Hobbes thought, it had its disadvantages. Men might be led by passion and interest to judge partially in their own cases, particularly in matters of property. "The preservation of their property," he wrote, "is the great and chief end . . . of men's uniting into Commonwealths." And though he believed that men were born equal, with an equal claim to the fruits of the earth, he also believed that by industry and frugality some could accumulate more property than others. It was to preserve this property, unequally divided, that men formed governments.

Men entered into political society by making a contract, one with another, to set up a legislature, which should make laws, and an executive, which should enforce law. This original contract implied majority rule, for the state is the collective body of the people. Locke, however, was no democrat, for he believed that the wage earner lacked the leisure to think or act politically. Not being fully rational, he must be excluded from the vote. Furthermore, since the end of government is the protection of property, he who possessed no property had no interest in it. Yet Locke was careful to protect the liberties of all. He argued that the laws of nature created rights which existed before man entered political society and which no government might violate. Among these he listed the right to life, health (meaning no man's health should be harmed), liberty, and possession. Not only was government limited by the laws of nature, but it might be dissolved if it neglected the ends for which it was created. If the executive, which might be in one person or a group, violated the terms of its trust, it would forfeit those rights; and if the legislators developed an interest separate from the people, they might be opposed. Revolution, in Locke's scheme, became the ultimate safeguard of the law.

When Locke first wrote down these ideas in 1679 and 1680 they were too radical to be published, but gradually they gained support from men of property. By the eighteenth century his *Two Treatises on Civil Government* had become a manual of orthodoxy. Newton's picture of an ordered universe, functioning according to observable laws, gave support to Locke's appeal to natural law. Locke's appeal to reason satisfied men and women in the age of reason, and his defense of property justified the oligarchy that had seized power in 1688. But beyond this he had written a classic defense of those two ideals for which the English had struggled throughout the seventeenth century and which they finally gained in 1689: individual liberty guaranteed by law and representative government expressed through Parliament.

FURTHER READING

*J.R. JONES. *Country and Court 1658–1714.* London, 1978. A sound, solid digest of current knowledge rather than a radical reinterpretation; chapters on administration, finance, and social trends precede the political narrative.

G.N. CLARK. *The Later Stuarts.* New ed., Oxford, 1961. Less exclusively political than other volumes in the Oxford History; contains illuminating chapters on overseas possessions, literature and thought, and arts and social life.

DAVID OGG. *England in the Reign of Charles II.* Two vols. Oxford, 1934. Contains an immense amount of information about Restoration England, about commerce, the army and navy, taxation, medicine, literature; written with urbanity and wit.

ROBERT S. BOSHER. *The Making of the Restoration Settlement: The Influence of the Laudians, 1649–1662.* Oxford, 1951. Explains why high Anglicanism triumphed after the Restoration.

DENIS T. WITCOMBE. *Charles II and the Cavalier House of Commons, 1663–1674.* New York, 1966. A scholarly examination of the relations of King and Parliament; explains why the Restoration monarchy failed to work.

K.H.D. HALEY. *The First Earl of Shaftesbury.* Oxford, 1968. A large-scale political biography, difficult to plow through but rewarding; excellent on the Popish Plot and Exclusion Crisis.

*J.R. JONES. *The Revolution of 1688 in England.* New York, 1972. An essay in historical revisionism; argues that James had intelligible reasons for adopting the policies he did and that their failure was not inevitable.

*PETER LASLETT. *The World We Have Lost.* New York, 1965. A stimulating but not definitive study of births, marriages, family, premarital pregnancy, illegitimacy, starvation, and death in Restoration England.

*RICHARD S. WESTFALL. *Never at Rest: A Biography of Isaac Newton.* Cambridge, England, 1980. A brilliant portrait of Newton the scientist, philospher, theologian, and public figure; the core of the book describes the development of his scientific ideas.

*KEITH THOMAS. *Religion and the Decline of Magic.* New York, 1971. A rich, fascinating study of prophecy, fortunetelling, thief-detection, miraculous healing, astrology, and alchemy, and their relation to religion and science.

16 War and Society

The Glorious Revolution made war with France inevitable, for William had not led an army to England merely to win the title of King; he had led an army there principally to bring England into the balance of power against France. This fact became clear in May 1689 when William, as King of England, with the support of Parliament, declared war on France. The war upon which England then embarked continued (with one short interruption between 1697 and 1701) until 1713. The nation was at war for twenty-one of the twenty-five years William and Anne reigned in England. It was a far-flung war. English armies fought in Ireland and Flanders, on the banks of the Danube and on the plains of Spain, at Port Royal in Acadia and at Port Mahon in Minorca. The fleet fought in the Channel, in the Mediterranean, and on the high seas. England maintained 40,000 men on the Continent, built and manned 323 ships of war, sent 9,000 men to Spain, and spent over £5 million a year to support its forces and subsidize its allies.

Such an effort could not fail to affect English society. Because of the war, Parliament met every year and became an indispensable part of the government. Because of the war, the royal administration grew in numbers and efficiency. Because of the war, new financial institutions emerged, which split propertied society into landed and monied interests. At the same time, the values of commerce permeated all ranks of society and helped shape English civilization. England entered the war a second-rate European power, divided from Scotland, unstable in its politics, and unsure of its colonies. It emerged a major European power, united with Scotland, politically stable, and set on the path of imperial greatness. England became Great Britain. A nation that had endured a century of discord and revolution now entered on a century of peace and stability.

THE WAR OF THE LEAGUE OF AUGSBURG

In 1667 the armies of Louis XIV invaded the Spanish Netherlands; in 1672 they attacked the Dutch, in 1681 they seized Strasbourg, and in 1688 they laid waste the Palatinate. These acts persuaded William to devote his public life to the task of curbing the power of France in Europe. They also drove the nations of Europe (Austria, Spain, Sweden, Bavaria, Saxony, and the Palatinate) to form the League of Augsburg in 1686 and to ally with the Dutch and the English in 1689 to resist French aggression. The English shared these fears that the greatness of France would endanger the liberties of Europe, but they had a further reason for declaring war: Louis XIV in March 1689 gave James II the men, money, and ships with which to return to Ireland to recover the Crown he had lost. For the English, the War of the League of Augsburg was also the War of the English Succession.

James landed in Ireland only to discover that the Irish were more intent on recovering the lands Cromwell had stolen from them than helping James recover the Crown of England. Ireland for the Irish was their program, "Now or Never" their motto. An Irish Parliament repealed the Act of Settlement of 1661 and confiscated the lands of 2400 Protestants who had fled to England. But the Presbyterians in Ulster did not flee; they sought safety behind the walls of Londonderry and Enniskillen. Their stubborn resistance, withstanding siege and assault, secured Ulster for William, thus providing him with a base from which, in the summer of 1690, he could lead 35,000 well-disciplined men south toward James's retreating and ill-equipped army of 21,000. Outnumbered, outmaneuvered, and outfought, the Irish could not prevent the English from storming across the river Boyne on the first of July. Among the first to flee the battlefield was James himself; a week later he took ship for France. His flight made the defeat of the Irish at the Battle of the Boyne the decisive engagement in the Protestant reconquest of Ireland.

In the next twenty years, the English reduced the Irish to a condition of virtual slavery. The Catholics, who composed four-fifths of the population, now owned but one-seventh of the land. A series of penal laws kept Catholics from public life. A Catholic could not hold office, sit in Parliament, vote in elections, serve on a jury, practice law, teach school, purchase land, or own a horse worth more than £5. And no Irishman whatever, not even the industrious Protestants, could export woolen cloth, sell cattle in England, or trade with the colonies. The Irish became, in Jonathan Swift's words, "hewers of wood and drawers of water" to their English conquerors.

In 1690 Ireland was the pivot of Europe; in 1692 the Channel was.

William III by Candlelight, portrait by Gottfried Schalcken (*the National Trust*).

Emboldened by a naval victory over the English at Beachy Head in 1690, Louis XIV in 1692 prepared to invade England. He assembled an army at Barfleur, which James II joined. But a French fleet sent to clear the Channel met defeat at La Hogue at the hands of a combined English and Dutch fleet that outnumbered the French fleet by 99 ships-of-the-line to 44. The French lost fifteen ships and Louis never again sent out the fleet. Seapower had saved England from invasion, as it had done once before when Philip II launched the Armada and as it was to do again when Napoleon and Hitler threatened to hurl their armies across the Channel.

Victory at the Boyne and victory at La Hogue secured the Protestant succession in England, but the war to lessen the power of France raged on in Flanders. Louis XIV won the battles but could not win the war. William was not a brilliant soldier, but what he lacked in brilliance he made up for in perseverance. Not until the sixth year of the war could the Allies hold their own against the French, but in that year, 1695, they captured the great fortress-city of Namur. The fall of Namur and the financial exhaustion of France led Louis XIV in 1697 to negotiate the Peace of Ryswick. Louis agreed to recognize William as King of England and to restore all the territories he had seized since 1678, except Strasbourg.

A contemporary engraving of the Battle of the Boyne (*Bettmann Archive*).

THE FINANCIAL REVOLUTION

The money that paid for the siege and capture of Namur came from the newly created Bank of England, the establishment of which marked a revolution in the financial affairs of England.

During the reigns of Charles II and James II the English government spent about £2 million every year; during the reigns of William and Anne, it spent nearly £6 million. The ability to tap the wealth of all Englishmen allowed this vast increase in public expenditure, and permitted a nation with less than 6 million inhabitants to send out a powerful fleet and support a formidable army. Two-thirds of the money needed for the war came from taxes, of which the land tax was the most important. Each year a Parliament elected by the landowners of England voted that the landowners of England should pay the government 4 shillings on the pound on the rents they collected, the equivalent of an income tax of 20 percent. When it came to raising money—the very sinews of war—the parliamentary monarchy of England proved far more effective than the royal absolutism of France.

Government borrowing provided for that part of the budget not met by taxes. In times of need both Charles I and Charles II had borrowed from wealthy individuals, often pledging crown revenues for repayment. But such loans were short-term, expensive, and destructive of future income. What England needed were long-term loans, secured by parliamentary revenues, and participated in by prosperous subjects from all walks of life. Such a loan Parliament devised in 1693, when it authorized the sale of life annuities, secured on an excise voted by Parliament for ninety-nine years. In effect, the government would not repay the principal, but would pay 14 percent interest on it until the holder died. The act of 1693 marks the beginning of a permanent national debt in England, one in which any person with a few extra pounds could participate. The Dean of Norwich, for one, rushed out to buy his daughter an annuity.

The idea of a permanent national debt gained a more solid foundation in 1694 with the establishment of the Bank of England. The idea for a bank arose from the fertile mind of William Patterson, son of a Scottish farmer, successful London merchant, and traveler to Holland (where he studied their bank) and to America (where he was, according to his friends, a missionary; according to his enemies, a buccaneer). But it was Charles Montagu, the brilliant Whig politician, who translated Patterson's idea into legislation and who steered it through Parliament. According to that legislation, a bank should be created that would lend the government £1.2 million. In return, the government would pay 8 percent interest on the money and would empower the bank to sell stock, receive deposits, make loans, and issue banknotes. The scheme was an immediate success; within twelve days subscribers bought up all the bank's stock. In the years that followed its notes retained their value, and the government found in the bank an indispensable source of further credit.

The Bank of England was the first joint-stock bank in England, but not the first bank. Private banking emerged in England during the 1650s, when the goldsmiths of London began to accept gold and silver for safekeeping and to lend out part of it at interest. Soon the receipts the goldsmiths gave for the gold and silver deposited with them began to circulate as paper money. By 1675 bankers were performing the three essential functions of banking: accepting deposits, lending money, and issuing notes. Soon economists saw that banks, by providing more generous credit and by increasing the supply of money, promoted new enterprises and thereby the employment of the poor. In the 1690s England needed credit and a circulating medium more than ever before, and the new Bank of England provided them.

The establishment of a stock exchange was the third step in the financial revolution of William III's reign. Stockbrokers were already gathering at Jonathan's and Garraway's coffeehouses in Exchange Alley and were dealing in company stocks and government securities. Because many brokers sold bogus stock or stock at double its price, Parliament decided in 1697 to limit their number to 100 and to require those selling government securities to register with the government. Pamphleteers continued to denounce "stock-jobbers," but without them there would have been no capital market.

THE POLITICS OF WAR AND PEACE

The authors of the revolution settlement did not intend that Parliament should meet every year, only every three years. But the insatiable demands of war forced William to summon it every year so it could vote the taxes and float the loans needed to pay for the war. William's dependence on Parliament had a profound influence on the development of the constitution, especially when coupled with the passions of party. Virtuous men decried the spirit of party, but they could not extinguish it. Division lists (that is, lists of how men voted on certain issues) survive for eight votes taken in the House of Commons during William's reign. They show that among those who voted, 85 percent cast votes solely on the Whig or solely on the Tory side. These party divisions were not fortuitous, for social differences and political principles divided people. Most squires were Tories, though not all, or else the Whigs would never have won an election. Most merchants and bankers were Whigs. The Tories favored the persecution of Dissenters, a naval war only, and the inviolability of the hereditary succession, which many of them placed in the House of Stuart. The Whigs favored religious toleration, a land war in Europe, and the revolution settlement.

William III desired to be King of all the English, not merely of the Whigs. He therefore chose to govern with a mixed ministry composed of statesmen from both parties or none. But the fury of the Whigs in 1690 drove him to turn to the Tories from 1690 to 1692. The Tories, however, failed to defend English shipping at sea, grew hostile to the land war, and proved unable to manage Parliament. Their failure gave the Whigs their opportunity. Gaining a predominant influence in Parliament, they gradually forced William to give them high office. By 1696 only Whigs sat in the Cabinet, that inner group of advisers who now replaced the Privy Council as the mainspring of government. It was the first party ministry in English history.

In 1697 William, who kept a tight grip on the reins of foreign policy, negotiated the Peace of Ryswick. The coming of peace spelled doom for the Whigs, for the Tories were now able to turn against them the country members' anger at the courtiers who had grown rich during the war. The split between Court and Country was as important in the politics of William's reign as the division between Whig and Tory. "If an angel came from Heaven that was a Privy Councillor," cried one member, "I would not trust my liberty with him for one moment." This spirit of distrust led Parliament in 1698 to deny William a standing army of more than 7000 men, for a standing army was seen as an instrument of tyranny. It also led the Commons in 1701 to impeach the Whig ministers who dared to negotiate treaties without first seeking the advice of Parliament. And it led Parliament that same year to add to the Act of Settlement (passed in order to settle the succession on the House of Hanover) a whole charter of liberties: no person who held an office of profit under the King should sit in the House of Commons; all resolutions taken in the Privy Council should be signed by the councilors; judges should be removable only upon the address of both Houses of Parliament; no pardon should be pleadable to an impeachment. Parliament in 1705 repealed the first two of these clauses, thus allowing the growth of cabinet government in England, but their passage in 1701 shows how deep was the countryman's distrust of the Court. The spirit of Eliot and Pym was not wholly dead.

The Tories, by exploiting the countrymen's fury against the Court, were able, between 1698 and 1700, to drive the Whigs from office. In the autumn of 1700 William was forced to bring the leading Tories into the Cabinet, but his mind was less absorbed by these domestic quarrels than by the question of the Spanish succession. Because the Treaty of Ryswick had made no provision for the succession to the Spanish crown after the death of Charles II, its sickly, childless, imbecile king, William had to negotiate two partition treaties with Louis XIV. The second of these allotted to the Austrian claimant Spain, its colonies, and the Spanish Netherlands, and to the French claimant Naples, Sicily, and Milan. But this treaty, which the merchants of London detested because it surrendered the Mediterranean to French dominance, never came into effect.

In 1700, Charles II left behind him a will that bequeathed to Philip, Duke of Anjou, Louis XIV's grandson, the entire Spanish empire. Most people, though not William, preferred the will and peace to partition and war. But Louis XIV then embarked on a series of arrogant actions that turned English public opinion in favor of war. He sent French armies into the Spanish Netherlands, seized the Dutch fortresses there, forced the Spanish to grant a French company the contract for supplying African slaves to Spanish America, and refused to demand from Philip a renunciation of his rights to the French crown. The threat posed to the balance of power no doubt alarmed the English, but many were even more alarmed at the threat posed to the markets for English cloth in Spain, the Netherlands, and the Mediterranean.

William in the summer of 1701 skillfully edged Parliament toward war and negotiated an alliance with the Dutch and the Emperor. This alliance was completed in September, several weeks before Louis XIV, standing at the deathbed of James II, recognized James's son, James III, as King of England. By this act Louis guaranteed that the English, Tories as well as Whigs, would rally behind the war. William, however, did not live to lead the armies of England once more against France. In February 1702, riding in the park of Hampton Court, his horse stumbled on a mole hole and pitched William to the ground. Two weeks later he died, leaving to others the prosecution of his life-long duel with Louis XIV.

THE WAR OF THE SPANISH SUCCESSION

Princess Anne, daughter of James II, ascended the throne in 1702. She was 37 years old, exceedingly fat, red and spotted in complexion, and wracked by gout. She had to be carried to her coronation. She was slow-witted, uninformed, obstinate, and narrow-minded; yet also pious, sensible, good-natured, and kind. She bore fifteen children and buried them all. She loved the Church and those who defended it, but had no interest in art, music, plays, or books. Her one hobby was eating; her husband's, drinking. This ordinary woman, whom the laws of hereditary monarchy raised to the throne, helped shape events during these years in two ways: first, by naming the Earl of Marlborough in 1702 to command her troops, and secondly by dismissing him from that command in 1711. By the first act she brought England unparalleled military victories; by the second she brought peace to her kingdom.

During the War of the Spanish Succession, John Churchill, Earl (later Duke) of Marlborough, waged ten campaigns, fought four major battles, and besieged over thirty towns. In all this fighting he never lost a battle or a skir-

Sarah Jennings, Dutchess of Marlborough
(*National Portrait Gallery*).

John Churchill, Duke of Marlborough
(*National Portrait Gallery*).

EUROPE IN THE LATE 17th AND
EARLY 18th CENTURIES

MILES

0 100 200 300 400

SWEDEN

SPANISH
NETHERLANDS

UNITED
NETHERLANDS

ENGLAND

London

PALATINATE

FLANDERS   THE

Rhine R.

Le Hogue

Namur

Heidelberg

Seine R.

Moselle R.

Blenheim

Danube R.

Strasbourg

BAVARIA

Vienna

FRANCE

AUSTRIA

Milan

SPAIN

MINORCA

Naples

Gibraltar

SICILY

mish or a siege. He was one of the great generals of history. His skill in war was no accident, for he had chosen the career of arms as a young man. The son of a royalist gentleman who had lost his lands fighting for Charles I, he was poor, obscure, and ambitious. He rose at Court through his own charm and through the charm of his sister, who was mistress to James, Duke of York. He rose in the army through his great courage and skill. He learned the French way of war when fighting for Louis XIV at Maestricht. He proved his own tactical genius by defeating the Duke of Monmouth at Sedgmoor. At Walcourt in 1689 he fought side by side with the Dutch, while at Kinsale in 1690 he displayed a keen strategic sense. To the skills of a soldier he added the talents of a courtier and diplomat. He was handsome, urbane, charming, never without a compliment, always persuasive, impossible to anger. Yet he was also crafty and dissimulating, kept his counsels to himself, and seized every opportunity to advance his family and fortune. Under William III he fell into disfavor, but the succession of Queen Anne saw his star rise again, for Sarah Jennings, whom he married in 1678, was the close confidante of the Queen.

Marlborough assumed command of the Allied armies at a moment when the nature of European warfare was changing profoundly. It was his genius to adapt his tactics to these changes; it was the misfortune of the French that they did not. Three technical innovations lay behind these changes: the flintlock musket, the prepacked paper cartridge, and the socket bayonet. The flintlock musket was several pounds lighter than its predecessor, the matchlock, misfired only twice in ten shots, and could be discharged eight times faster (about two shots a minute). The prepacked paper cartridge, containing powder and a one-ounce ball, simplified reloading. The socket bayonet, which allowed a soldier to fire his musket or stab with it, made the pike unnecessary. Marlborough saw that these innovations made the infantry a source of firepower, not blocks of resistance. He therefore placed his men in three lines, staggered, so that an entire platoon could fire at once. The French clung to the column, four or five deep, with only the front line firing. The French were equally old-fashioned in their use of the cavalry. Marlborough adopted the tactics of Gustavus Adolphus and Cromwell: the cavalry should ride hard against the enemy, disrupt them with the shock of the impact, and cut them down with naked steel. The French still regarded the cavalry as a mobile source of firepower, riding to within 30 paces of the enemy and discharging their pistols. The tactic cost them dearly at Blenheim.

Marlborough was equally innovative in his strategy. For forty years the armies of Europe had fought by siege. Having besieged and captured one town, an army would lay siege to the next. At this rate it would take thirty years to cross Flanders. Marlborough preferred a war of movement, leading to a decisive battle.

The supreme instance of such a war of movement occurred in 1704. Bavaria's entry into the war on the side of France posed a threat to Vienna and to Austria's continuance in the Grand Alliance. Marlborough resolved to save

Austria. With his usual painstaking attention to supply and with the gold of England behind him, he marched his army 250 miles across Europe, from the Netherlands to Bavaria. He momentarily paralyzed the French army by making a feint toward the Moselle; he then crossed the Rhine and marched on to Bavaria. At Heidelberg he had a new pair of shoes ready for each soldier. After driving the local Bavarian forces into Augsburg, he turned to face Marshall Tallard, who had pursued him at the head of a French army.

Though Marshall Tallard's army outnumbered that of the Allies by 56,000 men to 52,000, it was Marlborough, not Tallard, who sought battle. At the village of Blenheim, on the banks of the Danube, on August 13, Marlborough launched his attack. By bringing relentless pressure on the village itself, he caused the French to move troops there from the center. Sixteen English battalions thus pinned down twenty-seven French. Then late in the afternoon, with 81 squadrons of horse and 18 battalions of foot Marlborough attacked the center, where Marshall Tallard had only 64 squadrons of horse and 9 battalions of foot. The center broke and the English raced to the Danube, thereby encircling most of the French army. Before the day was done the English had destroyed two-thirds of the French army and captured its commander. The Battle of Blenheim ended forty years of continuous French victories, saved Vienna, preserved the alliance, and made Marlborough's name famous throughout Europe.

THE POLITICS OF VICTORY

The cost of victory was nearly £9 million a year. The task of raising this sum fell on Sidney, Earl of Godolphin, a loyal public servant, an astute financier, a compulsive gambler, and a breeder of racehorses. He raised one-third of the amount through loans; the other £6 million came from Parliament. This posed the central political problem of the age: the successful management of Parliament. The Queen solved it initially by relying on Tory ministers who enjoyed the support of a Tory Parliament. But the unrelenting fury of the High Church Tories against the Dissenters, and the Tories' dwindling zeal for waging war on the Continent, soon wrecked the Queen's scheme.

The High Church Tories directed their special anger against the practice of occasional conformity, a practice that allowed the Dissenters to circumvent the Test Act. That act denied state or municipal office to any person who did not take communion in an Anglican Church at least twice a year. The Dissenters circumvented the Act by taking communion as required, then worshipped every Sunday in their own chapels. The anger of the Tories at this practice arose less from a desire to correct religious error than from a desire for a monopoly of office. The religious fervor of the age of Cromwell had become the political passions of the age of Anne. In 1702 the extreme Tories carried through the House of Commons a bill against occasional conformity, but the Whigs and moderates in the House of Lords threw it out. In 1703 the Commons again passed the bill; the Lords again threw it out. The extreme Tories therefore sought in 1704 to tack it to a money bill, so that the Lords could not refuse it. But the Queen's servants and the Whigs joined forces to defeat it in the Commons. The Queen now turned away from the High Church Tories. By dividing her subjects, endangering bills of supply, and opposing the war on the Continent, the Tories had made their further employment impossible.

Though they had to rely on the Whigs, Marlborough and Godolphin did not intend to surrender power to them. They remained the managers, dispensing patronage, advising the Queen, governing the realm. But in order to manage Parliament they needed the help of the Whigs, who had increased their numbers in the 1705 elections: together with the Queen's servants, they now formed a majority in the Commons. It was Godolphin's plan to manage Parliament through an alliance of Whigs, courtiers, and moderate Tories; and it was the Queen's hope that such an alliance would allow her to retain the right to appoint ministers of her own choice. Both were to be disappointed. The passions of party swept away all such reconciling schemes. For the support they gave Godolphin in Parliament the Whigs demanded payment: the appointment of William Cowper as Lord Keeper in 1704, of the Earl of Sunderland as Secretary of State in 1706, of Lord Somers as President of the Council and Lord Wharton as Lord Lieutenant of Ireland in 1708, and of Lord Orford as First Lord of the Admiralty in 1709. Fiercely, stubbornly, then pathetically, Queen Anne opposed all these appointments. She was resolved not to become a prisoner of party. By 1709, however, she was. A Whig landslide in the general elections of 1708 left her no choice. The power of the purse allied to the passions of party had proved too strong for the royal prerogative.

The fact of party permeated all the politics of the reign of Queen Anne. Out of 1,064 members returned to Parliament between 1702 and 1714, only 71 cannot be clearly identified as Whig or Tory. And the rage of party flowed out from the Houses of Parliament to divide people in the counties, in the boroughs, in the city of London, in the Church, in the army, in coffeehouses, in the theater, in the journals, everywhere. The chief effect of party was to place political power in that party which prevailed at the polls and so won a majority in the House of Commons.

The House of Commons represented a narrow social elite, those who owned property, principally land. The ranks from which members of Parliament were drawn made up only 0.5 percent of Englishmen. Even then the country squires who crowded the benches of St. Stephen's—where the Commons met—protested against the chance army officer or merchant who strayed into the House. In an attempt to keep them out, they passed the Property Qualification Act of 1711, which required county members to own landed property worth £600 a year and borough members property worth £300—though the act was easily evaded by temporarily transferring land to a new member.

Those who had the right to vote for members of Parliament were more numerous, but still an elite. Only 4.3 percent of the population had the vote, about one adult male in five. And many of these voters were freehold tenants whom the landlord marshaled to the polls or townsmen in a borough where a great peer had a predominant influence. Of 513 seats in Parliament, perhaps 120 were at the nomination of a great magnate; another 20 were at the nomination of the Crown. In many constituencies a Whig or Tory family would have so firm a grip on the seat that the election would go uncontested. During Anne's reign only about 100 seats were contested in a general election, though in those contests the battle between Whig and Tory raged furiously.

The power of the squirarchy in local government was even greater than its power in the House of Commons. The squires, as justices of the peace, sat on the county bench, where they judged, administered, and taxed their countrymen. And the Revolution of 1688 had taught the Crown not to interfere in local government. In Cromwell's England the middle classes had endeavored to seize power; draymen, leather merchants, and the sons of butchers were found among those who governed England. The Restoration and the Glorious Revolution restored the rule of the wealthy. England became an oligarchy, in which the divine right of property replaced the divine right of kings.

THE NEW WORLD OF TRADE

The society over which this oligarchy ruled was one made rich by commerce. The hub of this new world of trade was London, with its half-million inhabitants. Below London Bridge the Thames was a forest of masts. Out of the Thames sailed the great East India ships, to bring back the tea that was to make the English a nation of tea drinkers. From North America came the beaver, with which to manufacture hats for gentlemen of fashion, and tobacco, with which to fill their pipes. From the Levant came coffee and cotton; from the African coast ivory and dyewood; from the Baltic hemp, tar, and timber. A steady stream of colliers brought coal from Newcastle, a trade which tripled in the seventeenth century. The small pinks, which carried more cargo and employed fewer men than the older ships, challenged the supremacy of the Dutch flyboat in the North Sea. By 1700 shipping owned in London reached 140,000 tons, and one in every four Londoners depended on the sea for a living.

Though London was the hub of trade, it did not dominate trade as it had under the Tudors. Merchants in London owned 140,000 tons of shipping, but those in the outports owned 183,000 tons. Every year 240 ships went in and out of Bristol harbor, carrying English manufactures to the colonies and bringing back tobacco and sugar. Exeter became a thriving port on the export of woolen cloth. Liverpool grew wealthy by refining the sugar its ships brought from the West Indies. The reexport of colonial products, principally tobacco, accounted for nearly a third of England's total exports. Once dangerously dependent on its trade to northern Europe, England now became a world entrepôt, one-third of whose imports came from America, the West Indies, and the East. The volume of trade also increased. English imports rose by £1.4 million a year, exports by £2.3 million. But what truly brought joy to the hearts of the mercantilists was the fact that during these same years a trade deficit of £300,000 a year became a trade surplus of £600,000. England now enjoyed a favorable balance of trade.

Large as England's foreign trade was, its domestic trade was three times greater. Ships and barges carried grain, coal, salt, bricks, and iron from port to port and up the navigable rivers. Cloth was still the greatest of English manufactures and was still organized according to the domestic system. But the salt panners on the Tyne, the sugar boilers on the Mersey, the tin smelters of Cornwall, the brewers of London, and the glass makers of Newcastle formed a semi-industrialized society. And each of these industries by 1700 had solved the problem of how to pan salt, boil sugar, smelt tin, brew beer, and make glass with coal rather than charcoal, thus escaping from the shortage of wood in England. Then in 1709, in Shropshire, a Quaker ironmaster, Abraham Darby, discovered how to smelt iron ore with coke (coal heated in an oven in order to drive off impurities). In time his discovery would transform the iron industry, but for the moment the greatest advances in manufacturing arose from an act of religious intolerance, not an advance in industrial technology. By revoking the Edict of Nantes in 1685, Louis XIV drove 15,000 Huguenots, mostly skilled artisans, to settle in London, at Spitalfields, Soho, and Bethnal Green. There they manufactured for peers and squires, for merchants and lawyers, the crystal, fine paper, cutlery, watches, and precision instruments the wealthy prized. Above all, the silk manufacturers of Spitalfields produced the velvets, satins, and brocades that an age of elegance required.

The spirit of commerce pervaded English society. Even the gentry engaged in economic activity. Sir John Lowther produced coal as well as corn on his Whitehaven estates. Thomas Foley, who founded a family in the West Midlands, mined iron ore on his property. Not all landlords had coal or iron on their land, but most of them produced timber or wool or woad for sale to the manufacturers of England. Angry squires might curse the monied men over tankards of October ale, but the Marquis of Tavistock had no qualms at marrying the granddaughter and heir of Sir Josiah Child, once a brewer, now an East India merchant, and one of the wealthiest men in England. Prosperous merchants, on their part, bought land and became gentlemen.

The growth of joint-stock companies permitted all men of wealth, whether great courtiers or successful landlords or wealthy lawyers or well-placed clergymen, to invest in the trade of England. In 1688 there were only fifteen joint-stock companies in all England; by 1696 there were over a hundred. One could invest not only in the great companies—the Bank of England, the East India Company, Hudson's Bay—but also in companies to manufacture gunpowder, smelt copper, produce hollow swordblades, and carry water from Hampstead to London. The luckiest of all were those who invested in William Philips's company to salvage a Spanish plate ship that had sunk off Hispaniola.

The company found gold and silver equal to that which Drake had brought home, and returned to each investor £100 for every £1 invested, a return of 10,000 percent!

This structure of trade and manufacturing rested securely on the agricultural wealth of England. This wealth was astonishing. Yields of wheat per acre in the seventeenth century were close to modern yields. In 1720 dairy cows gave a gallon and a third a day, only a little less than what they give today. Between the later Middle Ages and the end of the seventeenth century grain and grass yields rose about fourfold, and the increase in sheep and cattle was even greater. On the average, agricultural output rose fivefold between 1400 and 1700. Medieval agriculture was hardly able to support 3 million people; by 1700 England could feed 5 million and still export grain.

The explanation for this great increase in productivity lies in the agricultural revolution that occurred between 1560 and 1720. The heart of this revolution lay in the replacement of permanent tillage (with the arable lying fallow every third year) and permanent pasture with a system of alternation called up-and-down husbandry. Under this system, a farmer would grow wheat or barley on a piece of land for four or five years, then put it to grass for seven or eight years, then return it to tillage. This alternation preserved the fertility of the land, and though no more grain was produced, far more grass nutrients were. This meant more dairy products and more lamb, mutton, and beef. The introduction of up-and-down husbandry was accompanied by other changes. Turnips and clover were introduced as field crops and allowed the farmer to feed livestock during the winter. Permanent meadows were watered to give more and better grass. Marshes, such as the Fenland in East Anglia, were drained and their rich soil exploited. Marl, sand, lime, and manure were spread on fields to increase their fertility. Selective breeding improved cattle and sheep; during these years the Cotswold sheep were transformed—their legs shortened and their carcasses made larger and fleshier (for it was not their wool but their flesh that made them profitable). The sum total of these changes—themselves the product of the enterprise and ingenuity of English farmers—was to end the curse of widespread famine that hung over medieval England.

THE SOCIAL PYRAMID

The wealth this labor and enterprise produced was distributed among England's 5 million inhabitants in a highly inequitable manner. There was nothing new in this. What was new was the rise of "political arithmetic," a science that allowed the distribution of wealth to be measured. The greatest of the political arithmeticians was Gregory King, son of a Lichfield surveyor, a skillful mathematician, an ingenious statistician, and a minor civil servant who loved curious facts. During the reign of William III he described the structure of English society in table form.

At the apex of the pyramid were 160 noblemen, with an average income

Blenheim Palace, designed in the English baroque style by Sir John Vanbrugh and built at the public expense for the Duke of Marlborough (*The Central Press Photos Limited*).

of £3200 a year, and 26 bishops with incomes ranging from the bishop of Bristol's £360 a year to the bishop of Durham's £6000. The nobility used their opulent fortunes to build great country houses, to retain a phalanx of servants, to serve sumptuous meals, to purchase pictures from Italy, to buy furniture from France, to spend the season in London, and to wager vast sums at the gaming table.

Below the peers came the gentry, some 16,400 baronets, knights, esquires, and gentlemen, the richest of whom might be worth £2000 a year, the poorest only £200. Their average income was £354 a year. The rustic squire spent his business hours selling grain and buying livestock, his leisure hours hunting, shooting, and drinking. He spoke with a provincial accent, and his library had few books besides the Bible and Foxe's *Book of Martyrs*. He rarely visited London, but when he did he stood out in the crowd because of his old-fashioned coat without sleeves. The more prosperous among them built manor houses in the style of Wren, simple yet elegant. Paneling now replaced tapestries, and the sash window, often five feet high, replaced the mullioned windows of the Elizabethans. Their wives avidly collected chinaware brought from the East.

Below the gentleman came the yeoman, a man who owned the land he farmed, but who possessed no coat of arms and presumed to no gentility. Gregory King called them the freeholders of England and numbered them at 160,000. The better sort made, on average, £91 a year; the lesser sort only £55. To their numbers may be added 150,000 farmers, or husbandmen, who rented land as copyholders or leaseholders and who earned, on average, £42 a year. The squires showed their contempt for these classes by passing a law that prevented all freeholders worth less than £100 a year from killing game—even on their own land. The partridges were to be reserved for gentlemen.

Eltham Lodge, a modest country house built in the late seventeenth century (*Country Life*).

More numerous than the yeomen were those whom Gregory King called the laboring people and outservants. They worked in the fields as employees of the yeomen and farmers. They numbered some 364,000 families, and the average income of a family was about £15.

Life for these husbandmen and laborers as simple, arduous, but not intolerable. More of them ate wheaten bread than rye or barley bread. They saw roast meat on the table at least twice a week, perhaps oftener when beef fell to 2½ pence a pound and mutton to 2 pence. They had yet to learn to drink coffee and tea, but they drank enormous quantities of beer—between 2 and 4 pints a day. Foreigners were impressed with their clean, neat cottages. Hours of labor were long. The husbandmen returning from the fields, complained the pious, were too tired to say prayers. Child labor was common, and praised. Daniel Defoe rejoiced that around Halifax hardly anyone above the age of 4 was idle. Wages in the fields ran from 8 to 12 pence a day, too little to feed a wife and children. Only where the wife could earn 9 pence carding wool and the children 4 pence each spinning yarn could the working family fare well.

Trade, then as now, was where fortunes were made. Three million people earned £25 million in agriculture (or about £8 a person), while 300,000 earned £10 million in trade (or about £33 a person). According to Gregory King's calculation, some 2,000 eminent merchants earned £400 a year; another 2,000 merchants earned £198. Shopkeepers and tradesmen, of whom there were 50,000 families, earned £45 a year, while artisans, 60,000 in number, earned £38. The professions offered a second avenue to wealth. Lawyers earned £154 a year, eminent clergymen £72, lesser clergymen £50, naval officers £80, and army officers £60. Common seamen earned only £20, common soldiers £14. Great offices of state brought an income of £240 a year, lesser offices £120. These, then, were the classes—common seaman, soldier, and husbandman apart—who enjoyed the new wealth of England.

At the very base of the pyramid were 400,000 families of cottagers and paupers, the largest class of all and the poorest. Their yearly income averaged £6 10s. The terms "cottager" and "poor" were nearly synonymous, for a cottage was a small house or hovel with little or no land. Sir Francis Bacon called cottagers "but housed beggars." Since there was little regular employment on farms in the early eighteenth century, the squatters eked out a livelihood by squatting on the commons, keeping geese, cutting wood, and poaching. Their inadequate incomes often had to be supplemented by parish poor relief and private charity. The first provided about £900,000 a year; the second, about £200,000. Together they yielded about £1 per person a year for the poor— quite unevenly distributed. This was merely enough to stave off the worst hunger and cold. Each parish sought to exclude from its boundaries the poor from other parishes. By the Act of Settlement of 1662, a parish in which a man sought to settle could send him back to the parish from which he came if they thought he might someday be a burden. The true answer to this appalling problem of poverty, as Daniel Defoe saw, was not charity, but the employment of the poor. Sir Josiah Child, a governor of the East India Company and a writer on economics, even proposed that the government buy land, build workhouses, and set the poor to work. His advice went unheeded.

THE AUGUSTAN AGE

London, which was the center of trade, was also the center of a new middle-class culture. It was here that men conversed in their favorite coffeehouses, dined at taverns, read *The Spectator,* applauded the latest play, heard the new Italian opera, and purchased their waistcoats, cravats, and wigs (which even tradesmen now wore). The center of gravity in London moved westward as the great deserted the city and built townhouses in Bloomsbury, Piccadilly, and St. James's Square. Christopher Wren, after the Great Fire, had proposed rebuilding London with wide, straight streets meeting in a star-shaped open space. This was the principle of the *rond-point,* adopted by the French under Louis XIV. But Charles II, after a few days' thought, rejected the proposal. London's contribution to town planning in the seventeenth and eighteenth centuries was to be the square, a garden or field around which were built privately owned houses of similar design. These houses were usually of brick, of uniform height (three or four stories), sparsely decorated, the façade broken only by sash windows that diminished in size as they rose from story to story. As the *rond-point* reflected the majesty of an absolute monarch, so the London square reflected the wealth, power, good taste, and independence of the English gentleman.

Though the English in Charles II's reign had condemned coffee as useless, "since it serves neither nourishment nor debauchery," by Queen Anne's reign there were over 500 coffeehouses in London. Everyone had his favorite coffeehouse. Men of fashion went to White's in St. James's Street. Poets drank their coffee and chocolate at Will's, scholars at The Grecian. Merchants wrote marine insurance at Lloyd's and brokers traded in stock at Jonathan's. At coffeehouses great noblemen conversed easily with private gentlemen and men of all ranks learned the latest news from abroad and at home.

The theaters opened their doors at 6 P.M. In the London of Queen Anne there were two theaters—at Lincoln's Inn Field and in Drury Lane. Then in 1705 John Vanbrugh, soldier, playwright, and future architect of Blenheim Palace, built a theater in the Haymarket, called the Queen's Theater or the Italian Opera House. Though literary critics found Italian opera to be merely "nonsense well tuned," it conquered London during the reign of Queen Anne. England had its native composers, of whom Henry Purcell was the greatest. But even Purcell came under the Italian influence, bringing melodic expressiveness and dramatic declamation to his opera, *Dido and Aeneas.* Throughout Europe a new spirit entered music; the religious gave way to the secular.

Despite the power of Thomas Betterton's Hamlet, the theater did not flourish during the reigns of William and Anne. Most of the plays performed were comedies of manners by the Restoration dramatists. The plays were witty, cynical, and indecent, which led the clergy to denounce the immorality of the stage and the government to prosecute actors for lewdness. As a result of these attacks, the theater in Anne's reign grew more respectable and more sentimental.

The Augustan age of Queen Anne—so called because the greatness of its literary achievement resembled that of Rome under Augustus—was not an age of drama, nor of poetry, but of prose. Its characteristic literary forms were the newspaper, the pamphlet, and the review, all of which enjoyed a new freedom with the ending of the Licensing Act in 1695. An author could now, within the law of libel and sedition, write what he pleased. In the opening months of Queen Anne's reign the first daily newspaper in England, *The Daily Courant,* began; before she died the circulation of all newspapers had reached 67,000 a week. But the newspapers of that day, a single sheet printed on both sides, carried only news and advertisements; there was no editorial comment. The political pamphlet and the review provided that. The greatest of these pamphleteers and reviewers were Daniel Defoe and Jonathan Swift. Defoe's ironical attack on intolerance, in *The Shortest Way with the Dissenters,* led him to the pillory; and Swift's bitter denunciation of the Dutch in *The Conduct of the Allies* helped bring peace to England in 1713. For eight years Defoe wrote *The Review* to win men over to moderation and for two years Swift wrote *The Examiner* to make them Tories. Never before had the pen been so powerful, for never before had the politician so great a need to sway public opinion. The control of Parliament might depend upon it.

Swift and Defoe appealed to the public's interest in politics; Richard Steele and Joseph Addison to its interest in society. Richard Steele, at various times a captain in the Life Guards, playwright, theatrical manager, and projector of commercial schemes, began *The Tatler* in 1709 and *The Spectator* in 1711. He prevailed on his friend, Joseph Addison, a shy Oxford scholar, an undersecretary of state, and a literary genius, to contribute to both. *The Tatler* and *The Spectator* were instant successes, for their satire of vice and praise of virtue taught the newly enriched gentlemen, merchants, lawyers, and government servants how to act and how to spend their money.

The Spectator sought to reform the manners and quicken the moral life of English men and women. It prized good sense over great learning and preferred virtue to mere politeness. It satirized boorishness and ridiculed dueling. It directed men away from both political fanaticism and religious enthusiasm. "Reason," it urged, "should govern passion." It praised honesty above the affectation of good breeding: "The Tradesman who deals with me, in a commodity which I do not understand, with uprightness, has much more right to the character of a gentleman than the courtier who gives me false hopes or the scholar who laughs at my ignorance." It contrasted the "pride and beggary" of the European nobility with the willingness of English gentlemen to send their younger sons into trade. *The Spectator* was both a manual of deportment and a model of correct style. Its prose was balanced, graceful, polished, and clear—a style that suited an age which believed in reason, good sense, elegance, and sobriety.

The same spirit pervaded religion, where the fury of the High Churchmen against the Dissenters could not conceal the growth of moderation and toleration within the Church (a movement soon to be called Latitudinarianism). Under the influence of Newton and Locke, people began to emphasize the reasonableness of Christianity. They also sought a practical divinity, one that would teach people how to live. To this end, a group of clergymen founded the Society for the Reformation of Manners, which did much to reduce swearing and drunkenness, but perhaps did even more to promote the gloomy English Sunday. Even the Quakers grew more mellow, devoting their energies to the counting house rather than to the disruption of church services. As Daniel Defoe, the spokesman for the Dissenters, remarked, after riding through much of England, "the main affair of Life" is "getting money."

MARRIAGE, COURTSHIP, AND THE FAMILY

Public affairs loom large in works of history, but for most people public affairs are a very small thing compared to their private lives. And nothing is more central to a person's private life than the choice of a husband or wife. In the sixteenth century, among the landed classes, one's parents made that choice for one and based it on considerations of lineage, property, power, and honor. The family line must be continued, the estate augmented, political alliances cemented, and social degradation avoided. The system allowed little time for courtship, the bride and groom often seeing each other for the first time after the marriage had been negotiated. "People in my way," wrote the daughter of a marquess, "are sold like slaves."

This system of arranged marriages slowly decayed, weakened by the Protestant insistence on affection within a marriage, by the seventeenth-century emphasis upon personal liberty, and by the eighteenth-century celebration of sentiment. The change was slow and uneven. The great peers with great estates clung to arranged marriages the longest. Yet the forces of change were inexorable. In 1660 Parliament abolished the Court of Wards, where the Crown auctioned off the right to select husbands and wives for fatherless heirs and heiresses. In 1680 Aphra Behn, a zealous feminist, launched an attack upon arranged marriages. In 1705 Daniel Defoe denounced "marriages for the preserving of estates" as equivalent to rape. And Joseph Addison called for long courtships. By 1700 most children of squires and merchants possessed the right to veto their parents' choice; by 1800 they possessed the right of choice, with a veto left to their parents. This change made necessary opportunities for courtship, which were soon established. In the eighteenth century there grew up that world celebrated in the novels of Jane Austen, a world of balls, card parties, teas, assembly rooms, and the London and the Bath seasons.

Not all English men and women married and those that did often married late in life. The average age at marriage for daughters of the nobility was 20 in the sixteenth century, 23 in the eighteenth. The median age at marriage for the heirs of squires rose from 21 in the sixteenth century to 28 in the eighteenth, while younger sons in the eighteenth century did not marry until their thirties. The explanation for this trend lies in the turn towards choice in marriage, in the greater number of years spent at school and university, and in the need for younger sons to accumulate the wealth necessary to support a marriage. Many of these younger sons never accumulated that wealth, with the result that they chose to be bachelors. Their choice in turn increased the number of spinsters. In the sixteenth century 5% of the daughters of the landed classes never married; in the eighteenth century 25% never married. Because of their high social background they would not work, so they either served as housekeepers to a sister's family or existed in lonely lodgings on small pensions.

In the sixteenth and seventeenth centuries the children of shopkeepers, artisans, and yeomen enjoyed somewhat greater freedom in the choice of wives and husbands than did the children of the rich, but where there was property —a shop or a copyhold—parental control was exercised. By the eighteenth century that control had lessened; children from the lower middle class often married by free choice, even without their parents' consent. Among the propertyless poor, young men and women chose each other freely, with hardly any interference from parents. Courtship within the lower middle class tended to be decorous and the motives leading to marriage prudent. Courtship among the poor, who could afford few pleasures beyond sex and drink, was far less inhibited, as the figures for prenuptial pregnancies demonstrate. A prenuptial pregnancy was a pregnancy that resulted in the birth of a child 8½ months after the wedding, or earlier. In the sixteenth and seventeenth centuries recorded prenuptial pregnancies ran well below 20% of all first pregnancies; in the eighteenth century it shot up to 40%. In part this was a result of the revival between 1620 and 1720 of the belief that a betrothal (an exchange of promises to marry) justified the consummation of the sexual act, but many pregnancies occurred long before the wedding day and can only be explained by a decline in the moral, legal, and economic inhibitions against premarital sexual intercourse. The collapse of the Puritan movement lessened the moral inhibitions; the decay of Church courts lessened the legal impediments; and the rise of a landless laboring class able to find employment in cottage industries increased the opportunities. As a result, among the poor in the eighteenth century most brides had had sexual intercourse with their future husbands before marriage.

Once married, the bride was wholly subject to her husband. The principle of patriarchy held sway throughout the sixteenth and seventeenth centuries. In law, wrote Blackstone, "the husband and wife are one, and the husband is that one." Both their property and their children belonged to the husband alone. This subjection of the wife was accompanied by deference and distance; wives called their husbands "Sir," husbands their wives "Madam." The Reformation and the Renaissance state both deepened the subjection of women. Protestantism laid on the husband the duty, once exercised by the priest, to supervise the religious and moral conduct of the family—family prayers took the place of the confessional. The Renaissance state regarded deference to the father as a guarantee of law and order, the equivalent of obedience to the monarch. Not without reason did James I call himself "the politic father of his people." Among the lower middle classes the fact that marriage was an economic partnership gave the wife some leverage, but she was more often treated as a servant than as a partner. Among the laboring poor, wives were subjected to a crushing burden of toil and to beatings by their husbands.

During the eighteenth century, among the wealthier classes, a more intimate, more affectionate, more equal, and less patriarchal marriage appeared, a companionate marriage, in which wives and husbands addressed each other by their first names. The forces producing the companionate marriage were many. The decline in religious enthusiasm led to a decline in family prayers and to the authority the father exercised there. The growing belief in religious toleration and respect for the individual conscience furthered personal autonomy within the family. The Glorious Revolution, by discrediting patriarchy in the state, made it harder to justify it in the home. A growing revulsion against cruelty of all kinds led to the condemnation of wife-beating. In 1782 there was a public outcry when a judge sought to revive the doctrine that it was lawful for a husband to beat a wife, provided that the stick was no thicker than a thumb. But perhaps the most powerful force was the growing education of women. It was good conversation, wrote John Milton, that made for a good marriage, and it was education, asserted Dr. Johnson, that made for good conversation. In 1600 only one woman could sign her name to every eight men who could; by 1750 the ratio was one to two. And by then numerous boarding schools were turning out women well-versed in history, poetry, French, music, and dancing.

Parallel to these changes in marriage were changes in the attitude of men and women towards sexuality. Medieval theologians had condemned all sex as unclean and had made an ideal of virginity. The Protestant reformers replaced the ideal of virginity with that of holy matrimony, citing the Biblical injunction to be fruitful. But the Protestant theologians condemned all sexual activity that was not designed for procreation. There should be no sexual activity when conception is not possible, as during pregnancy. There should be no oral or manual sexual play. There should be no use of birth control practices, of which the commonest was *coitus interruptus.* There should be no expression of passionate love in marriage, which they regarded as no better than adultery. Actual practices may have differed considerably from these precepts, yet there were other obstacles to a high level of sexual activity in these years. Lack of personal hygiene, frequent illness, prudishness about appearing naked, and fear of pregnancy all inhibited sexual activity. During the eighteenth century, however, a desire to limit families and the new ideal of the pursuit of pleasure led to the liberation of sexuality among the upper classes. The new hedonism separated the pleasures of sex from the procreative function. Authors such as Aphra Behn, Mrs. Manley, Bernard de Mandeville, and John Wilkes unblushingly celebrated the pleasures of sex. From 1675 onwards the upper classes practiced birth control. And the bookstores of London freely sold pornographic books and pictures. But the new hedonism was largely for men. During these centuries, as during most of human history, there existed a double standard of sexual behavior. A bride was expected to be a virgin on her wedding night; a man was expected to have had some sexual experience. Fornication and adultery by men were regarded as minor sins; for women they brought the deepest dishonor.

This double standard was only possible because the bachelors and adulterous husbands of the upper classes found sexual partners in the actresses, milliners, maids, and whores of the lower classes. Promiscuity and prostitution among the poor supported female chastity among the rich. There is evidence to show that such promiscuity existed even in Elizabethan times. In Essex during Elizabeth's reign 15,000 persons out of a population of 40,000 adults were summoned before church courts for sexual offenses, which meant that an adult during those years had one chance in four of being summoned before a court for adultery, fornication, incest, or homosexuality. The rate of illegitimacy in Elizabethan England was 4 percent. Under the pressure of Puritan preaching a stricter standard of sexual morality was achieved in the seventeenth century; the rate of illegitimacy fell to 1½ percent. But in the eighteenth century both promiscuity and prostitution flourished, with the rate of illegitimacy rising to over 4 percent in 1760 and to 8 percent in the 1780s. London became the scene of a vast sexual underworld, made up of kept mistresses, high-class houses of assignation, general and specialized brothels, and common street whores. Men of all classes made use of prostitutes, the demand for which increased with the growing number of bachelors and late marriages. Poverty drove young girls to become prostitutes, in accordance with Francis Place's law that "chastity and poverty are incompatible." The growing culture of sexual promiscuity among the poor also helped swell the ranks of prostitutes. Many were recruited from unwed mothers. Prostitutes ranged in age from 15 to 22; the median age was 18; none was active after 22. They were an abject, wretched, hopeless class, the most pitiable class of persons in England.

The begetting of children was one of the principal purposes of marriage, though among the landed classes daughters were less welcome than sons (since the dowries needed to find them husbands could bankrupt a family). Among the poor few if any children were welcome (since it was a struggle to find the food to feed them). In the sixteenth and seventeenth centuries parents were negligent in the care of infants, with the result that infants were weaned from the mother's breast at a later date than they are today and were not subjected to severe toilet training. In other ways, though, they were more severely treated. In order to keep a child from breaking its leg or scratching out its eyes or tearing off its ears, it was wrapped tightly in bandages for the first four months of its life, a practice called swaddling.

Once the child had left infancy for childhood, he or she entered a world marked by formality, distance, deference, and obedience. Children of the upper classes saw little of their parents, being entrusted to a wetnurse as an infant, then to nurses and tutors, and finally, at about ten, to the master or mistress of a boarding school. Boys and girls lower in the social scale left home at about the same age to become domestic servants or apprentices. Not only deference but cruelty marked the years of childhood. This was in part a product of Puritanism, which taught the doctrine of Original Sin and regarded the child in the cradle as a sinner. His will must be broken, he must be taught obedience to God's commandments, he must be made virtuous; otherwise the dream of creating a Godly society on this earth could not be realized. To this end parents and masters used, not a system of rewards, but of physical punishment, to which was added the psychological terrors of death and Hell. The children's books of the time threatened divine vengeance on the sinner. It was even believed that schoolmasters could by flogging teach boys Latin grammar. The commonest form of punishment of an errant boy was to lay him over a bench and flog his naked buttocks with a bundle of birches until the blood flowed. Many apprentices were exposed to similar sadism from their masters. The one redeeming feature to the Puritan approach to childhood is that, unlike the earlier indifference shown children, it arose from a concern for the child's future.

During the eighteenth century this gloomy picture changed. Signs appeared of greater warmth, affection, intimacy, cheerfulness, and permissiveness within the family. Swaddling gave way to the use of loose clothing. Maternal breast feeding, which deepened the affection of the mother for the child, replaced wetnurses. More affectionate modes of address, as "Mamma" and "Papa" replaced "Sir" and "Madame." Symbolic acts of deference, such as kneeling or standing when in the presence of parents, faded away. Children's books that offered plain entertainment and fun replaced those that threatened divine vengeance. Toy shops sprang up in the towns and dolls with changeable clothing were mass produced. Parents limited the size of their families in order to have the means to educate their sons and marry off their daughters. Increasingly parents educated their children at home in order to save them from the brutality of the schools. But that brutality diminished as flogging students simply for academic lapses declined. The causes for these changes were many. John Locke provided the intellectual premise for them by arguing that man was not born evil, as Calvin taught, but a blank slate, a *tabula rasa*, upon which a favorable environment might inscribe virtue. This view, joined to the growing individualism of the age, made abhorrent the doctrine that the purpose of childrearing was to break the will of the child. Then there were those eighteenth-century ideals of the pursuit of happiness and the cultivation of sentiment, which inevitably led to a more cheerful, affectionate home. And finally there was that movement against cruelty that led not only to the abolition of the slave trade and the suppression of cockfighting but to the decline of flogging.

These changes took place first in the families of the urban, literate middle class, but they spread to the landed gentry, and later to the nobility. These new ideas had less influence upon the lower middle class, who were often Nonconformists. Such families became increasingly child-oriented but remained authoritarian. Among cottagers and artisans parents often treated their children brutally, but prized them as economic assets. Among the very poor, parents were careless, indifferent, and cruel. Where they could exploit their children's labor they did so; where they could not, they neglected them. Death by neglect contributed significantly to the child mortality of the eighteenth century. The new, affectionate, happy family was rarely to be found among the poor.

THE ACT OF UNION WITH SCOTLAND

The most important public act of Queen Anne's reign may well have been the Act of Union, which led the English and the Scots to bury centuries of strife. The Scotland of Charles II's reign was a monument to fanaticism. At the Restoration Scotland recovered its Parliament, which Cromwell had abolished, but that Parliament was subservient to the Privy Council in Edinburgh, which Charles II controlled from London. Charles used his power to restore episcopacy and to force the Presbyterians to renounce the Covenant. Unwilling to take the tests imposed on them, a third of the clergy—the Covenanters—left their churches and conducted religious services on lonely hillsides or in thick forests. The government sent the militia to suppress these conventicles; the fierce Covenanters answered with rebellion, which the government then ruthlessly crushed. But though the English denied the Scots political and religious independence, they forced on them an unwanted economic independence. By the Navigation Acts the Scots were forbidden to trade with the English colonies or to engage in the English coastal trade.

By no means did all Scots favor the Covenanters, for their tyranny was as dreaded as the Court's, but all did oppose the popish designs of James II. Thus when James withdrew his troops from Scotland to resist William, the government in Edinburgh found itself powerless. A group of Scots hurried south to persuade William to summon a convention in Edinburgh. It met in March 1689 and drew up a Claim of Right similar to the English Declaration of Rights, only more radical: Where the English said James had "abdicated," the Scots boldly said he was "deposed." The convention also forced William to reestablish the Presbyterian Church and to abolish the Lords of the Articles, the committee through which the Crown controlled Parliament. For the first time in centuries, the Scottish people enjoyed both religious and political independence.

But though a free Parliament quickened the political life of Scotland and a restored Presbyterianism calmed its religious quarrels, the Scots remained poor. A million inhabitants scratched a meager existence from the soil or engaged in a limited local trade. Scottish agricultural methods were medieval; no money was invested in the land; improvements proved impossible because of short leases and insecurity of tenure. The per capita wealth of Scotland was thought to be one-fifth that of England. What the Scots wanted most was a chance to participate in the English trading empire, but the English persisted in excluding them. The Scots therefore resolved to create their own commercial empire. In 1695 they founded a Company to Trade with Africa and the Indies, and in 1698 that company founded a colony at Darien, on the Isthmus of Panama. From here they hoped to dominate the trade of both Atlantic and Pacific. But the Darien adventure, in which so many people had invested, proved a fiasco. The company placed its colony in the center of a swamp, sent out woolens and Bibles the natives did not want, and offended Spain, then the ally of England. Disease, bankruptcy, and Spanish troops soon ended the life of the colony. The Scots now saw that their only salvation was to enter into a union with England, a union that would bring them within the Navigation Acts.

The Scots had sought such a union in the past—in 1667, in 1670, and again in 1689—but had always been repulsed. They now found a lever with which to pry open the English commercial empire. In 1703 the Scottish Parliament passed an Act of Security which provided that the Parliament should meet on Queen Anne's death and choose a successor. That successor would not be the person the English chose unless England had previously conceded Scotland freedom to trade with England and its colonies. The passage of the Act of Security forced the English to choose between the perpetual hostility of a separate Scottish kingdom or a union that guaranteed full reciprocity of trade.

The English chose union and reciprocity. In 1706 Queen Anne, with the consent of both Parliaments, named commissioners to negotiate a Treaty of Union. The treaty was a triumph of good sense and compromise. The two kingdoms became one, under a single Crown, with a single Parliament, and with trade laws that applied to all the inhabitants of "Great Britain," as the new kingdom was to be called. Though Scotland surrendered its Parliament, it retained its own system of law, so different from the English Common law, and the Presbyterian Church, whose privileges the treaty guaranteed for all generations to come. The taxation and tariff systems of Great Britain were to be one, though Scotland, in consideration of its poverty, was to pay only one-fortieth of the land tax.

The English Parliament ratified the treaty with little debate, but a bitter struggle ensued in the Scottish Parliament. Popular opinion in Scotland opposed the treaty, or did so until the Presbyterians saw that it offered adequate safeguards for their church. But the final decision rested with Parliament. In 1707 the Scottish Parliament ratified the treaty. Some English money no doubt lubricated the process, but bribery alone cannot explain ratification. The true explanation lies in economic interests. The Scottish merchants who hoped to trade with the colonies and the Scottish landlords who wished to export corn, cattle, and coal to England had the numbers and the power to persuade the Scottish Parliament to ratify the Treaty. Their calculations were not mistaken, for the Act of Union made possible the unprecedented prosperity of Scotland in the eighteenth century.

THE TREATY OF UTRECHT

The Act of Union was one of the most constructive acts carried out by the Whig ministers during these years. Their most destructive act was the failure to negotiate peace with France in 1709. The problem was Spain. In order to secure Portugal's adherence to the Grand Alliance, England in 1703 had promised not to make a peace that left Spain in the hands of the Bourbons. "No peace without Spain" became the slogan that imprisoned the minds of the Whigs. It proved particularly inappropriate when in 1707 a French and Spanish victory at the Battle of Almanza ended all hopes that Charles III, the Austrian claimant, could ever gain the Spanish throne. True, the next year Marlborough won another great victory and in 1709 France suffered the worst frost in living memory. A bankrupt Louis XIV even agreed to surrender Spain to Charles III, but when the English and Dutch demanded that he send French troops to drive his own grandson, Philip V, from Madrid, he refused. "If I must wage war," replied Louis XIV, "I had rather wage it against my enemies than against my children." The peace negotiations at Getruydenberg collapsed and the costly war dragged on.

In 1710 the nation grew weary of the war and Queen Anne grew weary of the Whigs. Not only did the squires groan under the heavy taxes, but shipping and trade suffered, as it had during William's war. Between May 1702 and Christmas 1709 the English lost 1146 merchantmen. The nation longed for peace, but the Whigs drove on the war. They then made a serious tactical error; they impeached Dr. Henry Sacheverell, an unimportant High Church clergyman, for preaching a sermon against the principles of the Glorious Revolution. In the ensuing trial the Whig lawyers duly exposed the fallacies of passive obedience and the Lords found Dr. Sacheverell guilty, but they only suspended him from preaching for three years. The sentence was in fact an acquittal. The long trial, the publicity that attended it, and the virtual acquittal of Sacheverell turned public opinion away from the Whigs and the Dissenters and toward the Church and the Tories.

At this very moment, Robert Harley, a country Whig in William's reign, a Speaker of the House in 1701, a Tory secretary of state under Queen Anne, and a politician famous for his skill in managing the Commons, found his way up the back stairs of Kensington palace. Winning the Queen's favor, he skillfully directed her actions and quietly undermined the power of Godolphin and the Whigs. In August the Queen dismissed Godolphin and in September removed the Whigs. Harley himself became Chancellor of the Exchequer, and moderate Tories filled the other offices. It was a splendid illustration of the power that remained in the Queen's hands, but Harley could not hope to remain in office unless he could manage Parliament successfully for her—and it was a Whig Parliament he must meet in the autumn. He therefore persuaded the Queen to dissolve Parliament and send out writs for the election of a new one. Desperate for peace and angered by the Sacheverell trial, the voters returned a Tory majority, a majority which Harley, himself a moderate Tory, skillfully managed to bring the country the peace it sought.

The greatest obstacle to peace lay with England's allies, particularly Austria, whose claims at the peace table far exceeded its contributions on the battlefield. To circumvent the allies, the new Tory ministry negotiated a separate peace. It began secret negotiations in August 1710 and reached a preliminary agreement with France in October 1711. It provided for a peace without Spain, which provoked the fury of the Whigs. Only by persuading the Queen to name twelve new peers was Harley able to win the support of the House of Lords for the preliminaries; and only by withdrawing English troops from combat in June 1712 could he force the allies to join in the negotiations at Utrecht. Britain undoubtedly deserted its allies and made a separate peace, but it is difficult to see how it could have made peace otherwise.

The resulting Treaty of Utrecht showed once again that most peace treaties reflect the disposition of military forces at the end of hostilities. The forces of Philip V had conquered Spain and the treaty acknowledged him as King of Spain, with the provision that the crowns of France and Spain should never be joined in one person. Marlborough had won that part of the Netherlands which is now Belgium; it became the Austrian Netherlands. The Dutch received the right to garrison the barrier fortresses in the Austrian Netherlands. Above all the treaty reflected the dominance of English seapower. Since 1694, the English fleet had wintered in the Mediterranean. In 1704, a week before the Battle of Blenheim, the fleet had seized Gibraltar, and four years later it captured Minorca, with its splendid harbor at Port Mahon. By the Treaty of Utrecht Britain retained both. In September 1710, 400 British marines and 1500 New Englanders captured Port Royal in Acadia, which was renamed Nova Scotia. The Treaty of Utrecht recognized it as English. The treaty likewise gave Britain a clear title to Newfoundland and the Hudson's Bay region, and granted to it the island of St. Kitt's in the West Indies. Finally, Britain wrested from Spain the Asiento, an agreement whereby Spain gave Britain the exlusive right to carry black slaves to the Spanish Indies and permission to send one English ship of 500 tons each year to trade at the annual fairs in the Caribbean.

Britain had not yet won Canada or gained India, but it was firmly set on the path of imperial greatness. The Treaty of Utrecht made that plain, but so did the demographic facts. In 1688 there were only 200,000 British settlers in North America; by 1713 there were 350,000.

THE HANOVERIAN SUCCESSION

The succession question dominated the last years of Queen Anne's reign, but intermingled with it was the question of the unity of the Tory party. Robert Harley, who became the Earl of Oxford in 1711, sought to govern above party, as Godolphin and Marlborough had tried to do in the early years of Anne's reign. But once again the managers came up against the insatiable demands of party. The Tories wanted every Whig thrown out of office and replaced with a Tory. These Tories found a leader in the brilliant and mercurial Henry St. John, Viscount Bolingbroke. Bolingbroke believed that a government could no more be carried on with mixed hands than a coach could be driven with unequal wheels. He vowed to drive every Whig from office, even the most minor. The Earl of Oxford, who as Lord Treasurer and the Queen's favorite controlled patronage, protested and delayed, but finally yielded. Gradually Tories replaced Whigs in the government, but not fast enough for Bolingbroke, who now sought to curry the Queen's favor behind Oxford's back.

Allied with Bolingbroke were the High Churchmen, who wished to suppress the Dissenters totally. In 1711 they secured an act against the practice of occasional conformity and in 1714 a Schism Act that would close down all Dissenting academies and schools. The hatred of the High Churchman for the Dissenter remained unabated to the bitter end.

But the time was running out for the Tories. The Queen's health declined and the prospect of the succession of the House of Hanover plunged the Tories into gloom, for they had offended Hanover. The Tories had on their right wing the Jacobites, so called because they supported the claims to the crown of James II and his son, James III, whose names in Latin would be Jacobus. Jacobitism was largely a sentimental movement, but the Jacobites were noisy and powerful enough in the Tory party, particularly among the Scottish members, to frighten Hanover. The Earl of Oxford, now descending into indolence and drink, probably remained loyal to Hanover, but Bolingbroke in the last few months of the Queen's reign appeared to cast his lot with the Jacobites. Winning the Queen's favor, he was able to engineer Oxford's dismissal and plan the admission of Jacobites to the Cabinet. But he had only two full days in power before the Queen died on August 1, 1714. Had she lived another six months, Bolingbroke might have sought to bring in the pretender, but he also might have shrunk from so hopeless an enterprise. It is almost certain that he could not have found a majority to repeal the Act of Settlement, and rebellion brought with it too many risks. The one certain fact is that Bolingbroke in these last months shattered the unity of the Tory party, thereby assuring that when the Whigs came to power under George I they would face a divided and discredited opposition. The Whig ascendancy of the eighteenth century was prepared in the last months of the Queen's reign.

FURTHER READING

DAVID OGG. *England in the Reigns of James II and William III.* Oxford, 1955. A narrative of political events, with chapters on law, government, religion, economics, and social thought; a lively, engaging book, offering a traditional interpretation of the Revolution.

HENRY HORWITZ. *Parliament, Policy, and Politics in the Reign of William III.* Manchester, England, 1977. Narrowly political; focuses on how the King's business was transacted in Parliament; not easy reading but incorporates in its narrative the most recent scholarly work on the reign.

GEORGE MACAULAY TREVELYAN. *England Under Queen Anne.* 3 vols. London, 1930, 1932, 1934. An epic survey of the reign, written with charm, acuity, and authority by a distinguished English historian.

GEOFFREY HOLMES. *British Politics in the Age of Anne.* London, 1967. A penetrating and vivid picture of the politics of the age, not only in Parliament but in the counties, coffee houses, theaters, and the press.

DAVID CHANDLER. *Marlborough as Military Commander.* New York, 1973. Not as limited as the title suggests; rather, a well-written biography by a leading authority on eighteenth-century warfare.

P.G.M. DICKSON. *The Financial Revolution in England: A Study in the Development of Public Credit 1688–1756.* London, 1967. A scholarly, technical, yet important study of the origins of the national debt, the money market, and the Stock Exchange.

ERIC KERRIDGE. *The Agricultural Revolution.* London, 1967. A study of alternate husbandry, fen drainage, the use of fertilizers, water meadows, and new crops such as turnips and clover; its thesis that these amounted to an agricultural revolution is controversial.

JUDITH HOOK. *The Baroque Age in England.* London, 1976. Discusses art and architecture during the whole seventeenth century, though the baroque, narrrowly defined, flourished only after 1690.

*JOHN LOCKE. *Two Treatises of Government.* Edited by Peter Laslett. Rev. ed., New York, 1960. Laslett shows that Locke wrote his classic work in 1680–83 to justify Shaftesbury's political program, not in 1689 to justify the Revolution.

LAWRENCE STONE. *The Family, Sex, and Marriage in England 1500–1800.* New York, 1977; abridged ed. in paperback, 1980. A pioneering work on an unexplored aspect of the past; written with verve and learning; though its arguments may be challenged its rich illustrative material remains.

Index